S0-DZG-998

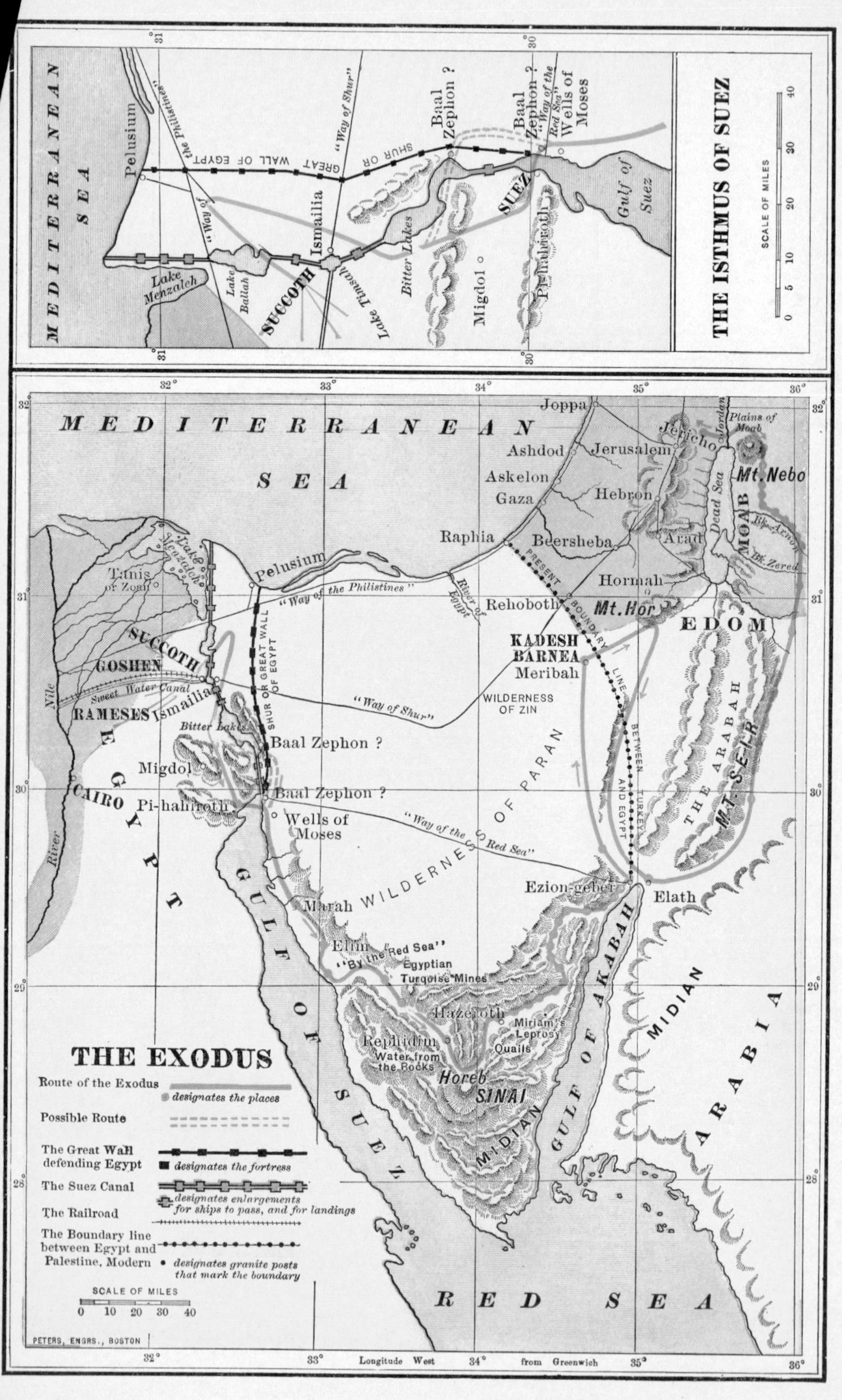

THE ISTHMUS OF SUEZ
SCALE OF MILES
0 5 10 20 30 40
MEDITERRANEAN SEA
Pelusium
"Way of the Philistines"
"Way of Shur"
GREAT WALL OF EGYPT
SHUR OR
Baal Zephon ?
"Way of the Red Sea"
Wells of Moses
Gulf of Suez
SUEZ
Pi-hahiroth
Migdol
Bitter Lakes
Ismailia
Lake Timsah
SUCCOTH
Lake Ballah
Lake Menzaleh
THE EXODUS
Route of the Exodus
designates the places
Possible Route
The Great Wall defending Egypt
designates the fortress
The Suez Canal
designates enlargements for ships to pass, and for landings
The Railroad
The Boundary line between Egypt and Palestine, Modern
designates granite posts that mark the boundary
SCALE OF MILES
0 10 20 30 40
PETERS, ENGRS., BOSTON
Longitude West from Greenwich
MEDITERRANEAN SEA
Joppa
Ashdod
Jerusalem
Jericho
Jordan
Plains of Moab
Mt. Nebo
Askelon
Gaza
Hebron
Dead Sea
MOAB
Bk. Arnon
Bk. Zered
Raphia
Beersheba
Arad
Hormah
Mt. Hor
EDOM
Rehoboth
KADESH BARNEA
Meribah
PRESENT BOUNDARY LINE BETWEEN TURKEY AND EGYPT
WILDERNESS OF ZIN
WILDERNESS OF PARAN
THE ARABAH
MT. SEIR
Pelusium
"Way of the Philistines"
River of Egypt
Lake Menzaleh
Tanis or Zoan
SUCCOTH
GOSHEN
Sweet Water Canal
Nile
RAMESES
Ismailia
Bitter Lakes
SHUR OR GREAT WALL OF EGYPT
"Way of Shur"
Baal Zephon ?
Migdol
CAIRO
Pi-hahiroth
Baal Zephon ?
Wells of Moses
"Way of the Red Sea"
River
EGYPT
Ezion-geber
Elath
Marah
Elim
"By the Red Sea"
Egyptian Turquoise Mines
Hazeroth
Miriam's Leprosy
Quails
Rephidim
Water from the Rocks
Horeb
SINAI
MIDIAN
GULF OF AKABAH
MIDIAN
ARABIA
GULF OF SUEZ
RED SEA
32° 33° 34° 35° 36°
31° 30° 29° 28°

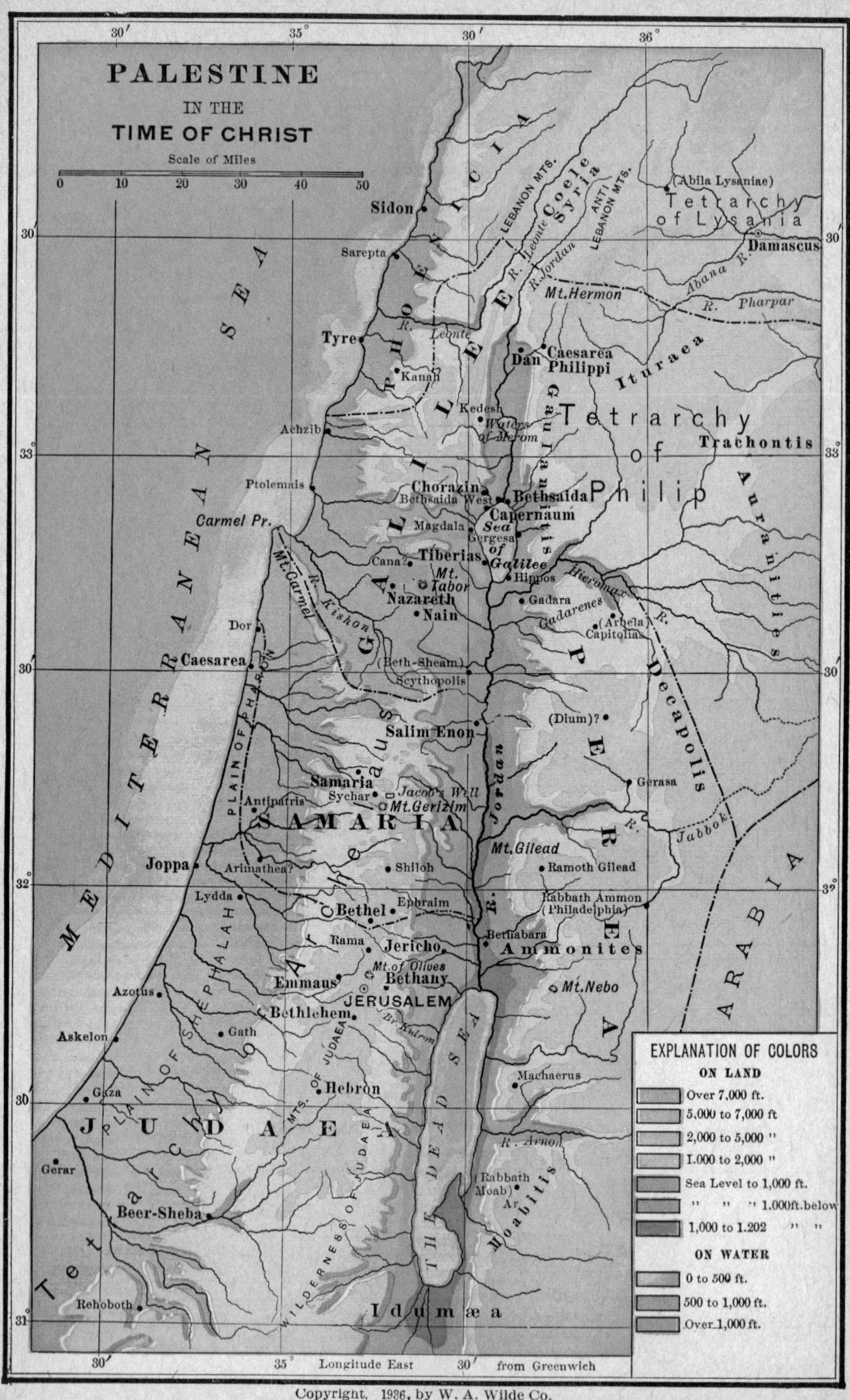

PALESTINE
IN THE
TIME OF CHRIST
Scale of Miles
0 10 20 30 40 50
30′ 35° 30′ 36°
MEDITERRANEAN SEA
PHOENICIA
LEBANON MTS.
Coele Syria
ANTI LEBANON MTS.
(Abila Lysaniae)
Tetrarchy of Lysania
Damascus
Abana R.
R. Pharpar
Mt.Hermon
R. Leonte
R. Jordan
Sidon
Sarepta
Tyre
Kanah
Achzib
Ptolemais
Carmel Pr.
Mt.Carmel
R. Kishon
Dan
Caesarea Philippi
Ituraea
Kedesh
Waters of Merom
Gaulanitis
Tetrarchy of Philip
Trachontis
Auranitis
GALILEE
Chorazin
Bethsaida West
Bethsaida
Capernaum
Magdala
Sea of Galilee
Gergesa
Tiberias
Cana?
Hippos
Mt. Tabor
Nazareth
Nain
Hieromax R.
Gadara
Gadarenes
(Arbela)
Capitolias
Dor
Caesarea
PLAIN OF SHARON
(Beth-Sheam)
Scythopolis
Decapolis
Salim Enon
(Dium)?
PEREA
Jordan
Gerasa
Samaria
Sychar
Jacob's Well
Mt.Gerizim
Antipatris
SAMARIA
Archelaus
R. Jabbok
Mt.Gilead
Ramoth Gilead
Joppa
Arimathea?
Shiloh
Lydda
Bethel
Ephraim
Rabbath Ammon (Philadelphia)
ARABIA
Rama
Jericho
Bethabara
Ammonites
SHEPHALAH
Mt.of Olives
Bethany
Emmaus
JERUSALEM
Mt.Nebo
Azotus
Bethlehem
Br. Kidron
MTS. OF JUDAEA
Gath
Askelon
Machaerus
PLAIN OF
Gaza
Hebron
JUDAEA
THE DEAD SEA
R. Arnon
Gerar
(Rabbath Moab)
Ar
Moabitis
Beer-Sheba
WILDERNESS OF JUDAEA
Tetrarchy of
Rehoboth
Idumæa
Longitude East from Greenwich
EXPLANATION OF COLORS
ON LAND
Over 7,000 ft.
5,000 to 7,000 ft
2,000 to 5,000 "
1,000 to 2,000 "
Sea Level to 1,000 ft.
" " " 1,000ft.below
1,000 to 1,202 " "
ON WATER
0 to 500 ft.
500 to 1,000 ft.
Over 1,000 ft.

FOUNDED BY REV. FRANCIS N. PELOUBET, D.D.

PELOUBET'S SELECT NOTES

ON THE

INTERNATIONAL SUNDAY SCHOOL LESSONS

IMPROVED UNIFORM SERIES: COURSE FOR

1943

The Gospel of John

Life and Letters of Peter and John

God in the Making of a Nation: Era of Moses

The Ten Commandments and the Teachings of Jesus

Four full-page colored pictures and 125 illustrations in the text.

BY

WILBUR M. SMITH, D.D.

Sixty-ninth Annual Volume.

BOSTON, MASS., U.S.A.

PUBLISHED BY W. A. WILDE COMPANY

131 CLARENDON STREET BOSTON, MASSACHUSETTS.

Printed in U. S. A.

TABLE OF CONTENTS.

MAP OF PALESTINE IN THE TIME OF CHRIST. THE MAP OF THE EXODUS.

INTRODUCTION: BIBLIOGRAPHY.

LIST OF LESSONS FOR THE YEAR.

FIRST QUARTER.

Gospel of John.

SECOND QUARTER.

Life and Letters of Peter and John.

THIRD QUARTER.

God in the Making of a Nation: Era of Moses.

FOURTH QUARTER.

The Ten Commandments and the Teachings of Jesus.

PUBLISHED SEPTEMBER, 1942. MADE IN U. S. A.

INTRODUCTION.

The author and publisher of this book are indeed grateful for the public favor which has carried it along for 69 years. As it is the oldest Sunday-school annual in the world, so it continues to enjoy the largest sale. We attribute this success to the unfailing evangelical purpose and method of the book. Its central aim has always been to exalt Jesus Christ, and maintain for him an ascendancy over human life. Biblical scholarship is a noble accomplishment. We seek it constantly for our book and its students. We try to keep fully abreast with discoveries in the rapidly enlarging field of Bible archæology, and to illuminate the Bible with whatever the best translators and the most thorough students of the life of the people of Bible lands can give us. But, with it all, our leading purpose is to lead souls to the world's Redeemer. We believe that Sunday school teachers and students recognize this aim of Peloubet's Select Notes, and heartily agree with it.

The main purpose of each volume of "Peloubet's Select Notes" has always been, and will continue to be, the exposition of the Scripture lesson in a way that will best help teachers to unfold it to their pupils.

Good teaching is the apex of a pyramid. It must have a broad and substantial base beneath it. A teacher is always likely to be confronted with questions outside the lesson, and if he does not know more, far more — than the lesson, he is sure to come to grief, losing his pupils' confidence. That is why these "Select Notes" are so full that no teacher can impart all the information they contain in the course of the recitation half-hour. That is why also they give the teacher more practical thoughts and more inspiring illustrations and quotations than he can possibly utilize. He is to fill his mind full to running over. He is to teach from an abundant reservoir. That is why also the teacher will always have on hand some book giving a wide view of the Bible or at least a section of the Bible covered by the year's study. A book on Bible geography, for example; a book on archæological discoveries in Bible Lands; a book treating Bible history in a comprehensive way; some theological treatise or volume on Christian evidences — such books as these, taken one at a time through a series of years, will so establish a teacher in the fundamentals of his great theme that he cannot be taken by surprise. He is like a general who has plenty of reserve troops.

All this serves not to confuse but to simplify. The more one knows about a subject, the more easily he can clarify it, the more directly he can present it. It is impossible to know too much for effective teaching.

These are "Select Notes." We believe that "all men are wiser than one man," and try to make this book a treasury of the best thoughts of the best Bible scholars.

The editor of this book has always felt that the editing of this volume was one of the greatest privileges in the field of Christian literature in the entire English Speaking world. Once thinking of it as a rare privilege, he now realizes also what a responsibility it is. He would truly covet the prayers of Sunday school teachers everywhere that the Spirit of God might definitely guide him, and instruct him in the writing of these lessons.

BIBLIOGRAPHIES.

LIVES OF CHRIST.

Alexander Patterson: *The Greater Life and Work of Christ.* pp. 418. This work, originally published nearly fifty years ago, has a comprehensiveness found in no other work of scholarly nature known to the editor. Its chapter headings clearly indicate the wealth of its contents, "Christ in the Eternal Past," "Christ in Creation," "Christ in the Old Testament Age," "Christ in His Earthly Life," "Christ in His Present State and Work," "The King of Kings and Lord of Lords," "Christ in the Eternal Future." The book has often been reprinted, and can be secured at a very low price.

J. Paterson-Smyth: *A People's Life of Christ.* pp. 505. 1920. Helpful, reverent, easily understood, in places quite suggestive; in spots too imaginative, and weak on our Lord's early self-consciousness.

Samuel J. Andrews: *The Life of Our Lord upon the Earth Considered in Its Historical, Chronological, and Geographical Relations.* New York, Charles Scribner's Sons, new edition, 1900. For historical, chronological and geographical matters, this volume has never been surpassed, though many discoveries have been made since Andrews wrote. Indispensable for a foundation study of the life of Christ.

A. B. Bruce: *The Training of the Twelve.* Numerous editions. Especially rich for character study. Dr. W. H. Griffith Thomas once spoke of it as "one of the greatest books of the nineteenth century, and one which may be read with unhesitating confidence and unfailing delight and profit by all Christian people."

Alfred Edersheim: *The Life and Times of Jesus the Messiah.* Eighth edition, revised, New York, London, 2 vols. A monument of learning, vividly written, with great reverence and insight; probably, everything considered, the most valuable life of Christ for general use in our language.

Frederick W. Farrar: *The Life of Christ*, 2 vols., various editions. First published in 1874. Brilliantly written, rich in historical details.

Cunningham Geikie: *The Life and Words of Christ.* London, 1883, 2 vols. Especially rich for the backgrounds which he paints for the various episodes in the Gospel narratives.

John Walter Good: *The Jesus of Our Fathers.* New York, The Macmillan Company, 1923. A massive, conservative, up-to-date volume, entirely trustworthy.

J. P. Lange: *The Life of the Lord Jesus Christ.* English translation, Edinburgh, 1872, 4 vols. By one of Germany's greatest New Testament scholars; profound, suggestive, theological; in some ways the greatest life of Christ ever written. To be used only by those who love to study and to have their minds lifted up into the highest realms of thought.

G. Campbell Morgan: *The Crises of the Christ.* Fleming H. Revell Company, New York, Chicago, 1903. Dr. Morgan's greatest work, and of superlative value in dealing with Christ's birth, baptism, temptation, transfiguration, crucifixion, resurrection, and ascension.

Augustus Neander: *The Life of Jesus Christ.* Various editions. By one of Germany's great scholars. First published almost a century ago, but still valuable; conservative.

David Smith: *The Days of His Flesh: The Earthly Life of Our Lord and Saviour Jesus Christ.* Numerous editions. Abreast of the most recent scholarship, rich in archaeological details, sometimes not as loyal to the inspiration of the Gospels as one would wish.

Robert E. Speer: *Studies of the Man Christ Jesus.* Many editions, first published in 1896. Helpful in the study of Christ's character.

Philip Vollmer: *The Modern Student's Life of Christ.* New York, Chicago, 1912. An invaluable work, similar to that of Andrews, but not so exhaustive, though with historical matters brought up to date.

Byron H. DeMent: *The Bible-Reader's Life of Christ.* A splendid elementary study, following a harmonistic arrangement of the Gospel records, with frequent richly suggestive paragraphs.

James Stalker: *The Ethics of Jesus.* New York, 1909.

R. A. Torrey: *The Real Christ.* 1920. Ten chapters on outstanding characteristics of Christ.

Alexander Whyte: *The Walk, Conversation, and Character of Jesus Christ Our Lord.* New York. Chicago. 1905. A book that stands altogether by itself on the subjects which it treats. A wonderfully suggestive exposition of various texts in the Gospel relating to the person of Christ, which are too frequently overlooked.

Charles E. Jefferson: *The Character of Jesus.* New York, 1908. Helpful, but not always to be trusted.

William E. McLennan: *In His Footsteps.* Revised edition, New York, 1911. "A record of travel to and in the land of Christ, with an attempt to mark the Lord's journeyings in chronological order from his birth to his ascension."

H. V. Morton: *In the Steps of the Master.* New York, 1934. One of the most fascinating, accurate, and suggestive volumes in the English language on the geographical background of the life and ministry of Jesus Christ. Should be in the hands of every Sunday-school teacher.

Gustaf Dalman: *Sacred Sites and Ways.* English translation, New York, 1935. A work altogether different from that of Morton, very scholarly and, in places, profound. Rich in historical references, more for the student than for the general Sunday-school teacher, but with light on some Gospel passages not to be found in any other published work.

BIBLIOGRAPHY.

JAMES STALKER: *The Life of Jesus Christ.* Edinburgh, 1879. A small book, far more valuable than its brevity would imply; brilliant, suggestive, reverent.

ARTHUR C. HEADLAM: *The Life and Teaching of Jesus the Christ.* New York, 1923. By an outstanding scholar of the Church of England, Bishop of Gloucester, Regius Professor of Divinity in the University of Oxford. Abreast of the most recent Christological thought. Often concerns itself with the hard problems of modern criticism.

OTTO BORCHERT: *The Original Jesus.* Translated by E. M. Stalker, New York, 1933. A very remarkable work, tremendously stimulating, with much new light on the entire Gospel narrative. Every Bible student will rejoice again and again as he reads these fascinating pages.

ADAM FAHLING: *The Life of Christ.* St. Louis, 1936. A large work (of some 770 pp.) strictly following a chronological order, with its material clearly divided into many clearly indicated sections; all historical, chronological, and geographical matters receiving particular attention. Based on a careful study of the important relevant literature. A worthwhile book for frequent reference.

EMIL SCHURER: *A History of the Jewish People in the Time of Christ.* English translation, 2 vols., published in five vols., Edinburgh, 1890–91; new edition, 1900. A standard work of vast learning, surveying all that was known in Schurer's time of the period just previous to and during the advent of Christ. A mine of rich material.

WILLIAM SANDAY: *Outlines of the Life of Christ.* 1905. A book that marked a new epoch in the study of the Gospel narratives. A good summary of the available material, though in some places too drastically critical.

ALFRED E. GARVIE: *Studies in the Inner Life of Jesus.* New York, London, 1907.

E. DEPRESSENSE: *Jesus Christ: His Times, Life and Work.* Seventh edition, London, 1879. By one of the greatest biblical scholars and preachers of France during the nineteenth century. Written in reply to Renan's rationalistic "Life of Jesus," and after half a century, still worth careful reading.

A. M. FAIRBAIRN: *Studies in the Life of Christ.* London, 1880, 4th edition, 1885. Masterly chapters on Christ's Temptation, the Kingdom of Heaven, the Later Teaching, Gethsemane, the Betrayer, the Crucifixion, the Resurrection, etc.

COMMENTARIES ON THE GOSPEL OF ST. JOHN.

F. GODET: *Commentary on the Gospel of John.* 2 vols. Translated from the French, with Notes, by Timothy Dwight, President of Yale College. (Masterly, profound, edifying.)

MARCUS DODS: *The Gospel of St. John.* 2 vols. (The Expositor's Bible.) (Invaluable, inexpensive, wonderfully suggestive.)

CHARLES R. ERDMAN: *The Gospel of John.* An Exposition. Philadelphia. 1917. (Brief, clear.)

S. D. GORDON: *Quiet Talks on John's Gospel.* New York. Chicago. 1915.

A. PLUMMER: *The Gospel According to St. John.* (The Cambridge Bible for Schools and Colleges.) Cambridge. 1886. (Exceptionally helpful.)

GEORGE REITH: *The Gospel According to St. John, with Introduction and Notes.* 2 vols. Edinburgh. n.d. (In *Hand-books for Bible Classes and Private Students.*) (In the mind of the editor the most valuable, illuminating work on John for its size in our language; amazingly rich notes.)

A. T. ROBERTSON: *The Divinity of Christ in the Gospel of John.* New York. London. 1916.

J. C. RYLE: *Expository Thoughts on the Gospels.* 3 vols. (Devotional, gives all the principal interpretations of most important passages.)

W. GRAHAM SCROGGIE: *St. John.* London and Edinburgh. n.d. (In the *Study Hour Series.*) (Brief, suggestive; good outlines.)

MELVIA THOMAS SHELFORD: *The Christ as John Knew Him. Lectures on the Gospel According to John.* London. New York. 1928.

ROBERT E. SPEER: *John's Gospel: The Greatest Book in the World.* New York. London. 1915. (A fine hand-book.)

B. F. WESTCOTT: *The Gospel According to St. John* (originally published in 1881 in *The Speaker's Commentary Series.* Many later impressions. (In many ways, the greatest commentary on the Fourth Gospel in English.)

J. RITCHIE SMITH: *The Teaching of the Gospel of John.* New York. London. 1903. (Theological.)

JOHN PETER LANGE: *The Gospel According to John* (revised, enlarged, and edited by Philip Schaff). New York. 1871 and later impressions. (Rich, better for those who read the Greek text.)

F. N. PELOUBET: *Suggestive Illustrations on the Gospel of John.* New York. 1898. (Exceptionally valuable for Sunday-school teachers.)

ARTHUR W. PINK: *Exposition of the Gospel of John.* 4 vols. Swengel, Pa. (Dispensational. In places quite original.)

JOHN CALVIN: *A Commentary on the Gospel According to John.* A new translation by William Pringle. Edinburgh. 1847. 2 vols.

ALBERT HUGHES: *The Glory of the Godhead in the Gospel of John.* Philadelphia. 1933. pp. 176.

WILLIAM MILLIGAN AND WM. F. MOULTON: *Commentary on the Gospel of St. John.* Edinburgh. 1898. pp. 36, 242. (A work, by two of the most distinguished Greek scholars of their day, now seldom seen, but containing some of the finest, clearest, most penetrating interpretations of the inexhaustible pages of this Gospel ever written.)

R. C. H. LENSKI: *The Interpretation of St. John's Gospel.* Columbus. 1931. pp. 1418. The most voluminous work on John of a scholarly nature ever published in this country. Never avoids any real problem. Conservative. Often the most satisfactory of all.

THOMAS WHITELAW: *The Gospel of St. John. An Exposition Exegetical and Homiletical.* Glasgow. 1888. Now rarely seen, but by one of the greatest commentators of his time, reverent, penetrating both theological and practical. Over 500 pages.

BIOGRAPHIES OF THE APOSTLE PETER.

A. T. ROBERTSON: *Epochs in the Life of Simon Peter.* New York. Chicago. 1933. (In some ways the best of all works on Peter; the result of years of labor in the text and with all the important literature on the subject.)

WILLIAM DALLMANN: *Peter: Life and Letters.* St. Louis, Mo. 1930. (Well arranged, beautifully illustrated, with many literary quotations and references to church history.)

F. B. MEYER: *Peter: Fisherman, Disciple, Apostle.* New York. Chicago. 1930. (Devotional, with all the virtues of this writer's famous books.)

W. H. GRIFFITH THOMAS: *The Apostle Peter: Outline Studies in His Life, Character, and Writings.* New York. Chicago. 1904. (Excellent for its outlines.)

F. J. FOAKES-JACKSON: *Peter: Prince of Apostles.* New York. 1927. (By a well-known scholar; somewhat critical; not of great help to Sunday-school teachers. In an appendix is "A List of Pictures in Which St. Peter Figures Prominently.")

ALBERT J. SOUTHHOUSE: *The Making of Simon Peter.* New York. n.d. (Practical, helpful.)

CLARENCE EDWARD MACARTNEY: *Peter and His Lord.* Sermons on the Life of Peter. Nashville. 1937. (A fresh treatment, by a distinguished preacher fully acquainted with the problems and needs of our time.)

CHARLES S. ROBINSON: *Simon Peter: His Early Life and Times.* Edinburgh. 1890. *Simon Peter: His Later Life and Labors.* New York. London. 1894. (Rich biographical studies; some of the author's pages are unsurpassed in Petrine literature for insight and application to our own lives.)

H. A. BIRKS: *Studies in the Life and Character of St. Peter.* London. 1887.

J. S. HOWSON: *Horae Petrinae: or, Studies in the Life of St. Peter.* London. 1883. (By a well-known New Testament scholar.)

W. T. P. WOLSTON: *Simon Peter: His Life and Letters.* Fourth edition. Edinburgh. 1926.

WILLIAM M. TAYLOR: *Peter the Apostle.* New York. 1875. (By one of the best expository preachers of his day; particularly valuable for Sunday-school teachers because of its practical applications.)

EDWIN HODDER: *Simon Peter: His Life, Times, and Friends.* London. New York. 1884. (A book that should be known more widely; independent, in places quite vivid.)

QUINTIN HOGG: *The Story of Peter from Bethsaida to Babylon.* London. 1900. (Sunday afternoon addresses to young men, delivered at the Polytechnic Institute, London.)

J. M. McInnis: *Simon Peter: Fisherman and Philosopher.* New York. London. 1930.
J. R. Macduff: *The Footsteps of St. Peter.* New York. 1877.
Harmon A. Baldwin: *The Fisherman of Galilee.* A Devotional Study. New York. 1923.
Abbe Constant Fouard: *St. Peter and the First Years of Christianity.* English translation. London. 1901. (Scholarly; written from the Roman Catholic viewpoint.)
E. Schuyler English: *The Life and Letters of Saint Peter.* 1941. pp. 271. (The latest life of St. Peter of genuine value. One great virtue of this book is that it frankly and sanely faces the great problems that arise in a study of the life and writings of the Apostle Peter.)

BIOGRAPHIES OF MOSES.

F. B. Meyer: *Moses, the Servant of God.* n.d. (An invaluable book from a devotional standpoint.)
J. B. Van Oosterzee: *Moses: A Biblical Study.* Translated from the Dutch. Edinburgh. 1876. (By one of the greatest theologians of the 19th century.)
M. G. Pearse: *Moses, His Life and Its Lessons.* 1894.
George Rawlinson: *Moses, His Life and Times* (in the Men of the Bible series). London. New York. 1887. (As excellent a life of Moses from the historical standpoint as we have.)
A. P. Stanley: *Lectures on the History of the Jewish Church.* Vol. 1, 92–183. (Brilliant.)
William M. Taylor: *Moses, the Law-giver.* N. Y. 1879. (A series of discourses by one of the outstanding preachers of his day. Practical, helpful, devotional, and historically correct.)
A. C. Gaebelein: *Moses, His First and Second Coming.* New York. 1940. A most remarkable book — some of its chapters are absolutely unique in the literature of Moses. The editor believes every Sunday-school teacher in America should purchase and carefully read this book for the lessons of this year.
Mildred Duff and Noel Hope: *Where Moses Went to School and Where Moses Learnt to Rule.* London. (A book for children.)
Alfred Edersheim: *The Exodus and the Wanderings in the Wilderness.*
Edmund Fleg: *The Life of Moses* (translated from the French). London. 1928.
Robert A. Hallen: *Moses: A Course of Lectures.* New York. 1869.
James Hamilton: *Moses, the Man of God.* London. New York. 1871.
John M. Lowrie: *The Hebrew Law-giver.* 2 vols. Philadelphia. 1865.
Percival Wood: *Moses, the Father of Preventive Medicine.* 1920. (Suggestive.)
It is not necessary to enumerate the great number of chapters in various books dealing with the life of Moses.

LITERATURE ON THE TEN COMMANDMENTS.

George Dana Boardman: *The Ten Commandments.* A Course of Lectures Delivered before the University of Pennsylvania. Philadelphia. 1889. (This is easily one of the most important volumes in the English language on this subject, the result of extensive research and full of richest material. The book concludes with three indexes of great value.)
John Calvin: *Commentaries on the Four Last Books of Moses,* Vol. 1, pp. 338–502; Vol. 2, p. 472; Vol. 3, pp. 5–201.
R. H. Charles: *The Decalogue.* Edinburgh. 1924. (By a distinguished Biblical scholar. Not only with valuable critical and historical notes, but also with excellent, practical applications to contemporary problems.)
Henry Sloane Coffin: *The Ten Commandments with a Christian Application to Present Conditions.* New York. 1915. (Fresh, helpful, somewhat liberal here and there, but with very suggestive pages.)
R. W. Dale: *The Ten Commandments.* Fourth Edition. London. 1884. (A series of messages delivered at Carr's Lane, Birmingham, on Sunday evenings late in 1870. A superb volume, with all the virtues of Dr. Dale's famous writings.)

J. OSWALD DYKES: *The Law of the Ten Words.* n.d. (Republished in "The Household Library of Exposition." Has a good chapter on "The Second Great Commandment," Lev. 19 : 18.)

ROBERT EYTON: *The Ten Commandments.* Sermons Preached at Chelsea, Holy Trinity. London. 1895. (Has two additional sermons on Matt. 19 : 17 and Matt. 19 : 16–21.)

F. W. FARRAR: *The Voice from Sinai.* The Eternal Bases of the Moral Law. London. New York. 1892. (A series of fifteen sermons preached at Westminster Abbey during November, 1891, and January, 1892. An absolutely indispensable volume with rich footnotes, brilliant applications, suggestive, profound, scholarly. Has additional sermons: "The Law Our Tutor," "The Manner of Keeping the Commandments," and "'Thou Shalt Not.'")

P. B. FITZWATER: *God's Code of Morals Applied to the New Day.* Chicago. 1926. A brief booklet of sixty-three pages. For sale by The Moody Press. Price, 30 cents.

H. J. FLOWERS: *The Permanent Value of the Ten Commandments.* London. 1927.

CHARLES HODGE: *Systematic Theology,* Vol. 3, 259–465.

W. L. HOOPER: *The Code of the Spiritual.*

GEORGE JACKSON: *The Ten Commandments.* New York. 1898.

STANLEY LEATHES: *The Foundations of Morality* (1882).

CLELAND BOYS MCAFEE: *The Mosaic Law in Modern Life.* New York. Chicago. 1906. (One of the best recent books, exceedingly practical, with many excellent applications to modern conditions.)

EDWARD BEECHER MASON: *The Ten Laws, a Foundation for Human Society.* New York. 1897.

J. G. MASSEE: *The Gospel in the Ten Commandments.* New York. Chicago. 1923. (A series of sermons preached by the distinguished pastor, at the time of their publication, of Tremont Temple, Boston; evangelical.)

F. D. MAURICE: *The Ten Commandments Considered as Instruments of National Reformation.* London. 1866. (Rather verbose.)

J. PARTON MILUM: *Do the Ten Commandments Stand To-day?* London. 1936. (Excellent, practical, takes account of modern thought.)

G. CAMPBELL MORGAN: *The Ten Commandments.* New York. Chicago. 1901. (With an additional chapter on "A New Commandment," John 13 : 34, 35. This book should be owned by every Sunday-school teacher. It is one of the briefest, yet one of the profoundest and most satisfactory and penetrating, works on this subject that is obtainable, much shorter than Boardman and Farrar, yet with much that these two men do not have.)

JOHN P. PETERS: *Jesus Christ and the Old Commandments.* New York. 1914.

B. W. RANDOLPH: *The Law of Sinai.* Devotional Addresses on the Ten Commandments. London. New York. 1896.

H. CLAY TRUMBULL: *The Ten Commandments as a Covenant of Love.*

ELIZABETH WORDSWORTH: *The Decalogue.* London. 1893. (Miss Wordsworth was, at the time this book was published, the principal of Lady Margaret Hall, Oxford.)

D. L. MOODY: *Weighed and Wanting. Addresses on the Ten Commandments.* 1898.

WM. MASSELINK: *Sermons on the Commandments.* Grand Rapids. 1934. (The best of recent books on the Ten Commandments. Excellent for its direct applications to contemporary life.)

TEMPERANCE LITERATURE.

BERTHA RACHEL PALMER: *A Syllabus in Alcohol Education.* National Woman's Christian Temperance Union, Evanston, Ill.

MARY LEWIS REED: "Alcohol — Its Physiological and Psychological Effects and Their Social Consequences" (a fifty-page booklet). From the author, Room 902, 468 Fourth Ave., New York City. 15 cents.

FRED D. L. SQUIRES: "The Truth about Alcohol in This Hour of National Emergency." American Business Men's Research Foundation, 111 W. Jackson Blvd., Chicago, Ill. 6 cents.

EMIL BOGEN, M. D., AND LEHMANN W. S. HISEY: *What About Alcohol?* 94 pages. Angels Press. 1240 S. Main St., Los Angeles. $1.50.

Temperance Facts. Minnesota Temperance Movement. 204 Hodgson Blvd., Minneapolis. 96 pages. 25 cents.

Quiz Book. Fundamental Facts Concerning Alcohol. Gray Printing Co., Fostoria, Ohio. 64 pages. 30 cents.

Paul C. Carter and Kenneth Cober: *An Old Fight in a New Arena.* Judson Press. 1940. 96 pages.

Howard E. Hamlin, "Alcohol Talks to Youth." National Woman's Christian Temperance Union.

Only the more recent literature has been given above — and generally the less expensive.

WILDE'S BIBLE PICTURE SET

Illustrating the International Uniform Sunday-School Lessons for 1943.

Sixty pictures, 90 cents, postpaid.

First Quarter.

Lesson 1

93 "I am the Light of the World." Holman Hunt.
43 John the Baptist Preaching. Titian.

Lesson 2

53 Nicodemus' Visit to Jesus. Artist unknown.

Lesson 3

55 Jesus and the Woman of Samaria. H. Hofmann

Lesson 4

60 Healing of the Impotent Man. Bida.

Lesson 5

83 Miracle of the Loaves and Fishes. Murillo.

Lesson 6

149 The Crucifixion. Munkacsy.

Lesson 7

593 Christ Healing the Blind Man. H. Richter.

Lesson 8

116 The Good Shepherd. Plockhörst.

Lesson 9

120 Raising of Lazarus. Rubens.

Lesson 10

806 The Statue of Laocoön.

Lesson 11

133 Jesus Washes the Disciples' Feet. Brown.
825 "In my Father's house are many mansions." C. Schonherr.

Lesson 12

535 Jesus in Prayer. Artist unknown.

Lesson 13

170 Thomas the Doubter. Guercino.

Second Quarter.

Lesson 1

46 "Behold the Lamb of God." Bida.
47 Christ and the Fishermen. Zimmermann.

Lesson 2

89 The Transfiguration. Raphael.

Lesson 3

136 Jesus in Gethsemane. Hofmann.

Lesson 4

538 Peter and John Hastening to the Sepulcher on the Morning of the Resurrection. Burnand.

Lesson 5

88 Christ's Charge to St. Peter. Raphael.
49 Miraculous Draught of Fishes. Raphael.

Lesson 6

599 Healing of the Lame Man by Peter. Nicolas Poussin.

Lesson 7

789 Simon Magus Comes to Peter and John. From an old Bible.

Lesson 8

271 Temperance. E. Burne Jones. (Temperance pours the pure water of life upon the fires of passion and appetite as she tramples them under her feet.)

Lesson 9

148 The Crucifixion. Hofmann.

Lesson 10

646 Christ or Diana. Long.

Lesson 11

453 St. Peter. Fra Bartolommeo.

Lesson 12

793 The Presence of the Lord. Hofmann.

Lesson 13

278 St. John the Evangelist. Carlo Dolci.

Third Quarter.

Lesson 1

804 Israelites in Bondage.

Lesson 2

381 Moses and the Burning Bush. Domenico. Feti.

Lesson 3

403 Moses. Michael Angelo.

Lesson 4

627 Three Members of a Temperance Society. Herring.

Lesson 5

577 The Israelites Going Out of Egypt. Paul Veronese.
383 Pharaoh Urging Moses to Leave Egypt. Doré.

Lesson 6

609 The Destruction of Pharaoh's Host. John Martin.
610 Miriam. W. Hensel.

Lesson 7

710 The Bread from Heaven.

Lesson 8

391 Giving of the Law on St. Sinai. Doré.

Lesson 9

580 Israelites Worshiping the Golden Calf. Raphael

Lesson 10

581 Moses and the Law. Phillippe de Champaigne.

Lesson 11

Map of the Exodus.

Lesson 12

387 Moses Striking the Rock. Murillo.

Lesson 13

794 Our Country's Flag and the Christian Flag.

Fourth Quarter.

Lesson 1

112. Christ and the Rich Ruler. Hofmann.

Lesson 2

64. The Sermon on the Mount. Hofmann.

Lesson 3

817 Jesus and His Disciples Going through the Wheatfield. Wehle.
598 The Man with the Withered Hand. Bida.

Lesson 4

39 In the Temple. Hofmann.
158 John and the Mother of Jesus. Wm. Dyce.

Lesson 5

670 Temperance Pledge.

Lesson 6

652 The Charity of St. Martin. Michel.

Lesson 7

728 Jesus and the Multitude of People.

Lesson 8

821 Zacchæus in the Sycomore. Artist unknown.

Lesson 9

122 "The Way, the Truth, and the Life."

Lesson 10

67 "Consider the Lilies." Henry Le Jeune.

Lesson 11

635 The Christ. Bida. "Love one another even as I have loved you."

Lesson 12

318 Head of Christ. Hofmann.

Lesson 13

691 The Star in the East. Doré.

RAPHAEL

THE TRANSFIGURATION

FIRST QUARTER.

JANUARY 3 — MARCH 28, 1943.

(First Half of a Six Months' Course.)

Aim: To lead the student through the teachings of the Gospel of John to achieve the aim as stated in John 20 : 31: " but these are written, that ye may believe that Jesus is the Christ, the Son of God; and that believing ye may have life in his name."

LESSON I. — January 3.

THE GLORY OF THE SON OF GOD. — John 1 : 1–18.

PRINTED TEXT, John 1 : 1–14.

GOLDEN TEXT. — ***And the Word became flesh, and dwelt among us (and we beheld his glory, glory as of the only begotten from the Father), full of grace and truth.*** John 1 : 14.

Devotional Reading: Colossians 1 : 9–18.
Beginner Topic: Two Happy Brothers.
  Lesson Material: John 1 : 1–18.
  Memory Verse: God . . . loved us, and sent his Son. 1 John 4 : 10.
Primary Topic: What John Said About His Friend.
  Lesson Material: John 1 : 1–28.
  Memory Verse: A friend loveth at all times. Proverbs 17 : 17.
Junior Topic: True to His Friend.
  Lesson Material: John 1 : 1–28.
  Memory Verse: A friend loveth at all times. Proverbs 17 : 17.
Intermediate and Senior Topic: God Dwelling Among Men.
Topic for Young People and Adults: Seeing God in Christ.

THE TEACHER AND HIS CLASS.

The Younger Classes will be able to comprehend a great deal of this lesson, even though it embraces one of the profoundest passages of the entire New Testament. If the teacher will write on a blackboard, or on a large sheet of paper, a list, say, of six or eight words, such as morning, breakfast, egg, book, home, mother, and then ask the pupils what these are, with the desire to lead them to recognize that these are *words*, he may then discuss with the pupils for a few moments what a word is. In this he should lead them to see that primarily it is first a thought, and then an expression of that thought from one person to another. In our lesson, Christ is called " the Word," and, as we proceed in our study, we will discover just what it means for Christ to be " the Word " from God to man.

The Older Classes will find in this passage one of the most amazingly rich passages to be found in any literature of the world, setting forth the inexhaustible, unfathomable, infinite glories of the Lord Jesus Christ. Of no *other* being in all the years could such lines as these be written. It would be well if the teacher should bring out, in his half hour of exposition, the vast differences between the Christ of this passage and men in general, and, at the same time, show how this infinitely glorious Person has desired, from eternity, to be a blessing to and an eternal companion of the fallen race of men, in His redeeming them from sin and death.

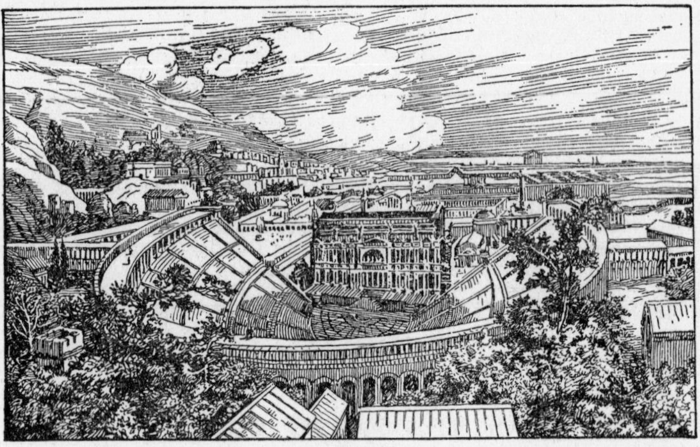

Ancient Ephesus.

THE LESSON IN ITS SETTING.

Time. — The Gospel of John was written about A.D. 90. Most of our passage cannot be chronologically identified, though our Lord's incarnation, set forth in verse 14, began 5 or 6 B.C.

Place. — No geographical area is mentioned in this entire passage. The Gospel of John was written probably in the city of Ephesus.

THE PLAN OF THE LESSON.

SUBJECT: The Trinity, the Deity, the Incarnation and the Work of Jesus Christ, the Son of God.

I. CHRIST THE ETERNAL WORD, VS. 1, 2.

II. CHRIST THE CREATOR OF ALL THINGS, V. 3.

III. CHRIST THE LIFE, V. 4 *a*.

IV. CHRIST THE LIGHT OF MEN, VS. 4 *b*–11.

1. The truth declared, v. 4 *b*.
2. The conflict of light with darkness, v. 5.
3. The witness of John the Baptist to Christ as Light, vs. 6–8.
4. The reaffirmation of the truth of Christ as Light, v. 9.
5. The rejection of the Light by the world, vs. 10, 11.

V. CHRIST THE ONLY ONE WHO CAN MAKE SINNERS TO BE THE SONS OF GOD, VS. 12, 13.

VI. CHRIST INCARNATE, VS. 14–17.

1. His incarnation.
2. His earthly abiding.
3. His divine glory.
4. His perfect manifestation of grace and truth.
   a. The fact stated.
   b. The testimony of John the Baptist.

VII. CHRIST THE REVEALER OF THE FATHER, V. 18.

THE TEACHER'S LIBRARY.

In addition to the great commentaries on John's gospel, a list of which is given in the bibliography in the Introduction to this volume, one should also consult on Christ as the Word, G. B. Stevens: *The Johannine Theology*, 74–101; J. P. Gloag: *Introduction to the Johannine Writings*, 167–189; J. J. Lias: *The Doctrinal System of St. John*, 33–64; the article "Logos," by E. F. Scott, in James Hastings: *Dictionary of Christ and the Gospels*, Vol. 2, 49–52 (rather unnecessarily technical), and, a much better one, by A. B. D. Alexander, in the *International Standard Bible Encyclopedia*, Vol. 3, 1911–1917; and an excellent article with extensive references, "The Word," by Prof. D. S. Talcott, in Smith's *Dictionary of the Bible*, Vol. 4, 3554–3557; also, J. R. Smith: *The Teaching of the Gospel of John*, 84–104.

All books devoted to the life of John the Baptist will, of course, have more or less extensive material on those verses of this passage which refer to the ministry of this prophet. For sermonic material, see on verse 1,

C. I. Scofield: *In Many Pulpits*, 23–40; B. B. Warfield: *Faith and Life*, 81–92. On verse 9, F. W. Robertson: *The Human Race*, 287 ff. On verse 10, see J. H. Bernard: *Via Domine*, 31 ff.; T. H. Darlow: *On Holy Ground*, 225–236; J. H. Jowett: *The Friend on the Road*, 139; C. I. Scofield: as above, 61–68. On verse 12, see G. Campbell Morgan, in the *Westminster Pulpit*, Vol. 6, 1–8; Phillips Brooks: *Sermons for the Church Year*, 18–34; Marcus Dods: *What Is a Christian?* 3; Hugh Black: *Christ's Service of Love*, 243–252. On verse 13, G. C. Morgan, as above, Vol. 10, 177–184. On verse 14, the same, Vol. 2, 265–272; James Hastings: *The Great Texts of the Bible — St. John, 1–12*, 26–68; Marcus Dods: *Footsteps in the Path of Life*, 19 ff.; William Taylor: *The Limitations of Life*, 15–29; John Kelman: *Things Eternal*, 245–249; F. F. Shannon: *The Soul's Atlas*, 52–67.

JOHN 1 : 1. In the beginning was the Word, and the Word was with God, and the Word was God.

THE PROLOGUE OF JOHN'S GOSPEL.

While it is true that the word "prologue," just like the word "eternity," does not occur in this passage, nor in any other Biblical passage, yet the first eighteen verses of John's Gospel have for centuries been designated as the Prologue of this Gospel. The word "prologue" comes from two Greek words meaning "that which goes before a speech," and thus comes to mean, "the preface or introduction to a discourse or performance; a preliminary discourse, preface, preamble."

"Starting with the divine genealogy or eternal divinity of Christ, the Evangelist presents, in a few bold outlines, the progress of revelation from the creation to the incarnation, a sort of miniature photograph of the history of preparation for Christ's coming in the flesh, and states the impression which His workings and personal appearance made upon the unbelieving world and the believing disciples. John the Baptist is mentioned as the representative of the Old Testament revelation which directly prepared the way for the Christian dispensation.

"We have here brought together the characteristic features of the fourth Gospel — its simplicity, sublimity, depth and ideality. We hear the sounds of thunder uttered by the 'son of thunder.' In the whole range of literature, ancient and modern, there is no passage or chapter that can at all compare with this Prologue. It is not poetic in form — yet, like the account of the creation in Genesis, to which it forms the New Testament pendant, it rises, by its calm dignity, simplicity and grandeur, to more than poetic beauty. The theme so far transcends the boundaries of time and sense, that the ordinary arts of rhetoric and poetry are struck with the silence of adoration and awe." — *Philip Schaff*.

A number of different outlines for this Prologue have been suggested, some of them quite radically different from others. Some scholars divide the passage into three parts, — verses 1–5, the eternal existence of Christ and His relation to God and the world; verses 6–13, Christ's activity from creation to the incarnation; verses 14–18, Christ's incarnation and activity in the Christian Church. Others divide the Prologue into two parts, making the period of His historic manifestation and working to begin with verse 6. We purposely have avoided in our own outline a *chronological* division (though we have used it in other places), and have, instead, used the various titles and attributes of Christ as a means of dividing the passage.

I. **CHRIST THE ETERNAL WORD,** vs. 1, 2. 1. **In the beginning.** "In Genesis 1 : 1 it is an act done 'in the beginning'; here it is a Being existing 'in the beginning,' and therefore prior to all beginning. 'In the beginning' here equals 'before the world was' (17 : 5; cf. 17 : 24; Eph. 1 : 4). Contrast 'the beginning of the gospel of Jesus Christ' (Mark 1 : 1), which is the historical beginning of the public ministry of the Messiah. 'The beginning' here is prior to all history." — *A. Plummer*.

Was the Word. The English word *word* here is a translation of the Greek word *Logos*, which "signifies in classical Greek both 'reason' and 'word.' Every word implies a thought. It is impossible to imagine a time when God was without thought.

2. The same was in the beginning with God.
3. All things were made through him; and without him was not anything made that hath been made.

Hence thought must be eternal as the Deity. The translation 'thought' is probably the best equivalent for the Greek term, since it denotes, on the one hand, the faculty of reason, or the thought inwardly conceived in mind; and on the other hand, the thought outwardly expressed through the vehicle of language. The two ideas, thought and speech, are indubitably blended in the term *Logos;* and in every employment of the word in philosophy and Scripture, both notions of thought and its outward expression are intimately connected. John the evangelist uses 'Logos' six times as a designation of the Divine pre-existence of Christ (John 1 : 1, 14; 1 John 1 : 1; Rev. 19 : 13), but he never puts it into the mouth of Christ. The Logos with whom the fourth gospel starts is a *Person.* Readers of the Synoptics had long been familiar with the term 'word of God' as equivalent to the Gospel; but the essential purport of John's Word is Jesus Himself, His Person." — *A. B. D. Alexander.*

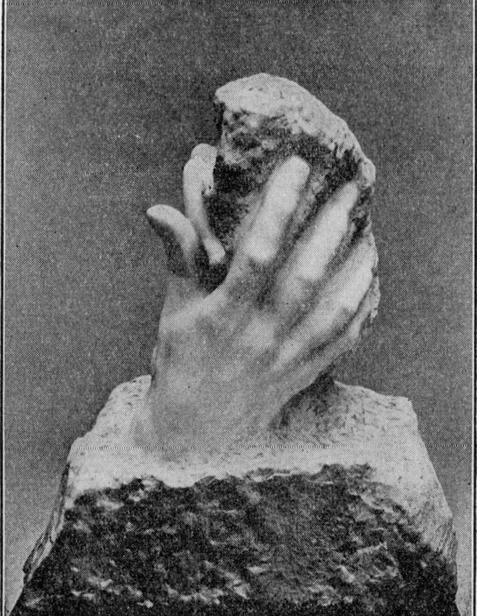
The Hand of God. Rodin.

"A 'word' is a *method of revelation.* By his words, a speaker exhibits both his intellectual caliber and his moral character. By our words, we shall be justified, and by our words, we shall be condemned. And Christ, as the Word, reveals the attributes and perfections of God. How *fully* has Christ revealed God! He displayed His power, He manifested His wisdom, He exhibited His holiness, He made known His grace, He unveiled His heart. In Christ, and nowhere else is God fully and finally told out." — *Arthur W. Pink.*

And the Word was with God. The following lines of Canon Westcott are profound, but should be mastered. "The phrase 'with God' is remarkable. It is found also in Matt. 13 : 56, Mark 6 : 3 and 9 : 19 and 14 : 49, Luke 9 : 41, 1 John 1 : 2. The idea conveyed by it is not that of simple coexistence as of two persons contemplated separately in company (as in 3 : 26, etc.), or united under a common concept (as in Luke 22 : 56), or so to speak, in local relation (as John 17 : 5), but of being directed towards and regulated by that with which the relation is fixed. The personal being of the Word was realized in active intercourse with and in perfect communion with God."

And the Word was God. This amazing declaration does not mean that the Word was the Father, but that the Word partook of the very nature of the Father, so that both the Father and the Son are identical in their nature and therefore both are divine; *i.e.,* Deity belongs to the Son as definitely as to the Father. Of all the verses of the New Testament, this supremely sets forth the deity of Him, Who later became known as Jesus of Nazareth.

2. **The same was in the beginning with God.** "This verse takes up the first two clauses of the preceding verse and combines them. Such recapitulations are characteristic of St. John." — *A. Plummer.*

II. **CHRIST THE CREATOR OF ALL THINGS,** v. 3. 3. **All things were made through him; and without him was not anything made that hath been made.**

4. In him was life; and the life was the light of men.
5. And the light shineth in the darkness; and the darkness apprehended it not.

"Three distinct words are used in the New Testament to convey the conception of creation, (1) to *create* (*ktizein*) and (2) to *make* (*poiein*), in reference to the Creator; and (3) to *become* (*gignesthai*), in reference to that which is created. The first word (Rev. 4 : 2, 10 : 6; Col. 1 : 16, etc.) suggests the idea of design, plan, purpose; the second (Rev. 14 : 7; Mark 10 : 6, etc.), of an actual result or object produced (comp. Eph. 2 : 10); the third, of the law fulfilled in the production of the object. The use of 'become' in verse 14, brings out its force as expressive of the unfolding of a divine order. The Word is described as the mediate Agent of Creation (*through* not *by*). (Cf. Col. 1 : 16; Heb. 1 : 2.)" —*B. F. Westcott.*

The Apostle wishes to make it understood that he who has become our Saviour is nothing less than the divine and personal Being who was associated with God in the work of Creation.

III. **CHRIST THE LIFE,** v. 4 *a*. 4 *a*. **In him was life.** "Life is one of John's characteristic words, used thirty times, denoting the highest blessedness from the creature's point of view. To *live* should mean to have an inexhaustible spring of felicity in one's self. God's life is the joy of His pure Being. The creature's life is the joy of being dependent on and finding its end in God. The end for which John writes is that men may have 'life in Christ's name.' This is the true spiritual and eternal life which consists in communion with God; comprehending all lower forms and phases, whether moral or rational or physical, which answer the purpose of God (cf. 5 : 26; 11 : 25; 14 : 6)." — *George Reith.*

"The only true life here noticed is that which, being eternal, is capable of enjoying, serving, and worshipping, suited to His presence and to be there forever. Believers have life; but it is in the Son, not in them, but in Him." — *Wm. Kelly.*

IV. **CHRIST THE LIGHT OF MEN,** vs. 4 *b*–11. 4 *b*. **And the life was the light of men.** "Here John passes from the relation of the Logos to the world at large and to his relation to men. As God the Father is in the absolute sense life and light (John 1 : 4 and 1 John 1 : 5) so is the Son likewise. Light, is a figurative expression for principle, divine truth both intellectual and moral, in opposition to darkness, which includes error and sin. Christ is not Light simply, but *the* Light, the only true Light." — *J. P. Lange.*

Holman Hunt.
"I am the Light of the World."

5. **And the light shineth in the darkness; and the darkness apprehended it not.** "This action of the Light is not to be limited to any one point. It is continuous from the creation to the consummation of things, though there have been times when it has flashed forth with peculiar splendour. Side by side with the light the darkness appears suddenly and without preparation. The perfect fellowship of man and God has been broken. Man in his self-will has separated, isolated himself. He has made for himself, so to speak, an atmosphere of darkness, by seeking to sever his life from the Source of life. After all that which is without God, apart from Him, is darkness. (Comp. 1 John 1 : 5.) The darkness comes down upon, enwraps men. As applied to light, this sense includes the further notion of overwhelming, eclipsing. The relation of darkness to light is one of essential antagonism." — *B. F. Westcott.*

For other references to darkness, see *e.g.*, John 3 : 19; 8 : 12; 12 : 35; Matt. 4 : 16; Luke 22 : 53; Acts 26 : 18; Romans 2 : 19; Eph. 5 : 8, 11; 6 : 12; Col. 1 : 13;

6. There came a man, sent from God, whose name was John.
7. The same came for witness, that he might bear witness of the light, that all might believe through him.
8. He was not the light, but *came* that he might bear witness of the light.
9. There was the true light, *even the light* which lighteth every man, coming into the world.
10. He was in the world, and the world was made through him, and the world knew him not.

---

and Rev. 16 : 10. The fact that hundreds of millions of people are, even now, living on this earth, nineteen hundred years after the Light of the world appeared among men, without salvation, is overwhelming testimony to the truthfulness of this passage.

6. **There came a man, sent from God, whose name was John.** 7. **The same came for witness, that he might bear witness of the light, that all might believe through him.** 8. **He was not the light, but *came* that he might bear witness of the light.** The writer of the fourth gospel at this point interjects the testimony of the last of Israel's great prophets, the forerunner of the Lord Jesus, John the Baptist, whose unusual and foreannounced birth is set forth so vividly by St. Luke (1 : 5-25, 57-80), and whose early ministry, before the baptism of our Lord, is found in all the Synoptic Gospels (Matt. 3 : 1-12; Mark 1 : 1-8; Luke 3 : 1-20). What the Synoptics say, John does not repeat, and the phrases used by John are not found in the Synoptics. John's testimony turned the thoughts of men to Christ, and, as it were, introduced Christ to Israel. The greatest of all the prophets of the generation of our Lord's advent lived exclusively to exalt, and glorify, and identify as the Lamb of God, the Light which had become incarnate, and was now about to shed His beneficent rays throughout the world, a world fearfully groping about in the midnight of the doubt, the wickedness, the skepticism and the despair of western civilization as it existed when our Lord appeared on earth.

John the Baptist. Titian.

9. **There was the true light, *even the light* which lighteth every man, coming into the world.** " The construction of this verse has been much disputed. Is the phrase ' coming into the world ' to be taken with ' every man,' as many ancient versions, and most of the ancient commentators affirm, or does it belong to the ' true light '? It is very questionable whether St. John ever spoke in any way to support the first of these interpretations. It seems then that we must join the phrase ' coming into the world ' with ' the true light.' But even then, three ways of rendering are apparently open to us. The phrase might mean, ' at its coming into the world '; the word ' coming ' might seem to be used as a word of future, that is, referring to one who was yet to come, but this would imply that the true Light had not yet come, which is manifestly not correct. We are then driven to the only legitimate rendering, which is to take 'was coming ' as equivalent to an imperfect ' came '; that is, at the time when John bore this witness, the true Light which lighteth every man came into the world." — *Henry Alford.*

" Out of Christ, there is no mental, moral, or spiritual illumination for men, and all any man has, whether recognized or not, is of Christ." — *George Reith.*

10. **He was in the world, and the world was made through him, and the world knew him not.** " Throughout the New Testament, it is most important to dis-

11. He came unto his own, and they that were his own received him not.
12. But as many as received him, to them gave he the right to become children of God, *even* to them that believe on his name:

---

tinguish the various meanings of 'the world.' It means (1) 'the universe'; (Rom. 1 : 20); (2) 'the earth' (v. 9; Matt. 4 : 8); (3) 'the inhabitants of the earth' (v. 29; 4 : 24); (4) 'those outside the church,' alienated from God (12 : 31; 14 : 17) and frequently in this verse, the meaning slips from (2) to (4)." — *A. Plummer.*

"This verse describes the unbelief of the whole world before Christ's incarnation. He 'was in the world' invisibly, before He was born of the Virgin Mary, as in the days of Noah. He was to be seen in His works and in His providential government of all things, if men had only had eyes to see Him. And yet, the very world which He had made, the work of His hands, did not acknowledge, believe, or obey Him. It knew Him not. At Athens, Paul found an altar 'to the unknown God.'" — *J. C. Ryle.*

11. **He came unto his own, and they that were his own received him not.** The phrase "his own" has in it a neuter noun, and is translated variously. Westcott says "to his own home." Others, "to his own things." In the second clause "his own" contains a masculine noun, and means "his own people," that is, the people of Israel.

"He came unto His own, land if you will, home if you will; or in the larger sense which reveals the economy and purpose of God, to His own creation; and His own people — in the midst of His own creation, those to whom after the flesh He did belong, those who constituted God's elect people for the purpose of revelation and who had so disastrously failed — received Him not. He came descended from David according to Jewish genealogy, to exercise His ministry among His own, these chosen people for the purposes of the Divine economy. With what result? 'His own received Him not.' . . . They tried to entangle Him in His talk, and His very own, the men of Nazareth, would fain have thrust Him headlong down the hill and destroyed Him; and at last, to make the whole tragedy brief in reverent statement, they delivered Him to Roman rule, and clamoured for His blood. The end, on the human side, of that which we celebrate at Christmas, the coming into human history of the Child Who lay in a manger, was the Cross." — *G. Campbell Morgan.*

Cliff above Nazareth.

V. **CHRIST THE ONLY ONE WHO CAN MAKE SINNERS TO BE THE SONS OF GOD,** vs. 12, 13. 12. **But as many as received him, to them gave he the right to become children of God, *even* to them that believe on his name.** "There were some who received Him. There were some who believed in His name. There were those who turned and followed Him imperfectly, but they followed; falteringly, but they followed; unworthily, but they followed! What of them? 'To them gave He the right to become children of God.'" — *G. Campbell Morgan.*

"Children are such as partake their father's nature. That is the infinite, profound mystery of the thing resulting from the coming of our Lord. He gave men the right to become children of God. He made those to whom He gave that right, partakers — and do not be afraid of the word, it is Peter's word in his letter — partakers of the Divine nature.

"Are you a child of God? Then already you are a partaker of His nature. I state it so because it is an amazing declaration. Sometimes the heart is tempted to be fearful and afraid in the presence of such revelations or statements of Scripture, because we are so conscious of being unlike God. Think again, and always think patiently of your own life as a believer, with God's patience. What is the Divine nature? It is essentially love. It is therefore holiness. It is also infinite wisdom. Every child of God partakes of these facts of the Divine nature. Every child of God becomes in measure love-centred, in measure holy, in measure wise with the wisdom of eternity." — *G. Campbell Morgan.*

13. Who were born, not of blood, nor of the will of the flesh, nor of the will of man, but of God.

14. And the Word became flesh, and dwelt among us (and we beheld his glory, glory as of the only begotten from the Father), full of grace and truth.

The phrase " believe on his name " occurs over thirty times in the Fourth Gospel. " Faith in or on Christ is the receiving or resting on Christ as God has given Him to men for salvation, implying the intellectual belief, the moral attitude of trust, the outflow of the heart's affection, and the act of volition by which surrender is made of the whole man over to Him (3 : 15). The element of personal trust in a personal Lord is the strongest (see 20 : 28), and this may be perfect when the complete intellectual conception of Christ is not so; but the more perfect the apprehension of Christ, His person, and work, the more unreserved the pure committal of all to Him. A man's *name* distinguishes him from others, and should indicate character and position, name and nature corresponding. God's name does so fully. Hence to believe in His ' name ' is to believe on Himself as known to us through the name He has revealed Himself by." — *George Reith.*

13. **Who were born, not of blood, nor of the will of the flesh, nor of the will of man, but of God.** " The threefold negation is an emphatic exclusion of all human and earthly origin and influence in every shape, — descent, privilege, will-power or natural attractions. Not by ordinary birth or by force of will can any man become a child of God. The chief idea here is that of the free grace of the Saviour, who conferred this wondrous dignity on all who received Him, whatever their past was; and who, though they might not be able to say they were born of Abraham, yet could say they were *born of God*, in the very act and fact of their reception of Jesus." — *George Reith.*

VI. **CHRIST INCARNATE,** vs. 14–17. 14. **And the Word became flesh.** " He became something which He had not been before; yet as it is implied that in ' flesh ' He revealed the life of God, He continued all He was. It was a voluntary act, not rendered necessary by any existing relation. And He came into flesh, not out of it. Human nature did not blossom into this flower; flesh did not become the Word, but the Word became flesh. God and man are indissolubly linked in His Person. *Flesh* is human nature in its entirety, though viewed on its outward and material side, and as opposed to the Divine nature, suggesting what is changing, weak, frail, corruptible; a use of the term borrowed from the Old Testament: not as Calvin, to indicate the *meanness* of the Incarnation — rather its reality and completeness. See 1 John 1 : 1; hence, *man* in full sense; cp. 1 John 4 : 2; 2 John 7; Rom. 1 : 3; and 1 Tim. 3 : 16. The Logos became not a *man*, but *man*." — *George Reith.*

And dwelt among us. " The Greek word here translated *dwelt*, means to pitch tent, to take up abode, and occurs in the New Testament in John's writings only, here, and four times in the Apocalypse; where it is used *twice* of the dwellers in heaven, 12 : 12; 13 : 6; and twice of God Himself, 7 : 15. The Greek word is the same as the Hebrew *shachan*, from which is derived the familiar term *shechinah*. The Logos dwelling in flesh was the fulfilment of the line of great promises; in fact, the fulfilment of the end for which the old economy existed, that God should take up His permanent abode with men, and be their God, Lev. 26 : 11 f.; Ezek. 37 : 27; and see Rev. 21 : 3. Our Lord's human nature is the ark of the New Testament, uniting God and man forever." — *George Reith.*

And we beheld his glory. " From time to time the Lord manifested His glory in the wilderness (Exod. 16 : 10; 24 : 16; 40 : 34, etc.); in the Temple of Solomon (1 Kings 8 : 11); and to the prophets (Isa. 6 : 3. Comp. Ch. 12 : 41; Ezek. 1 : 28, etc.; Acts 7 : 55); and even so Christ's glory flashed forth at crises of His ministry. It is not possible for us to define exactly in what way this majesty was shewn, by signs, by words, by events. Comp. Luke 9 : 31 f. It is enough that the Evangelist records his own experience. The Son of Man had a glory which corresponded with His filial relation to the Father, even when He had laid aside His divine glory (17 : 5)." — *B. F. Westcott.*

Glory as of. " This glory of the Incarnate Word is described as being ' glory as of an only son from his father,' a glory, that is, of one who represents another, being derived from him, and of the same essence with him." — *B. F. Westcott.*

The only begotten from the Father. Christ is One only Son, the One to whom the title belongs, in a sense completely unique and singular, as distinguished from that in which there are many children of God. The use of the word elsewhere in the New

Testament to describe an only child (Luke 7 : 12; 8 : 42; 9 : 38; Heb. 11 : 17) brings out this sense completely. — *B. F. Westcott.*

Full of grace and truth. " Among the Greeks *grace* included the conceptions both of personal charm — outward and inward, and of a generous, openhearted disposition. As used in the New Testament it is transfigured, and signifies the free, undeserved inclining of God to men, especially in the gospel of His Son; love uncaused by our love, mercy forgiving sins, and the free favour which takes no account of merit or demerit. *Truth* is not the faithfulness or veracity of God, but the perfect disclosure of His will for men, which is at the same time the disclosure of Himself (v. 18). This is full, compared with the partial views given in the old economy (v. 17); for all truth is embodied in Christ, who is the sum and substance of every prophecy, and therefore Himself ' the Truth ' (14 : 6). And it is reality and light contrasted with the plausible falsehoods, the darkness of this world, 8 : 12, 32; 1 John 2 : 20 f. Hence also it is truth in the sphere of the will, *i.e.* holiness, as well as in that of the intellect. Christ is full of grace for those who deserve nothing, and can claim and do nothing through sin; and He is full of truth for men who are dark and ignorant both in mind and morals. Truth is the light that exposes; grace the love that heals. See Rev. 3 : 7." — *George Reith.*

In point of time, thirty years elapse between the advent of Christ referred to in verse 14, and the testimony of John the Baptist to Christ, which, beginning here in verse 15, continues down through verse 36. Some harmonies of the Gospel make the prologue of John to extend through verse 18, but we believe it is more accurate to conceive of the prologue as ending with verse 14. (For other accounts of the early ministry of John the Baptist, see Matt. 3 : 1–12; Mark 1 : 1–8; Luke 3 : 1–20.)

In the four verses which conclude our lesson for this day, John says six things about the Lord Jesus: (1) That Christ is Himself to be preferred to the person of the Baptist, and must, in the minds of men, be set above or before him. (2) That Christ was in existence long before the Baptist. He was before Abraham, indeed he was before the foundation of the world. (3) That of His fulness we have all received (Comp. Col. 1 : 19; 2 : 9; Eph. 1 : 21; 3 : 19). As Christ possesses all the fulness of God, the Church and its various members are in turn filled with Him, and thus with His divine fulness. A cup of water is not an ocean of water, but contains the water that is in the ocean; so the believer is by no means the Son of God, but still he does have within him the life of God and becomes a child of God. (4) That grace and truth came through Christ, in contradistinction to the law that was given by Moses — this phrase has been expounded in our treatment of verse 14. (5) That Christ, the only begotten Son of God, is in the bosom of the Father. " The image is used of the closest and tenderest of human relationships of mother and child (Num. 11 : 12), and of husband and wife (Deut. 13 : 6), and also of friends reclining side by side at a feast (comp. 13 : 23) and so describes the ultimate fellowship of love. The exact form of the original words is remarkable. The phrase is not strictly ' in the bosom,' but ' into the bosom.' Thus there is the combination (as it were) of rest and motion, of a continuous relation, with the realization of it (comp. 1 : 1). The ' bosom of the Father ' (like heaven) is a state and not a place. It is more natural to take the words as an absolute description of the nature of the Son, so that the participle will be timeless. In fact the Ascension of Christ is essentially connected with the divine glory which he had ' before the foundation of the world.' " — *B. F. Wescott.*

VII. **CHRIST THE REVEALER OF THE FATHER,** v. 18. " He hath declared him." The word here translated declared is from a Greek root meaning *to lead the way*, preceded by a preposition meaning *forth*, and thus, originally, " to lead forth," and from this, ' to recount,' or ' to interpret,' to ' translate.' From this Greek word directly comes our word *exegesis*, meaning, an interpretation or explanation. " A form of this word was used by the Greeks of the expounder of oracles, of dreams, of omens, or sacred rites. John's meaning is that the Word revealed or manifested or interpreted the Father to men. The word occurs only here in John's writings. Wycliffe renders it ' He hath told out.' " — *M. R. Vincent.*

How many different titles do you find in these eighteen verses for the Lord Jesus Christ? How many different things has Christ accomplished according to these verses? In how many different ways is Christ in this Prologue revealed to be infinitely above mankind, even the highest type of men? In what primary way is Christ shown here also to be a true man? From a careful study of this Prologue, how many things are revealed here as being needed by man and incapable of being obtained except through Christ? Why does the testimony of John the Baptist con-

cerning the Messiah carry so much authority? Are the primary words of this passage, e.g., Light, Life, Truth, Grace, words that are of fundamental importance for men? In how many different ways is the grace of God toward or in Jesus Christ revealed in these verses?

LESSON II. — January 10.

JESUS INSTRUCTS A GREAT TEACHER. — John 3 : 1–16.

GOLDEN TEXT. — ***For God so loved the world, that he gave his only begotten Son, that whosoever believeth on him should not perish, but have eternal life.*** JOHN 3 : 16.

Devotional Reading: 1 John 3 : 1–10.
Beginner Topic: MATTHEW'S COMPANY.
Lesson Material: John 3 : 1–16; Luke 3 : 27–32; Mark 2 : 15.
Memory Verse: Jehovah is good to all. Psalm 145 : 9.
Primary Topic: NICODEMUS' FRIENDLY TEACHER.
Lesson Material: John 3 : 1–16.
Memory Verse: We know that thou art a teacher come from God. John 3 : 2.
Junior Topic: TWO FRIENDLY TEACHERS.
Lesson Material: John 3 : 1–16.
Memory Verse: Give diligence to present thyself approved unto God, a workman that needeth not to be ashamed, handling aright the word of truth. 2 Timothy 2 : 15.
Intermediate and Senior Topic: LEARNING FROM JESUS.
Topic for Young People and Adults: WHAT JESUS TAUGHT NICODEMUS.

THE TEACHER AND HIS CLASS.

The Younger Classes might be asked what kind of people they are to whom others would go for help; *e.g.*, a person ill would go to one who was skilled in diagnosing disease and capable of relieving pain, a good doctor; a person in financial difficulties would go to one who he thinks would have sufficient means for relieving him of his distress; another, who had been offered a famous painting, with the assurance that it was genuinely done by some great artist, *e.g.*, Rembrandt, would go to an expert in art for advice; one who wanted to become a master in music would sit at the feet of the finest music teacher available. So in our lesson, Nicodemus, already a man learned in the law, and living a truly righteous life, with deep longings for a richer spiritual life than he then possessed, went to the only one in all Palestine whom he thought would be able to help him — Jesus of Nazareth.

The Older Classes should have in this lesson one great truth emphasized, so rarely spoken of today, namely, the absolute necessity, if we are to be true Christians, of being born again, of having an experience of regeneration. This is the first time this great truth is mentioned in the Gospels, but throughout the New Testament it is found to be a fundamental aspect of Christian salvation. Many listening to this lesson will be hearing this truth for the first time in their lives. Let the teacher state at the very first that what Christ emphasized by introducing the passage, "Verily, verily," is something to which we are obligated to give the most careful consideration.

THE LESSON IN ITS SETTING.

Time. — The early part of April, A.D. 27.

Place. — Probably the city of Jerusalem.

THE PLAN OF THE LESSON.

SUBJECT: The Absolute Necessity for Every Man Being Born Again Who Will Ever Enter the Kingdom of God.

I. NICODEMUS' CONVICTION REGARDING JESUS, VS. 1, 2.
1. His high position.
2. His secret visit to Jesus.
3. His testimony concerning Christ.

II. CHRIST INSTRUCTS NICODEMUS AS TO THE NECESSITY OF BEING BORN AGAIN, VS. 3–12.
1. Christ's declaration concerning regeneration, v. 3.
2. Nicodemus' natural question, v. 4.
3. Jesus further expounds the truth of the new birth, vs. 5–8.
4. Nicodemus confesses his inability to comprehend this truth, v. 9.
5. Jesus' rebuke of Nicodemus, vs. 10–12.

III. CHRIST'S FURTHER TESTIMONY CONCERNING HIMSELF, VS. 13–16.

1. He came down from heaven, v. 13.
2. He was, even while on earth, present in heaven, v. 13.
3. The necessity for His death, v. 14.
4. The purpose of His death, vs. 15, 16.

THE TEACHER'S LIBRARY.

In addition to the standard lives of Christ, and the more important commentaries on John's Gospel, lists of which will be found in the bibliography in the Introduction to this volume, the following chapters on Nicodemus may be mentioned (we have yet to find for ourselves a complete and thoroughly satisfactory treatment of Nicodemus): A. B. Davidson: *The Called of God*, 249–271; W. M. Clow: *The Day of the Cross*, 355–368 (rather an unfavorable treatment); Alexander Whyte: *Bible Characters, Joseph and Mary to James the Lord's Brother*, 36 ff.; J. C. Morgan; *The Great Physician*, 35–72; L. R. Scarborough: *How Jesus Won Men*, 59–71, 195–199; George Matheson: *The Representative Men of the New Testament*, 109–130; A. T. Robertson: *Some Minor Characters in the New Testament*, 1–12; Adolph Saphir: *Conversion Illustrated by Examples Recorded in the Bible*, 181–216; F. A. Noble: *Typical New Testament Conversions*, 251–269; W. Boyd Carpenter: *The Son of Man Among the Sons of Men*, 187–208; James Jeffry: *The Personal Ministry of the Son of Man*, 47–59; Alfred Lee: *Eventful Nights in Bible History*, 236–249, James Hastings: *The Greater Men and Women of the Bible*, Vol. 5, *Mary to Simon*, 370–384; Norman MacLeod: *Night Scenes of Scripture*, 91–104; J. G. Greenhough: *Men of the New Testament*, 131–140; T. E. Miller: *Portraits of Men of the New Testament*, 23–34; L. A. Banks: *Great Saints of the Bible*, 276 ff.; J. D. Jones: *The Hope of the Gospel*, 126–138. There is one entire book devoted to a treatment of Nicodemus by John Reid: *Jesus and Nicodemus* (1906). By far the best article in any Bible dictionary on Nicodemus is the one by A. R. Fausset, in his *Englishmen's Critical and Expository Encyclopedia* (1884), 508, 509.

On the subject of regeneration as taught in this passage, see R. A. Torrey: *Fundamental Doctrines of the Christian Faith*, 206–224, and *Voice of God for the Present Hour*, 125–136; G. C. Morgan: *The Spirit of God*, 213–225; and, if it is available to the readers of this volume, by all means consult the 21 sermons on regeneration in Timothy Dwight's *Theology Examined and Defended*, 390–473.

E. Bickersteth: *The Spirit of Life*, 120–127; F. E. Marsh: *Emblems of the Holy Spirit*, 160–177; F. B. Meyer: *Five Musts of the Christian Life*, 9–20; J. R. Smith: *The Teaching of the Gospel of John*, 236–240; and the excellent article by J. Denney, "Regeneration," in James Hastings: *Dictionary of Christ and the Gospels*, Vol. 2, 485–489.

There is a vast amount of sermonic material on the verses of our lesson of which, we believe, the following is the more important: On verse 1, G. C. Morgan: *Westminster Pulpit*, Vol. 2, 393–400; on verse 2, A. Maclaren: *Expositions of Holy Scripture, John, 1–8*, 143–154; on verse 3, J. H. Jowett: *Brooks by the Traveler's Way*, 175–188; Phillips Brooks: *Seeking Life*, 193–209; F. W. Boreham: *A Handful of Stars*, 149–159; D. L. Moody: *The Way to God*, 38 ff.; A. J. Gordon: *Ecce Venit*, 85 ff.; James Hastings: *The Great Texts of the Bible, St. John, 1–12*, 148–180; D. J. Burrell: *The Verilies of Jesus*, 1–6. On verse 7 see A. C. Dixon: *Milk and Meat*, 1 ff.; Henry Drummond: *The Ideal Life*, 212–226; Gypsy Smith: *As Jesus Passed By*, 45–60. On verse 8 see H. P. Liddon: *University Sermons*, second series, 78–97; J. H. Jowett: *God Our Contemporary*, 181–193; A. Maclaren, as above, 154–162. On verse 14, D. J. Burrell: *The Gospel of Gladness*, 120 ff.; Joseph Parker: *The City Temple Pulpit*, Vol. 4, 12–18; A. Maclaren, as above; 162–180. On verse 16 see A. Maclaren, the same, 181–188; W. R. Nicoll: *The Lamb of Sacrifice*, 244–260, also, *The Lamb of God*, 21–36; F. W. Boreham: *A Handful of Stars*, 250–261; T. H. Darlow: *The Love of God*, 1–13; J. H. Jowett: *Brooks by the Traveler's Way*, 189–199; B. B. Warfield: *The Saviour of the World*, 103–130.

JOHN 3:1. Now there was a man of the Pharisees, named Nicodemus, a ruler of the Jews:

I. **NICODEMUS' CONVICTION REGARDING JESUS,** John 3:1, 2. George Whitefield wrote in 1752 a letter to his friend, Benjamin Franklin (who was then, and remained throughout his life emphatically an unbeliever), the following admonition: "As I find you growing more and more famous in the learned world, I would recommend to your diligent and unprejudiced study the mystery of the new birth. It is a most important study, and, when mastered, will richly answer all your pains. I bid you, my friend, remember that One, at whose bar we shall both presently appear, hath solemnly declared that without it we shall in no wise see His kingdom." If Benjamin Franklin had given heed to Whitefield's wise words he would have turned first to the passage which forms our lesson today. For some reason, this is the first time in several years that our Lord's conversation with Nicodemus has been assigned as a lesson in the International system.

1. **Now there was a man of the Pharisees, named Nicodemus, a ruler of the Jews.** Nicodemus is never referred to outside of the Gospel of John, but there he appears three times: at the beginning of our Lord's ministry, recorded in this passage; about a year and a half later, when he partially defends the Lord who was being bitterly denounced by his fellow-Pharisees (7:45–52); and, finally, at the end of our Lord's life (19:38–42), when we find him associated with Joseph of Arimathea, "bringing a mixture of myrrh and aloes, about a hundred pounds." Apart from these brief notices we know nothing of this man, but what we do know is significant. First of all, he belonged to the strictest sect of the Jews, the Pharisees, rigid legalists, attempting scrupulously every hour of the day to minutely observe not only the laws found in the books of Moses, but, in addition, the vast traditional, complicated interpretations of these laws which had been added after the close of the Old Testament. He belonged to a bigoted class which normally despised the

2. The same came unto him by night, and said to him, Rabbi, we know that thou art a teacher come from God; for no one can do these signs that thou doest, except God be with him.

Gentiles, counted themselves as the most superior group in the world, looked with more or less disdain upon the ignorant, the poor, and the defeated. They were custodians of the religious rites and legal interpretations of Judaism. Nicodemus, moreover, was a ruler among the Jews, and thus, a member of the Jerusalem Sanhedrin, the highest body in all Jewry, to which no man could be elected until he was forty years old, recognized as a true scholar, as a man of righteous habits, and well-spoken of in the community in which he lived. Thus, Nicodemus by his very position moved among the highest authorities in Israel in his day, an upright man who, as far as human effort went, would be counted as one righteous in the sight of the law. 2 *a*. **The same came unto him by night.** The fact that Nicodemus came to Christ at all, seemingly for instruction, is most significant. He is the only Pharisee who ever did so come to Christ, sympathetically, in the Gospels; later this very group of men would unite with others in condemning Christ to death. That he came not only would imply that he had a high conception of Christ, as we shall shortly see, but that a certain restlessness of soul must have been his experience at this time — a dissatisfaction with legalistic observances, a deep-seated conviction that if any one in Palestine could help him, this man Jesus could. That he came by night does not of necessity mean that he was timid, though most commentators so interpret. The late Bishop Boyd Carpenter suggestively remarks that " all his associations, opinions, and ideas are saturated with the Pharisaic thought of the day. His settled position, his place in public esteem, his habits of mind, are all more or less hostile to the influence of Christ. Natural prejudice, local jealousy, early training, and personal temperament are all obstacles in the way of the victory of Christ. . . . " Speculativeness, which was thoughtful, would suspect any teaching from an ignorant and uncultivated quarter like Galilee. Men of speculative mood are seldom without that fastidiousness which is prejudiced in favor of teaching which originates in the acknowledged centers of light. It naturally prefers opinions which spring from educated sources. It looks askance at doctrines which find favor among those who are deemed illiterate and vulgar." Dr. Caie, however, suggests that " night was practically the only time open to him for a calm and uninterrupted conversation." 2 *b*. **And said to him, Rabbi, we know that thou art a teacher come from God; for no one can do these signs that thou doest, except God be with him.** The word *rabbi* which Nicodemus uses was a title of late date, not having come into use till the time of Herod the Great. Like the word *master*, it comes from a root meaning *great*, and, on the lips of Nicodemus, was in itself the highest possible tribute he at that time could pay to our Lord. More than a master, Nicodemus recognizes him as a teacher come from God. In this he was right, but his conception of Christ was not

Christ and Nicodemus.

3. Jesus answered and said unto him, Verily, verily, I say unto thee, Except one be born anew, he cannot see the kingdom of God.

adequate. " Nicodemus was acquainted with the law, a student of the prophets; he had listened to the last voice of prophecy which had so startled Judæa, that of John the Baptist, and he was determined that there should be no voice to which he would not pay attention. His estimate of Jesus was that he was able to teach him something beyond what he already knew." — *G. Campbell Morgan.* Nicodemus was driven to this conclusion by his knowledge of the miracles which Christ had performed up to this time. It is noteworthy to observe that as far as our records go, we know of only one miracle performed before this conversation took place — that of changing the water into wine at Cana (2 : 1–11). Nicodemus thought that what he needed was more teaching: before the hour is closed he will know that what Jesus insists that he needs is not more knowledge but a new birth, complete regeneration.

II. **CHRIST INSTRUCTS NICODEMUS AS TO THE NECESSITY OF BEING BORN AGAIN,** John 3 : 3–12. Whether we believe the division is too fanciful or not, it is interesting at least to recall the threefold way in which Dr. G. Campbell Morgan divides the conversation we are now to study. He says that in verse 3 we have the record of these two persons face to face; in verses 4–8, we have them meeting mind to mind; and in verses 9–21, heart to heart. 3. **Jesus answered and said unto him, Verily, verily, I say unto thee, Except one be born anew, he cannot see the kingdom of God.** As we begin the study of this passage, let us go into the middle of this verse and take out one word and look at it for a moment, the word *anew.* In some versions the word is translated *again.* In the margin of the Revised Version (and in many other translations) the word is translated *from above.* Westcott insists that the last is the correct one, pointing out that in all other places in John's Gospel where the word occurs, it must so be translated (3 : 31; 19 : 11, 23). In favor of the other rendering *again,* or *anew,* Vincent reminds us that, "*from above* does not describe the fact but the nature of the new birth, which in the logical order would be stated after the fact but which is first announced if we render *from above.* If we translate *anew,* the logical order is preserved. Furthermore, Nicodemus clearly understood the word as meaning *again,* since in verse 4 he translated it *anew* a second time. Finally, it seems strange that Nicodemus should have been startled by the idea of the birth from heaven." We hold then to the word *anew* in our interpretation. What do we mean by a man being born anew, or born again? To begin with, it means something tremendously radical. What we are by nature we are because of what we were when *born.* At birth our sex is settled, the very frame of our body is already determined. No doubt our very temperament, our capacities, our habits, our inclinations, are all given to us at birth, at least fundamentally; indeed our very appearance. To be born *again* at least implies an absolutely new beginning, not a reformation of life, not a turning over of a new leaf, not the addition of some one new attribute or aspect or capacity, but something so radical that by it we are going to be something altogether different from what we have been. Of course, anyone knows that we cannot be born the second time physically. Therefore the reference here is spiritual, a rebirth not of body, but of soul, and mind, and character. Again, we should notice here and in verse 7 the universal inclusiveness and absolute necessity for such a miracle as this, if one is to be a member of the kingdom of God. No one is excepted, and no one can substitute something else for this tremendous reality. As Dr. R. A. Torrey years ago said, " Reformation will not take the place of the new birth. Morality is not enough — Nicodemus had morality but he needed something more, something deeper, something that underlies abiding morality. Baptism will not take the place of the new birth. Religion will not take the place of the new birth. Nicodemus was religious but he was unsaved until he was born again. Generosity in giving will not take the place of the new birth. Conviction of sin will not take the place of the new birth. Culture will not take the place of the new birth even though it be ethical culture or religious culture. Prayer will not take the place of the new birth. A man may spend hours a day in prayer and yet be a lost man."

Why is this miracle of the new birth so necessary? It is necessary because of that concerning which our Lord is speaking, namely, the kingdom of God. The kingdom of God is something spiritual, something holy, where God reigns, where God is loved, and obeyed, and worshiped, and honored, where His glory is lived for. It is not

4. Nicodemus saith unto him, How can a man be born when he is old? can he enter a second time into his mother's womb, and be born?

5. Jesus answered, Verily, verily, I say unto thee, Except one be born of water and the Spirit, he cannot enter into the kingdom of God.

6. That which is born of the flesh is flesh; and that which is born of the Spirit is spirit.

7. Marvel not that I said unto thee, Ye must be born anew.

---

necessary to be born again to make money. It is not necessary to be born again to have a high position in a university. It is not necessary to be born again to be a man of great political power. These achievements pertain to the earth, to the flesh, to the things that are visible, while the kingdom of God has to do with the Spirit, with the things invisible, with the heaven of God and the laws of heaven, the rule of heaven, an ultimate eternal abiding in heaven where the kingdom of God is perfected. Man is a fallen creature. By nature he is wicked; by nature he is rebellious; by nature he is without God, and without hope in the world; by nature he is an anarchist in the realm of moral law, an enemy of God, serving himself. No power on earth can change that nature, no power on earth has ever been able to change that nature, and the man with these tendencies and these characteristics, without the ability to change himself, or to be changed by some one else, will never have a right to enter the kingdom of God. He needs a new nature. He needs a complete regeneration of life. He needs what Jesus spoke of as being born again; not a second birth like his first, but a higher and different birth, the first one being of his parents, the second one being from God. This great profound doctrine of regeneration is frequently spoken of elsewhere by the Apostle John (1 John 2 : 29; 3 : 9; 4 : 7; 5 : 1–4, 18). It is referred to by the Apostle Peter (1 Pet. 1 : 23). It is frequently and in various ways referred to by the Apostle Paul (2 Cor. 5 : 17; Gal. 6 : 15; Eph. 2 : 10; 4 : 24; Titus 3 : 5).

4. **Nicodemus saith unto him, How can a man be born when he is old? can he enter a second time into his mother's womb, and be born?** "Nicodemus said to Him not that it was unnecessary, but that it was impossible. The very way in which Nicodemus stated his difficulty reveals the fact that at least he had grasped the profound significance of the word of the Teacher. That inquiry of Nicodemus reveals his recognition of the unity of personality. How can a man be born again? To begin again means to undo all the past, and what a man is today is the result of all the past. A man's personality is not merely his person, but it is the whole fact of him; not a day, not a moment, but the sum total of all the moments, hours, years. Christ said, Man must begin again. Nicodemus said, How are you going to undo the past, 'when he is old'? How can you take hold of a man and make him other than he is?" — *G. Campbell Morgan.*

5. **Jesus answered, Verily, verily, I say unto thee, Except one be born of water and the Spirit, he cannot enter into the kingdom of God.** 6. **That which is born of the flesh is flesh; and that which is born of the Spirit is Spirit.** 7. **Marvel not that I said unto thee, Ye must be born anew.** There has been no dispute among commentators and theologians as to the meaning of being born of the Spirit, all recognizing that this refers to none other than the Holy Spirit of God, the Third Person of the Trinity. But to what does "being born of water" refer? The editor is well aware that many will disagree with the interpretation here presented, but at least they will admit that almost all the outstanding authorities are unanimous in believing that the primary reference here is to baptism, though not exclusively to water baptism; nor do we mean to say that there is any regenerating power in the rite of water baptism. I think the words of the late Professor J. Ritchie Smith, of Princeton Theological Seminary (and therefore *not* of the Baptist communion), are as sane and sensible as any that have been written on this point. "The reference to baptism is too plain to be mistaken, though many attempts have been made to evade it. The natural sense of the words, which would suggest itself at once to Nicodemus, must not be forsaken unless some other meaning is clearly required by the course of the narrative or by the general character of New Testament teaching. If, then, water signifies baptism, in what sense are men born of water and the Spirit?

"Baptism is the sign and seal of repentance and the forgiveness of sins. The ordinance is not essential to regeneration, but that which it represents is essential.

8. The wind bloweth where it will, and thou hearest the voice thereof, but knowest not whence it cometh, and whither it goeth: so is every one that is born of the Spirit.

9. Nicodemus answered and said unto him, How can these things be?

10. Jesus answered and said unto him, Art thou the teacher of Israel, and understandest not these things?

11. Verily, verily, I say unto thee, We speak that which we know, and bear witness of that which we have seen; and ye receive not our witness.

12. If I told you earthly things and ye believe not, how shall ye believe if I tell you heavenly things?

The symbol is put for the fact. The old man dies in baptism, the new man is born of the Spirit. The primary reference of the words is probably to the baptism of John, though whether that or Christian baptism is meant is not important, for the significance of the rite is virtually the same. John preached ‘ the baptism of repentance ’; ‘ repent and be baptized,’ said Peter, ‘ unto the remission of your sins.’ And here, too, observe that baptism is associated with the work of the Spirit. ‘ Repent and be baptized . . . and ye shall receive the gift of the Holy Ghost ’ (Acts 2 : 38). The words mean then, unless men repent and are renewed by the Spirit, they cannot see the kingdom of God.

“ The same thought is presented in Titus 3 : 5, ‘ He saved us by the washing of regeneration and the renewing of the Holy Spirit ’ (cf. Eph. 5 : 26, ‘ Having cleansed it [the church] by the washing of the water with the word ’). In all these instances the reference to baptism is too obvious to be disregarded. Yet nowhere is it taught that baptism is essential to salvation.” And yet, the editor believes the last passage Professor Smith quotes (Eph. 5 : 26) only remotely refers to baptism, but emphatically to the cleansing power of the Word of God, and this is what many believe “ born of water ” must refer to.

8. **The wind bloweth where it will, and thou hearest the voice thereof, but knowest not whence it cometh, and whither it goeth : so is every one that is born of the Spirit.** The Greek word here translated *wind*, the word *pneuma*, is also and always the same word translated numerous times in the New Testament as *spirit.* “ Just as the power of the wind is beyond dispute by the evidences of its blowing that appeal to the senses, while the law of its coming and going abides a mystery, so the fact of the regenerating power of the Holy Spirit is proved by the phenomena of grace, while all the sacred mystery of its operation is beyond the discovery of any human mind.” — *G. Campbell Morgan.*

9. **Nicodemus answered and said unto him, How can these things be ?** 10. **Jesus answered and said unto him, Art thou the teacher of Israel, and understandest not these things ?** 11. **Verily, verily, I say unto thee, we speak that which we know, and bear witness of that which we have seen ; and ye receive not our witness.** The question of Nicodemus, “ How can these things be? ” goes deeper than the first question he asked, and the answer to it will occupy Christ throughout the rest of the discourse we are now studying — an answer which will lead straight to the cross. Note especially the significance of the article *the*, which is not to be found in the Authorized Version — “ *the* teacher of Israel.” If he was the outstanding teacher of Israel of his day, he ought to understand the things that the teacher come from God was uttering. In verse 11 we ought not to ignore the plural use of the first person “ we,” repeated three times, and the pronoun “ our ” used once. It may be He was referring to His testimony, and the testimony of the Holy Spirit, but probably by the use of this pronoun He meant to include all those who knew by experience the meaning of the new birth of which He was now speaking.

12. **If I told you earthly things and ye believe not, how shall ye believe if I tell you heavenly things ?** “ Here the phrase *earthly things* will mark those facts and phenomena of the higher life as a class which have their seat and manifestation on earth: which belong in their realization to our present existence: which are seen in their consequences, like the issue of birth: which are sensible in their effects, like the action of the wind: which are a beginning and a prophecy, and not a fulfillment. Heavenly things refers to those truths which belong to a higher order, which are in heaven, and are brought down thence to earth as they come back to men. Such was the full revelation of the Son, involving the redemption of the world and the

13. And no one hath ascended into heaven, but he that descended out of heaven, *even* the Son of man, who is in heaven.
14. And as Moses lifted up the serpent in the wilderness, even so must the Son of man be lifted up;
15. That whosoever believeth may in him have eternal life.

reunion of man with God, which is indicated in the three following verses." — *B. F. Westcott.*

III. **CHRIST'S FURTHER TESTIMONY ABOUT HIMSELF,** John 3 : 13–16.
13. **And no one hath ascended into heaven, but he that descended out of heaven, *even* the Son of man, who is in heaven.** That our Lord came down out of heaven, and this at the time of the incarnation, is frequently referred to in this Gospel, *e.g.*, 6 : 32 ff., 42; etc. " The phrase is used of the manifestation of God in the Old Testament (Exod. 19 : 11 ff.; Num. 11 : 17, 25; 12 : 5). The exact form of expression is very remarkable. It preserves the continuity of the Lord's personality and yet does not confound His natures." — *B. F. Westcott.* Some believe that the phrase " who is in heaven " is an early gloss and does not belong to the original narrative as John wrote it. If the phrase is genuine, then it would be similar to the phrase in 1 : 18, " who is in the bosom of the Father," indicating the kind of existence which Christ as the divine Son has ever had and continues to have. " The natural life of man, though derived from God, is not the life of God, which can only be quickened in us by the Holy Spirit. This great change is therefore not merely the improvement of any power or grace or gift which we naturally have: not merely amendment of life, not merely abandoning a sin. Flesh may be washed and adorned; but it is flesh still, and no matter whether flesh of Jew or Gentile. The whole man must be transformed: mind, heart, and will. And the Agent of transformation is the Spirit of God Himself acting directly and immediately on the spirit of man. *Born of the Spirit.* Hence such expressions: 'a new creature'; 'the new man'; 'the spiritual man'; see 2 Corinthians 5 : 17; Galatians 6 : 15; Ephesians 4 : 23; 1 Peter 1 : 23. Nothing, in fact, more striking can be said of it than Jesus here says: a new birth — a passing from one state of existence to another: from non-existence to existence (Hos. 2 : 23); from the law of sin and death to the law of the spirit of life in Christ Jesus. The new life may be feeble at first, growing very gradually; still it is new life, and will come to perfection in its time. It is not on a perfect state Jesus lays stress: it is on the kind of state the man is in; on the character of the life that is there, and not the vigor of it. As a matter of fact, in the regenerate there is always more or less of the power of the flesh; just as in the unregenerate there are often movements and strivings of the Spirit." — *George Reith.*

"As Moses Lifted up the Serpent in the Wilderness."

14. **And as Moses lifted up the serpent in the wilderness, even so must the Son of man be lifted up;** 15. **that whosoever believeth may in him have eternal life.** The reference here is to Numbers 21 : 5–9.

16. For God so loved the world, that he gave his only begotten Son, that whosoever believeth on him should not perish, but have eternal life.

" Jesus explains the nature and mode of this redemption by the lifting up of the serpent of brass in the wilderness to cure the Israelites bitten by the fiery serpent. . . . The serpent of brass transfixed on the pole meant the taking away of the cause of death by an act of divine judgment; it was the image of the thing that wrought their ruin, itself thereby brought to ruin. It said both that God was delivering them, and that He was delivering them *in such a way*. So the Son of Man lifted on the cross is at once the representation of man's destruction and sin, and of the divine judgment on sin by which sin is taken away. The crucifixion of the Son of God was the crowning act of human ungodliness; it was at the same time the descent of the curse on the Son of Man (man's one true representative) on account of sin, and so its complete removal; cp. 2 Corinthians 5: 21, ' He hath made him to be sin for us who knew no sin,' etc., and Galatians 3 : 13, ' Christ hath redeemed us from the curse of the law, having become a curse for us.' The cross is the symbol of God's salvation, but of salvation *in such a way*." — *George Reith.*

16. **For God so loved the world, that he gave his only begotten Son, that whosoever believeth on him should not perish, but have eternal life.** In the *British Weekly* for August 28, 1924, a small paragraph informed us that on the Sunday previous, the sainted F. B. Meyer, visiting in the Isle of Man, in preaching from this verse in the Wesleyan Methodist Church, in Ramsey, remarked that he had often wanted to preach from this text before, but never had, in all of his half century of ministry. He knew if he did not soon do it, he said, it would be too late, as he would have gone to heaven, and he would not like to have to tell the angels that he had never preached from that verse which contained the full gospel. Dr. James H. Snowden some years ago well remarked concerning this one sentence: " This contains the germs and roots of all theology and religion. It is the richest and most splendid verse in all the Bible. It sweeps the unbroken horizon of salvation. It mirrors the whole sky of redemption, thickset with stars. It gathers up all the notes of the gospel and strikes them in one massive chord. Calvary plants its blood-red cross in its center. It is full of infinities and eternities. It is ineffably bright with divine love, and yet it is edged with divine wrath. Heaven is in it, and so is hell."

Many believe that Dr. Alexander Maclaren's brilliant outline in his sermon on this verse is one of the finest masterpieces of expository division in our language. This is the way he opened his sermon: " I venture to say that my text shows us a lake, a river, a pitcher, and a draught. ' God so loved the world ' — that is the lake. A lake makes a river for itself — ' God so loved the world that he *gave* his . . . Son.' But the river does not quench anyone's thirst unless he has something to lift the water with: ' God so loved the world that he gave his . . . Son, that whosoever *believeth* on him.' Last comes the draught: ' shall not perish, but have *everlasting life*.' "

" The words ' God is love ' are not to be found in our catechism or in our confession. They do not occur, so far as I remember, in any of the confessions of the Reformed Church. No matter. We go back to the supreme standard, the Word of God, and we find the mystery there. God loves the world and each soul in the world. Each single soul is beloved as if there were no other. The worst and the most forgotten is strained to His bosom. Is it an easy thing to say? Nobody said it till Christ said it. Even after Christ said it, many of His most faithful servants have feared to repeat it. I shall never forget how Professor Elmslie, in the brief delirium before death, when his mind was wandering, came back over and over again to ' God is Love,' ' God is Love ' — I will go out and tell this to all the world. They do not know it." — *W. R. Nicoll.* Godet finely brings out the deeper implication of the word " give " when he says that " the choice of the verb is significant; it is the word for *giving*, and not only for sending; to give, to surrender, and that, if necessary, even to the last limits of sacrifice." But we must not forget a dreadful word in this verse, which is too often passed over or neglected. Unless this word is clearly looked at, and acknowledged to be true, then the verse itself loses its great significance. The word is *perish*. This great declaration of our Lord clearly implies that, unless men believe in Christ, and in Christ crucified, as God's gift of love to the world, then they are and will forever continue to be *perishing* creatures. To perish does not mean to become extinct, but to become useless, worthless, incapable of functioning in the way in which any instrument or organism is supposed to function. It is the word used for bread molding in the dew of the grass; it could equally be applied to a ship wrecked on the rocks, or to a watch smashed into bits — everything there but worthless forever. This is the program of God; this is the way of God. This is the secret of eternal life. This is that for which Christ died. This is how a man may be born again, by believing in the only begotten Son of God, and freely receiving the priceless merits of His holy death. This is the answer to Nicodemus' question, then, and now, and forever. Do you believe in this Person? Do you have eternal life? Do you know that you really have been born again?

THE ATTITUDE OF CHRIST TO NICODEMUS. "There is no excitement, no undue deference, nor eager politeness; no compromise, nor attempted persuasiveness; not even accommodation. Nor, on the other hand, is there assumed superiority, irony, or dogmatism. There is not even a reference to the miracles, the evidential power of which had wrought in His visitor the initial conviction, that He was a Teacher come from God. All is calm, earnest, dignified — if we may reverently say it — as became the God-Man in the humiliation of His personal teaching. To say that it is all un-Jewish, were a mere truism: it is divine. No fabricated narrative would have invented such a scene, nor so represented the actors in it." — *Alfred A. Edersheim.*

TO BELIEVE IN CHRIST AS A TEACHER FROM GOD COMPELS US TO ACKNOWLEDGE ALL OF HIS TEACHINGS AS TRUE. "If He is a Teacher, take His teachings, and what are they? These, that He is the Son of God; that 'He came from God'; that He 'went to God'; that He 'gives His life a ransom for many'; that He is to be the Judge of mankind; that if we trust in Him, our sins are forgiven and our nature is renewed. Do not go picking and choosing among His teachings, for these which I have named are as surely His as 'Whatsoever ye would that men should do to you, do ye even so to them,' or any other of the moral teachings which the world professes to admire. Take the whole teachings of the whole Christ, and you will confess Him to be the Redeemer of your souls, and the Lifegiver by whom, and by whom alone, we enter the kingdom of God." — *Alexander Maclaren.*

OUR OBLIGATION TO CARRY THE GOSPEL TO MEN IN HIGH POSITION. "This case of personal evangelism in which Jesus sought to win and probably did win this big moralist, the man in high position, ought to be a strong, burning lesson and message to preachers and soul-winners everywhere. It does not take courage for us to go into the downtown missions, in the jails, in the shops, factories and hospitals to speak about Christ and salvation to men and women who are down and out, or who are helpless behind prison bars, or on beds of disease, or men of the commoner walks of life; but it does take courage to approach men high in the social, political, commercial, professional, and official world. There are many thousands of them who are high in position and in popularity, but lost just the same; and they are neglected. We evade them. When we see them we talk about something else. We are afraid to boldly tell them of their sins, of their destiny in hell without Christ. We are afraid of offending them. This case of Nicodemus is a great lesson to all of us who meet our friends in the upper walks of life." — *L. R. Scarborough.*

How many different tributes did Nicodemus pay to Jesus? How is Christ shown to be superior to Nicodemus in this famous conversation? Why do you think Nicodemus came to Jesus by night? Can you explain why this passage gives one the impression of great earnestness? If Jesus really meant what He was here saying, and He surely did, what are some of the conclusions that must inevitably follow?

LESSON III. — January 17.

JESUS WINNING SOULS. — John 4 : 1–42.

PRINTED TEXT, John 4 : 27–42.

GOLDEN TEXT. — ***He that reapeth receiveth wages, and gathereth fruit unto life eternal.*** JOHN 4 : 36.

Devotional Reading : 2 Corinthians 5 : 14–20.
Beginner Topic : HAPPY NEIGHBORS.
Lesson Material : John 4 : 1–42.
Memory Verse : Let us love one another. 1 John 4 : 7.

Primary Topic: A WOMAN WITH GOOD NEWS.
Lesson Material: John 4 : 1–42.
Memory Verse: Go to thy house unto thy friends, and tell them how great things the Lord hath done for thee. Mark 5 : 19.
Junior Topic: TOO GOOD TO KEEP.
Lesson Material: John 4 : 1–42.
Memory Verse: Go to thy house unto thy friends, and tell them how great things the Lord hath done for thee. Mark 5 : 19.
Intermediate and Senior Topic: TELLING WHAT JESUS MEANS TO ME.
Topic for Young People and Adults: SEIZING OPPORTUNITIES FOR WINNING OTHERS TO CHRIST.

THE TEACHER AND HIS CLASS.

The Younger Classes might be easily introduced into an understanding of this lesson by being asked to tell what things they believe the morning the teacher is speaking to them, that they did not know about a week before, things which they believe simply because some one told them of the matter. For instance, that a brother has come to town to visit, that a house burned down ten miles out in the country, that someone's father has gone

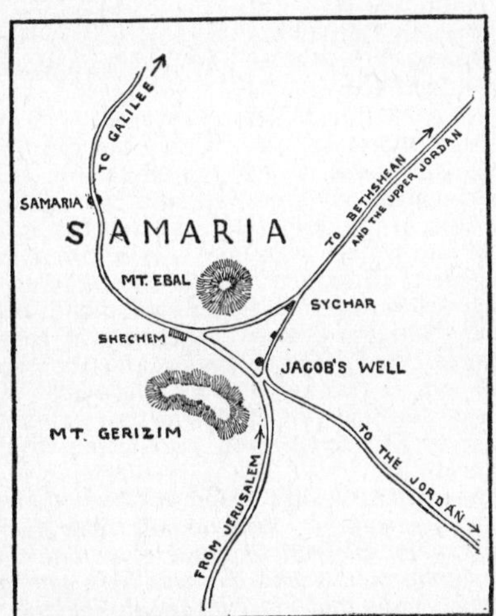

away to a big city on business, that a sister has been honored by election to a scholastic organization in college, etc., etc. Now if people believe thousands of things that others tell them, because they trust the one speaking, so will people believe us, when we tell them about the Lord Jesus Christ who is able to save, as the Samaritan woman did in our lesson.

The Older Classes will find in this lesson a great inspiration for personal work, a narrative from the life of the great Personal Worker Himself, showing us that no person has become so hardened with sin but that they still have within them longings for and a capacity for God; no person is so dull in being occupied with material things but that they can in the right way be lifted up quickly to think about the great spiritual eternities of God's revelation; no place is so difficult for the sowing of the gospel but that a harvest may be expected, if God so ordains and we are faithful.

THE LESSON IN ITS SETTING.

Time. — December, A.D. 27.

Place. — Jacob's well, near Sychar, in central Palestine.

THE PLAN OF THE LESSON.

SUBJECT: **How a Person Sunk in Sin and for Years Occupied with Material Things Only Can Be in One Afternoon Brought to Recognize Christ as the Messiah, Delivered from Sin, and Made a Power for Winning Others to Christ.**

I. CHRIST'S CONVERSATION WITH THE SAMARITAN WOMAN, John 4 : 1–27.
1. How He came to go through Samaria, and where He tarried, vs. 1–6.
2. His request for a drink of water at Jacob's well, and the astonishment of the one asked, vs. 7–9.
3. His declaration He could bestow living water is at first misunderstood, vs. 10–12.
4. He further expounds what He means by living water, and the woman expresses her desire to possess such a boon, vs. 13–15.
5. He is recognized as a prophet, vs. 16–19.
6. His great declaration about the spirituality of God and our worship of God, vs. 20–24.
7. He declares Himself to be the Messiah, vs. 25, 26.
8. The return of the disciples, v. 27.

II. THE REVIVAL IN SYCHAR, John 4 : 28–42.
1. The woman's testimony concerning Christ, vs. 28–30.
2. Christ's intervening teaching to His disciples, vs. 31–38.
   a. The meat of doing the Father's will, vs. 31–34.
   b. The ready harvest, v. 35.
   c. Some principles of spiritual harvest, vs. 36–38.
      (1) He that reaps receives wages.
      (2) In a spiritual harvest the fruit is unto life eternal.
      (3) Both sowers and reapers rejoice.
      (4) Some sow, others reap.

3. The belief of the Samaritans because of the woman's testimony, v. 39.
4. They request Christ to abide with them, v. 40.
5. Their later belief because of Christ's own words, vs. 41, 42.

THE TEACHER'S LIBRARY.

Commentaries vary in their value for the study of this lesson: Godet is very full on historical matters; Reith and Lenski are good for spiritual teaching; most others are only fair, for some strange reason. Of the lives of Christ, the best chapter is that in Edersheim. The most extensive treatment of this lesson with which the editor is acquainted is by R. C. Trench, in his *Studies in the Gospels*, 83–107. For geographical matters, see Gustaf Dalman: *Sacred Sites and Ways*, 209–220; William Thompson: *The Land and the Book*, Vol. 3, 148–151; and A. T. Schofield: *Where He Dwelt*, 65–90 (with beautiful pictures). For a study of the entire narrative, see A. T. Robertson: *Some Minor Characters in the New Testament*, 94–101; David Gregg: *New Epistles from Old Lands*, 75–96; F. A. Noble: *New Testament Conversions*, 67–83; James Jeffrey: *The Personal Ministry of the Son of Man*, 60–71; Adolph Saphir: *Conversions Illustrated by Examples Recorded in the Bible*, 217–252; A. Kuyper: *Women of the New Testament*, 31–33; W. F. Adeney: *Women of the New Testament*, 85–99; Isaac Williams: *Female Characters of Holy Scripture*, 221–232; G. Campbell Morgan: *The Great Physician*, 73–80; H. E. Lewis: *Women of the Bible*, 171–179; H. C. G. Moule: *From Sunday to Sunday*, 147–158; and a fine devotional booklet, *The Woman and Her Waterpot*, by Ethel Smith-McMichael. Above all, one should read the fervent pages on this scene in L. R. Scarborough: *How Jesus Won Men*, 72–87.

For sermonic material, on verse 24, see G. H. Morrison: *Wings of the Morning*, 154–163; on verse 35, J. D. Jones: *The Hope of the Gospel*, 205–217; G. H. Knight, *The Master's Questions to His Disciples*, 108–114; G. Campbell Morgan, in *The Westminster Pulpit*, Vol. 6, 337–344; on verse 36, the only sermon I have seen worth considering is that found in D. L. Moody's book, *Addresses and Prayers*, 16–24; on verses 36–38, W. M. Taylor: *The Limitations of Life*, 375–391; on verse 42, P. C. Ainsworth: *A Thornless World*, 55–64; G. Campbell Morgan, as above, Vol. 5, 345–352. On verses 4 and 44, two splendid sermons will be found in F. B. Meyer's, *Five Musts of the Christian Life*. On Jacob's well, one should also consult the interesting relevant pages in W. D. McCrackan: *The New Palestine*, 349–357.

I. CHRIST'S CONVERSATION WITH THE SAMARITAN WOMAN, vs. 1–27.

1. HOW HE CAME TO GO THROUGH SAMARIA, vs. 1–6. The Judæan ministry of our Lord began with the first cleansing of the temple (John 2 : 13–22), and is discussed almost exclusively in John's Gospel, terminating with verse 42 of our chapter, which opens with His departure from Judæa and His setting forth to Galilee, which necessitated His going through Samaria, a territory lying solidly between Judæa in the south and Galilee in the north, stretching across from the Mediterranean Sea to the Jordan. "The Jews, who were too scrupulous to pass through the Samaritan territory, were compelled to cross the Jordan twice and make a considerable detour if they wished to go to Galilee. Our Lord had no such scruples. He took therefore the great north road and one day at noon found Himself at Jacob's well where the road divides and where at any rate it was natural that a tired traveler should rest during the midday hours." — *Marcus Dods.* "The present day village 'Askar, with a well bearing the same name — about one and a half kilometers distant from Jacob's well — lying at the foot of Mount Ebal, reminds us of the name of this Sechar, which, however, seems to have been situated in close proximity to Jacob's well. . . . It was called Jacob's well probably because it was assumed that the ground round about was the piece of land which the patriarch purchased (Gen. 33 : 19; Josh. 24 : 32). . . . Apart from its position under Mount Gerizim, the peculiarity of Jacob's well is that it is near the crossing of the roads. To the east is the road running past the plain of 'Askar from south to north — a straight continuation of that which comes from Jerusalem, to end at Beth Shean and the lake of Tiberias.

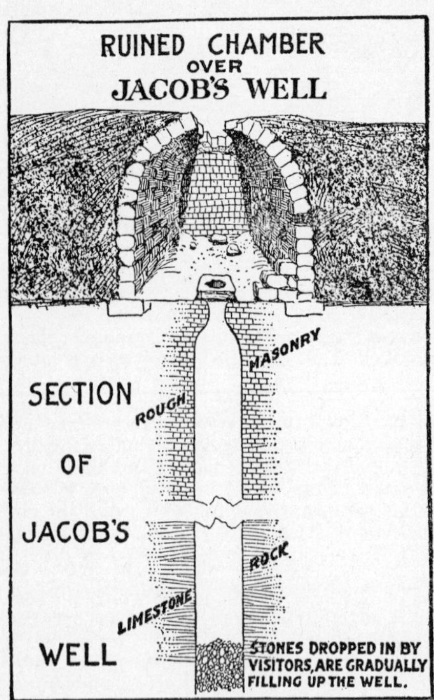

Ruined Chamber over Jacob's Well.

Palestine Exploration Fund.

Immediately south of the well runs, from west to east, the important route joining the Mediterranean and the Jordan valley, on which lay Neapolis, and from which the way led on toward western Galilee. Jacob's well has therefore the character of a road-cistern, which serves the convenience of travelers, and this, at any rate, fits in with the situation described in John 4." — *Gustaf Dalman.*

2. HIS REQUEST FOR A DRINK OF WATER, VS. 7–9. This paragraph opens with a most trivial, commonplace incident, a woman coming to a well to draw water. Yet, " if you had asked her as she left Sychem's gate, she would have answered, ' I come to draw water.' If you had asked her afterwards, her answer would have been different. For results of eternity, both for herself and many inhabitants of Samaria, depended on her coming that day, that hour, and to a large extent that portion of the hour during which the disciples were not with the Master, and there was thus no interruption or constraint in His conversing with her. . . . When He sat thus on the well, He knew that He had needs to go through Samaria and He knew that He was to be found there by one who sought Him not." — *Adolph Saphir.* The request of Christ astonished the woman because the Jews and the Samaritans bitterly despised each other. " The origin of the hostility of the two peoples, which lasts to the present day, may be traced to the Assyrian colonization of the land of Israel (2 Kings 17 : 24). From this followed the antagonism of the Samaritans to the Jews at the Return (Ezra 4; Neh. 6) which led to the erection of a rival temple on Mount Gerizim." — *B. F. Westcott.* The spirit of religious bitterness still lingers on the spot. Canon Tristran tells us that when near Nebulon his party asked drink from a woman who was filling her pitcher, " they were angrily and churlishly answered, ' The Christian dogs might get it for themselves.' "

From a photograph.

Jacob's Well.

3. CHRIST'S DECLARATION HE COULD BESTOW LIVING WATER, VS. 10–12. At once our Lord begins to lead the mind of this woman from the literal, material water which she had come to draw, for the quenching of the thirst of herself and her family, to an altogether different kind of water, a water of life, which would quench not the thirst of the body but the thirst of the soul. He begins to speak to her of " the gift of God." There have been many explanations of what Christ meant by " the gift of God," but personally, I believe Godet, following others, and followed by others, is right, when he identifies it as " eternal life, salvation, the full satisfaction of all the wants of the heart, and the possession of all the holy energies of which the soul is susceptible." Reith well remarks that it is impossible to draw distinctions between the gift of God, and who it was who was speaking to this woman, for " Jesus is both Gift and Giver." " Living water is a common expression for running spring water to distinguish it from water of a cistern or reservoir, and used as an emblem of spiritual blessings with great frequency in the Old Testament. And as all these are regarded as the result of the communication to men of the Holy Spirit of God, He Himself as a personal gift is specially pointed to." — *George Reith.* Christ, the Son of God, with only three years for doing all His great redemptive work on earth, had such a sincere concern for the soul of this almost abandoned, surely coarsened woman, that He would undertake to speak to her of the loftiest themes in the world, and of that which alone could satisfy her for time and for eternity. No soul that we ever

meet is common in God's sight — the tragedy is we make so many common in our own sight.

4. HE FURTHER EXPOUNDS WHAT HE MEANS BY LIVING WATER, vs. 13–15. " The water which the patriarch had drunk and given satisfied a want for the moment; the living water satisfied a want forever, and in such a way that a fresh and spontaneous source supplied each recurrent need of refreshment. The communication of the divine energy, as a gift of life, necessarily manifests itself in life. The blessing welcomed proves a spring of blessing, which rises towards and issues in eternal life; for this is as the infinite ocean in which all divine gifts find their end and consummation. The life comes from the Source of life and ascends to Him again. The image is developed in three stages. Christ's gift is as a spring of water, of water leaping up in rich abundance, and that not perishing or lost but going forth to the noblest fulfillment. . . . The original word translated *springing up into* describes the ' leaping ' of a thing of life, and not the mere ' gushing up ' of a fountain." — *B. F. Westcott.* " We have a magnificent symbolism of this, the life-giving power of these waters, in Ezek. 47 : 9 — ' Every thing shall live whither the river cometh '; that is, the river issuing from under the threshold of the House of God (v. 1; cf. Rev. 22 : 1; Joel 3 : 18; Zech. 14 : 8). . . . He is Himself the true fountain of Jacob (Deut. 33 : 28); this name He implicitly challenges as His own. There is only One, who can be what Christ here declares that He is, namely, ' a fountain of living waters ' (see Jer. 2 : 13; 17 : 13), and that is God. On the strength of this saying Augustine rightly claims Psalm 36 : 9, ' With thee is the fountain of life,' as fulfilled in Christ, and brings that passage into closest connection with this." — *R. C. Trench.*

Christ and the Woman of Samaria.

5. HE IS RECOGNIZED AS A PROPHET, vs. 16–19. " Jesus now drives the ploughshare of conviction of need and sin deeper down. He leaves the charm of parable and comes to unwelcome fact. The woman — like the stony ground hearer — has been receiving with joy the promises of a great good. Christ seeks now to make her understand the true nature of that good, and how much more she needs it than she thinks, and how much more is implied in receiving it than she thinks. Observe, first, Christ's self-respect. ' Go, call thy husband, etc.'; respect therefore even for the poor sinner before Him. The conversation had lasted long enough. Secondly, Christ refrains from pressing home personal truths, from extorting private confessions. Even He regarded the sacredness of human individuality when on earth (see Luke 7 : 48 ff.). Thirdly, He suggests the source of the woman's evil life in yielding to her own impulses — forgetful of ties binding to duty or love. ' Give me this water ' — that demand really symbolized her past vain life. A woman's impulse is her power and her weakness. Jesus says: Remember others who have claims on you. Fourthly, He sends a flash of light into the dark soul — an arrow into her conscience. A natural remark is at times the most embarrassing, especially where there is conscious guilt. It was a startling interruption, entirely unexpected.

" The impatient evasion was a suppression of truth amounting to suggestion of what was false. She meant that she had nobody to consider but herself; that was the sin and the sorrow of her life. She would rather have these pages unturned. Ah! what would she not have given to be able to fall back in the presence of this stranger, who penetrated every disguise, on the consciousness of a pure and innocent past! It could not be. The time is sure to come when sin is bitter indeed. Jesus shows her that He knows the kind of life she has led and is living — touching the painful subject gently but faithfully. What He had been offering her was as real as her immoral life; and was meant, if it meant anything for her, to save her from its degradation and curse; not to allure her with fine hopes only, but to cast the unclean spirit out of the heart. The woman had never been spoken to by men in this way. Those who knew her — as Christ did — avoided her, called her a depraved being; this man knew her thoroughly yet spoke gently to her. There is a lesson here for all Christian workers. . . . With a woman's dexterity and uneasy under the exposure, she seeks to turn the conversation into a less unpleasant channel. She can talk on religion, too, so long as the subject is kept away from her own life. She knows something about the famous standing controversy between Jews and Samaritans. Perhaps this Prophet will tell her more; what He thinks." — *George Reith.* "There is no abiding satisfaction which does not begin with a fair and frank consideration of our past, and which does not proceed from the actual facts of our own life. If this woman is to enter into a hopeful and cleansed life, she must enter through confession of her need of cleansing. No one can slink out of his past life, forgetting what is shameful. It is only through truth and straightforwardness we can enter into that life which is all truth and integrity. Before we drink the living water we must truly thirst for it." — *Marcus Dods.*

6. HIS GREAT DECLARATION ABOUT THE SPIRITUALITY OF GOD, VS. 20–24. The woman now reminds the Lord, and how little He needed reminding, that it was on Mount Gerizim, at the foot of which the well lies, that her ancestors had worshiped. "According to the Samaritan tradition it was on this mountain that Abraham prepared the sacrifice of Isaac, and here also that he met Melchisedek. In Deuteronomy 27 : 12, Gerizim is mentioned as the site on which the six tribes stood who were to pronounce the blessings for the observance of the law. And in the Samaritan Pentateuch, Gerizim and not Ebal is the mountain on which the altar was erected (Deut. 27 : 4)." — *B. F. Westcott.* Now, asked the woman, going as far away as she could from the matter of her own personal sinfulness and the wretchedness of her past life, how was it that Jesus was saying that in Jerusalem men ought to worship? (which does not mean necessarily that Jesus had even said this, but that all the Jews, of whom He was one, so insisted, and on this point the woman radically disagreed with them). There now comes from our Lord's lips one of the greatest statements in all the Word of God. He announced that the hour had come when those who truly worshiped God would "worship the Father in spirit and in truth," and then declared, "God is a Spirit: and they that worship him must worship in spirit and truth." "This great and glorious word settled everything: nature, form, and place of worship. For worship depends on the Being worshiped. A father's worship is the reverence, obedience, love of his children. This may and will receive certain outward expressions, for he would be a singular child who never cared to speak directly to his father; but it is shown in the whole spirit of the life. Then wherever there is a true child's heart, there is the sanctuary and shrine of the Father. By this word Jesus 'admits the woman to the very citadel of the faith' (Bengel). It was more important for her to know whom to worship than where: it would bring her to feel more acutely that whether Jew or Samaritan were right, she was all wrong. The conception of God as Father is the last and greatest revelation." — *George Reith.* By worshiping God in the Spirit we mean worshiping Him with our inner

From a photograph by Wilson.

Mt. Gerizim.

John 4 : 27. And upon this came his disciples; and they marvelled that he was speaking with a woman; yet no man said, What seekest thou? or, Why speakest thou with her?

28. So the woman left her waterpot, and went away into the city, and saith to the people,

29. Come, see a man, who told me all things that *ever* I did: can this be the Christ?

30. They went out of the city, and were coming to him.

---

being, not with hands and lips, with sacrifices, gesticulations, bowing down, crawling on our knees, or by any external devices (cf. Rom. 1 : 9; Eph. 6 : 18).

7. He Declares Himself to Be the Messiah, vs. 25, 26. "Something this poor sinner understands, but not much, of what has just been said to her. . . . We may take her words which follow, 'I know that Messias cometh, which is called Christ; and when he is come, he will tell us all things' — as a cry of helplessness. 'I see not my way in this new world into which Thou hast brought me; but One is coming, the Messias, the Prophet promised to our fathers; I can only wait in confidence that He will lead us into all truth, tell us all which it most concerns us to know.' At the same time there pierces through her words, as it seems to me, a timid presage and presentiment, such as she hardly dares own, much less ventures to utter, 'Thou perhaps art He whom we look for.'

"The word 'Messias' occurs only twice in the New Testament; here, and in Andrew's announcement to his brother Peter, of the Saviour whom he has found (John 1 : 41). It is there explained by the evangelist as 'being interpreted, The Christ,' or The Anointed; the title being drawn first from Psalm 2 : 2; and then from Dan. 9 : 25, 26." — *R. C. Trench.*

8. The Return of the Disciples, v. 27. 27. **And upon this came his disciples; and they marvelled that he was speaking with a woman; yet no man said, What seekest thou? or, Why speakest thou with her?** "The expression, 'No man said,' seems to imply that no man ventured to ask any question what was our Lord's reason for talking with the woman. It is not very clear why the sentence is introduced. The object probably is, as Cyril and Chrysostom remark, to show us the deep reverence and respect with which the disciples regarded our Lord and all His actions, even at this early period of His ministry. It also shows us that they sometimes thought things about Him to which they dared not give expression, and saw deeds of His which they could not understand, but were content silently to wonder at them. There is a lesson for us in their conduct. When we cannot understand the reason of our Lord's dealings with souls, let us hold our peace, and try to believe that there are reasons which we shall know one day. A good servant in a great house must do his own duty and ask no questions. A young student of medicine must take many things on trust." — *J. C. Ryle.*

II. **THE REVIVAL IN SYCHAR,** vs. 28–42.

1. The Woman's Testimony Concerning Christ, vs. 28, 29, 30. 28. **So the woman left her waterpot, and went away into the city, and saith to the people,** 29. **Come, see a man, who told me all things that *ever* I did: can this be the Christ?** It is almost a universal experience in every age, and among every type of people, that as soon as they have found the Messiah and Saviour, and know that their sins are washed away, and that they have the assurance of eternal life, they must go and tell others about it. Thus, our Lord's command to go into all the world preaching the gospel, and to bear testimony to Him, rests solidly upon the natural, normal urging of the Holy Spirit in the regenerated life. Some people are drawn to Christ by His teaching; some by His holy character; and some by His sacrificial death; some by the hope which He offers; others in other ways. This woman marveled at Christ because of His knowledge of all that she had ever done. 30. **They went out of the city, and were coming to him.** "We are astonished at the immediate effect of the woman's words. However, three causes may have, in a secondary sense, been at work. Her honest, enthusiastic, solemn manner; the circumstance that she felt the matter so important as to humble herself by alluding publicly to her sinful life; and lastly, the desire which many of them felt for the coming of the great Deliverer. But what would these and such like causes effect, were it not for the great and all-prevailing influence of the Father's drawing? 'All whom the Father hath given me shall come to me,' yet the three circumstances are of general importance. Earnest-

31. In the mean while the disciples prayed him, saying, Rabbi, eat.
32. But he said unto them, I have meat to eat that ye know not.
33. The disciples therefore said one to another, Hath any man brought him *aught* to eat?
34. Jesus saith unto them, My meat is to do the will of him that sent me, and to accomplish his work.
35. Say not ye, There are yet four months, and *then* cometh the harvest? behold, I say unto you, Lift up your eyes, and look on the fields, that they are white already unto harvest.
36. He that reapeth receiveth wages, and gathereth fruit unto life eternal; that he that soweth and he that reapeth may rejoice together.

---

ness and humility are the two great requisites in an evangelist; and often where we least expect it, God has prepared the way for the reception of His truth by creating in a soul a hunger and thirst after His righteousness. Think it therefore not useless or hopeless to speak to Samaritans about Israel's Messiah. Behold, how they came out unto Jesus!" — *Adolph Saphir.*

2. CHRIST'S INTERVENING TEACHING TO HIS DISCIPLES, VS. 31-38. 31. **In the mean while the disciples prayed him, saying, Rabbi, eat.** 32. **But he said unto them, I have meat to eat that ye know not.** 33. **The disciples therefore said one to another, Hath any man brought him *aught* to eat?** 34. **Jesus saith unto them, My meat is to do the will of him that sent me, and to accomplish his work.** "In these words we have a revelation of the true meaning of what He had been doing in connection with this woman. He had been doing the will of God, and accomplishing His work. He had found in her one whose life had been one of dissipation, and who had reached the moment of complete disillusionment, a disillusionment which had rendered her flippant and callous. He had so dealt with her as to bring her face to face with her past as to its reality, and leading her forward had given to her unquestionably the thirst-quenching water of life. This was the will of God; this was His work; and in the doing of the will, and the accomplishment of the work, He found the sustenance of His life. Having said this, He indicated to His disciples that this also was their work." — *G. Campbell Morgan.* On Christ's obedience to the will of God see, *e.g.*, John 5 : 30; 6 : 38-40; Matthew 26 : 42; Luke 22 : 42. For other references to work, see John 5 : 36; 6 : 29; 7 : 21; 9 : 4; 10 : 25, 32-38; 14 : 10-12; and especially, 17 : 4. 35. **Say not ye, There are yet four months, and *then* cometh the harvest? behold, I say unto you, Lift up your eyes, and look on the fields, that they are white already unto harvest.** "These words are arresting and appealing. They suggest victory, reward, accomplishment; fields white to harvest. The ploughing and preparing all over, the sowing and the long vigil done, and at last the fields ready for the reaper. The words are insistent and persistent. Two notes merge in them, those of opportunity and responsibility. Fields white to harvest constitute a call and a challenge. Is there any greater calamity in agriculture than harvest ungathered? . . .

"When He was sending forth the twelve, He said, 'The harvest truly is plenteous, but laborers are few' (Matt. 9 : 37). Yet again, when He sent the seventy, He made use of exactly the same figure, 'The harvest is plenteous, but the laborers are few' (Luke 10 : 2). And we affirm, without any hesitation, that standing in the midst of those who bear His name in every successive century and age of the Christian dispensation, He has been saying the same thing. At this very hour the living Lord, known no longer to His disciples in the world after the flesh, but intimately known by them in the life of the Spirit, is saying, 'Lift up your eyes, and look on the fields, that they are white already unto harvest.' Is there any greater tragedy in the redemptive purpose and process of God than harvest ungathered?

". . . It was in Samaria that Jesus said to these disciples of His, with all their Jewish prejudice and Hebrew narrowness, 'These fields are white to harvest.'

". . . Hopeless conditions constitute harvest in the economy of Christ. Distressed, oppressed, and broken humanity appeal to Jesus as the whitening and glory of harvest, waiting only the coming of the reapers." — *G. Campbell Morgan.*

36. **He that reapeth receiveth wages, and gathereth fruit unto life eternal; that he that soweth and he that reapeth may rejoice together.** Here is a verse which, though wonderfully rich in meaning, is almost utterly ignored by ministers of the

37. For herein is the saying true, One soweth, and another reapeth.
38. I sent you to reap that whereon ye have not labored: others have labored, and ye are entered into their labor.
39. And from that city many of the Samaritans believed on him because of the word of the woman, who testified, He told me all things that *ever* I did.
40. So when the Samaritans came unto him, they besought him to abide with them: and he abode there two days.
41. And many more believed because of his word;

---

gospel, so that one can hardly find anywhere an adequate interpretation of or a sermon of any importance on the truth it expresses. What could be more wonderful for any man, than to know that he is engaged in " gathering fruit unto life eternal "? This does not mean that we are ourselves enabled to bestow eternal life upon others, but that we are able, by faithful labor, in the power of the Holy Spirit, so to present Christ in His glorious salvation, to men who are dead in trespasses and sins, that they will receive Christ, and thus obtain eternal life. " The expression, ' to receive wages,' describes the joy with which these harvests are to be filled when gathering all souls and introducing them into the kingdom of heaven. And why must the reaper set himself at work without delay? Because there is something exceptional to happen on this day (' in order that '). God has intended in this circumstance to bring to pass a remarkable thing, namely; that both the sower and the reaper may once rejoice together." — *F. Godet.* 37. **For herein is the saying true, One soweth and another reapeth.** 38. **I sent you to reap that whereon ye have not labored: others have labored, and ye are entered into their labor.** " This plural, ' other men,' or ' others,' as it would be better rendered, must not lead us astray, as it has led so many, and induce us to refer this to the prophets and other principal laborers in the older covenant, who underwent their hard apprenticeship under the law (Gal. 4 : 3; Acts 15 : 10); as though the antithesis were between them and the apostles of the new. It is rather between Christ Himself and His apostles; between the Master and the servants, not between two different companies of the servants. He is the sower, they are the reapers; and as compared with His labors, theirs might be esteemed as none at all." — *R. C. Trench.*

3. THE BELIEF OF THE SAMARITANS BECAUSE OF THE WOMAN'S TESTIMONY, v. 39. 39. **And from that city many of the Samaritans believed on him because of the word of the woman, who testified, He told me all things that *ever* I did.** " Just this one woman had brought all this about. She had brought it about for the reason that she herself had been radically changed in character by the power of Christ, and filled with a high enthusiasm for souls. She was in dead earnest. Her acquaintances and neighbors understood and felt it. They knew what kind of woman she had been. They knew what kind of woman she had come to be. If the transformation in her had not been real and complete, she would have had no influence for good. Morally and spiritually she had been reconstructed. Her sense of obligation was quick and deep. She felt that she owed everything to Christ, and she was ready — more than ready, eager — to do everything she could for Christ. . . . This woman, just this one woman, this Samaritan woman, regenerated, converted, brought over from the fellowship of the world to the fellowship of the Christ, by her simple timeliness and activity in witnessing set a marked religious movement on foot, and led nobody knows how many souls out of darkness into light, and out of death into life." — *F. A. Noble.*

4. THEY REQUEST CHRIST TO ABIDE WITH THEM, v. 40. 40. **So when the Samaritans came unto him, they besought him to abide with them: and he abode there two days.** In reading this passage, we cannot but be reminded of a similar incident, not long before this, when John and Simon asked the Lord, " Where dwellest Thou? " with the result that " they abode with him that day." Our desire to abide with Christ is only the echo of His desire to have us abide with Him, and some day He is coming for all those who are His, taking them to Himself where He is, that where He is there they may be also.

5. THEIR LATER BELIEF BECAUSE OF CHRIST'S OWN WORDS, VS. 41, 42. 41. **And many more believed because of his word;** 42. **And they said to the woman, Now we believe, not because of thy speaking: for we have heard for ourselves, and know**

42. And they said to the woman, Now we believe, not because of thy speaking: for we have heard for ourselves, and know that this is indeed the Saviour of the world.

that this is indeed the Saviour of the world. "The simple title, 'the Saviour of the world,' is found once again in 1 John 4 : 14; and it is a significant fact that this magnificent conception of the work of Christ was first expressed by a Samaritan for whom the hope of the Deliverer had not been shaped to suit national ambition. The salvation sprang from the Jews and was recognized by the Samaritans." — *B. F. Westcott.* That is a great hour when a young man, brought up in a Christian home to believe in Christ as the Son of God, and the Saviour of the world, because of his faith in the testimony of his father or mother, or both, finally comes to know Christ in a very personal way, not because of what some one else has said, but because he has heard the Lord speak out of His own Word, and knows whereof he believes by a personal experience.

"Williams of Wern, the great Welsh preacher, had a gift of personal dealing, as well as of popular preaching. He was one day being entertained as a guest at an inn, and had gone to meditate in an orchard, where the servant maid came to the well to fetch water. He spoke to her, and offered her a reward if she would repeat, every time she came to the well, as a prayer, the words, 'Give me the living water, that I thirst not.' When Mr. Williams revisited the district some twelve months after, he missed her at the inn and inquired for her. 'We had to dismiss her,' the landlady told him. 'I am sorry to hear that,' he remarked. 'Oh, she did no wrong; but she became so changed, she used to speak to the men who came in about the evil of drinking; we would have lost all our custom had she remained.' So had the woman of Samaria reproduced her story in this humble sister and evangelist." — *H. E. Lewis.*

How many different titles of Christ do you find in this lesson? What would you say was the outstanding characteristic of Christ manifest in this lesson? What things did our Lord do in this lesson that He desires we also should do? What things did Christ say about Himself in this lesson that we cannot say about ourselves? What is there in this lesson that shows the true humanity of Christ, and what is there that shows His true deity? How many different obstacles can you think of that would immediately present themselves to this Samaritan woman as she started back to her home town to testify of Christ that would, naturally speaking, persuade her to remain silent? Do you think that every person whom we meet will as quickly respond to a message of salvation as this woman did? (The answer is certainly, No.) Do you think that if we asked the Lord every day to definitely guide us to those to whom we should speak about Christ we would frequently have the experience of seeing men brought to confess Jesus Christ? (The answer is an emphatic, Yes.)

LESSON IV. — January 24.

JESUS THE GREAT PHYSICIAN. — John 5.

PRINTED TEXT, John 5 : 2-17.

GOLDEN TEXT. — ***Wouldest thou be made whole?*** JOHN 5 : 6.

Devotional Reading: Psalm 116 : 1–8.
Beginner Topic: THE LAME MAN'S FRIEND.
  Lesson Material: John 5 : 1–15.
  Memory Verse: The Lord is my helper. Hebrews 13 : 6.
Primary Topic: THE FRIEND WHO STOPPED TO HELP.
  Lesson Material: John 5 : 1–15.
  Memory Verse: As ye would that men should do to you, do ye also to them likewise. Luke 6 : 31.
Junior Topic: AT THE POOL OF BETHESDA.
  Lesson Material: John 5 : 1–15.
  Memory Verse: Bear ye one another's burdens, and so fulfill the law of Christ. Galatians 6 : 2.
Intermediate and Senior Topic: HOW JESUS HEALS TODAY.
Topic for Young People and Adults: THE GREAT PHYSICIAN AT WORK TODAY.

THE TEACHER AND HIS CLASS.

The Younger Classes may be asked what they see when they go into a great city to visit. Well, they see its beautiful buildings, its parks, its zoological and botanical gardens, its museums, perhaps some manufacturing plants, etc. When Jesus went into a city, He saw the places where the sick were and the suffering. We go into a city to enjoy its sights. Jesus went into a city to relieve distress, burdens, and suffering humanity.

The Older Classes should be reminded that men and women can come out of almost any mood they may be in except the one of total hopelessness. When a person thinks he is beyond all redemption, all cure, past all help, then he is of all people the most miserable, and the light of life has gone out. It is to this kind of people that the Lord Jesus Christ comes. The man of our lesson had been in a state of hopelessness for years until he had actually believed he would never be any better. There is no person in the world so far down, so in bondage, so continuously defeated, but that the strong Son of God can bring deliverance and give a new life and a new beginning, and a victory that will abide.

THE LESSON IN ITS SETTING.

Time. — The Passover, April A.D. 28.
Place. — The pool of Bethesda in Jerusalem.

THE PLAN OF THE LESSON.

SUBJECT: Christ's Knowledge of, Love for, and Ability to Deliver the Most Powerless, Impotent, Hopeless Men and Women in the World.

I. MEN OF GREAT NEED, John 5 : 1–5.

1. The time.
2. The place.
3. The tragic group of incapacitated men.
4. The man who had been impotent for thirty-eight years.

II. THE SAVIOUR WHO SYMPATHETICALLY COMES TO THOSE IN NEED, 5 : 6, 7.

1. What He saw.
2. What He knew.
3. What He asked.

III. THE SAVIOUR WHO CAN PERFECTLY MEET OUR GREAT NEEDS, 5 : 8–15.

1. The command to the impotent man to arise, v. 8.
2. The miraculous healing of the impotent man, v. 9.
3. The testimony of the healed man, vs. 10–13.
4. Christ's final warning — "sin no more, lest, etc.," vs. 14, 15.

IV. CHRIST'S GREAT ASSERTION CONCERNING HIMSELF FOLLOWING THIS MIRACLE, 5 : 16–47.

1. The determination of the Jews to slay Jesus, v. 16.
2. Christ's first identification of Himself with the Father, v. 17.
3. The even deeper determination of the Jews to kill Jesus, v. 18.
4. Christ's great discourse about His relationship to His Father, vs. 19–47.

THE TEACHER'S LIBRARY.

All lives of Christ, and most of the larger works on John's Gospel, will be found to contain considerable material for the study of this lesson. All volumes likewise dealing with the miracles of our Lord will, of course, have chapters on this event, *e.g.*, R. C. Trench: *Notes on the Miracles of Our Lord;* W. M. Taylor: *The Miracles of Our Saviour;* T. B. Dover: *The Ministry of Mercy; The Miracles of Jesus,* by various authors; John Laidlaw: *The Miracles of Our Lord;* five sermons in Charles H. Spurgeon's *Sermons on Our Lord's Miracles,* Vol. 1; G. H. Hubbard, *Spiritual Messages of the Miracle Stories.* On the pool of Bethesda, see, especially, the excellent article, "Bethesda," by W. W. Moore, in James Hastings: *Dictionary of Christ and the Gospels,* Vol. 1, 193–195; also R. A. S. McAllister: *A Century of Excavation in Palestine,* 137–142; and Edward Robinson: *Biblical Researches in Palestine,* Vol. 1, 505–508.

For expository and sermonic material, of which, for some strange reason, there is no great abundance, see, for the entire passage, Albert Hughes: *The Glory of the Godhead in the Gospel of John,* 74–93; G. Campbell Morgan: *The Westminster Pulpit,* Vol. 3, 57–64; D. J. Burrell: *Christ and Men,* 158 ff. On verse 3, W. L. Watkinson: *The Duty of Imperial Thinking,* 229–233. On verse 4, Phillips Brooks: *The More Abundant Life,* 144 ff.; D. J. Burrell: *The Golden Passional,* 172–182. On verse 6, Andrew Murray: *Intercession,* 92 ff. On verse 7, A. J. Gossip: *From the Edge of the Crowd,* 223 ff.; and, on all the verses of our lesson, Alexander Maclaren: *Expositions of Holy Scripture, St. John* 1–8, 235–251.

GROWING UNBELIEF.

"Chapters 5–11 depict the growth of the unbelief of the Jews. In this part of the Gospel, three Judæan miracles and one in Galilee are related in full, and the impulse given by each to the hatred of the Jews is pointed out. These miracles are the healing of the impotent man (ch. 5), the miraculous feeding (ch. 6), the cure of the man born blind (ch. 9), and the raising of Lazarus (ch. 11). This section of the Gospel may be divided thus: 1. Chapters 5, 6, Christ manifests Himself as the Life first in Judæa, then in Galilee, but is rejected in both places. 2. Chapters 7–10 : 21, He attends the Feast of Tabernacles and manifests Himself by word and deed but is threatened by the mob and the authorities. 3. Chapters 10 : 22—11,

JOHN 5 : 2. Now there is in Jerusalem by the sheep *gate* a pool, which is called in Hebrew Bethesda, having five porches.

3. In these lay a multitude of them that were sick, blind, halt, withered.

Jesus withdraws from Jerusalem but returns to raise Lazarus; in consequence of which the authorities finally determine to slay Him." — *Marcus Dods*.

I. **MEN OF GREAT NEED,** vs. 1–5. There has been much dispute among scholars as to what feast this was to which John here has reference. It has been identified by some with the Passover, by others with Pentecost, and by others with the Day of Atonement. If this is the Passover feast, and this is what the majority of scholars today seem to believe, then many difficult problems in chronology immediately arise which are too complicated for discussion in this volume. We leave the problem here unsolved, because it makes no difference in the value and accuracy of this story as to which feast John here refers.

2. **Now there is in Jerusalem by the sheep *gate* a pool, which is called in Hebrew Bethesda, having five porches.** 3. **In these lay a multitude of them that were sick, blind, halt, withered.** For many centuries the identification of this particular spot was definitely in doubt, many different locations being proposed. However, the words of Professor W. W. Moore in his excellent article on this subject, written about 1905, can be depended upon as presenting the very latest data on this subject. "Now the sheepgate is known to have been north of the Temple, and 'the small cattle which entered Jerusalem came there certainly by the east; for it is on this side that the immense pastures of Judæa lie.' The modern St. Stephen's Gate answers to these data. It is at the northeast angle of the Temple area, and is the gate through which the Bedawin still lead their flocks to Jerusalem for sale. We must therefore look for the pool of Bethesda in this vicinity. . . . In 1872 it was pointed out by M. Clermont-Ganneau that 'the pool of Bethesda should be sought near the Church of St. Anne, where an old tradition has placed the house of the mother of Mary, calling it *Beit Hanna*, 'House of Anne.' This expression is exactly identical with *Bethesda*, both expressions signifying 'the house of mercy, or compassion.' Sixteen years later this anticipation was verified by the discovery of what is now very generally conceded to be the ancient pool of Bethesda, a short distance northwest of the present Church of St. Anne. In the autumn of 1888, 'certain works carried on by the Algerian monks laid bare a large tank or cistern cut in the rock to a depth of 30 feet, and Herr Schick recognized this as the pool of Bethesda. It is 55 feet long from east to west, and measures 12½ feet in breadth. A flight of twenty-four steps leads down into the pool from the eastern scarp of rock. Herr Schick, who at once saw the great interest of this discovery, soon found a sister-pool, lying end to end, 60 feet long, and of the same breadth as the first. The first pool was arched in by five arches, while five corresponding porches ran along the side of the pool. At a later period a church was built over the pool by the Crusaders, and they seem to have been so far impressed by the fact of five arches below that they shaped their crypt into five arches in imitation. They left an opening for getting

From a photograph by Bonfils.

The Pool of Bethesda near St. Stephen's Gate.

5. And a certain man was there, who had been thirty and eight years in his infirmity.

6. When Jesus saw him lying, and knew that he had been now a long time *in that case*, he saith unto him, Wouldest thou be made whole?

7. The sick man answered him, Sir, I have no man, when the water is troubled, to put me into the pool: but while I am coming, another steppeth down before me.

---

down to the water; and further, as the crowning proof that they regarded the pool as Bethesda, they painted on the wall of the crypt a fresco representing the angel troubling the water of the pool.' "

In the very earliest manuscripts of the Gospel of John, the entire passage, beginning with the word *withered*, and extending to the end of verse 4, is not found. And it is now unanimously agreed that these words were not written by St. John, but were a late insertion on the part of some copyists, who attempted by these words to explain why this great multitude of men was there, and to interpret the phenomenon of the moving of the waters. That the waters were agitated periodically we can easily believe, for in other places near Jerusalem such a phenomenon as this is known, even today, caused by certain natural siphoning, or in other cases, the result of the blowing of a strong wind upon the water. In fact, as Professor Laidlaw has said: " That the waters were beneficial and were moved at intervals are facts recognized in the narrative. It is only the description of the supposed cause — an angel visit — which disappears from the true text." " The five porches or covered colonnades were like a hospital, filled with a crowd of sufferers, four classes being mentioned. This number is often used for indicating completeness (Ezek. 14 : 21; Rev. 6 : 8; Matt. 15 : 31). The first group, the ' sick,' takes in all that are not included in other groups. The absence of the articles draws attention to the qualities indicated in the nouns. When so many sufferers are brought together they impress us much more than when we meet them singly; we then see more adequately all the wretchedness, the misery, the broken lives that form the result of sin among men." — *R. C. H. Lenski.* " Let me give you four other words, not that these are incorrect, but we get so familiar with the actual words of Scripture that it is good sometimes to translate by new words: strengthless, sightless, crippled, withered. I describe them all in one word — they were *unfit*, the people for whom Jerusalem had no use, perhaps giving charity occasionally, but still having no use for them because they were useless. There was no interest in the life of Jerusalem into which they could enter with any profit to the city." — *G. Campbell Morgan.*

5. **And a certain man was there, who had been thirty and eight years in his infirmity.** A few of us have been sick, perhaps for as long a time as six continuous weeks, and oh, the joy when sufficient strength comes back to enable us to walk. And how thrilled we were that first day when we went back to work, and knew that once again we could take our part in the life and activity of the world about us, and live a normal, satisfying, work-accomplishing life. But this man had been absolutely helpless, not for six weeks, but for 1976 weeks. He was not only helpless, but he was hopeless. When a man has been afflicted with any ailment for thirty-eight successive years, he is convinced he will never be well again. This man not only was conscious of all of his adult life being wasted, but every morning he awoke to realize that not only was the past a great barren wilderness, but all the future would be nothing but its prolongation. Death is better than a life like this.

6. **When Jesus saw him lying, and knew that he had been now a long time *in that case*, he saith unto him, Wouldest thou be made whole?** 7. **The sick man answered him, Sir, I have no man, when the water is troubled, to put me into the pool: but while I am coming, another steppeth down before me.**

II. THE SAVIOUR WHO SYMPATHETICALLY COMES TO THOSE IN NEED, vs. 6, 7. Into this unhappy gathering, over which perpetually hung an atmosphere of despair and depression, where the conversation must have been very common and often coarse and sordid (as it so often is in hospital wards where patients are thrown together for long periods of time and in other institutions which need not be mentioned) — into this place, where only the helpless came, but never one strong and well to encourage them, to investigate their cases, to attempt to heal them of their ailments, where none of the great of Jerusalem ever entered — into this group of forgotten men came, this day, the blessed Son of God. It was He who had announced at the very threshold of His ministry that He had come down "to preach the gospel to the poor; to heal the brokenhearted; to preach deliverance to the captives and recovering of sight to the blind, to set at liberty them that are bruised" (Luke 4 : 18). Why our Lord centered His attention upon one man in the group rather than upon all the men, or some other man, we do not know. This is the way of God's dealings; some are chosen, some are not. One reason, no doubt, why our Lord focused His attention this day on this man was because his was the worst case of all those who were there, and, if men were convinced He could deliver this man from his infirmity, they would know the Lord could save any man from whatever disease or affliction possessed him. Though the editor has looked at this passage for many years, he never noticed, until the other day, the particular significance of the phrase, "Jesus knew that he had been a long time in that case." Is not this a

J. Restout. — Louvre, Paris.

Christ Healing the Paralytic.

good word to read at the bedside of patients in hospitals, who have been confined for months at a time? Jesus knows! The Lord never performed healing miracles in the Gospels automatically. He could have laid His hand on this man without a word, lifted him up, and sent him home. He did not choose to do so. He first asked him a question, then He commanded him to do something, and then, later, He gave him a warning. He does not simply want this man automatically healed of a physical infirmity — He desires that there should be an act of faith, an exercise of will, an inner change, a transformation morally and spiritually as well as physically. So He asks him a question, "*Wouldest* thou be made whole?" Strange question, we might say. Yet, not so strange. The Lord was the perfect psychologist. "Not always are the miserable willing to be relieved. Medical men have sometimes offered to heal the mendicants' sores and their aid has been rejected. Even the invalid who does not trade pecuniarily on his disease is very apt to trade upon the sympathy and indulgence of friends, and sometimes becomes so debilitated in character as to shrink from a life of activity and toil. Those who have sunk out of all honest ways of living into poverty and wretchedness are not always eager to put themselves into the harness of honest labor and respectability. This reluctance is exhibited in its extreme form in those who are content to be spiritual imbeciles, because they shrink from all arduous work and responsible position. Life, true

8. Jesus saith unto him, Arise, take up thy bed, and walk.

9. And straightway the man was made whole, and took up his bed and walked.

Now it was the sabbath on that day.

10. So the Jews said unto him that was cured, It is the sabbath, and it is not lawful for thee to take up thy bed.

11. But he answered them, He that made me whole, the same said unto me, Take up thy bed, and walk.

12. They asked him, Who is the man that said unto thee, Take up *thy bed*, and walk?

13. But he that was healed knew not who it was; for Jesus had conveyed himself away, a multitude being in the place.

---

life such as Christ calls us to, with all its obligations to others, its honest and spontaneous devotion to spiritual ends, its risks, its reality, and purity, does not seem attractive to the spiritual valetudinarian. In fact, nothing so thoroughly reveals a man to himself, nothing so clearly discloses to him his real aims and likings, as the answer he finds he can give to the simple question, 'Are you willing to be made whole? Are you willing to be fitted for the highest and purest life?' The very answer showed that he was hopeless. It had become the established order of things with him that some one anticipated him. He speaks of it as regularly happening — 'another steps down before me.' He has no friend — not one that would spare time to wait beside him and watch for the welling up of the water." — *Marcus Dods.*

III. **THE SAVIOUR WHO CAN PERFECTLY MEET OUR GREAT NEEDS,** vs. 8–15. 8. **Jesus saith unto him, Arise, take up thy bed, and walk.** 9. **And straightway the man was made whole, and took up his bed and walked. Now it was the sabbath on that day.** Christ here is deliberately asking this man to do something which he not only had not done for thirty-eight years, but something which, for all that length of time, he had not been able to do. A command like this on the lips of anybody else would only have been words of torment, really words of mockery, and one does not mock helpless invalids or use foolish phrases in talking to them. Knowing our Lord to be gracious, compassionate, and truthful, we know also then that when He gives such a command as this He will give strength for its execution. He could have lifted this man up, without any exercise of will on the man's part at all, but He wanted this hopeless person to so manifest faith in Him the Saviour, that he would, in faith, exercise his will and deliberately attempt to obey the commandment of the One who stood before him. Salvation does take one thing *on our part*, our saying, "we will" — *i.e.*, we will believe, or we will trust the Saviour, or we will yield everything to Him, or we will obey Him whatever the consequences. There is no commandment in the Word of God for the obedience of which Christ will not give strength in the hour of need. The high ideals of the Christian life set forth in the New Testament are not for our continuous rebuke and discouragement, but for our attainment by the power of the indwelling Spirit of God. And there is no case of such long standing, so apparently helpless, but that Christ is able to deliver from whatever bondage, whatever habit, whatever doubt, whatever evil may have taken possession of any individual. Why did our Lord ask this man to take up his bed and walk, rather than to leave the bed there? Probably, as some one has said, that he might remove from the place of his long and fruitless waiting the very vestiges of a life of impotence and despair, so that he would never be tempted to go back again to the place where he had spent so many wasteful years. This man, walking out with his bed, proved to all others who were assembled there that he was completely and instantly healed. In like manner, one newly saved by Christ is to reveal the reality of his salvation by living that kind of a life which before was impossible for him — a life above the level of the world, a life manifesting divine strength, a life in which the power of God will be manifest. Westcott brings out the interesting point that the word here translated "bed" describes technically the bed of the poor, a pallet.

10. **So the Jews said unto him that was cured, It is the sabbath, and it is not lawful for thee to take up thy bed.** 11. **But he answered them, He that made me whole, the same said unto me, Take up thy bed, and walk.** 12. **They asked him, Who is the man that said unto thee, Take up *thy bed*, and walk?** 13. **But he that**

14. Afterward Jesus findeth him in the temple, and said unto him, Behold, thou art made whole: sin no more, lest a worse thing befall thee.
15. The man went away, and told the Jews that it was Jesus who had made him whole.
16. And for this cause the Jews persecuted Jesus, because he did these things on the sabbath.
17. But Jesus answered them, My Father worketh even until now, and I work.

---

was healed knew not who it was; for Jesus had conveyed himself away, a multitude being in the place.
14. Afterward Jesus findeth him in the temple, and said unto him, Behold, thou art made whole: sin no more, lest a worse thing befall thee.
15. The man went away, and told the Jews that it was Jesus who had made him whole.
16. And for this cause the Jews persecuted Jesus, because he did these things on the sabbath.
17. But Jesus answered them, My Father worketh even until now, and I work. No sooner had this man started home but the Jews laid hold of him, and told him that, because it was the Sabbath day, it was not lawful for him to take up his bed! "By 'the Jews' we understand here, as constantly in St. John, not the multitude but the Sanhedrists, the spiritual heads of the nation (1 : 19; 7 : 1; 9 : 22; 18 : 12, 14; cf. vs. 20 : 19). These find fault with the man, for had not Moses said, 'In it thou shalt not do any work' (Exod. 20 : 10), and still more to the point, 'Take heed to yourselves, and bear no burden on the Sabbath days' (Jer. 17 : 21); so that they seem to have words of Scripture to justify their interference and the offense which they took. But the man's bearing of his bed was not a work by itself; it was merely the corollary, or indeed, the concluding act, of his healing, that by which he should make proof himself, and give testimony to others of its reality. It was lawful to heal on the Sabbath day; it was lawful then to do whatever was immediately involved in, and directly followed on, the healing." — *R. C. Trench.* Instantly the man gives a reason for doing that for which they were, unjustly, condemning him. "He that made me whole, the same said unto me, Take up thy bed, and walk." The words of Marcus Dods here are superb: "Intuitively, the man lays down the great principle of Christian obedience. If Christ is the source of life to me, He must also be the source of law. If without Him I am helpless and useless, it stands to reason I must consider His will in the use of the life He communicates. This is the law which the Christian must still bear in mind when he fears to thwart any prejudice of the world, when he is tempted to abide his time among the impotent folk, and not fly in the face of established usage; when, though he has distinctly understood what he ought to do, so many difficulties threaten, that he is tempted to withdraw into obscurity and indolence." Note especially, that these Jews, who were so antagonistic to the Lord, and so scrupulous about obedience to the traditions of men, showed not one spark of joy, or appreciation, or amazement, as they beheld this man, impotent for thirty-eight years, walking in the full power of mature manhood. That is the way many people speak of the Lord Jesus — they try to accuse Him of this fault or that fault; they try to find contradictions in the Gospel narratives; they attempt to discover the irrationality of some expressions attributed to our blessed Lord. They talk about the impossibility of a life of regeneration; they attempt to trace many New Testament stories to some mythological origin, etc., etc., and live all their life unconscious of the glory, the greatness, the deity, the sublimity, the power, the loveliness of Christ Jesus the Son of God.

The conclusion of this episode in the life of this formerly impotent man (who never appears again in the Gospel story, and whose healing is recorded only in John's Gospel) carries with it a warning which every one of us surely need. "Behold, thou art made whole: sin no more, lest a worse thing befall thee." To begin with, these words definitely trace this man's impotency to some sinful indulgence in his life, the nature of which is not stated, but which can certainly be guessed at without much fear of going wrong. All disease and physical affliction certainly cannot be traced to any immediate transgression of moral law on the part of the one so afflicted, which even our Lord Himself clearly sets forth, in a later episode (John 9 : 3). Many true saints of God have suffered for years, not because of any moral transgression in their lives; while, on the other hand, thousands of men have lived for years in grossest wickedness and have never had an ache or a pain all that time. But this man's condition *was* due to some sin committed early in life. Undoubtedly he knew it. Tragic enough, to be a helpless invalid for nearly forty years; trebly tragic, to know every hour of the day and night that this invalidism is but the result of some hour's indulgence, of some deliberate flouting of the law of God. How he must have hated himself, and cursed the day when he gave way to his own evil inclinations, probably against the warnings of loved ones, and certainly with a knowledge that he was disobeying the law of God. Our Lord is interested, first of all, in a man's inner life, then his physical welfare. Healing him of his bodily infirmity, he wanted this man, in all the days to come, to reveal a spiritual soundness like to that of the soundness of body which had now been given to him. And may it not be that this warning, " Sin no more," was one which this man especially needed?

" Final punishment for one who persists in sin and fritters away his opportunities is sharper than the sharpest penalties of time. A worse thing than long years of weary, miserable, aborted life threatens the man who resists the grace which is visiting him. Spent nerve, decadent brain, aching limb, loneliness and neglect, the repugnance of bystanders, are retributions that do not traverse all the soul's susceptibilities to pain. These are the primitive elements out of which the complex, cumulative penalties of the hereafter will be built up, if we reject the Deliverer, and despise His admonitions.

" The dregs of the divine wrath are reserved for ungrateful and treacherous backsliding. For our quickening, and for our comfort, let us remember that the warning against repeated sin and the declaration of forgiveness are conjoined. The admonitory voice will speak in vain, unless it at the same time inspire us with hope. We must be made to feel that there is something worth taking care for, that we have indeed a gift and a blessing to keep." — *Thomas G. Selby.*

With this warning ringing in his ears, the man departed, telling the Jews that it was Jesus who had made him whole. " It is difficult to understand the motive of the man in conveying this information to the Jews since he knew the hostile spirit in which they regarded the cure. He was certainly not ungrateful for he still speaks of Jesus as having cured him. He may have wished to leave the responsibility of his illegal act with One who had power to answer for it; or it may be simplest to suppose that he acted in obedience to the instructions of those whom, as a Jew, he felt bound to obey." — *B. F. Westcott.*

THERE NEED BE NO WAITING FOR DELIVERANCE BY CHRIST OUR LORD.

" In the medical spring around which these porches were reared, the healing virtue was only intermittent. It was due, in some occult manner, to the troubling of the water, and only at that particular moment could the applicant receive benefit. But the efficacy of the blood of Christ is continuous. No one needs to wait a single moment for a cure from the Lord Jesus. He may have it at once if he will only apply, believingly, for it. Turn then, O sinner, from your evil way: and repair to Him. He will deliver you from your guilt; He will wash away your sin. He will give you salvation in the fullest significance of that word. ' He is able to save them to the uttermost that come unto God by him, seeing he ever liveth to make intercession for them '" (Heb. 7 : 25). — *William M. Taylor.*

A WORD OF EXHORTATION.

" I am here to say to you in this century, in this age, closer to you than any neighbor who sits at your side, closer than breathing, is this self-same Christ, with all the resources that are necessary for your remaking. You can be healed at the center of you, spiritually, and in the power of that spiritual remaking you can be master over the things that master you. If not, I have no gospel. I have no time to waste advising men to try. I know too well in my own life the hopelessness of trying. I am not here to advise men to join together in associations to help themselves to be better. There is no man to help me into the pool. The philosophy of life, if you take Christ out of it is, Each for himself and the devil take the hindmost. It is not always the hindmost in that race that the devil does take! Be patient with me, I am after one man it may be, a man who has drifted in here, who has happened to come in. You know full well you have been in the grip of infirmity for a year, five years, ten years, twenty years, you are in the grip of it now. Behind it all is the debasement of your spirit, the paralysis of your essential life, the weakening of your will, the deadening of the mind, the darkening of the intellect. You have sinned and the poison is in the very fiber of your mysterious spiritual personality. Christ is able to heal and to remake you. He can only do it in one way, in exactly the same way He did it with this man. . . . At the point where you are weakest begin to do the thing you say you cannot do, 'Arise.' You have been mastered by this habit, Arise, and let the arising begin here and now. Some man in agony looks into my face and says, What is the use of telling me that? That is no better than telling me to try. Quite so, unless you understand that when next you begin to obey and start out upon what seems to be the hopeless task of living the right life you must do it not as you have done it, but because He says do it, in obedience to Him yield the will and put yourself under His control.

I can but perish if I go,
I am resolved to try.
If I stay away I know
I must forever die.

In the moment that a man acts because Christ commands, trusting in Him, venturing on Him, in that moment Christ is able to touch the will with new strength, to touch the emotion with new feeling, to flood the intelligence with new light, to breathe through the pulses of desire His coolness and His balm." — *G. Campbell Morgan.*

IV. **CHRIST'S GREAT ASSERTION CONCERNING HIMSELF FOLLOWING THIS MIRACLE,** vs. 18–47. Time does not allow for the teacher to carefully consider the remaining portion of this chapter. It is one of those marvelous discourses of our Lord which few ministers ever preach from and few students ever sit down to carefully meditate upon. Let us see, in the very briefest way, what this remarkable address of our Lord teaches us. The editor believes he is safe in saying that in no one discourse in all the Gospels does Christ set forth His absolute deity as He does here. There are some critical schools that go so far as to say that the title "Son of God" was never used by Christ Himself, but only assigned to Him by Christians of a later generation. This chapter utterly repudiates such a false statement. Primarily, in this discourse, our Lord sets forth His relationship to the Father, and He enumerates at least nine fundamental features of that relationship as follows:

1. He does whatsoever the Father does, v. 19.
2. He is loved by the Father, v. 20.
3. He is shown all that the Father does, v. 20.
4. He quickeneth whom He will as the Father does, v. 21.
5. He has had all judgment committed to Him by the Father, vs. 22, 27.
6. He is to be honored as the Father is honored, v. 23.
7. He has life in Himself, as the Father has life in Himself, v. 26.
8. He seeks the Father's will, v. 30.
9. He is witnessed to by the Father, v. 31.

Four other truths are here set forth which we can only name. First, Christ says that whosoever heareth His Word and will believe on the Father who has sent Him, has now everlasting life (v. 24). Secondly, He makes the astonishing statement which only the Son of God could make, that the day will come when the dead shall hear the voice of the Son of God and live, that is, will be raised from the dead (vs. 25, 28, 29). Thirdly, toward the end of the chapter (v. 36), our Lord speaks of the testimony of His mighty works, His miracles, to the truth of His deity. Finally, He concludes with a comparatively long discussion of the testimony of the Scriptures to His deity, a profound passage which deserves the most careful study (vs. 37–47). No one in all the world but Christ has ever uttered such words as these. And of no one in all the world could they be true but of the Lord Jesus.

How many different characteristics of Christ are revealed in this lesson? Do you think it is possible for a man to be waited on and looked after for so long a period of time that he comes to the place where he would rather live that kind of an indolent life than to be active in daily work? Do you think there are men today who prefer to live in the wretchedness of their sin than to be delivered from sin and to walk in newness of life? What can you do for a man like that? Would Christ have spoken these words to this man, "Arise, and walk, and sin no more," unless He knew they could be fulfilled in this man's life? Do you not think that Christ will supply every day the strength we need to live that high and clean and victorious life to which He calls us by His Spirit through the teachings of the New Testament? In how many ways is Christ shown to be different from and superior to normal men, however good they might be? How can impotent, helpless, hopeless men today hear of the compassion of Christ and His desire and power to save them?

LESSON V. — January 31.

JESUS THE BREAD OF LIFE. — John 6.

PRINTED TEXT, John 6 : 8-14, 30-35.

GOLDEN TEXT. — ***Jesus said unto them, I am the bread of life.*** JOHN 6 : 35.

Devotional Reading: Psalm 63 : 1–8.
Beginner Topic: A BOY'S LUNCH.
  Lesson Material: John 6 : 1–14.
  Memory Verse: We . . . are helpers. 2 Corinthians 1 : 24.
Primary Topic: A BOY'S LUNCH.
  Lesson Material: John 6 : 1–14.
  Memory Verse: Give for alms those things which are within. Luke 11 : 41.
Junior Topic: A BOY AND HIS LUNCH.
  Lesson Material: John 6 : 1–14.
  Memory Verse: Give for alms those things which are within. Luke 11 : 41.
Intermediate and Senior Topic: HOW CHRIST SATISFIES YOUTH.
Topic for Young People and Adults: BREAD FOR SPIRITUAL HUNGER.

THE TEACHER AND HIS CLASS.

The Younger Classes may be asked what are the absolute essentials of life, without which even the meagerest existence is not possible? Well, we need air to breathe, water to drink, food to eat, shelter from the cold, from storms, and the dangers of the night, and clothes for covering our bodies, at least in western civilization. Food that we need is summed up in the word "bread." In this lesson Jesus recognizes that bread is essential, and that He desires men to have the elemental necessities of life, but, at the same time, after feeding the body, He shows men that there is something else they need, a food for their inner life, just as needful as the food for their physical body. As He had power to create the one so He alone has power to give the other. He is the Lord of life in every form.

The Older Classes should come away from this lesson with a double conviction, first, that the Lord Jesus is absolutely unique in His power to multiply food, apart from scientific processes, and thus He reveals Himself to be indeed the Sent One of God. In addition to this, one must rise from a study of this lesson conscious of the fact that the One who proves Himself to be sent from God so definitely emphasized the absolute need of all men for an inner nourishment, for food which would sustain a deeper life than the physical, partaking of which one would have abundant and eternal life. No other man in all the world could do what Jesus did in this chapter, and could rightly claim what Jesus here claims to be.

From a photograph by Bonfils.

Ruins of Capernaum.
Near the Sea of Galilee.

THE LESSON IN ITS SETTING.

Time.—All the events of this chapter fall in the month of April, A.D. 29.

Place. — The feeding of the five thousand took place at Bethsaida, on the shore of Galilee, while the walking on the sea was, of course, on the same body of water. The sermon on the Bread of Life was delivered in the synagogue of Capernaum.

THE PLAN OF THE LESSON.

SUBJECT: The Ability of the Lord Jesus to Satisfy Both the Physical and the Spiritual Elemental Needs of Men, Making Himself to Be Forever the Indispensable Christ of All Men.

I. THE MIRACLE OF THE FEEDING OF THE FIVE THOUSAND, John 6 : 1–14.

1. Christ's perfect knowledge, vs. 1–9.
   a. Of the needs of the multitude, vs. 1–5.
   b. Of what He Himself was about to do (in contrast to the perplexity of the disciples), vs. 6–9.
2. Christ's power manifested in the multiplying of bread and meat, vs. 10, 11.
3. Christ's plan for avoiding wastefulness, vs. 12, 13.
4. Christ recognized as the predicted Prophet, v. 14.

II. THE MIRACLE OF WALKING ON THE WATER, John 6 : 15–21.

III. CHRIST'S GREAT SERMON ON THE BREAD OF LIFE, John 6 : 22–59.

1. The attending circumstances, vs. 22–25.
2. The necessity for recognizing a bread of higher quality than that which perishes, vs. 26, 27.
3. The multitude ask Christ for a sign as evidence of His right so to address them, vs. 28–31.
4. Christ identifies Himself as the Bread of life, vs. 32–40.
   a. The True Bread from heaven.
   b. The Bread of God.
   c. The Bread of life.
   d. The bestower of life, vs. 36–40.
5. The murmuring of unbelief, vs. 41, 42.
6. Christ reasserts the truth that He is the Bread from heaven, vs. 43–50.
7. Christ explains that this Bread is His flesh given for the world, vs. 51–59.

IV. THE WINNOWING OF SUPERFICIAL FOLLOWERS FROM THE TRUE DISCIPLES OF CHRIST, John 6 : 60–66.

V. THE CONFESSION OF SIMON PETER, John 6 : 67–71.

THE TEACHER'S LIBRARY.

All commentaries on the Gospel of John, and most Lives of Christ, will be found helpful in the study of this lesson. In addition, one should consult all books on the miracles of our Lord, a list of which will be found in the Bibliography for January 24. For a discussion of the theological aspects of this chapter see George Smeaton: *The Doctrine of the Atonement as Taught by Christ Himself*, 270–283. On Christ the Bread of life, see Thomas Marjoribanks: *The Sevenfold "I AM,"* 85–100; A. C. Dixon: *The Glories of the Cross*, 119–126; Charles H. Spurgeon: *The Messiah — Sermons on Our Lord's Names and Titles, etc.*, 555–566. There is a very fine chapter on "The Lad with the Loaves and Fishes" in Joseph Hammond's *The Boys and Girls of the Bible*, Vol. 2, 144–153.

For sermonic material see Alexander Maclaren's *Exposition of Holy Scripture — St. John 1–8*, 251–279. On v. 10, Phillips Brooks: *Visions and Tasks and Other Sermons*, 226–243; on v. 12, Hugh Macmillan: *Two Worlds Are Ours*, 328–341; on v. 33, John Clifford: *The Dawn of Manhood*, 50–65; on v. 35, G. Campbell Morgan: *Westminster Pulpit*, Vol. 9, 89–96; J. S. Holden: *The Pre-eminent Lord*, 93–99; Andrew Murray: *The Full Blessing of Pentecost*, 107 ff.

I. **THE MIRACLE OF THE FEEDING OF THE FIVE THOUSAND,** vs. 1–14. This is the only miracle which is found in all the four Gospels, and is the only miracle recorded in John's Gospel that is found in any of the other Gospels (see Matt. 14 : 13–21; Mark 6 : 30–44; Luke 9 : 10–17). It marks, as it were, a dividing point in Christ's ministry, for at the end of the chapter we find that many walked no more with the Lord, after He interpreted to them the deeper meaning of this miraculous act. Exactly where the miracle took place we do not know, except near a mountain, close to the lake. When it says that He beheld a great multitude coming toward Him, "a day of teaching and healing must be intercalated before the miracle of the feeding was wrought. St. John appears to have brought together into one scene the first words spoken to Philip on the approach of the crowd, and the words in which they were afterwards taken up by Andrew, when the disciples themselves at evening restated the difficulty. It also appears from verse 15, that the Lord came down from the mountain before the miracle was wrought." — *B. F. Westcott.* Seeing the multitude, the Lord asked Philip with what means they would be able to purchase bread that this great multitude should be fed, which is in contrast to the earlier and rather heartless declaration of His disciples that the multitude should be sent away. "Christ takes men into the arms of His pity and sympathy (Heb. 4 : 15). The question was put to Philip, doubtless, as being a man of slower apprehension — cautious and hesitating. This was not to get the advice of Philip; Jesus is never presented in the Gospels in such an attitude. He ever gives, and receives nothing. Jesus observes the special characteristic of each disciple, and lovingly subjects each to the discipline best suited to him." — *George Reith.* Philip immediately replied that two hundred pennyworth, that is, two hundred denarii, equivalent to about forty dollars in our money, would not be sufficient to purchase bread for such a multitude as were before them.

JOHN 6 : 8. One of his disciples, Andrew, Simon Peter's brother, saith unto him,
9. There is a lad here, who hath five barley loaves, and two fishes: but what are these among so many?
10. Jesus said, Make the people sit down. Now there was much grass in the place. So the men sat down, in number about five thousand.
11. Jesus therefore took the loaves; and having given thanks, he distributed to them that were set down; likewise also of the fishes as much as they would.

---

8. **One of his disciples, Andrew, Simon Peter's brother, saith unto him,** 9. **There is a lad here, who hath five barley loaves, and two fishes: but what are these among so many?** "John also adds to Andrew's hopeless expression, 'What are these among so many?' As with the first question to Philip, so with this order to the disciples, these men think only that Jesus has in mind, by means of purchase, or by means of raking up supplies still available, to feed this vast crowd. So both times Jesus is told that His suggestions are hopeless. Barley bread was much used by the poorer classes. By the word here translated *fishes* is meant a cooked fish, eaten with thin flat cakes of bread, cakes which nobody thought of cutting since they were so easily broken for eating." — *R. C. H. Lenski.* (A teacher with a well-disciplined imagination will be able to make out a very vivid narrative, telling how this boy's mother packed his lunch when he told her he wanted to follow the crowd that was going to see Jesus.)

The Five Thousand Fed.

10. **Jesus said, Make the people sit down. Now there was much grass in the place. So the men sat down, in number about five thousand.** "The vast assemblage was thus sub-divided and broken up into manageable portions; there was less danger of tumult and confusion, or that the weaker, the women and the children, should be passed over while the stronger and ruder unduly put themselves forward. The apostles were able to pass easily up and down among the groups, and to minister in orderly succession to the necessities of all." — *R. C. Trench.*

11 *a.* **Jesus therefore took the loaves.** I have never seen any commentator dwell on this particular phrase, but I have always felt that it is definitely worth meditating upon. Christ certainly would not forcibly wrest something from this lad's hands, nor would He allow the disciples to do it. Are we not to assume that the lad had a real love for the Saviour, and wanted to contribute anything he had which he thought the Saviour could use? And after all, is not this just like a boy, at least a gentlemanly boy, to be generous even to the stinting of himself? One can bring out many lessons here, but certainly no teacher will want to neglect the opportunity of showing his or her pupils how, when we give all that we are and have to the Lord for His use, we not only have enough for our own needs, but our supply is thus made the means of the bestowal of a blessing upon countless others ministered to by the servants of the Lord Jesus. This, by the way, if the editor is not mistaken, is the only place in all the Gospels where a lad is spoken of.

12. And when they were filled, he saith unto his disciples, Gather up the broken pieces which remain over, that nothing be lost.

13. So they gathered them up, and filled twelve baskets with broken pieces from the five barley loaves, which remained over unto them that had eaten.

14. When therefore the people saw the sign which he did, they said, This is of a truth the prophet that cometh into the world.

---

11 *b*. **And having given thanks, he distributed to them that were set down; likewise also of the fishes as much as they would.** It is significant that John does not say that Christ broke the bread, as do the other Gospel writers, but of course, we know He did. I would assume that only through Christ's fingers was power manifested in multiplying the bread, but it may be, as others have suggested, that He conferred power that day on other disciples to also increase the supply of bread as they moved about in the crowd, though, personally, I do not think He did. On the anvil of this miracle rationalists have pounded their hammers for centuries, but they have never been able to destroy the testimony to the reality of the miraculous event taking place on this occasion. Even the extreme liberalists have been forced to say that the evidence for this miracle is overwhelmingly strong. Some have tried to show that Christ here only " hastened the processes of nature," even though they admit it to be a miracle, but Trench has a magnificent reply to this attempt to lessen the greatness of what Christ did. " That which finds place in the field is the unfolding of the seed according to the law of its own being. Thus, if the Lord had taken a few grains of corn and cast them into the ground, and if, a moment after, a large harvest had sprung up, to this the name of such a ' divinely-hastened process ' might have been fitly applied. But with bread it is otherwise; since before that is made, there must be new interpositions of man's art, and those of such a nature as that by them the very life, which up to this point has unfolded itself, must be crushed and destroyed. A grain of wheat left to itself could never, according to the laws of natural development, issue in a loaf of bread. And, moreover, the Lord does not start from the simple germ, from the lifeful rudiments, in which all the seeds of a future life might be supposed to be wrapped up, and by Him rapidly developed, but with the latest artificial product. The oak is folded up in the acorn, but not in the piece of timber hewn and shaped from itself. . . . We must be content to behold in this multiplying of the bread an act of divine omnipotence — not indeed now as at first, of absolute creation out of nothing, since there was a substratum to work on in the original loaves and fishes, but an act of creative accretion; a *quantitative*, as in the water turned into wine there was a *qualitative*, miracle, the bread *growing* in the Lord's hands, so that from that little stock all the multitude were abundantly supplied." — *R. C. Trench.*

12. **And when they were filled, he saith unto his disciples, Gather up the broken pieces which remain over, that nothing be lost.** 13. **So they gathered them up, and filled twelve baskets with broken pieces from the five barley loaves, which remained over unto them that had eaten.** Though we have already quoted an extended passage from Trench, we desire to insert one more paragraph from his wonderfully rich book on the miracles, because no one has expressed the meaning of this particular sentence quite so concisely. " With the Lord of nature, as with nature herself, the most-prodigal bounty goes hand in hand with the nicest and exactest economy; and He who had but now shown Himself God, again submits Himself to the laws and proprieties of His earthly condition, so that as in the miracle itself His power, in this command His humility, shines eminently forth. This which remained over must have immensely exceeded in bulk and quantity the original stock; and we thus have here a visible symbol of that love which exhausts not itself by loving; but after all its outgoings upon others, abides itself far richer than it would have done but for these; of the multiplying which there ever is in a true dispensing; of the increasing which may go along with a scattering (Prov. 11 : 24; cf. 2 Kings 4 : 1–7)."

14. **When therefore the people saw the sign which he did, they said, This is of a truth the prophet that cometh into the world.** John tells us later that he wrote his Gospel that men might believe that Jesus is the Christ, the Son of God, and that believing, they might have life through his name (20 : 31). All through his book he continually keeps in mind the effects of the miracles, and the matchless teaching of the Lord Jesus, upon those who behold His acts and hear His words. Here, they were willing to recognize Him as a prophet from God, but when He talks about the

30. They said therefore unto him, What then doest thou for a sign, that we may see, and believe thee? what workest thou?

necessity of His death they part from Him. So many want to hear something new, but do not want to kneel down and confess their sins, and ask for forgiveness through the blood of the Lord Jesus Christ.

II. **THE MIRACLE OF WALKING ON THE WATER,** vs. 15–21. To escape the crowd which, foolishly and impulsively, would make Him King, our Lord now departed into a mountain to be alone, no doubt for prayer. The disciples were accustomed to these silent disappearances of their Lord, and they took ship and set out for Capernaum with darkness fast coming upon them. Before their boat came into the harbor of this thriving city, a storm arose, in the midst of which, after hard rowing for a distance of perhaps four miles (the lake at its broadest is six miles across), they suddenly saw the Lord walking on the sea drawing nigh to the ship, and they were overwhelmed with fear. "But he saith unto them, It is I; be not afraid. They were willing therefore to receive him into the boat: and straightway the boat was at the land whither they were going." Inasmuch as our lesson is primarily concerned with the subject of Christ the Bread of life, we tarry to give only one paragraph on this (what might be called a) secondary miracle. "This, when we define its place among the nature miracles, must be held a work of power rather than of providence. A great take of fish, a sudden cessation of storm, occur within the ordinary course of events. They were notable miracles when they fell out in His hand and at His Word. But this is a direct act of control over natural law, carrying with it the suggestion of divine power, the power of Him 'who treadeth upon the waves of the sea' — divine power, in a form fitted to remind us of the Jehovah angel who parted the Red Sea and gave manna in the desert. The exact point of the act is not the suspension of natural law. The law of gravity is not suspended, so much as superseded, by the intervention of a higher law, viz., the liberation of a spiritual or glorified body from the bondage of earthly conditions. For Jesus Himself this act was (like the Transfiguration, say) a momentary antedating of the time when His body glorified should pass through shut doors, vanish and appear suddenly, and at length float upward, from the top of Olivet. Among other things He was proving here His right, and ours in Him through redemption, to a spiritual body, for which in His day of power this present body of our humiliation shall be at last exchanged." — *John Laidlaw.*

III. **CHRIST'S GREAT SERMON ON THE BREAD OF LIFE,** vs. 22–59. On the following day many who lingered, possibly in the hope of again seeing the Lord, or even of crowning Him King, took the boats that had come from Tiberias, and set sail for Capernaum. When they began to interrogate Him regarding such a simple thing as how He came to be in Capernaum, He, knowing their hearts even better than they themselves, told them frankly that this crowd was seeking Him not so much because they recognized in Him the Sent One of God, but because He had satisfied their physical hunger with the loaves which He had broken in their midst. From this He begins to lift their thoughts to a higher level, and to show them that they had a greater need in the depths of their lives than physical food could ever satisfy, the need of that food which would endure unto everlasting life.

By saying that God had "sealed" the Son of Man, Christ simply meant that the miracle of feeding the five thousand was a proof that He was indeed the One whom God had sent to bless them. Always ready to discuss religious topics, the multitude asked Him what they could do that they might work the works of God (cf. Mark 10 : 17), a natural question in the light of our Lord's preceding admonition that they should labor for the meat which endured unto life everlasting. "Works of God" are, of course, those things which we do that are pleasing to God. The answer of our Lord is a most remarkable one, penetrating into the very depths of gospel truth, into the foundation of the Christian system of revelation." "This is the work of God, that ye believe on him whom he hath sent." "The one great work required by God, and acceptable to God, and itself wrought by God, for gaining your acceptance with God, is faith in me (3 : 15 f., 36; 5 : 24, 40). This faith regards the Sent, the Sender, and the reason why He has been sent. This is the one 'good work' which is the spring out of which every other flows. Done in a moment, it continues on in its results through the whole life. For as 1 : 12 f. and 3 : 3 ff. show, faith implies regeneration and sonship. But faith in Christ is born of self-despair, which these Jews had not yet reached." — *George Reith.*

30. **They said therefore unto him, What then doest thou for a sign, that we may**

31. Our fathers ate the manna in the wilderness; as it is written, He gave them bread out of heaven to eat.

32. Jesus therefore said unto them, Verily, verily, I say unto you, It was not Moses that gave you the bread out of heaven; but my Father giveth you the true bread out of heaven.

33. For the bread of God is that which cometh down out of heaven, and giveth life unto the world.

34. They said therefore unto him, Lord, evermore give us this bread.

35. Jesus said unto them, I am the bread of life: he that cometh to me shall not hunger, and he that believeth on me shall never thirst.

---

see, and believe thee? what workest thou? 31. **Our fathers ate the manna in the**
wilderness; as it is written, He gave them bread out of heaven to eat. How so-called seekers after religious truth make innumerable foolish demands, postponing the hour of real decision, demanding evidence in the religious realm which they would never require in any other sphere of life! In spite of the fact that these people knew with certainty of the great miracle which Jesus had just performed in feeding the five thousand, they asked Him to produce *further* signs, which would be capable of proving that He was what He claimed to be, the Sent One of God. To support their demand they mentioned the great miracle of the wilderness wanderings in which their prophet Moses had obtained for them from the hands of God sufficient daily food (manna) for their sustenance during forty years (Exod. 16; Ps. 78 : 25).

32. **Jesus therefore said unto them, Verily, verily, I say unto you, It was not Moses**
that gave you the bread out of heaven; but my Father giveth you the true bread out
of heaven. 33. **For the bread of God is that which cometh down out of heaven, and**
giveth life unto the world. 34. **They said therefore unto him, Lord, evermore give**
us this bread. 35. **Jesus said unto them, I am the bread of life: he that cometh**
to me shall not hunger, and he that believeth on me shall never thirst. At this point our Lord attempts to lift up His listeners once again from the level of things material, to which their minds seem to be held, to higher levels of spiritual reality, telling them clearly that while under Moses they did have bread miraculously bestowed, yet it was only for their physical needs, but that now the Father was giving them "the true bread from heaven." This was none other than the Lord Jesus Christ, who had come down from heaven to give life unto the world. We probably should stop right here to notice the different phrases our Lord uses in this chapter in reference to this matter of bread. He calls Himself "the true bread from heaven," "the bread of God," and "the bread of life." Bread is the word which symbolizes the great elemental necessity of life called food. It is necessary for all men; it must be frequently partaken of, and, without it, death must inevitably follow. That food must be eaten by all men, if life is to be sustained, every one recognizes, but Christ also insists on another truth, that, as men with bodies must have physical food, so, because they have a soul, if they are to truly live and to have life that is eternal, a life that satisfies, a life that is rich, they must likewise partake of another bread, which is He Himself, the Bread of life. He is not *a* bread, but *the* Bread. Now we recognize that there are men today who do not confess to any spiritual hunger, and pretend to get on without God, without divine revelation, without prayer, without sacrifice, without the forgiveness of sins. There are millions of such men. But what we do say is this, that these millions of people do not have *hope;* they do not have abounding *joy;* they do not have *peace;* they do not have *light* in dark places; they do not have *deliverance from sin;* they do not *walk with God;* they do not look forward to *an eternal home.* They are not living abundant, rich, satisfying lives of peace, and power, and purity. In the moments when they allow themselves to think of their own condition, they find themselves restless, enslaved, working but never satisfied, studying but never coming to final truth, conceiving new social schemes but never living to see their fulfillment, and dying in disillusionment and despair. Life that is life, life that satisfies, is life that comes through the Lord Jesus Christ. Here, as in so many other places in the Gospels, our Lord continually talks about *life,* meaning fundamental spiritual life, and declares that that life is only to be found in Him. That He means life in all of its various manifestations, life that abides forever, is shown in His reference to the resurrection, and that it would be He who would raise up His own who believed in Him at the last day.

At this point, instead of appropriating the truth which Christ was now teaching, and rejoicing in the fact that at last the true Bread from heaven had appeared, the Jews murmured concerning the Lord, and said, "Is not this Jesus, the son of Joseph, whose father and mother we know? how doth he now say, I am come down out of heaven?" So instead of accepting the truth from the prophet of God, instead of allowing the miracle of the feeding of the five thousand to convince them of the reality of the words of Christ, they kept bringing up objections, which ultimately resulted in their not only rejecting the Lord Jesus, but in actually condemning and crucifying Him. Our Lord, however, instead of losing patience, gently rebukes them for their murmuring, and then, in a note of warning, clearly declares that no man could come to Him except the Father draw him, meaning that these men were not under the direct influence of God whom they claimed to know and love, nor were they taught of God, for all who had really heard the Father would come to Him. He then goes on to state the truth which drove them from Him, that it was His very flesh which He would give for the life of the world, and that if any man ate of that Bread he would live forever. Here, surely, our Lord is speaking of His atoning work, His flesh and His blood, without which no eternal life for dying man is possible.

"As in eating and drinking the body assimilates the nourishing properties of food, so this spiritual eating and drinking convey the fact that faith is an inner laying hold of Christ personally — a receiving Him, a resting on Him, an incorporation with Him. The eating His flesh and drinking His blood convey the fact that faith is the spiritual appropriation of Christ in respect of the great work which He was sent by the Father to do, namely, to shed His blood for sin; and taking to oneself the whole efficacy of this death. Eating and drinking is faith; eating and drinking the flesh and blood is faith in the atoning, propitiating power of Jesus. . . . Faith brings so absolute a union and communion with Christ, that there is but one common principle of life in the Saviour and the saved. The believer lives, moves, and has his being in Christ. . . . In the faith which so embraces and makes Christ one's own, there must go more or less of an intelligent apprehension of all that Christ is personally; of all that He claims; of all that as sent by the Father He has done for the world. Faith is not the sport of a devout but hazy and mystical imagination. It is a dealing with the real 'Son of man'; with the historic person of the man Christ Jesus, who appeared once in the world, and put away sin by the sacrifice of Himself, and went back to the glory of the Father. It is a receiving Him for the purpose for which the Father sent Him: to give us the life which in ourselves we do not have and never can apart from Him — the life eternal — the life of abiding in the Son and in the Father; and which life He has procured for us — made it possible for us to have — by dying in our behalf (1 : 29; 10 : 11; 1 John 2 : 2, etc.). Why it is Christ — as the propitiation for our sins — on whom faith needs to rest, is to be answered by unfolding the suggestion in the words, 'Ye have not life in yourselves.' The life which naturally we do have is a thing of condemnation and death, being hopelessly involved in the bonds of sin. Deliverance from it can be obtained only by the death of Christ, which was related to our sin, and which destroyed death in root and fruit." — *George Reith.*

"The one use of bread is to be eaten, and the one way of benefiting by it is to eat it. With food on the one side and a hungry man on the other, eating is the natural and necessary consequence. You get no good by seeing or smelling or touching bread; you can only benefit by eating it, living on it, making it part of yourself. This, as applied to our bodily life, seems almost childishly simple. But it is what many men completely fail to realize in the spiritual life. Once be sure that Christ is the Bread of life — the true, the living, the heavenly Bread — and then, surely, the only safe and sane course is to feed upon Him, to take His nature into yours, to fill yourself with His fullness, to assimilate Him and be partakers of Him. Yet that is where so many of us fail. We look, we hear, we touch, but we will not eat and live. We talk about Christ, read about Him, sing to Him, call ourselves by His name, associate ourselves with His Church; but we will not come to Him that we may have life; we will not let Him dwell in us, occupy us, transfigure us." — *Thomas Marjoribanks.*

IV. **THE WINNOWING OF SUPERFICIAL FOLLOWERS,** vs. 60–66. Often in the New Testament, we are reminded that the Cross of Christ is a stumbling-block to the Jews and foolishness to the Greeks, that of which men are ashamed (1 Cor. 1 : 18–23). So here, even before our Lord was crucified, we find these men stumbling at the truth of the atoning work of the Lord Jesus. Well did He know that in this multitude, so eagerly listening to Him, asking Him questions, and following Him about, there were many who did not and would not believe. " Upon this many of his disciples went back, and walked no more with him." They not only left Christ, but gave up what they had gained with Him. Bishop Ryle says: " No minister of the gospel should feel surprised if the same thing happens to him." We have known it to happen more than once that, when a minister who believed in the atoning work of Christ, came into a new congregation where Christ's saving work on the Cross had not been preached, or rather had been falsely interpreted, not only would many leave, but some would even ask for his resignation, and, in more than one case, the resignation was offered.

V. **THE CONFESSION OF SIMON PETER,** vs. 67–71. Here we have the first mention of the twelve apostles, as the Twelve, in the Gospel of John. Of them our Lord asks, " Will ye also go away? " to which Simon Peter, for all of them, gave one of the greatest confessions to be found anywhere in the Gospels. " His answer contains three reasons in logical order why they cannot desert their Master: (1) there is no one else to whom they can go even if they were to leave Him; (2) Jesus has all that they need; He has the ' sayings of eternal life '; and if there be other teachers who have them also, yet (3) there is but one Messiah, and Jesus is He." — *Alfred Plummer.* With this confession from the lips of Peter, the great scene closes with our Lord's announcement of the great tragedy, that of those twelve one was actually a devil, Judas Iscariot. So we find that, facing the great miracle of the feeding of the five thousand, and listening to this marvelous discourse of the prophet come from God, some believed, and some did not believe; some rejected Him, and some accepted Him; some stayed, many went away. And why? Who knows but God! This at least we do know, from Christ Himself, that the Father drew some, and some He did not draw; that some hearts were stubborn in unbelief, and others were yielded in loving obedience.

How many different titles do you find in this lesson which Christ gives to Himself? What titles of honor are ascribed by others to Christ in this lesson? In how many different ways does Christ in this chapter definitely declare Himself as of divine origin? What are those great elements in Christ's life and teachings, His work, and death, which make Him to be the only true Bread for man? If Christ's flesh had not been given up in death, would Christ have ever been able to bestow eternal life on man? What characteristics of our Lord are revealed in the miracle of the feeding of the five thousand? How can we do, spiritually, what the disciples did, materially, in this day, in distributing to hungry hearts the Bread of life? What is it in the death of Christ that divides men and leads so many to forsake the Lord, and look elsewhere for what their heart needs but will never find elsewhere?

LESSON VI. — February 7.

JESUS AFFIRMS HIS DEITY. — John 8 : 12–59.

PRINTED TEXT, John 8 : 12, 25–36, 56–59.

GOLDEN TEXT. — ***He that hath seen me hath seen the Father.*** JOHN 14 : 9.

Devotional Reading: Philippians 2 : 1–11.
Beginner Topic: SEVEN SISTERS.
  Lesson Material: Exodus 2 : 11–22.
  Memory Verse: We . . . are helpers. 2 Corinthians 1 : 24.
Primary Topic: BACK HOME IN NAZARETH.
  Lesson Material: John 8 : 12–59; Luke 2 : 46–52.
  Memory Verse: Children, obey your parents in all things, for this is well pleasing in the Lord. Colossians 3 : 20.
Junior Topic: BACK HOME IN NAZARETH.
  Lesson Material: John 8 : 12–59; Luke 2 : 46–52.
  Memory Verse: Children, obey your parents in the Lord: for this is right. Ephesians 6 : 1.
Intermediate and Senior Topic: WHAT JESUS TEACHES ABOUT HIMSELF.
Topic for Young People and Adults: WHAT JESUS TEACHES ABOUT HIMSELF.

THE TEACHER AND HIS CLASS.

The Younger Classes may be asked why we need light, and what happens when we do not have it. They will think first, of course, of physical light. Let the teacher then gradually bring them to see that, just as we need a light for guiding our steps on a dark road at night, or through the rooms of a house at night, so also we need a light for guiding us in our daily conduct, to keep us from stumbling, to show us the way in which we should walk. This will serve as a background for the first declaration of our lesson, that Christ came to be the Light of all men.

The Older Classes will find this entire lesson to be one of the most amazing passages of all the New Testament, revealing, on the one hand, the blackness, the wickedness, the bondage, the hopelessness of human hearts, apart from Christ, the great reasons why we should at once receive Christ, and then the consequent glories or tragic doom which respectively result from our accepting or rejecting the Messiah as the Son of God. These are not only the words of a great man which we find here. These are the eternally true words of the eternal and only begotten Son of God. Let us lean upon them heavily, and embrace them believingly, that the things that are promised here may be our daily possession and experience.

THE LESSON IN ITS SETTING.

Time. — Mid-October A.D. 29, shortly after the Feast of the Tabernacles.

Place. — This discourse, as indicated by verse 20, was spoken in the treasury of the Temple located in the court of the women, the most public part of the Temple, on Mt. Moriah, in the city of Jerusalem. Here the Sanhedrin ordinarily held its sittings.

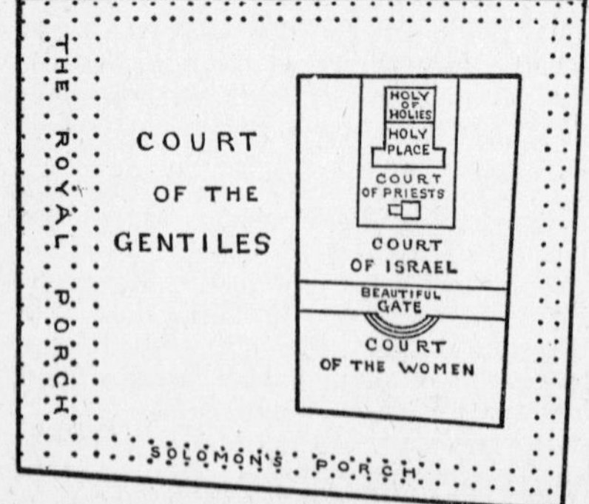

Plan of the Temple.

THE PLAN OF THE LESSON.

SUBJECT: The Lord Jesus Christ the Only Illuminator and True Emancipator of Mankind.

I. CHRIST THE LIGHT OF THE WORLD, v. 12.

II. THE TWOFOLD TESTIMONY TO CHRIST'S DIVINE ORIGIN, vs. 13–20.

III. "YE SHALL DIE IN YOUR SINS," vs. 21–24.

IV. CHRIST'S RELATIONSHIP TO THE FATHER, vs. 25–30.

1. The Father sent the Son.
2. The Father is true.
3. Christ speaks what He hears from the Father.
4. The Father was ever with Him.
5. Christ ever pleases the Father.
6. The sequence: many believed.

V. CHRIST THE TRUTH, vs. 31–59.

1. The freedom which the truth bestows, vs. 31, 32.
2. Sin enslaves but the Son can make us truly free, vs. 33–36.
3. The Jews who were seeking to kill Jesus were of their father the devil — the father of lies, vs. 37–44.
4. The terrible significance of refusing to believe the truth uttered by Christ, vs. 45–47.
5. Christ greater than Abraham, vs. 48–59.

THE TEACHER'S LIBRARY.

Inasmuch as this entire lesson is devoted to a spoken address of Christ, containing no particular action, it will be discovered that most Lives of Christ treat the chapter inadequately. However, great help will be found in some commentaries on John's Gospel. Then, of course, we have a series of sermons on Christ the Light and the Emancipator in Charles H. Spurgeon: *The Messiah. Sermons on Our Lord's Names, Titles and Attributes*, 103–114, 471–482. In addition, see a very scholarly article on "Christ the Truth" by James Moffatt, in Hastings's *Dictionary of Christ and the Gospels*, Vol. 2, 768–771; Thomas Marjoribanks: *The Sevenfold "I Am,"* 3–19; and S. H. Geisy: *The I Am's of Christ*, 83–102.

On those passages in this chapter which speak of Christ setting us free, see the magnificent addresses in Phillips Brooks's precious volume, *Addresses*.

Sermonic material is exceptionally rich on verse 12. See G. Campbell Morgan: *The Westminster Pulpit*, Vol. 3, 360–366; Phillips Brooks: *The Light of the World*, 1–23; J. H. Jowett: *The Silver Lining*, 69–70; J. D. Greenhough: *The Cross in Modern Life*, 88–95; L. A. Banks: *Christ and His Friends*, 254 ff. For verses 25 and 53, see John A. Bayne: *Questions Answered by Christ*, 166–172, and 173–178. On verses 31–36, see two powerful, brilliant sermons by R. C. Trench, in his *Westminster and Other Sermons*, 46–55, 269–280; D. J. Burrell: *The Verilies of Jesus*, 27–33; the same: *The Spirit of the Age*, 326–334. On verse 36, see H. C. G. Moule: *Christ Is All*, 43–54; C. I. Scofield: *In Many Pulpits*, 227–237; G. Campbell Morgan: as above, Vol. 9, 201–208. On verses 53–58, see G. Campbell Morgan: the same, Vol. 2, 217–224. Finally, one may consult the very rich passage in Alexander Maclaren's *Expositions of Holy Scripture, St. John, 1–8* — on verse 12, 319–330; on verse 30 and 31, 330–341; on verse 33, 341–350; on verse 35, 350–363.

JOHN 8 : 12. Again therefore Jesus spake unto them, saying, I am the light of the world: he that followeth me shall not walk in the darkness, but shall have the light of life.

I. **CHRIST THE LIGHT OF THE WORLD.** 12. **Again therefore Jesus spake unto them, saying, I am the light of the world: he that followeth me shall not walk in the darkness, but shall have the light of life.** Alexander Maclaren opens his brilliant sermon on this verse with the remarkable sentence so simple and yet so profound, "Jesus Christ was His own great theme." The words of Mr. Thomas Marjoribanks will form a fitting introduction to the study of this verse: "Probably nothing in all nature has been more constantly used to express spiritual ideas than light. This is perhaps owing to the fact that light, besides being a great blessing in itself, is the indispensable preliminary to a great many others. Light is so indispensable to our work, so closely associated with our knowledge, so necessary to our happiness, that even when we use the word figuratively we forget that it is a figure. Darkness becomes inevitably associated with ignorance, sorrow, sin; light with knowledge, truth, happiness. In the Bible, from Genesis to Revelation, we find light employed to signify the highest of blessings not only in the natural but in the spiritual world. On its very last page is the promise 'There shall be no night there.'" See Isa. 9 : 2; Luke 1 : 78, 79; John 1 : 4, 5.

Years ago the editor read a sermon of Dr. Jowett's on this text, which never fails to rise up in his mind when these words are read or heard, so suggestive and simple was Dr. Jowett's treatment of the verse: "If I interpret myself aright I am in need of three great primary things: I want to see the right way, I want to love it, and I want power to walk in it. The Light of Life will satisfy all those needs and equip me throughout my pilgrimage. How shall we interpret light? Let us begin here. Science tells us of the conversion of forces, how one force can be translated into another, how motion can become heat and heat become light; and this process of translation can be reversed. Our scientific papers have been recently telling us of a great experiment which has been tried in America. A vast machine was invented in the shape of a gigantic windmill, the arms being composed of reflectors catching the light of the sun. The concentrated light, in the form of heat, was then made to generate steam, and the steam was used to drive complicated machinery.

Byzantine Acrostic Forming the Two Greek Words, Life and Light.

(In the Metropolitan Museum of Art, New York.)

"When my Lord uses the figure of light I may find in its spiritual suggestion satisfaction for all other needs of my life. 'I am the light,' not only to make lucid but to make operative. The light illumines; the light kindles; the light empowers. The Lord brings to me light that I may know, warmth that I may feel, and power that I may do. He satisfies the mind, He inflames the desire, He communicates energy to the will."

II. **THE TWOFOLD TESTIMONY TO CHRIST'S DIVINE ORIGIN,** vs. 13–20. Of course, Christ's statement was nothing less than astonishing, so much so, that the Pharisees, who were determined not to receive Him as their Messiah nor to believe Him to be the Son of God, could only reply that Christ had no evidence with which to support such a rash statement, that He was speaking only for Himself, and that His record was not true. Christ's answer to this was twofold. First, He said, "Even if I bear witness of myself, my witness is true; for I know whence I came, and whither I go; but ye know not whence I come, or whither I go." "His own origin and destiny He knows; therefore also the origin and destiny of man. Hence He alone is the Light of men. Man's origin and destiny are clear in Christ, and clear nowhere else. We know in Christ that we are sons of God — though prodigal sons. We know in Christ that we can, if we will, have the old place in the Father's heart and home. Past and future lay unveiled to Christ's eye." — *George Reith.*

In the second place our Lord said that He was not alone in the testimony He was bearing up that the Father Who sent Him was also bearing witness of Him and that according to their own law, the testimony of two, when it agreed, was accounted as true (Deut. 17 : 6; 19 : 15). Of course, Our Lord meant that the very works He

25. They said therefore unto him, Who art thou? Jesus said unto them, Even that which I have also spoken unto you from the beginning.

26. I have many things to speak and to judge concerning you: howbeit he that sent me is true; and the things which I heard from him, these speak I unto the world.

27. They perceived not that he spake to them of the Father.

28. Jesus therefore said, When ye have lifted up the Son of man, then shall ye know that I am *he*, and *that* I do nothing of myself, but as the Father taught me, I speak these things.

---

was doing bore testimony to the fact that God was with Him, for no man could do such things as He did unless God enabled him to do them. His very teachings revealed the truth of God. His very life manifested the holiness of God. Everything about Him showed that God was with Him, and I suppose especially Christ had in mind the testimony of the Father at his very baptism when a Voice from heaven was heard saying " This is my beloved Son, in whom I am well pleased " (Matt. 3 : 17).

However, these Pharisees were not seeking the *truth*. They simply wanted to argue themselves out of the dilemma in which they found themselves to be, so they ask " Where is thy Father? " To this our Lord penetratingly replied, " Ye know neither me, nor my Father: if ye knew me, ye would know my Father also." " People who ask where the Father is, who want Him produced so that they can place Him on the witness stand, thereby demonstrate that they do not know Him at all, and no wonder then that they also do not know Him Whom God has sent. God is always on the witness stand of His written Word, where all who will may hear His testimony in full, and thus learn to know Him most intimately and adequately. Those who reject this testimony know neither the Father nor the Son — and the guilt of this ignorance is theirs alone." — *R. C. H. Lenski.*

III. **" YE SHALL DIE IN YOUR SINS,"** vs. 21–24. A new part of Christ's discourse on this great occasion begins with verse 21, in which He announces that soon He would go away, and when He had departed (not to come back again in their generation) they would die without believing Him and therefore die in their sins. They would die without their sins being forgiven. " When once they have rejected Him, heaven, whither He is about to return, will be closed to them; there will remain for them nothing but perdition. This declaration is a more emphatic repetition of 8 : 33, 34. The *seeking* of the Jews will not be that of faith; it will be only the longing for external deliverance. The words *in your sins*, indicate the state of inward depravity, and consequently of condemnation, in which both will overtake them; Jesus alone could have delivered them therefrom." — *F. Godet.*

The Jews, stubbornly refusing to take Christ's words for what they must have known He intended them to mean, asked if the reason why they could not come where He was going was because He was going to commit suicide. " By the Jews suicide was placed on the same level with murder, and the darkest regions of the world below were supposed to be reserved for those who were guilty of the claim. Thither indeed they could not follow Him." — *B. F. Westcott.*

IV. **CHRIST'S RELATIONSHIP TO THE FATHER,** vs. 25–30. 25. **They said therefore unto him, Who art thou? Jesus said unto them, Even that which I have also spoken unto you from the beginning.** 26. **I have many things to speak and to judge concerning you: howbeit he that sent me is true; and the things which I heard from him, these speak I unto the world.** 27. **They perceived not that he spake to them of the Father.** After all, this is the great question concerning Christ, " Who art thou? " Christ always recognized it to be the supreme question, for He was continually asking " Whom say ye that I am? " " It is incredible that the Jews can have failed to understand what Christ had just declared, that He was from above and not of this world. As in verse 19, they pretend not to understand, to contemptuously ask, '*Thou, who art thou?*' The pronoun is scornfully emphatic. The phrase ' even the same that I said unto you from the beginning ' is a passage of well-known difficulty, and the meaning will probably always remain uncertain. Of this six or seven Greek words, all excepting the words meaning ' unto you,' can have more than one meaning. ' What I from the beginning am also speaking to you of ' is perhaps as likely as any translation to be right." — *A. Plummer.*

28. **Jesus therefore said, When ye have lifted up the Son of man, then shall ye**

29. And he that sent me is with me; he hath not left me alone; for I do always the things that are pleasing to him.

30. As he spake these things, many believed on him.

31. Jesus therefore said to those Jews that had believed him, If ye abide in my word, *then* are ye truly my disciples;

---

know that I am *he*, and *that* I do nothing of myself, but as the Father taught me, I speak these things. 29. **And he that sent me is with me ; he hath not left me alone ; for I do always the things that are pleasing to him.** 30. **As he spake these things many believed on him.** In these five verses, Christ declares five things about the Father, four of them involving His relationship to the Father — the Son was sent by the Father, the Son speaks what He hears from the Father, the Son was ever conscious of the Father's presence with Him, the Son ever lived to please the Father. Finally, the Father in Himself is true. Of course in the phrase " When ye have lifted up the Son of man," our Lord has reference to His approaching death.

The Crucifixion. Murillo.

" Their moral and spiritual ignorance would lead them to make away with Him; and then they should know when too late for them, (1) that He was *He*, their very Christ, the very One they needed; (2) that He was sent from the Father, and not self-sent; (3) that He was the very revelation of the Father, teaching what the Father taught Him. The results of the cross, the glory at the right hand of God, and gift of the Spirit, through which Divine power went with the preaching of His name, are all included. The knowledge of Jesus was perfect as to all that should happen. The highest act of self-renunciation became the clearest proof that Jesus was all He claimed to be, the Son obedient unto death, even the death of the cross, and therefore highly exalted, Phil. 2 : 8 f. Either He was holy, harmless, and sinless, as He here claims, or the greatest impostor." — *George Reith.*

" What blasphemous effrontery would such a declaration ' I do always the things that are pleasing to Him ' be in the mouth of any but the Incarnated Deity. The theory that Jesus was the noblest and holiest of teachers, but nothing more, shatters against such words as these." — *A. Plummer.*

As a result of the wonderful words which came from our Lord's lips that day, many believed on Him. John's Gospel again and again gives us pictures of multitudes of people gathered around the Lord hearing His words, seeing His miracles, beholding His holy life, and when the hour of decision strikes, some going away to criticize, to repudiate, and ultimately to condemn to death, while others are convicted of their sin and of His truthfulness and deity, and, believing on Him, receive eternal life, and thereafter are known everywhere as the disciples of the Lord of glory.

V. **CHRIST THE TRUTH,** vs. 31–59.

1. THE FREEDOM WHICH THE TRUTH BESTOWS, vs. 31, 32. 31. **Jesus therefore said to those Jews that had believed him, If ye abide in my word, *then* are ye truly my disciples.** " The emphasis lies on the pronoun *ye* and not, as we are inclined to place it, on the verb *abide*. The sentence is a gracious recognition of the first rude beginning of faith. Even this, if it were cherished with absolute devotion, might become the foundation of better things. The *Word*, the revelation of Christ, is at once the element in which the Christian lives, and the spring of his life. He abides in the Word, and the Word abides in him (5 : 38; 1 John 2 : 14). Just so, in the language of St. Paul, the believer lives in Christ and Christ in the believer (Gal. 2 : 20)." — *B. F. Westcott.*

32. And ye shall know the truth, and the truth shall make you free.
33. They answered unto him, We are Abraham's seed, and have never yet been in bondage to any man: how sayest thou, Ye shall be made free?
34. Jesus answered them, Verily, verily, I say unto you, Every one that committeth sin is the bondservant of sin.
35. And the bondservant abideth not in the house for ever: the son abideth for ever.

---

32. **And ye shall know the truth, and the truth shall make you free.** These words express a fundamental law of life, even apart from their relationship to Christ. The whole world, *e.g.*, in the fifteenth and preceding centuries, believed that the earth was flat, and drew on their maps what was called the jumping-off place, that is, the edge of the earth beyond which there was nothing but an abyss of boiling water. When Columbus and Magellan proved that the earth was a sphere, men were delivered from this former error, and were free for further exploration and an understanding of the whole planetary system. This may work conversely also. Millions of people are deluded and deceived today, through a great many causes, into believing, *e.g.*, that there is no such thing as everlasting punishment. Only the truth, as revealed in the Word of God, can ever deliver them from such a dangerous delusion as this. In this way does the holy Word of God set us free from ignorance, from bondage to sin, from fear of man, and of death, from a false conception of how the favor of God may be secured, from low ideals, from the fascination of this world, from the allurements of sin, from the lies of the evil one, from death itself. And this Word is found incarnated, active, fulfilled, and eternally powerful, in the Truth Who is the Son of God.

Permission of The Sunday School Board, Nashville, Tenn.

2. SIN ENSLAVES BUT THE SON CAN MAKE US TRULY FREE, vs. 33–36. 33. **They answered unto him, We are Abraham's seed, and have never yet been in bondage to any man: how sayest thou, Ye shall be made free?** When Christ spoke of setting men free, His listeners, still in a critical mood, and refusing to accept His Words as true, made one of the most astonishingly inaccurate statements that could ever have been uttered by the Jews at any time, "We have never yet been in bondage to any man."

"The whole past history of their nation was the record of one bondage following hard on another, they for their sins having come at one time or another under the yoke of almost every people round about them. They had been, by turns, in bondage to the Canaanites, in bondage to the Philistines, in bondage to the Syrians, in bondage to the Chaldeans; then again to the Græco-Syrian kings; and now, even at the very moment when this indignant disclaimer is uttered, the signs of a foreign rule, of the domination of a stranger, everywhere met their eye. They bought and sold with Roman money: they paid tribute to a Roman emperor; a Roman governor sat in their judgment hall; a Roman garrison occupied the fortress of their city." — *R. C. Trench.*

34. **Jesus answered them, Verily, verily, I say unto you, Every one that committeth sin is the bondservant of sin.** The words of Archbishop Trench on this verse are simply powerful. "Any wilful sin, admitted into the heart, having once gained a footing there, cannot remain at a standstill, but must ever bring more and more the whole man under its dominion, laying ever new and ever stronger fetters upon him; so that the chains of evil habits which may have been but as spiders' threads at the first, so easily might they by a vigorous effort of the will have been snapped asunder, become links of iron at the last."

35. **And the bondservant abideth not in the house for ever: the son abideth for ever.** "The house is the kingdom of God, though the figure is not to be pressed

36. If therefore the Son shall make you free, ye shall be free indeed.

in its details. The chief point of contrast is the temporary place and the enduring place of the slave and the Son respectively in the house. As regards the Jews, the application was obvious. The kingdom was, so far as outward principles went, to be taken from them because they *would* reject the Sonship, the real and eternal privilege of the kingdom offered them, and remain in the slavery of sin. No one with the heart of a slave towards God can possibly be within His eternal house; and the heart of a sinner unpardoned is the heart of a slave." — *George Reith.*

36. **If therefore the Son shall make you free, ye shall be free indeed.** " Theoretically, we are free politically. Actually, we are the slaves of party, of the caucus, of the bosses and the trusts. The very minute I give over into the hands of a convention the right to formulate my political creed I am no longer absolutely free. When I allow a habit to dominate my life, I am no longer free. When I allow pride, or vanity, or ambition, or pleasure to control my life, I am the basest of slaves. The very fact that I do not, can not, cease from sin proclaims me a slave. Jesus Christ came into a world of slaves.

" It is interesting to note that His first formal announcement of His mission on earth touched life at that very point. In the synagogue at Nazareth there was handed to Him the book of the Prophet Isaiah, and he found the place where it was written: ' The spirit of the Lord is upon me, because he hath anointed me to preach . . . deliverance to the captives " (Luke 4 : 18). — *C. I. Scofield.*

3. THE JEWS WHO WERE SEEKING TO KILL JESUS WERE OF THEIR FATHER THE DEVIL — THE FATHER OF LIES, VS. 37–44. These Jews were boasting that because they were the descendants of Abraham, they were free. What they meant by this, it is difficult to say, for they certainly could not have reference to political freedom. It may mean they were free from all condemnation, thinking themselves to be in favor with God, because of their mere physical descent from the father of the Hebrew race. " But," says our Lord, " though you are Abraham's seed, you are seeking to kill me, and inasmuch as what I have told you I have heard from God and yet you would kill me, which Abraham never would and never did, you are not true children of Abraham. You have another father, morally and spiritually, not God, but the devil, a murderer from the beginning, who had no truth in him, who is a liar, and the father of lies and speaketh a lie." This is indeed a tremendous and terrible accusation. But it is true, not alone for the Jews, to whom Christ was then speaking, but for all men who likewise reject the Lord, and would put Him to death. Christ taught that the devil was a real person. He it was who brought about the fall of man, and thus brought death into the world. He it was who lied to Eve, and persuaded her to disobey God. A passage that throws a great deal of light on these words of our Lord, though seldom referred to by commentators, for some strange reason, is Romans 6 : 16: " Know ye not, that to whom ye present yourselves as servants unto obedience, his servants ye are whom ye obey; whether of sin unto death, or of obedience unto righteousness? " — Two things the Jews themselves could not deny: First, that they refused to believe what Christ was saying, and secondly, they were plotting to put Him to death. By this they proved themselves not to be seeking the truth of God, because they were rejecting it, nor were they looking for *the* prophet of God, because they were plotting to put Him to death. In fact, what they were doing was not simply a proof of their stubbornness, their ignorance, their willfulness, but it revealed them to be, though they denied it, inspired by, energized by, deluded by, and enslaved by Satan himself, the enemy of God, and the enemy of Christ.

4. THE TERRIBLE SIGNIFICANCE OF REFUSING TO BELIEVE THE TRUTH UTTERED BY CHRIST, VS. 45–47. Our Lord, continuing His accusation, lays down a great principle, which all must recognize to be true, whatever they think of the Lord Jesus, " He that is of God heareth the words of God," and the supplementary truth, " for this cause ye hear them not, because ye are not of God."

" All men are *of God* in the sense of having His image, and therefore having so far a capacity for the truth of Christ; for if it were not so, the gospel could not appeal to them. And (v. 44) all men are *of the devil* in the sense of having a principle of evil in them, that mars and tends to obliterate the image of God. There are not *sorts* of human natures. Accordingly, it is the moral attitude men take up, when conscious of the opposing forces that war within them, the determination of will toward one side or other, which marks them as being, or not being, *of God — of the*

56. Your father Abraham rejoiced to see my day; and he saw it, and was glad.

57. The Jews therefore said unto him, Thou art not yet fifty years old, and hast thou seen Abraham?

58. Jesus said unto them, Verily, verily, I say unto you, Before Abraham was born, I am.

59. They took up stones therefore to cast at him: but Jesus hid himself, and went out of the temple.

---

truth; cf. 3 : 21, 'He that doeth truth is coming to the light.'" — *George Reith.* (Cf. John 10 : 4.)

5. CHRIST GREATER THAN ABRAHAM, vs. 48–59. All that the Jews could now say was that Christ was a Samaritan, demon-possessed. They could not answer His accusations. There was no reply to His arguments, so they simply threw names at Him, as many have done since. Christ does not reply to the charge that He is a Samaritan. "For Him it contained nothing offensive, for He knew that Samaritans might equal or excel Jews in both benevolences and gratitude" (Luke 10 : 33; 17 : 16). — *A. Plummer.* He did deny that He was demon-possessed, and reasserted that in everything He did, or said, He honored the Father. Then, instead of walking away from them, utterly provoked by their diabolical hardness of heart, He threw out one final, tremendous promise, perchance a few might come to see the truthfulness and the preciousness of what He was saying, "If a man keep my word, he shall never see death." By this, of course, our Lord meant that such a man would never see death as a punishment of sin, he would never see death as the ultimate dreadful experience of the eternal wrath of God in judgment. At once the Jews cried out that now they *knew* He had a demon, for their father Abraham was long ago dead, and all their prophets, and by such a saying as this, Christ was making Himself greater than their father Abraham. Christ picks up this statement and insists that He is greater than their father Abraham, for said He

56. **Your father Abraham rejoiced to see my day; and he saw it, and was glad.** "Christ's day was the day of promise fulfilled; when the new age of gospel grace began in the advent of the Son of God in flesh. More or less consciously, Abraham rejoiced in the Messianic hope; and his joy grew deeper, truer, just in proportion as by the discipline of his faith other hopes clinging to this were stripped off, and the Messianic reality stood out. In heaven he saw its realization in Christ's descent to earth; cf. Luke 9 : 31. If not this, the seeing of Christ's day must refer to some vision of faith at some one or other crisis in his life, such as Isaac's sacrifice, that struck out new channels of aspiration in Abraham's breast." — *George Reith.*

57. **The Jews therefore said unto him, Thou art not yet fifty years old, and hast thou seen Abraham?** 58. **Jesus said unto them, Verily, verily, I say unto you, Before Abraham was born, I am.** Here is one of the most significant passages in the New Testament, setting forth the great doctrine of Christ's pre-existence. The words of G. Campbell Morgan are profound, and worth the most careful consideration: "I cannot stand at any fixed point and say, I am. Everything is changing, and I am changing and passing. I am, in a second, becomes I was, and no human being can finally use that word, I am. It is the very word by which God unveiled the supreme fact of His own nature to the great law-giver. Whom shall I say sent me? asked Moses, and the answer came 'I am' (Exodus 3 : 14). As Moses perhaps was waiting for something to be added, for some explanation unveiling, or interpretation, the word was repeated, '— that I am.' It is the express and essential word of absolute Deity. It is a word which can only be uttered by a Being of underived existence, living in the essential fact of life, uncreated and unending. This is what Christ said in the presence of these men. Before Abraham appeared, began to be, 'I am.' There is no past tense to His being, and no future. He is at the centre of all life, never having derived, consequently His influence is not traditional, but inspirational. The Hebrew today, the devout Hebrew, is influenced by Abraham; but it is a traditional influence. The Christian of today is influenced by Christ, but it is not a traditional influence. I am not influenced by the Christ of nineteen hundred years ago, but by the Christ of this hour and this place and this life. 'I am,' not I was. Therein is the absolute difference between Abraham and Christ, between Hebraism and Christianity."

59. **They took up stones therefore to cast at him: but Jesus hid himself, and**

went out of the temple. And so, not content with calling Him all sorts of foul names, refusing to heed His warnings, morally unable to recognize Him to be the Sent One of God, refusing to acknowledge their own bondage to sin, unalarmed and unmoved at the terrible accusation of Christ, that they were doing the work of the evil one, and even though they must have known that never before had man spoken as this man, even though His life testified to the truthfulness of His works, they, not content with going away to discuss what He said, not content with refusing Him, *took up stones to stone Him*, the Son of God. The Prophet of God, the Holy One of God, Who went about doing good, Whose lips knew no words but those of grace, Who came to lay down His life for them, Who offered them eternal life, Whose blood could wash away their sins, Whose resurrection could give them the hope of everlasting life, Him they took up stones to stone.

How many different titles do you find given to Christ in this lesson? What were some of the things Christ said about Himself in this discourse which no mere man could ever truly say about himself? What reasons can you think of why the Jews appearing in this particular event of our Lord's life did not believe on Him? In what ways does Satan today persuade men to reject the revelation of Christ in the New Testament? Are we helping men to believe on Christ, or are we doing Satan's work by helping men to reject Christ?

LESSON VII. — February 14.

JESUS HEALS A MAN BORN BLIND. — John 9.

PRINTED TEXT, John 9 : 18–38.

GOLDEN TEXT. — ***One thing I know, that, whereas I was blind, now I see.*** JOHN 9 : 25.

Devotional Reading: Psalm 27 : 1–6.
Beginner Topic: TWO GOOD EYES.
Lesson Material: John 9.
Memory Verse: Let us love one another. 1 John 4 : 7.
Primary Topic: NOT AFRAID.
Lesson Material: John 9.
Memory Verse: For my mouth shall utter truth. Proverbs 8 : 7.
Junior Topic: WHAT THE BLIND MAN NEEDED MOST.
Lesson Material: John 9.
Memory Verse: My God shall supply every need of yours according to his riches in glory in Christ Jesus. Philippians 4 : 19.
Intermediate and Senior Topic: WHAT THE BLIND MAN LEARNED.
Topic for Young People and Adults: THE MEANING OF THE BLIND MAN'S EXPERIENCE.

THE TEACHER AND HIS CLASS.

The Younger Classes should be led in a very simple way to realize that while there are thousands and thousands of things each man does not know, and will not know, there are a few great fundamental things that each man does know. For instance, even a child knows his mother from all other women in a large group; a young boy in school soon knows where his classroom is, and what subjects are to be recited upon during the different hours of the day. We know what we like to eat, and what we do not like to eat; we know what we like to do and what we do not like to do. So in our spiritual experience we *know* whether or not Christ has come into our heart; we *know* if God is our Father or not; we *know* whether or not we believe the Bible. Our lesson today is about a man who had a glorious experience with Christ, from which certain great realities became his, and nothing in the world could ever deprive him of the knowledge of what Jesus had done for him, and of the change that had come over him.

The Older Classes will here find a remarkable study in personal testimony to the Lord Jesus Christ, contrasted with fierce opposition to Christ. We have plenty of opposition to the Lord Jesus today, sometimes expressed in definite antagonism; sometimes in sheer indifference, but do we also have the strong clear testimony to Christ by those who know Him that we ought to have, that we need for these critical days? The man in this lesson rebukes most of us by his confounding of all Christ's critics, and his strong loyalty to the One who had given him sight.

THE LESSON IN ITS SETTING.

Time. — Mid-October, A.D. 29.

Place. — Somewhere in the city of Jerusalem.

THE PLAN OF THE LESSON.

SUBJECT: The Reality of a Definite Experience with Christ Which No Argument and No Opposition Can Ever Take Away from Us.

I. JESUS DISCUSSES THE STATE OF THE BLIND MAN WITH HIS DISCIPLES, John 9 : 1–5.

II. THE HEALING OF THE BLIND MAN, vs. 6, 7.

III. THE UNBELIEVING NEIGHBORS AND PHARISEES REFUSE TO ACKNOWLEDGE THE MIRACLE, vs. 8–34.

1. The Question of *Identity*, vs. 8, 9.
2. The Question of *How* his eyes were opened, vs. 10–15.
3. The Question of *Who* could perform such miracles, vs. 16–23.
4. The Clear Testimony of the one once Blind, vs. 24, 25.
5. The Question of *How* is again debated, vs. 26, 27.
6. The One Once Blind Declares his Conviction that Jesus was of God, vs. 28–33.
7. He is cast out though his words could not be contradicted, v. 34.

IV. JESUS MEETS THE RESTORED MAN AND LEADS HIM TO BELIEVE IN HIM AS THE SON OF GOD, vs. 35–38.

V. JESUS' FINAL WORDS TO THE PHARISEES, vs. 39–41.

THE TEACHER'S LIBRARY.

The standard lives of Christ will not be found adequate in the treatment of this lesson, and larger commentaries on John's Gospel will be found to be less satisfactory here than on other chapters. Thus Lenski, who devotes thirty-five pages to a discussion of the entire ninth chapter of John, but devotes sixty-eight pages to the same number of verses of chapter 10. All books on the miracles of Christ will also have chapters on this episode in our Lord's life, but most of them seem quite weak, with the exception of the magnificent twenty-five page discussion in Trench's work. Biographical chapters are, for some strange reason, exceedingly scarce, and what we have is quite superficial. See F. A. Noble: *Typical New Testament Conversations*, 103–118; A. T. Robertson: *Minor Characters in the New Testament*, 119–126; G. Campbell Morgan: *Westminster Pulpit*, Vol. 3, 161–168; Albert Hughes: *The Glory of the Godhead in the Gospel of John*, 133–152. On the pool of Siloam, see the brief article by W. Ewing, in James Hastings: *Dictionary of Christ and the Gospels*, Vol. 2, 628; and Gustaf Dalman: *Sacred Sites and Ways*, 309–313. For sermonic material on verse 25, see L. A. Banks: *Christ and His Friends*, 277 ff.; Charles H. Parkhurst: *The Blind Man's Creed*, 1 ff.; on verse 29, H. S. Coffin: *University Sermons*, 192–210, 243–256; on vs. 35–38, Phillips Brooks: *The Light of the World*, 194–215; on verse 37, Alexander Maclaren: *Triumphant Certainties*, 119–127. Above all see *ten sermons* by Charles H. Spurgeon, in his *Sermons on Our Lord's Miracles*, Vol. 2. There are two chapters on this miracle in an old, and not well known work, W. B. Stevens, *The Sabbaths of Our Lord*, 218–256.

In the Gospels there are three different occasions when our Lord opened the eyes of the blind, once in Capernaum, when two blind men were healed, recorded only in Matthew 9 : 27–31; again, near Jericho, when two other blind men were healed, recorded in all three of the Synoptics (Matt. 20 : 29–34; Mark 10 : 46–52; Luke 18 : 35–43), and this occasion, recorded only by John.

I. **JESUS DISCUSSES THE STATE OF THE BLIND MAN WITH HIS DISCIPLES,** vs. 1–5. Palestine, in the time of our Lord, was a place where theological discussions were the order of the day, and where, while men did not seem to be very seriously concerned about the alleviation of suffering, they raised difficult questions and entered into fruitless speculations upon almost every occasion. The disciples were not free from this spirit of the age in the early days of their discipleship. Seeing a man born blind, and there were many at that time, they asked whose sin it was that brought this about, whether his own or that of his parents. After all, quite a foolish question because the man was *born* blind, so how could the blindness be the result of any sin of his, unless one believed in the transmigration of souls, and this was hardly considered in Jewish theology. Our Lord never was asked a question that He could not immediately answer, because of his infinite and divine wisdom. Here He at once replies that this blindness was due to the sin of neither the man him-

From a sketch.

Blind Leading the Blind.

self nor his parents, but that through him, and his miraculous recovery, the works of God should be made manifest. Before He proceeds to perform the miracle, he makes two declarations concerning Himself, that He must work the works of the Father who sent Him, and that while He is in the world He is the light of the world. Both of these assertions refer directly to the miracle that is about to take place. "To enter into the plan of God for the bringing of this man to the light of everlasting life, that he should thus for a while be dark outwardly; that so at once upon this night, and upon the night of his heart, a higher light should break, and the Sun of righteousness arise on him, with healing in his wings for all his bodily and all his spiritual infirmities; which, but for that long night of darkness and sorrow, might have never been: while again this was part of a larger whole, and fitted in, according to His eternal counsels, to the great scheme for the revelation of the glory and power of the Only Begotten to the world (cf. 5 : 20; 9 : 17; 11 : 25, 32, 33)." — *R. C. Trench.*

II. **THE HEALING OF THE BLIND MAN,** vs. 6, 7. One of the certain proofs for the genuineness and authenticity of the Gospels is seen in the constantly manifested characteristic of the records of the miracles, namely, that the miracles are not strung out with great details; that is, what our Lord does is recorded with the greatest brevity, without adornment, and without elaboration. Thus, in this chapter, while twenty-seven verses are devoted to the debate which arose because of this miracle, it takes only two verses to record what our Lord *did.* Finishing His introductory pronouncement, Christ spat on the ground, made some clay, which He placed on the eyes of the blind man, and told him to go wash in the pool of Siloam. This he immediately did, with the instant result that he returned seeing. It does not say that he returned to Christ. In fact, the record would seem to indicate that Christ disappears from the scene for a considerable length of time, and of course, was not present during the long debate that followed. Why did our Lord anoint this man's eyes with clay? "There was no value in the clay. About that I think we are all in agreement. Christ healed blind men without clay upon another occasion. Christ never dealt with two people in the same way. There was no virtue in the clay. Clay will never open a man's eyes. There is no virtue in the waters of Siloam. You may pour all the waters of Siloam over blind eyes today — this is one of the things that remain, you can find the ancient pool still there — but no sight will come. Christ did not by His touch make the clay magical with medicine. Christ did not will into the waters of Siloam some property that mysteriously healed the man. The man did not gain his sight by clay and Siloam. What, then, did happen? Christ put clay upon his eyes, and told him to go, and in that moment He created the opportunity for the exercise of faith. The man went. Why did he go? He went because he believed. If you say he went in obedience, I reply that obedience is the demonstration of belief. There is no belief that is not expressed in obedience. There is no obedience that is not based on faith. His going was the activity of faith." — *G. Campbell Morgan.*

Photograph by Bonfils.

Pool of Siloam.

The pool of Siloam is outside Jerusalem, at the mouth of the Tyropœon valley, on the slope south of the Temple area, where "in New Testament times, a covered arcade within the pool 22½ feet high and 12 feet wide ran around the four sides. The spring is intermittent. During the rains it may flow twice a day, but in late summer, once in two days. On the last day of the Feast of Tabernacles, water from this fountain was poured on the altar. The handful of poor inhabitants who live in the village of Siloam on the east slope of the valley still use the impure water for domestic purposes." — *W. Ewing.*

III. **THE UNBELIEVING NEIGHBORS AND PHARISEES REFUSE TO ACKNOWLEDGE THE MIRACLE,** vs. 8–34.

1. THE QUESTION OF *IDENTITY*, vs. 8, 9. A miracle like this, of course, could not help but create an enormous amount of discussion among the people who lived

JOHN 9 : 18. The Jews therefore did not believe concerning him, that he had been blind, and had received his sight, until they called the parents of him that had received his sight,

19. And asked them, saying, Is this your son, who ye say was born blind? how then doth he now see?

20. His parents answered and said, We know that this is our son, and that he was born blind:

---

where this man begged. (One whole chapter, in the most remarkable book in the world, the Gospel of John, devoted to one day's experience in the life of an obscure, unnamed beggar!) That the person walking around in their midst could now see, everyone had to admit, but somehow there was a unanimous reluctance on the part of these neighbors to recognize that a miracle had been performed, so they tried to explain the phenomenon some other way. Foolishly, they began to ask whether this man now seeing was the same beggar who had been blind during all the years they had known him. The whole discussion was rather stupid, like some discussions in philosophy, and it was brought to an abrupt and final end, by the man simply saying, "I am he." He knew he was the man born blind, now seeing, and his testimony could not be contradicted.

2. THE QUESTION OF *HOW* HIS EYES WERE OPENED, vs. 10–15. Instead of frankly and joyfully acknowledging that this man had experienced a wonderful cure, and seeking out the Lord to thank Him for what He had done, these stubborn unbelievers, so deliberately antagonistic to the claims of Christ, raised a second question: "*How* then were thine eyes opened?" The man told all that he knew, namely, that one called Jesus had made clay, anointed his eyes, told him to go to Siloam and wash, which he had done, and immediately he had received sight. Note carefully the little article "the" — "the" man that is called Jesus, implying that this person was the pre-eminently discussed individual of that hour. When they asked him where this person Jesus was, he told them he did not know. Some things the man knows, and some things he does not know. He gladly tells what he does know; he does not even guess at what he does not know. This is a good principle for all of us. So they brought him, whose eyes had just been opened, to the Pharisees, and they likewise began to ask *how* he had received his sight, and he repeated the story of his glorious deliverance.

3. THE QUESTION OF *WHO* COULD PERFORM SUCH MIRACLES, vs. 16–24. The third problem is now raised, and this time by the Pharisees, who were skilled in theological discussions and who had a score of supposed and worthless reasons for not accepting Christ as the Sent One of God. Realizing that this miracle had been performed on the Sabbath day, they said that settled the question, the one who did this could not be of God. "We cannot be sure whether this is the last day of the Feast of the Tabernacles (7 : 37) or the next Sabbath. There were seven miracles of mercy wrought on the Sabbath: (1) withered hand (Matt. 12 : 9); (2) demoniac at Capernaum (Mark 1 : 21); (3) Simon's wife's mother (Matt. 8 : 14, 15); (4) woman bowed down eighteen years (Luke 13 : 14); (5) dropsical man (Luke 14 : 1); (6) paralytic at Bethesda (John 5 : 10); (7) man born blind." — *A. Plummer.* Others said, that a man who was a sinner could not possibly perform such a miracle as this, recognizing that such a deliverance from blindness could only be by the power and with the approval of God. So they turned to the blind man again, to ask him what *he* thought of the person who had so graciously and undeniably given him his sight. This time we discover that the man's conception of the One who healed him is higher than at first, for he answered: "He is a prophet." "Not yet the Messiah; not yet the Son of God; of these higher dignities of his benefactor the man as yet has no guess; but what he believes Him he boldly declares Him, 'a prophet' — one furnished with a message from above, and attesting that message by deeds which no man could do, except God were with him (John 3 : 2; 4 : 19; 6 : 14). They who asked this cared not in the least for the judgment of the man, but they hoped to mold him into an instrument for their own wicked purposes. . . ." — *R. C. Trench.*

18. **The Jews therefore did not believe concerning him, that he had been blind, and had received his sight, until they called the parents of him that had received his sight,** 19. **and asked them, saying, Is this your son, who ye say was born blind? how then doth he now see?** 20. **His parents answered and said, We know that this is our son, and that he was born blind:** 21. **but how he now seeth, we know not;**

21. But how he now seeth, we know not; or who opened his eyes, we know not: ask him; he is of age; he shall speak for himself.
22. These things said his parents, because they feared the Jews: for the Jews had agreed already, that if any man should confess him *to be* Christ, he should be put out of the synagogue.
23. Therefore said his parents, He is of age; ask him.
24. So they called a second time the man that was blind, and said unto him, Give glory to God: we know that this man is a sinner.
25. He therefore answered, Whether he is a sinner, I know not: one thing I know, that, whereas I was blind, now I see.

---

or who opened his eyes, we know not: ask him; he is of age; he shall speak for himself. How stubborn the human heart can be when it is determined that, no matter how great the evidence, it will not recognize Jesus of Nazareth to be the Son of God, and believe in Him for salvation and eternal life. If these interrogators were looking for dependable evidence on which to base their decision about Christ, they had it now in abundance; but no, they are not going to be forced to acknowledge what they have determined they will not believe, so they call this man's parents, and interrogate them. They confess that this was their son, that he was born blind, that now he could see, and that, if they wanted any further information they should ask him for he was of age. After all, this was about everything they could say, and yet they refused to bear witness to the grace and power and deity of this person Christ, because a decree had gone forth that if any man should confess Jesus to be the Christ, he should be excommunicated from the synagogue. 22. **These things said his parents, because they feared the Jews: for the Jews had agreed already, that if any man should confess him *to be* Christ, he should be put out of the synagogue.** 23. **Therefore said his parents, He is of age; ask him.** "There were two, or as some say three, kinds of excommunication among the Jews, greatly differing in degrees and intensity; and Christ often speaks of them as among the sharpest trials which His followers would have to endure for His name's sake (John 16 : 2). The mildest form was exclusion for thirty days from the synagogue. To this period, in case the excommunicated showed no sign of repentance, a similar or a longer period, according to the will of those that imposed the sentence, was added. In other ways too, it was made sharper; it was accompanied with a curse; none might hold communion with him now, not even his family, except in cases of absolute necessity. Did the offender show himself obstinate still, he was in the end absolutely separated from the fellowship of the people of God, cut off from the congregation — a sentence answering, as many suppose, to the delivering to Satan in the Apostolic Church (1 Cor. 5 : 5; 1 Tim. 1 : 20)." — *R. C. Trench.* Now we begin to see why these Pharisees refused to acknowledge the truth concerning Christ to which the evidence overwhelmingly led, because, long before this, they had taken their stand against Christ, denouncing Him, and now they were, through sheer pride of office, and reputation for wisdom, determined not to acknowledge their fault, by changing their verdict.

4. THE CLEAR TESTIMONY OF THE ONE ONCE BLIND, VS. 24, 25. 24. **So they called a second time the man that was blind, and said unto him, Give glory to God: we know that this man is a sinner.** 25. **He therefore answered, Whether he is a sinner, I know not: one thing I know, that, whereas I was blind, now I see.** "The phrase, 'Give glory to God,' is a solemn charge to declare the whole truth (cf. Josh. 7 : 19). The man by his former declaration had really, so they implied, done dishonor to God. He was now required to confess his error: to recognize in the authoritative voice of the Jews his own condemnation, and to admit the truth of it. At the same time, under this thought of the rendering of glory to God by the confession of error, lies the further idea that the cure was due directly to God, and that to Him, and not to the man called Jesus, was gratitude to be rendered." — *B. F. Westcott.* They tried to help the man to such a confession by dogmatically declaring that they absolutely knew that his man Jesus was a sinner. Well, the man formerly blind is not going to discuss something he knows nothing about. He keeps away from theology, but he remains true to what he knows — once he was blind, now he sees. No one can deny that. "Find some man who has been a drunkard or habitual gambler, or given up to unclean, shameful ways, and is now thoroughly and permanently changed,

26. They said therefore unto him, What did he to thee? how opened he thine eyes?
27. He answered them, I told you even now, and ye did not hear; wherefore would ye hear it again? would ye also become his disciples?
28. And they reviled him, and said, Thou art his disciple; but we are disciples of Moses.
29. We know that God hath spoken unto Moses: but as for this man, we know not whence he is.
30. The man answered and said unto them, Why, herein is the marvel, that ye know not whence he is, and *yet* he opened mine eyes.
31. We know that God heareth not sinners: but if any man be a worshipper of God and do his will, him he heareth.
32. Since the world began it was never heard that any one opened the eyes of a man born blind.

---

reformed, redeemed, by the action of faith and the power of Jesus' love. Tell him that the Bible is an untrustworthy book, that the Christian doctrines are unproved, that Christ's saving power is only an imagination. Read out to him a long catalogue of difficulties, discrepancies, and contradictions; pile up before him all the arguments which have been used to prove miracles impossible. He will hardly listen to you — or he will hear you with impatience, perhaps with a laugh of derision. It is as if you flung puff darts, or set yourselves to prove that the sun gives no light. He has one big, momentous, living fact to set against all your talk. He knows that he was once a vulgar, degraded being, an animal hardly conscious of a soul, a lecherous, swinish, uncontrollable beast, chained, led captive by his lusts, possessed with seven devils, without hope and without shame, sinking down to deeper depths and to very hell. *Now* the devils are gone out of him, the chains are broken, he is clothed and in his right mind, his infernal passions are subdued; his life, which was all foul disease, has been restored to health. He is a free man. And Christ has done it. Christ's cross, Christ's love, Christ's mighty spirit within him. You cannot move this man by sophistical word-fencing and sneers. He will answer as the seeing man did in the story: I know nothing about all your objections and your clever reasonings; one thing I know that whereas I was blind, now I see." — *J. G. Greenhough.*

5. THE QUESTION OF *HOW* IS AGAIN DEBATED, vs. 26, 27. 26. **They said therefore unto him, What did he to thee? how opened he thine eyes?** 27. **He answered them, I told you even now, and ye did not hear; wherefore would ye hear it again? would ye also become his disciples?** The repeating of the question of *how* the man was healed simply reveals the fact that these stubborn men were finding the testimony of the beggar too strong and clear for denial. He no more than answers one of their questions but that, refusing to accept the testimony, they turn to another problem. Every Christian minister has met this type of people who begin arguing about some problem in the Bible, *e.g.*, where Cain got his wife, the universality of the Flood, the virgin birth of Christ, the so-called contradictions of the Gospels, etc., etc., and as soon as the believer clears up one point, they drop the matter and turn to something else, simply determined not to believe.

6. THE ONE ONCE BLIND DECLARES HIS CONVICTION THAT JESUS WAS OF GOD, vs. 28–33. 28. **And they reviled him, and said, Thou art his disciple; but we are disciples of Moses.** 29. **We know that God hath spoken unto Moses: but as for this man, we know not whence he is.** 30. **The man answered and said unto them, Why, herein is the marvel, that ye know not whence he is, and *yet* he opened mine eyes.** The skeptical Pharisees now bring up another subject. They knew that God had spoken to Moses, but they do not know whence this man Jesus is; that is, they do not know that He is from God, at which confession of ignorance the one once blind shows his astonishment. "Here is one evidently clothed with powers mightier than man's, able to accomplish a work like this; and you, the spiritual rulers of our nation, you that should try the spirits, should be able to pronounce of each new appearance whether it be of God or not, here acknowledge your ignorance, and cannot decide whence He is, whether of earth or of heaven." — *R. C. Trench.*

31. **We know that God heareth not sinners: but if any man be a worshipper of God, and do his will, him he heareth.** 32. **Since the world began it was never**

33. If this man were not from God, he could do nothing.
34. They answered and said unto him, Thou wast altogether born in sins,
and dost thou teach us? And they cast him out.
35. Jesus heard that they had cast him out; and finding him, he said,
Dost thou believe on the Son of God?
36. He answered and said, And who is he, Lord, that I may believe on
him?
37. Jesus said unto him, Thou hast both seen him, and he it is that
speaketh with thee.
38. And he said, Lord, I believe. And he worshipped him.

---

heard that any one opened the eyes of a man born blind. 33. **If this man were not from God, he could do nothing.** "The blind man, seeing that there is a wish to argue with him, becomes more and more bold, and sets himself also to the work of arguing. If he has not studied dogmatics, he at least knows his catechism. Is there an Israelite who is ignorant of this theocratic axiom: that a miracle is an answer to prayer; and that the prayer of a wicked person is not answered?" — *F. Godet.* "The Pharisees actually have only furthered the beggar's thinking: for while at first he is not ready to discuss whether Jesus is an open sinner, now he proves conclusively that he must be the very opposite, a God-fearing person who does God's will. The logic in the little lecture is invincible. It deals with premises which are axiomatic to all Jews. Hence the conclusion is inevitable." — *R. C. H. Lenski.*

7. HE IS CAST OUT THOUGH HIS WORDS COULD NOT BE CONTRADICTED, v. 34. 34. **They answered and said unto him, Thou wast altogether born in sins, and dost thou teach us? And they cast him out.** "Defeated by his pitiless logic, the adversaries of Jesus give way to rage. Their driving him out cannot designate an official excommunication; for this could not be pronounced except in a regular meeting. They expelled him violently from the hall, perhaps with the intention of having the excommunication pronounced afterward by the Sanhedrin." — *F. Godet.*

IV. **JESUS MEETS THE RESTORED MAN AND LEADS HIM TO BELIEVE IN HIM AS THE SON OF GOD,** vs. 35–38. 35. **Jesus heard that they had cast him out; and finding him, he said, Dost thou believe on the Son of God?** "The emphasis of the pronoun is remarkable and may be contrasted with v. 34. *Dost thou,* the outcast, thou that hast received outward sight, thou that hast borne a courageous testimony, *believe on the Son of Man* — cast thyself with complete trust on Him who gathers up in Himself, who bears and who transfigures all that belongs to man? The thought of 'the Son of Man' stands in true contrast with the selfish isolation of 'the Jews.' The new society, seen here in its beginning, rests upon this foundation, wide as humanity itself." — *B. F. Westcott.* 36. **He answered and said, And who is he, Lord, that I may believe on him?** 37. **Jesus said unto him, Thou hast both seen him, and he it is that speaketh with thee.** "Did you ever notice how exquisitely beautiful the addition in my text is to the words which He used to the woman of Samaria? To her He simply said, 'I that speak unto thee am he.' To the man who had only had a pair of eyes that could see anything for some four and twenty hours, He said, 'Thou hast *seen* Him.' And was not that enough to prove His claim? 'Thou hast seen him.' He gave you the eyes to see; now He has given you the Christ to look at. 'Thou hast both seen him, and it is he that talketh with thee.' . . . Be sure of this, that the perception of Christ's real presence and work with us and on us, which is made ours through faith, is as real, as direct, and I believe a great deal more reliable, than the thing that we call 'sight,' which is secured by the play of a material beam of light upon nerves that may be diseased, and may carry erroneous messages to the brain." — *Alexander Maclaren.* 38. **And he said, Lord, I believe. And he worshipped him.** This man, of course, did not have a full conception of all that the Sonship of Christ involved, for even the Apostles themselves were slow in coming to realize the full meaning of Christ's deity. But this man did believe that Christ had come from God, and He was the Sent One of God, that He was God's prophet, that He was God's Son, that He was doing God's work, that His words were true. A man who believes this much will believe all else that he finds concerning Christ in the Word of God. This man had not yet been trained in the theological formulations of the great creeds of the Church, but he knew Christ to be the Son of God, he loved Him, and bore testimony to Him. The fact that he worshiped him " shows that his idea of the Son of God includes attributes of divinity." The word for worship occurs elsewhere in this Gospel only in 4 : 20–24; 12 : 20, always of the idea of the worship of God." — *A. Plummer.*

V. **JESUS' FINAL WORDS TO THE PHARISEES,** vs. 39–41. " In its closing verses the chapter brings us back to the truth with which it opened, and shows us one parting flash of its obverse side. The Light of the world is Healer of the blind, but also Judge and Condemner of those who think they see. ' Are we then among the blind so meant? ' said the Pharisees. But Jesus answers with an unexpected irony: ' Would God you were so! for in that case you might receive your sight.' '*Now ye say, We see;* therefore your sin remaineth.' This whole chapter, it has been remarked, shows modern criticism its own portrait. The defenders of Judaic Sabbatism reasoned thus: God cannot lend His power to a violator of our Sabbath law; hence the cure alleged did not take place. Modern opponents of the supernatural in the gospel history reason after exactly the same fashion, merely substituting a scientific axiom for a religious statute. ' Miracles do not happen; therefore, however well attested this cure of one born blind, it did not occur.' But the fact holds good against the statute, of whatever kind it be, and will in the end force it to abdicate." — *Thomas Laidlaw.*

BELIEVING AND REFUSING TO BELIEVE THE MIRACLES OF CHRIST.

" The opponents of the supernatural have frequently said, that no one of the wonderful works performed by Jesus was ever thoroughly investigated; but in view of the narrative which we have just outlined, that statement cannot be substantiated. This man was questioned, and cross-questioned, as to whether he had really been born blind, and how he came to see; but no influence could make him waver, or shake a single statement which he made. His parents also testified to the fact of his blindness, and we may be sure that if any other means could have been used to discredit the miracle, they would have been employed by the Pharisees. But the more they were convinced in their own hearts that a miracle had really been wrought, the more bitter became this antagonism to Him who wrought it.

" The truth is, as we have formerly said, that the effect of the miracle depends on the intellectual pre-possessions and moral proclivities of the spectator. If intellectually he had adopted the philosophy which declares that miracles are impossible, he will not believe one though it should be wrought before his own eyes; and if morally he is antagonistic to the Christ, the sight of a miracle will only aggravate that antagonism. So the miracles were as really tests of those who witnessed them as proofs of the divine commission of Him who performed them; and those who reject them now, as they read of them in these Scriptures, would not have been convinced by them if they had seen them performed. We need not be surprised, therefore, at the conflicts that are waged over them in these days." — *William M. Taylor.*

WHY THE APOSTLE JOHN GIVES SO MUCH SPACE TO THIS MIRACLE.

" It is asked what is the aim with which John related this fact with so much of detail. No striking testimony of Jesus respecting His person marks it as worthy of attention. It refers far more, as it seems, to the history and conduct of a secondary personage, than to the revelation of Jesus Himself. Evidently John accords this fact this honorable place because it marks a decisive step in the progress of Israelitish unbelief. For the first time, a believer is, for his faith, cast out of the theocratic community. It is the first act of the rupture between the Church and the synagogue. We shall see in the following chapter that Jesus really regards this fact in this light." — *F. Godet.*

How many different things did this man once blind say about the Lord Jesus? How many different wicked things did the opponents of Christ on this occasion say concerning the Lord? How do you account for the fact that on the same day, in the same place, resulting from the same miracle, one man becomes convinced that Jesus is the Son of God, while others denounce Jesus as a sinner and worthy of condemnation? How does the record of this man's testimony illustrate the profound truth that as we publicly testify to Christ our faith is strengthened and our knowledge of Christ is increased? Who, as far as the things of this life are considered — that is, money, learning, reputation, power, religious position — who was the more fortunate, the group of Pharisees or the beggar? Do you think that the possession of so many

coveted objects on the part of the Pharisees had something to do with their refusal to believe in the Lord Jesus, and if so, how? What are we, who have experienced redemption by the grace of God through Jesus Christ, to do in an unbelieving world like ours today?

LESSON VIII. — February 21.

JESUS THE GOOD SHEPHERD. — John 10.

PRINTED TEXT, John 10 : 1-5, 11-16, 27-30.

GOLDEN TEXT. — *I am the good shepherd: the good shepherd layeth down his life for the sheep.* JOHN 10: 11.

Devotional Reading: Psalm 23.
Beginner Topic: MY ANIMAL FRIENDS.
Lesson Material: John 10 : 1–5; Luke 15 : 3–6.
Memory Verse: Be ye kind. Ephesians 4 : 32.
Primary Topic: LIKE A SHEPHERD.
Lesson Material: John 10.
Memory Verse: He calleth his own sheep by name. John 10 : 3.
Junior Topic: THE GOOD SHEPHERD.
Lesson Material: John 10.
Memory Verse: Jesus therefore said . . . I am the good shepherd: the good shepherd layeth down his life for the sheep. John 10 : 7, 11.
Intermediate and Senior Topic: FOLLOWING OUR SHEPHERD.
Topic for Young People and Adults: WHAT THE GOOD SHEPHERD DOES FOR US.

THE TEACHER AND HIS CLASS.

The Younger Classes will probably enter more quickly and intelligently into comprehending this lesson if the teacher is able to secure a large colored picture, depicting a flock of sheep being led toward the sheepfold by the trusted shepherd. The herding of sheep in this country is so different from what it was, and still is, in Palestine, that something like this will be necessary to bring the pupils immediately into the right frame of mind for comprehending the precious truths of this chapter.

The Older Classes will here discover once again the absolute uniqueness, the infinite superiority, the divine wisdom characterizing all that Christ here utters — words on the lips of anyone else that must be counted utter foolishness, but from His lips words of comfort, of confirmation, of assurance. Behind the words there ever stands the omnipotent Son of God to make them real and true.

THE LESSON IN ITS SETTING.

Time. — The first half of this chapter, through verse 21, records a message uttered by our Lord in mid-October A.D. 29. The words recorded in verses 22–39 were uttered late in December of that year; within a few days after, the event recorded in the last two verses took place.

Place. — Each of the discourses recorded in this chapter was uttered in Jerusalem, but of course, the event spoken of in the last three verses occurred in Bethany beyond Jordan.

THE PLAN OF THE LESSON.

SUBJECT: The Perfect Knowledge of Christ Concerning His Death, the Needs of His Own Sheep, and the Eternal Future.

I. CHRIST THE GOOD SHEPHERD, John 10 : 1–21.
1. The true and the false shepherds contrasted, vs. 1, 2.
2. The true shepherd is known by his sheep, vs. 3–6.
3. Christ the Door of the sheep, vs. 7–9.
4. Christ the Good Shepherd, vs. 10–14.
5. The Shepherd announces His death for the sake of the sheep, vs. 15–18.
6. The argument among the Jews over this teaching, vs. 19–21.

II. THE ETERNAL SAFETY OF CHRIST'S OWN, John 10 : 22–29.

III. CHRIST ASSERTS THAT HE AND THE FATHER ARE ONE, John 10 : 30–39.
1. The assertion, v. 30.
2. The opposition, v. 31.
3. The question, v. 32.
4. The argument, vs. 33–36.
5. The appeal, vs. 37, 38.
6. The renewed opposition, v. 39.

IV. CHRIST RETURNS TO THE PLACE WHERE HE WAS BAPTIZED, John 10 : 40–42.

THE TEACHER'S LIBRARY.

On the entire subject of shepherd life in Palestine see Anna F. Mamreov: *A Day with the Good Shepherd* (1910); Stephen A. Haboush: *My Shepherd Life in Galilee* (1917); W. M. Thomson: *The Land and the Book*, 201–205; and the article by Frank Richards, "Sheep-Shepherd," in James Hastings's *Dictionary of Christ and the Gospels*, Vol. 2, 620–621. On Christ as Shepherd see three sermons by Charles H. Spurgeon, in his *The Messiah, Sermons on Our Lord's Names and Titles and Attributes*, 255–290; Samuel H. Geisy: *The I AM'S of Christ*, 259–286; T. Marjoribanks: *The Sevenfold "I AM,"* 65 ff.; Ada R. Habershon: *The Study of the Types*, 135–142; David Gregg: *Studies in John's Gospel*, 162–177.

Very few of the standard lives of Christ will be found of any particular value for the study of this lesson, but many of the commentaries on John's Gospel do contain helpful material. If one wishes to read a profound theological discussion of the major subjects involved in this chapter, he should certainly consult the magnificent discussion in Godet's superb commentary on this Gospel. For sermonic material on verse 3, see J. H. Jowett: *Brooks by the Traveller's Way*, 265–280; W. R. Nicoll: *Sunday Evening*, 217–223; on verse 11, H. P. Liddon, *Easter in St. Paul's*, 312–322; G. Campbell Morgan: *Westminster Pulpit*, Vol. 6, 297–304; on verse 12, Percy Ainsworth: *The Pilgrim Church*, 235 ff.; on verse 15, Phillips Brooks: *Visions and Tasks and Other Sermons*, 280–296; on verse 16, one should especially read the great missionary address of Alexander Maclaren, "Other Sheep," occupying twenty-five pages in his *Expositions of Holy Scripture, St. John 9–14*, 40–74; on verses 17, 18, G. Campbell Morgan: *The Teaching of Christ*, 252–254; the same, in the *Westminster Pulpit*, Vol. 10, 105–112; on verses 27, 28, J. H. Jowett: *Brooks by the Traveller's Way*, 59–66; W. R. Nicoll as above, 225–232.

The connection between chapters 9 and 10 is worthy a moment's consideration. In reality, Christ's remarks to the Pharisees, occasioned by their conduct when the man born blind had been healed, is continued in the great discourse we are now to study. They excommunicated this man and thereby showed themselves to be false spiritual guides. "The subject of verses 1–21 is the contrast between these false guides of the people and Jesus Himself, the true Guide." — *George Reith.* Before we even enter into the discussion of our lesson, anticipating the subjects that will arise for consideration, it might be well to quote a compact paragraph, by Professor Richards, on the entire subject of the sheep and shepherd life of Palestine. "The

A Shepherd in Palestine.

sheep of Palestine are still the broad-tailed breed of Biblical times (Exod. 29 : 22; Lev. 3 : 9, 11, R. V. 'fat tail'). The tail is from five to fifteen inches wide, and weighs from ten to fifteen pounds, sometimes even as much as thirty pounds, supplying ten pounds and upwards of pure fat, which is packed for winter use. The sheep are white, though some have brown faces; only the rams have horns. They 'find pasture' (John 10 : 9) in the lower lands in winter and on the mountains in summer, the best pastures being in South Palestine (the Negeb and Gerar) and on the plain to the east of the Jordan; but even 'the pastures of the wilderness' (Ps. 65 : 12; Joel 2 : 22) are welcome in spring, when the grass and flowers have grown which are burnt up in summer. The shepherd leads his sheep (John 10 : 4) during the day in the cool months, but in the hotter part of the year from sunset to early morning, when he brings them back to the fold (John 10 : 1, 16), or leaves them to lie under a prepared shelter under the bushes. The fold is a low flat shed or series of sheds, with a yard surrounded by a wall (John 10 : 1; cf. Num. 32 : 16; Judg. 5 : 16; Zeph. 2 : 6); on cold nights the flocks are shut in the buildings. The wall is surmounted by a fence of sharp thorns to keep out the wolves (John 10 : 12) and other wild beasts

JOHN 10 : 1. Verily, verily, I say unto you, He that entereth not by the door into the fold of the sheep, but climbeth up some other way, the same is a thief and a robber.

2. But he that entereth in by the door is the shepherd of the sheep.

3. To him the porter openeth; and the sheep hear his voice: and he calleth his own sheep by name, and leadeth them out.

(Isa. 31 : 4; 1 Sam. 17 : 34); jackals and hyenas prey almost up to the walls of Jerusalem, while leopards and panthers often leap over the high fence of the fold, and the shepherd is still at times known 'to lay down his life for the sheep' (John 10 : 11). Robbers are as great a source of danger; a lamb or a kid is sometimes carried off by a bird of prey, and there are deadly snakes in the limestone rocks. The Gospel parable does not exaggerate the rejoicing of the shepherd when he has recovered a sheep that has gone astray upon the mountains (Matt. 18 : 12; Luke 15 : 4)."

I. **CHRIST THE GOOD SHEPHERD,** vs. 1–21.

1. THE TRUE AND THE FALSE SHEPHERDS CONTRASTED, VS. 1, 2. 1. **Verily, verily, I say unto you, He that entereth not by the door into the fold of the sheep, but climbeth up some other way, the same is a thief and a robber.** We have here the beginning, not of a parable, but of what we might truly call an allegory. Allegories are found only in the Fourth Gospel, here, and in chapter 15, whereas no true parables are found anywhere in the Fourth Gospel. Our Lord's teaching begins, as it were, negatively, rather than positively, pointing out for us the characteristics of the false shepherd, and then giving the picture of the true shepherd. "The oriental sheepfolds are commonly walled or palisaded with one door or gate. Into one of these enclosures several shepherds drive their flocks, leaving them in charge of an under-shepherd or porter, who fastens the door securely inside, and remains with the sheep all night. In the morning the shepherds come to the door, the porter opens to them and each calls away his own sheep." — *A. Plummer.* "There is a shade of difference between the word translated *thief* and the word translated *robber;* the second term suggests a more marked degree of violence and audacity than the first. The one steals, the other slaughters. Jesus means to describe here the audacity full of cunning with which the Pharisees had succeeded in establishing their authority in the enclosure of the people of God, beyond the limits of any charge instituted by God. Nothing in the law justified the despotic power which this charge exercised." — *F. Godet.*

The Sheepfold.

2. **But he that entereth in by the door is the shepherd of the sheep.** The shepherd is known to the porter and therefore is allowed to enter as soon as he appears. Thieves would not want the porter even to know of their presence. A thief comes among the sheep to steal them, for his own selfish purposes, whether to make money, or to increase his own flock, or for immediate consumption; the shepherd is continually watchful over the welfare of the sheep.

2. THE TRUE SHEPHERD IS KNOWN BY HIS SHEEP, VS. 3–6. 3. **To him the porter openeth; and the sheep hear his voice: and he calleth his own sheep by name, and leadeth them out.** "The relations of shepherd and sheep in the East are peculiarly intimate and tender. The shepherd's call is recognized by his own sheep, for each of which he has a name; they follow him as he leads them from the fold to the pasture, or from one pasture to another; and him only they will follow; from a stranger's call they will flee, not recognizing the voice. The hearing implies the recognition of a familiar and loving voice. There is no compulsion or violence, as in the case of a thief or robber (Ps. 110 : 3). As all the sheep know the shepherd, the shepherd **knows each sheep.** The tie is personal. The history of each sheep, its state, quali-

4. When he hath put forth all his own, he goeth before them, and the sheep follow him: for they know his voice.
5. And a stranger will they not follow, but will flee from him: for they know not the voice of strangers.

ties, worth, age, are known to the shepherd, and its special name suggests his knowledge, interest, and affection towards itself." — *George Reith.*

4. **When he hath put forth all his own, he goeth before them, and the sheep follow him: for they know his voice.** "The verb here translated 'hath put forth' designates an energetic and almost rough act by which the shepherd helps the sheep, which still hesitates, to break away from the other sheep of the fold, and to give itself up to the chances of the new existence which the shepherd's call opens before it." — *F. Godet.*

From a photograph by Wilson.

A Druse Shepherd.

They are very faithful to their flocks, attending them night and day through sunshine and storm, never forsaking them in their hour of danger.

5. **And a stranger will they not follow, but will flee from him: for they know not the voice of strangers.** "All along the way which the sheep follow, strange voices make themselves heard, on the right hand and the left, seeking to turn them aside from the steps of the shepherd. They are those of thieves who, not being able to play openly the part of robbers, use means of seduction or intimidation. The sheep is for the future made familiar with the voice of the shepherd, so that every voice which is not his produces upon it a strange and rebellious effect." — *F. Godet.* The editor himself will never forget an experience he had in Palestine, some years ago, in the very valley where, it is thought, David wrote the Twenty-third Psalm. He carefully listened to the shepherds as they called their own sheep, with a strange guttural sound, which seemed quite simple; but when he himself tried to utter the same sound, the sheep, instead of being utterly indifferent to the new voice, actually got up and ran away. They not only knew I was a stranger, and not their shepherd, but they were afraid of me. This is why a Christian, truly saturated with the Word of God, flees from so-called religious teachers who deny the deity of Christ, who are enemies of His Cross, who repudiate supernaturalism, who wish to synthetically unite all different religions into one vast undefined, acceptable mass of various ethical and moral precepts.

3. Christ the Door of the Sheep, vs. 7–9. Our Lord now moves from one figure of speech to another. First He calls Himself the Good Shepherd, now he calls Himself the Door of the sheep. "He did not use His words at random, and this at least is contained in them. He gathers men around His person, and assures us that He holds the key to life; that if He admits us, words of exclusion pronounced by others are but idle breath; that if He excludes us, the approval and applause of a world will not waft us in. No claim could possibly be greater." — *Marcus Dods.* Sir Wilfred Grenfell in his book, *Labrador Looks at the Orient,* gives us an excellent illustration from his own experiences of what our Lord meant when he called Himself the Door. "One of our party, as we climbed, noticed a shepherd driving his sheep into a large kind of cave with an open mouth. In reply to her question, he said: 'I am putting them away for the night to be safe from jackals and dogs.' But she objected: 'There is no door to the cave.' He replied simply: 'I am the door.' It is the Eastern shepherd's custom to lie down across the doorway of such caves, and with his own life to protect the sheep." But what did our Lord mean when He said that all who ever came before Him were thieves and robbers, which the sheep did not hear? "The thieves and robbers were those who claimed an authority of their own over God's heritage; who did not act as if they were only in possession of a delegated power; who opened the door of the kingdom, or shut it, according to their own fancy; (Luke 11 : 52) 'Ye have taken away the key of knowledge.' Any-

11. I am the good shepherd: the good shepherd layeth down his life for the sheep.

12. He that is a hireling, and not a shepherd, whose own the sheep are not, beholdeth the wolf coming, and leaveth the sheep, and fleeth, and the wolf snatcheth them, and scattereth *them:*

---

one claiming to stand between Christ and men is therefore a thief or a robber. . . . From the million voices of earth His voice is heard in the quiet of conscience, in the convictions of truth and duty, in the hour of sickness and of death." — *George Reith.*

4. CHRIST THE GOOD SHEPHERD, VS. 10–14. There is hardly a more remarkable verse in the entire Gospel of John than verse 10 of this chapter, though it is not designated as a part of the printed text. By the thief here I would think that Christ first, of course, meant the Pharisees, who continually were thinking of their own enrichment and of the maintenance of their high position, rather than the welfare of the people, who were being spiritually crushed under the dead weight of a vast mass of traditions. But ultimately, I think the thief here is none other than Satan. He steals from men their character, their high ideals, the peace and joy of heart, the purity of love, the instincts for helping others, and ultimately he does his best to actually extinguish the very life that is in us, bringing us into that horrible condition of enslavement to sin which can be likened to nothing else than death itself, a living death. But our Lord came that we might have life, abundant life; life in its greatest fullness; life that satisfies; life that permeates every part of our being; life that is rich in joy and peace and power and purity; life that knows a love for God and rests in God; life that is free because of redemption; life that has a purpose because Christ is the ideal life that grows increasingly rich because it is eternal life; life without regrets; life that is pleasing to God, free from fear, filled with confidence and courage and hope. Sometime ago, I remember reading in a work of science by Professor Joseph Mayer, not a Christian, some words that show the cry of the human heart to be exactly that which Christ is here speaking of: "To live happily and to live more abundantly, either personally or in offspring and loved ones, is a desire that evidently permeates the whole of animal creation."

Plockhörst.

The Good Shepherd.

11. **I am the good shepherd: the good shepherd layeth down his life for the sheep.** "The word translated 'good' cannot be adequately translated: it means 'beautiful, noble, good,' as opposed to 'foul, mean, wicked.' It sums up the chief attributes of ideal perfection. Christ is the Perfect Shepherd, as opposed to His own imperfect ministers; He is the true Shepherd, as opposed to the false shepherds, who are hirelings or hypocrites; He is the Good Shepherd, who gives His life for the sheep, as opposed to the wicked thief who takes their lives to preserve his own. Thus in Christ is realized the ideal Shepherd of the Old Testament (Ps. 23; Isa. 40 : 11; Jer. 23; Ezek. 34, 37 : 24; Zech. 11 : 7). . . . The phrase 'layeth down his life' is a remarkable one and peculiar to St. John, whereas 'to *give* his life' occurs in the Synoptics (Matt. 28 : 20; Mark 10 : 45). 'To *lay* down' perhaps includes the notion of 'to *pay* down,' a common meaning of the words in classical Greek; if so, it is exactly equivalent to the Synoptic phrase 'to give as a *ransom*.' It occurs again in vs. 15, 17; 13 : 37, 38; 15 : 13; 1 John 3 : 16. (Cf. Gen. 13 : 5; 14 : 12; 31 : 39, 40; 32 : 7, 8; 37 : 33; Job 1 : 17; 1 Sam. 17 : 34, 35.)" — *George Reith.*

12. **He that is a hireling, and not a shepherd, whose own the sheep are not,**

13. *He fleeth* because he is a hireling, and careth not for the sheep.
14. I am the good shepherd; and I know mine own, and mine own know me,
15. Even as the Father knoweth me, and I know the Father; and I lay down my life for the sheep.
16. And other sheep I have, which are not of this fold: them also I must bring, and they shall hear my voice; and they shall become one flock, one shepherd.

---

beholdeth the wolf coming, and leaveth the sheep, and fleeth, and the wolf snatcheth them, and scattereth ***them:*** 13. ***he fleeth*** **because he is a hireling, and careth not for the sheep.** "Beyond question this hireling portrays all false religious teachers in the outward church. The portrait is extreme in order to cover also the worst teachers of this type. The lesser and partial types are thereby not excluded. Jesus undoubtedly meant the Pharisees as a class, some of whom stood before him at the moment; he meant the Sadducees as well, for their effect on the people was equally pernicious. The hireling character of the Sanhedrin and its leaders is plainly brought to view in 11 : 48; even Pilate saw it, Matthew 27 : 18; Mark 15 : 10. . . . We are constrained to hold that the wolf does mean the devil. Nothing also does he like better than to find a hireling with God's sheep, instead of some shepherd sent by Jesus and made courageous by Him. Then he can complete what the hireling has begun: snatch with his fangs and kill, by destroying the faith in the hearts of God's children; scatter helplessly those not at once spiritually crushed, by making them shift for themselves in the wilderness of this world, till he either snatches them too or till their spiritual life faints and dies out of itself." — *R. C. H. Lenski.* (Lenski devotes almost seven pages to this one verse and is very helpful.)

14. **I am the good shepherd; and I know mine own, and mine own know me.** "It is the knowledge of mutual love, trust, sympathy. Christ's knowledge of His sheep is perfect, as are His love to them and sympathy with them. It is a knowledge embracing and determining all their past and future; their gift by the Father to Him, their call, their faith, and repentance, their experiences in search for and finding the kingdom, their present walk and conflict, their future glory. And this knowledge is individual and discriminating. He knows each one, calls each, cares for each, disciplines him, watches over him, prepares a place in glory for him (cf. Rev. 3 : 12; 2 : 17). . . . On the other hand, there is the reciprocal knowledge of Christ by His sheep. In one sense imperfect, in another sense perfect, for it is based on the personal experience of His grace and love by which their faith is awakened, and the conscious relationship established between Him and them. The response to His call; the assurance that it is a call for them; the assurance that each responding to it has, that he himself is before the eye and under the rod of Him that telleth the flock; the deepening trust; the repose on Christ's wisdom and love; the sense of His indispensableness in all hours of this frail and sinful existence; the quickened apprehension of His will and purpose in the teaching of the Holy Spirit and of all providences; the absolute confidence toward which the soul strives and in measure attains, confidence even that failure and sin will not quench Christ's love — these are the fruits and proofs of the knowledge of their Shepherd by the sheep. And we know ourselves truly only in Christ's knowledge of us." — *George Reith.*

5. THE SHEPHERD ANNOUNCES HIS DEATH FOR THE SAKE OF THE SHEEP, vs. 15–18. 15. **Even as the Father knoweth me, and I know the Father; and I lay down my life for the sheep.** 16. **And other sheep I have, which are not of this fold: them also I must bring, and they shall hear my voice; and they shall become one flock, one shepherd.** Before discussing the great theme which Christ here enters upon, concerning His vicarious death, let us first think for a moment of this great sentence wherein our Lord speaks of His "other sheep." The outline of Alexander Maclaren is superb. First, he says, we here have Christ teaching us how to think of the heathen world. "The sheep whom He sees while He speaks are not only men of that generation. These mighty words are world-wide and world-lasting. The whole of the ages are in His mind. All nations are gathered before His prophetic vision." Secondly, says the famous expositor, we have here Christ teaching us how to think of His work and ours — "Them also I must bring." "The Cross of Christ and it alone gathers men into a unity; for it alone draws men to Christ. His death as the constraining motive of life in the hearts which receive it, draws them away

27. My sheep hear my voice, and I know them, and they follow me:
28. And I give unto them eternal life; and they shall never perish, and no one shall snatch them out of my hand.
29. My Father, who hath given *them* unto me, is greater than all; and no one is able to snatch *them* out of the Father's hand.

---

from their own ways by the Cross of love and points them to Him." Finally, we have here our Lord teaching us how to think of the certain issues of His work and ours. "There is to be but one Shepherd and over all the earth a great unity of obedience to Him. Here is the knell of all authority that does not own Him, and the subordination of all that does. The hirelings, the blind guides, that have misled and afflicted humanity for so many weary ages, shall be all sunk in oblivion."

Note now what our Lord says about His death: (1) It was for His sheep that He would lay down His life. (2) Because He would lay down His life for His Sheep, the Father loved Him. (3) No man compels Christ to lay down His life, He does it of His own volition. (4) Laying it down of His own power, He is able to take it up again by His own power. Of these words, Dr. Liddon once said: "In no other passage of the Gospels is the majesty of our Lord's divine person more plainly revealed in His words than here." You and I do not lay down our lives when we please. When death comes we have no power with which to resist it. Christ foresaw His death and could have escaped it but that He came to die for the sins of the people. More than that, once having suffered death there is no man in the whole universe who is able to pick up that life again once having been separated from it, no one but the Son of God, so that everything He did centered in His death. By that death He pleased the Father, and by that death He won for us our eternal redemption. The Cross was central in the purpose of the Trinity in the advent of Christ, in the work of the Saviour, and when Christ's death is given a subordinate place in modern thought or totally ignored, or weakened into an act of unexpected martyrdom, or is looked upon as a tragic, unexpected error, then we do not have the mind of God and we are outside of the reach of God's redeeming purposes."

6. THE ARGUMENT AMONG THE JEWS OVER THIS TEACHING, VS. 19–21. Every time our Lord spoke of His death (see, for example, John 6 : 52, 60, 66), there was furious opposition on the part of many of His listeners, who may be counted as the first "enemies of the cross of Christ" (Phil. 3 : 18). It is true even down to this present day that that above all in the Christian faith which many find to be a stumblingblock and foolishness, is the vicarious death of the Lord Jesus.

II. **THE ETERNAL SAFETY OF CHRIST'S OWN,** vs. 22–29. "Between verses 21 and 22 there is an interval of about two months; for the Feast of Tabernacles would be about the middle of October, and that of the dedication toward the end of December. In this interval some would place Luke 10 : 1–13. If this be correct, we may connect the sending out of the Seventy both with the Feast of Tabernacles and also with John 10 : 16." — *A. Plummer.*

27. **My sheep hear my voice, and I know them, and they follow me:** 28. **and I give unto them eternal life; and they shall never perish, and no one shall snatch them out of my hand.** 29. **My Father, who hath given *them* unto me, is greater than all; and no one is able to snatch *them* out of the Father's hand.** Our Lord now repeats in part some of the things He had previously said concerning the close relationship that exists between His sheep and Himself as the Shepherd. He reveals that the reason they do not believe Him is because they are not of His sheep, for His sheep know His voice, and, trusting Him, they follow Him, as these people would, if they were really His sheep. What infinite privileges are granted to the true sheep of the Good Shepherd: they are given eternal life; they shall never be taken out of the safe-keeping of the Shepherd; they are the gift of the Father to the Son; they are forever safe in the Father's hands. All the power of the Godhead is here revealed as more than sufficient for the eternal preservation of those whom the Father has given to the Son. "All that the sheep are, and all that they shall be, flows out of this original gift of them by the Father to the Son (6 : 37). They are dear to the Son as the Father's original possession and gift; and as such they will have all done for them that the subjects of such divine forethought and love deserve. They will be well cared for: they have the Almighty God for their Father, and in His hands they shall ever remain. Jesus returns them to the Father's hands, from which He received them, with the object accomplished for which they were entrusted to Him.

30. I and the Father are one.

The allusion to the excommunication of the man born blind is probable." — *George Reith.* The editor has always felt that a passage quite parallel with this is the glorious conclusion of the eighth chapter of Romans (Rom. 8 : 38, 39). Our salvation originates from the heart of God; our salvation is secured to us by the death of Christ; our salvation instantly involves the gift of eternal life which will never, never, never be taken away from us, and our ultimate, final glorification is also in the purpose of God and by His power will be accomplished.

III. **CHRIST ASSERTS THAT HE AND THE FATHER ARE ONE,** vs. 30–39.

30. **I and the Father are one.** " Every word in this pregnant clause is full of meaning. It is *I*, not *the Son; the Father*, not *my Father;* one essence, not one person; *are*, not *am*. The revelation is of the nature of Christ in the fullness of His double nature, of the incarnate Son in the fullness of His manifested being, and that in relation to *the Father*, to God as He is Father at once of the Son and of men. The incarnation was the proof of the complete unity of the Father and the Son. Through that was shown the true connection of God and man. And so it is that the union of believers together is made dependent on the union of the Father and the Son (17 : 22, according to the true reading).

" It seems clear that the unity here spoken of cannot fall short of unity of essence. The thought springs from the equality of power (*my hand, the Father's hand*); but infinite power is an essential attribute of God; and it is impossible to suppose that two beings distinct in essence could be equal in power. (Cf. Rev. 20 : 6; 22 : 3)." — *B. F. Westcott.*

Once again (cf. John 8 : 59), the Jews took up stones to stone Him, leading Christ to ask for what one of the many good works He had accomplished in their midst they were attempting to put Him to death? " No," said these crafty Jews, " not for any of your good works, but for blasphemy, ' because that thou, being a man makest thyself God.' " They well knew that everything He had been saying implied Deity, which lifted Him up to a plane of absolute equality with the Father. Now the answer of Christ has given a great deal of trouble, and we must not treat this difficult passage superficially. The words which our Lord quotes are taken from Psalm 82 : 6. The words of Marcus Dods here should be carefully considered: " The contrast our Lord draws between Himself and those who had in Scripture been called ' gods ' is significant. It is the Eighty-second Psalm He cites; and in it the judges of Israel are rebuked for abusing their office. It is of these unjust judges the psalm represents God as saying, ' I have said, Ye are gods, and all of you are children of the Most High. But ye shall die like men, and fall like one of the princes.' To these judges this word of God, ' Ye are gods,' had come at their consecration to their office. Having been occupied with other work they were now set apart to represent to men the authority and justice of God. But, argues our Lord, if men were called gods, *to* whom God's word came — and they are so called in Scripture, which cannot be broken — appointing them to their office, may He not rightly be called Son of God who is Himself sent to men; whose original and sole destiny it was to come into the world to represent *the Father?* The words are overweighted with manifold contrast. The judges were persons ' to whom ' the word of God came, as from without; Jesus was a person Himself ' sent into the world ' from God, therefore surely more akin to God than they were. The judges represented God by virtue of a commission, received in the course of their career — the word of God *came* to them: Jesus, on the other hand, represented God because ' sanctified,' that is, set apart or consecrated for this purpose before He came into the world, and therefore obviously occupying a higher and more important position than they. But, especially, the judges were appointed to discharge one limited and temporary function, for the discharge of which it was sufficient that they should know the law of God; whereas it was ' the Father,' the God of universal relation and love, who consecrated Jesus and sent Him into the world, meaning now to reveal to men what lies deepest in His nature, His love, His fatherhood. The idea of the purpose for which Christ was sent into the world is indicated in the emphatic use of ' the Father.' He was sent to do the works of the Father (v. 37); to manifest to men the benignity, tenderness, compassion of the Father; to encourage them to believe that the Father, the Source of all life, was in their midst accessible to them. If Jesus failed to reveal the Father, He had no claim to make. ' If I do not the works of My Father, believe Me not.' But if He did such works as declared the Father to be in their midst, then, as bearing the Father in Him and doing the Father's will, He might well be called ' the Son of God.' ' Though ye believe not Me, believe the works; that ye may know, and believe, that the Father is in Me, and I in Him.'

" There can be no question, then, of the conclusiveness with which our Lord rebutted the charge of blasphemy. By a single sentence He put them in the position of presumptuously contradicting their own Scriptures." — *Marcus Dods*. The answer of our Lord only the more infuriated His enemies, who sought to seize Him that they might immediately put Him to death, but He suddenly escaped out of their hand.

IV. **CHRIST RETURNS TO THE PLACE WHERE HE WAS BAPTIZED,** vs. 40–42. See John 1 : 28. " The hostility of the hierarchy being invincible and becoming more and more dangerous, Jesus retires into Peræa for quiet and safety before His Passion. This interval was between three and four months, from the latter part of December to the middle of April. But some portion of this time was spent at Ephraim (11 : 54) after going to Bethany in Judæa to raise Lazarus. Nothing is told us as to how much time was given to Bethany or Bethabara in Peræa, how much to Ephraim." — *A. Plummer*. Godet has some beautiful words on this concluding portion of our lesson. " We feel from the Apostle's tone, that this sojourn was not without pleasure for Jesus and for His first disciples. There is a charm in finding oneself, on finishing one's career, in the places where it was begun. Jesus had, moreover, the joy of gathering a harvest here which had been prepared by the faithful labor of His forerunner. It would be difficult not to recognize in this description the personal recollection of the evangelist." — *F. Godet*.

How many different titles does our Lord ascribe to Himself in this lesson? What other titles are given to Christ by His enemies in this lesson? What characteristics of the Lord Jesus are revealed in this wonderfully rich chapter of John's Gospel? How many treasures do we have in Christ as recorded in the utterances of this lesson? Would you say that the portrait which Christ here draws of Himself would normally attract men or repel men? Why do we need a Shepherd? In how many different ways does Christ in this lesson reveal Himself to be infinitely superior to all men who have ever lived on this earth? Realizing that most of His audience at this time refused to believe what He said, do you think there was anything else Christ could have said or could have done in their midst that would have delivered them from this spirit of unbelief and led them to recognize Him to be the Sent One of God? Would you say that the story of the Prodigal Son in any way illustrates Christ's statement that the thief cometh to steal and to kill and to destroy? Do you think there are some religious people in the world today, some who are even called religious leaders, who instead of guiding the people into green pastures and leading them beside the still waters, impoverish them materially, spiritually, and intellectually?

LESSON IX. — February 28.

JESUS RESTORES LAZARUS TO LIFE.

PRINTED TEXT, John 11 : 20-29, 32-35, 38-44.

GOLDEN TEXT. — *I am the resurrection, and the life.* JOHN 11 : 25.

Devotional Reading: 1 Peter 1 : 3–12.
Beginner Topic: WHEN JESUS BLESSED THE CHILDREN.
  Lesson Material: Mark 10 : 13–16.
  Memory Verse: I love thee, O Jehovah. Psalm 18 : 1.
Primary Topic: MARY AND MARTHA'S BEST FRIEND.
  Lesson Material: John 11.
  Memory Verse: Thou art nigh, O Jehovah. Psalm 119 : 151.
Junior Topic: IN A BETHANY HOME.
  Lesson Material: John 11.
  Memory Verse: Yea, though I walk through the valley of the shadow of death, I will fear no evil; for thou art with me. Psalm 23 : 4.
Intermediate and Senior Topic: JESUS MASTER OF LIFE.
Topic for Young People and Adults: JESUS MASTER OF LIFE AND DEATH.

THE TEACHER AND HIS CLASS.

The Younger Classes might be asked whom most of them like to see come into their home? They will mention, first, their grandmother, and then, perhaps, an uncle or aunt, and then, in a time of real sickness, they will want a doctor, and perhaps some kind neighbor, who knows how to nurse a mother who is ill. In other words, we like those to come into our home who in some way brighten the day, relieve distress, and make our hearts glad. Into the home at Bethany, on the day described in our lesson, Jesus came bringing more than comfort or relief from pain — He actually raised a loved one up from the grave and gave him back to his mourning family. This is what Jesus will do some day for all the children of God, restoring us to all our friends and loved ones, for eternity.

The Older Classes should have emphasized especially the utter supernaturalness of this stupendous miracle, and for this the teacher ought to take care that that material is presented which will convince the class beyond all contradiction that this is a true record of something that actually happened in the life of our Lord, which marks Him as truly the Resurrection and the Life.

THE LESSON IN ITS SETTING.

Time. — January, A.D. 30.

Place. — The home of Mary and Martha, in the village of Bethany, which is over the ridge on the eastern slope of the Mount of Olives, opposite Jerusalem.

THE PLAN OF THE LESSON.

SUBJECT: The Love of Christ for His Own Which Includes His Perfect Knowledge of Our Conditions and Our Griefs, His Compassionate Sympathy with Us in Our Sorrows, and His Ability to Deliver Us in His Own Perfect Time from Every Cause of Grief and from Death Itself.

I. CHRIST'S PERFECT POISE IN AN HOUR OF SORROW AND APPARENT DANGER, VS. 1–10.

1. He knows that Lazarus' illness will glorify God, vs. 1–6.
2. He knows no harm can come to Him while He has work to do, vs. 7–10.

II. CHRIST'S CHARACTERIZATION OF DEATH AS SLEEP, VS. 11–16.

III. CHRIST'S CONCERN FOR THOSE WHO MOURN, VS. 17–32.

1. The unsatisfying comfort of some friends, vs. 17–19.
2. His words of hope to Martha, vs. 20–27.
   a. The certainty of Lazarus' resurrection.
   b. Christ Himself is the resurrection and the life.
   c. True death will never be the experience of those who believe in Christ.
3. His compassion for Mary in her sorrow, vs. 28–36.
4. The question, v. 37.

IV. CHRIST'S VICTORY OVER DEATH, VS. 38–44.

1. Approaching the grave.
2. The command concerning the stone.
3. The prayer of thanksgiving.
4. The call to Lazarus to come forth.
5. The dead Lazarus lives again.

V. THE TWO OPPOSITE CONSEQUENCES THAT FOLLOWED THIS MIRACLE, VS. 45–47.

1. Many believed, v. 45.
2. Some stir up opposition and scheme to kill Him, vs. 46–57.

THE TEACHER'S LIBRARY.

All lives of Christ, all commentaries on John's Gospel, and all books dealing with our Lord's miracles will, of course, have much material on this inexhaustible chapter. The forty pages in Godet, and the forty-five pages in Trench are especially valuable. On the last ten verses, Marcus Dods, in his work on John, has a brilliant chapter, which he calls, "Jesus the Scapegoat." There is one modern book of sermons devoted exclusively to this chapter, by that famous preacher of England, J. D. Jones, *The Lord of Life and Death.* (Beware, however, of a tendency in this book to Universalism.) The following books will be found to contain large sections on the raising of Lazarus: James Culross: *The House at Bethany;* J. R. MacDuff: *Memories of Bethany;* J. R. Miller: *Mary of Bethany;* W. M. Clow: *The Idylls of Bethany* (1919), on vs. 1, 5, 11. There are two excellent chapters on the grief of Mary and Martha in R. S. Candlish: *Scripture Characters,* 217–243. Two hundred pages of Hugh Macmillan's exhaustive work, *Our Lord's Three Raisings from the Dead,* are devoted to a consideration of this miracle.

On Lazarus himself, there is not as much material as one would expect; but see A. T. Robertson: *Some Minor Characters in the New Testament,* 177–182; T. R. Williams: *Men of the New Testament,* 195–204; an article by A. Plummer, in James Hastings's *Dictionary of the Bible,* Vol. 3, 85–88; an article by E. H. Plumptre, in William Smith's *Dictionary of the Bible,* Vol. 2, 1612–1617; and a characteristically brilliant treatment, in Alexander Whyte's *Bible Characters: Joseph and Mary to James,* 78–86.

I have purposely chosen not to give much sermonic material, because of the abundance of other material. But on vs. 25 and 26, see Alexander Maclaren's *Expositions of Holy Scripture, St. John, 9–14,* 81–91; J. H. Knight: *The Master's Questions to His Disciples,* 213–219; F. W. Boreham: *A Handful of Stars,* 44–56; A. J. Gossip: *The Galilean Accent,* 151–160; T. Marjoribanks: *The Sevenfold "I AM,"* 123 ff.; S. H. Geisy: *The "I AM'S" of Christ,* 289–310; on v. 35, A. H. Strong: *Miscellanies,* Vol. 2, 310–327; G. H. Morrison: *The Wind on the Heath,* 189–197; L. R. Scarborough: *The Tears of Jesus,* 13–24, and *How Jesus Won Men,* 262–267; the article, "Tears," by A. P. Sym, in Hastings: *Dictionary of Christ and the Gospels,* Vol. 2, 706–707; James Hastings: *Great Texts of the Bible, St. John, 1–12,* 484–493; on vs. 30–45, see Maclaren, as above, 92–107; and then, of course, if one has time, there are ten wonderfully rich sermons on this chapter in Charles H. Spurgeon's *Sermons on Our Lord's Miracles,* Vol. 1.

INTRODUCTORY.

The great German commentator, H. A. W. Meyer, has well said of this chapter: "No narrative of the New Testament bears so completely the stamp of being the opposite of a later invention. The very artistic style of representation, which in the account of this last and greatest miracle is most strikingly prominent, is only comprehensible from the personal, profound, and sympathizing recollection which had preserved and cherished, even in its finest traits, the truth and reality of the event with peculiar vivacity, fidelity, and inspiration." Canon Westcott, in his great commentary on this Gospel, reminds us that the numerous minute touches "mark the fullness of personal knowledge or the impression of an eye-witness, as for example, the relation of the family to Jesus, the delay of two days, the exact position of Bethany, the presence of Jews, the secret message, the poise of Jesus, the following of the Jews and their weeping, the prostration of Mary, the successive phases of the Lord's emotion, and the appearance of Lazarus." Bayle, in his famous *Dictionary* (Vol. 5, p. 17), tells us that the great philosopher Spinoza once said that "if he could have persuaded himself of the resurrection of Lazarus, he would have broken in pieces his whole system and embraced the ordinary faith of Christians." There are two other miracles of raising the dead recorded in the Gospels (but not found in John, as the raising of Lazarus is not found in any of the Synoptics), namely, the raising of the daughter of Jaïrus (Matt. 9 : 18, 19, 23–26; Mark 5 : 22–24, 35–43; Luke 8 : 41, 42, 49–56), and the raising of the widow's son (recorded only in Luke 7 : 11–17).

I. CHRIST'S PERFECT POISE IN AN HOUR OF SORROW AND APPARENT DANGER, vs. 1–10.

1. HE KNOWS THAT LAZARUS' ILLNESS WILL GLORIFY GOD, vs. 1–6. Bethany was a small village on the eastern slope of the Mount of Olives, near enough to Jerusalem to make it easily accessible, but far enough away to assure one of absolute quiet and freedom from the disturbing noises of surging crowds. This was the home, above all others in Palestine, which Jesus loved. "We know not how often

Siemiradzki.

Christ with Mary and Martha.

the Lord had been an inmate of that house at Bethany. One memorable occasion, with its word of warning to one of its inmates, we know of before this time (Luke 10 : 41, 42); and when later than this during the Great Week, He lodged in Bethany (Matt. 21 : 17; Mark 11 : 11, 19), returning thither for the night after the task of the day in the unfriendly city was over, and again repairing with the early morning to the city, he can scarcely have honored any other roof than this with His presence. Now, therefore, when there is sorrow there, they turn in their need to Him whom they may have themselves already proved an effectual helper in the day of trouble, who at any rate has shown Himself such in the extremest necessities of others." — *R. C. Trench.* The three members of this home, we are told, Jesus especially loved. "The word used in v. 3, *philein*, denotes a passionate, emotional warmth, which loves and cares not to ask why; the affection of lovers, parents, and the like. The word used in v. 5, *agapan*, denotes a calm, discriminating attachment, which loves because of the excellence of the loved object; the affection of friends. *Philein* is the stronger, but less reasoning; *agapan* the more earnest, but less intense. The sisters naturally use the more emotional word, describing their own feeling toward their brother; the evangelist equally naturally uses the loftier and less impulsive word." — *A. Plummer.* "Without love people may adorn their dwelling places as they please, but they remain houses, not homes; but when love is present a cottage becomes a home dearer and more precious to those who dwell within than all the palaces of kings. But to perfect the happiness of a home, one other love is necessary, and that is the love of Christ. It deepens and enriches all other love, and it flows when other loves get wounded and torn, a love from which nothing can ever separate us." — *J. D. Jones.*

In this home one member, Lazarus, was desperately sick, and at once the sisters sent a messenger to Jesus, informing Him of the shadow that has come over the home where He often loved to visit. The moment He heard of it (and of course, He knew of it before), He remarked that the sickness was not unto death but for the glory of God, that the Son of God might be thereby glorified. "Jesus, foreseeing all that would happen, intended these words to act as consolation to the sisters in the hour of trial, when their brother had died, and as a test of their faith in His love and truth. He refers to this in His interview with Mary, at the grave (v. 40) recalling this message. They are words which are fitly spoken over every Christian deathbed, now that Jesus is Himself dead and risen. The limits of the divine and human in our Lord are not easily defined, but the impression left on the mind here is that of absolute omniscience, as everywhere in this Gospel; and the simplest explanation is the profoundest after all, that Jesus spoke in full consciousness of the future, of the miracle, and of the results in the culmination of unbelief against Himself on the cross, through which His mission should be accomplished to the glory of His Father (12 : 23; 13 : 32; 17 : 1, 5)." — *George Reith.* Strange to say, our Lord upon hearing of Lazarus' sickness, instead of hurrying immediately to Bethany from the Jordan where He was tarrying, "abode two days still in the same place where He was." "This tarrying was a part of the severe yet gracious discipline of divine love. It is often thus. He intervenes with mighty help, but not till every other help, not until, to the weak faith of man, even His own promise, is seen utterly to have failed." — *R. C. Trench.*

2. HE KNOWS NO HARM CAN COME TO HIM WHILE HE HAS WORK TO DO, vs. 7–10. When our Lord suggested to His disciples that they should return to Judæa where not long before they had taken up stones to stone Him (10 : 31, 39), and His disciples remonstrated with Him because they were afraid harm would ultimately come to their Master, to them Jesus replied, "Are there not twelve hours in a day," by which He meant that His life was ordered of God and that what work God intended Him to do that He should do, and until that work was finished the evil purposes of men would remain unaccomplished.

II. **CHRIST'S CHARACTERIZATION OF DEATH AS SLEEP,** vs. 11–16. Disposing of this objection on the part of the disciples, Jesus now turns to the matter of Lazarus' illness. Our Lord spoke of this death as a "sleep," a beautiful word, often used in the Scriptures for what normally must be considered as life's greatest tragedy. "Sleep as an image of death is common from the dawn of literature; but the Gospel has raised the expression from a figure to a fact. (Cf. Matt. 27 : 52; Acts 7 : 60; 13 : 36; 11 : 30; 15 : 6, 18; 1 Thess. 4 : 13; 2 Pet. 3 : 4.) The thoroughly Christian term 'cemetery' (sleeping place), in the sense of a place of repose for the dead, comes from the same Greek root. The exact time of Lazarus' death cannot be determined, for we do not know how long Christ took in reaching Bethany. Christ calls him '*our* friend,' as claiming the sympathy of the disciples, who had shown unwillingness to return to Judæa." — *A. Plummer.* Now our Lord gives one of the reasons why He had not immediately proceeded to the home at Bethany, that He in raising this man from the grave might present to His followers a new opportunity for believing Him to be the Son of God.

III. **CHRIST'S CONCERN FOR THOSE WHO MOURN,** vs. 17–32.

1. THE UNSATISFYING COMFORT OF SOME FRIENDS, vs. 17–19. Before John brings Christ into actual contact with the mourners of this beloved family, he gives us a few intimate details concerning the immediate situation. The distance from Bethany to Jerusalem (fifteen furlongs) was something under two miles, "and is mentioned to account for the many Jews who came to condole with the sisters. It

JOHN 11 : 20. Martha therefore, when she heard that Jesus was coming, went and met him: but Mary still sat in the house.

21. Martha therefore said unto Jesus, Lord, if thou hadst been here, my brother had not died.

22. And even now I know that, whatsoever thou shalt ask of God, God will give thee.

23. Jesus saith unto her, Thy brother shall rise again.

24. Martha saith unto him, I know that he shall rise again in the resurrection at the last day.

25. Jesus said unto her, I am the resurrection, and the life: he that believeth on me, though he die, yet shall he live;

26. And whosoever liveth and believeth on me shall never die. Believest thou this?

27. She saith unto him, Yea, Lord: I have believed that thou art the Christ the Son of God, *even* he that cometh into the world.

---

was part of the Jewish ceremonial of mourning that many (ten at least) should come and console (cf. 2 Sam. 12 : 17; Job 2 : 11). It is said that the usual period of mourning was thirty days; three of weeping, seven of lamentation, twenty of sorrow." — *A. Plummer.* "From the fact that Lazarus had already been four days in the tomb, it is apparent that he was dead when Jesus received the message. It is uncertain how long the journey took. The Jews interred on the evening of the day one died." — *George Reith.*

2. HIS WORDS OF HOPE TO MARTHA, VS. 20–27. 20. **Martha therefore, when she heard that Jesus was coming, went and met him: but Mary still sat in the house.** 21. **Martha therefore said unto Jesus, Lord, if thou hadst been here, my brother had not died.** The characteristics of these two sisters are here at once evident. Mary, the quieter of the two, and the more meditative, remains in the home, while Martha, as soon as she hears that the Lord is coming, goes out to meet Him. The first thing she said to Him has probably a double implication — it is on the one hand an acknowledgment on her part that Christ's presence would have prevented the death of her brother; on the other hand, it is possibly somewhat of a rebuke, implying that the Lord *ought* to have been there, to have prevented her brother dying. She adds that she knows that whatever Christ might ask of God, He would grant, which certainly means that she believes Christ, even now, can raise her brother from the dead. 22. **And even now I know that, whatsoever thou shalt ask of God, God will give thee.**

23. **Jesus saith unto her, Thy brother shall rise again.** 24. **Martha saith unto him, I know that he shall rise again in the resurrection at the last day.** 25. **Jesus said unto her, I am the resurrection, and the life: he that believeth on me, though he die, yet shall he live.** In His quiet confidence, the Lord assures her that her brother will rise again, though He does not even hint that that would be then. To this Martha replies that, of course, she knows this, believing in the doctrine of the resurrection at the last day. Then our Lord gave one of those great statements concerning Himself, which has been the source of comfort and strength and hope to His people down through the ages. "I am the Resurrection, and the Life." "The words are in a paradoxical form. The resurrection is not a blessing apart from Him. Nor has He only power to raise from the dead and give life (5 : 21 ff.). He is personally the substance of the resurrection and the life. The word resurrection is to be taken in its widest sense, so that it is true to say life results from resurrection, and resurrection from life, to the believer. He must share Christ's life in order to have the power within him of the resurrection from the grave to the endless life, and by sharing Christ's risen life now in faith, he is in fact risen with Christ, and independent of every future change, death of the body itself, and shall be kept from the endless death, v. 24." — *George Reith.* "The resurrection is one manifestation of the Life. It is involved in the Life. It is a personal communication of the Lord Himself, and not a grace which He has to gain from another. He *is* that which men need. He does not *procure* the blessing for them." — *B. F. Westcott.* 26. **And whosoever liveth and believeth on me shall never die. Believest thou this?** 27. **She saith unto him, Yea, Lord: I have believed that thou art the Christ the Son**

28. And when she had said this, she went away, and called Mary her sister secretly, saying, The Teacher is here, and calleth thee.

29. And she, when she heard it, arose quickly, and went unto him.

32. Mary therefore, when she came where Jesus was, and saw him, fell down at his feet, saying unto him, Lord, if thou hadst been here, my brother had not died.

33. When Jesus therefore saw her weeping, and the Jews *also* weeping who came with her, he groaned in the spirit, and was troubled,

34. And said, Where have ye laid him? They say unto him, Lord, come and see.

35. Jesus wept.

---

of God, *even* he that cometh into the world. " To believe ' this ' is to believe what He says of Himself, and thus believe ' in Him.' It is one thing to hear it, to reason and argue on it; and quite another thing to believe, embrace, trust it. To believe is to receive, hold, enjoy the reality and power of it, with all that lies in it of joy, comfort, peace, and hope. In what sense Martha addresses Jesus as ' Lord ' is shown by the titles she at once adds. In ' I have believed ' note the emphatic pronoun. Others have not believed, others have charged Jesus with blasphemy (10 : 33) for calling Himself ' the Son of God ' — Martha ' has believed,' has done so this long while, and is believing now." — *R. C. H. Lenski.* Note particularly how Christ seems to emphasize, above everything else, the importance of believing in *Him.*

3. HIS COMPASSION FOR MARY IN HER SORROW, VS. 28–36. 28. **And when she had said this, she went away, and called Mary her sister secretly, saying, The Teacher is here, and calleth thee.** 29. **And she, when she heard it, arose quickly, and went unto him.** 32. **Mary therefore, when she came where Jesus was, and saw him, fell down at his feet, saying unto him, Lord, if thou hadst been here, my brother had not died.** Immediately upon her great confession of Christ, Martha went back to the home to tell Mary that the Master was nearby, and was calling for her, which must mean that Christ had sent a special message of this nature to the other sister. She arose at once, and went to the place where Jesus seems to have been tarrying for the time being, outside of the village of Bethany, probably that He might have an opportunity for speaking privately to the sisters without the inconvenient noisiness of a crowd of nearby mourners. No doubt, Mary and Martha had continually talked about the Lord's coming to the house, before Lazarus had died, and had both concluded that, should the Lord come, their brother would be healed. This accounts for the fact that her words to Christ are identical with those of her sister. 33. **When Jesus therefore saw her weeping, and the Jews *also* weeping who came with her, he groaned in the spirit, and was troubled.** " The *spirit* is the seat of the religious emotions, as the *soul* is that of the natural affections. Thus in 12 : 27 Jesus says: *My soul is troubled*, because the foreseeing of His suffering makes His nature shudder, while here and in chapter 13 it is in His *spirit* that He is agitated, because in both cases He sees Himself in immediate contact with evil in its blackest form, and because with a holy horror he feels the nearness of the invisible being who has taken possession of the heart of Judas, and (in our passage) of that of His declared enemies. This parallel throws light on the groaning of Jesus in verse 33. This internal revolution terminated in this sudden and brief question: *Where have you laid him?* " — *F. Godet.* " The word here translated *groan* occurs five times in the New Testament, here and verse 38; Matthew 9 : 30; Mark 1 : 43; 14 : 5. In all cases, as in classical Greek, to express not sorrow but indignation or severity." — *A. Plummer.* 34. **And said, Where have ye laid him? They say unto him, Lord, come and see.** 35. **Jesus wept.** " The term *to weep* does not indicate, like the word weeping in verse 33, sighs, but tears; it is the expression of a calm and gentle grief. It is a strange fact that it is precisely the Gospel in which the divinity of Jesus is most strikingly affirmed, that leads us also best to know the profoundly human side of His life." — *F. Godet.* Hugh Macmillan once said: " I am strongly tempted to do nothing more than to repeat the words: for I feel that to comment upon them is to gild the sunshine and paint the lily. . . . The dead are raised to life by no callous philosopher with a hard eye and unfeeling heart; by no magician who simply waves his hand and accomplishes with no cost or effort to him-

38. Jesus therefore again groaning in himself cometh to the tomb. Now it was a cave, and a stone lay against it.

39. Jesus saith, Take ye away the stone. Martha, the sister of him that was dead, saith unto him, Lord, by this time the body decayeth; for he hath been *dead* four days.

40. Jesus saith unto her, Said I not unto thee, that, if thou believedst, thou shouldest see the glory of God?

41. So they took away the stone. And Jesus lifted up his eyes, and said, Father, I thank thee that thou heardest me.

---

self the mighty miracle; by no God who stands afar off in the heavens and issues His commandments to the dead to rise as He issued His commandment to light to appear at the creation; but by One who is very near with the tender weakness that is more moving and majestic than all our strength, and the sorrowful experiences that are more beautiful and precious than all our gladness."

Reputed Tomb of Lazarus.

4. THE QUESTION, v. 37. Already, before the miracle takes place, we see a line of demarcation separating those who are drawn to Christ, by His power and personality and grace, from those who are determined that He should be put to death: some are moved with the love they see manifested in our Lord's tears; others critically ask, Could not the one who opened the eyes of the blind have delivered this man Lazarus from the illness which brought him to the grave?

IV. **CHRIST'S VICTORY OVER DEATH,** vs. 38, 39. 38. **Jesus therefore again groaning in himself cometh to the tomb. Now it was a cave, and a stone lay against it.** 39. **Jesus saith, Take ye away the stone. Martha, the sister of him that was dead, saith unto him, Lord, by this time the body decayeth; for he hath been *dead* four days.** "This, like many other touches in the narrative, indicates the social position of the Bethany family. It was not a common burial place among many, but like what we call a family vault. These were caverns, partly natural, partly artificial, in some rocky hill, probably in imitation of the ancestral cave of Machpelah, to which the Jew looked back with such reverence. These vaults usually had a stone at the entrance, either like a cover or trough-stone, when the cave was vertical, or like a door when it was horizontal, to keep out beasts of prey; often used also as a memento of the dead. Jesus bids roll it away, when a significant incident occurs. Martha interposes. It is she, so attentive to all proprieties, so observant and so active, that even grief cannot absorb her incessant care. Perhaps, she surmises that after all Jesus means to do something; but a feeling of the glaring impossibility of the thing gets the better of her, and she cries out, as if protesting against any attempt on the part of Jesus to grapple with Death's power. It is just her former cry, 'Lord, if thou hadst been here' something might have been done then, but, alas! nothing can be done now. It is all over; he has been dead four days." — *John Laidlaw.* 40. **Jesus saith unto her, Said I not unto thee, that, if thou believedst, thou shouldest see the glory of God?** These words, while addressed first to Martha, because she is the one that raised the objection, must surely have been uttered for the benefit of all who were near, and were spoken to remind those who had confessed their faith in Him that in ordering the stone to be removed He was only initiating an act which would reveal the glory of God, and should thus persuade them to do what He commanded them to do. 41 *a.* **So they took away the stone.** "He employed natural means to remove natural obstructions, that His divine power might come face to face with the supernatural element. He puts forth supernatural power to do just that which no less power could accomplish; but all

42. And I knew that thou hearest me always: but because of the multitude that standeth around I said it, that they may believe that thou didst send me.

43. And when he had thus spoken, he cried with a loud voice, Lazarus, come forth.

44. He that was dead came forth, bound hand and foot with grave-clothes; and his face was bound about with a napkin. Jesus saith unto them, Loose him, and let him go.

---

the rest — removing the stone beforehand, loosening the grave clothes afterwards — He bids men do in the ordinary way. No doubt the power which could call Lazarus from the sleep of death included power to rend the rocks, roll away the stone, strip off the gravebands without human aid." — *George Reith.* 41 *b.* **And Jesus lifted up his eyes, and said, Father, I thank thee that thou heardest me.** 42. **And I knew that thou hearest me always: but because of the multitude that standeth around I said it, that they may believe that thou didst send me.** "If the human side of Christ's personality be presented to us in the previous clause, the divine side is presented in this. The communion which Jesus had with His Father was complete and continuous. He was ever the Son in the bosom of the Father (1 : 18). It was not to be supposed that Jesus had to ask special help in the doing of this miracle, as if it were harder for Him to do; the Jews themselves present thought differently (v. 37); and there is no request for aid — simply thanksgiving for the assurance that He was heard. It was well, therefore, that this emphatic assertion of His unbroken communion with God, and of His personal confidence that His will and God's were always in accordance, should follow the utterance of thanks. . . . In the calm consciousness of His unity with God, of fulfilling the Father's mission and purpose, . . . He thanks the Father for the opportunity given Him of setting forth the glory of God." — *George Reith.* 43. **And when he had thus spoken, he cried with a loud voice, Lazarus, come forth.** 44. **He that was dead came forth, bound hand and foot with grave-clothes; and his face was bound about with a napkin. Jesus saith unto them, Loose him, and let him go.** "More exactly what He cried was, 'Lazarus! hither! forth!' without a verb at all. The simple grandeur, brevity, and force of this resurrection call corresponds with the mighty effect. The great voice or shout, from One who was wont to speak so gently and quietly, thrilled the heart of every listener. Every eye was riveted on the dark mouth of the open sepulchre. The echo of the loud cry had hardly ceased when a figure stood sharply outlined against the gloom, in its swathing of white linen, and in a moment more sprang forward, struggling with the gravebands, and eager to throw himself at his Redeemer's feet. We can almost share the mingled pulse of fear and joy that throbbed through that crowd as he '*that had been dead*' came forth. The instinctive shudder and recoil — just for an instant — from what seems a walking corpse. Then, the forward wave, the rush of joyous recognition, when they saw that it was Lazarus alive. Next, eagerly clustering round, they help him off with the grave-clothes. They unbind the napkin from his face. At the word of Jesus, and almost

The Raising of Lazarus. Frederic Shields.

as soon as it was spoken, '*they loose him, and let him go.*' The significance of this mighty deed we cannot over-estimate, for it is on the one hand, a profoundly significant symbol of Christ's redemption, and on the other, a signal testimony to His right and power to redeem." — *John Laidlaw.*

We believe that Lazarus at this time did not receive a resurrection body, but that his spirit simply returned to that ordinary fleshly body in which he had lived up to the hour of his death. Thus, Lazarus died again. How long he lived after being raised from the dead we do not know. It is significant that he says absolutely nothing about any experience of his between the hour when his spirit left his body and the hour when it returned to his body at the command of Jesus. If this narrative had been written a century or two later, it would have been adorned with all sorts of fanciful things, including a long discourse from Lazarus about what he saw on the other side of death. The remarkable absence of all such statements in this chapter testify to its historical truthworthiness.

V. **THE TWO OPPOSITE CONSEQUENCES THAT FOLLOWED THIS MIRACLE,** vs. 45–57. John tells us near the close of his Gospel that the purpose for which he had written the book was that men might believe that Christ was the Son of God, and throughout the pages of his wonderful narrative of our Lord's life he especially emphasized the act of belief on the part of those who beheld our Lord's miracles. But, and how strange we have to put a "but" at the end of such a mighty manifestation of Christ's deity — but many went and reported these things to the Pharisees, and the Pharisees called a council together and decided that because it was expedient that one person should die for the nation, that the whole nation should not be destroyed by the Romans, Christ should be put to death! Bishop Ryle, in a very practical chapter on this wicked determination of Christ's enemies, says we should observe at least three things in reading these concluding verses: the desperate wickedness of man's heart in refusing to be convinced by overwhelming evidence; the blind ignorance with which God's enemies often act and reason, as here, when they said if they let Christ alone they would be ruined, but if they put Him to death they would be saved, whereas later history showed that by putting Him to death they finally brought down upon them tragedy and ruin; and, finally, the importance that bad men sometimes attach to outside ceremony, while their hearts are full of sin, as here, when the Jews went up to Jerusalem before the Passover to purify themselves, when, at the same time, they were ready to do the will of the Pharisees, and to put their own Messiah to a violent death. Of course, Caiaphas was not aware of the full truthfulness of what he said in declaring that one man must die for the whole nation. We must understand that the comment in verses 51 and 52 is by John the Apostle, and not a continuation of the speech of Caiaphas.

CONCLUSION.

There are, it seems, three great truths to be drawn from this chapter: (1) that Christ by His omniscience and omnipotence proves Himself to be the Son of God in conquering, what no other being who ever lived on earth has been able to conquer by his own volition and strength, the enemy Death. (2) Do we not have here a clear picture, in allegorical form, of our spiritual resurrection? "The sinner, like Lazarus, is dead, buried, we may say already corrupt and loathsome. Christ comes Himself to the sinner's tomb. He bids, 'Take away the stone.' He calls His servants to ply all preliminary means. He sends His agents to warn and teach. But there is no life till He calls. He cries with a loud voice. It is the 'effectual call' of His word and spirit. The man hears, the dead lives, the soul is converted. Then, once more, comes in the use of means. Remove hindrances; explain to the restored soul the way of life more perfectly." — *John Laidlaw.* (3) Finally, we certainly have here the assurance of our own resurrection, by the power of Him who not only said He was the Resurrection and the Life, but who was able to deliver from death and the grave this man, from whose body his spirit had departed. What Christ did then, He did in an even greater way when He raised Himself from the dead not many months later; and what He proved Himself able to do then, in the body of His humiliation, He certainly will be able to do in the body of His glory, when He comes for His own, and all believers, of all ages, buried in every part of the world, will come forth from the earth and the sea, in glorified bodies, to be with the Lord forever. Love and power here are perfectly interwoven in the raising of Lazarus, and love and power are the two great forces that guarantee to us our resurrection on the day of His appointment. (Cf. John 5 : 25, 28; 1 Thess. 4 : 16.)

How many different characters appear in this chapter, and what are the different parts that each plays? How many differences do you discern between our Lord's disciples and His friends, and the Lord Himself? What are the indications in this lesson of Christ's supernatural knowledge? Why does our Lord put so much emphasis upon the experience of believing in Him? How many different characteristics of Christ are here set forth? Do you think if Mary and Martha had not sent this message to Jesus, He would have come to Bethany anyway and raised Lazarus from the dead? How many different reasons can you suggest why Christ did not heal Lazarus (even though He was not present in Bethany) instead of allowing Him to die?

LESSON X. — March 7.

BIBLE TEACHINGS AGAINST DRUNKENNESS. — 1 Samuel 30 : 16, 17; Isaiah 28 : 1–4, 7; Galatians 5 : 19–21.

GOLDEN TEXT. — *Strong drink shall be bitter to them that drink it.* ISAIAH 24 : 9.

Devotional Reading: Psalm 5 : 1–7.
Beginner Topic: THE QUESTION THOMAS ASKED.
  Lesson Material: John 14.
  Memory Verse: God is love. 1 John 4 : 8.
Primary Topic: WHAT JESUS FOUND TO DO.
  Lesson Material: John 13.
  Memory Verse: Through love be servants one to another. Galatians 5 : 13.
Junior Topic: WHEN JESUS WASHED THE DISCIPLES' FEET.
  Lesson Material: John 13.
  Memory Verse: Whatsoever thy hand findeth to do, do it with thy might. Ecclesiastes 9 : 10.
Intermediate and Senior Topic: A SHORT CUT TO FAILURE.
Topic for Young People and Adults: BIBLE TEACHINGS AGAINST DRUNKENNESS.

THE TEACHER AND HIS CLASS.

The Younger Classes might have their interest aroused in this lesson by having the teacher put on the board a series of four line drawings of a man in four stages of intoxication.

The Older Classes need to be reminded of the terrible and constantly growing menace of intoxication in our country. Probably education in these matters, showing the disastrous consequences of alcoholic intoxication, will be of some help in restoring to our country a sense of shame and fear in these matters. But I frankly think what we need most of all is to hear what the Word of God has to say and be guided thereby. Millions of people in this country do not even know that the Bible definitely, frequently, and uncompromisingly classifies drunkenness with the worst crimes and sins. This is where it belongs.

THE LESSON IN ITS SETTING.

Time. — The event recorded in 1 Samuel occurred possibly 1056 B.C.; Isaiah 28 was written not far from 725 B.C.; Paul probably wrote his Epistle to the Galatians in A.D. 58.

Place. — The city of Ziklag has not yet been definitely identified, but it was somewhere south of Gaza, in southern Palestine. Ephraim is the name of that part of Palestine which can be generally located in the central western section of the Holy Land; here it is probably a synonym for all of Samaria. Galatia was a province in Asia, an area today known as Asia Minor.

THE PLAN OF THE LESSON.

SUBJECT: The Perverting and Demoralizing Effect of Alcoholic Intoxication.

I. DRINKING AND CAROUSING RENDER AN ARMY OPEN TO ATTACK AND DESTRUCTION, 1 Sam. 30 : 16, 17.

II. THE BEAUTY DOOMED TO FADE AND THE BEAUTY THAT ABIDES FOREVER, Isa. 28 : 1–4.

III. THE EFFECT OF STRONG DRINK UPON THOSE WHO MINISTER IN HOLY THINGS, Isa. 28 : 7.

IV. THE WORKS OF THE FLESH WHICH PRACTICED BAR MEN FROM THE KINGDOM OF GOD, Gal. 5 : 19–21.

1. Sins of sensuality (3).
2. Sins connected with pagan religion (2).
3. Sins of an antisocial nature (4).
4. Sins of personal excess (2).

THE TEACHER'S LIBRARY.

On the particular verses chosen from 1 Samuel, the only commentary with which I am acquainted that can be said to give any definite help is that by H. D. M. Spence, in *The Bible Commentary for English Readers*. For an historical background of the entire occasion see the excellent chapter in W. G. Blaikie's volume in *The Expositor's Bible*, 416–428; and William J. Deane: *David: His Life and Times*, 65–80. As far as the editor knows, there are absolutely no worth-while sermons on this text. For the passage taken from Isaiah, one should consult especially the two commentaries on this book by Albert Barnes and T. R. Birks. See also Hugh C. McCook: *The Gospel in Nature*, 311–329; a sermon in the *Preacher's Monthly*, Vol. 4, 314 ff., by A. Maclaren, "The Judgment of Drunkards and Mockers"; and another, "A Crown of Pride or a Crown of Glory," in his *Expositions of Holy Scripture, Isaiah 1–48*, 125–136. On the Galatian passage one should consult the commentaries on this epistle by John Eadie, J. B. Lightfoot, E. H. Perowne (in the *Cambridge Bible for Schools and Colleges*); P. B. Huxtable (in the *Pulpit Commentary*); and, for an exhaustive consideration of most of the Greek words, the work by Ernest De-Witt Burton (in the *International Critical Commentary*). I find nothing of any importance, of a sermonic nature, on Galatians 5 : 19–21. Other temperance literature will be referred to in later temperance lessons in this volume, but the editor would especially call attention now to a very valuable booklet, of approximately a hundred pages, *Temperance Facts*, compiled by W. G. Calderwood, which may be purchased for twenty-five cents from the Minnesota Temperance Union, 205 Hodgson Building, Minneapolis, Minn.

---

1 SAMUEL 30 : 16. And when he had brought him down, behold, they were spread abroad over all the ground, eating and drinking, and dancing, because of all the great spoil that they had taken out of the land of the Philistines, and out of the land of Judah.

17. And David smote them from the twilight even unto the evening of the next day: and there escaped not a man of them, save four hundred young men, who rode upon camels and fled.

I. **DRINKING AND CAROUSING RENDER AN ARMY OPEN TO ATTACK AND DESTRUCTION,** 1 Sam. 30 : 16, 17. 16. **And when he had brought him down, behold, they were spread abroad over all the ground, eating and drinking, and dancing, because of all the great spoil that they had taken out of the land of the Philistines, and out of the land of Judah.** 17. **And David smote them from the twilight even unto the evening of the next day: and there escaped not a man of them, save four hundred young men, who rode upon camels and fled.** David, at this time of his life, had fled from Saul and the Israelitish army to the camp of the Philistines, and was assisting these warlike people in their attacks upon nearby enemy tribes, though, of course, he would never co-operate with the Philistines in their war against Israel. He had been living for some time at Ziklag, in southern Palestine, and, as captain of the bodyguard of king Achish, it was necessary for him to be away from Ziklag for certain (longer or shorter) periods. The chapter opens with David coming back from one of these military adventures to find Ziklag burned to the ground. "It is probable that David's return to Ziklag, and the expedition in which he had to engage to recover his wives and his property, took place at or about the very time when Saul made his journey to Endor, and when the fatal battle of Gilboa was raging. . . . It appears from the chapter now before us that, in the absence of David and his troop, severe reprisals had been taken by the Amalekites for the defeat and utter destruction which they had lately inflicted on a portion of their tribe. We must remember that the Amalekites were a widely dispersed people, consisting of many tribes, each living separately from the rest, but so related that in any emergency they would readily come to one another's help. News of the extermination of the tribes whom David had attacked, and whom he had utterly destroyed lest any of them should bring word to Achish of his real employment, had been brought to their neighbors; and these neighbors determined to take revenge for the slaughter of their kinsmen. The opportunity of David's absence was taken for invading Ziklag, for which purpose a large and well-equipped expedition had been got together; and as they met with no opposition, they carried everything before them. Happily, however, as they found no enemies they did not draw the sword; they counted it better policy to carry off all that could be transported, so as to make use of the goods, and sell the women and children into slavery, and as they had a great multitude of beasts of burden with them (v. 17) there could be no difficulty in carrying out this plan. It seems very strange that David should have left Ziklag, apparently without the protection of a single soldier. . . . It was probably one of the bitterest of the many bitter hours that David ever spent." — *W. G. Blaikie.* Providentially, an Egyptian who knew the place to which the Amalekites had fled, appeared just at the time when David first became aware of what had happened to his property and his wives, and guided them to the place where these marauders were drinking and carousing in celebration of their victory. Discovered in such a state, totally surprised and unprepared, reeling about because of their gluttony and drinking, the whole Amalekite host that had destroyed Ziklag was destroyed by David and his soldiers. Many a battle has been lost for the same reason. It is very interesting to note that Mr. Malcolm de Sieyes, Washington representative of General de Gaulle of the French Free Government, recently made the following report: " Though they (the Germans) were big and tough and hard enough for anybody, I can't understand how they got that way on the food they had. In the morning they got a sort of tea made out of acorns or something with a crumbly, meal bread. Their only hot meal was at noon — a kind of thin stew with little pieces of meat about as big as your fingernail. In the French army, *we got one quart of wine every day*, but for the Germans, anything alcoholic is ' *verboten.*' For supper, they had the same bread with some margarine or jam." Senator Sheppard, in his last public address delivered January 16, 1941, made the following sober remarks regarding the evil effects of drinking in armies: " Mr. President, the armies of young men now training to preserve democracy and peace must be physically fit. Their bodies must be strong. Their muscles must be able to respond to the instantaneous call of will and mind and soul. Their brains must not be dull, and their eyes must not be dimmed by alcohol.

" The men who man our ships must be alert to the perils that surround them, below the surface of the ocean as well as above. And men of perfect control of body and mind will be needed to pilot our aircraft. To these objectives, alcohol is a frightful menace.

" Mr. President, I condemn beverage alcohol as a threat to the health, happiness, and prosperity of our citizenship.

" I condemn it because an alcohol-drinking democracy cannot develop the maximum strength for national defense." — *Sunday School Times.*

What Delayed Marshal Ney?

The battle of Waterloo, one of the great turning points of history, was fought near Brussels in June, 1815. The allied armies of Prussia, England, and the Netherlands, under the Duke of Wellington, were on one side, and the French under Napoleon on the other. Before the three armies had united, Napoleon hoped to meet and overcome them separately. Hearing that Wellington had ordered the English and Dutch forces to concentrate at a place called Quatre Bras, where four roads joined, Napoleon ordered Marshal Ney to get there at once and keep the allies from taking the place. For some reason which Napoleon never understood, Marshal Ney did not march to Quatre Bras until it was too late. The Duke's forces arrived first and held the place. It is said that Napoleon at St. Helena often asked why the heroic Ney had lost so decisive a morning before giving the order to attack. Recently, an Italian periodical, the *Corriere della Sera*, published an explanation that was found in a small pamphlet discovered by an antiquarian in Belgium. It was entitled, ' The Influence of Burgundy on the Belgian Campaign in 1815.' The author of this pamphlet, who was most certainly not influenced by any preconceived anti-alcohol ideas, reported that when Marshal Ney returned to his headquarters on the evening of the fifteenth, he was feeling thirsty and accepted the offer of a glass of old Burgundy wine. But the Burgundy, like other alcoholic liquors, instead of quenching his thirst, only made it worse. The wine, says the Italian paper, affected the first Marshal of the empire exactly as it would have affected a common soldier. After drinking more of the wine, Ney fell into a deep and prolonged sleep. When he awoke his head was heavy and his ideas confused; he found himself absolutely unable to give orders or to reach any decision. In fact, it is doubtful if he had read Napoleon's order, for he acted as if he did not know about it. When he finally recovered his senses and his mental and physical faculties, it was too late to head off the meeting of the Duke's armies at the crossroads. Napoleon had to rearrange his plans, and the battle was lost.

II. **THE BEAUTY DOOMED TO FADE AND THE BEAUTY THAT ABIDES FOREVER,** Isa. 28 : 1–4. 1. **Woe to the crown of pride of the drunkards of Ephraim,**

ISAIAH 28 : 1. Woe to the crown of pride of the drunkards of Ephraim, and to the fading flower of his glorious beauty, which is on the head of the fat valley of them that are overcome with wine!

2. Behold, the Lord hath a mighty and strong one; as a tempest of hail, a destroying storm, as a tempest of mighty waters overflowing, will he cast down to the earth with the hand.

3. The crown of pride of the drunkards of Ephraim shall be trodden under foot:

4. And the fading flower of his glorious beauty, which is on the head of the fat valley, shall be as the first-ripe fig before the summer; which when he that looketh upon it seeth, while it is yet in his hand he eateth it up.

---

and to the fading flower of his glorious beauty, which is on the head of the fat valley of them that are overcome with wine! 2. **Behold, the Lord hath a mighty and strong one; as a tempest of hail, a destroying storm, as a tempest of mighty waters overflowing, will he cast down to the earth with the hand.** 3. **The crown of pride of the drunkards of Ephraim shall be trodden under foot:** 4. **and the fading flower of his glorious beauty, which is on the head of the fat valley, shall be as the first-ripe fig before the summer; which when he that looketh upon it seeth, while it is yet in his hand he eateth it up.** The words of T. R. Birks, of Cambridge, in his excellent, but today not well-known commentary on Isaiah, are worth quoting here in their entirety: "The crown of pride, or proud crown, of the drunkards of Ephraim is Samaria, the metropolis of the kingdom. It stood on a hill in the midst of a rich and fruitful valley. . . . The figure alludes doubly to the elevated site of Samaria, and to the chaplet or garland of flowers, often worn by revellers in their joyous banquets. . . . It is compared not only to a crown, but to a fading flower, a chaplet or wreath already withering, because its fall was so near. The sensuality and drunkenness of the city are denounced by other prophets. Some take drunkards literally, others for those drunk with worldly pride. Both ideas may well be included in the warning. Revelling and drunkenness imply spiritual blindness and stupor, and increase it, and make men senseless to the approach of the divine judgments. The mighty and strong one of the Lord, or appointed by Him for the work of judgment, is the king of Assyria, Shalmaneser, by whom the siege was begun, with his successor, Sargon, who completed the overthrow. He is described in chapter 10, as the tool or instrument to execute the warnings of God. He would soon pluck this proud and beautiful garland from the head of the drunkards of Ephraim, and cast it down to the earth with his hand, as a fierce tempest or flood sweeps everything away before it. The union of two metaphors, each separately striking, adds double force to the prophet's warning. . . . The proud crown or garland of the drunkards, when the spoiler has torn it from their brows, and cast it on the ground, will be trodden under his feet. Samaria, the glorious beauty or ornament of Ephraim, would be indeed like a fading flower, a wreath withering away; and also like the early fig, which drops when the tree is shaken, and which he who sees it no sooner sets his eyes upon than he devours it with greedy haste." — *T. R. Birks.* "The gathering of figs takes place about August. Now, if any one sees a fig as early as June, he fixes his eyes upon it, and hardly touches it with his hands before he swallows it, and that without waiting to masticate it long. Like such a dainty bit will the

Stone Monument Commemorating the Wars of King Shalmaneser.

7. And even these reel with wine, and stagger with strong drink; the priest and the prophet reel with strong drink, they are swallowed up of wine, they stagger with strong drink; they err in vision, they stumble in judgment.

luxuriant Samaria vanish. The fact that Shalmaneser, or his successor Sargon, did not conquer Samaria till after the lapse of three years (2 Kings 18 : 10), does not detract from the truth of the prophecy; it is enough that both the thirst of the conqueror and the utter destruction of Samaria answered it." — *F. Delitzsch.*

III. **THE EFFECT OF STRONG DRINK UPON THOSE WHO MINISTER IN HOLY THINGS,** Isa. 28 : 7. 7. **And even these reel with wine, and stagger with strong drink; the priest and the prophet reel with strong drink, they are swallowed up of wine, they stagger with strong drink; they err in vision, they stumble in judgment.** By far the best comment on this verse with which the editor is acquainted is that by Albert Barnes, in his old but still profitable work on Isaiah. " In the previous verses the prophet had said that the kingdom of Judah should be saved while that of Ephraim should be destroyed. Yet he does not deny that they also were guilty of crimes for which punishment would come upon them. To portray these crimes, and to declare the certain judgment which awaited them, is the design of the remainder of the chapter. The word rendered ' have erred ' refers usually to the fact that men *stagger* or *reel* through wine, and is applied commonly to those who are intoxicated (Prov. 20 : 1). The subsequent part of this verse shows, however, that it does not refer merely to the fact that they stagger and reel as intemperate men do, but that it had an effect on their ' vision ' and ' judgment '; that is, it disqualified them for the discharge of their duties as priests and as prophets. In this part of the verse, however, the simple idea is, that they reel or stagger through wine, *i.e.*, they are addicted to intoxication. In the subsequent part of the verse the prophet states the effect in producing indistinctness of vision and error of judgment. . . . Probably the priest and the prophet are specified to denote the higher classes of society. It is probable that the prophet also designs to indicate the enormity of the sins of the nation, from the fact that those who were specially devoted to religion, and who were supposed to have immediate communication with God, were addicted to intemperance. . . . They are completely absorbed by wine; they not only themselves indulge in its use, but they are themselves, as it were, swallowed up by it, so that their reason, and strength, and virtue are all gone — as a vessel is absorbed in a maelstrom or whirlpool. . . . It was the office of the prophets to declare the will of God; probably also to explain the sense of the sacred Scriptures, and to address the people on their duty. Here the prophet says that the effect of their intemperance was that they had themselves no correct and clear views of the truth, and that they led the people into error. . . . There were many important subjects on which the priests sat in judgment among the Hebrews, particularly in all matters pertaining to religion. By the influence of intoxicating liquors they were disqualified for the high and holy functions of their office; and the consequence was that the nation was corrupt, and was exposed to the heavy judgments of God." — *Albert Barnes.*

As every one knows, the Apostle Paul says, in a famous passage (Eph. 5 : 18) that all believers are not to be drunk with wine, but to be filled with the Spirit. This ought to be especially true with those whose life work it is to interpret the Scriptures, to deal with the souls of people, and to be continually engaged in holy tasks — the administration of the sacraments, visiting the sick, praying with the dying, and so on, because the Christian ministry is distinctly one in which the presence and illumination, the sanctification, the wisdom and power of the Holy Spirit are constantly needed. A minister who is not doing his work in the power of the Holy Spirit is the most miserable of all creatures, and his life, whatever else it is, is barren of the fruit that God looks for. Certain it is that a minister addicted to alcoholic beverages, bringing him to intoxication, is one in whom the Holy Spirit is not abiding in sovereign power. We have known many ministers ourselves whose whole life work has been wrecked because they could not leave this fiery stuff alone. And is it not true, though of course the consequences are not quite so evident or so terrible, that enslavement to tobacco on the part of the clergymen does result in a definite loss of spiritual power and a beclouding of the soul? If you look about the country, you will generally notice that the men who are bringing men and women into the presence of Christ for conviction and conversion — the ministers who have

Galatians 5 : 19. Now the works of the flesh are manifest, which are *these:* fornication, uncleanness, lasciviousness,

20. Idolatry, sorcery, enmities, strife, jealousies, wraths, factions, divisions, parties,

21. Envyings, drunkenness, revellings, and such like; of which I forewarn you, even as I did forewarn you, that they who practise such things shall not inherit the kingdom of God.

---

a real passion for souls (not always, but generally), are those who walk in freedom from this nicotine habit.

IV. **THE WORKS OF THE FLESH WHICH PRACTICED BAR MEN FROM THE KINGDOM OF GOD,** Gal. 5 : 19–21. 19. **Now the works of the flesh are manifest, which are *these:* fornication, uncleanness, lasciviousness,** 20. **idolatry, sorcery, enmities, strife, jealousies, wraths, factions, divisions, parties,** 21. **envyings, drunkenness, revellings, and such like; of which I forewarn you, even as I did forewarn you, that they who practise such things shall not inherit the kingdom of God.** This is the first time that these three verses, so dark in their enumeration of the sins of men, have ever appeared as a part of the printed text of the International Sunday School Lessons. The editor ventures to suggest that not one of his readers has ever heard a sermon from this particular passage. And yet it is a part of the Word of God, a very sober part of the Word of God. It is a word of warning, and it should be heeded. The mere examination of this passage with some care will bow any heart before God, asking for cleansing when it is conscious of being guilty of any of these sins, asking, too, for divine deliverance from each and all of them throughout the years that remain. (Other catalogues of sins may be found in Rom. 1 : 29–31; 13 : 13; 1 Cor. 6 : 9, 10; 2 Cor. 12 : 20, 21; Eph. 5 : 3–5; 1 Pet. 4 : 3.)

1. Sins of Sensuality. Gal. 19. **Now the works of the flesh are manifest.** The word *manifest* means "open, evident," so that any one may see, the appeal being to common knowledge. **Which are *these:* fornication, uncleanness, lasciviousness,** 20. **idolatry, sorcery, enmities, strife, jealousies, wraths, factions, divisions, parties,** 21. **envyings, drunkenness, revellings, and such like; of which I forewarn you, even as I did forewarn you, that they who practise such things.** *Fornication* — the Greek word here refers to all illicit sexual intercourse in general, a sin which was universally practiced throughout the Roman empire at the time Paul was writing; in fact, it had even become a part of temple rituals in most of the Greek cities, like Corinth and Ephesus. Any such intercourse outside of the marriage state is absolutely condemned without any excuse or compromise, throughout the New Testament. *Uncleanness* — in some writers the Greek word here is used to indicate uncleanness of a sore or wound; in the Septuagint it is sometimes used of ceremonial impurity (Lev. 5 : 3, etc.), and sometimes of moral impurity or wickedness (Prov. 6 : 16; Ezek. 9 : 9, etc.). In the New Testament (in every case except Matthew 23 : 27) it is used of moral impurity, and in the seven out of the nine occurrences of the word in Paul's epistles it stands in association with fornication, or some other word denoting sexual vice.

Babylonian Idols.

Lasciviousness — the derivation of the Greek word Paul used here is doubtful. It may be defined as "the self-asserting propensity indulged without check or regard to ordinary propriety, especially in libidinous gratification." — *John Eadie.*

2. Sins Connected with Pagan Religion. *Idolatry* — this word, of course, refers to the worship of images or false gods which were found everywhere throughout the Roman world in Paul's time. It was said that it was easier to behold a statue of some god or goddess on the streets of Athens than to see a man. There were

really hundreds of deities worshiped in different parts of the Roman empire at this time, and practically every aspect of life, and every important element in nature, had its god or goddess. Idolatry not only was false, and kept men from the worship of the true God, but it was also degrading — intellectually, physically, and morally. Men become like that which they worship. Idolatry in Europe, as such, may be said to have been forever banished with the advent of Christianity after four centuries of struggle. However, it is tragically prevalent throughout India, and in most of Africa, and we are sorry to say it forms a large part of the worship practiced by the Roman Catholic Church, not so much in the worship of false gods, of course, as in the *worship* of the Virgin Mary and the saints of long ago. *Sorcery* — the word which Paul used here is *pharmaxia*, the classical word for a drug, whether harmful or wholesome, and, as any reader will at once realize, it is from this that our word "pharmacy" is derived. "In Demosthenes, Aristotle, and the Septuagint it is used of witchcraft because witches employ drugs (Exod. 7 : 11, 22); in Isaiah 47 : 9 it is a synonym of enchantment. In the present passage the reference is to witchcraft, sorcery, magic of any kind, without special reference to the use of drugs." — *E. D. Burton.*

3. SINS OF AN ANTISOCIAL NATURE. *Enmities* — this common word is found many times in the New Testament, meaning, simply, hatred, or that which is hateful, or the act of hating and opposing others. This has no reference, of course, to political opposition, but to that antagonism toward others, whether individuals or organized groups, involving bitterness and hate, driving one to undertake that which will work for the harm of those hated. *Strife* — this also means contention or rankling, and, as Eadie remarks: "In such strife, love by which the law is fulfilled, becomes wholly lost, for it springs out of these 'hatreds' and is nursed by them." *Jealousies* — "The common element in all the uses of the word in Greek literature is its expression of an intense feeling, usually eager desire of some kind. Sometimes it means an intense devotion for persons or things (Ps. 69 : 10; Rom. 10 : 2, etc.); sometimes it means anger, perhaps always with the thought that it arises out of devotion to another person or thing (Ezek. 33 : 25; Acts 5 : 17, etc.); and then it means jealousy, the unfriendly feeling excited by another's possession of goods, or envy, the eager desire for possession created by the spectacle of another's possession (Rom. 13 : 13; 1 Cor. 3 : 3; James 1 : 14, 16). In the present passage it is clearly used in the last-named sense." — *E. D. Burton.* *Wraths* — this word in classical literature meant breath, soul, spirit, heart, as the seat of emotion, and then temper, courage, or anger. In the New Testament it is sometimes used to indicate the wrath of God (Rev. 14 : 10, 19; 15 : 1, 7, etc.). Frequently it means the anger of men (Luke 4 : 28; 2 Cor. 12 : 20; Eph. 4 : 31, etc.). Here it simply means a passionate outburst of hostile feeling. These four words that we have just studied, all closely related, are types of sin which all of us are at one time or another so prone to commit. How frequently home life is almost ruined because of anger; labor unions today are guilty of these very sins in a most terrible way. Political opponents can so easily fall into these sins; people working for corporations or in institutions can become jealous of others when they find them advanced over them. We are especially prone to be inflamed with bitterness and wrath when we feel an injustice has been done to us. *Factions* — "This word means, first of all, labor for hire, then intriguing or canvassing for office, and then it comes naturally to signify party spirit. In Philippians 2 : 3 it means vain glory. (See also 2 Cor. 12 : 20 and Romans 2 : 8.) It may thus be defined as direct, selfish intriguing that alike sacrifices peace and truth to gain its end." — *John Eadie.* In this day of the collapse of international law, we need not search very far for illustrations of this sin. *Divisions* — This is generally taken to mean "the decided and violent taking of a side on selfish and unyielding grounds." (See Rom. 16 : 17.) *Heresies* — The Greek word here is actually spelled *haireseis*, from which, as we can see at once, comes the very root of our English word heresy. It means, literally, the act of taking, the capturing, or storming of a city, then, that which is chosen, a chosen course of thought and action, "hence one's chosen opinion, and according to the context, an opinion varying from the true exposition of the Christian faith. It may then come to mean a body of men separating themselves from others, and following their own tenets, as the Sadducees (Acts 5 : 17), or the Pharisees (Acts 15 : 5), or the Christians (Acts 24: 5, 14); and thus it came to mean, as here, dissension arising from diversity of opinions and aims." — *J. H. Thayer.* (For those who care to investigate this word further there is an exhaustive study of its meaning in the *Pulpit Commentary.*) *Envyings* — this means simply the desire to appropriate what another possesses.

Before passing on to the last group of words, may it not be truly said that the secret of victory for all of us over each and every one of these sins, is to be found in our being yielded to the Lord Jesus Christ, and allowing His Spirit of love, tenderness, forgiveness, long-suffering and kindness to prevail and dominate in every aspect of daily life.

4. Sins of Personal Excess. *Drunkenness* — The word which Paul uses here occurs elsewhere in the New Testament only in Luke 21 : 34 and Romans 13 : 13, and simply means intoxication resulting from imbibing intoxicating drink. Drunkenness was common in the Roman world, because, in a time of universal despair, it seemed to be the means of transporting one's spirit into another world, artificial and unreal as it might be, of joy, laughter, and supposed strength and virility. There must be, though the editor does not know anything of this from personal experience, tremendous exhilaration in these intoxicating beverages, and when a person feels that life has become hopeless, when one seems surrounded with troubles, and overwhelmed with disaster, when one is frantic with loneliness, or seeking to indulge in the wildest pleasures of sin, how natural then to turn to these stimulating, but at the same time, destructive liquids. Drunkenness is a sin for many reasons. In the first place, it is a defilement of the body, definitely working for the destruction of its organs, and therefore the weakening of the very temple of God. It is a sin because, in the grip of intoxication, a man is both foul and dangerous — even in the politest society he will use the vilest and most suggestive phrases, and, when aroused, he will attack his best friend, as is clearly evidenced in the vast number of murders committed in our country by men under the influence of liquor. It is a sin because it makes men careless of the welfare of other people, rendering them selfish, so that they do not mind smashing into other cars on the highway, or destroying property in some wild evening's carousal. It is a sin because it results in the beclouding of the mind, in the dulling of one's judgment, in the deadening of one's spiritual faculties, all of which results in drawing men away from God. *Revellings* — the word here used is also found in Romans 13 : 13 and 1 Peter 4 : 3, and may be said to unite in it both the notion of riot and of revelry. It is often used of the company of revelers themselves; and generally implies a condition of drunkenness. Any one who lives in a large city and has to listen to the noise and coarseness and yelling that are characteristic of wild parties in a nearby apartment or hotel, know what this word means. 21. **Shall not inherit the kingdom of God.** To inherit the kingdom of God is, of course, to have eternal life. It involves all that is ever thought of in the idea of heaven, of eternal peace and joy, of a home above in the presence of the Lord Jesus Christ. To be shut out of the kingdom of God means nothing less than to be confined to darkness and everlasting suffering. Even the words make one's heart almost stop, and yet this is what the Word of God says. Ah, but let us be reminded of this, the text does not say that any one who has ever been guilty of any of these sins will never inherit the kingdom of God, for then all of us would be hopelessly lost. No matter what sin any man has been guilty of, the blood of Jesus Christ His Son can wash that sin or can make atonement for that sin and reconcile that soul to God. What it does say is that those who practice and continue in these sins, who persistently embrace them and indulge in them, these will never enter the kingdom of God. There is a difference between a man who lives in sin day after day, and a Christian who in some sudden moment of temptation falls into sin, only to cry to God to be immediately delivered therefrom.

A Greek Symposium.

The editor believes that questions on this lesson are not called for and that the teacher will most effectively convey to his or her class the truths in these passages if he or she, filled with the subject, possibly using a blackboard, certainly prepared with definite, recent, convincing facts regarding the terrible consequences of intoxication in our modern life, will press these things earnestly and convincingly upon the hearts of those who are listening. Let this be a solemn occasion when the whole class rises up to leave the room, determined by the grace of God to live delivered from these destructive, divinely-condemned, sorrow-begetting sins.

LESSON XI. — March 14.

IN THE UPPER ROOM. — John 13, 14.

PRINTED TEXT, John 13 : 12-20; 14 : 1-6.

GOLDEN TEXT. — *Jesus saith unto him, I am the way, and the truth, and the life: no one cometh unto the Father, but by me.* JOHN 14:6.

Devotional Reading: 1 Peter 5 : 1-11.
Beginner Topic: MY FRIEND JESUS.
Lesson Material: John 17.
Memory Verse: I will pray unto Jehovah. Jeremiah 42 : 4.
Primary Topic: JESUS' PRAYER FOR HIS FRIENDS.
Lesson Material: John 17 : 1-20.
Memory Verse: The blessing of Jehovah be upon you; we bless you in the name of Jehovah. Psalm 129 : 8.
Junior Topic: DID JESUS PRAY FOR ME?
Lesson Material: John 17 : 1-20.
Memory Verse: Pray one for another. . . . The supplication of a righteous man availeth much in its working. James 5 : 16.
Intermediate and Senior Topic: JESUS OUR EXAMPLE AND THE WAY.
Topic for Young People and Adults: THE SECRET OF GREATNESS.

THE TEACHER AND HIS CLASS.

The Younger Classes might be asked what would be the nature of a conversation between two people who, bound together with ties of deepest love, are about to part, knowing that they will not see each other again in this life. Well, of course, there would be words of comfort, words of assurance, words of hope, and, from the older to the younger, or, from the superior to the inferior, words of admonition and commands. So in our Lord's last great discourse with His own beloved disciples, we find all these elements set forth in vivid reality, a discourse richer, deeper, more meaningful, more precious, more capable of universal application than any farewell discourse delivered by any other person who ever lived on this earth.

The Older Classes, while they may feel in their hearts that the passage for study this Lord's day is familiar, should apprehend, at the close of the teaching

From a photograph by Wilson.

Mount Moriah. The Temple Area.

Reputed upper room in the group of buildings on the right of the picture.

of this lesson, as never before, the lofty ideals which the Lord set before His own disciples to guide them in life here on earth while He was absent, the greatness of His own personality, and the adequacy of His grace and power to meet every need for all of His own during the days while He would be away. There are no words in all the literature of the world to compare in depth of meaning, and richness of potential blessing, with these words which we are about to study this morning.

THE LESSON IN ITS SETTING.

Time. — Thursday evening, April 6, A.D. 30.

Place. — In the upper room where the Last Supper was held, somewhere in the city of Jerusalem.

THE PLAN OF THE LESSON.

SUBJECT: The Marvelous Love of Christ for His Own as Manifested in What He Did for His Disciples and What He Said to His Disciples the Last Night They Were Together.

I. JESUS WASHES HIS DISCIPLES' FEET, John 13 : 1–17.

1. The mind and heart of Christ the night of His betrayal, v. 1.
2. Christ washes the disciples' feet, vs. 2–5.
3. Peter remonstrates with Christ, vs. 6–11.
4. Christ interprets the meaning of what He has just done, vs. 12–17.

II. JESUS FORETELLS HIS BETRAYAL BY JUDAS, 13 : 18–30.

1. The preliminary announcement, vs. 18–20.
2. The definite prediction, v. 21.
3. The disciples' inquiry, vs. 22–25.
4. Judas receives the sop and leaves the upper room, vs. 26–30.

III. CHRIST ADMONISHES HIS DISCIPLES TO LOVE ONE ANOTHER, 13 : 31–35.

IV. OUR LORD FORETELLS PETER'S DENIAL, 13 : 36–38.

V. CHRIST'S GREAT WORDS OF COMFORT, John 14.

1. He is coming again to receive us to Himself, vs. 1–5.
2. He is the Way, the Truth, and the Life, v. 6.
3. He is the perfect revelation of the Father, vs. 7–11.
4. Those who believe will be enabled to do greater works than Christ, v. 12.
5. The promise regarding prayer, vs. 13, 14.
6. Love and obedience, v. 15.
7. The promise of the Holy Spirit, vs. 16–18.
8. The new life we have in Christ, vs. 19, 20.
9. Beloved by the Father and the Son, vs. 21–23.
10. The significance of Christ's words and their interpretation by the Holy Spirit, vs. 24–26.
11. The bestowal of peace, v. 27.
12. Some consequences that should follow in the hearts of the disciples because of Christ's words, vs. 28–31.

THE TEACHER'S LIBRARY.

The material for the study of this lesson is simply enormous, and the editor can only point out the more important volumes. All of the better commentaries on John's Gospel, and most of the larger lives of Christ, will be found to have rich material for the understanding of these inexhaustible verses. Then one ought to consult, as far as time and opportunity permit, the great books which are exclusively devoted to an exposition of this final discourse of our Lord, most of all, T. D. Bernard: *The Central Teaching of Jesus Christ* (1892); then A. E. Garvie: *The Master's Comfort and Hope* (1917); H. L. Pass: *The Glory of the Father* (London, 1935). See also, especially for these two chapters, E. R. Hendrix: *Christ's Table Talk*, 83–146; William Evans: *From the Upper Room to the Empty Tomb*, 39–52. There is an excellent article on the word *sop*, by J. C. Lambert, in James Hastings: *Dictionary of Christ and the Gospels*, Vol. 2, p. 665. There is at least one volume devoted entirely to an exposition of the fourteenth chapter of John, namely, J. H. Dunham: *John Fourteen: The Greatest Chapter of the Greatest Book*.

Sermonic material need hardly be consulted. On 13 : 12, G. H. Knight: *The Master's Questions to His Disciples*, 248–254; T. H. Darlow: *Via Sacra*, 7 f.; on 13 : 17, Andrew Murray: *The Inner Chamber and the Inner Life*, 56–60; on 14 : 1, James Hastings: *Great Texts of the Bible, St. John 13–21*, 40–58; Alexander Maclaren: *Expositions of Holy Scripture, St. John 9–14*, 253–262; F. F. Shannon: *The Enchanted Universe*, 29–45; on 14 : 2, G. G. Findlay: *The Things Above*, 187 ff.; Alexander Maclaren, as above, 263–281; James Hastings, as above, 60–103; W. R. Nicoll: *The Lamp of Sacrifice*, 155–171; David Smith: *The Pilgrim's Hospice*, 97–106; on v. 3, W. R. Nicoll: *Ten-Minute Sermons*, 123–129; J. D. Jones: *The Unfettered Word*, 108 ff.; on v. 5, H. P. Liddon: *Christmastide Sermons*, 18–37; on v. 6, James Hastings, as above, 106–126; G. Campbell Morgan: *Westminster Pulpit*, Vol. 9, 369–376; H. P. Liddon: *Advent in St. Paul's*, 587–599; James Marjoribanks: *The Sevenfold "I AM,"* 43–62; S. H. Geisy: *The "I AM'S" of Christ*, 57–102.

SOME INTRODUCTORY REMARKS CONCERNING OUR LORD'S FAREWELL DISCOURSE.

"The five chapters of this Gospel, 13–17 inclusive, are marked off as a distinct section of the book, first by their historical setting, and then by their special character. The importance of that special portion of our Lord's ministry on which we enter here is evident from the space which it occupies, being little less than a fourth of the entire Gospel. The twelve previous chapters cover a period of nearly three years; these five are records of a single evening. In those we range through Judæa, Samaria, Galilee; we are in the wilderness, on the seaboard, in streets and synagogues, and most often in the temple itself. In these we remain in a single chamber of the private house; in those we are in the presence of the multitudes, all classes of disciples, hearers, observers, opponents. In these we are in the inner circle, which may be called the Lord's own family." — *T. D. Bernard.*

I. JESUS WASHES HIS DISCIPLES' FEET, 13 : 1–17.

1. THE MIND AND HEART OF CHRIST THE NIGHT OF HIS BETRAYAL. 1. "Now before the feast of the passover, Jesus knowing that his hour was come that he should depart out of this world unto the Father, having loved his own that were in the world, he loved them unto the end." Christ's death was not an accident, or a miscarriage of His own plans, as some hold today, but was in the eternal program of God. The very time, the nature, and the consequence of His death were perfectly known to our Lord from the beginning. He knew that this was His last night on earth before His death on the Cross, and one great passion filled His whole being these closing hours — a love for His own which He is now about to manifest in a twofold way — by what He did for them, and by what He is about to say to them. Love is the theme and the source of all that our Lord is about to say to His own disciples. "He had loved them, and He loved them still. It was their condition which had brought Him into the world and His love for them was that which would carry Him through all that was before Him." — *Marcus Dods.*

2. CHRIST WASHES THE DISCIPLES' FEET, vs. 2–5. Here we have set before us, unintentionally we would almost say, one of the most powerful contrasts in all the Word of God — the heart of the Saviour and the heart of the traitor. In the heart of the Saviour there wells up the eternal sacrificing love of God; in the heart of Judas there reigns, for the most iniquitous of all deeds, Satan himself. Christ, knowing full well that He had come from God, that all things in the universe were in His hands, and that He was about to depart to God, desiring to teach His disciples, just before He left, the necessity of love for one another, the glory of serving one another, and the need for true humility, put aside His outer garments, and, girding Himself with a towel, began to stoop down and to wash His disciples' feet, wiping them with the towel with which He was girded. "In Palestine, as in other countries of the same latitude, shoes were not universally worn, and were not worn at all within doors; and where some protection to the foot was worn, it was commonly a mere sandal, a sole tied on with a thong. The upper part of the foot was thus left exposed, and necessarily became heated and dirty with the fine and scorching dust of the roads. Much discomfort was thus produced, and the first duty of a host was to provide for its removal. A slave was ordered to remove the sandals and wash the feet. And in order that this might be done, the guest either sat on the couch appointed for him at the table, or reclined with his feet protruding beyond the end of it, that the slave, coming round with the pitcher and basin, might pour cool water gently over them.

"On ordinary occasions it is probable that the disciples would perform this humble office by turns, where there was no slave to discharge it for all. But this evening, when they gathered for the last supper, all took their places at the table with a studied ignorance of the necessity, a feigned unconsciousness that any such attention was required. As a matter of course, the pitcher of cool water, the basin, and the towel had been set as part of the requisite furnishing of the supper chamber; but no one among the disciples betrayed the slightest consciousness that he understood that any such custom existed. . . . For any one to wash the feet of the rest was to declare himself the servant of all; and that was precisely what each one was resolved he, for his part, would not do. No one of them was sensitive enough to be ashamed of showing such a temper in Christ's presence. There they sat, looking at the table, looking at the ceiling, arranging their dress, each resolved upon this — that he would not be the man to own himself servant of all." — *Marcus Dods.*

3. PETER REMONSTRATES WITH CHRIST, vs. 6–11. We must recognize that Peter did more talking, and said more foolish things (in the Gospels) than any other one of the disciples of our Lord. Again and again, Christ had to rebuke him for his foolish statements which arose out of a heart that often failed to comprehend what Christ was saying and doing. Here, when the Lord comes to bathe Simon's feet, the fisherman, well knowing how infinitely above him the Lord was in every way, at first deliberately refused to allow Him to wash his feet. Peter believed he knew better what the Lord ought to do on this occasion than the Lord Himself knew. Whenever we get to the place where we think we are wiser than the Lord, be sure of it we are of all men most foolish. Christ simply tells him that if he does not allow the Saviour to wash his feet, then Simon can have no part with Him. "Submission is needful even to what is dark and unintelligible. Obedience is the great badge of discipleship; submission also to Christ's personal cleansing, in order to have

JOHN 13 : 12. So when he had washed their feet, and taken his garments, and sat down again, he said unto them, Know ye what I have done to you?
13. Ye call me, Teacher, and, Lord: and ye say well; for so I am.
14. If I then, the Lord and the Teacher, have washed your feet, ye also ought to wash one another's feet.
15. For I have given you an example, that ye also should do as I have done to you.
16. Verily, verily, I say unto you, A servant is not greater than his lord; neither one that is sent greater than he that sent him.

Christ's personal fellowship." — *George Reith.* If Peter refused to allow the Lord to do what He knew Peter needed, then Peter, automatically, was separating himself from close communion with his Saviour. Peter, at once realizing this, cried out, "Lord, not my feet only, but also my hands and my head." "No thought was so terrible to him as that of forfeiting communion with his Master. He will submit to anything rather than lose his Lord's fellowship. He flies from the extreme of resistance to the extreme of compliance. There spoke a true and noble soul." — *George Reith.* This leads our Lord to utter one of His profoundest assertions, namely, that he that is washed needs not to be washed again except his feet. "In the Greek we have quite a different word from the one rendered 'wash' elsewhere in these verses: the latter means to wash part of the body, this to bathe the whole person. A man who has bathed does not need to bathe again when he reaches home, but only to wash off the dust from his feet: then he is wholly clean. So also in the spiritual life, a man whose moral nature has once been thoroughly purified need not think that this has been all undone if in the walk through life he contracts some stains: these must be washed away, and then he is once more wholly clean." —*Alfred Plummer.* Yet, added our Lord, they were not all clean. There was one in their midst who would betray Him, and he was not washed at all — Judas Iscariot.

Jesus Washes the Disciples' Feet.

4. CHRIST INTERPRETS THE MEANING OF WHAT HE HAS JUST DONE, VS. 12–17. 12. **So when he had washed their feet, and taken his garments, and sat down again, he said unto them, Know ye what I have done to you?** 13. **Ye call me, Teacher, and, Lord: and ye say well; for so I am.** 14. **If I then, the Lord and the Teacher, have washed your feet, ye also ought to wash one another's feet.** 15. **For I have given you an example, that ye also should do as I have done to you.** 16. **Verily, verily, I say unto you, A servant is not greater than his lord; neither one that is sent greater than he that sent him.** "It will be observed that the example of Christ is always offered in connection with some form of self-sacrifice. . . . The custom of feet-washing has been continued in various forms in the Church. By a decree of the Seventeenth Council of Toledo it was made obligatory on the Thursday in Holy Week 'throughout the churches of Spain and Gaul.' In 1530 Wolsey washed, wiped, and kissed the feet of fifty-nine poor men at Peterborough. The practice was continued by English sovereigns till the reign of James II; and as late as 1731 the Lord High Almoner washed the feet of the recipients of the royal gifts at Whitehall on

17. If ye know these things, blessed are ye if ye do them.
18. I speak not of you all: I know whom I have chosen: but that the scripture may be fulfilled, He that eateth my bread lifted up his heel against me.
19. From henceforth I tell you before it come to pass, that, when it is come to pass, ye may believe that I am *he*.
20. Verily, verily, I say unto you, He that receiveth whomsoever I send receiveth me; and he that receiveth me receiveth him that sent me.

'Maundy Thursday.' The present custom of the feet-washing in St. Peter's is well known. The practice was retained by the Mennonites; and also by the United Brethren, among whom it has now fallen into disuse." — *B. F. Westcott.* It is *still* continued by these two Christian communions in our country. What our Lord was really laying upon the disciples as a command was their willingness to serve others in the humblest and most menial ways, and to be glad to serve in this way whenever they knew it was the Lord's will; to manifest a spirit of humility; to reveal their willingness to take the low place among men. What our Lord here desires is not so much some physical act of footwashing as true humility of heart. 17. **If ye know these things, blessed are ye if ye do them.** The principle enunciated here is of profound significance. Strange that more men do not preach on this text! Its truthfulness is to be seen in every major sphere of life — when we know what is right, what the Lord demands of us, we will never have true joy until we are doing those very things. Never!

II. **JESUS FORETELLS HIS BETRAYAL BY JUDAS,** 13 : 18–30. 18. **I speak not of you all: I know whom I have chosen: but that the scripture may be fulfilled, He that eateth my bread lifted up his heel against me.** 19. **From henceforth I tell you before it come to pass, that, when it is come to pass, ye may believe that I am *he*.** 20. **Verily, verily, I say unto you, He that receiveth whomsoever I send receiveth me; and he that receiveth me receiveth him that sent me.** The scripture to which our Lord here refers is the Hebrew text of Psalm 41 : 9. "The metaphor here is of one raising his foot before kicking, but the blow is not given. This was the attitude of Jesus at this moment. It has been remarked that Christ omits the words of the psalmist, 'Mine own familiar friend whom I trusted.' He had not trusted Judas and had not been deceived as the psalmist had been." — *Alfred Plummer.*

Our Lord now definitely announces that one of the twelve sitting there in the upper room would that night betray the Master. The word here translated *betray*, means "to pass into other hands, and is translated sometimes 'betray,' sometimes 'deliver' or 'deliver up,' according (it appears) as the idea of treachery is or is not in the mind of the translators. It is a prominent word throughout these transactions, occurring fifteen times in this Gospel and often also in the others. This emphatic repetition offers two suggestions. First, the delivering up is not casual, but necessary, or falls, at least, under the providential fitness of things. The Gentiles have no power against Jesus till the Jews deliver Him up. The Jews have no possession of Him till He is delivered up by a disciple. The other suggestion is that of the self-abandonment of Him who suffers Himself to be thus betrayed and delivered. There is no resistance, defense, or flight. Men do unto Him 'whatever they list,' as He said they would (Matt. 17 : 12). He leaves Himself in their hands when the hour is come to do so. They take their responsibility in what they do; He fulfills His in what He suffers." — *T. D. Bernard.*

Amazed at what the Lord has said, and not knowing which one of the twelve it could be who would prove traitor, Simon Peter, generally the first to start anything, suggested to John, who was leaning on the bosom of the Lord, that he should ask Jesus to which one He was referring. This he did. Christ did not *name* Judas, of course, but He did say that it was he to whom, after dipping it, he would give the sop. Following the word by an immediate act, He dipped and gave the sop to Judas. The word here translated *sop* occurs in its English form only in this chapter. "It is akin to the words *soap*, and *soup*, and denotes food soaked in liquid before being eaten. (See Ruth 2 : 14; Job 31 : 17.) It seemed probable that this sop was not the specific passover sop passed around to the company by the host, but a particular sop that Jesus offered to Judas on purely personal grounds. At an oriental feast the host sometimes presented the guest with a special tidbit from the food on the table as a distinguishing mark of his favor. And it was not by any accident of Judas' position at the table, but because of a deep purpose in the heart of Jesus that this sop was given. What was commonly understood to be a token of hospitable good-will was without doubt meant in this case to be the expression of a feeling deeper than any ordinary human affection, and at the same time to be a last appeal to the better nature of this erring disciple." — *J. C. Lambert.* "At that moment the conflict was decided. It is to be noticed that the pronoun here and in verse 30 isolates Judas and sets him as it were outside the company. The work was in essence already begun. Therefore, the Lord now removes the traitor from His presence. Repentance is no longer possible; and Christ welcomes the issue for Himself." — *E. F. Westcott.* "As Satan made suggestions to him (v. 2), and Judas listened to them; now Satan takes full possession of him." — *Alfred Plummer.*

The Last Supper. Bida.

III. **CHRIST ADMONISHES HIS DISCIPLES TO LOVE ONE ANOTHER,** 13 : 31–35. It is impossible for us to enter with any fulness into the rich teachings of these verses, so let us emphasize one fundamental truth here set forth; namely, that as Christ has loved us, so ought we also to love one another, by which all men will know that we are Christ's disciples. "The commandment was not entirely strange to the Old Testament (Lev. 19 : 18), but the example embodied in the Lord Jesus Christ of a love not seeking its own and going to the extreme sacrifice for its object — and its object unworthy — was new. Hence, the 'as' includes both *fact, measure, manner, and motive* (15 : 12 ff.). He had just given them an instance (v. 15). To love God with all the heart, and the neighbor as oneself, is the sum of the old covenant. To love one another as Christ has loved us, is the sum of the new covenant. The two are essentially one; but love, God's love, has been now manifested (1 John 3 : 16; 4 : 10). The more they loved one another for Christ's sake, and in Christ's way, they should realize Himself as among them." — *George Reith.*

IV. **OUR LORD FORETELLS PETER'S DENIAL,** 13 : 36–38. What a dark night this was for the Lord Jesus, fully conscious that one of His own who had lived with Him and had been trusted by Him for three years, would now actually betray Him at the instigation of the devil; conscious that Simon Peter, who had said so many fine things and had done so much good work during the preceding three years, would, through sheer cowardice, deny that he even knew the Lord this night; fully aware that He would begin to suffer within a few hours the brutal beating of Roman soldiers, and, within twenty-four hours, would be dying upon the Cross, yet at the same time, tender, considerate, loving toward His own — perfect Man and Son of God indeed! We need not tarry here with this discourse with Peter, which is given in all the four Gospels, except to point out that here once again Peter did not know his own heart, and, swollen with a false sense of his own courage, he was preparing himself for the manifestation of cowardice which would soon be his humiliating experience.

JOHN 14 : 1. Let not your heart be troubled: believe in God, believe also in me.

2. In my Father's house are many mansions; if it were not so, I would have told you; for I go to prepare a place for you.

3. And if I go and prepare a place for you, I come again, and will receive you unto myself; that where I am, *there* ye may be also.

V. **CHRIST'S GREAT WORDS OF COMFORT,** John 14. "The Speaker in this chapter is the Son of Man, acting in contingent circumstances, and conversing with individual persons, but embracing in the vastness of divine intention the whole race of mankind. Hence it is that a wonderful combination of the personal and immediate with the universal and perpetual distinguishes all the words of Jesus, and pre-eminently those which are here." — *T. D. Bernard.* 1. **Let not your heart be troubled: believe in God, believe also in me.** "'Let not your heart be troubled,' is the first word of the discourse. It will recur at the end. The reasons are supplied by the intervening words. 'Troubled' is the best English equivalent we can give for the Greek; but as generally employed, its force is fainter. The verb Jesus uses is used often of the agitation of waters, the heaving and surging of the sea, aptly represents the deeper agitations of the soul, painful to strong natures, dangerous to the weak. Thrice it is used of our Lord Himself in some access of vehement emotion. So He shared the experiences which in us He would comfort and control. Such a condition needs control, tending as it does to confusion of judgment and suspension of faith. 'Let not your heart be troubled' was then not only a word of sympathetic kindness, but a needful counsel; and it is so still, falling with composing power on many an agitated mind. 'Troubled' we must be in the trying times of this changeful, sinful mortal life, but not as helpless victims of circumstances or feelings; not as losing the higher consciousness which should restore composure and minister support." — *T. D. Bernard.* This verse has given some difficulty to commentators, but Westcott is probably right in declaring that both of the words "believe" in this verse are imperatives. Note particularly how Christ places Himself in immediate relationship with the Father, asserting He is equally worthy of being believed, which certainly would imply that He was convinced He was God the Son in a way that no other person has ever been or ever will be. 2. **In my Father's house are many mansions; if it were not so, I would have told you; for I go to prepare a place for you.** The word here translated *mansions* is from a Latin word meaning *a resting place*, especially, a station on a great road where travelers found refreshment. This is also probably the meaning of the Greek word which our Lord used. The idea or "the impression given is restful, one of settled continuance and secure possession. These mansions are 'many.' One can scarcely take this to mean merely that there would be room for those disciples, or for any number of inmates. Not the inmates, but the mansions, are many. Variety of appropriation is suggested, though not asserted." — *T. D. Bernard.* The very phrase, "in my Father's house," is fragrant with love springing from an intimate relationship between Christ and the Father, and is certainly born of a profound knowledge of heaven, concerning which no *man* knows anything except through divine revelation. 3. **And if I go and prepare a place for you, I come again, and will receive you unto myself; that where I am, *there***

"In My Father's House Are Many Mansions."

4. And whither I go, ye know the way.
5. Thomas saith unto him, Lord, we know not whither thou goest; how know we the way?
6. Jesus saith unto him, I am the way, and the truth, and the life: no one cometh unto the Father, but by me.

---

ye may be also. (Cf. John 12 : 26; 17 : 24; 2 Cor. 5 : 8; Phil. 1 : 23.) Here is the clearest possible announcement of what is known in the Church as the second advent of our Lord. It is strange how some men have tried to twist the Scriptures into teaching something else. Christ promised to come back for us because He wants us to be with Him. Here again is the manifestation of infinite love. He is going away. They will be separated, but it will not be permanent. He who created the universe can traverse all space; He who made our bodies, and then came in a body of His own, died, and rose again — can raise us from the dead, and bring us to Himself, forever. This is a consummation; this is a hope; this is a promise of glory such as the lips of no religious leader, no prophet, no seer could ever utter concerning himself and his own except the Lord Jesus Christ. He will not come for any but His own, and no one else will ever come for those who are not Christ's. Mohammed will not come for his own; Buddha will not come for his; Moses will not come for his.
4. **And whither I go, ye know the way.**
5. **Thomas saith unto him, Lord, we know not whither thou goest; how know we the way?** 6. **Jesus saith unto him, I am the way, and the truth, and the life: no one cometh unto the Father, but by me.** In Latin the entire sixth verse can be expressed alliteratively by the three words *via, veritas, vita.* "He is the way to the truth, and the way to the life. He is the truth of the way, and the truth of the life. He is the life of the way, and the life of the truth." Westcott's words here are especially rich: "Christ is the way by which the two worlds are united, so that men may pass from one to the other (Heb. 9 : 8; 10 : 20; Eph. 2 : 18). Hence, perhaps the Christian faith is spoken of as the Way (Acts 9 : 2; 19 : 9, 23, etc.)." Christ is the truth unchangeable and eternal concerning the fundamentals of existence. Note carefully, He does not say He *brings* the truth, or *teaches* the truth, but He *is* the truth. In Him is the truth concerning God; in Him is the truth concerning love; in Him is the truth of holiness; in Him is the truth of sacrifice; in Him is the truth of life; in Him is the truth of creation; in Him is the truth of the ultimate sovereignty of righteousness.

Hofmann.
"The Way, the Truth, and the Life."

Christ next declares Himself to be the perfect revelation of the Father summed up in the phrase, "He that hath seen me hath seen the Father." "The revelation of Christ is the full revelation of God. It is but the inference from the other great assertion: 'I and the Father are one' (10 : 30). The true apprehension of Christ is the apprehension of God." — *George Reith.* It may be said without fear of contradiction that not only is Christ the revelation of God, but, apart from Christ, men do not know the true God in His fullness, in the love His Fatherhood manifests, and in His saving grace.

Turning from His own works, Christ now tells His disciples that they themselves, after he has gone, will do even greater works than those of which He had been speaking. These greater works are those which are done, not by men generally, but by those who believe on the Lord Jesus. "These greater works are not in higher measures of miracle or teaching, for who could surpass those of Jesus? The preaching of the apostles, having for its subject a dying and a risen Christ, was more effectual than Christ's personal ministry involving the building up of the Church, the conversion of individual souls, the spiritual miracles of regeneration, saving men from sin and sanctifying them." — *George Reith.*

There follows now a series of precious promises which it would take whole volumes to expound. There is the promise that whatever His disciples would ask in His name the Father would grant. And how many things they would have to pray for in their life of conflict with evil, in the hour of temptation and trial, in the desire to know the will of God, and in all that pertains to a godly life on earth! There follows, then, the promise of the Holy Spirit the Comforter, the Spirit of truth, who would indwell them, enable them, and sanctify them. The word here translated *Comforter* is found in the New Testament only in the writings of John (John 14 : 16, 26; 15 : 26; 16 : 7; 1 John 2 : 1). Properly the word means, "one called to the side of another, and then, one counselling, supporting, or aiding another; it is used technically for the advocates, for the defense of a party." — *B. F. Westcott.* The subsequent verses of this chapter reveal how the Holy Spirit aids and guides and strengthens our life. There follows then the promise of new life in Christ. We abide in Him as the vine abides in the branches (which Christ will soon talk about), and He abides in us.

A theme which is almost never spoken of in our pulpits these days is one which our Lord speaks of more frequently in these closing hours of His earthly ministry than in all the other three years of His teaching, namely, obedience to His commandments. In verse 15, He says if we love Him we will keep His commandments. Now He declares that if we keep His words in love, the Father will love us and both the Father and the Son will take up their abode in us. In the next chapter He says that if we do what He commands us, we are His friends. These words are spoken to believers, to true disciples. They do not concern the fact of salvation, but the life of the redeemed after salvation. What a difference it would make with every one of us if, every morning when we awoke, we determined in our heart that day to obey the commandments of the Lord Jesus! May God deliver all of us, especially those who claim to be believers in every great doctrine of the Christian faith, from thinking that the Christian life is only one of intellectual assent, and not one also of the loving obedience of the heart.

Our Lord now returns again to the work of the Holy Spirit in particular relationship to the later exposition of His teaching. The Holy Spirit is to refresh our memories with the words Christ uttered when on earth.

"This is the guarantee that the apostolic witness to Christ is reliable. We are not at the mercy of mere human impressions of Christ's person and word, however trustworthy in themselves these might be (cf. 1 John 2 : 20, 27; 1 Cor. 2 : 10)." — *George Reith.* Promises and gifts seem to pour forth one after another from the lips of our Lord in these precious hours of sacred communion. Here He bestows on His own a peace which passeth all understanding. "The peace which Christ desires His disciples to enjoy is that which characterized Himself; the same serenity in danger, the same equanimity in troublous circumstances, the same freedom from anxiety about results, the same speedy recovery of composure after anything which for a moment ruffled the calm surface of His demeanor. This is what He makes over to His people; this is what He makes possible to all who serve Him. . . . *It is not outward things which can give peace of mind, no more than it is a soft couch which can give rest to a fevered body. Restfulness must be produced from within.*" — *Marcus Dods.*

Finally, our Lord reminds the disciples of some of the things they should be experiencing in their own hearts, because of what He has been telling them: they should rejoice because He was going to His Father; later, as they began more fully to apprehend what He has been telling them, they will believe more truly than ever that He was and is indeed the very Son of God. But the time has come for Christ to enter into His passion, which means that they must all leave the holy atmosphere of this upper room, and begin to wend their way toward the garden of Gethsemane. It is probable that the contents of chapters 15 and 16 were spoken on the way from the upper room to the garden.

How many different characteristics of our Lord do we find revealed in this lesson? In how many different ways does Christ show His deep love for His disciples in these two chapters? Why did our Lord put so much emphasis upon the iniquitous betrayal of Judas soon to take place? How many different things are said in this lesson about the relationship of Christ the Son of God to God the Father? What is the difference

between Peter's denial of Christ and Judas' betrayal of Christ? How many different titles of Christ do you find in this lesson? Why is it necessary for the disciples of Christ to be taught divine truth by the Holy Spirit? Looking over this lesson carefully, would you say that Christ emphasized material prosperity and "social welfare," or did He emphasize most man's moral and spiritual life here on earth?

LESSON XII. — March 21.

OUR LORD'S INTERCESSORY PRAYER. — John 17.

PRINTED TEXT, John 17 : 1-8, 18-26.

GOLDEN TEXT. — *Holy Father, keep them in thy name which thou hast given me, that they may be one, even as we are.* JOHN 17 : 11.

Devotional Reading: Hebrews 7 : 23-28.
Beginner Topic: A GLAD SURPRISE.
Lesson Material: John 20, 21.
Memory Verse: Thou, Jehovah, hast made me glad. Psalm 92 : 4.
Primary Topic: THE GLAD SURPRISE.
Lesson Material: John 20.
Memory Verse: The Lord is risen indeed. Luke 24 : 34.
Junior Topic: A HAPPY SURPRISE.
Lesson Material: John 20.
Memory Verse: The Lord is risen indeed. Luke 24 : 34.
Intermediate and Senior Topic: PRAYING FOR OTHERS.
Topic for Young People and Adults: THE MINISTRY OF INTERCESSION.

THE TEACHER AND HIS CLASS.

The Younger Classes might be asked what they would do if, on opening the door of a room, they unexpectedly found a loved one on his or her knees, earnestly praying to God from the depths of the heart. Well, of course, they would quietly close the door, and tiptoe away, private prayer is such an intimate matter. Yet on this one occasion, when our Lord poured out His heart to the Father in glory, He allowed some of His disciples, among whom was probably John, to overhear Him pray. What He prayed that night is what we find in this beautiful, holy, and sacred page of the Word of God.

The Older Classes would surely obtain a firm grasp of much of the wealth of this particular chapter if, the week before it is taught, the teacher would assign different subjects pertaining to the chapter to the pupils, *e.g.*, What did our Lord in this prayer say about the Word of God? What did He say about the relationship of Christians to the world? What definite petitions did He offer for His own? How many different things did He say about Himself? How many different things did He say about His Father in heaven? etc., etc.

THE LESSON IN ITS SETTING.

Time. — Thursday evening, April 6, A.D. 30.

Place. — Not definitely known, possibly in the upper room, possibly in the court of the Temple; hardly on any street in Jerusalem which had to be traversed on the way to the garden of Gethsemane.

THE PLAN OF THE LESSON.

SUBJECT: The Requests of the Son of God to His Father in Heaven the Night Before He Was to Be Crucified and Die.

I. CHRIST'S PRAYER FOR HIMSELF, John 17 : 1-5.
   1. The request to be glorified by the Father, v. 1.
   2. The relationship of the Son to the Father, vs. 2-4.
      a. The Son receives power over all flesh from the Father, v. 2.
      b. The Son is sent by the Father, v. 3.
      c. The Son glorifies the Father, v. 4 *a.*
      d. The Son has finished the work which the Father gave Him to do, v. 4 *b.*
   3. The request for glorification is repeated, v. 5.

II. CHRIST'S PRAYER FOR HIS DISCIPLES, vs. 6-26.
   1. His relationship to His own, vs. 6-10.
      a. They were given to Christ by the Father, vs. 6, 7.

b. They were persuaded of Christ's divine origin, v. 8.
c. They are mutually the Father's and the Son's, vs. 9, 10 *a*.
d. In them Christ is glorified, v. 10 *b*.

2. His requests for His own, vs. 11–24.
a. That they might be kept through the Father's name, vs. 11, 12.
b. That they might have Christ's joy fulfilled in them, v. 13.
c. That they might be kept from the evil one, vs. 14–16.
d. That they might be sanctified through the truth, vs. 17–19.
e. That they all should be one, vs. 20–23.
f. That they should behold His glory, v. 24.

III. CHRIST'S CONCLUDING REASSERTION OF HIS PURPOSE FOR HIS OWN, VS. 25, 26.

1. They believe Christ was sent by the Father, v. 25.
2. Christ has declared unto them the Father's name, v. 26 *a*.
3. The purpose of all this is that the love of the Father and the Son might abide in them, v. 26 *b*.

THE TEACHER'S LIBRARY.

Biographies of the Lord Jesus Christ will not be found very satisfactory in the study of this particular lesson. Some commentaries will be found to be very helpful, *e.g.*, Reith, Westcott, Lange, and Lenski. The pages in Bernard's *Central Teaching of Jesus Christ* will be found quite rich. There are three books with which the editor is acquainted which are devoted entirely to the exposition of this one chapter, J. S. Stone: *The Prayer Before the Passion* (London, 1911); H. C. G. Moule: *The High-Priestly Prayer* (not as satisfactory as Bishop Moule's other works, in the mind of the editor); Marcus Rainsford: *The Lord's Prayer for Believers*, frequently reissued, and, without doubt, one of the greatest devotional classics in the English language. In addition, one might consult G. Campbell Morgan, *The Westminster Pulpit*, Vol. 8, 217–224.

Homiletic material is not generally satisfying for an understanding of this chapter. See, however, on v. 3, H. P. Liddon: *Passiontide Sermons*, 268–270; G. Campbell Morgan, as above, Vol. 10, 353–360; J. D. Jones: *The Unfettered Word*, 253 ff.; on v. 9, J. H. Jowett: *Brooks by the Travelers Way*, 189–199; on v. 15, J. H. Jowett: *Apostolic Optimism*, 47–58; on vs. 16–19, an excellent passage in H. A. Ironside's *Holiness, the False and the True*, 67–78; on v. 17, J. S. Holden: *A Voice from God*, 257–275; Andrew Murray: *The Inner Chamber and the Inner Life*, 133–137; the same: *Holy in Christ*, 142–148; on v. 19, W. R. Nicoll: *Ten-Minute Sermons*, 235–241; Andrew Murray: *Holy in Christ*, 150–156; Alexander Whyte: *Lord Teach Us to Pray*, 116–129; on v. 24, Andrew Murray: *With Christ in the School of Prayer*, 214–220; on v. 26, Andrew Murray: *Love Made Perfect*, 36–73; Alexander Maclaren: *Expositions of Holy Scripture, St. John 15–21*, 210–219.

JOHN 17 : 1. These things spake Jesus; and lifting up his eyes to heaven, he said, Father, the hour is come; glorify thy Son, that the Son may glorify thee:

INTRODUCTION.

"This prayer of Jesus is in some respects the most precious relic of the past. We have here the words which Christ addressed to God in the critical hour of His life — the words in which He uttered the deepest feeling and thought of His Spirit, clarified and concentrated by the prospect of death. Even among the prayers of Christ this stands by itself as that in which He gathered up the retrospect of His past and surveyed the future of His Church; in which, as if already dying, He solemnly presented to the Father Himself, His work, and His people. Recognizing the grandeur of the occasion, we may be disposed to agree with Melanchthon, who, when giving his last lecture shortly before his death, said: 'There is no voice which has ever been heard, either in heaven or in earth, more exalted, more holy, more fruitful, more sublime, than this prayer offered up by the Son of God Himself.'" — *Marcus Dods.*

"In this prayer, He embraces all that from chapter 13 : 31 He has said, and sets His seal to all things already done, looking to things past, present, and future. It is a tacit intimation of the new Pentecost at hand. Who would not rejoice that these things which Jesus spoke with the Father are written and remain? In all the Scripture, this chapter is in words most easy, in their meanings most profound." — *J. A. Bengel.*

Tholuck, the great German theologian, said: "If in human speech divinity is manifest and sublimity is joined to condescending humility it is in this prayer." Luthardt well remarks: "Neither in the Scripture nor in the literature of any nation can there be found a composition which in simplicity and depth, in grandeur and fervor may be compared to this prayer."

I. **CHRIST'S PRAYER FOR HIMSELF**, vs. 1–5.

1. THE REQUEST TO BE GLORIFIED BY THE FATHER, v. 1. 1. **These things spake Jesus; and lifting up his eyes to heaven.** "In prayer the eye of faith is always instinctively directed to heaven, as heaven is everywhere open, and angels are ascending and descending. Heaven is the abode of the Hearer of prayer and Giver of every good gift. Every prayer of faith is a spiritual ascension." — *Philip Schaff.* **He said, Father.** It is strange that in almost all of our great theological works,

2. Even as thou gavest him authority over all flesh, that to all whom thou hast given him, he should give eternal life.

when the doctrine of God is expounded, almost nothing is said about God as Father, and the Christian Church has because of this been robbed of much spiritual truth and comfort proceeding from such truth. The very word Father expresses the most intimate relationship, far more than the word Lord, or God, or even Redeemer. This intimate relationship is one manifested in love. It is also a term implying a superiority of position (not necessarily of character or essence), and the one who uses the term at once takes a place of obedient submission to the one addressed. **The hour is come.** "The hour fixed by God in which 'the Lamb slain from the foundation of the world' should be offered up; the supreme hour of the world's history, the striking of which rang out the old and rang in the new; the hour to which all the previous dispensations were preparatory. Time measures all things, yet the measure of time itself is the unfolding of God's eternal purpose of grace for sinners. All that happens in time is under God's rule; but time itself happens in order that God's end in creation and redemption may be reached; and 'time shall be no longer' when the mystery of God shall be finished, when this prayer of the Lord shall be fulfilled in the perfecting of His mystical body. Time is for purposes of salvation; the Lord Jesus Christ is the Beginning and the End." — *George Reith.* **Glorify thy Son, that the Son may glorify thee.** This glorification includes "the acceptance of the sacrifice, the atonement made and redemption achieved, the reversal of death and overthrow of Satan, and all the history to follow — resurrection, ascension, session at the right hand, the gift of the Holy Spirit, the mediatorial reign, the coming in of the kingdom. All are the gifts of the Father, by which He glorifies the Son. They are desired for the further end, 'that the Son may glorify thee.' For it is the will, the work, the wisdom, righteousness, and love of the Father which, through this divine economy, are to be manifested in heaven and in earth." — *T. D. Bernard.*

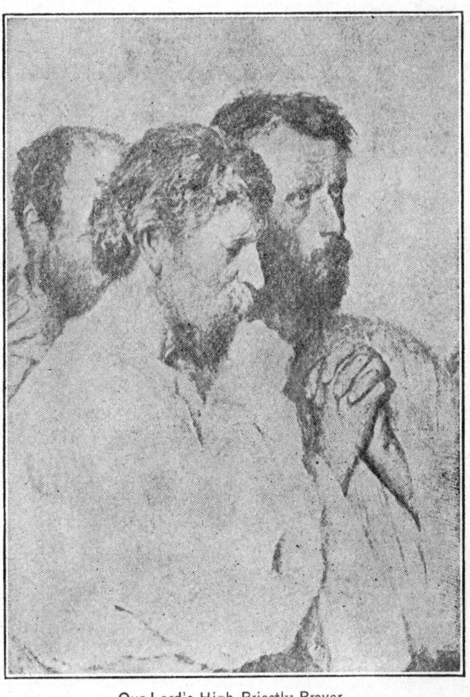

Our Lord's High-Priestly Prayer.
Detail from the painting by E. Burnand in the Lausanne Gallery.

"Glorify Thy Son by enthroning Him at Thy right hand, and crowning Him as Head of the Church, and Head over all things to the Church; glorify Thy Son by sending down the Holy Spirit to those on whose behalf He suffers, that He may comfort them, that He may quicken them, that He may unite them to their risen Head, and be in them 'a well of water springing up into everlasting life'; glorify Thy Son by putting all their foes under His footstool; glorify Thy Son by gathering together Thy people to Him, as it is written, 'unto Him shall the gathering of the people be'; glorify Thy Son by granting Him by and by in the midst of His redeemed and glorified Church to sing praises unto Thee and say — 'Behold, I, and the children which God hath given me.'" — *Marcus Rainsford.*

2. THE RELATIONSHIP OF THE SON TO THE FATHER, VS. 2–4. 2. **Even as thou gavest him authority over all flesh, that to all whom thou hast given him, he should**

3. And this is life eternal, that they should know thee the only true God, and him whom thou didst send, *even* Jesus Christ.

4. I glorified thee on the earth, having accomplished the work which thou hast given me to do.

5. And now, Father, glorify thou me with thine own self with the glory which I had with thee before the world was.

---

give eternal life. "The complete elevation of the incarnate Son to His divine glory was necessarily presupposed in His mission. He received a legitimate authority the over humanity as its true Head, and this could only be exercised in its fullness after ascension. . . . Nothing is said or implied as to the sovereignty of the Son over other created beings. His office is regarded primarily in relation to man fallen. . . . The phrase is the rendering of a Hebrew phrase which describes mankind in their weakness and transitoriness, as contrasted with the majesty of God (Gen. 6 : 12; Ps. 44 : 2; 145 : 21; Isa. 40 : 5; 49 : 26; 66 : 16, 23; Joel 2 : 28; Ezek. 20 : 48; 21 : 5; Jer. 12 : 12; 25 : 31; Job 12 : 10; 34 : 15); and from that side of their nature in which they are akin to, and represent, the lower world (Gen. 6 : 19; 7 : 15, 21; 8 : 17; 9 : 11, 15; Ps. 136 : 25; Jer. 32 : 27; 45 : 5). (Cf. Matt. 24 : 22; Luke 3 : 6; Acts 2 : 17; 1 Pet. 1 : 24; Rom. 3 : 20; 1 Cor. 1 : 29; Gal. 2 : 16.)

"At the same time the universality of the gospel is laid open. Not all Israel only (Luke 2 : 10, *all the people*, Matt. 15 : 24), but all humanity are the subjects of Messiah (Matt. 28 : 19)." — *B. F. Westcott.* 3. **And this is life eternal, that they should know thee the only true God, and him whom thou didst send, *even* Jesus Christ.** This is the only actual definition of life we find proceeding from our Lord's lips, and should be carefully compared with the parallel definition of life uttered by the Apostle Paul, a full generation later (Phil. 1 : 21; Gal. 2 : 20). The knowledge Christ speaks of here is not a mere intellectual comprehension of the attributes of God, but a knowledge arising from experience with God, from an understanding of God's revelation to men. For instance, it is one thing to read a love story of other people, it is an altogether different thing to be in love oneself. Love can only truly be understood, not from reading a book about it, but from experiencing it. No one can fully enter into the glory of a sunset from seeing it partially portrayed in an oil painting as they can from beholding an actual sunset. The knowledge here spoken of, then, is our personal experience of the power of God, the love of God, the grace of God, the holiness of God — all these manifested in Jesus Christ our Lord. But when we come to know God, love fills our hearts, the future glows with hope, we are redeemed from the power of sin. This is life, and there is no life worthy the name except that which is centered in a knowledge of the only true and living God as revealed in His only begotten Son Jesus Christ. 4. **I glorified thee on the earth, having accomplished the work which thou hast given me to do.** "'Glory to God in the highest' sounded from heaven when Jesus was born into the world; and now that He will leave it, glory has been rendered upon earth. It has been rendered by the perfect devotion of a holy human life, by word and deed, by character and by service. It has been rendered by accomplishment of the work which was given to be done. Many works are finished, by coming to an end, though partial and imperfect. Not so this. The word employed means, not merely ended, but achieved and perfected. 'My meat is to do the will of him that sent me, and to accomplish his work' (4 : 34)." — *T. D. Bernard.*

3. The Request for Glorification Is Repeated, v. 5. 5. **And now, Father, glorify thou me with thine own self with the glory which I had with thee before the world was.** "The apostle who had been in the third heaven tells us that 'it pleased the Father that in Him should all the fullness dwell.' There is the full answer to His prayer; 'glorify thou me with thine own self, with the glory which I had with thee before the world was.' And what saith the Spirit? What an object for hope, for triumph, for praise, and for glory is our Emmanuel! 'It pleased the Father that in Him should all fullness dwell'; and all fullness *doth dwell in Him.* And the soul that receives Him is complete in Him, who is the head of all principality and power; and 'of his fullness we all received, and grace for grace.' The glorifying of the Son of Man and His assumption into the glory He had with His Father before the world, began with His resurrection!" — *Marcus Rainsford.*

6. I manifested thy name unto the men whom thou gavest me out of the world: thine they were, and thou gavest them to me; and they have kept thy word.
7. Now they know that all things whatsoever thou hast given me are from thee:
8. For the words which thou gavest me I have given unto them; and they received *them*, and knew of a truth that I came forth from thee, and they believed that thou didst send me.

II. **CHRIST'S PRAYER FOR HIS DISCIPLES,** vs. 6–24.

1. HIS RELATIONSHIP TO HIS OWN, vs. 6–10. 6. **I manifested thy name unto the men whom thou gavest me out of the world: thine they were, and thou gavest them to me; and they have kept thy word.** "The manifestation of God's name may be said to be in part the condition of gathering disciples: the susceptible responded to the revelation (cf. v. 2). On the other hand, to such responsive souls alone could this revelation, in its deepest reaches (13–17) be made. The *name* of God, an Old Testament idiom (12 : 28, vs. 11 f., 26), stands for the whole nature and will of God as disclosed to men through the Son; the fullness of His grace and truth to sinners (see 1 : 18). . . . In what sense did the disciples belong to God before coming to Jesus? They were God-fearing men, Israelites indeed; listening to God's voice in conscience and Scripture, and longing for more of God in heart and mind: they were 'of God'; 'hearing and learning of the Father.' So they 'came to Christ.' *Thou gavest them Me.* The attraction of the disciples to Jesus, and their acceptance of Him as Lord, He ascribes to the power of the Father upon them. The believer belongs to the Father before He belongs to the Son, and is led by the Father to the Son when the Son manifests the Father to Him. There is in this reciprocal influence of Father and Son on the human heart (14 : 23) a striking verification of the prayer: 'Glorify thy Son, that thy Son also may glorify thee.' The Father gives and draws to the Son just as the Son in turn manifests the name of the Father (Matt. 11 : 27)." — *George Reith.* 7. **Now they know that all things whatsoever thou hast given me are from thee.** The disciples apprehended this truth because the Lord had continually emphasized it to them, and by His prayers of thanksgiving to the Father and His obedience to the Father's will, and His frequent petitions of the Father He had made this truth vividly known to the disciples. 8. **For the words which thou gavest me I have given unto them; and they received *them*, and knew of a truth that I came forth from thee, and they believed that thou didst send me.** "The 'words' imply all the separate utterances of Christ as personal revelation of the character and will of God, convincing the believing receiver of them that Christ is divine in origin and person, and His mission divine. Deeper and assured knowledge and faith follow obedience. Christians can be regarded from each of these three great points of view: (1) as the Father's gift to the Son (it is evident how dear to the heart of Jesus such tokens of His Father's love were, vs. 2, 6, 9, 11, 12, 24); (2) as men who obey the Word of God; (3) as men who repose faith in their divine Lord." — *George Reith.*

When the Son says that He prays not for the world but for them whom the Father had given Him, He surely means that it is not on this particular occasion that He would pray for the world. "The exclusion of 'the world' from Christ's prayer is no limitation of the extent of His love (cf. v. 21), but a necessary result of the immediate circumstances of the prayer. His work is fulfilled in ever-increasing circles of influence. At present He is interceding for those who have been prepared beforehand to continue His work; and in their behalf He pleads a request of which the fulfillment is guaranteed (so to speak) by a threefold claim." — *B. F. Westcott.* Christ is glorified in us when we manifest forth His graces, His love, His compassion, His very character so that Christ is living in and through us. The Lord will be supremely glorified in us when we are made conformable to the image of the Son of God, and when we have bodies like unto His glorious body and will forever be at the footstool of His throne, serving Him day and night forever and forever. Every thought of love and honor and praise directed to Christ; every prayer uttered in His name; every deed done for His sake; every manifestation of His character reveals the meaning of this phrase that Christ is glorified in us.

2. HIS REQUESTS FOR HIS OWN, vs. 11–24. Here begins a series of six wonderful petitions uttered by our Lord this night for the disciples who were then His own,

18. As thou didst send me into the world, even so sent I them into the world.

---

and for all the disciples yet to arise, who would continue to form the ever-growing family of God's children. First, our Lord asks that we might be kept through the Father's name. We should remember that Christ here is only praying for His own, not for people out in the world in the grip and power of Satan, not for unbelievers, not for those who love sin. "The unique phrase of address (*Holy Father*, cf. Rev. 6 : 10; 1 John 2 : 20; v. 25, *righteous Father*) suggests the main thought. The disciples hitherto had been kept apart from the corruption of the world by the present influence of Christ. The revelation of holiness which He had made had a power at once to separate and to unite. He asks that God, regarded under the separate aspects of purity and tenderness, may carry forward to its final issue (*that they may be one even as we are*) that training which He had Himself commenced, and that too in the same way (*keep in thy name*, cf. 17 : 12). The 'name' of the Father, the knowledge of God as Father, is regarded as an ideal region of security in which the disciples were preserved. It is the ground of their safety and not of Christ's power." — *B. F. Westcott.*

The second petition is that we might have the joy of Christ fulfilled in us. It is very interesting to note that the words *joy* and *rejoice* are more frequently on the lips of our Lord this last night of His earthly life, this night of darkness, of Satanic manifestation, of denial, betrayal, and suffering, than in all the rest of His three years of ministry together, as far as the Gospel records indicate (John 14 : 28; 15 : 11; 16 : 20–24, and here). The very fact that Christ desires that the hearts of His own should be filled with joy would seem to definitely imply that that is the kind of life every believer may live, and should live, and that, if we fully enter into the meaning, the preciousness, and the power of the words Christ uttered this one night as found in these chapters of John's Gospel, the joy of Christ will be fulfilled in us.

The third specific petition for His own is that they should be kept from the evil one. Note carefully the relation of the believer here to the world: (1) he is hated by the world; (2) he, like his Lord, is not of the world; (3) it is not the will of the Father that we should be taken out of the world; (4) it is the will of Christ that while in the world we should be kept from evil. There is some difference among commentators as to whether the conclusion of verse 15 should read "the evil" or "the evil one," but the general consensus of opinion is that it is the evil one himself to whom this passage refers. "He does not pray only that they may be delivered from the outward assault of the evil one (2 Thess. 3 : 3), but that they may be preserved from resting within his domain." — *B. F. Westcott.* "The prayer that God will keep His servants who must encounter the subtle efforts of the enemy teaches believers forever to rely on this keeping or guarding grace."

The fourth petition, which we seldom hear referred to, and yet which is one of infinite depth and significance, was that all believers might be sanctified by God through the truth, the truth being His Word. "To sanctify is to consecrate to a religious use what hitherto had appertained to the common life, without the idea of sin (cf. Exod. 40 : 13; Lev. 22 : 2, 3; Matt. 23 : 17). . . . From the Old Testament point of view, the consecration was an external, ritual act; in the new covenant, where all is spiritual, the seat of consecration is above all the heart, the will of the consecrated person. Jesus, therefore, in saying, 'sanctify them,' asks for them a will entirely devoted to the good — that is, to God and to His service, and consequently to the task which God gives them to discharge in the world. All their forces, all their talents, all their life, are to be marked with the seal of consecration to this great work, the salvation of men; a thing which implies the renouncing of all self-gratification, however lawful it may be, the absence of all interested aims, of all self-seeking." — *F. Godet.* 18. **As thou didst send me into the world, even so sent I them into the world.** For what purpose did the Father send the Son into the world? He sent the Son to reveal the Father, to condemn sin, to hold forth the Word of eternal life, to reveal His saving grace, to provide a way of salvation, to make eternal life the gift of God fulfilled for men. As the Son came on this divine mission, so do we, in our human, and limited way, also have given to us a divine mission, definitely related to that of Christ. He came to make the gospel possible; we are permitted to live in the world to proclaim that gospel. He came to love and redeem men: we are to have that same love for men and point them ever to the same Redeemer. He came to save: we are ever to set forth His salvation to lost men.

19. And for their sakes I sanctify myself, that they themselves also may be sanctified in truth.

20. Neither for these only do I pray, but for them also that believe on me through their word;

21. That they may all be one; even as thou, Father, *art* in me, and I in thee, that they also may be in us: that the world may believe that thou didst send me.

22. And the glory which thou hast given me I have given unto them; that they may be one, even as we *are* one;

23. I in them, and thou in me, that they may be perfected into one; that the world may know that thou didst send me, and lovedst them, even as thou lovedst me.

---

19. **And for their sakes I sanctify myself, that they themselves also may be sanctified in truth.** "The self-sanctifying of our Lord found place through His whole life, but culminates and comes out in special distinctness in His crucifixion. Wherein it consists is made clear by the words from the Epistle to the Hebrews. The Messiah spake: 'Lo, I come to do thy will.' And then it is added, 'In the which will we have been sanctified through the offering of the body of Christ.' It was the offering of the body of Christ that was the will of God: in doing that will He sanctified us. It was of the doing that will in the offering His body that He spake, 'I sanctify myself, that they themselves also may be sanctified in truth.' The giving up of His will to God's will in the agony of Gethsemane, and then the doing of that will in the obedience unto death, this was Christ's sanctifying Himself and us too. . . . He sanctified Himself for us, that we ourselves also might be sanctified in truth. Yes, our sanctification rests and roots in His, in Himself." — *Andrew Murray.*

Carrying the Cross.

The fifth petition of our Lord's occupies more space in the record of this prayer than any other one petition which He offered, namely, that we should be one in Him.
20. **Neither for these only do I pray, but for them also that believe on me through their word;**
21. **that they may all be one; even as thou, Father, *art* in me, and I in thee, that they also may be in us: that the world may believe that thou didst send me.**
22. **And the glory which thou hast given me I have given unto them; that they may be one, even as we *are* one;**
23. **I in them, and thou in me, that they may be perfected into one; that the world may know that thou didst send me, and lovedst them, even as thou lovedst me.** Notice the three stages in this prayer in regard to the Word of God. In verse 8, the Father is said to have given the words to the Son. In verse 14, the Son acknowledges He has given God's Word to His disciples. In verse 20, the Word becomes our Word, and, through this, many are brought to believe. So we have the Word from the Father to the Son; from the Son to His disciples; from the disciples to an unbelieving world.

24. Father, I desire that they also whom thou hast given me be with me where I am, that they may behold my glory, which thou hast given me: for thou lovedst me before the foundation of the world.
25. O righteous Father, the world knew thee not, but I knew thee; and these knew that thou didst send me;
26. And I made known unto them thy name, and will make it known; that the love wherewith thou lovedst me may be in them, and I in them.

"This text is often cited by those who seek to promote the union of churches. But we find it belongs to a very different category and much higher region. That all churches should be under similar government, should adopt the same creed, should use the same forms of worship, even if possible, is not supremely desirable; but real unity of sentiment towards Christ and of zeal to promote His will is supremely desirable. Christ's will is all-embracing; the purposes of God are wide as the universe, and can be fulfilled only by endless varieties of dispositions, functions, organizations, labors. Whether churches abide separate or are incorporated in outward unity, the desirable thing is that they be one in Christ, that they have the same eagerness in His service, that they be as regiments of one army fighting a common foe and supporting one another, diverse in outward appearance, in method, in function, as artillery, infantry, cavalry, engineers, or even as the army and navy of the same country, but fighting for one flag and one cause, and their very diversity more vividly exhibiting their real unity." — *Marcus Dods.* Such a perfect union prevails in the Trinity of the Godhead — the same character, the same essence, the same holiness, the same purpose, the same truth; a unity of desire, a unity in plan, a unity in purpose, a unity in joy possesses and unites the Father and the Son and the Holy Spirit. So also, when we receive the truth as it has been divinely revealed to us, when we rejoice in the things in which God rejoices, when we have the compassion that possessed the heart of Christ, when our will is in perfect union with Christ's will, when the Holy Spirit is leading us in all things, then are we one in Christ. It is sad to think, and yet how can one deny it, that those who do not believe in Christ as He is revealed in His Word, those who do not receive His precious blood for atonement for sin, those who do not trust Him as the Saviour and the Son of God, those who are not in obedience to Him are not one with Christ. They may talk about Him, but there is no true fellowship and oneness there. 24. **Father, I desire that they also whom thou hast given me be with me where I am, that they may behold my glory, which thou hast given me: for thou lovedst me before the foundation of the world.** This is what we may call the last petition of Christ in this prayer for His own. . . . "The expression of Christ's self-consciousness in the word 'I will' is sublime. The love of Christ's heart can be satisfied with nothing less than this, that His people, the Father's gift to Him, be with Him forever, sharing His blessedness. . . . Two main elements in the future life are the presence and the glory of Christ, to which is added the third, 'that they may behold . . . the world.' The contemplation of Christ's glory is the condition of being changed into the same image from glory to glory. Christ's deepest desire is to have His people with Him. He interprets their deepest desire in praying that they may behold, and so receive into themselves, His glory (1 John 3 : 2; Rom. 8 : 17)." — *Alexander Maclaren.* That glory, as stated above, is the Father's love to Him; that eternal love as ground of all the communication of Himself which the Father has made to the Son (see Eph. 1 : 4; 1 Pet. 1 : 20).

III. **CHRIST'S CONCLUDING REASSERTION OF HIS PURPOSE FOR HIS OWN,** vs. 25, 26. 25. **O righteous Father, the world knew thee not, but I knew thee; and these knew that thou didst send me;** 26. **and I made known unto them thy name, and will make it known; that the love wherewith thou lovedst me may be in them, and I in them.** "Must we not feel that if these words, or anything like them, really came from the lips of Jesus Christ, we are here in the presence of something other than a holy life of a simple humanity, which might help men to climb to the apprehension of a God who was perfect love; and that when He says 'He that hath seen me hath seen the Father,' we stand before 'God manifest in the flesh.' . . . If this Christ in His weakness and humanity, with pity welling from His eyes, and making music of His voice, with the swift help streaming from His fingertips to every pain and weariness, and the gracious righteousness that drew little children and did not repel publicans and harlots, is our best image of God, then love is the center of divinity, and all the rest that we call God is but circumference and fringe of that central brightness. . . . How can it be that the love of Christ to me shall be identical with the love of God to Christ? There is only one answer. If Christ dwells in me, then God's love to Him falls upon me by no transference, but by my incorporation into Him. I am more and not less myself because 'I live, yet not I, but Christ liveth in me.'" — *Alexander Maclaren.*

SOME PRACTICAL LESSONS FROM THIS PRAYER.

"One inestimable treasure we have here already in this great Orison of the Lord, the treasure of a supreme example and encouragement to pray, to pray for others and for ourselves, to speak in simplicity to the invisible God, to tell out our desires, across all mystery, to Him. One great antidote to a prayerless slumber on the Enchanted Ground is to read again the Scripture records of prayer, and above all of our Master's prayers. Within sound of the praying voice of Jesus the infidel misgiving will expire and the Christian will recover his first simplicity. When Jesus, the Jesus of this great gospel, He who has approved Himself to the soul as the veritable 'Son of God with power,' lifts up His eyes to the heaven, the Christian is thankful to look thither also, with the simplicity of a child, believing with a happy repose of thought that 'beyond, beyond this lower sky' shines the radiant reality of the heaven of the immediate, blissful, all-loving Presence, 'the high and holy place.' When 'this same Jesus,' looking up thither, speaks, the Christian thankfully knows and owns, in deepest reassurance, that the utterances of human lips are no vanity, no thing of nought, in that region, to that supreme Personality; the expression of our longings, the explanation of our fears, the confession of our sins, is what God looks for and approves. When Jesus says, 'Father,' and the Christian stands by His side and listens, then across a thousand subleties and sophisms, nay, amidst innumerable mysteries impervious to his intellect, baffling the finite mind as it attempts to comprehend fully its own relations with the Infinite, he knows that the Eternal and Ultimate is Personal." — *H. C. G. Moule.*

From a painting by Albrecht Dürer.

Praying Hands.

In how many ways is the relationship of Christ the Son to His Father set forth in this wonderful chapter? What lessons concerning our own prayer life do you derive from a study of this prayer of our Lord's? What great truths uttered in this prayer pre-eminently bring hope and comfort to the hearts of Christian people? What are some of the things in this prayer that no other person in the world could ever say to God the Father? What are the sentences in this chapter which reveal Christ's absolute confidence in the ultimate success of the preaching of the gospel and the ultimate perfection of His own? How many different petitions uttered by Christ in this chapter for His own are you finding fulfilled in your own life day by day?

LESSON XIII. — March 28.

THE APPEARANCES AFTER THE RESURRECTION. — John 20 : 18—21 : 25.

PRINTED TEXT, John 20 : 19-31.

GOLDEN TEXT. — ***I am alive for evermore.*** REVELATION 1 : 18.

Devotional Reading: Psalm 16.
Beginner Topic: BREAKFAST WITH JESUS.
Lesson Material: John 21 : 1–14.
Memory Verse: Thou, Jehovah, hast made me glad. Psalm 92 : 4.

Primary Topic: JOHN'S BOOK ABOUT JESUS.
Lesson Material: John 1, 3, 20, and previous lessons for the quarter.
Memory Verse: Oh give thanks unto Jehovah, call upon his name; Make known among the peoples his doings. Psalm 105 : 1.
Junior Topic: THE BOOK JOHN WROTE.
Lesson Material: John 1, 3, 20, and previous lessons for the quarter.
Memory Verse: But these are written, that ye may believe that Jesus is the Christ, the Son of God; and that believing ye may have life in his name. John 20 : 31.
Intermediate and Senior Topic: A DOUBTER CONVINCED.
Topic for Young People and Adults: CHRIST STILL WITH US.

THE TEACHER AND HIS CLASS.

The Younger Classes might be asked what conclusion could be drawn if two children said to another friend, "We saw your father on the street today," and the one spoken to would say, "I do not believe what you say. My father is supposed to be in such and such a city today, on business." Well, for one thing it would mean that the one spoken to had a conflict in his mind. On the one hand, he had heard his father was in this distant city on business; on the other hand, he has the testimony of his two friends that his father was seen in his own city. It might be that the lad spoken to was just of a skeptical turn of mind, and refused to believe hardly anything that he heard. When he got home that night he discovered that his father had unexpectedly come back to the city. Now something like that happens in our lesson. Thomas believes that Jesus is dead in the tomb. The disciples tell him they have seen the Lord. He refuses to believe them, but he wanted to believe, and so he tells them what evidence would be necessary to persuade him to believe that Jesus had been raised from the dead. The evidence is given, and Thomas believes.

The Older Classes will here find a wonderful portrait of our Lord Jesus — constantly concerned that His disciples should be absolutely convinced of the reality of His resurrection; bestowing peace and the power of the Holy Spirit upon His disciples for the enrichment of their lives; so directing their secular work that it is attended by phenomenal success; seeking the love of His own. Every word He utters, and every deed He performs, is for the enrichment, the deepening, the blessing, of those who belong to Him. His heart toward us today is as His heart was toward the disciples then.

THE LESSON IN ITS SETTING.

Time. — The first appearance to the assembled disciples was on Easter night, April 9, A.D. 30. The second appearance was the following first day of the week, April 16. The appearance to the disciples at the sea of Galilee was sometime later in the month of April.

Place. — The two appearances to the assembled disciples were in an upper room in Jerusalem, possibly the room in which the Lord's Supper was instituted. The appearance to the disciples engaged in fishing was, of course, on the sea of Galilee in Northern Palestine.

THE PLAN OF THE LESSON.

SUBJECT: The Desire of Christ to Convince His Disciples Forever of the Reality of His Resurrection and to Give Them Power and Guidance for Their Work Which Would Begin upon His Ascension.

I. THE REPORT OF MARY MAGDALENE, John 20 : 18.

II. CHRIST APPEARS TO THE TEN ON EASTER NIGHT, 20 : 19–23.
1. The fear of the disciples.
2. The subsequent joy of the disciples.
3. The preliminary enduement.
4. The commission given the disciples.

III. CHRIST APPEARS TO THE ELEVEN EIGHT DAYS LATER, 20 : 24–29.
1. The preceding conversation of the disciples with Thomas, vs. 24, 25.
2. Christ's words to Thomas, vs. 26, 27.
3. Thomas' faith and confession, v. 28.
4. The blessedness of those who believe having not seen, v. 29.

IV. JOHN'S PURPOSE IN WRITING HIS GOSPEL, 20 : 30, 31.

V. CHRIST'S APPEARANCE TO THE DISCIPLES AT THE SEA OF GALILEE, John 21 : 1–25.
1. Obedience to Christ's commands results in failure being followed by phenomenal success, vs. 1–11.
2. Christ's presence means the provision of life's necessities, vs. 12–14.
3. The supremacy of love, vs. 15–17.
4. Christ's final words of admonition for Peter vs. 19–24.
5. The unrecorded miracles of Christ, v. 25.

THE TEACHER'S LIBRARY.

All lives of Christ will be found somewhat helpful in the study of our lesson, but especially one should consult books particularly devoted to the resurrection of our Lord, *e.g.*, H. B. Sweete: *The Appearances of Our Lord After the Passion;* J. C. Massee: *After His Passion;* F. W. Krummacher: *The Risen Redeemer;* G. D. Boardman: *Our Risen King's Forty Days;* Henry Latham: *The Risen Master;* B. F. Westcott: *The Revelation of the Risen Lord;* Boyd Carpenter: *Forty Days of the Risen Life;* James Orr: *The Resurrection of Jesus;* C. C. Dobson: *The Risen Lord and His Disciples.* Then one also may profitably consult most of the standard biographies of Peter, and of course, all of the larger commentaries on John's Gospel. Above all, though perhaps the teacher will not be able to secure it, there is a very precious and exceedingly rich volume devoted exclusively to an exposition of the two chapters assigned to our lesson: *Jesus and the Resurrection,* by H. C. G. Moule.

On the entire passage, see also the relevant passages in A. B. Bruce: *The Training of the Twelve,* 488–531; S. D. Gordon: *Quiet Talks on John's Gospel,* 243–256; David Gregg: *Studies in John's Gospel,* 333–348. For expository material see Alexander Maclaren: *Expositions of Holy Scripture, St. John 15–23,* 308–338. For sermonic material, we mention only the following more important sermons: G. Campbell Morgan, in the *Westminster Pulpit,* on verse 21, Vol. 10, 409–416; on verses 21–23, Vol. 4, 137–144; on verse 28, Vol. 5, 129–136; on verse 27, 249–256; on verse 19, see G. H. Morrison: *The Unlighted Luster,* 112–121; H. P. Liddon: *Easter in St. Paul's,* 217–229; Alexander Smellie: *Out of the Desert a Gift,* 11 ff., 195 ff.; J. S. Holden: *The Pre-eminent Lord,* 103–109; on verse 25, H. P. Liddon: *Christmastide in St. Paul's,* 1 17; an article "Print" in James Hastings: *Dictionary of Christ and the Gospels,* Vol. 2, 419–420; on verse 29, Dinsdale T. Young: *The Crimson Book,* 53–70. On the very interesting conversation of our Lord, though it does not appear in the printed text, John 21 : 15–17, see W. G. Ballentine: "Lovest Thou Me?" in *Bibliotheca Sacra,* 1889, 524–542; George B. Stevens: *The Johannine Theology,* 270–272; R. C. Trench: *Synonyms of the New Testament,* 84–86; B. B. Warfield: *Biblical Doctrines,* 589–592; James Moffatt: *Love in the New Testament,* 277, 278, 307.

JOHN 20 : 19. When therefore it was evening, on that day, the first *day* of the week, and when the doors were shut where the disciples were, for fear of the Jews, Jesus came and stood in the midst, and saith unto them, Peace *be* unto you.

I. **THE REPORT OF MARY MAGDALENE,** John 20 : 18. It was to Mary Magdalene that our Lord first appeared on Easter morning, an appearance filled with beautiful lessons, but one that does not come within the scope of our lesson today. The conclusion of our Lord's conversation was a command for her to go to Jerusalem and to announce to His brethren the Lord's approaching ascension. She immediately obeyed, declaring to the disciples that she had seen the Lord, and repeating what He had said to her. Thus she was the first preacher of the resurrection. She never appears again in the gospel story.

II. **CHRIST APPEARS TO THE TEN ON EASTER NIGHT,** John 20 : 19–23. This is the only portion of our entire lesson which is reported by any of the Synoptic writers (see Mark 16 : 14; Luke 24 : 36–48). 19. **When therefore it was evening, on that day, the first *day* of the week, and when the doors were shut where the disciples were, for fear of the Jews, Jesus came and stood in the midst, and saith unto them, Peace *be* unto you.** Where the disciples were gathered together on the night of the day when our Lord rose from the dead we cannot be sure. Many have thought that it was in the same room in which Christ instituted the Lord's Supper, on Thursday evening of the preceding week. From Mark's account we gather that the ten had dined together, and that the meal was finished. This was what we might call a secret meeting, for the ten had attempted to secure themselves from intrusion by locking the doors of the house in which they met, not knowing but that the Jews who had murdered Jesus would now attempt to do bodily harm to the well-known followers of the Lord. While they were seated at the table the Lord suddenly stood in their midst. The narrative certainly implies that He came into the room without opening any door, or having a door opened for Him. "In His risen and glorified state time, space, and rock of the tomb, the walls and doors of buildings, no longer hampered the body of Jesus. He appears where He desires to appear, and His visible presence is gone when He desires to have it so. This is wholly supernatural, and to our minds, wholly incomprehensible. . . . 'He came and stood in their midst' is all that human thought and language say. The disciples did not see Him take so many steps from the door or wall to their midst. He was there, and that was all." — *R. C. H. Lenski.* How beautiful are the first words which Christ speaks to these more or less frightened disciples, "Peace be unto you." "When then our Lord appeared with His 'Peace be unto you,' He restored peace, because He restored the sense, however indefinite as yet, of pardon for past sin, and of reconciliation with God. Without this there can be no true peace for the soul of man. We need a peace which the world cannot give. We need this prerogative gift of Christ; His great Easter blessing. Its presence is traceable in the quiet resolve which is never disturbed by the ever varying circumstances of the passing years; in the well-compacted harmony

20. And when he had said this, he showed unto them his hands and his side. The disciples therefore were glad, when they saw the Lord.
21. Jesus therefore said to them again, Peace *be* unto you: as the Father hath sent me, even so send I you.
22. And when he had said this, he breathed on them, and saith unto them, Receive ye the Holy Spirit:
23. Whose soever sins ye forgive, they are forgiven unto them; whose soever *sins* ye retain, they are retained.

---

of the faculties; in the undertone of thankfulness and praise which is proof against the tragical possibilities of the days to come. This peace is no more touched by the troubles of life than the depths of the ocean are stirred by the storm which sweeps its surface." — *H. P. Liddon.* 20. **And when he had said this, he showed unto them his hands and his side. The disciples therefore were glad, when they saw the Lord.** Christ showed them His hands and side "to convince them He was the very same Person who had been crucified, having the same body; as the words just uttered would assure them, His heart was still the same to them (cf. Luke 24 : 39)." — *George Reith.* For the first time since before the crucifixion, the disciples' hearts were filled with joy, and we believe we are not exaggerating when we say that their hearts never lost that joy, from the night when they first knew their Lord was truly risen from the grave to the hour when, for His sake, years later, one after the other they laid down their lives. 21. **Jesus therefore said to them again, Peace *be* unto you: as the Father hath sent me, even so send I you.** Compare with this commission the almost identical words uttered in a prayer on Thursday night (John 17 : 18). "The Greek word for *sent* is not the same in both clauses: in the first it is the verb *apostellein;* in the second it is the verb *pempein.* The latter is the most general word for sent, implying no special relation between sender and sent; the former adds the notion of a delegated authority constituting the person sent, the envoy or representative of the sender. (It is from this word that apostle is derived.) Both verbs are used both of the mission of Christ and of the mission of the disciples (see, for example, for the use of the first word, John 1 : 6, 19, 24; 4 : 38; 17 : 18; and for the use of the second, John 4 : 34; 5 : 23, 24, 30, 37; 7 : 16, 18, 28, 33, and in all the passages in chapters 12–16)." — *A. Plummer.* 22. **And when he had said this, he breathed on them, and saith unto them, Receive ye the Holy Spirit: 23. whose soever sins ye forgive, they are forgiven unto them; whose soever *sins* ye retain, they are retained.** The meaning of this passage has been variously interpreted, and we believe Professor Reith's full exegesis should be quite fully quoted. "The Holy Spirit is represented in Scripture as the Breath of God which, indeed, the word Spirit itself means. He is the breathing of God — the essence and life of God, breathed by Father to Son, and

Courtesy of H. W. Fishmuth.

The Christ.

"Peace be unto you."

24. But Thomas, one of the twelve, called Didymus, was not with them when Jesus came.
25. The other disciples therefore said unto him, We have seen the Lord. But he said unto them, Except I shall see in his hands the print of the nails, and put my finger into the print of the nails, and put my hand into his side, I will not believe.

---

by Father and Son to men. Breathing is the most manifest token of life; so that, in breathing on the disciples, our Lord was giving them to share His own life — the life of God. He was so possessed with the Spirit that the very breath of His body was spiritual — communicating divine life. He had not done this before, though the Father had given Him the Spirit without measure (3 : 34). As Creator, He breathed into man's nostrils the breath of life at the first (Gen. 2 : 7), and man became a living soul. And now He breathed on His disciples as Redeemer; Himself the glorified Man, the quickening Spirit, giving life, and life more abundantly to overcome the death of sin. This private act of Christ, before His ascension, would convince His disciples all the more that the public outpouring of the Holy Spirit at Pentecost was truly His own gift to the Church, His own very life, was no mere external equipment, was no alien power — nothing new, strange, unknown, but the symbol of the great fact that they henceforth lived in their Lord's life. . . . Our Lord gave the disciples first their *work*, then the needful *endowment* for it, and now *authority* in the carrying of it out." "In this remarkable gift there is implied the institution of the Church of Christ as a visible, organized society, with its methods of procedure, laws, office-bearers, and discipline. Our Lord had already made the same promise of authority to them (Matt. 16 : 19; 18 : 18) in a form taken from the rules of the synagogue communions. 'Binding' and 'loosing' were familiar terms applied to the discipline exercised by the elders of synagogues over the members. The disciples therefore would understand that their Master was calling them to organize a society on earth of those believing in His name, and to exercise all needful discipline in connection with it — to determine who should, and who should not, be within its fellowship. It is implied, further, that their fellowship shall be a fellowship of those who have had their sins forgiven, who enjoy that peace with the Father which He had just declared to themselves. The second appearance (vs. 24-29) is peculiar to John." — *George Reith.*

III. **CHRIST APPEARS TO THE ELEVEN EIGHT DAYS LATER,** 20 : 24-29. 24. **But Thomas, one of the twelve, called Didymus, was not with them when Jesus came.** 25. **The other disciples therefore said unto him, We have seen the Lord. But he said unto them, Except I shall see in his hands the print of the nails, and put my finger into the print of the nails, and put my hand into his side, I will not believe.** Why Thomas was not with the disciples the first time they were gathered together in the upper room, the evening of Easter, we do not know with certainty. He was of a morose disposition, always looking on the darker side of things, and, as is usual with a person of such a temperament, demanding evidence before he received as fact anything unusual. Certainly Thomas did not believe he would see the Lord Easter night, as probably none of the others did. More than that, he did not want to be in the company of the apostles. He wanted to be alone with his own grief. A person whose mind is filled with doubt does not enjoy the companionship of others, especially in an hour of great crisis. It should be carefully noted that the disciples did not part from Thomas. They did not cast him out of their fellowship; they were gracious and tender to him, telling him through the week that followed what they had seen and what they had heard, all of which made a tremendous impression on Thomas. Thomas wanted to believe. He did not say he would never believe, as some men do, neither did he say, "I don't care what has happened — it makes no difference to me." What Thomas needed was overwhelming proof of the reality of Christ's resurrection, and there certainly is nothing wrong in a man wanting that kind of evidence. When he needs it, Christ is willing to give it. By the end of the week, the disciples had persuaded Thomas to join with them on the second Sunday night. Here is a great lesson for Christians. You have many members in your church who have been absent for a long time. Has church been a blessing to you? Have you found the Lord truly present in its services? Then, why not deal with these absent members through the week, speaking graciously to them, and cordially, sincerely, lovingly, earnestly urging them to come to the house of the Lord the follow-

26. And after eight days again his disciples were within, and Thomas with them. Jesus cometh, the doors being shut, and stood in the midst, and said, Peace *be* unto you.
27. Then saith he to Thomas, Reach hither thy finger, and see my hands; and reach *hither* thy hand, and put it into my side: and be not faithless, but believing.
28. Thomas answered and said unto him, My Lord and my God.
29. Jesus saith unto him, Because thou hast seen me, thou hast believed: blessed *are* they that have not seen, and *yet* have believed.

---

ing week, to see if it is not true that the Lord will be there to bless them. What if the disciples had actually parted company with Thomas? It may be that he never would have gone into their company again, and never would have seen the risen Lord, humanly speaking. "The worst thing that a man can do when disbelief, or doubt, or coldness shrouds his sky and blots out the stars, is to go away alone and shut himself up with his own, perhaps morbid, or, at all events, disturbing, thoughts. The best thing that he can do is to go among his fellows. If the sermon does not do him any good, the prayers and the praises and the sense of brotherhood will help him. If a fire is going out, draw the dying coals close together, and they will make each other break into a flame." — *Alexander Maclaren.* 26. **And after eight days again his disciples were within, and Thomas with them. Jesus cometh, the doors being shut, and stood in the midst, and said, Peace *be* unto you.** 27. **Then saith he to Thomas, Reach hither thy finger, and see my hands; and reach *hither* thy hand, and put it into my side.** Nothing is said here about any preliminary conversation between Christ and Thomas. The narrative implies that our Lord supernaturally knew not only of the doubt in Thomas' heart, but the words which he had previously spoken to the disciples in demanding physical proof of Christ's resurrection. Our Lord takes up these very words from Thomas' lips, uttered at some previous time, and challenges him to do that which previously he had insisted he would have to do before he believed that Jesus had truly risen from the dead. This is what we call scientific proof. It is the evidence of things seen, and it is as valid today as the day when our Lord stood before those disciples. The old commentator Wordsworth has a wonderful paragraph in his commentary on this verse: "The wounds which Satan inflicted in malice and scorn on our Lord's crucified body, have been converted by His controlling power and wisdom into proofs of His resurrection, and marks of His personal identity. They have become indelible evidence of His power, graven as it were with an iron pen on the Rock of Ages, to be read by the eyes of angels and men for eternity; and they remain forever as glorious trophies of His victory over death and sin and over Satan himself." **And be not faithless, but believing.** "Although I do not believe that the words . . . were intended to convey that Thomas was of an incredulous turn, and that this was made a matter of reproach, still there was much apparent in Thomas that was amiss, and which might easily get worse — and the words with which our Lord ends the colloquy contain a note of warning, and a call to self-searching." — *Henry Latham.* "Thomas was not faithless, but he was on the way to be faithless." — *B. F. Westcott.* 28. **Thomas answered and said unto him, My Lord and my God.** "Everything combines to show that Thomas did not employ the test which he had himself proposed. The presence of the Lord enabled him to feel at once that what he had unconsciously desired was something more than could be assured to him by mere sensible testing. He recognized the Lord, but he knew also that his Lord was more than man. Having set before himself distinctly the extent of his hope, he was better able than others to perceive how the revelation of the Lord went beyond it. His confession undoubtedly was addressed to Christ. The discipline of self-questioning, followed by the revelation of tender compassion and divine knowledge, enabled Thomas to rise to the loftiest view of the Lord given in the Gospels. This confession forms the appropriate close to John's narrative." — *B. F. Westcott.* "By one of those frequent reactions in the moral life, Thomas rises by a single bound from the lowest degree of faith to the highest, and proclaims the divinity of his Master in a more categorical expression than all those which had ever come forth from the lips of any of his fellow apostles. . . . The apostolic faith as it has just risen to the full height of its object, will be able henceforth to re-echo throughout the world by means of the testimony of the chosen messengers so as incessantly to reproduce itself." — *F. Godet.* 29. **Jesus saith unto him, Because thou hast seen me,**

30. Many other signs therefore did Jesus in the presence of the disciples, which are not written in this book:
31. But these are written, that ye may believe that Jesus is the Christ, the Son of God; and that believing ye may have life in his name.

thou hast believed: blessed *are* they that have not seen, and *yet* have believed. "Thomas himself ought to have believed in the testimony of the rest, confirmed by all he had known and experienced of Christ in past days. Certainty cannot be too clear; but certainty does not depend on evidence of sight and sense. Our Lord does not mean that faith has not its solid reasons, or that the less evidence we have for our belief the more blessed we are if we do believe. He does not mean that to believe much is better than to believe little. That depends on the object of our faith. Credulousness is as objectionable as unbelief. Both spring from the same root. The heart has its reasons, and faith has its evidence. Faith is not submission to authority that demands our conscience. Faith is not blind acceptance of truth. Faith is not the opposite of reason. No man believes without intelligent grounds for his belief. Faith is the opposite of sight, because it asserts what is not seen; the opposite of reason *in this sense*, that it compels belief in an object which reason alone cannot apprehend. But faith in the unseen has its own proofs, which satisfy the believing mind and heart that there is an unseen and eternal. Our Lord does not call us to believe in Him on less substantial or plain evidence than would convince us in other matters. We cannot meet with the risen Saviour now — He has gone to the right hand of God; but in place, we have the testimony of the apostles in this Gospel record; and that, with the promised aid and testimony of the Holy Spirit both there and in our own spirits, is solid ground of belief for all the world." — *George Reith.*

IV. **JOHN'S PURPOSE IN WRITING HIS GOSPEL,** 20 : 30, 31. 30. **Many other signs therefore did Jesus in the presence of the disciples, which are not written in this book:** 31. **but these are written, that ye may believe that Jesus is the Christ, the Son of God; and that believing ye may have life in his name.** "John is glancing back over his whole work — 'this book'; and 'signs' here, as elsewhere in this Gospel, are miracles generally. (Cf. especially, 12 : 37.) The expression 'many and other' points the same way; many in number and different in kind from those related. The signs of the resurrection from the nature of the case were all similar in kind. . . . On the one hand there were many unrecorded; but on the other hand some have been recorded. It was not John's purpose to write a complete 'Life of Christ'; it was not his purpose to write a 'Life' at all. Rather he would narrate just those facts respecting Jesus which would produce a saving faith in Him as the Messiah and the Son of God. John's work is 'a Gospel and not a biography . . . that those who read this record may be convinced of two things — identical in the divine counsels, identical in fact, but separate in the thoughts of men: (1) that Jesus, the well known Teacher and true man, *is the Christ*, the long looked for Messiah and Deliverer of Israel, the fulfiller of type and prophecy; (2) that He is also *the Son of God*, the divine Word and true God. Were He not the latter He could not be the former, although men have failed to see this. Some had been looking for a mere Prophet and Wonder-worker — a second Moses or a second Elijah; others had been looking for an earthly King and Conqueror — a second David or a second Solomon. These views were all far short of the truth, and too often obscured and hindered the truth. Jesus, the Lord's anointed, must be and is not only very man but very God." — *Alfred Plummer.* Right here we might ask a question. If John's Gospel is written for the purpose of convincing men that Jesus is the Christ, the Son of God, whose fault is it if when an unbeliever reads this Gospel he is not thereby convinced that Jesus is the Son of God? It is his own fault for the proof here is overwhelming.

V. **CHRIST'S APPEARANCE TO THE DISCIPLES AT THE SEA OF GALILEE,** 21 : 1–25. Dr. Henry Latham, late scholar of Cambridge University, says that probably "the company of the apostles left Jerusalem immediately after the octave of the resurrection day; on their return to Galilee they would naturally betake themselves to their ordinary mode of gaining a livelihood. We do not find that the apostles had been directed to remain together and they may have gone separately to their respective homes. Nathanael, on his way to Cana, might stay for a day or two on the lake side with the sons of Zebedee and the rest. I suppose that it was at Capernaum that they went on board."

1. OBEDIENCE TO CHRIST'S COMMANDS RESULTS IN FAILURE BEING FOLLOWED BY PHENOMENAL SUCCESS, VS. 1–11. In the first part of our lesson today, ten of the

apostles were together; later we find all the eleven together. Here it would appear that seven of them were together. There always has seemed something out of place about these disciples going back to their nets, but possibly that is what they should have done until they had further directions from the Lord as to what to do. One would have thought they would have come frequently together for prayer, and talking about the Lord, but apparently they did not do this. The fact that on the particular day, the events of which are described in this chapter, the apostles had caught absolutely nothing, would seem to indicate that they were not enjoying success in their work, because it was not done under the definite direction of the Lord, not even His permission. When morning was come, unknown to them the Lord approached the fishermen and asked if they had any meat, that is, if they had gathered any fish. Being told that they had not, He commanded them to cast the same net they had been using all night, in the very spot where they were then located, on the right side of the ship. When they had done so, such a great multitude of fishes were found in the net that they were unable to draw it, that is, to lift it up into the boat. In this net were found 153 fish, apparently of a considerable size. A great many things have been said about the number of fish that were caught, and why the number should be recorded sixty years after the event took place. Latham's remarks here are very good. "The crew and the owners of the boat were paid by shares of the fish; when these fish were of all sorts and sizes, they were set out in heaps, and one heap went for a share; but, in this immediate case, the fish were all large, and so nearly of a size that, roughly speaking, a share would be so many apiece. Consequently, as soon as the fish were taken out of the net, they were counted and laid on the grass." . . . "By this miracle He gave the apostles to understand that not only when with them in the flesh could He give them success. Even now after His resurrection and when they did not recognize Him on the shore He blessed their labor, that they might even when they did not see Him believe in His nearness and in His power most effectually to give them success." — *Marcus Dods.* For an earlier, miraculous draught of fishes, see Luke 5 : 1–11.

2. CHRIST'S PRESENCE MEANS THE PROVISION OF LIFE'S NECESSITIES, VS. 12–14. This is undoubtedly one of the most exquisite passages in all the Word of God. Our Lord was actually preparing breakfast for His disciples and partaking of it with them. We should carefully note that "a feeling of respectful fear prevents the disciples from approaching this mysterious person. Jesus invites them to eat; but even then they do not dare to address Him. It is no longer the familiar relation of former days." — *F. Godet.* "Christ graciously provides for the disciples' present wants and invites them to be His guests: why but to show them that in their work hereafter they should never want but He would provide." — *Henry Alford.*

3. THE SUPREMACY OF LOVE, VS. 15–17. Inasmuch as these verses reappear in the printed text of the lesson for May 2, all remarks have been left for that lesson.

4. CHRIST'S FINAL WORDS OF ADMONITION FOR PETER, VS. 19–24. "After accepting Peter's love and publicly reinstating him as an apostle, the Lord prophesies what kind of a death shall crown his career. We recall 13 : 36, 'But thou shalt follow me afterwards.' Once Peter rashly disregarded the word of Jesus that he could not then follow Jesus, and that rash disobedience had ended in denial. But then already Jesus told Peter that he should follow Him, namely, into death 'afterward.' And now, when Peter is again fully restored to his former place, the Lord amplifies the word spoken before Peter's denial, the word about dying for his Lord. It is a mistake then to assume that now Jesus is still testing Peter and as much as asking whether he will furnish the highest proof of love. Nor are these words only an admonition to patience and resignation. No, as John states, these words are direct prophecy. Peter is to know the kind of death he is to die, and knowing this in advance he will not only go forward joyfully to meet it, but will also devote himself most zealously to the flock entrusted to him while his life lasts. Paul was also told in advance, 'how great things he must suffer for my name's sake' (Acts 9 : 16)." — *R. C. H. Lenski.*

What is next related of Peter is singularly characteristic. "There is in him a peculiar kind of curiosity, which we find in people of very active minds. He wants to have everything fully made out. Of this we find another example in Peter. He it is, who when the 'Lord had said one of you shall betray me,' beckoned to John at the supper and said unto him, 'Tell us who it is of whom He speaketh.' There is one other question of curiosity in the Gospels which may very well have come from Peter, although his name does not appear. It is, 'Lord, are there few that be saved?' (Luke 13 : 23). This boldness in asking what he had no business to ask is more like what we should expect of Peter than of any one else, and our Lord's way of dealing with the question is characteristic. He points to what men who would be saved would have to *do*. They are to strive in order to enter. . . . Our Lord gives him in fact no answer, for, 'If I will that he tarry till I come,' is only saying, 'If a lot ever so improbable awaits him, what business is that of yours? Keep to the duty that is before yourself. Follow thou me.' " — *Henry Latham.*

5. THE UNRECORDED MIRACLES OF CHRIST, v. 25. "The purpose of this verse seems to be to assert and vindicate the fragmentary character of the Gospel, considered merely as a historical narrative — for that the doings of the Lord were so many — His life so rich in matter of record — that, in a popular hyperbole we can hardly imagine the world containing them all, if singly written down; thus setting forth the superfluity and cumbersomeness of anything like a perfect detail, in the strongest terms, and in terms which certainly look as if fault had been found with this Gospel for want of completeness, by some objectors." — *Henry Alford.*

What was the principal purpose of the appearance of Christ to His disciples after His resurrection? Why did Christ, as far as we know, appear exclusively after His resurrection to those who believed in Him and not to the unbelieving Jewish officialdom and the scoffing multitude who had repudiated His claims that He was the Messiah? Was Thomas an honest doubter, or not? How many different results do you find in this lesson accruing from a knowledge on the part of the disciples that their Lord had risen from the dead? How many different characteristics of Christ do you find in the passages assigned for this lesson? Have you told the Lord all this week that you love Him? Do you think our lives are as definitely planned by God as the lives of these apostles? Why was it so tremendously important to convince the eleven apostles of the great truth of the resurrection? What would have happened if the apostles had not been convinced?

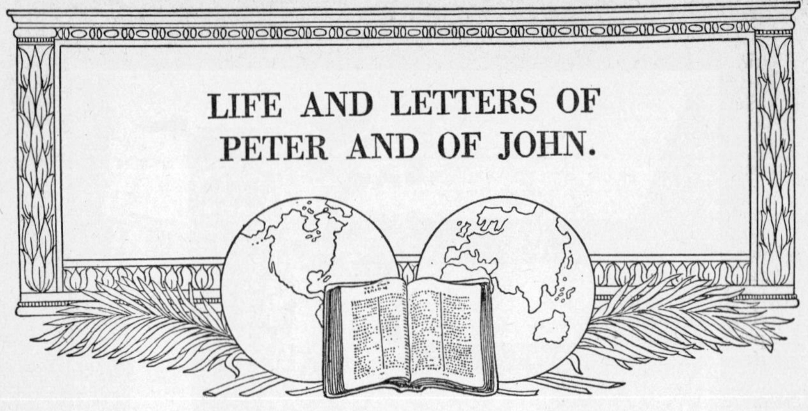

SECOND QUARTER.

APRIL 4—JUNE 27, 1943.

(SECOND HALF OF A SIX MONTHS' COURSE.)

AIM: To find, through a study of the lives and letters of Peter and John, help for Christian living today.

LESSON I. — April 4.

PETER AND JOHN BECOME DISCIPLES OF JESUS. — John 1 : 29–42; Mark 1 : 16–20.

GOLDEN TEXT. — ***And Jesus said unto them, Come ye after me, and I will make you to become fishers of men.*** MARK 1 : 17.

Devotional Reading: Romans 10 : 6–15.
Beginning Topic: JESUS' FRIEND ANDREW.
Lesson Material: John 1 : 35–42; Mark 1 : 16–18.
Memory Verse: Let us love one another. 1 John 4 : 7.
Primary Topic: PETER'S BROTHER ANDREW.
Lesson Material: John 1 : 35–42; Mark 1 : 16–18.
Memory Verse: We have beheld and bear witness that the Father hath sent the Son to be the Saviour of the world. 1 John 4 : 14.
Junior Topic: PETER'S BROTHER ANDREW.
Lesson Material: John 1 : 35–42; Mark 1 : 16–18.
Memory Verse: We have beheld and bear witness that the Father hath sent the Son to be the Saviour of the world. 1 John 4 : 14.
Intermediate and Senior Topic: WON — AND WINNING OTHERS.
Topic for Young People and Adults: WON — AND WINNING OTHERS.

THE TEACHER AND HIS CLASS.

The Younger Classes might be asked what are those experiences in life which you want to go and tell about to your dearest loved ones immediately. Well, probably for one thing the coming of a little baby into your home; the return of an older brother who has been absent for a long time. Then a child wants to tell all of his playmates at once of some wonderful trip his parents are planning for the entire family; or about some new gift which has come into their possession. This was what the first disciples did when they came to recognize in Jesus of Nazareth their Messiah, their Saviour.

The Older Classes should receive from a study of this lesson a new conviction concerning the seriousness of this business of thinking about coming to know Christ as the Son of God, the Lamb of God, believing in and proclaiming the Lord Jesus Christ. These men were

LEONARDO DA VINCI.

THE LAST SUPPER.

looking for the truth, and when they found Christ they knew that here was the Sent One of God. The trouble with the world today is that it is not concerned with the divine Saviour; it is not concerned with the problem of sin; it is not concerned about the One who can save. And when the world is not concerned about these things, then the world is not going to discuss or investigate these things, and when such truths are ignored, then the deepest and most vital problems of life remain unsolved, and men abide in their bondage, their restlessness, their hopelessness, their despair.

THE LESSON IN ITS SETTING.

Time. — The events described in the passage taken from John occurred in February, A.D. 27; the call of the four disciples, recorded by Mark, occurred in April, A.D. 28.

Place. — The testimony of John the Baptist and the first call of the three disciples probably took place near Bethany, beyond Jordan; the latter call of the four disciples took place, as the text clearly indicates, at the sea of Galilee, near Capernaum.

THE PLAN OF THE LESSON.

SUBJECT: The Power of Christ to Attract Men and the Great Changes Which Christ Achieves in the Lives of Men Who Sincerely Follow Him.

I. THE TESTIMONY OF JOHN THE BAPTIST, John 1 : 29–34.

1. Christ is the Lamb of God.
2. Christ existed previous to and is superior to John the Baptist.
3. Christ identified by His being anointed by the Holy Spirit.
4. Christ's mission to baptize with the Holy Spirit.
5. Christ is the Son of God.

II. THE FIRST THREE DISCIPLES, John 1 : 35–42.

1. The attraction to Christ.
2. The interrogation by Christ.
3. The invitation of Christ.
4. The conviction concerning Christ.
5. The compulsion to witness to Christ.
6. The prediction of Christ concerning Simon.

III. THE LATER CALL OF FOUR DISCIPLES, Mark 1 : 16–20.

1. Their original occupation.
2. The call to follow Christ.

St. Peter and St. John. Dürer.

3. The promise of Christ for those who would answer the call.
4. Their immediate response to the call.

THE TEACHER'S LIBRARY.

All lives of Christ and most commentaries on John's Gospel and Mark's Gospel will be found helpful for the study of this lesson. Especially should one consult the relevant chapters in A. B. Bruce: *The Training of the Twelve.* Here Reith's classic, though a small commentary, very difficult these days to secure, will be found exceptionally rich. In addition, all volumes devoted to the twelve apostles will be found helpful, especially biographies of John the Baptist and Simon Peter. The following books on John the Baptist are commended: J. Feather: *The Last of the Prophets;* H. R. Reynolds: *John the Baptist* (a masterly study); A. T. Robertson: *John the Loyal;* W. C. Duncan: *The Life and Character of John the Baptist;* F. B. Meyer: *John the Baptist.* There is some magnificent material in Alexander Maclaren's *Expositions of Holy Scripture, St. John,* Vols. 1–8, 40–73. Maclaren was never better than in these rich pages. For sermonic material see, on John 1 : 29, L. S. Banks: *Christ and His Friends,* 27–39; F. W. Boreham: *A Bunch of Everlastings,* 39–50; William Taylor: *The Silence of Jesus,* 17 ff.; B. B. Warfield: *The Saviour of the World,* 69–100; W. R. Nicoll: *The Lamb of God,* 3–18; on verses 35–42, D. J. Burrell: *Christ and Men,* 40 ff.; on verses 38, 39, John A. Bain: *Questions Answered by Christ,* 119–126; G. Campbell Morgan: *Westminster Pulpit,* Vol. 2, 353–360; on verses 41, 42, G. C. Morgan, as above, 369–376; J. S. Holden: *The Gospel of the Second Chance,* 86–102; J. D. Jones: *The Glorious Company of the Apostles,* 23 ff.; T. H. Darlow: *The Upward Calling,* 90 ff.

Before beginning our studies in this new quarter, it might be best to definitely locate the passage we are about to study in the life of our Lord. Christ's ministry was introduced by the initiatory work of John the Baptist, which will be found in Matthew 3 : 1–2, Mark 1 : 1–8, and Luke 3 : 1–20; this was followed by our Lord's baptism, not recorded in John, but found in Matthew 3 : 13–17, Mark 1 : 9–11, and Luke 3 : 21, 22. Immediately after the baptism Christ entered upon His great temptation in the wilderness, likewise recorded in all the Synoptic Gospels (Matt. 4 :

JOHN 1 : 29. On the morrow he seeth Jesus coming unto him, and saith, Behold, the Lamb of God, that taketh away the sin of the world!

30. This is he of whom I said, After me cometh a man who is become before me: for he was before me.

1–11; Mark 1 : 12, 13; Luke 4 : 1–13). The next event in our Lord's life, according to almost all the Gospel harmonies, was John's testimony to Christ before the priests and Levites, found in John 1 : 19–28. Our lesson today begins with the events of the day following the giving of the testimony just referred to. All that is recorded from John 1 : 19 through John 2 : 12 is found exclusively in John's Gospel. The call of the four, which is also assigned to our lesson, took place about fourteen months after John's first testimony to Christ as the Lamb of God.

I. **THE TESTIMONY OF JOHN THE BAPTIST,** John 1 : 29–34.

1. CHRIST IS THE LAMB OF GOD, v. 29. 29. **On the morrow he seeth Jesus coming unto him, and saith, Behold, the Lamb of God, that taketh away the sin of the world!** Christ was coming, probably, direct from the Temptation. It was fitting that His active ministry should begin with this solemn recognition by His forerunner. "It seems likely, from the abrupt definiteness of the form in which the phrase 'the Lamb of God,' is introduced, that it refers to some conversation of the Baptist with the disciples, springing out of the public testimony given the day before. The reference which he had made to Isaiah might naturally lead to further inquiries as to the general scope of the prophet; and there can be no doubt that the image is derived from Isaiah 53 (cf. Acts 8 : 32). But the idea of vicarious suffering endured with perfect gentleness and meekness, which is conveyed by the prophetic language (cf. Jer. 11 : 19), does not exhaust the meaning of the image. The lamb was the victim offered at the morning and evening sacrifice (Exod. 29 : 38 ff.), and thus was the familiar type of an offering to God. And yet more, as the Passover was not far off (2 : 12, 13), it is impossible to exclude the thought of the Paschal Lamb, with which the Lord was afterward identified (19 : 36; cf. 1 Pet. 1 : 19). The deliverance from Egypt was the most conspicuous symbol of the Messianic deliverance (Rev. 15 : 3; Heb. 3 : 3 ff.; Ezek. 20 : 33 ff.); and 'the lamb' called up all its memories and its promises. And it has been plausibly conjectured that this thought may have been brought home by the sight of the flocks of lambs passing by to Jerusalem as offerings at the coming Feast. However this may have been, the title as applied to Christ, under the circumstances of its utterance, conveys the ideas of vicarious suffering, of patient submission, of sacrifice, of redemption, not separately or clearly defined, but significant according to the spiritual preparation and character of those before whom the words were spoken." — *B. F. Westcott.*

Note particularly the phrase "of the world." Christ is everywhere in the New Testament recognized not only as the Creator of the world, the Upholder of the world, but the Saviour of the world. He it is who will draw all men unto Himself. It is He who came declaring that God loved the world. The whole universe will some day bow before Him who once was scoffed at as He hung upon a tree. The world today may be under the domination of sin, but sin is a usurper, and Christ came into the world to save men from this foreign, galling, enslaving power. "If, as is obviously the tendency in many quarters today, Christianity be thought of as being mainly a means of social improvement, or if its principles of action be applied to life without that basis of them all, in the Cross which takes away the world's iniquity, then it needs no prophet to foretell that such a Christianity will only have superficial effects, and that, in losing sight of this central thought, it will have cast away all its power.

"I beseech you, dear brethren, remember that Jesus Christ is something more than a social reformer, though He is the first of them, and the only one whose work will last. Jesus Christ is something more than a lovely pattern of human conduct, though He is that. Jesus Christ is something more than a great religious genius who set forth the Fatherhood of God as it had never been set forth before. The gospel of Jesus Christ is the record not only of what He said but of what He *did*, not only that He lived but that He died; and all His other powers, and all His other benefits and blessings to society, come as a result of His dealing with the individual soul when He takes away its guilt and reconciles it to God." — *Alexander Maclaren.*

2. CHRIST EXISTED PREVIOUS TO AND IS SUPERIOR TO JOHN THE BAPTIST. 30. **This is he of whom I said, After me cometh a man who is become before me: for he was before me.** It is very strange that almost all commentators simply

31. And I knew him not; but that he should be made manifest to Israel, for this cause came I baptizing in water.

32. And John bare witness, saying, I have beheld the Spirit descending as a dove out of heaven; and it abode upon him.

33. And I knew him not: but he that sent me to baptize in water, he said unto me, Upon whomsoever thou shalt see the Spirit descending, and abiding upon him, the same is he that baptizeth in the Holy Spirit.

---

ignore this verse. Undoubtedly, John means by these words that Christ first, in point of time, existed before John the Baptist; that he was, in other words, none other than the Eternal Son of God. In addition to this He was to be preferred before John because he was in character superior to John, in origin superior to John, in His very nature superior to John, in His mission superior to John. John the Baptist was by far the greatest prophet of his day, but when he stood before Christ he could sincerely say that he was not even worthy to unloose the Saviour's shoe latchet. You can judge the character and the greatness of any man by what he says about the Lord Jesus Christ.

3. Christ Identified by His Being Anointed by the Holy Spirit. 31. **And I knew him not; but that he should be made manifest to Israel, for this cause came I baptizing in water.** " The Baptist had known Jesus personally since childhood, and may have had his own personal convictions regarding who Jesus really was. All this is here brushed aside, for a prophet's certainty must come from a higher source, that is beyond all question. . . . All along in the past, the Baptist was without the knowledge that was vouchsafed to him eventually in such a wonderful manner. But the Baptist could not be left in this ignorance and uncertainty, for God had sent him as the Messiah's forerunner in order to make the Messiah known to Israel. The absolute certainty regarding who and what the Messiah was thus had to be given to the Baptist." — *R. C. H. Lenski.* " It had never (before) occurred to him that this simple village Carpenter, so closely related to himself, whose course of life was apparently so absolutely ordinary and commonplace, could be He of whom Moses in the Law and the Prophets did write. In this sense John could truly say, 'I knew him not.' " — *F. B. Meyer.* 32. **And John bare witness, saying, I have beheld the Spirit descending as a dove out of heaven; and it abode upon him.** The Greek word here translated " beheld " implies a certain intention, not an accidental look. " The word used of the Spirit ' moving on the face of the waters ' (Gen. 1 : 2), describes the action of a bird hovering over its brood, and the phrase is explained in the Talmud, ' The Spirit of God was borne over the water as a dove which broods over her young.' The dove, as a symbol here, suggests the notion of tenderness, innocence (Matt. 10 : 16), gentle and tranquil movement." — *B. F. Westcott.* " Of course, this visible descent of the Spirit made no change in the nature of Christ. It served two purposes: (1) to make the Messiah known to the Baptist and through him to the world; (2) to mark the official announcement of the ministry of the Messiah like the announcing of a king. The whole incident is very parallel to the transfiguration. In both, Christ is miraculously glorified previous to setting out to suffer; in both a voice from heaven bears witness to Him; at both ' the goodly fellowship of the prophets' is nobly represented." — *Alfred Plummer.* I do not know of anything on this verse so simply wonderful as the profound words of Godet, which thrilled me when I first came upon them years ago, and which still continue to bless my soul. " This emblem was admirably adapted to the decisive moment of the baptism of Jesus. It was a matter, indeed, of nothing less than the new creation, which was to be the consummation of the first creation. The creative Spirit which had of old brooded with His life-giving power over chaos, to draw from it a world full of order and harmony, was going, as if by a new incubation, to transform the first humanity into a heavenly humanity. But that which here must be observed is the *organic* form which the illuminous apparition assumes."

4. Christ's Mission to Baptize with the Holy Spirit. 33. **And I knew him not: but he that sent me to baptize in water, he said unto me, Upon whomsoever thou shalt see the Spirit descending, and abiding upon him, the same is he that baptizeth in the Holy Spirit.** " This expression has something solemn and mysterious in it; John evidently means to designate thereby God Himself who had spoken to him in the desert and given him his commission. This commission included: (1) the command to baptize; (2) the promise to reveal to him the Messiah on the

34. And I have seen, and have borne witness that this is the Son of God.
35. Again on the morrow John was standing, and two of his disciples;
36. And he looked upon Jesus as he walked, and saith, Behold, the Lamb of God!
37. And the two disciples heard him speak, and they followed Jesus.

occasion of the baptism; (3) the indication of the sign by which He should be manifested to him; (4) the command to bear testimony to Him in Israel." — *F. Godet.* "Why, again, should John use this phrase for Christ? It was suggested probably by the voice that sounded from heaven. 'Son of God' was a familiar designation of the Messiah. It was founded on the promise made to David regarding his posterity (2 Sam. 7 : 14), 'I will be to him a Father, and he shall be to me a son'; and it is nothing but the echo of that promise which we find in Psalm 2 : 7; 89 : 27; Isa. 7 : 14; 9 : 6, where the conception of sonship of God is applied to the anointed king." — *George Reith.*

5. CHRIST IS THE SON OF GOD. 34. **And I have seen, and have borne witness that this is the Son of God.** At the baptism a voice from heaven was heard saying, "Thou art my beloved Son" (Mark 1 : 11; cf. Ps. 2 : 7; Isa. 7 : 14; 9 : 6). By this phrase John certainly meant to designate Christ as being lifted up above all other beings who had ever appeared on earth — human or superhuman, whether men or angels. The phrase implies the most intimate relationship and identity of nature and the likeness of character.

On the value of the testimony of John the Baptist, Marcus Dods finely says: "It is the testimony of a contemporary, of whom we know from other sources that he was generally reckoned a prophet — a man of unblemished and inviolable integrity, of rugged independence, of the keenest spiritual discernment. There was no man of larger size or more heroic mold in his day. In any generation he would have been conspicuous by his spiritual stature, his fearless unworldliness, his superiority to the common weaknesses of men; and yet this man himself looks up to Jesus as standing on quite a different platform from his own, as a Being of another order. He can find no expressions strong enough to mark the difference: 'I am not worthy to loose His shoe latchet'; 'He that is of the earth' (that is, himself) 'is earthly, and speaketh of the earth: He that cometh from heaven is above all.' He would not have used such expressions of Isaiah, of Elijah, of Moses. He knew his own dignity, and would not have set so marked a difference between himself and any other prophet. But his own very greatness was precisely what revealed to him the absolute superiority of Christ. These crowds that gathered round him — what could he do for them more than refer them to Christ? He was not that light, he could but bear witness of that light. And this he did, by pointing men to Jesus, not as a brother prophet, not as another great man, but as the Son of God, as One who had come down from heaven.

"It is, I say, impossible that we can make nothing of such a testimony. He was one who knew, if any man ever did, spotless holiness when he saw it; who knew what human strength and courage could accomplish; who was himself certainly among the six greatest men the world has seen; and this man, standing thus on the highest altitudes human nature can reach, looks up to Christ, and does not only admit His superiority, but shrinks as from something blasphemous, from all comparison with Him. What is the flaw in his testimony, or why are we not accepting Christ as our light, as able to take away our sins, as willing to baptize us with the Holy Ghost?" — *Marcus Dods.*

II. **THE FIRST THREE DISCIPLES,** John 1 : 35–42. "The difference between this narrative and that of the Synoptics (Matt. 4 : 18; Mark 1 : 16; Luke 5 : 2) is satisfactorily explained by supposing this to refer to an earlier and less formal call of these first four disciples, John and Andrew, Peter and James. Their call to be apostles was a very gradual one." — *Alfred Plummer.* Schaff speaks of the events recorded in this paragraph as "the cradle of the Christian Church." 35. **Again on the morrow John was standing, and two of his disciples;** 36. **and he looked upon Jesus as he walked, and saith, Behold, the Lamb of God!** Note carefully that John shows how sincere he was in his remarkable testimony to the person and character and mission of Christ by actually introducing his own personal disciples to the Lord Jesus Christ, knowing, as he did so, that he would be losing them, but, while it would be, as it were, his loss, it would be their gain, and of course, Christ's gain. 37. **And the two disciples heard him speak, and they followed Jesus.** "The word here trans-

38. And Jesus turned, and beheld them following, and saith unto them,
What seek ye? And they said unto him, Rabbi (which is to say, being
interpreted, Teacher), where abidest thou?
39. He saith unto them, Come, and ye shall see. They came therefore
and saw where he abode; and they abode with him that day: it was about
the tenth hour.

lated *follow* expresses the single act as their choice was made once for all." — *B. F. Westcott.* "When the Baptist uttered the same words on the previous day, these two disciples also heard, and yet they did not act. It is idle to speculate; yet we may recall in our own cases how we did often need a second or third invitation." — *R. C. H. Lenski.* Notice that the first followers of Christ were won to Him as they recognized He was the One who would shed His blood for their sins, *the* Lamb of God. When a person accepts Christ as the Lamb of God, you can generally depend upon it that that person is a sinner truly saved by grace. In these days too many are asking young people simply to receive Christ as a Teacher, as an Example, as a Man of high ethical ideals, as a revelation of God's love, etc. Commentators do not seem to notice this, but how significant it is that the first disciples came because they saw in Christ the sin-bearer. 38. **And Jesus turned, and beheld them following, and saith unto them, What seek ye?** "The question put by Jesus to the following disciples, 'What seek ye?' was the first breath of the winnowing fan which the Baptist had warned them the Messiah would use. It was not the gruff interrogation of one who would not have his retirement invaded, nor his own thoughts interrupted, but a kindly invitation to open their minds to Him. It was meant to help them to understand their own purposes, and to ascertain what they expected in following Jesus. 'What seek ye?' Have you any object deeper than mere curiosity? For Christ desires to be followed intelligently, or not at all. So many follow because a crowd streams after Him and carries them with it; so many follow because it is a fashion, and they have no opinion of their own; so many follow experimentally, and drop off at the first difficulty; so many follow under misapprehension, and with mistaken expectations. Christ turns away none for mere slowness in apprehending what He is and what He does for sinful men. But by this question He reminds us that the vague and mysterious attraction which, like a hidden magnet, draws men to Him, must be exchanged for a clear understanding at least of what we ourselves need and expect to receive from Him. He will turn from none who in response to His question can truly say, We seek God, we seek holiness, we seek service with Thee, we seek Thyself." — *Marcus Dods.* **And they said unto him, Rabbi (which is to say, being interpreted, Teacher), where abidest thou?** "This question seems to imply a desire for conversation and private communion as though they would say, 'We would fain need more of Thee. We are drawn to Thee by John the Baptist's proclamation. We would like to go aside with Thee from the crowd, and inquire more of Thee more privately and quietly, at Thy dwelling, about the things which are upon our hearts.'" — *J. C. Ryle.* 39. **He saith unto them, Come, and ye shall see. They came therefore and saw where he abode; and they abode with him that day: it was about the tenth hour.** "We cannot tell what passed that day between Andrew and Jesus. We may imagine some of the things he said; we do not know. In all likelihood he sat and asked questions out of the perplexity with which his heart was filled, concerning the age in which he lived, as seen through the ministry of John. Perhaps he asked questions concerning the mystery of Jesus in relation to the ancient prophecies. Perhaps he asked Him some question concerning that last word of John, 'Behold, the Lamb of God, which taketh away the sin of the world.' These are but speculations. I will not follow them further, for I want to say this, I am profoundly glad there is no record of the conversation. The truth revealed is that Jesus will take a man or two men and give Himself to them specially, wholly, alone, when no one else intrudes." — *G. Campbell Morgan.* "In this 'Come and see' there is a distinct call to the personal act of faith. Both of these words, 'come' and 'see,' are used in the New Testament as standing emblems of faith. Coming to Christ is trusting Him; trusting Him is seeing Him, looking unto Him. 'Come unto me and I will give you rest,' 'Look unto me, and be ye saved, all ye ends of the earth.' There are two metaphors, both of them pointing to one thing, and that one thing is the invitation from the dear lips of the loving Lord to every man, woman, and child. 'Come and see!'" — *Alexander Maclaren.* "The tenth

40. One of the two that heard John *speak*, and followed him, was Andrew, Simon Peter's brother.

41. He findeth first his own brother Simon, and saith unto him, We have found the Messiah (which is, being interpreted, Christ).

42. He brought him unto Jesus. Jesus looked upon him, and said, Thou art Simon the son of John: thou shalt be called Cephas (which is by interpretation, Peter).

---

hour" here means either ten o'clock in the morning, or four o'clock in the afternoon, "and while the antecedent probability that St. John reckons time like the rest of the evangelists will incline us to four P.M., the fact that a good deal remains to be done on this day makes 10 A.M. rather more suitable." — *Alfred Plummer.* "The mention of time is one of the small traits which mark St. John. He is here looking back upon the date of his own spiritual birth." — *B. F. Westcott.* 40. **One of the two that heard John *speak*, and followed him, was Andrew, Simon Peter's brother.** 41. **He findeth first his own brother Simon, and saith unto him, We have found the Messiah (which is, being interpreted, Christ).** "Andrew is more particularly described as the brother of Simon Peter on account of the subsequent distinction of Peter. He appears again as mediator and pioneer in John 12 : 22. The text leads us to suppose that this finding occurred on the same day that the disciples were with Jesus. We may easily imagine that Andrew found his brother on returning in a common lodging place." — *J. P. Lange.* The word *Messiah* is a Hebrew word, appearing in the Old Testament as the word *Maschach*, meaning "to anoint," and is transliterated, in the Greek, by the word *christos*, which means exactly the same thing, the Anointed One. The word Messiah is found only twice in the New Testament (here, and John 4 : 25); in both places with the Greek equivalent. "The word was applied originally to the king or priest anointed with the holy oil of consecration, the symbol of the Spirit of God, and gradually came to be exclusively applied to the promised king who should deliver Israel from all enemies and sorrow, and reign in righteousness and peace forever. Compare these passages where the reference is to the mere earthly king (1 Sam. 12 : 3; 2 Sam. 22 : 51; Ps. 20 : 6; 84 : 9; 132 : 10); and those where the references, though primarily applicable to an earthly, rises to a heavenly object (1 Sam. 2 : 10; Ps. 2 : 2; and cf. Dan. 9 : 25)." — *George Reith.* Andrew's testimony clearly implies that this group of fishermen often spoke together of the coming Messiah before they ever saw the Lord Jesus. They wanted the Messiah to come. They knew that in Him and through Him God's will would be perfectly achieved. In fact, it was the greatest discovery that they ever made. It is with difficulty that we can put ourselves in the place of these men, for they were saturated with the Messianic expectations of the Old Testament, whereas today, we, of course, do not live in the Old Testament, and realize that its predictions of Christ's advent have been fulfilled. Men have somehow lost the sense of wonder that the heavens have ever opened, and that the Son of God came down to give His life a ransom for many. We do not find it stated in any commentary, though no doubt it has been so stated, that the men who were most active in laying the foundations of the Church in the apostolic period were those who came to Christ at the beginning of His ministry, and who, when they saw Him, at once recognized Him to be the Sent One of God. 42. **He brought him unto Jesus.** "Andrew was a quiet, honest, unobtrusive man. . . . Do not forget that Christ's first disciple was not Peter but Andrew. Until this hour Christ's first need is a strong quiet soul who is always content to remain largely out of sight. This is not to undervalue Peter, but it is rightly to estimate Andrew. It is not to undervalue any man whom Christ calls to the place of prominence, and if God is calling you there, have done with the miserable cowardliness of Saul, who hid away among the stuff when he ought to have gone to the throne. It is mock modesty that hides when God would thrust to the front. When you have come to the front, however, do not imagine you are a great man, and that Andrew does not count. A great succession has followed, and is still following, but Andrew, comparatively unknown, led the way." — *G. Campbell Morgan.* **Jesus looked upon him and said, Thou art Simon the son of John: thou shalt be called Cephas (which is by interpretation, Peter).** The word *Cephas* is the Aramaic word for *stone*, just as the word *Petras* is the Greek word for *stone*. "The root of Peter's character was firmness, which, however, needed to be chastened before Simon could be the man of rock. He did not always show this

MARK 1 : 16. And passing along by the sea of Galilee, he saw Simon and Andrew the brother of Simon casting a net in the sea; for they were fishers.
17. And Jesus said unto them, Come ye after me, and I will make you to become fishers of men.
18. And straightway they left the nets, and followed him.

---

firmness, but it was in him to be the thing, and Jesus holds up to him his ideal, that he may ever aspire to it and believe in himself because Christ believed in him. Of this new name Jesus made use when receiving those confessions (6 : 68; Matt. 16 : 16), which were a fulfillment of this prophecy (cf. Acts 2). Great importance was attached to names among the Hebrews. The new name was the emblem of the future life taken into abiding relation with God. To give a new name meant therefore a complete knowledge of the man; power to give the character and relation which the name represented, and adoption into personal service. Name and nature must correspond at last (Rev. 3 : 12)." — *George Reith.* "If I had to search the New Testament through I could not discover a more beautiful illustration of the charity and hopefulness of our blessed Lord than I find in these His first words to Peter. For when Simon came to Him that day he was anything but a 'rock' man. He was a man of sand that day, and for many a day after that. It took months, it took years, it took a lifetime to turn Simon into Peter — the man of sand into the man of rock. For long it seemed as if Christ's prophecy and hope would be disappointed. For Simon in the Gospels is a weak and vacillating creature. It is the man of sand you see in the man who ran away in the garden and who denied Christ with oaths and curses in the Judgment Hall at the taunt of a serving maid. Yet Christ bated not a jot of heart or hope for His fallen disciple. Yes, he is the man of sand all through the Gospels; but in the Book of the Acts, on the day of Pentecost, at the gate of the Temple called Beautiful before the Sanhedrin — he is Peter the Rock. And yet I will not say that Simon never turned coward after Pentecost — that he was always a man of rock after Pentecost." —*J. D. Jones.*

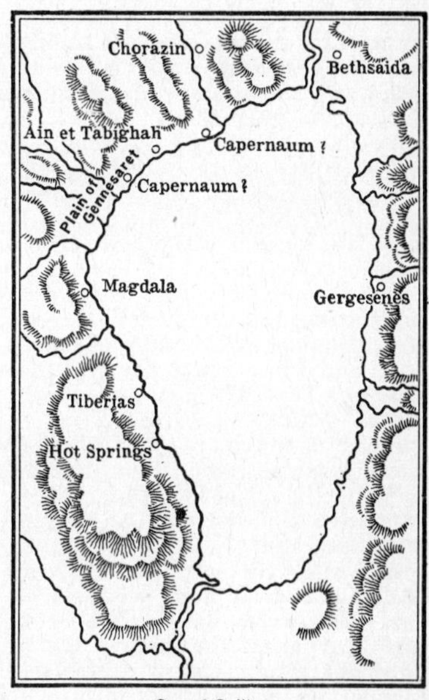

Sea of Galilee.

III. **THE LATER CALL OF FOUR DISCIPLES,** Mark 1 : 16–20. Around the sea of Galilee in Northern Palestine more events of the Gospel narratives take place than in any other portion of the Holy Land, not excluding the city of Jerusalem. This lake, which is 12½ miles long, and nearly 7 miles broad, is 682 feet below the level of the Mediterranean Sea, a fact which was never known until the early nineteenth century. It is sometimes called the sea of Chinneroth, from a word meaning a harp, because of its harp-like contour. It is generally known as the sea of Galilee because Galilee was the name of the province on its western shore. It is also called the sea of Gennesaret, which may be a corrupt form of Chinneroth. Sometimes it is simply known as the sea (Matt. 4 : 15). Finally, it is called the sea of Tiberias, from the city of that name on its western shore. "The western shore of the lake was the busiest and most populous part of Galilee, while the eastern was for the most part a solitude." — *Thomas M. Lindsay.* Around this lake most of the disciples lived, and Capernaum at its northern end is the one city of all those mentioned in the Gospels designated in reference to Christ as "His city." Here most of His miracles were performed, and much of His teaching was uttered. 16. **And passing along by the sea of Galilee, he saw Simon and Andrew the brother of Simon casting a net in the sea; for they were fishers.** 17. **And Jesus said unto them, Come ye after me, and I will make you to become fishers of men.** 18. **And straightway they left the nets, and followed him.**

19. And going on a little further, he saw James the *son* of Zebedee, and John his brother, who also were in the boat mending the nets.
20. And straightway he called them: and they left their father Zebedee in the boat with the hired servants and went after him.

19. **And going on a little further, he saw James the *son* of Zebedee, and John his brother, who also were in the boat mending their nets.** 20. **And straightway he called them: and they left their father Zebedee in the boat with the hired servants and went after him.** "This was by no means the first meeting between Jesus and these two pairs of brothers.

. . . "in addition to the testimony of John, they had been eye witnesses of some of Christ's wonderful works. The turning of the water into wine at Cana, the healing of the nobleman's son, the miraculous draught of fishes, are all probably to be dated before this incident. Faith had been for weeks and possibly months maturing in their hearts — first the blade, then the ear, then the full corn in the ear.

"These men followed Christ because they had already discovered that He was worth following. . . .

"What an exaltation this is! From fishers to fishers of men. But that is ever Christ's way. He does not destroy the qualities of watchfulness and alertness these men had gained by their business as fishermen. He turns them to higher uses, 'Henceforth ye shall catch men.'

"What is your gift — song? You shall sing for Him! You shall become a preacher of salvation. Sympathy? You shall minister to His sick and poor. What are you — a builder? You shall help to build the temple of God. A soldier? You shall fight the good fight of faith. A servant? You shall be a bond servant of Christ. Our Lord never destroys a faculty. He consecrates and exalts it.

"'Fishers of men!' And that is what we all ought to be; we are saved that we may become saviours. Notice how these men at once began to fish for others. Andrew went and called his own brother Simon; John went off and fetched James. Have we begun to fish for men? Have we ever laid hold of a soul for Christ? The joy of 'catching a man alive' — there is nothing on earth to equal it.

"How shall we become 'fishers of men'? Not by our own cleverness or skill. 'I will make you to become fishers of men,' says our Lord. 'I *will make* you' — that is the equipment. If we want to be successful fishers of men, we must go to Jesus Christ for the necessary qualifications." — *J. D. Jones.*

Christ and the Fishermen. Zimmermann.

The question is often asked why Christ, for the most part, chose *fishermen*, and not men in political power, or great scholars. Well, for one thing these men were not bound by the traditions of Judæa, and the Pharisees who dominated there; for another thing, they were men of robust health and rugged nature, who would be able to endure the greatest hardships in their preaching ministry, during the years that would follow our Lord's ascension, and terrible hardships indeed they did endure, all of them finally becoming martyrs. Moreover, there must have been about these men a certain simplicity, and transparency of character, which would not only commend them to the Lord, but mark them as excellent channels for the outpouring of God's grace upon the Roman world; men who, once coming to a conviction, would be willing to endure everything to maintain it. Christ, both in His own life and in His teachings, seemed to have the greatest appreciation of the dignity of manual labor.

How many different things do you think there were about the Lord Jesus which drew these disciples to Him? Exclusively from the passages of Scripture which we have studied in this lesson, what would you say were the major successive steps in the growth of the faith of these men? In how many different ways is Christ here marked out as superior to all men? Why did Christ want these disciples near Him during His earthly ministry? Do you think that these disciples realized what a tremendous step they were taking when they forsook their secular occupations? Do you think Christ called some who refused to respond? (The answer is, Yes.) Do you think that Christ often calls men to Himself by human agencies?

LESSON II. — April 11.

PETER AND JOHN WITNESS CHRIST'S GLORY. — Mark 9 : 2–8; 2 Peter 1 : 16–18.

GOLDEN TEXT. — ***There came a voice out of the cloud, This is my beloved Son: hear ye him.*** Mark 9 : 7.

Devotional Reading: 2 Corinthians 3 : 12–18.
Beginner Topic: The Shepherd's Story.
  Lesson Material: 2 Peter 1 : 16–18; Luke 2 : 1–20.
  Memory Verse: God . . . loved us, and sent his Son. 1 John 4 : 10.
Primary Topic: A Happy Secret.
  Lesson Material: Mark 9 : 2–8; 2 Peter 1 : 16–18.
  Memory Verse: Thou hast put gladness in my heart. Psalm 4 : 7.
Junior Topic: At the Foot of the Mountain.
  Lesson Material: Mark 9 : 2–25; 2 Peter 1 : 16–18.
  Memory Verse: We have our hope set on the living God, who is the Saviour of all men. 1 Timothy 4 : 10.
Intermediate and Senior Topic: Seeing the Glory of Christ.
Topic for Young People and Adults: The Meaning of the Transfiguration.

THE TEACHER AND HIS CLASS.

The Younger Classes should be reminded of how many things we are convinced of because of what our eyes see. If we see a man helping an elderly woman across the street in the midst of heavy traffic, we say he is kind and thoughtful. If we observe a farmer rising early every morning and working hard all day until after sunset, year after year, we say he is a hard working man. If we see a man beginning a business in a small way, in a small store, and, after ten or fifteen years, find the store growing, the building enlarged, the stock increased, we say that the man is successful in business. Now in our lesson today, three disciples *saw* something concerning the Lord Jesus, which marked Him out as a person different from every one else in the world, and what they saw helped to convince them that this person Jesus was indeed the Son of the living God.

The Older Classes may possibly enter upon the study of this lesson with more or less ignorance concerning the facts it contains and their significance. We are very familiar with the birth story, with many of the miracles and parables of Jesus, with His death and resurrection, but for some strange reason, in modern times the transfiguration has been comparatively ignored. The teacher now has an opportunity to bring before the class a body of evidence regarding the deity and uniqueness of Christ, which will come in more or less of a fresh and convincing way to the minds of those who listen. Let him make the most of it.

THE PLAN OF THE LESSON.

SUBJECT: How the Son of Man Was Manifested to Be the Son of God to His Three Closest Disciples on the Mount of Transfiguration, and the Effect of This Experience on Their Later Ministry.

I. The Attending Circumstances, Mark 9 : 2 *a*.
1. The time.
2. The men who accompanied Jesus.
3. The place.

II. THE TRANSFIGURATION ITSELF, Mark 9 : 2 *b*, 3.
1. The fact.
2. The visible manifestation of the fact.

III. THE CONVERSATION OF MOSES AND ELIJAH, Mark 9 : 4.

IV. THE FOOLISH PROPOSAL OF PETER, Mark 9 : 5, 6.

V. THE VOICE FROM HEAVEN, Mark 9 : 7.

VI. ALONE — WITH CHRIST, Mark 9 : 8.

VII. PETER'S SUBSEQUENT USE OF THE FACT OF THE TRANSFIGURATION IN CONTENDING FOR THE TRUSTWORTHINESS OF THE CHRISTIAN MESSAGE, 2 Peter 1 : 16–18.
1. The Christian message not a fable.
2. The apostles themselves were eyewitnesses of Christ's glory.
3. The apostles had heard a voice from heaven concerning Christ.

THE LESSON IN ITS SETTING.

Time. — Autumn, A.D. 29.

Place. — Not specifically designated, but undoubtedly Mount Hermon, far north in Palestine.

THE TEACHER'S LIBRARY.

All lives of Christ, a list of which will be found in the Introduction to this volume, will carry a chapter on this episode in our Lord's life. There are four books known to the editor devoted exclusively to a discussion of the transfiguration: J. A. Beet: *The Transfiguration of Jesus* (1905); F. W. Gunsaulus: *The Transfiguration of Christ* (1886); W. E. Evill: *The Son of Man and the Transfiguration* (1925); Archibald Allan: *The Transfiguration of Jesus* (1923). Of course, all lives of Peter will contain chapters on this experience of the three disciples. In addition to commentaries on the Gospel of Mark, which generally will not be found satisfactory for the study of this particular lesson, one should consult the material in G. Campbell Morgan's *The Crises of the Christ*, 215–267; R. C. Trench: *Studies in the Gospels*, 184–214; William Evans: *Epochs in the Life of Christ*, 93–125; and an article by A. S. Martin, in James Hastings's *Dictionary of Christ and the Gospels*, Vol. 2, 742–746; a very scholarly, critical article, but of a definitely conservative nature, by Dr. W. J. Moulton in *Biblical and Semitic Studies*, by Members of the Semitic and Biblical Faculty of Yale University (New York, 1902), 159–210. If the editor may be permitted to say so, there is a very full chapter on this subject in his recently published *The Supernaturalness of Christ*, 163–185. For shorter studies, see John MacBeath: *The Hills of God*, 73–85; W. R. Polhamus: *Mountain Scenes from the Bible*, 254–268. On the subject of the visit of Elijah, see F. B. Meyer: *Elijah and the Secret of His Power*, 205–213; W. M. Taylor: *Elijah the Prophet*, 195–209; J. R. MacDuff: *The Prophet of Fire*, 313–351. On the subject of Moses on the Mount of Transfiguration, there seems to be practically no material at all; I do not find the matter discussed in any of the standard lives of Moses. For expository material see especially Alexander Maclaren: *Expositions of Holy Scripture, St. Mark 9–16*, 1–12. For sermonic material, see, first of all, A. B. Davidson: *Waiting Upon God*, 139–159; on Mark 9 : 2, W. M. Clow: *The Secret of the Lord*, 165–177; on verse 5, the same, 216–228 (half of this volume, 165–241, is occupied with sermons on the Transfiguration); on verses 5, 6, Phillips Brooks: *Sermons for the Church Year*, 336–351; on 2 Peter 1 : 16, H. F. Henderson: *The Eyewitnesses of Christ*, 1 ff.; on verses 16–18, D. J. Burrell: *The Spirit of the Age*, 104–122. For works on 2 Peter, see especially E. H. Plumptre, in the *Cambridge Bible for Schools and Colleges;* J. R. Lumby, in the *Expositor's Bible;* Charles Bigg, in the *International Critical Commentary Series;* N. M. Williams, in the *American Commentary on the New Testament;* and the excellent chapter, "*The Transfigured Jesus*," in John Henry Jowett: *The Redeemed Family of God*, 249–263.

From a photograph by Wilson.

Mount Hermon from the Damascus Road.

INTRODUCTION.

The transfiguration of our Lord is found not only in Mark, but in Matthew (17 : 1–13) and in Luke (9 : 28–36). The word transfiguration is derived directly from the Latin word *transfiguratio*, meaning "a transformation"; this word is from the Latin verb *transfiguro*, meaning "to transform" or "to transfigure." Thus in the Latin Vulgate, the phrase in Matthew's account, "he was transfigured," reads "*transfiguratus est*." We shall consider the meaning of the Greek words used here when we discuss the opening verse of our lesson. This same subject was assigned for a lesson (March 29) in last year's cycle, and it may be a little difficult to give material for a whole lesson on the same subject which is entirely new. If there is anything in this lesson's treatment that is to be found in the treatment of the same lesson for last year, it is entirely accidental.

MARK 9 : 2. And after six days Jesus taketh with him Peter, and James, and John, and bringeth them up into a high mountain apart by themselves: and he was transfigured before them;

3. And his garments became glistering, exceeding white, so as no fuller on earth can whiten them.

I. **THE ATTENDING CIRCUMSTANCES,** Mark 9 : 2 *a*. 2 *a*. **And after six days Jesus taketh with him Peter, and James, and John.** These are the three disciples who were in Christ's innermost circle of friends. They are the only ones whom He allowed to be with Him at the raising of Jaïrus' daughter; and they are the only ones who were allowed to accompany Him into the innermost part of the garden of Gethsemane the night He was betrayed. Probably He chose these three disciples to be His closest friends because, in the first place, they had the greatest ability; and this means, in the second place, that they would be the most prominent members of the apostolic church after the Lord's ascension, most of the teaching and framing of apostolic truth depending upon them (with the single addition of the Apostle Paul). **And bringeth them up into a high mountain apart by themselves.** There have been many different suggestions as to the exact location of this mountain. Some have even thought it was the Mount of Olives; others that it may have been Mount Tabor; but it seems that the general opinion has been that it can be nowhere else than Mount Hermon. "But whatever mountain it was, it certainly is not for nothing that this and so many other of the most memorable events in Holy Scripture find place upon mountains; as the offering of Isaac (Gen. 22 : 14), the giving of the old Law (Exod. 19; Deut. 33 : 2), and of the new (Matt. 5 : 1), the last decisive conflict between Jehovah and Baal (1 Kings 18), the apparition of the risen Lord (Matt. 28 : 16); from 'a very high mountain' the vision of the New Jerusalem is vouchsafed to Ezekiel (40 : 2), and to John (Rev. 21 : 10). It was not by accident that in the days of His flesh the Lord was wont to withdraw to a mountain for prayer (Matt. 14 : 23; Luke 21 : 37; John 6 : 15), even as, according to Luke, it was for prayer that He retired to this the mount of His transfiguration. Towering above the smoke and stir of this dim and lower earth, advancing their heads into a purer atmosphere and one nearer to heaven, they have in them a sort of natural *Sursum corda*, which constitutes them fittest spots for such nearer commerce with God, or special communication from Him." — *R. C. Trench.*

The Transfiguration. Fra Angelico.

II. **THE TRANSFIGURATION ITSELF,** Mark 9 : 2 *b*, 3. 2 *b*. **And he was transfigured before them.** The word here translated transfigured is the Greek word *metamorphoo*, from which comes our word, as one can at once see, *metamorphosis*. The root of this word *morphoo* means to mold into a form, so that the compound word, which here appears, means to change the form of, to alter. It is found referring to our own transformation, which is spiritual (and not physical as the Lord's) in 2 Corinthians 3 : 18, and Romans 12 : 2. The word does not simply mean an external change, but an actual inner and external change. 3. **And his garments became glistering, exceeding white, so as no fuller on earth can whiten them.** The comments of Professor Joseph Addison Alexander, though made nearly ninety years ago, are

4. And there appeared unto them Elijah with Moses: and they were talking with Jesus.

still of value, and we repeat them in our lesson. " *Raiment*, in the Greek is a plural form corresponding to our clothes, but in the sinuglar denoting the outer garment of the oriental dress. *Shining*, a still more expressive term in the original, applied by Homer to the glistening of polished surfaces and to the glittering of arms, by Aristotle to the twinkling of the stars, and by Euripides to the flashing of lightning, which last idea Luke (9 : 29) expresses by a different verb. *White exceedingly as snow*, a poetical expression, even in its form, and even in translation, when the order of the words is left unchanged. . . . The word translated *white* means originally clear and bright, as applied by Homer to pure water, the sense of color being secondary and indefinite, comprehending a variety of shades from gray to pure white. Here the word no doubt expresses more than the mere neutral sense of whiteness, namely, that of an effulgent white light without shade or spot; but that the notion of color was meant to be conveyed at the same time, is clear from the comparison that follows. *So as* (or, retaining the strict sense of the original, *such as*, *i.e.*, such garments as) *a fuller*, *i.e.*, any fuller, cloth-dresser, literally, carder, one who cleansed woollen cloth by carding or combing it. *On the earth* may either be a strong universal expression, meaning in the world, in the universe, in existence, or contain a more specific reference to the heavenly source from which alone such brightness could proceed. . . . What is said is not merely that no fuller upon earth could whiten *those clothes* so, but that no one could produce such whiteness." " The veil of the flesh which had concealed the glory of the Godhead was, as it were, withdrawn and the full blaze of ineffable light broke forth from within, while even His garments caught the wondrous rays and shimmered with the dazzling brightness of sun-smitten snow." — *H. M. Luckock*. " The Transfiguration was a transaction between the Father and His beloved Son incarnate, who always received everything from that Father. Jesus did not ask to be transfigured, just as He did not ask to have the Spirit descend upon Him as a dove. But knowing the Father's intention, Jesus came up the mountain and brought the needed witnesses. . . . The noun *morphe*, from which the verb is formed, always denotes the essential form, not a mask or transient appearance, but the form that goes with the very nature. So here the actual *morphe* of Jesus was changed; He underwent an actual metamorphosis. God did this to Him right before them, in the actual presence of the disciples. . . . The three aorists in Matthew and the two in Mark report objective facts, actual changes in Jesus Himself, and not something merely subjective, only in the eyes and minds of the three disciples. All the natural explanations of rationalists, that the rays of the sun lit upon the face and clothes of Jesus, while He was standing on an elevation higher than the disciples, are puerile efforts to dodge another miracle. When the disciples looked at the countenance of Jesus they looked at a refulgence as brilliant and dazzling as the sun itself. And this extended to His entire form, for His very garments had the translucent whiteness of pure light." — *R. C. H. Lenski*.

III. **THE CONVERSATION OF MOSES AND ELIJAH,** Mark 9 : 4. 4. **And there appeared unto them Elijah with Moses: and they were talking with Jesus.** The words of Professor Lenski are exceptionally helpful in this connection: we quote them in part. " The question is inevitable, why just these two, Moses and Elijah. The best answer seems to be, Moses as the great representative of the law, Elijah as the great representative of prophecy. Moses stands at the head of Israel's history, Elijah appears when Israel had declined so that only 7,000 remained who had not bowed to idolatry.

" How did the three disciples recognize Moses and Elijah? Certainly not by the correspondence of their features and dress to ideas the disciples and the Jews had formed concerning their looks. Nor do we hear that the disciples had to wait till Jesus afterwards told them who these two glorified men were. A far better answer is that the saints in heaven need not be introduced and named to us, but are known at once through an intuition wrought by God. If anything beyond this is needed, it is that when God makes a revelation he makes it fully, by conveying to the beholder all that he is to know. Elijah ascended bodily to heaven, and thus undoubtedly appeared here in his glorified body. Much speculation appears in regard to Moses. According to Deuteronomy 34 : 5, 6, he died and his body was buried by God Himself in an unknown place. We know of no transfer of his body to heaven. Only the soul of Moses had entered heaven."

5. And Peter answereth and saith to Jesus, Rabbi, it is good for us to be here: and let us make three tabernacles; one for thee, and one for Moses, and one for Elijah.
6. For he knew not what to answer; for they became sore afraid.
7. And there came a cloud overshadowing them: and there came a voice out of the cloud, This is my beloved Son: hear ye him.

IV. **THE FOOLISH PROPOSAL OF PETER,** Mark 9 : 5, 6. 5. **And Peter answereth and saith to Jesus, Rabbi, it is good for us to be here: and let us make three tabernacles; one for thee, and one for Moses, and one for Elijah.** 6. **For he knew not what to answer; for they became sore afraid.** "Peter and his fellows were so taken with the sight of that which they saw that they desired to abide on the mount with Jesus and the saints. What moved them shows what will delight us when this transient world is over and God will gather His people to Himself. Here was Mount Hermon, and there will be heaven; here were but two saints, there the multitude no man can number; here was but Christ transfigured, there He will sit at the right hand of God, enthroned in the majesty of heaven; here was a representative for a brief interval, there a gift and permanent possession of blessedness. When the apostle Peter speaks of tabernacles, he means those little booths or huts such as were constructed for the Feast of Tabernacles, made out of branches of trees or bushes." — *Thomas M. Lindsay.* There are some fine Bible students who believe that Peter spoke wisely here, and that in some way we have here a symbol of the coming of the kingdom of God, but it definitely says that Peter *did not know* what to answer, and it should be clearly noted that our Lord, as far as the record goes, paid no attention whatever to Peter's word. It was as though He just let him talk on and on. The late Professor W. M. Clow, commenting on this desire of Peter to remain with these saints on the mount, makes a very fine point when he says that, "The curse of the cloistered life lies heavy and desolating on the history of Christianity. There are devoted men and women who think that they are never at their best and highest, and never entirely religious, unless they are attending conferences on the state of the soul and meetings for the deepening of religious life. They run from one convention to another, and they have an inward belief that if life could only be a constant succession of Bible reading and hymn singing and prayer, they would become pleasing to God. They lose perspective in Christian doctrine and begin to lay stress on some rite or ceremony or detail of the faith. They often become Pharisaic and censorious, and are very eager in reviving and quickening their fellow believers, whose interest in Christ they often openly question, to a more zealous faith."

From a photograph by Wilson.
Booths of Tree Branches upon the Houses.

V. **THE VOICE FROM HEAVEN,** Mark 9 : 7. 7. **And there came a cloud overshadowing them: and there came a voice out of the cloud, This is my beloved Son: hear ye him.** "The essential difference between this voice and that which was heard at the baptism, is the phrase, 'Hear ye him.' The words are from Deuteronomy 8 : 15, 19, and seem to be suggested by the appearance of Moses. The Prophet like unto Moses is identified with the Christ, the beloved or elect Son; the allegiance due to Moses is now, with Moses' concurrence, transferred to Jesus." — *H. B. Swete.* "In the words themselves of this majestic installation there is a remarkable honoring of the Old Testament, and of it in all its parts, which can

8. And suddenly looking round about, they saw no one any more, save Jesus only with themselves.

---

scarcely be regarded as accidental; for the three several clauses of that salutation are drawn severally from the Psalms (Ps. 2 : 7), the prophets (Isa. 42 : 1), and the Law (Deut. 18 : 5); and, as we shall see, they do together proclaim Him concerning whom they are spoken to be the King, the Priest, and the Prophet of the New Covenant. Peter therefore might very fitly declare that in this voice from heaven, 'he received from God the Father honor and glory' (2 Pet. 1 : 17). And first, 'This is my beloved Son'; but the King's Son is Himself the King; 'yet have I set my King upon my holy hill of Sion' (Ps. 2 : 6). And then, 'in whom I am well pleased'; holy, harmless, and undefiled, fairer than the children of men (Ps. 45 : 2), the scepter of whose kingdom is a scepter of righteousness (Heb. 1 : 8), for in no other could God take a perfect pleasure; and thus the Priest who could and should offer Himself without spot to God (Heb. 9 : 14; 1 John 3 : 5). But then, further, He is the One whom all are commanded to obey, 'Hear ye him'; therefore henceforth the sole Prophet of His Church; Moses, or the Law, has passed away, for that was the shadow and outline of good things to come (Col. 2 : 17; Heb. 8 : 5; 10 : 1), while in Him is the substance of good things actually present; Elias, or the prophets, has passed away, for in Him all prophecy is fulfilled (Luke 16 : 16; 1 Cor. 13 : 8)." — *R. C. Trench.*

VI. **ALONE WITH CHRIST,** Mark 9 : 8. 8. **And suddenly looking round about, they saw no one any more, save Jesus only with themselves.** "The vision vanished suddenly and things returned to their natural condition. The adverb *suddenly* belongs with the participle *looking round*, so that we should say, 'suddenly they looked round and saw,' not, 'they looked round and suddenly saw.' *Suddenly* denotes the quick transition from the heavenly vision to ordinary conditions." — *Ezra P. Gould.*

THE TRANSFIGURATION NATURALLY BELONGS IN THE STORY OF OUR LORD'S EARTHLY MINISTRY.

"There is no more significant experience in Christ's life. It touches our needs and hopes more closely than we think. To any one who remembers who Jesus Christ is, and what He has been and will be to men, no incident of His life is more credible. In all likelihood Jesus was often transfigured in His nights of lonely prayer, although there were no eyes to see Him. No experience set down in the Gospels more entirely becomes the Lord of glory. To one who walked with God and spoke face to face with Him as a child to a father, round whom God's angels continually hovered, on whom the thoughts of all God's saints were set, it is only natural that the fashion of His face should alter, His raiment become as white as snow, and men of God commune with Him." — *W. M. Clow.*

THE SUPERNATURALNESS OF THE TRANSFIGURATION.

No other person in all history has been transfigured, and concerning no other person has a voice from heaven ever been heard to say, "This is my beloved Son, hear ye him." If these things actually happened, Christ is none other than the Son of God; we cannot escape from that conclusion. The voice must be either the voice of God the Father, or the voice of Christ Himself, or the voice of an angel, or the voice of Satan, or the voice of one of the disciples. If it was the voice of Christ, then He performed an act of ventriloquism to deliberately deceive the disciples, and this is utterly contrary to everything we know of the holy Son of God. Whatever we think of Jesus, every rational person knows that He would never stoop to a trick like that. It is impossible that the voice should be the voice of an angel, for no angel could say, unless he lied, that Christ was his begotten Son, and if angels are unfallen angels, they do not lie. The voice could never have been the voice of Satan, because that is the one thing that Satan, during our Lord's life on earth never wanted to admit, namely, that Christ was the Son of God. It is the last thing he would ever say. Certainly the disciples did not say this, for they were so frightened they hardly knew what to say. The only record that we have of any of them speaking is the record of Peter, and it would have been better if he had said nothing, for his words were foolish, needing to be rebuked by Christ.

2 PETER 1 : 16. For we did not follow cunningly devised fables, when we made known unto you the power and coming of our Lord Jesus Christ, but we were eyewitnesses of his majesty.

Let it be repeated, if the record is true, and there is every reason for believing it to be true, and there is no reasonable explanation accounting for these things except on the basis that they actually took place, then the Transfiguration reveals Christ to be none other than the only begotten Son of God.

No orator at the height of his greatest oration, no general of any army about to receive the sword from his defeated enemies, no traveler beholding for the first time the majesty of the Alps, or the dazzling beauties of the tropics, no young man ever walking to the altar of a church to be wedded to the one whom he deeply loves, no man at any time of history has ever been known to undergo such an experience of physical transfiguration as Jesus underwent this day. I do not mean to be sarcastic, but I wish that some scholars who make light of this event and who deny its historicity, would take three companions whose testimony could be depended upon, up on to a high mountain and be transfigured before them, and then have this experience followed by a voice from heaven actually saying, "This is my beloved Son in whom I am well pleased." When someone else has an experience like this, we can begin to discuss its naturalness. Until one does, it remains strictly a manifestation of the supernatural.

THE SIGNIFICANCE OF THE TRANSFIGURATION.

"Christ was granted a glimpse among the children of men, winning redemption for them, and an earnest likewise of the joy that was set before Him. From the vantage ground of the Mount of Transfiguration He descried the consummation which awaited Him beyond the hill of Calvary. Nor was that the only consolation which was vouchsafed to Him. His heart had been grieved by the dullness of the Twelve, the folly of the multitude, and the hostility of the rulers, and in that transcendent hour it was revealed to Him how His work was viewed by God and the glorified saints. Though He stood alone on earth, misunderstood, forsaken, and persecuted, He had heaven's sympathy and approval.

"And the Transfiguration had a purpose also in relation to the disciples. It was designed to reconcile them to the incredible and repulsive idea of Messiah's sufferings by revealing to them the glories that should follow. What did they hear as they listened to the converse betwixt those two glorified saints who bore the greatest names on Israel's roll of honor? They heard them talking of 'the decease,' or as it is in Greek, 'the Exodus,' which He was about to accomplish at Jerusalem. In the judgment of Moses and Elijah that issue, which seemed to the disciples an intolerable ignominy and a crushing disaster, was a splendid triumph, like the mighty deliverance which God had wrought for Israel when He brought her by the hand of Moses out of the land of bondage and made her a free nation." — *David Smith.*

VII. **PETER'S SUBSEQUENT USE OF THE FACT OF THE TRANSFIGURATION IN CONTENDING FOR THE TRUSTWORTHINESS OF THE CHRISTIAN MESSAGE,** 2 Peter 1 : 16–18. The Second Epistle of Peter was written about thirty-five years after his experience on the mount beholding our Lord's transfiguration. It seems to have left a powerful and permanent impression in his life, and now, when he comes to write his last epistle, in which he wishes to strengthen the faith of those to whom he is writing, persuading them once again of the truthfulness of the great Christian convictions, he introduces, not the resurrection of Christ as he did on the day of Pentecost and often subsequently, but the transfiguration of the Lord. 16. **For we did not follow cunningly devised fables.** F. W. Farrar, in his invaluable but now seldom read series of Hulsean Lectures for 1870, *The Witness of Christ to History*, translates this last phrase, "Not on the false track of myths, artificially elaborated," and continues, "in such words more than 1800 years ago, did St. Peter anticipate and reject the gnostic theories which began so early to trouble the Church, and which have sprung up in modern times, thick and rank as grass upon the housetops. The expression agrees with the calm declaration of St. Paul (2 Cor. 2 : 17) that they, the apostles, were not as the many who trafficked with, who adulterated, that is, who falsified, mutilated, misrepresented the Word of God — but as of sincerity, but as of God, in the sight of God, so spake they in Christ." **When we made known unto you the power and coming of our Lord Jesus**

17. For he received from God the Father honor and glory, when there was borne such a voice to him by the Majestic Glory, This is my beloved Son, in whom I am well pleased:
18. And this voice we *ourselves* heard borne out of heaven, when we were with him in the holy mount.

Christ. Many scholars believe that the word *coming* here refers to the first advent of our Lord, but probably Dean Plumptre is right in saying that "the 'coming' here, as in every other passage of the New Testament in which the word occurs, is the second advent, not the first. The mind of the Apostle goes back to what he had witnessed in the glory of the Transfiguration, as the pledge and earnest of that which was afterwards to be revealed. The word does not occur in the first epistle, but the fact is implied in 1 Peter 1 : 7, 13; 4 : 13; 5 : 4." **But we were eyewitnesses of his majesty.** "Both words are significant. That for 'eyewitnesses' (not found elsewhere in the New Testament, but used of God as the all-seeing in 2 Macc. 7 : 35; 3 Macc. 2 : 21), was applied in classical Greek to the highest order of those who were initiated as spectators of the Eleusinian mysteries. It would, perhaps, be too much to say that that association was definitely present to the Apostle's mind, but the choice of an unusual and suggestive word at least implies that he looked on himself as having been chosen to a special privilege. It deserves notice also, as bearing on the authorship of the epistle, that the verb derived from the noun had been used by the writer of 1 Peter 2 : 12; 3 : 2. The word for 'majesty' also has the interest of having been used in the Gospel narrative in close connection with the healing of the demoniac boy which followed the Transfiguration (Luke 9 : 43), and, as found there, may fairly be taken as including, as far as the three disciples who had seen the vision of glory were concerned, what had preceded that work of healing, as well as the work itself. The only other passage in the New Testament in which it is found is in Acts 19 : 27, where it is used of the 'magnificence' of the Ephesian Artemis." — *E. H. Plumptre.* 17. **For he received from God the Father honor and glory, when there was borne such a voice to him by the Majestic Glory, This is my beloved Son, in whom I am well pleased:** 18. **and this voice we *ourselves* heard borne out of heaven, when we were with him in the holy mount.** Professor J. R. Lumby very aptly remarks, in commenting on these verses, that "we learn here why the apostles were taken with Jesus to witness His transfiguration. Just before that event we find (Matt. 16 : 21; Mark 8 : 31; Luke 9 : 22) it recorded by each of the synoptists that Jesus had begun to show unto His disciples how He must suffer and die at Jerusalem. To Peter, who, as at other times, was the mouthpiece of the rest, such a declaration was unacceptable; but at his expression of displeasure he met the rebuke, 'Get thee behind me, Satan.' He, and the rest with him, felt no doubt that such a death as Jesus had spoken of would be, humanly speaking, the ruin of their hopes. Now these three representatives of the apostolic band behold Moses and Elias appearing in glory, and Christ glorified more than they; and the subject of which they spake was the very death of which they had so disliked to hear; the decease which He was about to accomplish in Jerusalem (Luke 9 : 31). The verb which the evangelist uses tells of the fulfillment of a prescribed course, and thus Peter was taught, and the rest with him, to speak of that death afterwards as he does in his former letter. 'Christ was verily foreordained' to this redeeming work 'before the foundation of the world.' They heard that He who was to die was the very Son of God. God's voice had been heard there attesting the divinity of their Lord and Master; the place whereon they had thus stood was for evermore holy ground."

The editor trusts he will be pardoned if he lifts from his discussion of this great episode in his recent book, referred to in the bibliography for this lesson, the following two paragraphs: To me it would almost seem that the voice which was heard is in some ways even more significant than the physical change which was undergone by our Lord. I must confess that, from the earliest days of my ministry, this sentence spoken from heaven has fascinated me. You and I hear according to the same laws that all the disciples heard when they were on earth. Almost invariably we know, when answering the telephone, if the voice is that of our employer, father, son, or a dear friend. What is more important, we know what that voice is saying. When the housewife orders two loaves of bread sent to the house, she does not expect two dozen loaves of bread when the order is delivered. Two means two, and not two dozen. When the agent at the railroad station says that the train for New York will leave from Chicago at 5 P.M., he is not misunderstood to have said "8 P.M.," or "10 P.M." Thousands and thousands of people make train connections every day in this country because of information received by them through the ear.

How many different characters appear in this lesson? How did each of these characters reveal that Christ is infinitely superior to all? Why did our Lord want these disciples to behold His transfiguration? Do you believe what the voice from heaven said about the Lord Jesus Christ? How can we practically carry out day by day in our own life, the admonition heard that day and remembered through the years, "Hear ye Him"? Is there any other religion in the world, ancient or modern, which can point to such an experience as this with the historical evidence supporting the claim, occurring in the life of the founder of that religion? (The answer is an absolute No.) How many different truths, related to our own hope and confidence for the future, are revealed to us in this lesson?

LESSON III. — April 18.

PETER AND JOHN IN GETHSEMANE. — Matthew 26 : 36–46; John 18 : 10–12.

GOLDEN TEXT. — ***Watch and pray, that ye enter not into temptation.*** Matthew 26 : 41.

Devotional Reading: Hebrews 2 : 17, 18; 4 : 14–16.
Beginner Topic: When I Pray.
Lesson Material: Matthew 26 : 41; John 17.
Memory Verse: I will pray unto Jehovah. Jeremiah 42 : 4.
Primary Topic: Surprised Peter.
Lesson Material: Matthew 26 : 36–46; John 18 : 10–12.
Memory Verse: Be ye kind one to another. Ephesians 4 : 32.
Junior Topic: Surprised Peter.
Lesson Material: Matthew 26 : 36–46; John 18 : 10–12.
Memory Verse: Jehovah is merciful and gracious, slow to anger, and abundant in lovingkindness. Psalm 103 : 8.
Intermediate and Senior Topic: Standing by Christ Today.
Topic for Young People and Adults: Standing by Christ Today.

THE TEACHER AND HIS CLASS.

The Younger Classes might be reminded that when a friend or a loved one is sick we try to do everything they want done, to heed every request, to meet every need, as far as we are able. Most of all, this is true when we know our loved one is about to die, desiring to refuse them nothing. In the lesson which we study today, our Lord asked three of His disciples to watch and pray with Him the last night He was on earth; instead of doing what He asked they fell sound asleep, not once or even twice, but three times in one evening.

The Older Classes will find here one of those gospel pictures presenting, in a most unintentional way we would say, the vast contrast that we continually find to exist between our Lord's life of perfect holiness, and obedience to the will of God, and our lives of shallowness, fleshliness, and selfishness. Yet, throughout this narrative, we hear the gracious voice of the Lord urging His disciples to watch and pray; as though recognizing their weaknesses, He encourages them to more exalted spiritual experiences. So, today, though we have often failed the Lord, we can hear His voice through the day's trial and defeat, urging us on to better and holier things tomorrow. When He tells us to watch and pray, we may be sure it is essential that we do so, and that He will enable us to do so.

THE PLAN OF THE LESSON.

SUBJECT: How Two of Christ's Closest Disciples Failed Him in an Hour of Great Need.

I. The Lord Leads Peter and John to Gethsemane, Matt. 26 : 36, 37.
1. With the other disciples.
2. Later alone with the Lord.

II. The Command to Watch, Matt. 26 : 38.

III. THE DISCIPLES SLEEP WHILE JESUS PRAYS, Matt. 26 : 39–44.
1. The first petition, v. 39.
2. The first rebuke, vs. 40, 41.
3. The second petition, v. 42.
4. The second failure, v. 43.
5. The third petition, v. 44.

IV. THE FINAL WORDS IN THE GARDEN, Matt. 26 : 45, 46.
1. The hour of betrayal has come.
2. It is time to go.

V. PETER FOOLISHLY THINKS HE MUST DEFEND CHRIST WITH A SWORD, John 18 : 10, 11.
1. The foolish act.
2. The rebuke of Peter.
3. The decision of Christ.

VI. THE ARREST OF JESUS, John 18 : 12.

THE LESSON IN ITS SETTING.

Time. — Thursday evening, April 6, A.D. 30.

Place. — Gethsemane, a garden on the western slope of the Mount of Olives, opposite Jerusalem.

THE TEACHER'S LIBRARY.

All lives of Christ, worthy of the name, will be found to contain some material on the experience of Christ in Gethsemane. For our lesson especially, most commentaries on Matthew's Gospel will be found helpful, but especially those by Broadus, G. Campbell Morgan, J. P. Lange, and Alfred Plummer.

On the entire Gethsemane experience, see J. R. MacDuff: *Memories of Olivet*, 300–329; K. Schilder: *Christ in His Suffering*, 289–392 (especially for verse 49, see pp. 379–392); Alexander Whyte: *Lord Teach Us to Pray*, 130–142; G. Campbell Morgan: *The Westminster Pulpit*, Vol. 7, 201–208; A. M. Fairbairn: *Studies in the Life of Christ*, 239–257; J. C. Cox: *Six Meditations on the Gardens of Scripture*, 95–118; David M'Intyre: *The Prayer Life of Our Lord*, 117–123; William Evans: *From the Upper Room to the Empty Tomb*, 109–145; F. W. Krummacher: *The Suffering Saviour*, 95–118 (these pages are wonderfully rich; nothing else like them anywhere that we know of); A. Tholuck: *Light from the Cross*, 125–140; A. E. Garvie: *Studies in the Inner Life of Jesus*, 374–388; three sermons by G. H. Morrison, W. L. Walker, and W. J. Townsend in *God's Garden*, 1–14, 137–148, 215–228; and Alexander Maclaren: *Expositions of Holy Scripture, St. Matthew 18–28*, 262–270.

On the particular experience and conduct of Simon Peter in Gethsemane we are surprised to find that practically all the lives of Peter are here most inadequate, with the single exception of the three splendid chapters in Charles S. Robinson's *Simon Peter: His Later Life and Labors* (New York, 1894), 82–108. We know of nothing worth consulting on the experience of John in the garden of Gethsemane, except a few paragraphs in James M. MacDonald's *Life and Writings of St. John* (London, 1877), 92–94, and even this is not at all adequate.

For sermonic material, on Matthew 26 : 39 see F. F. Shannon: *The Infinite Artist*, 26–39; F. W. Robertson: *Sermons Preached at Brighton*, 644–651; on verses 40, 41, see the unusually fine chapter in G. H. Knight: *The Master's Questions to His Disciples*, 290–296; on verse 45, J. S. Holden: *Life's Floodtide*, 152–177; on John 18 : 11, see G. H. Knight, as above, 311–317; J. S. Holden: *Redeeming Vision*, 126–134. On the geographical and historical aspects of Gethsemane, see Gustaf Dalman: *Sacred Sites and Ways*, 261–268, 320–327; W. D. MacCrackan: *The New Palestine*, 163–167; and, of course, articles on Gethsemane in all the more important Bible dictionaries.

INTRODUCTION.

The experience of our Lord in the garden of Gethsemane the night of His betrayal is recorded in detail in all three of the Synoptic Gospels (see also Mark 14 : 26, 32–42; Luke 22 : 39–46), and is referred to in John's Gospel (18 : 1). Inasmuch as this particular lesson falls in a quarter in which we are to particularly study the lives of the apostles Peter and John, the editor believes that in the interpretation of this week's lesson most of the emphasis should be placed upon the actions and conduct of the two disciples, rather than upon Christ's own agony in the garden. For those who wish a full consideration of Christ's own experience, see the exposition of the lesson for March 10, in the volume of *Peloubet's Select Notes* for 1940. In his very rich chapters on this event in our Lord's life, Krummacher expresses exactly the mood of every reverent Bible student when he approaches this particularly sacred page: "I confess that whenever I am called upon to treat of the sacred mysteries of Gethsemane, I cannot divest myself of a certain degree of awe. I feel as if there stood at the gate of that garden a cherub, who, if not with a flaming sword, yet with a repelling gesture, refused admittance, and emphatically repeated our Lord's injunction to tarry outside, while He retires to pray. . . . But the gospel brings the mysterious narrative before us for consideration, and hence it is incumbent upon us to enter into its sacred gloom, and seek to comprehend as much of it as human apprehension is capable of." — *F. W. Krummacher.*

Dr. Alfred Plummer very aptly reminds us: "Perhaps the evangelist had no such intention, but they exhibit a tragic irony in placing our Lord's prayer in the garden immediately after the confident boasting of Peter and his companions. The apostles are so sure of their own strength that they will not allow the possibility of failure, even when they are forewarned of it by Christ. The Son of Man is so conscious of the weakness of humanity that He prays to the Father that He may be spared the approaching trial. He feels the need of being strengthened by prayer, and although He at other times followed His own rule (6 : 6) of praying in retirement (14 : 23), here He seems to have desired the company and sympathy of His three most intimate disciples."

Matthew 26 : 36. Then cometh Jesus with them unto a place called Gethsemane, and saith unto his disciples, Sit ye here, while I go yonder and pray.

37. And he took with him Peter and the two sons of Zebedee, and began to be sorrowful and sore troubled.

I. **THE LORD LEADS PETER AND JOHN TO GETHSEMANE,** Matthew 26 : 36, 37. 36. **Then cometh Jesus with them unto a place called Gethsemane, and saith unto his disciples, Sit ye here, while I go yonder and pray.** "The name Gethsemane means oil-press. But the place was not simply an oil-press, for John calls it a garden or orchard, probably containing fruit trees and flowers, as well as vegetables. Gethsemane is now shown as a small enclosure lying just where the three roads across the Mount of Olives branch off at its base (see on 21 : 1), and between the central and southern roads, both of which lead to Bethany. This enclosure is of somewhat less than an acre, and contains several very old olive trees, looking at a distance like large old apple trees. These identical trees appear to be traced back for many centuries. But they cannot have existed in our Lord's time, for Josephus tells us that the Romans, in order to build their mounds about the walls, cut down all the trees for ten or twelve miles around the city, so that the region that had been so beautiful with trees and gardens was now desolate on every side, and a pitiable, mournful spectacle. . . . The real Gethsemane was probably quite near this enclosed place. As 'Jesus ofttimes resorted thither with his disciples,' so that Judas knew the place, we naturally think of it as near the way to and from Bethany. If not a small public garden or park, it was owned by a public-spirited man who allowed visitors to enter at will, particularly during the great festivals, or else by some friend of Jesus, like the owner of the house in which He had eaten the passover." — *J. A. Broadus.* No doubt all the eleven disciples were with our Lord as He approached Gethsemane, Judas having already separated from them and being at this time in the company of those who were about to arrest Jesus. 37. **And he took with him Peter and the two sons of Zebedee, and began to be sorrowful and sore troubled.** These three disciples — Peter, James, and John — are always named in the first group of four among the Twelve (see Matt. 10 : 2); they alone had accompanied our Lord when He raised the daughter of Jaïrus from the dead (Matt. 9 : 18, 19, 23–26, etc.); and they alone were with our Lord on the mount of transfiguration (Matt. 17). "There is something remarkable in Matthew's expression, 'He began to be sorrowful,' as if a sudden wave of emotion, breaking over His soul, had swept His human sensibilities before it. The strange word translated by the Revisers 'sore troubled' is of uncertain derivation, and may possibly be simply intended to intensify the idea of sorrow; but more probably it adds another element, which Bishop Lightfoot describes as 'the confused, restless, half-distracted state which is produced by physical derangement or mental distress.' A storm of agitation and bewilderment broke His calm, and forced from His patient lips, little wont to speak of His own emotions, or to seek for sympathy, the unutterably pathetic cry, 'My soul is exceeding sorrowful' — compassed about with sorrow, as the word means — 'even unto death.' No feeble explanation

From a photograph by Wilson.

The Garden of Gethsemane.

38. Then saith he unto them, My soul is exceeding sorrowful, even unto death: abide ye here, and watch with me.

39. And he went forward a little, and fell on his face, and prayed, saying, My Father, if it be possible, let this cup pass away from me: nevertheless, not as I will, but as thou wilt.

---

of these words does justice to the abyss of woe into which they let us dimly look. They tell the fact, that, a little more and the body would have sunk under the burden. He knew the limits of human endurance, for 'all things were made by him,' and, knowing it, He saw that He had grazed the very edge. Out of the darkness He reaches a hand to feel for the grasp of a friend, and piteously asks these humble lovers to stay beside Him, not that they could help Him to bear the weight, but that their presence had some solace in it. His agony must be endured alone, therefore He bade them tarry there; but He desired to have them at hand, therefore He went but 'a little forward.' They could not bear it with Him, but they could 'watch with' Him, and that poor comfort is all He asks. No word came from them. They were, no doubt, awed into silence, as the truest sympathy is used to be, in the presence of a great grief." — *Alexander Maclaren.*

II. **THE COMMAND TO WATCH,** Matthew 26 : 38. 38. **Then saith he unto them, My soul is exceeding sorrowful, even unto death: abide ye here, and watch with me.** "There are times when even a little child would be a defense for a strong man. There are hours of fear in which, could we but feel a child's little touch, we should be men again. Christ would have with Him the very men who were going to flee away from Him. He would have these men remain to give Him such little comfort as was in the power of man to give under circumstances so tragic." — *Joseph Parker.*

The Sleep of the Disciples.

III. **THE DISCIPLES SLEEP WHILE JESUS PRAYS,** Matthew 26 : 39–44. 39. **And he went forward a little, and fell on his face, and prayed, saying, My Father, if it be possible, let this cup pass away from me: nevertheless, not as I will, but as thou wilt.** "Three elements are distinguishable in our Lord's prayer. There is, first, the sense of Sonship, which underlies all, and was never more clear than at that awful moment. Then there is the recoil from 'the cup,' which natural instinct could not but feel, though sinlessly. The flesh shrank from the Cross, which else had been no suffering; and if no suffering, then had been no atonement. His manhood would not have been like ours, nor His sorrows our pattern, if He had not thus drawn back, in His sensitive humanity, from the awful prospect now so near. But natural instinct is one thing, and the controlling will another. However currents may have tossed the vessel, the firm hand at the helm never suffered them to change her course. The will, which in this prayer He seems so strangely to separate from

40. And he cometh unto the disciples, and findeth them sleeping, and saith unto Peter, What, could ye not watch with me one hour?
41. Watch and pray, that ye enter not into temptation: the spirit indeed is willing, but the flesh is weak.

the Father's, even in the act of submission, was the will which wishes, not that which resolves. His fixed purpose to die for the world's sin never wavered. The shrinking does not reach the point of absolutely and unconditionally asking that the cup might pass. Even in the act of uttering the wish, it is limited by that 'if it be possible,' which can only mean — possible, in view of the great purpose for which He came. That is to be accomplished, at any cost; and unless it can be accomplished though the cup be withdrawn, He does not even wish, much less will, that it should be withdrawn. So, the third element in the prayer is the utter resignation to the Father's will, in which submission He found peace, as we do." — *Alexander Maclaren*. 40. **And he cometh unto the disciples, and findeth them sleeping, and saith unto Peter, What, could ye not watch with me one hour?** I think the words of Alexander Whyte buried away in a now little read periodical of forty years ago, are powerfully pathetic. "His three disciples were indeed within a stonecast of the scene of His agony, but they were fast asleep, that the Scripture might be fulfilled, 'I have trodden the winepress alone and of the people there was none with me.' . . . Had He, after rising from His vigil, with His face pouring sweat of blood, found Peter on his knees, it would have been more to Him than an angel from heaven strengthening Him. Instead He found that disciple three times fast asleep — Peter who had sworn at the table that the others might do as they pleased, but he would die with his Master." "They were to watch *with* Him, not *over* Him. He had to go through *this* agony, as all others, alone. He never at any time asked His disciples to pray *for Him*. He never even prayed *with* them, though He constantly prayed *for* them. He does not now ask them to intercede for Him, only to pray for themselves. All life through He was as One apart, doing a work in which none could bear Him company. He often asked their *faith;* He asked their *love;* He asked their *sympathy;* but He never asked their *prayers*. He only showed them, by word and by example, how to pray. . . . But the secret of their unwatchfulness is clear enough. They had never yet completely taken in what He had so often said to them about the coming *cross*. They could not even yet bring themselves to believe that He would really die — die so awfully, die so soon. And they were also completely ignorant of their own weakness. They credited themselves with a valiant faith that existed only in their own imaginations. They were full of the self-security and self-confidence that always precede a fall. . . . I sleep sometimes from self-indulgence, not from weariness. I sleep because I cease to *feel* acutely the danger that may be near. My sleep is too often the sleep of earthly-mindedness, in which I have pleasant dreams, but they are all of earthly, and not of heavenly, things; visions indeed, but not visions of a glory that excelleth, only of the world that passeth away. When I think of my indolence in my Master's service, of my indifference to His glory, of my self-indulgence when He is calling for the sacrifice of self in His behalf, I am forced to feel that I am not *living* my life, but *sleeping it away*. Well for me that my Master does not sleep when caring for *my* interests, as I do when entrusted with *His!* If my Lord were not more mindful of His promises to me than I am of mine to Him I would be undone forever." — *G. H. Knight*. 41. **Watch and pray, that ye enter not into temptation: the spirit indeed is willing, but the flesh is weak.** "That the disciples struggled to be wakeful need not be doubted. They had been charged to watch, and at such a time they would be anxious to be loyal to the Lord's commands. Moreover, the saying, 'The spirit is willing, but the flesh is weak,' implies that the disciples had been willing to obey but had been overcome by frailty of the flesh. If Christ needed to be strengthened by prayer, how much more His faulty disciples! He had entered into temptation and had felt the full strain; He desires therefore that they may be protected as He has been by prayer." — *Alfred Plummer*. "We are never told anything about the *object* of watching. We cannot watch Satan, who is too elusive; nor can we watch our circumstances which are so variable. We cannot watch our sins, because we have no conception of their real character. We cannot watch ourselves because of our lack of understanding and control. It is therefore probable that absence of any object of watching is intended to suggest our watching Christ, for by 'looking off unto Jesus' and being occupied with Him we are guarded against sudden circumstances, sin, and self. Then with watching comes prayer, and as we are told of the

42. Again a second time he went away, and prayed, saying, My Father, if this cannot pass away, except I drink it, thy will be done.
43. And he came again and found them sleeping, for their eyes were heavy.
44. And he left them again, and went away, and prayed a third time, saying again the same words.
45. Then cometh he to the disciples, and saith unto them, Sleep on now, and take your rest: behold, the hour is at hand, and the Son of man is betrayed into the hands of sinners.

---

danger we are enabled to meet it in divine strength. These two combining, as we have seen, spiritual alertness and spiritual dependence, may be summed up in the one word faith, or trust, in the Master. Such faith would have given them fortitude, insight, knowledge of self and spiritual experience. The more we trust the more we know, the more we see, the more we feel, the more we do." — *W. H. Griffith Thomas.*

42. **Again a second time he went away, and prayed, saying, My Father, if this cannot pass away, except I drink it, thy will be done.** 43. **And he came again and found them sleeping, for their eyes were heavy.** There is something almost inconceivably tragic in the contrast set forth in these two verses. Our Lord's day had been more exhausting, more fatiguing than that which the disciples had just come through. Yet they yield to the weakness of flesh, while He deliberately resists the call of the flesh to rest. More than that, they had not asked Him to pray; He had asked them to pray, and we would have thought that even if they had first yielded to the temptation to fall asleep, now once rebuked by Him, they would have used every conceivable device for keeping awake and praying with Him that night. How truly here, and so often in our own lives, does the flesh dominate the spirit, and do we give way to the baser demands of our nature, even when we know we are disappointing the Lord Jesus Christ! Certainly the disciples *could* have kept awake, if they were *determined* enough to do so.

Head of Christ. Hofmann.
From "Christ in Gethsemane."

44. **And he left them again, and went away, and prayed a third time, saying again the same words.** We are reminded here of Paul praying three times for the Lord to take from him the thorn which was so agonizing to his flesh (2 Cor. 12 : 8). Of course, it was our Lord who was facing death, not the disciples, and thus He was more conscious of the terribleness of the suffering He faced and of the need for strength to endure them, than the disciples. They could not die the death He was about to die, but they could have strengthened Him for this terrible experience if they had that night been faithful to Him. It should be remembered that when the night is gone, the opportunity is over; the next night our Lord's body was cold in the tomb of Joseph of Arimathea. Opportunities to help others, to strengthen others, to encourage others, in times of great spiritual distress and agony, are soon over; if we are not faithful in the hour we are needed, the hour will soon come when nothing we can do will be of any help.

IV. **THE FINAL WORDS IN THE GARDEN,** Matthew 26 : 45, 46. 45. **Then cometh he to the disciples, and saith unto them, Sleep on now, and take your rest:**

46. Arise, let us be going: behold, he is at hand that betrayeth me.

John 18 : 10. Simon Peter therefore having a sword drew it, and struck the high priest's servant, and cut off his right ear. Now the servant's name was Malchus.

---

behold, the hour is at hand, and the Son of man is betrayed into the hands of sinners. There are two different opinions regarding the exact meaning of our Lord's words found in this sentence. We take the privilege of presenting both of them. "A great many of the old expositors declare that when He spoke to them of taking their rest He spoke satirically. That is impossible. Satire had its place in His method; it had often played like summer lightning, clearing the atmosphere. But this was no satire. Then what did He mean? We must put a break between verses 45 and 46. He came back to them, His own triumph won, and they were still drowsy, and opened their eyes as He came perchance, and He quietly said to them, There is little time left, sleep on now. And they went back to sleep and He watched over them." — *G. Campbell Morgan*. The words of Dr. Schilder, whose three monumental volumes on the suffering of our Lord form the greatest contribution to an understanding of these hours that has been written in the last quarter of a century, has written some words that, while somewhat mystical and profound, yet are worth our most careful consideration. "Ironically, He looks upon these who are able to sleep amid the alarm which hell is sounding against heaven, amid the ringing of bells whose heaven-sent sounds reverberate through the spheres. Jesus endures it now, without toleration, but with perfect calm, without perturbation. He knows now, For such as these I shall die. He knows His death will not be the futile sacrifice of friendship for friendship, but one born of the perfect will to fulfill the demands of justice, through love. He knows now that Gethsemane and Golgotha are so awfully sublime because the Bridegroom can only give Himself to a bride who can give nothing, but can only receive. He knows there is a heavenly irony; He knows that, as He looks upon those sleeping disciples. The covenant of grace, like every covenant, has two parties; and yet, in a sense, there is only one party, for the Church is the sleeping beauty who cannot even remain awake in the hour of the Bridegroom's coming. Now He knows that He is the Bridegroom who will buy His bride; but He knows, too, that only by purchase can He make her His bride.

"Sleep on now and rest. . . .

"The phrase expresses a unification of desires by virtue of the fear of God's name. It expresses a unique victory on the part of the perfect man who labored in prayer as man never labored before. With these words He who was undone in the depths strides to His heights again." — *K. Schilder*. 46. **Arise, let us be going: behold, he is at hand that betrayeth me.** Christ here means, Let us go and meet this peril. He knew that the hour of His betrayal and arrest had come, and He was prepared to meet it, and knew that it could not now be postponed. Of course, there is no suggestion here that our Lord was tempted to escape from the garden or to avoid the arrest that He knew would take place immediately. The calm of our Lord, the confidence, the strength, the perfect wisdom and perfect poise are in contrast to the confusion and dullness and weakness, and it seems, the pathetic silence, of the three apostles. "Whether Jesus heard the approach of the betrayer with the crowd around Him, or saw the lights, or just felt the proximity of the traitor before he was there, we do not know and it matters little. The scene is pictured as it happened, with lifelike power." — *A. T. Robertson*.

V. PETER FOOLISHLY THINKS HE MUST DEFEND CHRIST WITH A SWORD, John 18 : 10. **Simon Peter therefore having a sword drew it, and struck the high priest's servant, and cut off his right ear. Now the servant's name was Malchus.** Though the editor has not exactly seen it so stated in any commentary on this passage, it is yet almost axiomatic, definitely proved in this particular incident, that when we do not do what Christ wants us to do for Him, we are sure, sooner or later, and generally sooner, to do something He does not want us to do. Peter did not stay awake, as the Lord told him to, and now he is going to do something he thinks for the Lord, which was directly contrary to Christ's will. Peter's rashness on this occasion is recorded by all the four evangelists, but John alone mentions the name of Malchus. "It is impossible to tell what position the servant held, or why the evangelist records the name, which was not an uncommon one. The servant's prominent action evidently marked him out for St. Peter's attack." — *B. F. Westcott*. 11. **Jesus therefore said unto Peter, Put up the sword into the**

11. Jesus therefore said unto Peter, Put up the sword into the sheath:
the cup which the Father hath given me, shall I not drink it?
12. So the band and the chief captain, and the officers of the Jews, seized
Jesus and bound him.

---

the sheath: the cup which the Father hath given me, shall I not drink it? "Christ's aside to Peter is in a sense the same as in Matthew 26 : 52, but in terser and more graphic words. The act was an impulse, unreasoning but natural, and only too likely to be followed by the swing of the pendulum to the other side." — *George Reith.* The cup to which our Lord here refers is a symbolic expression, by which is meant all the suffering, the bitterness, the loneliness of the entire passion episode, culminating in Christ's death upon the cross. Christ this night had discovered in the agony of His prayer, that this path of suffering could never be avoided if He was to remain in the will of God, and remain He would, however terrible the cost. When a strong man's will is made up nothing can change it. This little, feeble attempt of Peter, this flurry of superficial courage, does not in any way arouse some false hope in Christ's heart that they might be able to fight their way out of the garden. Where Peter was ignorant, Christ's knowledge was abundant. "This blow was aimed in reality at the entire plan of redemption. If Peter meant to accomplish anything, he meant to liberate Christ from arrest. If he had succeeded, how could this mission of our Redeemer have been fulfilled? If there should be no death of the Surety, there could be no sacrifice made for the sinner; then there would fail all hope of atonement; then the seed of the woman could never bruise the serpent's head. It is an amazing fact in Simon Peter's history that twice before he had forgotten such considerations, and been stingingly rebuked for his officious sympathy and interference with divine purposes. Yet here he is again! . . . This blow of Peter was reckless. For what could that little band of disciples hope to do? If they intended to fight, two swords were too few; if they desired conciliation, one sword was quite too many. The assault which was made so rashly must have roused those soldiers into wrathful excitement. It was the majesty of the Master's calmness which threw them down to the ground backward. They were superstitious, and easily controlled through their fears. But this rough appeal to arms surrendered every advantage. Use of the sword was just in their line; it presumed that Jesus had nothing else to use but iron weapons. And that many a blade flashed back the torchlight, as these military men sprang to such a challenge, it needs no effort to imagine. The entire Church on earth might have been swept out of existence in a swift instant of madness, but for the presence of its divine Head." — *Charles S. Robinson.*

VI. **THE ARREST OF JESUS,** John 18 : 12. 12. **So the band and the chief captain, and the officers of the Jews, seized Jesus and bound him.** Westcott says that the Greek of this verse could be paraphrased, "therefore the band," etc., meaning that seeing there was no longer any resistance the officers could arrest the Lord. "All combine to take the willing prisoner. In particular, it will be observed that the action of the Roman guard is now noticed. They probably secured the Lord and delivered Him to the priest's servants 'bound' (cf. v. 24). It was the policy of the priestly party to represent Christ as a dangerous enemy to public order; and perhaps they really feared a rescue by the people (Matt. 26 : 5)." — *B. F. Westcott.* Inasmuch as this verse does not belong directly to the account of our Lord's being forsaken by the disciples, which is what we have been studying today, we do not comment further upon it.

There are four souls participating in the drama of this hour; our Lord, and three of His own disciples, we might say, the best three. Around these four souls crowd the temptations of the evil one. This is the beginning of that great day when once and for all the redemption of man will be wrought out by the sacrifice of Christ, God's Son. If failure should mark the work of this hour, then man remains forever hopeless, bound and lost. As far as mere men are concerned, Satan won. The flesh was dominant. Spiritual things were submerged, but there was another Man there, Son of Mary, Son of Man, the Man from heaven, the Second Man, the Last Adam, and He by prayer, by fully entering into the eternal purposes of the Godhead, by love, by the suppression of the flesh, by the indwelling of the Spirit of God, by the sovereignty of holiness — this Man, God and Man, defeated Satan at every point, and alone, forsaken, His sorrow unshared, His suffering unheeded, His request for companionship ungranted — this Man, our Saviour and Redeemer, continued to be ever triumphant over evil, continued to abide in the will of God; and by that will, and that death, and that holiness, hath saved and sanctified all those who put their trust in Him. There have been great battles on earth between the forces of righteousness and the armies of wicked nations, but there has never been a conflict with such enormous consequences for the welfare and the liberty, and the hope and the life of men as the conflict this night, which beginning will end before another day is passed, in the defeat of principalities and powers, in the casting down of Satan, in the offering up of a sacrifice which is sufficient to save every man from his sins forever.

Why did our Lord take the three disciples into the garden of Gethsemane? What would have been different if the disciples had done what our Lord asked them to do — to watch and pray? Fundamentally, what are some of the reasons you can suggest why our Lord remained awake and continued to pray while Peter, James, and John fell asleep, and as far as we know, did not pray at all? Why do you think Peter is so silent this hour when normally we find him fluent of speech? Do you think by our faithfulness in prayer we can help those who are severely tested with temptation to go through an hour of testing triumphantly?

LESSON IV. — April 25.

THE RISEN LORD (EASTER SUNDAY). — John 20 : 1–17.

GOLDEN TEXT. — *He is risen.* MARK 16 : 6.

Devotional Reading: 1 Corinthians 15 : 50–58.
Beginner Topic: MARY'S GLAD STORY.
Lesson Material: John 20 : 1–18.
Memory Verse: Thou art nigh, O Jehovah. Psalm 119 : 151.
Primary Topic: A GLAD, GLAD DAY.
Lesson Material: John 20 : 1–18.
Memory Verse: The Living One; and I was dead, and behold, I am alive for evermore. Revelation 1 : 18.
Junior Topic: MARY MAGDALENE'S GLAD TIDINGS.
Lesson Material: John 20 : 1–18.
Memory Verse: We bring you good tidings of the promise made unto the fathers, that God hath fulfilled . . . in that he raised up Jesus. Acts 13 : 32, 33.
Intermediate and Senior Topic: WHAT JOHN FOUND AT JESUS' TOMB.
Topic for Young People and Adults: WHAT THE TOMB REVEALED TO JOHN.

THE TEACHER AND HIS CLASS.

The Younger Classes may be reminded that when they come into a city for a visit it is their loved ones whom they wish to see, or, perhaps, some dear friend, while the other thousands and thousands of people or casual acquaintances are not visited. Those who are close to us are given the choicest things of our life, both materially and socially. We love to show favors to those who are near to us, and especially to those who have in some way manifested their love for us. Here our Lord, rising from the dead on Easter morning, showed Himself first, and spoke first, to one who had faithfully ministered to Him for over two years, and who, when others had left the tomb, remained to find out, if possible, what had happened to the body of her Lord.

The Older Classes will here find one of the most exquisite narratives in all the Word of God. Especially will this prove of greatest value in the teaching of women's Bible classes, for it seems that nowhere else perhaps in the Word of God, except in the birth of our Lord of Mary of Nazareth, was womanhood ever quite so honored as on this day when Christ appeared, first of all, not to one of the eleven disciples, nor to any great one, but to her out of whom He had cast seven demons. The entire narrative is a perfect illustration of the tenderness, the compassion, the thoughtfulness, and understandingness of our Lord.

THE LESSON IN ITS SETTING.

Time. — The resurrection of our Lord took place on Sunday morning, April 9, A.D. 30.

Place. — We do not know exactly where the burial and resurrection of our Lord took place, but we do know that he was buried in the rock tomb of Joseph of Arimathea outside the city wall of Jerusalem, which undoubtedly means north of the city and near the place where He was crucified.

THE PLAN OF THE LESSON.

SUBJECT: The Comfort, the Certainty, and the Commission Found in Our Lord's First Words to a Human Individual After He Arose from the Dead.

I. MARY DISCOVERS THE TOMB IS EMPTY AND REPORTS HER DISCOVERY TO THE DISCIPLES, 20 : 1, 2.

II. PETER AND JOHN CONFIRM MARY'S REPORT, 20 : 3–10.

1. What they did when they heard what Mary reported.
2. What they saw.
3. What they concluded.
4. What they did after their visit to the tomb.

III. OUR LORD'S FIRST APPEARANCE AFTER HIS RESURRECTION — TO MARY MAGDALENE, 20 : 11–17.

1. Mary's sorrow, v. 11.
2. Mary's words to the angels, vs. 12, 13.
3. Mary beholds the risen Lord, vs. 14–17.
   a. Jesus' question.
   b. Jesus calls Mary by name.
   c. Jesus' prohibition.
   d. Jesus' commission.

THE TEACHER'S LIBRARY.

All lives of Christ will have some material on this lesson, but most will not be found very adequate. Commentaries will be found indispensable, especially the remarks by Reith and Westcott, and the very full material (30 pages) in Lenski's (comparatively) recent volume. Lange here is poor; others are fair. For a study of Mary Magdalene, see G. Campbell Morgan, in the *Westminster Pulpit*, Vol. 4, 161–168; Walter F. Adeney: *Women of the New Testament*, 195–208; W. M. Mackay: *The Woman of Tact*, 303–314; Abraham Kuyper: *Women of the New Testament*, 23–25; A. T. Robertson: *Some Minor Characters in the New Testament*, 74–86; Alexander Whyte: *Bible Characters: Joseph and Mary to James the Lord's Brother*, 95–103; T. H. Davies: *The Inner Circle*, 149–169; George Milligan in *Women of the Bible*, 217–224.

On this particular event of our Lord's appearance to Mary Magdalene there is nothing to be compared, for richness and devotional value, to a small, rarely-seen volume by that great saint and scholar, Bishop H. C. G. Moule, *Jesus and the Resurrection;* also, see G. H. Morrison: *Footsteps of the Flock*, 281–284; and the relevant chapters in such works on the resurrection as the following: B. F. Westcott: *The Revelation of the Risen Lord;* Henry Latham: *The Risen Master* (very full on the significance of the grave clothes); G. D. Boardman: *Our Risen King's Forty Days;* F. W. Krummacher: *The Risen Redeemer;* H. B. Sweete: *The Appearances of Our Lord After the Passion.* There are many other books on the resurrection of Christ that could be named, but most of them are weak on this particular event. On verse 2, see some excellent words in B. B. Warfield: *Biblical Doctrines*, 586–588; on verse 7, Hugh MacMillan: *The Mystery of Grace*, 312–329; on verses 11–14, G. H. Morrison: *The Ever Open Door*, 109–112; on verses 11–18, the same, *Wings of the Morning*, 97–107 (a beautiful sermon on "Love and Grief"); on verse 13, J. S. Holden: *Life's Flood Tide*, 89–105; H. P. Liddon: *Easter in St. Paul's*, 12–24; on verse 15, G. H. Knight: *The Master's Questions to His Disciples*, 318–324; on verse 17, W. R. Nicoll: *Sunday Evening*, 181–188; Alexander Maclaren: *After the Resurrection*, 1–14. For a more or less full consideration of the overwhelming evidence for the resurrection of our Lord, and the consideration of many of the modern theories that have been proposed to explain the empty tomb without recognizing the Lord's resurrection, the editor would take the liberty of referring to his chapter, "The Historical Reality of Christ's Resurrection," in his volume, *The Supernaturalness of Christ.*

INTRODUCTORY.

THE MARY OF OUR LESSON.

The Mary of our lesson appears on only three occasions in the gospel history, and never again after Easter Sunday. Her condition before conversion, her deliverance from demon possession, and her devotion to the Lord, as together with other well known women she ministered unto Christ of her substance, are recorded in Luke 8 : 1–3. The implication here is that Mary Magdalene, which means Mary of Magdala (a town on the western shore of the sea of Galilee), was a woman of means. She is next seen at the Cross, and near the tomb of our Lord, together with the women who had accompanied her in ministering to our Lord's needs throughout His fatiguing journeys, preaching and teaching in Palestine (Matt. 27 : 56, 61; Mark 15 : 40, 47; Luke 23 : 49, 55, 56). The appearance to Mary Magdalene on Easter morning is recorded only in John's Gospel. Mary's conversion led her to a life of devotion to the Lord. Her devotion kept her at the Cross when all the disciples had fled, and kept her at the tomb after the other disciples had gone home, and the recognition of this devotion is certainly the reason for our Lord's first appearance to this woman. It is a terrible tragedy in Biblical interpretation that Mary Magdalene should have ever been identified with the sinful woman of Luke 7 : 35–50. Any large dictionary will say that a woman of unchaste habits is sometimes called a "Magdalene," which rests upon this tragic misinterpretation of the Gospels. These two women are absolutely distinct characters.

THE CIRCUMSTANCES ATTENDING OUR LORD'S APPEARANCE TO MARY.

The exact sequence of the events recorded in the Gospels as occurring on Saturday night and Easter morning is very difficult to determine. The following is suggested by Canon Westcott: "Just before 6 P.M., Saturday, Mary Magdalene and Mary

John 20 : 1. Now on the first *day* of the week cometh Mary Magdalene early, while it was yet dark, unto the tomb, and seeth the stone taken away from the tomb.

2. She runneth therefore, and cometh to Simon Peter, and to the other disciple whom Jesus loved, and saith unto them, They have taken away the Lord out of the tomb, and we know not where they have laid him.

3. Peter therefore went forth, and the other disciple, and they went toward the tomb.

4. And they ran both together: and the other disciple outran Peter, and came first to the tomb;

---

the mother of James go to view the sepulchre (Matt. 28 : 1). Soon after that there is the purchase of spices by Mary Magdalene and Mary the mother of James (Mark 16 : 1). Very early on Sunday morning the resurrection occurs, followed by the earthquake, the descent of the angel, and the opening of the tomb (Matt. 28 : 2–4). About 5 A.M., Mary Magdalene, Mary the mother of James, and Siloam, probably with others, start for the sepulchre in the twilight. Mary Magdalene goes before the others and returns at once to Peter and John (John 20 : 1 ff.). About 5 : 30 A.M., Mary's companions reach the sepulchre when the sun had risen (Mark 16 : 2). Then occurs a vision of an angel and the message to the disciples (Matt. 28 : 5 ff.). About 6 : 30 A.M., Peter and John visit the tomb (John 20 : 3–10). Then occurs the vision of two angels to Mary Magdalene, and finally the appearance of the Lord Himself to Mary Magdalene (John 20 : 11–18; Mark 16 : 19)."

Schönherr.

At the Tomb on Easter Morning.

I. **MARY DISCOVERS THE TOMB IS EMPTY AND REPORTS HER DISCOVERY TO THE DISCIPLES,** vs. 1, 2. 1. **Now on the first *day* of the week cometh Mary Magdalene early, while it was yet dark, unto the tomb, and seeth the stone taken away from the tomb.** 2. **She runneth therefore, and cometh to Simon Peter, and to the other disciple whom Jesus loved, and saith unto them, They have taken away the Lord out of the tomb, and we know not where they have laid him.** "What Mary Magdalene saw at the tomb all the rest of the women saw too with the same dismay. They were all convinced that the body of Jesus had been stolen by the Jews. Mary Magdalene's quick thought and her acting instantly on that thought, prevented any of the other women from joining her in running back. We cannot tell where the two disciples, Peter and John, were, nor where the rest of the eleven were. If Mary Magdalene knew where the others were, she knew too where to find these two, and felt that she could count on them, and so flew to where they were. By the pronoun 'they' she means the Jews. Who but they would rifle the grave; not being satisfied with killing Jesus, their hate for Him has now desecrated even His dead body. Although Mary Magdalene thinks He is dead and all His work for nought, she cannot but still call Him 'Lord.' It is a little touch, yet how genuine!" — *R. C. H. Lenski.*

II. **PETER AND JOHN CONFIRM MARY'S REPORT,** vs. 3–10. 3. **Peter therefore went forth, and the other disciple, and they went toward the tomb.** 4. **And they ran both together: and the other disciple outran Peter, and came first to the**

5. And stooping and looking in, he seeth the linen cloths lying; yet entered he not in.
6. Simon Peter therefore also cometh, following him, and entered into the tomb; and he beholdeth the linen cloths lying,

tomb. We have never seen this referred to in any commentary, but the editor has always felt that there was a remarkable parallel between the report concerning the birth of our Lord in Bethlehem, and the report of the empty tomb, which really was the report of His resurrection. When the chief priests and scribes of the people told Herod, and the wise men, that Christ would be born in Bethlehem, not one of them went down to see if this were true, though the Wise Men did. So, likewise, when the guard came back to the city to report to the Sanhedrin that the tomb was empty (Matt. 28 : 11-15), we do not read that any of the Sanhedrin went to the tomb to corroborate this amazing declaration, but Peter and John, disciples of the Lord, hastened to see if this thing was true. " John, being the younger and more agile, arrives first. But his emotion is so strong that he timidly stops at the entrance to the sepulchre, after having looked in. Peter, of a more masculine and practical character, resolutely enters. These details are so natural and so harmonious with the personality of the two disciples, that they bear in themselves the seal of their authenticity." — *F. Godet.*

Peter and John at the Empty Tomb.

5. **And stooping and looking in, he seeth the linen cloths lying; yet entered he not in.** 6. **Simon Peter therefore also cometh, following him, and entered into the tomb; and he beholdeth the linen cloths lying.** The original word used by John, translated " stooping down and looking in," conveys the thought of " looking intently with eager desire and effort at that which is partially concealed." — *B. F. Westcott.* The thing which John makes to be the astonishing phenomenon seen by the disciples is " the linen cloths lying." " Nothing whatever had been done with them, they were merely lying. We are not to imagine that they had been unwound from the body as was done with the grave bands of Lazarus when he came to life (John 11 : 44), neither had they been cut or stripped off in some other way. They lay just as they had been wound about the limbs and body, only the body was no longer in them, and thus the wrappings lay flat. All the aromatic spices were exactly as they had been strewn between the layers of linen, and these layers, one wound over the other, were numerous, so that all these spices could be held between them. No human being, wrapped round and round with bands like this, could possibly slip out of them without greatly disturbing them. They would have to be unwound, or cut through, or cut and stripped off. They would thus, if removed, lie strewn around in disorder or heaped on a pile, or folded up in some way. If the body had been desecrated in the tomb by hostile hands, this kind of evidence would appear. But hostile hands would have carried off the body as it was, wrappings and all, to get it away as soon as possible, and to abuse it later and elsewhere. But here the linen bands were. Both their presence and their undisturbed condition spoke volumes. Jesus was risen from the dead." — *R. C. H. Lenski.* 7. **And the napkin,**

7. And the napkin, that was upon his head, not lying with the linen cloths, but rolled up in a place by itself.

8. Then entered in therefore the other disciple also, who came first to the tomb, and he saw, and believed.

9. For as yet they knew not the scripture, that he must rise again from the dead.

10. So the disciples went away again unto their own home.

11. But Mary was standing without at the tomb weeping: so, as she wept, she stooped and looked into the tomb;

---

that was upon his head, not lying with the linen cloths, but rolled up in a place by itself. "The napkin which had been on the head of Jesus, bound around it to envelop the head, lay in a place apart from the wrappings, neatly folded up, or we might say, rolled up. It had not been snatched off and thrown aside. The perfect participle is passive: somebody had carefully folded this cloth and laid it there in the most orderly way, that it should act as a second witness to testify to the resurrection of Jesus. If both the headcloth and the bands had been folded up, neither would indicate the miracle of the resurrection. Then Peter and John would conclude only that friendly human hands had unclothed the dead body for some strange reason and had taken it away. What these disciples saw was vastly more. One may ask why Jesus had not left the cloth like the bands, simply passing out of it and leaving the fastenings undisturbed. One answer is that then both the cloth and the bands would have uttered the same testimony; then Jesus would have left but one witness. He left two. Folding up the cloth and placing it apart from the bands betrays an ordering hand." — *R. C. H. Lenski.* 8. **Then entered in therefore the other disciple also, who came first to the tomb, and he saw, and believed.** "The exact interpretation of the word 'believed' is difficult. It is not likely that it means simply 'believed that the body had been removed as Mary Magdalene reported.' Such a conclusion was rather a matter of natural and immediate inference from what he saw. The use of the word absolutely rather points to the calm patient acceptance of a mystery as yet in part inexplicable with full confidence in the divine love. The threefold sign of the stone removed, the empty sepulchre, the graveclothes leisurely arranged, indicated something still to be more fully shown, and the Apostle waited in trustful expectation for the interpretation. Perhaps the word may have even a fuller sense, and imply that John believed in some way that the Lord was alive." — *B. F. Westcott.* 9. **For as yet they knew not the scripture, that he must rise again from the dead.** "The disciples had never understood the signification of Scripture with which they were familiar, such as Psalm 2; 16 : 10; Isaiah 53, etc. The Lord had endeavored to enlist their sympathies on the point, had even directly told them that He would die and rise again the third day (Matt. 16 : 21; Mark 8 : 31; Luke 9 : 22)." — *George Reith.* We believe that commentators here have not satisfactorily considered the full implications of this verse. There are many other indications in the Old Testament that resurrection would occur on the third day, as for example: Genesis 1 : 9–13; 40 : 12–20; 42 : 17, 18; Exodus 10 : 22, 23; Leviticus 7 : 17, 18; 19 : 6, 7; Jonah 1 : 17; Hosea 6 : 2. 10. **So the disciples went away again unto their own home.** We have not seen it so referred to, but is there not in the return of the disciples to their home, and the remaining of Mary Magdalene at the tomb, something of a parallel to the end of the seventh chapter of this Gospel, and the beginning of the eighth, "And every man went to his own house; Jesus went unto the mount of Olives"?

III. **OUR LORD'S FIRST APPEARANCE AFTER HIS RESURRECTION TO MARY MAGDELENE,** vs. 11–17.

1. Mary's Sorrow, v. 11. 11. **But Mary was standing without at the tomb weeping: so, as she wept, she stooped and looked into the tomb.** "She was denied the poor comfort even of weeping over His corpse, and paying the last tender rites of reverence and love. Reluctant to abandon all hope, clinging, as we all do, to the outward form which has contained the dear object of love, as if by clinging to it we could bring back what is no longer there, with a woman's persistence and affection, refusing to believe but that still, even after the scrutiny of the two men, some trace might be found of that beloved object, she lingered in the garden; and she once again stooped down, and through her tears looked into the sepulchre." — *George*

12. And she beholdeth two angels in white sitting, one at the head, and one at the feet, where the body of Jesus had lain.

13. And they say unto her, Woman, why weepest thou? She saith unto them, Because they have taken away my Lord, and I know not where they have laid him.

14. When she had thus said, she turned herself back, and beholdeth Jesus standing, and knew not that it was Jesus.

Reith. "There is a kind of love that faces facts, and it is a noble and courageous love. It opens its eyes wide to dark realities, and bowing the head it says, 'I must accept them.' But there is an agony of love that does not act so; it hopes against hope and beats against all evidence. It is only women who can love like that, and it was a love like that which inspired Mary. No one will ever doubt John's love to Jesus. No one will ever doubt the love of Simon. 'Yea, Lord, Thou knowest that I love Thee.' But the fact remains that on that Easter morning Peter and John went to their homes again, and only a woman lingered by the grave. I have not the least doubt that they urged her to go with them. They had been too long with Jesus not to be true gentlemen. It was cold and raw there, and the grass was wet, and it was dangerous for a woman with these Roman soldiers. But Mary simply replied, 'I cannot go.' She must linger and watch in the teeth of all the facts. And I say that measured by a test like that, there is not a disciple who can match the love of Mary." — *G. H. Morrison.*

2. MARY'S WORDS TO THE ANGELS, VS. 12, 13. 12. **And she beholdeth two angels in white sitting, one at the head, and one at the feet, where the body of Jesus had lain.** "In each of the accounts of the resurrection an angelic appearance is recorded — in every case an appearance to the woman who came to the tomb: no angels had been seen by Peter and John (vs. 5, 6); The 'white' garments are the symbol of purity and glory (see the references in the margin, and also Rev. 3 : 4, 5; 6 : 11; 19 : 14, etc.). That one of the angels was 'at the head' and the other 'at the feet where the body of Jesus had lain' is to be regarded as expressive of the fact that the body was wholly under the guardianship of heaven." — *William Milligan.* 13. **And they say unto her, Woman, why weepest thou? She saith unto them, Because they have taken away my Lord, and I know not where they have laid him.** "Love is, as a rule, supremely indifferent to criticism. It has ears and eyes for one object only; it moves straight forward to that on which its heart is fixed; it passes by all other objects — not with pride or disdain — not even with effort. It heeds not their existence. Mary was at that very time gazing on an angelic form, so splendid and so unearthly 'that for fear of him' the soldier-keepers of the grave 'did shake and became as dead men.' To Mary, in that moment of supreme sorrow, this glorious angel was as nothing. All that she cared for, and hoped for, all her purest feeling, all her loftiest thought, had been buried some thirty-five hours ago in that rocky tomb along with the mangled body which they bore away in the evening from the hill of Calvary.

"She does not mean to sit down there in the garden, wring her hands and beat her breast, and cease to inquire and to hope. She will persevere; she will cross-question anyone that she meets, whether it be an angel or a gardener, till she knows the truth. The disappointment does not overmaster her love; her love is still the motive power of her soul; she has her grief, so to say, well in hand and does not mean to despair because she has hitherto met with failure." — *H. P. Liddon.*

3. MARY BEHOLDS THE RISEN LORD, VS. 14–17. 14. **When she had thus said, she turned herself back, and beholdeth Jesus standing, and knew not that it was Jesus.** A great deal has been brought out of this verse that possibly was not originally intended to be taken from it. Now it may be that our Lord was greatly changed, because we read elsewhere that the two who walked with Him on the Emmaus road did not know Him (Luke 24 : 16) but we must not place too much emphasis upon the failure of the disciples at times to recognize their Lord. Is it not true, even in the days before His resurrection when He walked to the disciples on the water, that they seemed not to have recognized that it was the Lord, but thought it was His spirit (Matt. 14 : 26, etc.)? I think C. C. Dobson, in his splendid book, *The Empty Tomb and the Risen Lord*, has excellently summed up some of the reasons why Mary did not at once recognize her Lord. "She fails to recognize Him because her eyes are dim with tears, because she is stooping down, because she sees His form outlined

15. Jesus saith unto her, Woman, why weepest thou? whom seekest thou? She, supposing him to be the gardener, saith unto him, Sir, if thou hast borne him hence, tell me where thou hast laid him, and I will take him away.

16. Jesus saith unto her, Mary. She turneth herself, and saith unto him in Hebrew, Rabboni; which is to say, Teacher.

---

against the rising sun, so that His face is in shadow, because she is not expecting to see Him, because He is perhaps wearing a different kind of cloth, for His old robes had been divided among the soldiers. She is, moreover, only half turned towards Him as is apparent from the fact that in verse 16 she completely turns toward Him. She is simply aware of a man behind her and is too much preoccupied with her thoughts to look closely." 15. **Jesus saith unto her, Woman, why weepest thou? whom seekest thou?** These are the first words of our Lord, as far as we know, spoken to any human being after He had been raised from the dead. "They are an echo of the words of the angel: an echo and something more; for He does not pause at their inquiry. He adds a clause which half interprets the mourner's sorrow, and the mourner's error. The question, 'Why weepest thou?' is deepened, explained, invested with a power of sympathy by the further question, 'Whom seekest thou?' Such sorrow, so the words imply, must be for a person and not for a thing; rightly understood, for the living, and not for the dead." —*B. F. Westcott.* "I am often weeping over losses that turn out to have been no losses at all. The tears that fall at the grave of my affections, or at the grave of my ambitions, may often be, like Mary's, only tears of ignorance; and I may soon discover that 'God, having provided something better for me,' gives me what not merely compensates for the loss, but goes infinitely beyond it, too." — *G. H. Knight.* **She, supposing him to be the gardener, saith unto him, Sir, if thou hast borne him hence, tell me where thou hast laid him, and I will take him away.** "She supposed Him to be the gardener, not because He had on the gardener's clothes, nor because He held the spade, as represented in some pictures, but because no one else was likely to be there at that early hour, and to question her as to her reason for being there. Her answer shows that she thought it possible that it had been found inconvenient to have the body of Jesus in the tomb and that it had been removed to some other place of sepulchre." — *Marcus Dods.* 16. **Jesus saith unto her, Mary.** "We cannot doubt that there would be more of the old tenderness of Jesus in the pronunciation of her name than in the words as yet spoken to her. The very mark, indeed, of the relation between Jesus and His people, when that relation is conceived of in its most tender form, is that

The Risen Lord and Mary Magdalene. Plockhörst.

17. Jesus saith to her, Touch me not; for I am not yet ascended unto the Father: but go unto my brethren, and say to them, I ascend unto my Father and your Father, and my God and your God.

'he calleth his own sheep by name' (10 : 3). We are not to imagine that it is only the sound of the voice that is now recognized by Mary. By the name, by the tone in which the name is uttered, a whole flood of recollections is brought up. All the deepest and most solemn impressions that had been produced upon her by her former intercourse with Jesus are reawakened in power. She recalls not merely what was most human but what was most divine in Him." — *William Milligan.* **She turneth herself, and saith unto him in Hebrew, Rabboni; which is to say, Teacher.** The Authorized Version reads *Master,* which is to be preferred. "This word *Rabboni* occurs also in Mark 10 : 51. It is strictly, 'My Master.' Here only is the term Master applied to the Lord after the resurrection. The preservation of the form is one of those little touches which stamp the evangelist as a Jew of Palestine." — *B. F. Westcott.* 17. **Jesus saith to her, Touch me not; for I am not yet ascended unto the Father: but go unto my brethren and say to them, I ascend unto my Father and your Father, and my God and your God.** The word here translated "touch me not" does not simply mean to touch lightly with the fingers, but to hold, to retain, to cling to. Frequently it is asked why the Lord told Mary not to touch Him, but told Thomas that he might touch Him (John 20 : 27). The incidents are altogether different. The Lord's invitation to Thomas was simply to reach hither his finger to touch His wounds, that he might be convinced of the reality of His resurrection body, whereas with Mary it was her desire to cling to Christ, to hold Him on earth, that she might never lose sight of Him again, and this was utterly contrary to our Lord's purposes for His post-resurrection life and ministry. The prohibition was especially appropriate just at this hour, for Christ must then, that day, ascend to His Father above. I personally believe that our Lord ascended to heaven on the very day on which He arose from the dead, and frequently repeated His ascensions, unseen by the disciples between His various appearances to them during the forty days preceding the final Ascension. "There is in the expressions, 'My brethren,' 'My Father,' 'your Father,' a foretaste, as it were, of the future communion. These terms set forth the indissoluble solidarity which will unite them to Him in the glorious state into which He now enters. He had not until now called them *His* brethren. (The same expression is found again in Matt. 28 : 10.) He calls them His brethren as sharing in the divine adoption which He has acquired for them; they will enjoy with Him filial communion with God Himself. In the name of 'Father' there is filial intimacy; in that of 'God' complete dependence, and this for the disciples as for Jesus Himself. But within this equality, so glorious for the believers, there remains an ineffaceable difference. Jesus does not and cannot say, 'our Father,' 'our God,' because God is not their Father, their God, in the same sense in which He is His Father and His God." — *F. Godet.* Mary Magdalene was not one of the apostles, neither did she, as far as we know, and as far as the custom of the early Church would seem to imply, become a great preacher or herald of the gospel, but she was used by the Lord to bring the first message of His resurrection to the disciples, thus confirming their faith and establishing their hope. So, many a godly woman, while not appearing in pulpits, or moving great multitudes with powerful preaching, has been enabled, by teaching her own children, or teaching a Sunday School class, to be the divinely chosen agent through whom Christ has implanted in the heart of some one who will become a mighty preacher of the Word an abiding conviction of the glory of the risen Lord.

THE WONDER OF CHRIST'S APPEARING FIRST TO MARY MAGDALENE.

"The unceasing wonder of it all is this, that to her *first* He should have showed Himself. Simon Peter had been at the tomb that morning, and 'on this rock,' said Jesus, 'I will build my church.' John had been at the sepulchre that morning — the disciple who had leaned upon Christ's bosom; yet neither to John nor to Peter had there been a whisper — no moving of pierced feet across the garden — all that was kept for a woman out of whom there had been cast seven devils. It is very notable that the first word of Christ after He had risen from the dead was *Woman.* 'Woman, why weepest thou' — these are the first words which fell from the lips of Christ when He arose. And they tell us that though everything seemed different, yet there was one thing which death has failed to alter, and that is the eyes of Christ for those who love Him, and the sympathy of Christ for those who weep. You remember how when Christ was in the wilderness, He was tempted to cast Himself down from the Temple. He was tempted to reveal Himself in startling fashion, as the Jews expected that Messiah would. But Christ resisted that spectacular temptation, and showed Himself quietly to kindred hearts; and now after the grave has done its work, He is the very same Jesus as had His home in Nazareth. There are some arguments for the resurrection of the Lord which I confess do not appeal to me. They are too elaborate and metaphysical; they always leave some loophole of escape. But there is one argument that is irresistible, and to me is overwhelming in its artless evidence, and that is the argument of this sweet incident. I could have believed the story was a myth if Christ had shown Himself upon the Temple steps. Had He appeared to Pilate and said, 'Behold the Man,' I could have believed it was an idle story. But that He should pass by Pilate and the people, and His mother and John and James and Simon Peter; that He should show Himself first and foremost to a woman, who had nothing to her credit but love, I tell you that even the genius of a Shakespeare could never have conceived a scene like that. The strange thing is that what Christ did that morning, He has been constantly doing ever since. The first to see Him in all His power and love have been the very last the world expected. Do not pride yourself on your apostolate. There are things that you may miss for all your privileges. And some poor Magdalene, to whom you send the missionary, may be the first to hear the footfall on the grass." — *G. H. Morrison.*

Christ and Mary. Hofmann.

"At what point shall the presence of Christ break through and quicken expectation and faith? Shall He go to the high priest's palace or to Pilate's Praetorium and triumph over their dismay? Shall He go and lay busy plans with this and that group of followers? On the contrary, He appears to a poor woman who can do nothing to celebrate His triumph and might only discredit it, if she proclaimed herself His friend and herald. But thus continuous is the character of Jesus through death and resurrection. The meekness, the true perception of the actual sorrows and wants of men, the sense for spiritual need, the utter disregard of worldly powers and glory, characterize Him now as before." — *Marcus Dods.*

How many different characters appear in this lesson, and how many of them speak? What is the difference in tone and mood conveyed between the word spoken by Mary and the words uttered by the Lord? In how many different ways is our Lord in this lesson shown to be high and lofty, up above all other beings on earth? In how many ways does Christ show His abiding compassion and love for His own? What are the different affirmations for our own hearts which may be with certainty derived from the events and conversations involved in this hour of our Lord's life?

LESSON V. — May 2.

CHRIST'S CHARGE TO PETER. — John 21.

PRINTED TEXT, John 21 : 15-24.

GOLDEN TEXT. — *Greater love hath no man than this, that a man lay down his life for his friends.* JOHN 15 : 13.

Devotional Reading: 1 John 3 : 13-18.
Beginner Topic: BREAKFAST OUTDOORS.
  Lesson Material: John 21.
  Memory Verse: O give thanks unto Jehovah; for he is good. Psalm 136 : 1.
Primary Topic: BREAKFAST OUTDOORS.
  Lesson Material: John 21.
  Memory Verse: O give thanks unto Jehovah; for he is good. Psalm 136 : 1.
Junior Topic: BREAKFAST BY THE SEA.
  Lesson Material: John 21.
  Memory Verse: The Lord . . . reigneth. Let us rejoice and be exceeding glad, and let us give the glory unto him. Revelation 19 : 6, 7.
Intermediate and Senior Topic: PROVING OUR LOVE FOR CHRIST.
Topic for Young People and Adults: LOVE THE MASTER MOTIVE.

THE TEACHER AND HIS CLASS.

The Younger Classes might be asked what they would rather have from their father or mother than any other one thing in the world, something that would last as long as life endured, and something which would bring with it almost every other treasure of life, and without which life would hardly be worth calling life, yet, something that millions of children know nothing about, either because they have lost their parents, or because their parents seemingly never bestow this gift upon them. What is the greatest thing? Of course, it is love. Our Lord said that the *first* commandment was to love the Lord with all our being, and the second one was to love our neighbor as ourselves. He wants our love, for that means everything, and in our lesson we have the story of Jesus asking one of His disciples if he really loved Him.

The Older Classes will find here a perfect illustration of what we might call the practical side of love. We so often think of love as a mere sentiment, connected with moonlight and roses (and these things are all right), but in the New Testament, love is recognized when there are definite expressions of that love. The Lord Jesus, for instance, said that if we loved Him we would keep His commandments (John 14 : 15, 23). Here in our lesson, when Christ hears Peter say that he truly loves the Lord, the Lord gives him *work* to do, which should be prompted by that love. Let us never talk about loving God, and our fellow men, unless there are real manifestations of this love in our daily conduct.

THE LESSON IN ITS SETTING.

Time. — April, A.D. 30.
Place. — The Sea of Galilee.

THE PLAN OF THE LESSON.

SUBJECT: The Power and Mercy of Christ to Restore a Man, Who Had Flagrantly Denied Him, to Perfect Communion with Him and to a Place of Trust.

I. THE DISCIPLES' UNSUCCESSFUL FISHING WITHOUT CHRIST, John 21 : 1-3.

II. THE DISCIPLES' PHENOMENAL OBEDIENCE TO CHRIST, vs. 4-8.

III. THE BREAKFAST TOGETHER, vs. 9-14.
1. The prepared meal.
2. The command.
3. The invitation.
4. The fellowship.

IV. CHRIST'S PERSONAL COMMISSION TO SIMON PETER, vs. 15-23.
1. The three questions, three declarations, and threefold command, vs. 15-17.
2. The prediction of Simon Peter's death, vs. 18, 19 *a*.
3. The first command to follow Christ, v. 19 *b*.
4. The second command to follow Christ, vs. 20-22.
5. The misinterpretation of Christ's words by some, v. 23.

V. THE CONCLUSION OF JOHN'S GOSPEL, vs. 24, 25.

THE TEACHER'S LIBRARY.

The literature on this chapter is simply enormous. First, there are to be considered the commentaries on John's Gospel, of which by far the most exhaustive is the 30-page section in Lenski. Then there are the standard lives of Christ, some of which, at about this period of our Lord's life, get rather weak. Books devoted to the post-resurrection appearances of Christ, are, for some strange reason, not particularly strong in their treatment of this particular episode. Then, of course, there are the books dealing with the miracles of Christ (for this lesson one should particularly consult Trench). Of the many lives of St. Peter, a list will be found in the Introduction to this volume. Especially rich, however, are the pages in Charles S. Robinson's, *Simon Peter: His Later Life and Labors* (1894), 175–267. Superior to all is the precious little volume by Bishop Moule: *Jesus and the Resurrection.* For other chapters, see, L. L. Nash: *Early Morning Scenes in the Bible*, 195–209; J. R. MacDuff: *Memories of Gennesaret*, 343–370. For expository material, see Alexander Maclaren: *Expositions of Holy Scripture, St. John 15–21;* on verse 15, 372–381; verses 18, 19, 382–390; verses 21, 22, 391–401. For sermonic material, on verse 15, see G. H. Knight: *The Master's Questions to His Disciples*, 353–359; on verses 15–17, T. H. Darlow: *The Upward Calling*, 319–322; H. C. G. Moule: *The Secret of the Presence*, 143–154; Andrew Murray: *The Children for Christ*, 328–336; James Hastings: *Great Texts of the Bible, St. John, 13–21*, 416–436; John Henry Jowett: *The Preacher — His Life and Work*, 75–109; on verse 21, John A. Bain: *Questions Answered by Christ*, 235–240; on verses 21, 22, G. H. Knight: *as above:* 360–367; on verse 22, J. Stuart Holden: *Supposition and Certainty*, 117–126; on verse 23, James Hastings: *as above:* 439–458; D. J. Burrell: *God and the People*, 167–177; P. B. Powers: *The "I Wills" of Christ*, 283–300; W. M. Taylor: *The Limitations of Life*, 63–77. On the significance of the various words for love used by Jesus in this passage, see, R. C. Trench: *Synonyms of the New Testament*, 84–86; B. B. Warfield: *Biblical Doctrines*, 589–592.

I. **THE DISCIPLES' UNSUCCESSFUL FISHING WITHOUT CHRIST,** vs. 1–3. The last appearance of our Lord following His resurrection, preceding the one we are about to study, is that which occurred on the Sunday night after Easter, when the eleven disciples were gathered together in the upper room (John 20 : 26–29). How long a period intervened between that appearance and the one of our lesson we have no way of determining. Inasmuch as the entire period between our Lord's resurrection and His ascension was only forty days in length, this seemingly must have been within three or four weeks after Easter Sunday. Those of the apostolic group who were engaged in fishing, before the Lord had called them into His constant companionship, had returned to the sea of Galilee, waiting, it would seem, for further directions from their risen Master. Some have thought it was a mistake to go back to Galilee, but we do not know that in any way they were actually going contrary to the Lord's will at this specific time. "When Peter said, 'I go a fishing,' it is hardly probable that the disciples thought of anything but the supply of their temporal wants. In Peter's being the first to make the proposal, we can hardly fail to see the elements of that character which gave him the prominence he afterward had in the Church of the Redeemer." — *William Milligan.* It has been pointed out by a number of exegetes that the word here translated *took* means, "to lay hold of," and does not seem to be elsewhere used in the sense of catching fish. The whole night long they caught nothing — wasted labor, depressed spirits, and coming to the morning without anything for the supply of the day's needed food.

Fishing Boats on the Sea of Galilee.

II. **THE DISCIPLES' PHENOMENAL SUCCESS IN FISHING WHEN IN OBEDIENCE TO CHRIST,** vs. 4–8. In His own beautiful and gracious way, the Lord Jesus, unrecognized at the moment by His disciples, for reasons which we cannot accurately ascertain, came to where they were laboring, and quietly asked them, in a tone of true solicitousness, "Children, have ye aught to eat?" "The original word here translated *children* marks the difference of age or position, and not the tie of relationship (cf. 1 John 2 : 13, 18). The form of the question in the original suggests a negative answer." — *B. F. Westcott.* "The question which He asks is important, especially the word which is rendered in the Authorized Version 'meat,' but which we have rendered by 'to eat.' For thus we observe the true point of the question — not, ' Have you *caught* fish? ' but, ' Have you fish *to eat?* ' The term, however, was commonly used of fish. Here it seems to refer to provision of fish taken by them for eating when they started. It ought to be carefully noted also that, as is shown by the particular form of the question, it is the *meal* that is before the mind of Jesus. Only when we see this do we gain the true point of view from which to contemplate the whole narrative." — *Milligan* and *Moulton*. Hearing them confess that they had really nothing to eat, our Lord commanded them to cast the net on the right side of the boat, assuring them that they would find what heretofore they had failed to find. Not only was the net immediately full of fishes, but so utterly packed with fishes, that they were not at first able to draw it up into the land. Just at what point we are to say this event was a miracle, it is difficult to

The Draught of Fishes.

determine. In the first place, our Lord certainly showed divine omniscience when He told them that their net would be full if they would cast it on the right side of the ship. But, no doubt, they had been casting that net on both sides of the ship all night. In some miraculous way, our Lord apparently brought this great school of fish at that moment into close proximity at the right side of the boat. We do not think it is necessary to say that Christ at this moment *created* these fish, but He did bring them to the side of the boat, which, of course, is something far beyond the power of any mere man to accomplish.

III. **THE BREAKFAST TOGETHER,** vs. 9–14. What now follows is one of the most delicately beautiful episodes of the entire Gospel history. When the disciples stepped out of the boat on to the shore, they saw " a fire of coals there, and fish laid thereon, and bread." Many explanations have been suggested as to the source from whence Christ derived the fish and bread which He had prepared for their breakfast. It would seem, as Godet, and Westcott, and others admit, that He had, somehow, in a supernatural way, provided them Himself. With Bishop Ryle no doubt we would all agree when he says: " I cannot doubt that this verse records a miracle (Ps. 78 : 19). The burning fire, the fish lying on it, the bread, were all the creation of Him who had but to will a thing and it was done. Ever compassionate, our Lord thought good at this appearing, to show His poor, toiling disciples that He cared for their bodies, as well as their souls, and remembered that they were men." Before breakfast was eaten, Jesus commanded the disciples to bring of the fish which they had taken, a command which Simon Peter immediately obeyed. Drawing the net to the land he found it full of great fishes, to the number of 153. A great deal has been said about the significance of this number, but we have never seen any attempt to symbolically interpret the number that seemed sane and sensible. The verse would seem simply to indicate that these men who had been fishermen for years, were accus-

JOHN 21 : 15. So when they had broken their fast, Jesus saith to Simon Peter, Simon, *son* of John, lovest thou me more than these? He saith unto him, Yea, Lord; thou knowest that I love thee. He saith unto him, Feed my lambs.

16. He saith to him again a second time, Simon, *son* of John, lovest thou me? He saith unto him, Yea, Lord; thou knowest that I love thee. He saith unto him, Tend my sheep.

17. He saith unto him the third time, Simon, *son* of John, lovest thou me? Peter was grieved because he said unto him the third time, Lovest thou me? And he said unto him, Lord, thou knowest all things; thou knowest that I love thee. Jesus saith unto him, Feed my sheep.

---

tomed to counting, and perhaps weighing the fish that were caught, and did so on this occasion according to habit. One should here compare the similar miracle occurring at an earlier period in our Lord's ministry (Luke 5 : 4–7), where, in contrast to what is said here, the net was found to be breaking. "The contrasts all point to the difference between a ministry of trial with the suffering Lord, and a ministry of triumph with a glorified Lord."

Now the disciples hear the Lord invite them to break their fast with the risen Master Himself as host. Whether our Lord Himself partook of the bread and fish we are not told. Wherever Christ is found at a table, He at once becomes the host. He is the One who breaks the bread. He is the One who knows and supplies our every need. When we read in the concluding sentence of this paragraph that, "This is now the third time that Jesus was manifested to the disciples after that he was risen from the dead," we must recognize that this does not limit to three the number of appearances of Christ to different people from the time He was raised from the dead, for of these this would be the seventh; but it is the third time He appeared to the *assembled disciples*, — once on Easter night, once on the Sunday night following, and now, for the third time.

IV. **CHRIST'S PERSONAL COMMISSION TO SIMON PETER,** vs. 15–23. Food is important, drink is important, sleep is important, rest is important, health is important. All these things our Lord knows about, and arranges the circumstances of life so that they may be obtained. But our Lord did not come *primarily* to provide for the inescapable physical needs of a normally healthy person, who is taking his rightful place in the life and work of the world. When He did specifically minister to such needs, He did it always with spiritual ends in view. So now, breakfast being over, Christ turns to Simon Peter and interrogates him about something infinitely higher than food and drink; *e.g.*, his love for the Lord. 15. **So when they had broken their fast, Jesus saith to Simon Peter, Simon, *son* of John, lovest thou me more than these? He saith unto him, Yea, Lord; thou knowest that I love thee. He saith unto him, Feed my lambs.** There was a time, not many days before this, when Peter was boasting of how loyal he was to the Lord Jesus, but all of his boasting proved vain and empty. Christ wants to know from Peter's own lips whether Peter really and truly now loves the Lord and Master. "But now, let me take this as my Master's question to myself; and see how deep it goes, not only into my feelings, but into my life. For it is not, 'Believest thou Me?' or 'Understandest thou Me?' or even, 'Servest thou Me?' It goes closer home. It is, '*Lovest* thou Me?' and all these other things may be where *love* is not. Again, He does not ask, 'Lovest thou My word?' or 'Lovest thou My work?' or 'Lovest thou My brethren?' He asks, 'Lovest thou *Me?*' And yet again, He does not ask, 'Art thou in the company of those that love Me?' He will not let me shelter myself by losing myself in a crowd who all profess to love Him. He brings me out into the light, to stand alone, and asks, 'Lovest *thou* Me?'" — *G. H. Knight.*

16. **He saith to him again the second time, Simon, *son* of John, lovest thou me? He saith unto him, Yea, Lord; thou knowest that I love thee. He saith unto him, Tend my sheep.** 17. **He saith unto him the third time, Simon, *son* of John, lovest thou me? Peter was grieved because he said unto him the third time, Lovest thou me? And he said unto him, Lord, thou knowest all things; thou knowest that I love thee. Jesus saith unto him, Feed my sheep.** "The address of the Lord, thrice repeated, recalls the first words addressed to St. Peter (1 : 42), when he received the surname Cephas (Peter).

" The three questions could not but recall the three denials; and the form of this last question could not but vividly bring back the thought of the failure of personal devotion at the moment of trial. So Peter was grieved not only that the question was put again, but that this third time the phrase was changed; that the question was not only put once again, but at the same time put so as to raise a doubt whether he could indeed rightly claim that modified love which he had professed. His ' grief '

" He saith unto him, Tend my sheep." Raphael.

lay in the deep sense that such a doubt might well be suggested by the past, even if it were at the time ungrounded. Men might reasonably distrust his profession of sincerity after his fall, but he appealed to the Lord (' Thou knowest ')." — *B. F. Westcott.*

It is a very interesting point, one I think I have never seen pointed out in any commentary on John's Gospel, that, up to this time, while we frequently read of the Lord's definitely and specifically loving others, we do not once read of any one's saying that they loved the Lord. May it not be that Christ, before He ascended, really longed for such an expression from the heart of one of His disciples? This is not the first time Christ had seen Peter since the denial, for the Evangelist Luke tells us that the Lord had appeared to Simon somewhere, the circumstances not being recorded, on Easter day (Luke 24 : 34). He is already restored, but now Christ wishes to draw from these lips which had denied Him thrice, a threefold expression of love. " The word for love in verses 15 and 16 is *agapan.* Peter in all three answers uses *philein*, and our Lord uses *philein* in the third question (v. 17). The change is not accidental; and once more we have evidence of the accuracy of the writer; he preserves distinctions which were actually made. Peter's preference for *philein* is doubly intelligible: (1) it is the less exalted word; he is sure of the natural affection which it expresses; he will say nothing about the higher love implied in *agapan;* (2) it is the warmer word; there is a calm discrimination implied in *agapan* which to him seems cold. In the third question Christ takes him at his own standard; he adopts Peter's own word, and thus presses the question more home. . . . Peter had professed to be ready to die for his Master (13 : 37) and had declared that though all the rest might deny Him, he would never do so (Matt. 26 : 33). Jesus recalls this boast by asking him whether he *now* professes to have more loyalty and devotion than the rest. . . . It is Peter's modesty that speaks, and his sense of shame at his own shortcomings. . . . Not only does he change the word for ' love ' from *agapan* to *philein*, says nothing about ' more than these '; he will not venture any more to compare himself with others. Moreover he makes no professions as to the future; experience has taught him that the present is all that he can be sure of. The ' thou ' in ' thou knowest ' is emphatic. This time he will trust the Lord's knowledge of him rather than his own estimate of himself. Not only is he not degraded on account of his fall, he receives a fresh charge and commission. The work of the fisher gives place to that of the shepherd: the souls that have been brought together and won need to be fed and tended. And this Peter must do. . . . The

18. Verily, verily, I say unto thee, When thou wast young, thou girdedst thyself, and walkedst whither thou wouldest: but when thou shalt be old, thou shalt stretch forth thy hands, and another shall gird thee, and carry thee whither thou wouldest not.

19. Now this he spake, signifying by what manner of death he should glorify God. And when he had spoken this, he saith unto him, Follow me.

20. Peter, turning about, seeth the disciple whom Jesus loved following; who also leaned back on his breast at the supper, and said, Lord, who is he that betrayeth thee?

---

word rendered 'feed' means 'supply with food.' The word used here means rather 'be shepherd to.' Tending implies more of guidance and government than feeding does. The lambs, which can go no distance, scarcely require guidance, their chief need is food. The sheep require both. The third time Jesus makes a further concession: He not only ceases to urge the 'more than these,' but He adopts Peter's own word, *philein*. The apostle had rejected Christ's standard and taken one of his own, about which he could be more sure; and Christ now questions the apostles' own standard. This is why 'Peter was grieved' so much; not merely at the threefold question recalling his threefold denial, not merely at his devotion being questioned more than once, but that the humble form of love which he had professed, and that without boastful comparison with others, and without rash promises about the future, should seem to be doubted by his Lord." — *Alfred Plummer.*

"It is as if 'the Shepherd and Bishop of our souls' comes to Peter now leading his entire flock. First he says: 'Look at these lambs in the flock; I am placing them into thy care. They specially need feeding; do thou feed them aright!' Then he points to the whole flock, as if to say: 'Look at all this flock; I am placing the whole of it into thy care. It needs all that shepherding means; be thou its true shepherd!' And even this is not enough for the heart of Jesus. A third time (v. 17) he bids Peter look at the flock, now to impress most deeply upon him what lies in the possessive 'my,' which is used thrice. For now Jesus calls the flock *little sheep*, using the tender, loving diminutive 'my dear sheep,' *i.e.*, my little precious ones, for whom my heart goes out, who need care so much. 'I place them into thy hands; feed them all as I bade thee to feed my lambs!' Thus all the affection Peter has for Jesus is to flow out for the flock which is so precious to Him. As he feeds and shepherds this flock, so will he prove his affection for his Lord. What is so near and dear to the heart of Jesus will be equally near and dear to Peter's heart. . . . The dealings of Jesus with Peter are no special exaltation of Peter, but a serious reminder of his grave defection. The Lord nowhere places Peter over the other apostles." — *R. C. H. Lenski.* 18. **Verily, verily, I say unto thee, When thou wast young, thou girdedst thyself, and walkedst whither thou wouldest: but when thou shalt be old, thou shalt stretch forth thy hands, and another shall gird thee, and carry thee whither thou wouldest not.** 19. **Now this he spake, signifying by what manner of death he should glorify God.** "We now well know what the Lord meant, whatever at the moment these first hearers understood in detail. John at once applies them to his friend's death, and to that death as a special occasion of the glorification of God, and as evidently caused by man — that is, a martyr death. . . . It is practically quite certain that many years before this narrative was written at Ephesus, Peter had died unto the Lord: the prophecy had been fully expounded by the event. And we need not doubt that the death was by crucifixion; indeed, the words here about the outstretched hands may asssure us of this. . . . It is remarkable indeed, this solemn prophecy of suffering, so closely connected with the joy of love and restoration. In one way or another it will surely be thus with every true disciple of our beloved Saviour. To each of us without exception He will assign some cross to bear for Him; to each He will say, in one way or another, 'If you love Me, serve Me; and you shall *suffer for Me*.' Only, the suffering is the 'accident,' the joy the 'substance.' First the pardon, the love, the gladness; then the allotment of the cross, which that deep joy will make so much better than bearable." — *H. C. G. Moule.* **And when he had spoken this, he saith unto him, Follow me.** "The end of martyrdom having now been shown, the Lord repeated the command given before under different circumstances to others (1 : 43; Matt. 8 : 22; 9 : 9; 19 : 21)." — *B. F. Westcott.* 20. **Peter, turning about, seeth the disciple whom Jesus loved following; who also leaned back on his breast at the supper, and said, Lord, who is**

21. Peter therefore seeing him saith to Jesus, Lord, and what shall this man do?

22. Jesus saith unto him, If I will that he tarry till I come, what *is that* to thee? follow thou me.

23. This saying therefore went forth among the brethren, that that disciple should not die: yet Jesus said not unto him, that he should not die; but, If I will that he tarry till I come, what *is that* to thee?

---

he that betrayeth thee? 21. **Peter therefore seeing him saith to Jesus, Lord, and what shall this man do?** "It was a natural question. Although Peter did not know the full meaning of the words just addressed to himself, he felt that they betokened trial, sorrow, perhaps even prison and death. When, therefore, he saw John following Jesus, nothing would more readily occur to him than to ask, And what, Lord, shall be his fate? The answer of Jesus evidently implies that there was something not altogether to be commended in the spirit or in the tone of Peter's question. There was probably impatience of the calm spirit of John, of that calmness which had immediately before contrasted so strikingly with his own impetuosity — for when he had thrown himself into the sea to hasten to his Master's feet, John had remained in the boat dragging to the shore the net with fishes." — *William Milligan.* 22. **Jesus saith unto him, If I will that he tarry till I come, what *is that* to thee? follow thou me.** "What needs to be emphasized in our Lord's answer is that He tells Peter John's course of life and his destiny are matters which Peter has no need to concern himself about so far as to think that he should modify his own action by them. If God has a different career for John, that is not Peter's concern. Peter himself is an individual with a direct personal responsibility to God. And he must decide his course of action as a personal matter between God and himself. 'What is that to thee? Follow thou me.' The words have a similar application to us all. Every course of action which presents itself to us must be decided on directly between ourselves, our conscience, and God." — *John A. Bain.* No doubt the phrase, "till I come," refers to our Lord's second advent. Jesus did not say that He would come during John's lifetime, but He simply laid down the principle that what if He did come it was Peter's business to see that he himself, Simon Peter, was following the Lord. "If you will follow Christ, your old age will be saved from the bitterest pangs that afflict the aged, and will be brightened by future possibilities. Instead of shrinking from the end, we shall put our hands quietly and trustfully into His, as a little child into its mother's soft warm palm, and shall not ask whither He leads, assured that since it is He who leads, we shall be led aright." — *Alexander Maclaren.* 23. **This saying therefore went forth among the brethren, that that disciple should not die: yet Jesus said not unto him, that he should not die; but, If I will that he tarry till I come, what *is that* to thee?** "Only when Peter was actually crucified in the year 64, was the prophecy spoken by Jesus concerning his martyrdom fully and positively understood. So with John — the event would finally make clear just what the Lord's will concerning him was. The statement here made, therefore, means only one thing: it calls upon all to wait till such time as the Lord Himself will make plain what His will concerning John is. In Peter's

Peter Leaps from the Boat to Meet Jesus.

24. This is the disciple that beareth witness of these things, and wrote these things: and we know that his witness is true.

case, Jesus pronounced an actual prophecy; in John's he declined a prophecy, and left John's career and end wholly in the secrecy of His will. Verse 23 is of decisive importance for the genuineness and the authorship of the Fourth Gospel. The report: 'This disciple does not die,' was spread among the brethren when chapter 21 was being written. But this report could not stand a single day beyond the date of John's death. The moment John died, the words of Jesus concerning John would either have to be abandoned as containing a prophecy about John, or some other meaning than this that John is not to die would have to be connected with Jesus' words. With John dead, nobody could say: 'He dies not.' With John dead, nobody could write that brethren are reporting: 'He dies not,' unless he should add: 'But he died nevertheless.' This proves most completely that when verse 23 was written, John was alive, and John as well as the writers of this chapter were waiting to see what the Lord's will would be concerning him. With John alive when chapter 21 was written, he certainly was equally alive when the previous twenty chapters were written. And thus once more, in the most decisive way, the Gospel itself settles its genuineness and its authorship." — *R. C. H. Lenski.*

V. **THE CONCLUSION OF JOHN'S GOSPEL,** vs. 24, 25. 24. **This is the disciple that beareth witness of these things, and wrote these things: and we know that his witness is true.** This verse is "an addition obviously by another, and probably later, man, attesting the identity of the writer of this Gospel with John, and therefore the authenticity of the foregoing record and the credibility of the writer of it. It is usually ascribed to one, or more, or all, of the elders of the church at Ephesus. We cannot tell for certain; but that these verses are an integral portion of the Gospel is indisputable." — *George Reith.* (Cf. for the phraseology here used, 1 John 1; 13 : 14; 5 : 18–20; 3 John 12.) "This plural 'we know' cannot possibly be reduced to a singular. It is no mere editorial or a majestic plural, for John never uses such a plural. He could not do so here by way of exception, for no writer could possibly call himself 'this disciple,' and then in the same breath add 'we know,' meaning 'I know.' Even those who think John himself penned or dictated 21 : 1–23 admit that others are responsible for verses 24 and 25. Who these persons are will never be known; their names can never be recovered. All that we can say is that they must have been the presbyters of Ephesus, the prominent leaders of the churches associated with John. 'We know' is weighty, and in writing this down through the hand of one of their number they fully realize what weight this their attestation will have for all the other churches to whom this new Gospel record is brought. They know on direct and certain evidence. John has been in their midst for many years, they know his entire history. Their knowledge reaches back to other apostles, with whose testimony they could and did compare that of John. These apostles need not all have been in Ephesus itself, for the presbyters could have known and conferred with them elsewhere. Finally, they had the other evangelists. Thus the weight of 'we know' is ample. The testimony of the presbyters is not added to John's Gospel as though without such certification the veracity of John's Gospel would be subject to doubt." — *R. C. H. Lenski.*

"And there are also many other things which Jesus did, the which if they should be written every one, I suppose that even the world itself would not contain the books that should be written." Of course, this is a figure of speech, a hyperbole expressing a great truth that thousands and thousands of volumes would not exhaust a complete record of all that Jesus did during His life on earth. "The attempts which century after century continue to be made to write the 'Life of Christ' seem to prove that even the fragments that have come down to us of that 'Life' have been found in their many-sidedness and profundity to be practically inexhaustible. After all that the piety and learning of eighteen hundred years have accomplished, Christians remain still unsatisfied, still unconvinced, that the most has been made of the very fragmentary account of scarcely a tenth portion of the Lord's life on earth. What would be needed to make even this tenth complete? What, therefore, did complete the whole?" — *Alfred Plummer.*

Peter did not know when the morning sun rose this day that he had come to one of the great crises of his life, and that from this time on he would be an altogether different man. He beheld one more miracle, no, two, performed by his blessed Lord. His own lips had framed a confession of love. He had heard the Lord entrust to him a more solemn task than ever the Lord had previously designated as his life work. He had even heard that day that he was to die a martyr, crucified as the Lord had been crucified for him. From this day on we behold a courageous Peter in place of the cowardly one of a few days ago. We behold a humiliated Peter in place of the boastful one we so often saw previous to this time. We behold one forgetting self and utterly devoted to Christ, never again denying Him, never again cursing and lying — the Rock which Christ once predicted he would be, the apostle worthy of the name which he was now for a full generation to bear.

What different aspects of Christ's character do you find manifested in this lesson? How many different things does Peter do in this lesson? What is the difference between Peter's words on this occasion and the words that he spoke to the Lord on Thursday evening of Passion Week? How does this lesson manifest the faithfulness of Christ to those whom He has called, even when they have failed Him? What hope of ultimate fruitfulness in service does this lesson give for any man, who united to Christ and truly belonging to Him, having fallen into grievous sin, is mercifully restored by the Lord to full communion with Him?

LESSON VI. — May 9.

PETER AND JOHN LEADERS IN THE EARLY CHURCH. — Acts 2 : 37–41; 3 : 1–8; 4 : 13, 18–21.

GOLDEN TEXT. — ***Now when they beheld the boldness of Peter and John, and had perceived that they were unlearned and ignorant men, they marvelled; and they took knowledge of them, that they had been with Jesus.*** ACTS 4 : 13.

Devotional Reading : Psalm 33 : 12–22.
Beginner Topic : ON THE WAY TO CHURCH.
Lesson Material : Acts 3 : 1–26; 4 : 1–37.
Memory Verse : We . . . are helpers. 2 Corinthians 1 : 24.
Primary Topic : AT THE BEAUTIFUL GATE.
Lesson Material : Acts 3 : 1–8.
Memory Verse : Our help is in the name of Jehovah, who made heaven and earth. Psalm 124 : 8.
Junior Topic : INSIDE THE BEAUTIFUL GATE.
Lesson Material : Acts 3 : 1–8.
Memory Verse : In the midst of the congregation will I sing thy praise. Hebrews 2 : 12.
Intermediate and Senior Topic : TWO DARING PREACHERS.
Topic for Young People and Adults : ESSENTIALS OF CHRISTIAN LEADERSHIP.

THE TEACHER AND HIS CLASS.

The Younger Classes may be introduced to this lesson by being reminded of the importance of the *beginnings* of things; *e.g.*, if we are driving to a distant city, how important that we begin the journey on the right road, for, if we just turn the wrong corner within five minutes after leaving home, we may find ourselves, after hours of driving, further from the city than when we began. So in building a house, how important that the foundations should be strong, and their lines straight and accurate, lest, when the building is completed, and all the money set aside for it has been spent, it should collapse. In the beginning of the early Christian Church, how important that everything should be done according to the leading of the Spirit of God, soundly and sanely, so that the first lines taken in teaching and preaching and dealing with new converts should make for a strong foundation on which could be erected the great superstructure of the Christian Church.

The Older Classes will find the Apostle Peter in this lesson quite a new man, yet, still Peter. The one who so frequently was the mouthpiece for the apostles in the Gospels, is found here also to be the first speaker on almost every occasion; but the boastfulness of Peter before the resurrection is gone. He now is occupied wholly with Christ. The cowardice of Peter at the time of our Lord's passion is gone, and we find him now a man of constancy and courage. The man who formerly made foolish suggestions now becomes the man of great wisdom and foresight. The resurrection of Christ, and the descent of the Holy Spirit, transformed this man, until he was the Rock which Christ predicted three years ago he would be.

THE LESSON IN ITS SETTING.

Time. — Pentecost occurred May 28, A.D. 30. The healing of the lame man at the Temple occurred a few weeks later. Exactly when Peter and John were arrested, and brought before the Sanhedrin, we cannot specifically say. It may have been late in A.D. 30, or early A.D. 31.

Place. — Jerusalem, and, in part, the Temple.

2. The double instruction, v. 38 *a*.
   a. Repent.
   b. Be baptized.
3. The promise — Ye shall receive the Holy Spirit, vs. 38 *b*, 39.
4. Additional instruction, v. 40.
5. The first Christian baptism, v. 41.

II. THE FIRST APOSTOLIC MIRACLE, Acts 3 : 1–8.

1. The place where it occurred — the Temple. v. 1.
2. The needy lame man, vs. 2, 3.
3. The words of Peter, vs. 4–6.
4. The miracle, v. 7.
5. The manifested joy, v. 8.

III. THE BOLDNESS OF PETER AND JOHN IN THE FIRST CHRISTIAN PERSECUTION, Acts 4 : 13, 18–21.

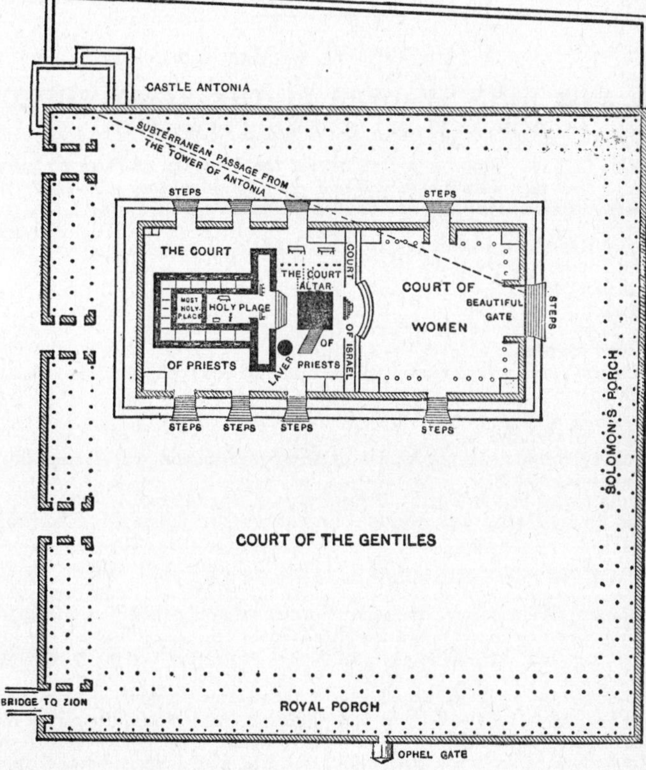

THE PLAN OF THE LESSON.

SUBJECT: The Manifestation of Divinely-Given Wisdom and Divinely-Bestowed Power in the Ministry of the Early Apostles at the Beginning of the Christian Church.

I. PETER INSTRUCTS THE FIRST CHRISTIAN CONVERTS, Acts 2 : 37–41.

1. Their conviction of crucifying the Son of God, v. 37.

1. The impression which Peter and John made upon their persecutors, v. 13.
2. The reply of Peter and John when commanded to cease proclaiming the name of Jesus, vs. 18–20.
3. The apostles are released, v. 21.

THE TEACHER'S LIBRARY.

All of the larger commentaries on the Book of Acts will be found helpful for the study of this lesson, but especially, for minute details, do we recommend the works by Rackham and Furneaux. For profound, historical exposition and application, see especially the rich pages in the work by Stokes in the *Expositor's Bible*. For some strange reason, biographies of the Apostle Peter are here for the most part inadequate. However, there are some good pages in F. B. Meyer, in the work on Peter by Quinton Hogg, and especially, in the biography of Peter by W. M. Taylor. In working over the material again for the life of Simon Peter, the editor has about come to the conclusion that there is not a really exhaustive life of Peter in the English language. For expository material see, on 3 : 1–8, Alexander Maclaren: *Expositions of Holy Scripture, Acts, 1–12*, 98–104; on 4 : 13, the same, 136–144. There seems to be really no sermonic material of importance on the five verses in this lesson taken from the second chapter of Acts. On the miracle of the healing of the lame man, see Marcus Dods: *How to Become Like Christ*, 121 ff.; Joseph Parker: *The People's Bible*, Vol. 23, 80–87; Hugh Macmillan: *The Gate Beautiful*, 1–13; on 3 : 6, Phillips Brooks, *The Law of Growth*, 99–114; the same, in *New Starts in Life*, 124–140; Andrew Murray, *The Ministry of Intercession*, 91 ff.; and, if teachers are able to discover a copy, see the great sermon by Dean Charles R. Brown, "Such As I Have," which won the $500.00 prize offered by the *World's Work* in 1925, published in pamphlet form. On 4 : 13, see John H. Jowett: *The Transfigured Church*, 169–180; on chapter 4, W. B. Riley: *The Bible of the Expositor and the Evangelist — Acts*, 85–100; on 4 : 20, W. M. Taylor: *The Silence of Jesus*, 203 ff. On the subject of baptism in the early church, see the very long article by A. J. Maclean in James Hastings: *Dictionary of the Apostolic Church*, Vol. 1, 128–136; on repentance, see the article by W. F. Lofthouse, in the same work, Vol. 2, 316–317.

ACTS 2 : 37. Now when they heard *this*, they were pricked in their heart,
and said unto Peter and the rest of the apostles, Brethren, what shall we
do?
38. And Peter *said* unto them, Repent ye, and be baptized every one of
you in the name of Jesus Christ unto the remission of your sins; and ye
shall receive the gift of the Holy Spirit.
39. For to you is the promise, and to your children, and to all that are
afar off, *even* as many as the Lord our God shall call unto him.

I. **PETER INSTRUCTS THE FIRST CHRISTIAN CONVERTS,** Acts 2 : 37–41. The verses here assigned to our lesson describe the events which took place immediately following Peter's powerful sermon delivered on the day of Pentecost, which may rightly be called the first sermon ever preached in the Christian Church. The result of the sermon was exactly what the Lord intended, indicative of what we all should expect to result from preaching to unsaved people, if such preaching is done in the name of Christ and in the power of the Holy Spirit. 37. **Now when they heard *this*, they were pricked in their heart, and said unto Peter and the rest of the apostles, Brethren, what shall we do?** The word here translated "pricked" means, originally, "to pierce, to sting sharply, to stone, to smite. Homer used it of horses denting the earth with their hoofs. The sermon went home, they felt the sting of Peter's words." — *A. T. Robertson*. 38. **And Peter *said* unto them, Repent ye, and be baptized every one of you in the name of Jesus Christ unto the remission of your sins; and ye shall receive the gift of the Holy Spirit.** "John's baptism had been a baptism of repentance for the remission of sins, but the work of Peter and his fellow apostles was no mere continuation of that of the Baptist (cf. 19 : 4, 5). Their baptism was to be in the name of Jesus Christ. Peter's address had been directed to the proof that Jesus was the Christ, and it was only natural that the acknowledgment of the cogency of that proof should form the ground of admission to the Christian Church; the ground of the admission to baptism was the recognition of Jesus as the Christ." — *R. J. Knowling*. Repentance literally means a "turning around," and in the New Testament, a turning around or a change of mind; that is, to have another mind regarding God, and Christ, ourselves, and sin. "Repentance is that change of a sinner's mind which leads him to turn from his evil ways and live. The change wrought in repentance is so deep and radical as to affect the whole spiritual nature and to involve the entire personality. The intellect must function, the emotions must be aroused, and the will must act. There may be a knowledge of sin without turning from it as an awful thing which dishonors God. The change of view may lead only to a dread of punishment. There must be a consciousness of sin and its effect on man and its relation to God before there can be a hearty turning away from unrighteousness. There can be no external substitute for the internal change. Repentance is only a condition of salvation and not its meritorious ground." — *Byron H. Dement*. Baptism follows belief, and certainly is not a saving ordinance. Only faith can save us. Baptism is a sign of the washing away of our sins, a public acknowledgment that we are henceforth to be identified with Jesus Christ, an external rite symbolizing our being identified with the body of Christ. If 1900 years of the teaching of the Holy Spirit in the Church means anything, it means that the believer should be baptized. 39. **For to you is the promise, and to your children,**

40. And with many other words he testified, and exhorted them, saying, Save yourselves from this crooked generation.
41. They then that received his word were baptized: and there were added *unto them* in that day about three thousand souls.

and to all that are afar off, *even* as many as the Lord our God shall call unto him. "Peter knew from the first, we see, that the Gentiles were to be admitted to the same privileges as Israel. But Christ's commission said they were to preach first in Jerusalem and Judæa. Peter needed the vision of the great sheet let down from heaven to tell him *when* God's time was come for the extension of the work." — *R. J. Lumby.* Compare Ephesians 2 : 13. 40. **And with many other words he testified, and exhorted them, saying, Save yourselves from this crooked generation.** "This shows that Luke did not profess to give more than the substance of what was said." — *W. M. Furneaux.* What Peter here meant was that these people should accept the the Lord Jesus Christ as their Saviour, and thus be saved from the doom which was to fall upon Israel because of its rejection of Christ, climaxing in the destruction of the city of Jerusalem some forty years later (cf. 1 Cor. 11 : 32; Gal. 1 : 4). 41. **They then that received his word were baptized: and there were added *unto them* in that day about three thousand souls.** "The number need cause no surprise. The death of Jesus was recent, and the consciousness that a national crime had been committed might easily be roused. Moreover, the remembrance of His teaching and of His miracles was still fresh; and many of these new converts may have been in a sense believers already, but had been restrained by timidity or irresolution from an open profession of their faith. We must not credit the church in Jerusalem with this full increase. Probably many of the three thousand were pilgrims who returned from their homes after the Feast. Nor must we assume that all became genuine Christians. The episode of Ananias and Sapphira shows that men might, as in other revivals, be carried away by their feelings without any real and permanent transformation of character." — *W. M. Furneaux.*

The Vision of Peter. Julius von Schnorr.

II. **THE FIRST APOSTOLIC MIRACLE,** Acts 3 : 1-8. We could not begin the study of this particular part of our lesson any more appropriately than by quoting Professor James Stalker's excellent words about the friendship of Peter and John. "In those days John and Peter became so closely associated as to be inseparable. In every scene in which John is mentioned in the Acts, Peter is mentioned along with him. . . . The origin of this friendship was, indeed, far earlier. John and Peter were natives of the same town. As boys they learned the same trade, and in manhood they were partners in business. They, in all probability, went together to Jerusalem to the feasts and they both were involved in the movement of the Baptist. They were introduced to Christ on the same day. Not only were both among the twelve apostles, but both belonged to the chosen three. . . . In this friendship, Peter was, to outward appearance, the predominant partner. In the first half of the Book of Acts he is always the leader; and John retires behind his

ACTS 3 : 1. Now Peter and John were going up into the temple at the hour of prayer, *being* the ninth *hour*.

2. And a certain man that was lame from his mother's womb was carried, whom they laid daily at the door of the temple which is called Beautiful, to ask alms of them that entered into the temple;

3. Who seeing Peter and John about to go into the temple, asked to receive an alms.

4. And Peter, fastening his eyes upon him, with John, said, Look on us.

5. And he gave heed unto them, expecting to receive something from them.

6. But Peter said, Silver and gold have I none; but what I have, that give I thee. In the name of Jesus Christ of Nazareth, walk.

---

more prominent figure, playing an altogether subordinate part. But it is one of the finest peculiarities of a time like Pentecost that all engaged in the work of God forget themselves, being too concerned with the work itself to have time to spare for estimating the magnitude of their own share in it or contrasting it with that of others; and we may be certain that the heart of John would have been the last to envy the honor vouchsafed to another." 1. **Now Peter and John were going up into the temple at the hour of prayer, *being* the ninth *hour*.** "We read in Scripture of three specified hours of prayer in accordance with which the psalmist speaks of his own custom, 'evening, and morning, and at noon, will I pray' (Ps. 55 : 17). And in like manner, Daniel prayed 'three times a day' (Dan. 6 : 10). The evening prayer was this to which Peter and John were going up; at such a time the ninth hour would be at half past four." — *J. R. Lumby.* The Apostle John does not appear again in the Book of Acts after this scene. Notice that these apostles had not broken from the habit of going up to the Temple. They were good Jews but they were also supremely devoted Christians, and they found there was nothing to prevent them continuing the worship of God in the Temple, which had been sacred to them from their youth. 2. **And a certain man that was lame from his mother's womb was carried, whom they laid daily at the door of the temple which is called Beautiful, to ask alms of them that entered into the temple.** "The blind and crippled, the halt and maimed, are sure to be found where they can best excite the pity of pious people. The particular spot at which this lame man lay cannot be identified. 'Beautiful' is not a name that was given to any one of the gates; but it was a description of several. It may have been the Gate of Nicanor, so called because the hand of Nicanor, the great enemy of the Maccabees, had been nailed to it as a trophy by Judas after his victory over him. More likely, perhaps, it was the gate Shushan, called sometimes the Corinthian Gate, towering to the height of nearly ninety feet, and covered with lilies in silver and gold. It is generally associated with Susa, the capital of Persia, but we must look for its appellation to the fact that Shushan is the Hebrew for a lily, and that the lily was the Hebrew type of beauty." — *H. M. Luckock.* 3. **Who seeing Peter and John about to go into the temple, asked to receive an alms.** This man was just a beggar. He had no way of making a living, or at least he did not choose to seek a way, and no doubt, for all his life, he had found the gifts thrown at him at this temple gate sufficient for all his needs. 4. **And Peter, fastening his eyes upon him, with John, said, Look on us.** Normally, one becomes not only accustomed to seeing beggars, but somewhat impatient with them. They are the people with whom we almost never stop to talk. Not so Peter. Like his Lord, he saw into the inner life of this poor creature, and apprehended that he not only should be delivered of his lameness but that he should know the Lord Jesus Christ. 5. **And he gave heed unto them, expecting to receive something from them.** 6. **But Peter said, Silver and gold have I none; but what I have, that give I thee. In the name of Jesus Christ of Nazareth, walk.** "Wealth is not the standard of worth. Mankind has been primarily beholden to those who have possessed little of this world's goods, but have abounded 'in faith, and utterance, and knowledge, and in all earnestness and in love.' Through the poverty of Christ we have been enriched with all spiritual treasures and entitled to an inheritance that fadeth not away. There are bags in the heavens that wax not old, and treasures in the heavens that fail not, where no

7. And he took him by the right hand, and raised him up: and immediately his feet and his ankle-bones received strength.

thief draweth nigh, neither moth destroyeth. Yonder a little girl is sobbing piteously on the grave of her mother! I am touched, and offer her a gold piece! She snatches it from my hand, flings it into the open grave, and continues to sob convulsively! What more can I do? That is all that I had to give, and it was unavailing! Presently a poor woman, in plain and shabby clothes, kisses the child, strokes the little head, presses her to her bosom, and comforts her with gentle crooning! See the eyes droop in sleep, and the little one is soothed and quieted! That woman had neither silver nor gold, but she possessed what was infinitely more precious, and that she gave without stint. This is what the world needs today. Would that men and women of all classes in society realized it, and instead of the giddy race for wealth and pleasure they would possess themselves of, and impart to others, treasures compared with which the mines of Crœsus offer a miser's dole.

Julius von Schnorr.

Peter Cures a Lame Man.

"In the present case, Peter communicated the inspiration of his own strong faith in Jesus of Nazareth. He summoned him to act on such faith as he had. He called on things that apparently were not as though they were. He mingled a drop of his own soul-tincture into the clouded uncertainty and questioning of the cripple's soul, and it suddenly crystallized with the daring act of faith." — *F. B. Meyer*. There is one marked difference between the manner of our Lord's performing miracles and the manner in which the apostles performed them. "Jesus effected cures Himself by merely speaking a word from His own personality and in His own power. His disciples effected cures by speaking in His Name (John 16 : 23, 24). Only a few weeks before the temple courts had been thronged by crowds of blind and lame seeking to be healed by Jesus (Matt. 21 : 14). The Healer had been crucified and buried, and the maimed were content to ask alms only. He now came again in His disciples gifted with the presence and power of His Spirit, and the wonders of healing were again performed. The man felt that there was no mockery in the command. Its words were interpreted to him by the look and touch of Peter, by the rush of new life through him, and perhaps by some memory of Jesus." — *T. M. Lindsay*. Professor Stokes has some very fine comments on this chapter from which we can choose only the following few lines: "Peter's words are typical of the spirit which should ever animate the Christian preacher or teacher. They turn the attention of his hearers wholly away from himself and exalt Christ Jesus alone. Such has ever been and ever must be the secret of successful preaching. The preacher of Christian truth who thinks of himself rather than of the great subject of his mission, who only preaches that he may be thought clever or eloquent, debases the Christian pulpit and must be an awful failure in that day when God shall judge the secrets of men by Jesus Christ." 7. **And he took him by the right hand, and raised him up: and immediately his feet and ankle-bones received strength.** "The unusual Greek word, here translated 'ankle-bones,' is a medical term found in Hippocrates. It is one of the details which betray Luke, the physician. See how he notes in the word 'immediately' that the months of the ordinary cure were compressed into a moment; that the man was lame from his birth, so that it was not a case of nervous debility; that he had reached an age (4 : 22) when such cures no longer occur." — *W. M.*

8. And leaping up, he stood, and began to walk; and he entered with them into the temple, walking, and leaping, and praising God.

ACTS 4 : 13. Now when they beheld the boldness of Peter and John, and had perceived that they were unlearned and ignorant men, they marvelled; and they took knowledge of them, that they had been with Jesus.

Furneaux. 8. **And leaping up.** "Not leaping out of his couch (as has sometimes been supposed), of which there is no mention, but leaping up for joy (cf. Isa. 55 : 12; Joel 2 : 5)." — *R. J. Knowling.* **He stood, and began to walk; and he entered with them into the temple, walking, and leaping, and praising God.** "Such vivid details may have been derived from Peter himself, and they are given here with a vividness characteristic of Mark's Gospel, of which Peter may reasonably be regarded as the main source." — *R. J. Knowling.* Professor Lumby suggests that the lame man entered with the apostles into the temple because "he doubtless felt that this was the best visit he could make with his new powers and he would be the more anxious to go there as Peter and John were going too." We have known many people desperately sick to pray to God that if He would restore them to health again they would begin to be truly faithful in attendance at the house of the Lord, but upon recovery their vows were soon broken, and sometimes they became more hardened than ever in their indifference. It would be a good habit for all of us if, every Lord's day morning, we would remember the sicknesses from which God has delivered us, the problems which the Lord has solved for us, the bondage from which He has set us free, the fears which He has taken out of our hearts.

THE CHURCH'S OPPORTUNITY.

"The Church's opportunity is lame humanity, lame from its birth. It is waste of time to discuss how humanity came to be lame; it is lame, and that is the trouble. The Church's opportunity is not to build schools and erect forums where we shall discuss how men were born lame. The disciples of old came to Jesus with a question, a wonderfully tempting metaphysical and psychological question, 'Rabbi, who sinned, this man, or his parents, that he should be born blind?' He dismissed their question: 'Neither did this man sin, nor his parents; but that the works of God should be made manifest in him: we must work the works of him that sent me.' Lame humanity is the Church's opportunity. This is indeed a pathetic story and picture; lame humanity at the Beautiful Gate, but outside! There at the gate, with all the mountain's far-flung splendors encircling the city; there, where the steps went up to the temple, he lay; but outside. That is humanity's position, in the midst of beauty, but not of it; in the realm of things lovely and of good report, but excluded. That is the position of humanity everywhere; it sighs and sobs and is in agony at the Beautiful Gate; but it cannot get in. There is the Church's opportunity." — *G. Campbell Morgan.*

III. **THE BOLDNESS OF PETER AND JOHN IN THE FIRST CHRISTIAN PERSECUTION,** Acts 4 : 13, 18–21. The miracle of healing the lame man brought together a great crowd of the curious, and Peter took this opportunity of preaching to them concerning Christ and the resurrection, which so aroused the Jewish hierarchy of the city and the religious leaders of that day, that continuing their vicious animosity toward Christ and everything connected with Christ, they determined that this new religion should not grow, and they laid hands on the apostles and put them into prison. On the morrow they were brought before Annas, the high priest, and Caiaphas, John, and Alexander, and, no doubt, the entire Sanhedrin (cf. John 18 : 13). The apostles being set before this august body, the most powerful body of Jews in the world at that time, were asked by what power or by what name they had performed this miracle of healing the lame man. Peter at once spoke for the apostolic group, giving a marvelous testimony to the centrality, the essentiality, the preeminence of the Lord Jesus Christ, whom he deliberately charged his hearers with having crucified. Our lesson begins as this testimony of the Apostle Peter terminates. 13. **Now when they beheld the boldness of Peter and John, and had perceived that they were unlearned and ignorant men, they marvelled; and they took knowledge of them, that they had been with Jesus.** "The effect produced upon the Sanhedrin was astonishment: first at the boldness of Peter and John in thus accusing them; then at their use of Scripture, when it was obvious that they had not

18. And they called them, and charged them not to speak at all nor teach in the name of Jesus.

19. But Peter and John answered and said unto them, Whether it is right in the sight of God to hearken unto you rather than unto God, judge ye:

20. For we cannot but speak the things which we saw and heard.

21. And they, when they had further threatened them, let them go, finding nothing how they might punish them, because of the people; for all men glorified God for that which was done.

---

been trained in the technical learning of the rabbinical schools. This is the meaning of *unlearned;* and in this sense the Lord Himself had never learned. Nor had they any professional status. They were *ignorant:* the Greek word is *idiots,* and an idiot was a private person who possessed no official position or special ability. So in 1 Corinthians 14 : 16 the word is used for an ordinary member of the congregation. It had been adopted into Hebrew, and gradually the idea of ignorance began to cling to it. At the same time they recognized they had been of Jesus' company. We are surprised that this fact was not known to the Sanhedrin from the first. The word, however, denotes personal recognition. Hitherto the Sadducean rulers had been indifferent to the doings and the persons of the followers of the enthusiastic prophet of Nazareth. Now, however, they recognized Peter and John as having been in the immediate company of Jesus in the temple in that last week, or even as present in the high priest's house on that last night. They were then the ringleaders of the sect. John himself was known to Caiaphas, but it was an acquaintanceship which the high priest might find it convenient to forget at this juncture." — *R. B. Rackham.* The word here translated " unlearned " means " unlettered men without technical training in the professional rabbinical schools of Hillel or Shammai. Jesus Himself was so regarded (John 7 : 15). The word translated ' ignorant ' means a layman, a man not in office (private person), a common soldier and not an officer; a man not skilled in the schools, and therefore very much like the word translated ' unlearned.' The word is from the Greek word *idios,* meaning one's own, and our word idiosyncrasy is one with an excess of such a trait, while idiot is one who has nothing but his idiosyncrasy." — *A. T. Robertson.*

In their astonishment, which confused them, and being unable to contradict the fact that the lame man stood before them healed, they commanded the apostles to go outside of the council room, and then conferred among themselves as to what they should do to these men who were so boldly preaching and teaching in the name of the Lord Jesus, coming to the conclusion that they should threaten them, and command that they should no longer speak in that name. 18. **And they called them, and charged them not to speak at all nor teach in the name of Jesus.** This has been the experience of the Church in different parts of the world in every age. First, the Jews attempted to keep the apostles from speaking in the name of Jesus; then Roman emperors and the officers of provinces set about the impossible task of suppressing the Christian faith; later Mohammedanism attempted to put to death all those who preached in the name of Christ; later this was carried out, though only for a brief time, by non-christians, *e.g.,* in the terrible Chinese Boxer uprising, and in islands and various parts of the seas, in Tibet, in Africa, among the Indians of South America. Leaders of false religions have attempted to stop the mouths of those who were bringing in light and truth, love and redemption. Behind all this opposition is the arch-enemy of God, Satan himself. 19. **But Peter and John answered and said unto them, Whether it is right in the sight of God to hearken unto you rather than unto God, judge ye:** 20. **for we cannot but speak the things which we saw and heard.** 21. **And they, when they had further threatened them, let them go, finding nothing how they might punish them, because of the people; for all men glorified God for that which was done.** " These two men can claim spiritual descent from the three children before Nebuchadnezzar: ' Our God, whom we serve, is able to deliver us. . . . But if not, be it known unto thee, O king, that we will not serve thy gods ' (Dan. 3 : 17, 18). So Socrates had declared to his judges: ' I will obey God rather than you, O Athenians. If you would dismiss me and spare my life, on condition that I should cease to teach my countrymen, I would rather die a thousand times than accept the proposal.' They had not been required to unsay what they had affirmed, but only to desist from affirming it in the future. But they accept no such compromise. In this first conflict between the Church and earthly authority, they assert a great principle — that the Christian conscience is the supreme court of appeal. They say with Micaiah (1 Kings 22 : 14), 'As the Lord liveth, what the Lord saith unto me, that will I speak.' So their words have become sacred watchwords, to which men, who had powers, civil or ecclesiastical, arrayed against them, have turned for comfort. The answer of Bunyan, when imprisoned and forbidden to preach was, 'I am at a point with you. If I were out of prison again today, I would preach the gospel again tomorrow, by the help of God.' 'The powers that be are ordained of God,' says Paul (Rom. 13 : 1), and it is my duty to obey them; but if there comes a time, when the soul is hemmed in between the mandate of an earthly ruler and the Word of God — when the alternative is to follow Babylon, or to refuse to bow at the sound of cornet, flute, and dulcimer — then to a Christian man a higher duty overrides the lower." — *W. M. Furneaux.* "The same appeal is made by John, both in his Gospel (1 : 14) and in his First Epistle (1 : 1, 2) in vindication of his teaching; and here the final answer is that of St. John and St. Peter jointly." "Opposition to Christ is always opposition in spite of conclusive evidence. There is the healed man, oh ye men of the Sanhedrin, confronting you! In God's name, why waste time accounting for him, why not let this thing go on? The healed man has been multiplied in all the centuries. The healed man is in all the world today. The healed man is here, healed mentally, spiritually, physically, in proportion as he is true to the great spiritual truths to which he has submitted himself. . . .

"Finally, opposition on the part of the material to the spiritual eventuates in the destruction of the material. Dr. John Hall, for so many years the minister of Fifth Avenue Presbyterian Church, New York, once illustrated that in this way. He said: 'A serpent fastens upon a steel file and attempts to gnaw it through; it is at first gratified at the evidences of apparent success; but presently blood is there, and the serpent finds that the file has been destroying its tooth rather than its tooth the file.' If Christianity is becoming materialized, God have mercy on us and the world. It must be the Christianity of men and women filled with the Holy Spirit, knowing the power of the one Name, and bringing men to deliverance through it, which alone can be victorious." — *G. Campbell Morgan.*

How many different characters do you find in the lesson which we have just studied, and what are some of the differences between them? Putting all these different characters together, what would you say was the influence of believing in Christ over those who identify themselves with Christ and the consequences in the characters of men when they rejected Christ, as for instance, the Sanhedrin? How many different things does the Apostle Peter in this lesson teach about the Lord Jesus Christ? Would you say after studying this lesson, that men were primarily drawn to Simon Peter or to the Lord Jesus? In how many different ways is Peter here at the beginning of his public ministry carrying out the commands of the Lord Jesus Christ? What are some of the reasons you can think of why Christ has given the Church the sacrament of baptism? How do Christians reveal to an unbelieving world that they are in the constant companionship of Jesus Christ their Lord?

LESSON VII. — May 16.

PETER AND JOHN PREACH TO SAMARITANS. — Acts 8 : 4–25.

PRINTED TEXT, Acts 8 : 14–25.

GOLDEN TEXT. — ***Lift up your eyes, and look on the fields, that they are white already unto harvest.*** John 4 : 35.

Devotional Reading: Psalm 96 : 1–9.
Beginner Topic: How Philip Helped.
  Lesson Material: Acts 8 : 4, 5, 26–40.
  Memory Verse: The Lord is my helper. Hebrews 13 : 6.
Primary Topic: Why a City Was Glad.
  Lesson Material: Acts 8 : 4–12, 25.
  Memory Verse: Go ye into all the world, and preach the gospel to the whole creation. Mark 16 : 15.

Junior Topic: WHY A CITY WAS GLAD.
Lesson Material: Acts 8 : 4-12, 25.
Memory Verse: Ascribe unto Jehovah the glory due unto his name: Bring an offering, and come into his courts. Psalm 96 : 8.
Intermediate and Senior Topics: COMRADES IN SERVICE.
Topic for Young People and Adults: CHRISTIANITY CROSSING RACIAL LINES.

THE TEACHER AND HIS CLASS.

The Younger Classes may be asked what things can never be bought with money, as, for instance, spiritual power, real love, character, purity; then they may be asked what things ought *not* to be bought for money (but sometimes are) *e.g.*, a political position, and, in some cases, places of preferment in the church. Our lesson concerns the case of a man who tried to buy from the apostles the power of the Holy Spirit.

The Older Classes will discover in this lesson a picture of the purity, the power, and the passion of the early church in preaching the gospel, in maintaining high spiritual ideals, in winning souls, in casting out demons, and in moving whole cities. The church was never supposed to be a weak institution, spiritually speaking, but dynamic, breaking down the strongholds of evil, and setting men free from every evil bondage. How wonderful it would have been if the power manifest here in this revival in Samaria had always remained as the outstanding characteristic of the church throughout the ages!

THE LESSON IN ITS SETTING.

Time. — A.D. 36.
Place. — The city of Samaria, in Central Palestine, northwest of Sychar and Shechem.

THE PLAN OF THE LESSON

SUBJECT: What Happens when the Divinely Empowered Disciples of the Christian Faith Come Face to Face with the False Pretensions of Paganism and Demon-possessed Men.

I. THE RESULT OF THE SCATTERING OF THE EARLY DISCIPLES, Acts 8 : 4.

II. PHILIP'S MINISTRY IN THE CITY OF SAMARIA, VS. 5-8.

III. SIMON THE SORCERER, VS. 9-24.

1. His earlier history, vs. 9-11.
2. His professed belief, vs. 12, 13.
3. His offer to purchase spiritual power with money, vs. 14-19.
   a. What Simon saw that led him to make this offer, vs. 14-17.
   b. The offer itself, vs. 18, 19.
4. His rebuke by Peter, vs. 20-23.
   a. The rebuke.
   b. The command to repent.
   c. The warning.
5. His request for prayer, v. 24.

IV. SUBSEQUENT EVANGELIZING LABORS, V. 25.

THE TEACHER'S LIBRARY.

Some commentaries on the Book of Acts will be found rather worthless for the study of this lesson, but we would recommend the great pages by G. T. Stokes in the *Expositor's Bible;* J. R. Lumby in the *Cambridge Bible for Schools and Colleges;* and R. J. Knowling, in the *Expositor's Greek Testament,* together with others that will be quoted in this lesson. Philip does not appear in the printed text itself, so we do not give a list of references to him. Most biographies of Simon Peter say practically nothing about this episode, but see W. M. Taylor: *Peter the Apostle,* 253-267; J. R. MacDuff: *The Footsteps of St. Peter,* 381-406; A. T. Robertson: *Epochs in the Life of St. Peter,* 209-219.

On Simon, called Simon Magus, see A. T. Robertson: *Some Minor Characters of the New Testament,* 102-110; James Hastings's *Greater Men and Women of the Bible, St. Luke to Titus,* 136-152; Alexander Whyte: *Bible Characters, Joseph and Mary to James the Lord's Brother,* 197-207; William Ramsay: *The Bearing of Recent Discoveries on the Trustworthiness of the New Testament,* 117-131; A. C. Headlam, in James Hastings's *Dictionary of the Bible,* Vol. 4, 524-527; J. E. Roberts, in James Hastings's *Dictionary of the Apostolic Church,* Vol. 2, 493-498. On the city of Samaria, see the articles by James Strahan, in James Hastings's *Dictionary of the Apostolic Church,* Vol. 2, 447-448; by W. Ewing, in the *International Standard Bible Encyclopedia,* Vol. 4, 2671-2672; and, George Adam Smith: *The Historical Geography of the Holy Land,* 323-363.

For expository material, see Alexander Maclaren: *Acts of the Apostles, 1-12,* 242-248; Joseph Parker: *The People's Bible,* Vol. 23, 182-209 (the same as the work later called *Apostolic Life*). Sermonic material on this passage is practically non-existent. See, however, a great sermon, "Imperialism and Service," in J. G. Simpson: *Christian Ideals,* 245-260. On the entire episode, see D. J. Burrell: *Home Sanctuary,* 284-295; on verse 21, J. C. Ryle: *Old Paths,* 217 ff.; and some excellent remarks in Andrew Murray's little book, *Money.*

I. THE RESULT OF THE SCATTERING OF THE EARLY DISCIPLES, Acts 8 : 4. The first three verses of this chapter briefly summarize the terrible persecution of the early Church undertaken by Saul, and our lesson opens with the consequence of this persecution, namely, the forcing out from Jerusalem of the Christians, that they might, scattered everywhere, sow the seed of the gospel in areas not heretofore touched.

II. **PHILIP'S MINISTRY IN THE CITY OF SAMARIA,** Acts 8 : 5–8. Among those scattered abroad was Philip the evangelist, who had previously been chosen to have the oversight of the daily ministration of the poor in the Christian community of Jerusalem (Acts 6 : 5). He must be clearly distinguished from Philip one of the twelve Apostles, who belonged to Bethsaida of Galilee (John 1 : 44; 12 : 21). We not only find Philip the dominating personality of the events recorded throughout this chapter, but, twenty years later, we find him still active in the Christian Church (Acts 21 : 8, 9).

The city of Samaria was the capital of the northern kingdom of Israel from the time of Omri to the end of the Israelitish kingdom, 722 B.C. It is located on an oblong hill northwest of Shechem, having a position of great charm and beauty, and, in the days of ancient warfare, because of the precipitous sides of the hill on which it was located, it was a city of great strength. Alexander the Great took the city in 331 B.C. It suffered greatly under John Hyrcanus, who attempted to utterly destroy it in 119 B.C. It was rebuilt by Pompey, and then by Herod the Great, who not only restored its former glory, but extended and strengthened and adorned it on a scale of great magnificence. Ruins of the city to be seen today silently testify to its greatness many centuries ago. How the city finally was destroyed, we do not know. It is the traditional burying place of John the Baptist. "If Philip's home was at Cæsarea where he ended his preaching tour and where he was living twenty years later (21 : 8), his choice of Samaria may have been determined by his familiarity with the district. Moreover, he was probably safer there than in more distant places, for the Jews had no synagogues there, nor the Sanhedrin any power. And the opposition which Stephen's teaching had excited among the Jews would incline the Samaritans to give a refuge and a welcome to one who taught on the same lines. The Samaritans worshiped Jehovah, practiced circumcision, and observed the Sabbath; but rejected all the Scriptures except the Pentateuch, and regarded Gerizim, not Jerusalem, as the Holy City. The Jews looked upon them with abhorrence. The Gentiles they regarded only as exiles from the Covenant, the Samaritans as schismatics and apostates. 'Thou art a Samaritan' was the most injurious reproach which they could utter against Jesus (John 8 : 48). Though the Lord had forbidden the apostles (Matt. 10 : 5) to preach to the Samaritans during His ministry, which was specially directed to the Jews, the prohibition had been removed by Him before His ascension (1 : 8); and the parable of the Good Samaritan and the episode of the Samaritan leper (Luke 17 : 16) may have helped Philip to conquer any religious antipathy which, as a Jew, he may have felt. But as a Hellenist he would be comparatively free from the bitter prejudices of the native Jews." — *W. M. Furneaux.*

From a photograph by Wilson.

Samaria.

Ruins, Church of St. John.

Joseph Parker has a great paragraph opening his chapter on this episode. "Look first of all at the *condition* in which Philip found the city or the region of Samaria. You find there the condition of the *whole world* represented in one pregnant sentence. Samaria was (1) *diseased,* (2) *possessed,* and (3) *deluded.* These are the conditions in which Christianity has always to fight its great battle. Christianity never finds any town *prepared* to co-operate with it. All the conquests of Christianity imply a long siege, stubborn hostility, inveterate prejudice, and the victory of right over wrong. We are none of us by nature prepared to give the Christian teacher a candid hearing. We 'hate the fellow, for he never prophesies good of us.' The literary lecturer pays homage to his audience, but the preacher rebukes it, humbles it, pours upon it holy despite and contempt. The *world* is no better today than Samaria was when Philip went down. And these three words, whole categories in themselves, include the moral condition of the race. *Diseased* — there is not a man in this house who is thoroughly and completely well, nor in any house, nor in all the world. . . . The world is not only diseased, it is *possessed.* Possessed with demons, possessed with unclean spirits, possessed with false ideas. Why make a marvel or a mystery about demoniacal possession when we are all so possessed? Why push this idea back some twenty centuries or more, as if it were an ancient anecdote? We are all devil-ridden. We had better give the right names to our mental conditions, lest we be attaching the wrong label and mistaking ourselves utterly. Out of Christ, out of the Cross, self-centered, self-poised, self-seeking, we are mad! . . . Samaria was also *deluded.* She was bewitched. The sorcerer had flung his charms upon her mind, and she was led as the sorcerer's will suggested or desired. Understand that *somebody* has to lead the world. My question is, who is to be the *man* of the future, the *life*, the *Sovereign*, the *King* of the future? This Man, Christ, or Barabbas? "

Notice especially the resultant joy from the great revival that swept over this city. " They rejoiced because their souls had found the truth, which can alone satisfy the cravings of the human heart and minister a joy which leaves no sting behind, but is a joy pure and exhaustless. The joys of earth are always mixed, and the more mixed the more unsatisfying. The joy of a Christian soul which knows Christ and His preciousness, which has been delivered by Christ from deceit and impurity and vice, as these Samaritans had, and which feels and enjoys the new light thrown on life by Christ's revelations, that joy is a surpassing one, ravishing the soul, satisfying the intellect, purifying the life." — *G. T. Stokes.* A fascinating study would be to examine the passages in the Old Testament which speak of joy coming to a nation or to a city, and it will always be noticed that such an experience is the result never of idolatry, but always of a return to God and a real manifestation of a religious revival (see, *e.g.*, 2 Kings 11 : 20; 2 Chron. 24 : 10; 29 : 27, 30; 30 : 23, 26; Ezra 6 : 22; Neh. 8 : 10, 12; 12 : 43).

III. **SIMON THE SORCERER,** Acts 8 : 9–24.

1. HIS EARLIER HISTORY, VS. 9–11. Though this particular passage, the only one in which Simon the sorcerer appears in the New Testament, would never lead one to believe that this character would play a great part in subsequent tradition and medieval lore, we find more attention was paid to the later history of this man in subsequent Christian literature than to the history of most of the apostles themselves. " The old religions of paganism had lost most of their power in the age in which our Lord appeared. Skepticism, and its usual accompaniment, gross superstition, abounded throughout the Roman empire. Hence multitudes of sorcerers abounded, and most great men had a diviner or reader of the future in their households. Elymas the sorcerer was in attendance on the governor of Cyprus (Acts 13 : 6, 7); and Simon was the great wizard of Samaria. Simon Magus may be looked on as the type of this numerous class of religious teachers, who were partly sincere in their belief in the power of the supernatural and in their capacity to wield its influence, and were partly fraudulent quacks working on the ignorance and credulity of their fellows. Most scholars agree in making this Simon the same as the Simon mentioned by Josephus who, a professed magician, was employed by Felix to persuade Drusilla, daughter of Herod Agrippa I, to desert her husband Azizus and marry him; for wizards or magicians were used to execute shameless deeds." — *T. M. Lindsay.* " We shall probably understand Simon Magus best, if, to skill in the art of magic, we add a tacit claim to be an incarnation of the divine. He was first a magician, then a pseudo-Messiah. It was to the wonderful performances which he effected through magic that he owed his earliest influence over the Samaritan mind. Ignorant and superstitious people, who find the whole world about them to be full of unknown powers, and whose chief longing is to break the bonds of material, commonplace nature, so as to reach the occult, the superhuman, or the divine, lend greedy and credulous ears to any one who seems to have a spiritual power which others have not, to be able to lay his finger on those secret springs which influence events, or, by some mysterious force, to effect the desired and achieve the marvelous. It is of the essence of magic, at its best, to depend for its wonders upon secret powers, superhuman or divine, which obey other than moral laws. It never aims at moral results, never works through moral processes. A pure heart or penitent will is no condition of its power. It lends itself as fast to the foulest as to the holiest ends. It serves spiritual pride, or passion, or revenge, or covetousness, equally with the

ACTS 8:14. Now when the apostles that were at Jerusalem heard that Samaria had received the word of God, they sent unto them Peter and John:
15. Who, when they were come down, prayed for them, that they might receive the Holy Spirit:

---

noblest thirst for goodness. It is, therefore, essentially irreligious, because unethical. Besides, it professes to discover laws, or charms, or hidden fates, which compel the divine will and make the power of God an involuntary minister to the desires of man. Instead of serving God, it thinks to make God serve human caprice. Thus it is again irreligious." — *J. O. Dykes.*

2. HIS PROFESSED BELIEF, vs. 12, 13. Simon was no dullard. He was ever eager to discover new ways for impressing people with his greatness. He was very anxious to pick up new ideas and to master new devices for exciting, influencing, and mastering others. So when he beheld the great power which Philip exercised, which he recognized no doubt to be genuine, a power greater probably than he had ever seen before, he felt he must align himself with such a group as this and so he "believed, and being baptized continued with Philip." The question has always been debated if this was genuine faith, and the answer must be, No. "The faith of Simon rested on the outward miracles and signs, a faith which ended in amazement — but it was no permanent, abiding faith, just as the amazement which he had himself inspired in others, gave way before a higher and more convincing belief. He may have believed in the Messianic dignity of Christ, and in His death and resurrection, constrained by the miracles which Philip wrought in attestation of his preaching, but it was a belief about the facts, and not a belief in Him whom the facts made known, a belief in the *power* of the new faith, but not an acceptance of its *holiness*." — *R. J. Knowling.* "He was convinced from the works which Philip did, that Philip was in league with some powerful Spirit; he viewed baptism as the initiation into communion with that Spirit, and expected that he should be able to make use of the higher power thus gained for his own purposes, and unite this new magical power to his own. All were baptized who professed faith in Jesus as the Messiah; there was therefore no reason for rejecting Simon, considering besides that from the nature of the case he would for the time have given up his magical practice." — *A. Neander.*

3. HIS OFFER TO PURCHASE SPIRITUAL POWER WITH MONEY, vs. 14–19. 14. **Now when the apostles that were at Jerusalem heard that Samaria had received the word of God, they sent unto them Peter and John.** The late Professor Stokes has some wonderfully rich words on the purpose of the visit of John and Peter to Samaria, now under the power of a real revival. "They were doubtless sent to inspect the work, and see whether the apostolic approval could be given to the step of evangelizing the Samaritans. They had to form a judgment upon it; for no matter how highly we may rate the inspiration of the apostles, it is clear that they had to argue, debate, think, and balance one side against another just like other people. It is clear, from the simple fact that controversy and debate held a prominent place in the early Christian Church, that there was no belief in the existence of infallible guides, local and visible, whose autocratic decisions were final and irreversible, binding the whole Church. It was then believed that the guidance of the Holy Spirit was vouchsafed through the channel of free discussion and interchange of opinion, guided and sanctified by prayer. The apostles duly discharged their mission, and by their ministry the converts received the gift of the Holy Spirit, together with some or all of those external signs and manifestations which accompanied the original blessing on the day of Pentecost at Jerusalem." "The step implied no jealousy of Philip, or any idea that his ministry was defective. When, shortly after, he 'went about preaching the glad tidings to all the cities' (v. 40), we hear of no such commission to supplement his work. And, later still, it was Barnabas, and not any of the Twelve, who was dispatched on a precisely similar mission to Antioch (11:22). It is sometimes said that we have in this passage the origin of the later rite of confirmation. But Luke's language does not support the idea that the work of the evangelist needed to be supplemented by the apostles. It is true that the Samaritans were circumcised, and no such objection appears to have been raised as was subsequently urged in the case of Cornelius. But many Christian Jews would be scandalized by the admission of Samaritans; and, as the responsible leaders of the Christian society, the apostles felt it to be their duty to examine and sanction the new departure." — *W. M. Furneaux.*
15. **Who, when they were come down, prayed for them, that they might receive the**

16. For as yet it was fallen upon none of them: only they had been baptized into the name of the Lord Jesus.
17. Then laid they their hands on them, and they received the Holy Spirit.
18. Now when Simon saw that through the laying on of the apostles' hands the Holy Spirit was given, he offered them money,
19. Saying, Give me also this power, that on whomsoever I lay my hands, he may receive the Holy Spirit.

Holy Spirit: 16. **for as yet it was fallen upon none of them: only they had been baptized into the name of the Lord Jesus.** 17. **Then laid they their hands on them, and they received the Holy Spirit.** "In a book so marked by the working of the Holy Spirit that it has received the name of the 'gospel of the Spirit,' it is difficult to believe that St. Luke can mean to limit the expression *might receive* here and in the following verse, to anything less than a bestowal of that divine indwelling of the Spirit which makes the Christian the temple of God, and which St. Paul speaks of in the very same terms as a permanent possession (Gal. 3 : 2; Rom. 8 : 15). St. Paul's language in 1 Corinthians 12 : 30 makes it plain that the advent of the Holy Spirit was not of necessity attested by any peculiar manifestations, nor were these manifestations essential accompaniments of it. There cannot be any reason to doubt the validity of Philip's baptism, and it is therefore evident that the laying on of hands is here distinct from baptism. But both here and in 19 : 6, it follows closely upon baptism and is performed by apostles. We should remember that Acts does not describe baptism as being completed by laying on of hands; the baptism was not invalid. The Samaritan converts became by its administration, members of the church; and the laying on of hands was not so much a completion of baptism as an addition to it." — *R. J. Knowling.* The words of A. T. Robertson here are sane and sensible. "The laying on of hands did not occur at the great Pentecost (2 : 4, 33), nor in 4 : 31; 10 : 44, nor is it mentioned in 1 Corinthians 12 and 14. It is mentioned in Acts 6 : 7 about the deacons, and in 13 : 3 when Barnabas and Saul left Antioch. And in Saul's case, it was Ananias who laid his hands on him (9 : 17). Hence it cannot be concluded that the Holy Spirit was received only by the laying on of the hands of the apostles or by the hands of any one." 18. **Now when Simon saw that through the laying on of the apostles' hands the Holy Spirit was given, he offered them money,** 19. **saying, Give me also this power, that on whomsoever I lay my hands, he may receive the Holy Spirit.** "The ambition or cupidity of Simon had slumbered for a time, but was now aroused at the sudden prospect of obtaining a power which would enable him to gratify his selfish desires, which would place at his command unbounded wealth and influence. He had seen Philip perform miracles, but had seen no instance until now in which that power had been transferred to others. The interval between this development of his true character and his

Simon Magus. From an old print.

"He offered them money."

20. But Peter said unto him, Thy silver perish with thee, because thou hast thought to obtain the gift of God with money.

21. Thou hast neither part nor lot in this matter: for thy heart is not right before God.

22. Repent therefore of this thy wickedness, and pray the Lord, if perhaps the thought of thy heart shall be forgiven thee.

---

profession of the Christian faith was probably not long." "This act originated our word *simony*, which Webster defines as 'the crime of buying or selling ecclesiastical preferment,' or the 'corrupt presentation of any one to an ecclesiastical benefice for money or reward.' It is fortunate for us that our religious institutions in this country require us to obtain our knowledge of the term from a lexicon." — *H. B. Hackett.* Dean C. J. Vaughan has some very remarkable paragraphs on this tragic episode, but we can here quote only one. His entire chapter is eminently worth reading. "We are all in danger of too much worshiping power. Money is power, and talent is power, and rank is power, and office is power, and knowledge (above all) is power. But all these things are of the earth, and will perish with the earth. Be not ye led astray. Power-worship is too often devil-worship: this Simon, with all his show, was a creature groveling and crawling and creeping among things of time and sense. Let the power you worship be all God's power. You will know it by its signs. You will know it by its pointing upward; by its drawing you toward holiness, toward good, toward charity, toward heaven, toward God; you will know it by its making the unseen world real to you, and the world of show and semblance less attractive. That is the effect of God's power, as it is reflected even in the poor imperfect characters of His children below. How much more, as it shines in the Holy Book, or streams upon us from the mercy-seat above *in the face of Jesus Christ*."

4. HIS REBUKE BY PETER, VS. 20–23. 20. **But Peter said unto him, Thy silver perish with thee, because thou hast thought to obtain the gift of God with money.** 21. **Thou hast neither part nor lot in this matter: for thy heart is not right before God.** Here is a double revelation, first of Peter's own heart, and then of Simon's heart. Peter had many faults, but a love for money was not one of them. This was the tragedy of Judas Iscariot. Peter may have made many blunders, and at times proved himself a coward, but one thing he knew, that the gospel of Christ was the gospel of holiness, and that whatever power he had, or anybody else would have, in the name of Christ, must be by a divine bestowal, through the Holy Spirit, in the name of Christ, not something mechanical, not something to be bought, not something which could be passed automatically from man to man. It is one thing to *ask God* for divine power, that we may use it for His glory in saving souls; it is another thing to seek spiritual power for ourselves, that we ourselves may be exalted among men, that our own reputation may be enhanced, or, worst of all, that our income might be multiplied. This man's *heart* was wrong. He did not know the true God, and he was not seeking the will of God. Joseph Parker has a powerful page on this phrase of Peter's, "Thy money perish with thee," in which he says, in part: "The church had not then become a machine. Ordination was not then a thing to be arranged. It was *inspiration*. It was the sudden seizing of the mind, and its transformation into spiritual dignity and majesty. We do not understand this now. Men are now 'prepared' for the ministry. Now we 'educate' men for the pulpit. By all means be educated, be instructed; but educate the *man*, and the *citizen*, and let the pulpit alone. You do not educate the poet. You educate the men; and too much education we cannot have; there is no virtue in ignorance; ignorance is always weakness; therefore would I uphold strenuously the education of the *citizen*, the *subject*, the *man*, the *individual*, but let the pulpit *receive the gift of God*." 22. **Repent therefore of this thy wickedness, and pray the Lord, if perhaps the thought of thy heart shall be forgiven thee.** "On the condition of prayer and repentance not only could the stern wish of Peter be averted, but the anger of God also. But the phrase seems to imply that to Peter's mind there was not much hope of such repentance. The word rendered *thought* is found in the New Testament only here, and gives the idea of a matured plan. The Apostle sees how full the mind of Simon has been of the scheme which he has conceived, and the knowledge of this seems expressed in the "if perhaps" with which the clause begins. He will not declare that there is not, not even for such an offender, but the covetousness, which is idolatry, makes repentance almost impossible." — *J. R. Lumby.* 23. **For I see that**

23. For I see that thou art in the gall of bitterness and in the bond of iniquity.

24. And Simon answered and said, Pray ye for me to the Lord, that none of the things which ye have spoken come upon me.

25. They therefore, when they had testified and spoken the word of the Lord, returned to Jerusalem, and preached the gospel to many villages of the Samaritans.

---

thou art in the gall of bitterness and in the bond of iniquity. " The preposition *in* makes a great difficulty in this verse, for the word in the original means *into*, and it seems best to regard the preposition as used with the sense of motion toward a place or state, and subsequent rest there (so in Luke 11 : 7). For the expression ' gall of bitterness ' compare Deuteronomy 29 : 18. The second expression ' bond of iniquity ' is also found in Isaiah 58 : 6. The whole sentence would thus imply that Simon had gone from one evil to another till he had reached, and was remaining in a stage which deserved the reprobation spoken against idolatry in the Old Testament; he had allowed evil to make him its prisoner." — *J. R. Lumby.* The word here translated *gall* is found in the Septuagint of Job 20 : 14, where it is used to translate a Hebrew word meaning the gall of vipers, that is, the poison of vipers, which the ancients supposed to lie in the gall. It may also refer to the gall plant, or wormwood.

5. HIS REQUEST FOR PRAYER, v. 24. 24. **And Simon answered and said, Pray ye for me to the Lord, that none of the things which ye have spoken come upon me.** " The sordid sorcerer, spared a more fearful doom which might have righteously overtaken him, seemed for the moment to be covered with confusion and remorse. The rebuke was not without effect; the barbed dart of the Apostle had reached his guilty heart; and smarting under it, perhaps with a knowledge of the swift and powerful retribution that had been visited on the other two victims of lying and avarice in Jerusalem, he importunately entreats his reprover to pray to the Lord for him, that none of the things spoken might come upon him. It seems, however, to have been only a momentary flash of conviction, a momentary selfish dread of punishment — the cry of terror without the pang of genuine penitence." — *J. R. MacDuff.* Alford says that Simon here speaks much as Pharaoh (Exod. 8 : 28; 9 : 28), who yet hardened his heart afterwards. " It is observable also, that he wishes merely for the averting of the punishment. The words seem remarkably to set forth the mere terror of the carnal man without any idea of the *me* becoming another man in thoughts and aims."

IV. SUBSEQUENT EVANGELIZING LABORS, Acts 8 : 25. 25. **They therefore, when they had testified and spoken the word of the Lord, returned to Jerusalem, and preached the gospel to many villages of the Samaritans.** " What they had seen convinced them of the fitness of the Samaritans to receive the gospel, and they felt that the time had come to act upon their Lord's command (1 : 8). But the message cannot have been very widely accepted, since we find the Samaritans later in collision with the Christians. They were so severely punished by Zeno and Justinian for murdering Christians and destroying churches, that they never afterwards recovered. One fact, however, of importance we do know about the Christian Church in Samaria — that it produced Justin Martyr, the first considerable writer in the early Church." — *W. M. Furneaux.*

SOME THINGS MONEY CANNOT BUY.

" Simon had that mercenary mind which St. Paul calls the *root of all evil.* He thought that money could do anything. He deified money. Knowing what it was to him; how he taught for money, and practiced sorcery for money, and aimed at popularity for money, and set himself up as *some great one* for money; he took it for granted that every one else regarded money in the same way. Alas, what an idolatry of money is there in a Christian land, in the Christian Church! What revelations are daily made of the light in which we look at money. If there are none now who seek to buy God's gifts with money, at least are there not some who consent to sell their own souls for money? Oh, these dishonesties in trade, in speculation, in trusts, yes, even in charity! If we really cared for God's gifts, I can even fancy that some of us might offer money for them. If we do not offer money for God's gifts, is it not because we care ten thousand times more for things which money can purchase?

Money can get a luxurious table, a well-furnished house, a gay equipage; or, if there is not enough for these, at least it can buy us a humbler or a coarser kind of bodily indulgence. It can do more; it can buy consideration, it can buy flattery, it can buy fawning and cringing, it can buy a thousand attentions while we live, and a few crumbs of gratitude when we lie low in death. But I will tell you what no money can buy; it cannot buy any one of God's highest gifts; it cannot even buy health, or eyesight, or comeliness; it cannot buy the affection of one human being; it cannot buy repose of conscience, hope in death, or a single ray of the sweet and secret and supporting love of God. And therefore a man who learns by long habit to think that money is everything is as much what the Scripture calls a fool as he is what the Scripture counts a sinner. That thoroughly mercenary mind is one of the very lowest and most debased types of the fallen human character. That is the real sin of Simony." — *C. J. Vaughan.*

How many different characters appear in our lesson, and what are some of the fundamental differences distinguishing each from the other? What is the difference between the power which drove Philip to go up to Samaria to preach, and the passion which prompted Simon's request for power? What are some of the things which a father can pass on to his son, and what are some of the things which a father cannot pass on to his son? Do you think that there are today places where the gospel has been heard just as little as in Samaria before Philip went there to preach? (The answer is, Yes; even in our own country there are many hamlets where people have never heard a real gospel sermon, except, thank God, many are now hearing the gospel over the radio.) What is the difference between the reaction of this sorcerer to Philip's preaching in Samaria, and the reaction of many of the Ephesians who were practicing magical arts, to Paul's preaching in their city (Acts 19: 18–20)? How could this vice of simony be practiced even in some ecclesiastical circles today?

LESSON VIII. — May 23.

BIBLE TEACHINGS ON WINE'S DECEITFULNESS. — Proverbs 20 : 1; 23 : 29–35; Matthew 24 : 45–51.

GOLDEN TEXT. — ***At the last it biteth like a serpent, and stingeth like an adder.*** PROVERBS 23 : 32.

Devotional Reading: Galatians 6 : 7–10.
Beginner Topic: AS JESUS GREW UP.
 Lesson Material: 1 Peter 2 : 9–25; Luke 2 : 39–52.
 Memory Verse: Children, obey your parents. Colossians 3 : 20.
Primary Topic: JESUS' FRIEND PETER.
 Lesson Material: 1 Peter 1 : 1; 2 : 11–25.
 Memory Verse: By this shall all men know that ye are my disciples, if ye have love one to another. John 13 : 35.
Junior Topic: MORE LIKE HIS MASTER.
 Lesson Material: 1 Peter 1 : 1; 2 : 11–25.
 Memory Verse: By this shall all men know that ye are my disciples, if ye have love one to another. John 13 : 35.
Intermediate and Senior Topic: JUDGING DRINKS BY WHAT THEY DO.
Topic for Young People and Adults: ALCOHOL THE DECEIVER.

THE TEACHER AND HIS CLASS.

The Younger Classes will not be too young to understand what is meant by the importance of *ultimate consequences.* It may be according to our own lazy dispositions not to do our home work and not to study our lessons, and to neglect them may be very nice for a day or two, or a week or two. Suddenly, however, an examination falls upon us, and, not having our lesson, we flunk, and then we are kept back in school. This means that we are not growing in knowledge, that we will not some day be equipped for the work we ought to do, etc., etc. So, in the matter of eating, we sometimes gorge ourselves at the table because the food tastes good, and then, before another day comes, we are violently sick and the doctor is at the bedside. Our acts must be considered in the light of their *ultimate consequences.* This is what our lesson attempts to set forth, in relation to the matter of intoxicating beverages.

The Older Classes. We are, of course, living in a time when drinking is considered smart, when it is practiced on a vast scale. We are also living in a time when our nation needs all the strength, the intelligence, the wealth, the courage it can command. Now, the whole business of liquor robs men of strength, leads them to squander money on that which has no permanent value, incapacitates men for tasks demanding great endurance, and greatly weakens a nation's fidelity, as some of the notes in this lesson will reveal. This is supremely the time for our country to be emphatically temperate.

THE LESSON IN ITS SETTING.

Time. — The book of Proverbs was written somewhere between 1000 B.C. and 1025 B.C. Our Lord's words on the Mount of Olives were uttered Tuesday, April 4, A.D. 30.

Place. — The book of Proverbs may have been written in the city of Jerusalem; the parable taken from our Lord's discourse was uttered on the Mount of Olives opposite and east of Jerusalem.

THE PLAN OF THE LESSON.

SUBJECT: A Word from God Warning Us Against Indulging in Those Things Which Lead to Wickedness and Foolishness.

I. THE EVIL CONSEQUENCES OF HABITUALLY DRINKING INTOXICATING BEVERAGES, Prov. 20 : 1; 23 : 29–35.
1. Wine deceives those who drink it, 20 : 1.
2. It results in sorrows of heart, 23 : 29, 30.
3. Finally it brings a sting, 23 : 31, 32.
4. It arouses sensual desires, 23 : 33 *a*.
5. It stupefies one's senses, 23 : 34, 35.

II. TWO KINDS OF SERVANTS, Matt. 24 : 45–51.
1. The faithful and wise servants, vs. 45–47.
2. The evil servant, vs. 48–51.

THE TEACHER'S LIBRARY.

Many works on the book of Proverbs are of really no value in the study of the particular verses of our

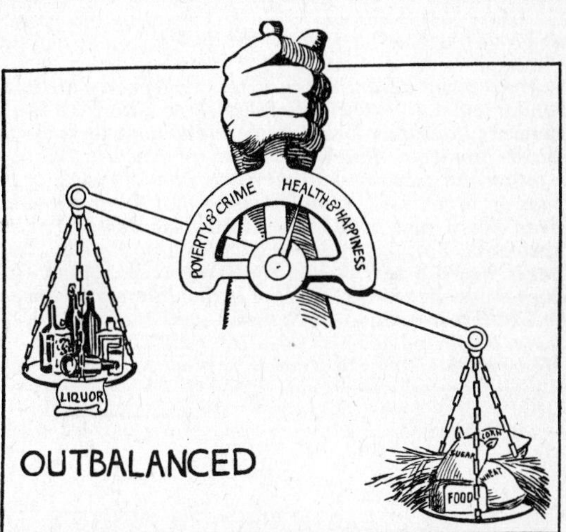

lesson, but see the commentaries by Adolf Zöckler in *Lange's Commentary*, the work by Moses Stuart, and, especially, Charles Bridges: *An Exposition of the Book of Proverbs* (New York, 1847); and E. H. Plumptre in the *Bible Commentary*. Sermonic material is scarce, especially recent material; see William Stevens Perry: *Life Lessons from the Book of Proverbs*, 207–224; H. M. Wharton: *Gospel Talks* (Baltimore, 1886), 133–143; Alexander Maclaren: *Expositions of Holy Scripture, Esther to Ecclesiastes*, 256–263; W. R. Riley: *The Bible of the Expositor and the Evangelist, Proverbs*, 209–222. One may also consult T. R. Lees and Dawson Burns: *The Temperance Bible Commentary* (6th edit., 1894), 133–139.

On the parable taken from Matthew's Gospel many commentaries on Matthew will be found to be of really no value, and most books on the parables of our Lord, for some strange reason, do not include a treatment of this passage. See, however, the relevant pages in G. Campbell Morgan: *The Gospel According to St. Matthew;* and the work by J. M. Gibson in the *Expositor's Bible;* as well as Alexander Maclaren: *Bible Class Expositions, St. Matthew*, Vol. 2, 132–140.

PROVERBS 20 : 1. Wine is a mocker, strong drink a brawler; and whosoever erreth thereby is not wise.

I. THE EVIL CONSEQUENCES OF HABITUALLY DRINKING INTOXICATING BEVERAGES, Prov. 20 : 1; 23 : 29–35.

1. WINE DECEIVES THOSE WHO DRINK IT, 20 : 1. 1. **Wine is a mocker, strong drink a brawler; and whosoever erreth thereby is not wise.** "The spirit of wine or strong drink appears here personified or represented as in a sense an evil demon, which excites to frivolous wantonness, to wild and boisterous action, and by the confusion

PROVERBS 23 : 29. Who hath woe? who hath sorrow? who hath contentions? who hath complaining? who hath wounds without cause? who hath redness of eyes?
30. They that tarry long at the wine; they that go to seek out mixed wine.
31. Look not thou upon the wine when it is red, when it sparkleth in the cup, when it goeth down smoothly:
32. At the last it biteth like a serpent, and stingeth like an adder.

---

of the senses into which it plunges man, robs him of all clear self-possession." — *Otto Zöckler.* "The Hebrew word here translated *mocker* is from a verb frequently applied to men who scorn or contemn that which is good (Prov. 9 : 7, 8; 13 : 1, etc.). Here it denotes their character. As applied to the wine that intoxicates, this word symbolizes the effect of such wine upon the drunkard; either inclining him to mock at serious things, or in the mockery, it may, by a figure, be said to make such of the good resolutions he forms before partaking of it. The statement that strong drink is raging teaches that it causes disturbances internally to those who drink it — this is to the latter physically true — and through them externally to their families and society at large. Nor are vocal signs of this disturbing agency often absent." — *F. R. Lees.* May it not be that wine also deceives in this, that it promises a pleasure which does not abide, a strength it cannot communicate, a joy it cannot sustain.

2. IT RESULTS IN SORROWS OF HEART, 23 : 29, 30. 29. **Who hath woe? who hath sorrow? who hath contentions? who hath complaining? who hath wounds without cause? who hath redness of eyes?** "The trouble here spoken of is strictly anxious care, complaint; the wounds without cause are wounds received in causeless or wholly unprofitable disputes, wounds and stripes such as come of the brawls of drunken men; finally the dark redness of the eyes is the revolting effect of excessive wine as it shows itself in the face (see Gen. 49 : 12)." — *Otto Zöckler.* 30. **They that tarry long at the wine; they that go to seek out mixed wine.** "Mixed wine is that which is flavored with aromatic spices that increase its stimulating properties. There is a touch of sarcasm in the phrase 'go to seek.' The word elsewhere used of diligent search after knowledge (Job 11 : 7; Prov. 25 : 2) is here used as if ironically, of the investigations of connoisseurs in wine, meeting to test its qualities." — *E. H. Plumptre.*

3. FINALLY IT BRINGS A STING, 23 : 31, 32. 31. **Look not thou upon the wine when it is red, when it sparkleth in the cup, when it goeth down smoothly.** "The wine of Lebanon is said to be of a rich golden color like Malaga or the darker sherries. Sometimes the color is heightened by saffron. In the Hebrew, the phrase translated 'goeth down smoothly' describes the pellucid stream flowing pleasantly from the wine skin or jug into the goblet or the throat." — *E. H. Plumptre.* "The whole sentence blends the attractiveness to the senses of the wine in color, effervescence, and taste." — *Alexander Maclaren.* 32. **At the last it biteth like a serpent, and stingeth like an adder.** "Did wine bite first, who would touch it? Did Satan present the cup in his own naked form, who would dare to take it? If poison was seen in the cup, who would venture upon it? Yet is the poison less dangerous because it is unseen? The adder's sting is concealed, yet most fatal." — *Charles Bridges.* The headaches, the stupefying consequences, the sins of remorse, the loss of strength for work, the inability to undertake one's normal daily tasks, the nausea which often follows, the ulcerated condition of stomachs, the bloated face, the bleary eye, all these things are involved in the sting which follows the so-called pleasure of drinking.

4. IT AROUSES SENSUAL DESIRES, 23 : 33 *a.* **Thine eyes shall behold strange things.** It will be noticed that in the Authorized Version this phrase concludes, "Behold strange women," and so does it read in the margin of the Revised Version, and it is that translation which we retain in our discussion. That drinking leads to sensuality all history testifies. The lascivious pictures hung in drinking places, the coarse language that follows even partial intoxication, the connection of taverns and saloons with shameful institutions, all testify to the fact that alcohol sensually inflames men and women and drives them to an abandonment of all moral restraint, so that, under the influence of this accursed stuff, hardly anything is counted impure or vile or unclean. Sins do not stand alone, one leads to another, one embraces another.

33. Thine eyes shall behold strange things, and thy heart shall utter perverse things.
34. Yea, thou shalt be as he that lieth down in the midst of the sea, or as he that lieth upon the top of a mast.
35. They have stricken me, *shalt thou say*, and I was not hurt; they have beaten me, and I felt it not: when shall I awake? I will seek it yet again.

---

5. IT LEADS MEN TO SAY FOOLISH THINGS, 23:33 *b*. **And thy heart shall utter perverse things.** There are two conditions under which a man's words are not counted as of any value, and he is not held accountable for them; namely, the condition of insanity, and the condition of intoxication. When a man is intoxicated, his words become boastful, arrogant, brutal, foul, foolish, and often false. He thinks he is ten times the man that he really is. He talks about achievements he has never accomplished; he allows himself to indulge in coarse conversation, which at other times, uninflamed by drink, he would even shudder to hear. The editor himself had an experience of such a fact not long ago when traveling from New York to Paoli. He was sitting in the parlor car late one night when a group of only five men remained, and so coarse did the conversation of two of these men become, loud at the same time, that the pullman conductor, knowing the editor to be a clergyman (from his clergy certificate), came up to him and said: " This is no place for you, nor for me either. I will let you sit in a private bedroom until you get to your destination." What is the good of all this? Men only think less of us; we think less of ourselves, and our nature is vulgarized by the outpouring of such stuff.

6. IT STUPEFIES ONE'S SENSES, 23 : 34, 35. 34. **Yea, thou shalt be as he that lieth down in the midst of the sea, or as he that lieth upon the top of a mast.** " A man who would try to lie down and go to sleep in the heart of the sea, or on the masthead of a ship, would be a manifest fool and would not keep life in him for long. One has seen drunken men lying down to sleep in places as exposed and as ridiculous as these; on public roads or on railway tracks, or anywhere where the fancy took him. The point of the verse seems to be the drunken man's utter loss of fitness and complete incapacity to take care of himself. He cannot estimate dangers. The very instinct of self-preservation has forsaken him. There he lies though as sure to be drowned as if he were in the depth of the sea, though on as uncomfortable a bed as if he were rocking on a masthead where he could not balance himself." — *Alexander Maclaren.* Strange to say, the night before writing this very lesson, the editor here in Chicago saw a poor fellow propped up against a water hydrant, sound asleep, in bitter winter, on the corner of one of the most heavily traveled streets of our city, near his pushcart piled up with junk which he had gathered together from the alleys. He would certainly catch cold sleeping there for hours in the chill of the night; anyone could steal the result of his day's hard work; and he could easily be run over by a careless driver. You could not get within ten feet of him but you knew what was wrong; he simply reeked with the cheapest kind of whiskey. The man that sells this kind of stuff is a criminal. 35. **They have stricken me, *shalt thou say*, and I was not hurt; they have beaten me and I felt it not: when shall I awake? I will seek it yet again.** " The fool returns to his folly craving foolish indulgences. So lost and ashamed his reason, so tyrannized by his appetite, that he longs to be bound again and only seeks relief from his temporary awakening to a sense of his misery by yielding himself up again to his ruinous sin (see Jer. 2 : 25)." — *Charles Bridges.* " The inebriate does not apprehend any danger. His friends warn him of sickness and blows and wounds; but he derides them saying, I have felt no bruises, I will not hear your advice, but as soon as I have slept I will again seek the cup. What he says is in contempt or ridicule of his friends." — *Moses Stuart.* " The tyranny of desire which awakes into full activity before the rest of the man does, and the inevitable will which in spite of all bruises and discomforts yields at once to the overmastering desire, make the tragedy of a drunkard's life. There comes a point in life's fleshly indulgence in which the craving seems to escape from the control of the will altogether. Doctors tell us that the necessity for drink becomes a physical disease. Yes, but it is a disease manufactured by the patient himself, and he is responsible for getting himself into such a state." — *Alexander Maclaren.*

There is one phrase here we ought to emphasize, " Look not thou upon the wine when it is red." The whole passage is full of warning, but there is only one definite admonition, one thing for men to *do*, and that is to take this matter of drinking in

MATTHEW 24 : 45. Who then is the faithful and wise servant, whom his lord hath set over his household, to give them their food in due season?

46. Blessed is that servant, whom his lord when he cometh shall find so doing.

47. Verily I say unto you, that he will set him over all that he hath.

48. But if that evil servant shall say in his heart, My lord tarrieth;

49. And shall begin to beat his fellow-servants, and shall eat and drink with the drunken;

50. The lord of that servant shall come in a day when he expecteth not, and in an hour when he knoweth not,

51. And shall cut him asunder, and appoint his portion with the hypocrites: there shall be the weeping and the gnashing of teeth.

---

hand before it becomes one's master, and not even go where these things will be put in the way to tempt us. There are times when we cannot avoid eating in places where liquor is served because it is served almost everywhere, but we do not have to stand up at the bar with some friend; we do not have to sit at the table where cocktails are being served; we do not have to mingle with company that must drink; we do not have to let our nostrils breathe the odors of these intoxicating beverages; we do not have to let our eyes rest upon the sparkle of these colored liquids. If we are not near the poison, we will not then be tempted to partake of it. The further away we keep from everything involved in this whole horrible business, the safer we will be. And, if God has so ordained that you have never been tempted by these flaming beverages, thank God, but be patient with those who are its slave, speak to them about a Saviour who can deliver from every evil thing.

II. **TWO KINDS OF SERVANTS,** Matt. 24 : 45–51. This parable of our Lord's has been seldom commented upon, for some strange reason. 45. **Who then is the faithful and wise servant, whom his lord hath set over his household, to give them their food in due season?** 46. **Blessed is that servant, whom his lord when he cometh shall find so doing.** 47. **Verily I say unto you, that he will set him over all that he hath.** 48. **But if that evil servant shall say in his heart, My lord tarrieth;** 49. **and shall begin to beat his fellow-servants, and shall eat and drink with the drunken;** 50. **the lord of that servant shall come in a day when he expecteth not, and in an hour when he knoweth not,** 51. **and shall cut him asunder, and appoint his portion with the hypocrites: there shall be the weeping and the gnashing of teeth.** The best practical comments I have seen anywhere on this paragraph are those by Dr. G. Campbell Morgan, and we take the liberty of quoting quite fully from his superb exposition. " In the parable of the household, the word itself is suggestive. Jesus said: ' Who then is the faithful and wise servant, whom his lord hath set over his *household?* ' The Greek word here translated household is only once again used. In Revelation (22 : 2) we read that ' the leaves of the tree were for the *healing* of the nations.' What relation can there be between healing and household? This question can only be answered by an understanding of what this word household really signifies. It is the word from which we derive our word *therapeutic*, and the basal idea of it is healing. The word household refers to all such in the house as serve. That first word, ' Who then is the faithful and wise *servant?* ' is the word bond-slave; but the word household comes from another term for servant, which is other than the word bond-slave. It is a word that signifies a loving service, a purpose of healing in service. This word, then, suggests the picture of a great house, and one Lord; and of all those in the house under His control, as thinking of His interests, while serving under His command. He used the word that indicated the love principle in service, the tender healing ministry that only grows out of love. Thus in a word, flaming and flashing with meaning, we discover our Lord's conception of His Church, during the time of His absence. His household all serve, but all serve by love, and the ministry is a healing ministry. Now let us very carefully notice His word: ' Who then is the faithful and wise servant, whom his lord hath set over his household? ' Service is the condition of greatness. The servant is ' set over.' Why ' set over '? Because he is a servant. This is not a picture of the priesthood, or of the ministry according to many modern conceptions of these. There is no sense in which any priesthood or ministry is set over the Church of God, save by their ministry. 'Whosoever would be first among you, shall be servant of all.' Here is Christ's picture of one servant set over the rest, because he serves all the rest. It is not a picture of any man in the household, it is not a picture of one in official authority; it is the picture of each one in the exercise of the ministry of healing and of love. Now, in the parable we see two attitudes. First that of the faithful and wise servant. His attitude is simply that of bringing forth meat in due season, and feeding the rest; the attitude of caring for all the other members of the household during the lord's absence, for the sake of the absent lord. But there is another servant here, and Jesus speaks of him as 'that evil servant.' He says, 'My lord tarrieth.' He is not returning yet; and with that sense of the Master's absence, he turns to evil courses within the household, beating his fellow servants instead of feeding and caring for them; turning aside to the companionship of drunken men, instead of standing in the place of loyalty to the absent lord. In the parable we have two results. When the lord returns, the servant who has been loyal to the service of his fellow servants, for the sake of his absent lord, is promoted and put into the place of a new authority; while the evil servant is cut asunder and cast out."

"This portrait presupposes that a long period will elapse before Christ comes. The secret thought of the evil servant is the thought of a time far down the ages from the moment of our Lord's speaking. It would take centuries for such a temper to be developed in the Church. What is the temper? A secret dismissal of the anticipation of the Lord's return, and that not merely because He has been long in coming, but as thinking that He has broken His word, and has not come when He said He would. This unspoken dimming over of the expectation and unconfessed doubt of the firmness of the promise is the natural product of the long time of apparent delay which the Church has had to encounter. It will cloud and depress the religion of later ages, unless there be constant effort to resist the tendency and to keep awake. The first generations were all aflame with the glad hope 'Maranatha' — 'The Lord is at hand.' Their successors gradually lost the keenness of expectation, and at most cried, 'Will not He come soon?' Their successors saw the starry hope through thickening mists of years; and now it scarcely shines for many, or at least is but a dim point, when it should blaze as a sun. It was an 'evil' servant who said so in his heart. He was evil because he said it, and he said it because he was evil; for the yielding to sin and the withdrawal of love from Jesus dims the desire for His coming, and makes the whisper that He delays a hope; while, on the other hand, the hope that He delays helps to open the sluices, and let sin flood the life. So an outburst of cruel masterfulness and of riotous sensuality is the consequence of the dimmed expectation. There would have been no usurpation of authority over Christ's heritage by priest or pope, or any other, if that hope had not become faint. If professing Christians lived with the great white throne, and the heavens and earth fleeing away before Him that sits on it, ever burning before their inward eye, how could they wallow amid the mire of animal indulgence? The dreadful doom of the unwatchful servant is cast into a form of awful severity. The cruel punishment of sawing asunder, which, tradition says, was suffered by Isaiah, and was not unfamiliar in old times, is his. What concealed terror of retribution it signifies we do not know. Perhaps it points to a fate in which a man shall be, as it were, parted into two, each at enmity with the other. Perhaps it implies a retribution in kind for his sin, which consisted, as the next clause implies, in hypocrisy, which is the sundering in twain of inward conviction and practice, and is avenged by a like but worse rending apart of conscience and will. At all events, it shadows a fearful retribution, which is not extinction, inasmuch as, in the next clause, we read that his portion — his lot or that condition which belongs to him by virtue of his character — is with the hypocrites. He was one of them, because, while he said 'my lord,' he had ceased to love and obey, having ceased to desire and expect; and therefore whatever be their fate shall be his, even to the dividing asunder of soul and spirit, and setting eternal discord among the thoughts and intents of the heart. That is not the punishment of unwatchfulness, but of what unwatchfulness leads to, if unawakened. Let these words of the King ring an alarm for us all, and rouse our sleepy souls to watch, as becomes the children of the day." — *Alexander Maclaren.*

"Heavy smoking has a positive and demonstrably bad effect on longevity, physical and nervous energy, and general health. With every puff, heavy smokers shorten their own lives. Dr. Raymond Pearl of Johns Hopkins found that among 100,000 heavy (over ten cigarettes a day) smokers, 53,774 die before the age of 60. Among the same number of nonsmokers, only 43,436 die before that age. 'Smoking,' he announced, 'is associated with definite impairment of longevity. This impairment is proportional to the habitual amount of tobacco used.' Even if you smoke moderately, you have much less chance of reaching 60 than if you don't smoke at all. It's a slow count, but it gets you finally. . . . Under the flogging of the nicotine whip, the body burns up sugar faster; heart action, respiration and blood pressure are kept at a ding-dong pitch. At the end of a two-pack day, the smoker's system has received an unmerciful beating. Impoverished nerves and body cells cry out with fatigue and irritation. The chain-smoker suffers from a chronic 'tired feeling.' He is an energy bankrupt and must borrow new energy at the outrageous interest rate of still heavier smoking. Meanwhile, his food tastes like a motorman's glove, and a hacking cough keeps his throat as raw as a sandpapered blister. Some fun, smoking! . . . Too many people accept their craving for tobacco as a commonplace social habit. But I maintain that heavy smoking is a *disease symptom*. Whenever I see a chain-smoker in action I know at once that he is plain sick and should submit to a searching medical examination to discover the underlying cause of his smoking. On the physical side, this may range from a thyroid deficiency to a faulty diet or lack of exercise. Or there may be an emotional factor. My psychiatrist friends tell me that most of their patients are frantic smokers. When their lives get straightened out, the craving for tobacco falls away. I have always opposed the pernicious advertising that extols the 'benefits' of tobacco-using. While I was training for my second fight with Jack Dempsey I was offered $15,000 to endorse a certain brand of cigarettes. I didn't want to be rude, so, in declining, I merely said I didn't smoke. Next day the advertising man came back with another offer: $12,000 if I would let my picture be used with the statement that 'Stinkies must be good, because all my friends smoke them.' That compelled me to say what I thought — that cigarettes were a foul pestilence, and that advertising which promoted their use was a national menace. I am here reminded of the Metropolitan Opera tenor whose picture was blazoned on billboards with this joyful declamation: 'Gaspies Do Not Hurt My Throat.' When asked about it, he laughed and replied: 'It is true, Gaspies never hurt my throat. I don't smoke.' Such misleading advertising I cannot rap too hard. It is dangerous, particularly to our 35,000,000 young people. To contract the tobacco habit when the growth factors of the body are exerting themselves to their maximum is to handicap oneself physically and mentally for life. To me the ugliest of advertising is that which features soldiers or sailors smoking cigarettes. As Director of the Navy's Physical Fitness Program, I can bluntly say that few things could be worse for physical fitness than promoting the cigarette habit." — *Gene Tunney* (from a remarkable article of his, "Nicotine Knockout, or the Slow Count," in *The Reader's Digest*, December, 1941; by the kind permission of the Reader's Digest Association, Inc.).

A word concerning our young people and their drinking habits. That liquor is getting a terrific hold upon our young people there is no question. What are we going to do about it? Well, there are a number of things to do. In the first place, we must set them the right kind of an example. No father or mother has any right to complain about children drinking if they themselves drink. A friend told me recently that he told his two boys, who are away at school: "You boys have a right to do anything you see your father do, and he hopes you will not do those things which you know he does not do." That is a fine ideal to set before our children. In the second place, we should provide the very best, cleanest, most satisfying social life for our young people, places for them to meet, entertainment for them to enjoy, forms of clean sport in which they can actively and enthusiastically participate. In the third place, they should at least be given the facts about this cursed business of drinking. It does not make any difference how vividly the facts are presented providing nothing is exaggerated. A visit to a ward in some hospital where one will find men broken with liquor, would not be a bad thing. Watching men stumble out of some saloon at night might help, though the watching should be done from the outside. The strong clear statements of our doctors regarding the wretched physical consequences of periodic indulgence in liquor should be known to our young people. In the fourth place, they should, as far as possible, have the highest ideals, great objectives, set before them, something worth living for, the desire to be men of power, men of culture, men of refinement, men of wholesome influence, men whose lives are counting in this world. That is the tragedy with so many of our young people, they do not seem to have anything noble to live for — a few hours' work, a pay check at the end of the week, and a gay time until the next work day begins. Finally, what we need is a great revival. So many millions of our young people are not believers in the Lord Jesus Christ, are not regularly in church on the Lord's day, and are not indwelt by the Holy Spirit. The heaviest drinking, no matter what one says to the contrary, is outside of Christian circles. Where you find young people doing things for Christ, testifying to Christ, in love with Christ, you find the liquor question solved.

Fundamentally, what do you think are the major reasons for men drinking when most of them know the terrible consequences which will result? In how many different ways is a man in his entire nature, weakened and debased by intoxication? What are we going to do for our young people who are drinking so tragically today?

LESSON IX. — May 30.

PETER'S COUNSEL TO SCATTERED CHRISTIANS. — 1 Peter 1 : 1; 2 : 9–25.

PRINTED TEXT, 1 Peter 1 : 1; 2 : 11-25.

GOLDEN TEXT. — *Honor all men. Love the brotherhood. Fear God. Honor the king.* 1 PETER 2 : 17.

Devotional Reading: Romans 12 : 1–8.
Beginner Topic: MOSES' BIG SISTER.
Lesson Material: 1 Peter 3 : 13; 5 : 6, 7; Exodus 2 : 1–10.
Memory Verse: He careth for you. 1 Peter 5 : 7.
Primary Topic: PETER IN PRISON.
Lesson Material: 1 Peter 3 : 13–15; 5 : 6, 7; Acts 12 : 1–17.
Memory Verse: God . . . careth for you. 1 Peter 5 : 6, 7.
Junior Topic: PETER IN PRISON.
Lesson Material: 1 Peter 3 : 13–15; 5 : 6, 7; Acts 12 : 1–17.
Memory Verse: A cheerful heart is a good medicine. Proverbs 17 : 22.
Intermediate and Senior Topic: HOW A CHRISTIAN OUGHT TO LIVE.
Topic for Young People and Adults: THE CHRISTIAN AS A CITIZEN.

THE TEACHER AND HIS CLASS.

The Younger Classes might be introduced to this lesson by being reminded that different things are expected of different people, according to the position they hold in life, the honor that men give them, and the influence which they exert. For instance, a woman would be more careful than ever of what she said and did, and where she went, when she had her own precious children to bring up, than in the days before she had any children. A minister surely should live without spot and without blemish before his people, because of the high privilege which he has of preaching to them the Word of God. A school teacher, because of his or her influence, has a far greater obligation resting upon him or her to live nobly and strongly and uprightly than, say, some one who is driving a truck, who will never influence children, or a chemist who is shut up in his laboratory all day. Our lesson tells us of the high and exalted position which all Christians have in Christ, and then tells us the kind of a life we ought to live because of our exalted privileges.

The Older Classes, in these bewildering days, will find here a voice from God regarding the things we ought to do, and the things we ought not to do. But before these, what we might call Christian commandments, are dwelt upon, the teacher should be careful to make clear the fact, which is so often ignored, that such a life as is depicted here is never to be attempted or expected, except it springs from the spiritual, dynamic relationship that we have to Jesus Christ, made possible by His redeeming work for us. Such a life as is set forth in this passage is never to be presented to unbelieving men for their attainment, but to Christians, who are energized by divine power.

THE LESSON IN ITS SETTING.

Time. — Probably about A.D. 60.

Place. — See the extended note at the beginning of the lesson for June 6, under "Place."

THE PLAN OF THE LESSON.

SUBJECT: The Exalted Place into Which Christ Has Brought Us and the Life We Ought to Be Daily Living Because of This Exalted Position.

I. THE APOSTLE'S SALUTATION, 1 Peter 1 : 1.

II. OUR EXALTED POSITION BY DIVINE GRACE, 1 Peter 2 : 9, 10.

1. An elected race.
2. A royal priesthood.
3. A holy nation.
4. A purchased people.
5. A people called out of darkness into light.
6. A people who have obtained mercy.

III. THE LIFE WE SHOULD BE LIVING BECAUSE OF OUR EXALTED POSITION, 1 Peter 2 : 11–20.

1. A life of abstention from fleshly lusts, vs. 11, 12.
2. A life of obedience to civil law, vs. 13–16.
3. A life in which all men are honored, v. 17.
4. A life of love for our brethren, v. 17.
5. A life manifesting fear of God, v. 17.
6. A life of cheerful subjection to our masters, vs. 18–20.

IV. CHRIST OUR EXAMPLE IN HIS SUFFERING, 1 Peter 2 : 21–24.

1. The fact of His being our Example, v. 21.
2. His sinlessness, v. 22.
3. His unrevengefulness, v. 23.
4. His vicarious death for us, v. 24.

V. CHRIST THE SHEPHERD AND BISHOP OF OUR SOULS, 1 Peter 2 : 25.

THE TEACHER'S LIBRARY.

There are a number of excellent commentaries on First Peter, including the one by E. H. Plumptre (in the *Cambridge Bible for Schools and Colleges*); the very full and excellent notes by A. J. Mason, in the *Bible Commentary for English Readers;* F. C. Cook, in the *Bible Commentary;* J. R. Lumby (in the *Expositor's Bible*); G. F. C. Frönmueller in the Lange series of commentaries; and, for those who follow the Greek text, Charles Bigg, in the *International Critical Commentary* series; J. E. Huther, in the famous series of *New Testament Commentaries* edited by H. A. W. Meyer; J. H. A. Hort, in the *Expositor's Greek Testament.* For expository material, see the superb work by F. B. Meyer: *Tried by Fire;* and the not so definite, but in places helpful, volume, *The Redeemed Family of God*, by J. H. Jowett. For sermonic material on 1 : 1 see Alexander Maclaren: *Expositions of Holy Scripture, Epistles of 1 and 2 Peter, 1 John*, 1–7; on 2 : 16, H. P. Liddon: *Easter in St. Paul's*, 371–380; on 2 : 17, F. W. Farrar: *Bells and Pomegranates*, 181 ff.; H. P. Liddon: *University Sermons*, First Series, 54–78; J. D. Jones: *The Unfettered Word*, 86–93 (a magnificent sermon); W. L. Watkinson: *The Bane and the Antidote*, 285–304; on 2 : 19, H. P. Liddon, *as above*, 335–345; on 2 : 20, Andrew Murray: *Like Christ*, 27–33; on 2 : 21, Alexander Maclaren, *as above*, 107–116; James Hastings: *Great Texts of the Bible, James to Jude*, 80–99; F. W. Farrar, *as above*, 133 ff.; H. P. Liddon, *as above*, 346–358; on 2 : 24, James Hastings, *as above*, 102–113; Joseph Parker: *The People's Bible*, Vol. 27, 305–313; A. T. Pierson: *The Hopes of the Gospel*, 85 ff.; J. G. Simpson: *Christian Ideals*, 263 ff.; George Smeaton: *The Apostles' Doctrine of the Atonement*, 430–438; on verses 24, 25, an unusually fine exposition in James M. Gray's *Salvation from Start to Finish*, 35–52.

On Christ our Example, see a magnificent article by J. R. Van Pelt, in James Hastings: *Dictionary of Christ and the Gospels*, Vol. 1, 555–558; Charles Gore: *Belief in Christ*, 174–183; H. P. Liddon: *Sermons on Some Words of St. Paul*, 223–225.

1 PETER 1 : 1. Peter, an apostle of Jesus Christ, to the elect who are sojourners of the Dispersion in Pontus, Galatia, Cappadocia, Asia, and Bithynia.

THE FIRST EPISTLE OF PETER.

The following introductory words of Charles R. Erdman are distinctly worth considering, as we begin this first lesson in the series on the writings of Peter. "Peter was a prominent figure in the world of literature; this 'unlettered layman,' as the rulers regarded him, was one of the authors of the New Testament, one of the immortals among the writers of the Christian era. His abiding influence is linked to the two epistles which bear his name. The first of these letters was written to Christians dwelling in portions of what is now known as Asia Minor. Many of these readers were converts from Judaism, and Peter writes with continual reference to the Old Testament; but the large number were Gentiles, and frequent mention is made of their former mode of life. More important is the fact that all these converts were in the midst of cruel hardships and temptations. They were not suffering from a persecution instituted by the state, but from social ostracism, and from the enmity of fanatical Jews and hostile pagans. They were compelled to endure slander, violence, hatred, suspicion, loss of goods, worldly ruin. To those in distress and trials so bitter and fiery, Peter writes to give counsel and comfort, to strengthen faith and to inspire courage. This is an epistle of hope. It points the believer to the blessed issues of trial, and teaches him to regard present darkness in the light of a future which is radiant with the visible glory of Christ."

I. THE APOSTOLIC SALUTATION, 1 Peter 1 : 1. 1. **Peter, an apostle of Jesus Christ, to the elect who are sojourners of the Dispersion in Pontus, Galatia, Cappadocia, Asia, and Bithynia.** "The authoritative tone of this epistle is shown at the outset. The writer assumes his full titles — the Rock-name which Christ had given him, and the official dignity of an 'apostle of Jesus Christ' — *i.e.*, one

1 PETER 2 : 11. Beloved, I beseech you as sojourners and pilgrims, to abstain from fleshly lusts, which war against the soul;

12. Having your behavior seemly among the Gentiles; that, wherein they speak against you as evil-doers, they may by your good works, which they behold, glorify God in the day of visitation.

charged with full legatine authority from Christ (John 17 : 18; 20 : 21) — a vicar of Christ to the Church, and not only a representative of the Church Godward. . . . The persons for whom the letter is destined are very clearly specified. In John 7 : 35, we have 'the dispersion of the Greeks,' where it clearly means 'those of the dispersed Jews who live among the Greeks,' so here 'the dispersion of Pontus,' or 'the Pontine dispersion,' will mean 'those of the dispersed Jews who live in Pontus.' (See James 1 : 1.) The word rendered 'sojourners' means people who are resident for a time among strangers: it might, for instance, describe English people who have taken houses in Paris without becoming naturalized. . . . The apostle of the circumcision is writing to those of the circumcision. The addition of the words 'the blood of Jesus Christ' is the only thing which shows that they are *Christian* Jews. The provinces named make up the whole, or nearly so, of what we call Asia Minor, are given in no order that can be assigned a meaning. At any rate, the churches of Galatia and Asia owed their origin to Paul. Of the founding of the rest we know nothing; perhaps they were founded by Silas; but Jewish settlers from Cappadocia and Pontus had heard Peter's first sermon on the Church's birthday (Acts 2 : 9). A few years later, and Pliny finds the whole upper shore of Asia Minor overrun and swallowed up by Christians." — *A. J. Mason.*

II. **OUR EXALTED POSITION BY DIVINE GRACE,** 1 Peter 2 : 9, 10. "But ye are an elect race, a royal priesthood, a holy nation, a people for God's own possession, that ye may show forth the excellencies of him who called you out of darkness into his marvelous light. Who in time past were no people, but now are the people of God: who had not obtained mercy, but now have obtained mercy." We regret that these two verses were not included in the printed section of our lesson because they are exceedingly rich. The phrase "an elect race" comes from Isaiah 43 : 20; the phrase "royal priesthood" is derived from the Septuagint of Exodus 19 : 6. "As priests we worship in near proximity to God; as kings we rule over men with a rule born of love which blesses and saves." The phrase "a people for God's own possession" is derived from Deuteronomy 7 : 6, and, probably Isaiah 43 : 21. "Love yearns for proprietorship; nor can the heart of God be satisfied unless it can speak of some as its own. Oh, happy they who have obeyed His summons, and have made a complete surrender of themselves to Him! He has already taken them for His own possession. Enclosed as a garden; tilled as a field; inhabited as a home; guarded, kept, used, loved, with an emphasis none others know. Nor is there anything in God Himself which is not at the disposal of those who hold nothing back from Him." — *F. B. Meyer.* "The word for 'show forth,' which is nowhere else found in the New Testament, means by rights 'to proclaim to those without what has taken place within.' This strict signification is very suitable here. Peter says that God has taken us for a people peculiarly near to Him, and the purpose is, not that we may stand within His courts and praise Him, but that we may carry to others the tidings of what we have been admitted to see." — *A. J. Mason.*

III. **THE LIFE WE SHOULD BE LIVING BECAUSE OF OUR EXALTED POSITION,** 1 Peter 2 : 11–20.

1. A LIFE OF ABSTENTION FROM FLESHLY LUSTS, vs. 11, 12. 11. **Beloved, I beseech you as sojourners and pilgrims.** "In the Septuagint version of Psalm 39 : 12, we find both the words and the thoughts to which Peter now gives utterance." — *E. H. Plumptre.* **To abstain from fleshly lusts, which war against the soul.** "The negative aspect of the Christian life is put forward first, as being prior, both in order of thought, and often in that of time, to its more positive development. The entreaty rests upon the character implied in the previous words. Travelers in a strange land, yet more in the land of enemies, do not care commonly to adopt all its customs. They retain their nationality. . . . The words 'fleshly lusts' have, perhaps, a somewhat wider range than the English term suggests, and take in all desires that originate in man's corrupt nature, as well as those directly connected with the appetites of the body (compare Paul's list of the 'works of the flesh' in Galatians 5 : 19–21). 'Soul' stands here, as in 1 : 9, for the higher element of man's nature." — *E. H. Plumptre.* 12. **Having your behavior seemly among the Gen-**

13. Be subject to every ordinance of man for the Lord's sake: whether to the king, as supreme;

14. Or unto governors, as sent by him for vengeance on evil-doers and for praise to them that do well.

15. For so is the will of God, that by well-doing ye should put to silence the ignorance of foolish men:

---

tiles; that, wherein they speak against you as evil-doers, they may by your good works, which they behold, glorify God in the day of visitation. "The seemly conduct of believers must be continuous, or it will fail of its effects. It is not one display of Christian conduct, nor occasional spasmodic manifestations thereof, which will win men to love the way of Christ. And this is the result without which Christ's people are not to rest satisfied. The evil reports of the adversaries are ill-grounded, but they do not think so; and the only means of removing their perverse view is by a continuous revelation of the excellence of Christ's service. They may rail, but we must bless; they may persecute, we must not retaliate, but returning good always for their evil, make them see at length that this way which they are attacking has a character and a power to which they have been strangers. This enlightenment is implied in the word 'behold': *They behold your good works.* It denotes initiation into a mystery. And to unbelievers Christ's religion must be a mystery. The clearing of the vision leads them up to faith. The word in every place where it occurs in the New Testament is Peter's own, and he employs it once (2 Peter 1 : 16) to describe the vision, the insight, into the glory of Christ which he and his fellows gained at the transfiguration. Such a sight removes all questionings, and constrains the enlightened soul to join in the exclamation, 'Lord, it is good for us to be here.' The victory for Christ is to be won on the very ground where the opposition was made. In the very matter over which the enemy reviled, there shall they praise God for that which they erewhile maligned." — *J. R. Lumby.* There have been many different interpretations of the phrase "in the day of visitation," and the words of Professor Plumptre are perhaps as satisfactory as any. "The day in which God visits men is one of outward blessings, as in Job 10 : 12, Luke 1 : 43, or of chastisement, as in Isaiah 10 : 3. In Luke 19 : 44 it is manifestly applied to the 'accepted time,' the season in which God was visiting His people, it might be by chastisements, as well as by the call to repentance and the offer of forgiveness. And this, we can scarcely doubt, is its meaning here also."

2. A LIFE OF OBEDIENCE TO CIVIL LAW, VS. 13–16. 13. **Be subject to every ordinance of man for the Lord's sake: whether to the king, as supreme;** 14. **or unto governors, as sent by him for vengeance on evil-doers, and for praise to them that do well.** 15. **For so is the will of God, that by well-doing ye should put to silence the ignorance of foolish men.** "They are to submit, but not because of the original source from which the authority flows, but because of the practical consequences of not submitting. It must be done 'for the Lord's' (*i.e.*, Jesus Christ's) 'sake,' *i.e.*, in order not to bring discredit upon His teaching, and persecution upon His Church. This difference of treatment, in the midst of so much resemblance, shows that at the date of Peter's letter there was much more immediate cause for laying stress on political subordination." — *A. J. Mason.* (Cf. Rom. 13 : 1; Ephesians 5 : 21—6 : 9; Titus 2; Colossians 3 : 18—4 : 1.) "The world from the first hated the religion of Jesus, and professed to suspect it, as inimical to itself. It was a favorite charge against the early Christians that they were plotting the overthrow of the empire, and the dethronement of Cæsar, in favor of 'one Jesus.' Their private meetings were supposed to be convened for unlawful political purposes. It was therefore necessary that men's minds should be disabused of the impression that any violence subversive of existing society was contemplated. For this purpose the early Christians were specially exhorted to conform, so far as they could, to the demands and usages of the people among whom they sojourned as pilgrims and strangers. They were to render to Cæsar the things that were Cæsar's. If they accepted the order, and safety, and privileges of a settled national and corporate life, they were to bear their quota of its cost, and yield homage to the form of government which they found in vogue, agreeing to modify or alter it only by orderly and constitutional methods. They were therefore called upon to render to all their dues, tribute to whom tribute, custom to whom custom, fear to whom fear, honor to whom honor. A quiet and peaceable life was to be their model; submission

16. As free, and not using your freedom for a cloak of wickedness, but as bondservants of God.

17. Honor all men. Love the brotherhood. Fear God. Honor the king.

18. Servants, *be* in subjection to your masters with all fear; not only to the good and gentle, but also to the froward.

19. For this is acceptable, if for conscience toward God a man endureth griefs, suffering wrongfully.

20. For what glory is it, if, when ye sin, and are buffeted *for it*, ye shall take it patiently? but if, when ye do well, and suffer *for it*, ye shall take it patiently, this is acceptable with God.

---

to their law; well-doing their purpose. Thus, in the process of time, they would disarm prejudice, and conciliate their foes, by the exhibition of the graces of an inoffensive, tender, and beneficent life." — *F. B. Meyer.* 16. **As free, and not using your freedom for a cloak of wickedness, but as bondservants of God.** "Peter reminds the Christians that, although they are truly free, indeed the only truly free men — a point ever present to the minds of the apostles — yet that freedom did not imply license to break the laws of men, being in fact another word for subjection to God. What he warns them against most specially was making that liberty a pretext for maliciousness, a word which designates any kind of evil, most frequently malignity, malice; here it evidently refers to the evil and refractory spirit shown in violation of law. False teachers inculcated two main errors. Judaizers claimed exemption from human law; Gentile sophists confounded liberty with libertinism, and held that grace implied deliverance from the restraints and penalties of divine law." — *F. C. Cook.*

3. A LIFE IN WHICH ALL MEN ARE HONORED, v. 17. 17 *a*. **Honor all men.** "It is that word *all* that constitutes the difficulty of this demand. It is the universality involved in it that makes it so hard. The people in New Guinea as well as the people in England! The denizens of darkest Africa as well as our fellow citizens! *All* men! The dwellers in Whitechapel as well as the inhabitants of Mayfair, the poor of Bethnal Green as well as the rich in Belgravia! The servant as well as the master, the maid as well as the mistress; the employed as well as the employer; the illiterate peasant as well as the college don; the sinner as well as the saint! It is the uncompromising sweep of the demand that makes it so hard to obey. We find no difficulty in honoring some men. Men of high character and obvious worth — we delight to honor them. But *all* men! Who is sufficient for this? The tramp, the drunkard, and the criminal — how can we honor them? The vicious and the filthy, the profligate and the harlot — how are we to honor them? . . . All men were made in the image of God. In multitudes of them the image has been sadly defaced, overlaid with selfishness and sin, but in none was it entirely destroyed or wholly lost." — *J. D. Jones.*

4. A LIFE OF LOVE FOR OUR BRETHREN, v. 17. 17 *b*. **Love the brotherhood.** "Within the Christian society in which all were brothers, as being children of the same Father, there might well be a warmer feeling of affection than that which was felt for those who were outside it. The special love of the brethren does not shut out other forms and degrees of love, and our Lord's words 'Love your enemies' (Matt. 5:44) are therefore left in all their full force of obligation." — *E. H. Plumptre.*

5. A LIFE MANIFESTING FEAR OF GOD, v. 17 *c*. **Fear God. Honor the king.** (Cf. 1 Peter 1:17; 5:6.) It may be the apostle is here referring to Proverbs 24:21. "This is a command not only of the Old but of the New Testament, inasmuch as a lowly awe before the holy God is an essential of the filial relation to God." — *J. E. Huther.* The last clause of this verse is simply a reiteration of that which was already commanded in verse 13.

6. A LIFE OF CHEERFUL SUBJECTION TO OUR MASTERS, vs. 18–20. 18. **Servants, *be* in subjection to your masters with all fear; not only to the good and gentle, but also to the froward.** 19. **For this is acceptable, if for conscience toward God a man endureth griefs, suffering wrongfully.** 20. **For what glory is it, if, when ye sin, and are buffeted *for it*, ye shall take it patiently? but if, when ye do well, and suffer *for it*, ye shall take it patiently, this is acceptable with God.** "In urging upon his readers conduct becoming to Christians in the various relations of life, Peter

21. For hereunto were ye called: because Christ also suffered for you, leaving you an example, that ye should follow his steps:
22. Who did no sin, neither was guile found in his mouth:

first emphasizes the duties of citizens to the State. He next dwells upon the relation of servants to their masters. He does not address them as slaves, the word employed by Paul, but as ' household servants,' a term, which, in that day, included free men and women, even clerks and musicians and teachers and physicians; thus the passage applies to the attitude of all employees toward their employers and bears upon the vexed modern problems of labor and capital. The one comprehensive exhortation is to submission. It implies not only obedience but also loyalty; servants are not only to submit but to be faithful and to advance the interests of their masters. The ' fear ' is not of punishment, but denotes anxious fidelity and deference under all circumstances, the desire to avoid all offense. As submission to a cruel tyrant like Nero was a special test of loyalty to the State, so the proof of faithfulness in servants was found in their obedience not only to masters, who were kind and considerate, but also to the froward, the unreasonable, the cruel, and the unjust. It would be specially acceptable to God, if for His sake, because of obligation to Him and strengthened by the thought of His presence, they would endure patiently sufferings which were undeserved, blows and scourgings even when they had merited praise." — *Charles R. Erdman.* Literally, the phrase, " this is acceptable," should read, as the margin of the Rev. Ver. indicates, " This is grace." " The best of masters hardly feels grateful to the best of servants for doing his duty, though he will be grateful for the spirit and manner in which it is done. Here the ' thanks ' are put quite generally, as in the first passage in Luke: ' This is a matter of thanks.' It does not say as yet who is to pay the thanks, and we may naturally conclude that the master so served, and all who are cognizant of the service, are the persons meant." — *A. J. Mason.*

IV. **CHRIST OUR EXAMPLE IN HIS SUFFERINGS,** 1 Peter 2 : 21–24.

1. The Fact of His Being Our Example, v. 21. 21. **For hereunto were ye called: because Christ also suffered for you, leaving you an example, that ye should follow his steps.** " The Greek word here translated *example* is not found elsewhere in the New Testament. It seems to have been a technical word for the drawing which was set before young students of art for them to copy. Such a picture of patience under suffering Peter now paints, as with a few vivid touches, and sets it before those who were novices in the school of the Christ-like life that they may become artists worthy of their Master." — *E. H. Plumptre.* " Wherever Scripture presents Christ as an example, it does so almost always with reference to His self-abasement in suffering and death (Phil. 2 : 5; John 13 : 15; 15 : 12; 1 John 3 : 16; Heb. 12 : 2). Only in 1 John 2 : 6 is Christ presented as an example in the more general sense." — *J. E. Huther.* " My brethren, the difference between Jesus Christ and ourselves is indeed infinite; it is the difference between the Creator and the creature. And yet He is also truly Man; and for the purposes of imitation the truth of His manhood secures all that we require. There are many actions, many words, many silences of a father which the child can understand; they are quite independent of the father's superiority, and they have the same significance whether the father is their author or the child. Our Lord Jesus Christ Himself bids us be perfect even as our Father which is in heaven is perfect. Certainly we cannot imitate Jesus Christ when He heals the sick, or raises the dead. But we can enter into and cherish the spirit of those high works of mercy. We can do the natural kindnesses which are akin to them. And there are deeds and words of His which we can copy in the letter as well as the spirit." — *H. P. Liddon.*

2. His Sinlessness, v. 22. 22. **Who did no sin, neither was guile found in his mouth.** This testimony of the Apostle Peter to the sinlessness of Christ is very significant. With it we should compare the words of Peter's companion for many years, the Apostle John (1 John 3 : 5), and the words of the Apostle Paul (2 Cor. 5 : 21). Peter had lived in the companionship of Christ for three years; he had watched Him on every conceivable occasion, publicly and privately; he saw Him under every circumstance, favorable and adverse; he saw Him at times of great success and times when everyone turned against Him; he saw the Lord at meals; when He was weary; he knew of the nights He spent out on the mountain praying; he saw Him dealing with souls, and knowing his Lord perfectly and intimately, yet he could bear testimony thirty years later that there was no sin in the life of Jesus of Nazareth.

23. Who, when he was reviled, reviled not again; when he suffered, threatened not; but committed *himself* to him that judgeth righteously:
24. Who his own self bare our sins in his body upon the tree, that we, having died unto sins, might live unto righteousness; by whose stripes ye were healed.

---

3. HIS UNREVENGEFULNESS, v. 23. 23. **Who, when he was reviled, reviled not again; when he suffered, threatened not; but committeth *himself* to him that judgeth righteously.** "Christ had met taunts and revilings with a silent patience. They in their passionate indignation too often threatened revenge in some near or distant future. He, though He might have asked His Father for twelve legions of angels, had uttered no threats of judgment, but had committed Himself (as in the words on the Cross, 'Father, into thy hands I commend my spirit,' Luke 23 : 46), to the righteous Judge. So should the slaves who suffered wrongfully commit their cause to God in the full assurance that they will one day have righteous judgment." — *E. H. Plumptre*. (Cf. Isa. 53 : 7.)

4. HIS VICARIOUS DEATH FOR US, v. 24. 24. **Who his own self bare our sins in his body upon the tree, that we, having died unto sins, might live unto righteousness; by whose stripes ye were healed.** "The primary meaning of the verb translated *bare* is, 'to carry up,' 'to bear upwards.' From that primary signification arises a secondary or metaphorical sense in the most natural way, viz., 'to offer in sacrifice.' It is used in its primary signification, when it is said that the Israelites, at the exodus from Egypt, brought up the bones of Joseph (Josh. 24 : 32); when David brought up the bones of Saul and Jonathan from Bethshan (2 Sam. 21 : 13); when our Lord brought up the disciples to the mount of transfiguration (Matt. 17 : 1); when He was carried up to heaven at His own ascension (Luke 24 : 51). In the secondary signification, naturally derived from the former, it denotes to offer in sacrifice; the allusion being to the fact that the victim was carried up to the altar, which was always erected on a raised or elevated spot (James 2 : 21; Heb. 7 : 27). . . . The language must be taken as affirming that sin was taken away in His own body on the tree. Sin was thus taken away by a fact in connection with Christ's cross, and this virtually amounts to expiation. It will not do to say, that the cross, as it persuades men to believe and lead a virtuous life, is followed in due course by the taking away of sin. They must be understood of a result effected in His own body. . . . The words imply that Christ, by His own act as well as by God's appointment, bore our sins in His own body, connecting Himself with sinful humanity, and taking our sins in such a way as to incorporate them with Himself, or conjoin them with His own body. He made our sins His own, in such a way that they adhered to Him in the only sense in which they could adhere to the sinless humanity of the incarnate Son — by suretyship and imputation. That is brought out in the words, 'who his own self.' He became personified guilt: it was made His by His own act and His Father's will." — *George Smeaton*. Dr. James M. Gray has an excellent illustration of the profound truth of this verse in the following story: "In Dr. Bainbridge's *Around the World Tour of Christian Missions*, written now twenty years ago, there is a curiously interesting and suggestive incident. When in his journey he had reached Tokio, Japan, intending to remain there some little time, he was waited upon one morning by an official, with this singular inquiry: 'Who stands for you?' Supposing it to be a question of passports, he presented his, but that was not what was wanted. He then offered some letters of introduction he had, but they also were unsatisfactory, and the question was repeated, 'Who stands for you?' It was finally explained that there was an ordinance in that city to the effect that no foreigner could take up his residence there for any length of time, unless he provided himself with a 'substitute.' As a matter of fact, there were natives who hired themselves out to foreigners for this purpose. If the foreigner transgressed any law the substitute suffered the penalty for it. If the penalty were even death, the substitute suffered death. Dr. Bainbridge secured a substitute, and was thereafter permitted to remain in peace and security as long as he chose."

"In what sense is Christ said to have 'died to sin'? Evidently, in the sense that sin (not His own sin, for He was sinless, but our sin which He bore), caused Him to be crucified; and that when once He paid its penalty by death, it lost the power to bring Him into the place of penalty again. There is a man in prison, let us say, awaiting the gallows or the electric chair to expiate the crime of murder.

25. For ye were going astray like sheep; but are now returned unto the Shepherd and Bishop of your souls.

But when he has once expiated it, when he once dies in accordance with the law, the crime can never again bring him to judgment. He is dead to it forever, even though afterward, were it possible, he should arise from the dead. So in the case of Christ, when He expiated human guilt He did so once and forever, and became dead to it thereafter. But the believer on Jesus Christ, as we learn from this, and even more plainly from other Scriptures, is so identified with Christ in God's purpose, is so entirely one with Him as his representative and substitute, that when Christ died to sin upon the cross the believer also died in Him. And if sin cannot again bring his substitute into the place of penalty, neither can it bring the one whose representative He was. Hence the significance of that word in Romans 8 : 1: 'There is therefore now no condemnation to them which are in Christ Jesus.' This means no judgment, no penalty, no guilt to them that are in Him, *i.e.*, bound up with Him in identity and substitution. But Peter's phrase is in the plural, 'dead to sins'—it is not 'sin'; and this is even better yet, and more gracious and more satisfying to the soul. 'Sin' refers to our sinful nature, while 'sins' refers to the consequences or fruits of that nature in the actual transgressions of our lives."—*Dr. James Gray.* Many have tried to make out, from the last phrase, "by whose stripes ye were healed" (cf. Isa. 53 : 6; Ps. 119 : 176), the idea that this verse teaches a healing of all physical ailments through Christ's work upon the cross. This phrase has nothing to do with the healing of the body but with the healing of the soul, with spiritual healing.

The Lost Sheep. Alfred Soord.

V. CHRIST THE SHEPHERD AND BISHOP OF OUR SOULS, 1 Peter 2 : 25. 25. **For ye were going astray like sheep; but are now returned unto the Shepherd and Bishop of your souls.** We have often in this lesson made use of the compactly constructed paragraphs of the late Dean Plumptre, and we know of nothing better in the interpretation of this verse than his words. "The sequence of thought is suggested by the 'all we like sheep have gone astray,' but the imagery could scarcely fail to recall to the mind of the apostle the state of Israel 'as sheep that had no shepherd' (Matt. 9 : 36), and the parable of the lost sheep (Matt. 18 : 12, 13; Luke 15 : 4). The image had been a familiar one almost from the earliest times to describe the state of a people plunged into anarchy and confusion by the loss of their true leader (Num. 27 : 17; 1 Kings 22 : 17). We can scarcely fail to connect the words with those which Peter had once heard as to the 'other sheep' who were not of the fold of Galilee and Jerusalem (John 10 : 16). In the 'strangers of the dispersion' he might well recognize some, at least, of those other sheep. In the thought of Christ as the Shepherd we have primarily the echo of the teaching of our Lord just referred to, but the name at least suggests a possible reference to the older utterances of prophecy and devotion (Ps. 23 : 1; Isa. 40 : 11; Ezek. 34 : 23; 37 : 24).

In the word for Bishop (better, perhaps, looking to the later associations that have gathered round the English term, guardian or protector), we may, possibly, find a reference to the use of the cognate verb in the Septuagint of Ezekiel 34 : 11. The Greek noun is often used in the New Testament in special association with the thought of the Shepherd's work. (Cf. Acts 20 : 28; 1 Peter 5 : 4.) There is, perhaps, a special stress laid on Christ being the Shepherd of their souls. Their bodies might be subject to the power and caprices of their masters, but their higher nature, that which was their true self, was subject only to the loving care of the Great Shepherd."

How many different titles for the Lord Jesus do you find in this passage? What do you think, of all the work and teaching of Christ with which Peter was so thoroughly acquainted, did he count as of pre-eminent and central importance? Why should Christians want so to live that their lives will commend the gospel which they proclaim and bear wholesome testimony to the Lord whom they profess to follow? Do you think that the characteristics of a Christian's life mentioned in verses 11–20, come naturally to Christians, or are they the consequences of continual discipline and self-control? Is there any other religion in the whole world that can truly assure or promise its followers that they are an elect nation, etc.? (The answer is an emphatic "No.") As far as you can recall, in how many different ways was Christ's earthly life characterized by those virtues which are here set forth as goals for which we are to strive?

LESSON X. — June 6.

PETER COMFORTS PERSECUTED CHRISTIANS. — 1 Peter 3 : 13–17; 4 : 12–16; 5 : 6–10.

GOLDEN TEXT. — *For it is better, if the will of God should so will, that ye suffer for well-doing than for evil-doing.* 1 PETER 3 : 17.

Devotional Reading: Hebrews 11 : 32—12 : 2.
Beginner Topic: LITTLE SAMUEL.
Lesson Material: 1 Samuel 3.
Memory Verse: Thou art nigh, O Jehovah. Psalm 119 : 151.
Primary Topic: GOD'S BEST PROMISE.
Lesson Material: 2 Peter 1 : 1–11.
Memory Verse: Blessed be Jehovah . . . there hath not failed one word of all his good promise. 1 Kings 8 : 56.
Junior Topic: PROMISES THAT CANNOT FAIL.
Lesson Material: 2 Peter 1 : 1–11.
Memory Verse: Blessed be Jehovah . . . there hath not failed one word of all his good promise. 1 Kings 8 : 56.
Intermediate and Senior Topic: FAITHFUL UNDER FIRE.
Topic for Young People and Adults: FACING PERSECUTION TODAY.

THE TEACHER AND HIS CLASS.

The Younger Classes might be introduced to this lesson with a story. The editor remembers hearing some one tell of a colored woman down south, who, after carrying a heavy basket for two miles, came to the railroad station where she boarded a train for a town some thirty miles away. She was carrying a supply of provisions, but when she got on the train, instead of putting the basket on the floor, and resting from the burden, she thought she still had to carry it and so held it all the thirty miles. If she had only let the train carry that basket, as well as herself, she would not have been nearly so exhausted. Our lesson tells us how we are to cast our cares upon the Lord, and thus be relieved of the exhaustion which comes from constant anxiety and worry.

The Older Classes will find here a subject which is rarely touched upon in our churches these days, something we seldom think about, namely, suffering with Christ. The New Testament is full of this subject. No doubt one of the reasons why we do not enter more fully into the deeper aspects of Christian experience, is because we do not know what it is to suffer with Christ. It may be that the terrible war which is upon us will drive us into these experiences, and out of it, if we are chastened therein, will come some precious fruits in our Christian life never before borne by the most of us.

THE LESSON IN ITS SETTING.

Time. — The exact time for the writing of this Epistle cannot be determined, but it was probably not far from A.D. 60.

Place. — In the last chapter of this Epistle, the writer refers to "She that is in Babylon," which has led some to believe that First Peter was written from the great city on the Euphrates River bearing that name; others have suggested that, because the city now known as Cairo, Egypt, was anciently called Babylon, the Epistle was written from there. A majority of scholars, however, believe that Peter used the word Babylon to designate the city of Rome.

THE PLAN OF THE LESSON.

SUBJECT: The Conduct of Christians in a Time of Persecution and Some of the Blessings That Are Promised for Those Who Are Faithful in Such an Hour.

I. PRINCIPLES OF CONDUCT IN TIMES OF PERSECUTION, 1 Peter 3 : 13–17.

1. Normally when we do good we will not be liable to punishment, v. 13.
2. If we suffer when living righteously we need not be terrified, v. 14.
3. We should sanctify Christ in our hearts, v. 15 *a*.
4. We should ever be ready to give a reason for our belief, v. 15 *b*.
5. Thus we will put to shame those who falsely accuse us, v. 16.
6. We are to be sure our suffering is not for an evil we have done, v. 17.

II. SOME COMFORTING TRUTHS TO REMEMBER IN TIMES OF PERSECUTION, 4 : 12–16.

1. We may even rejoice because we are partakers of Christ's sufferings, vs. 12, 13.
2. We have in such a time the opportunity to glorify God, vs. 14–16.

III. THE CHARACTERISTICS OF CHRISTIAN LIFE ESPECIALLY WHEN BESET BY SATAN, 5 : 6–10.

1. A life of humility, v. 6.
2. A life whose anxieties are cast upon God, v. 7.
3. A life of sobriety and vigilance, v. 8 *a*.
4. A life of resistance to the devil, vs. 8 *b*, 9.
5. A life of increasing strength and stability, v. 10.

THE TEACHER'S LIBRARY.

For a list of commentaries on First Peter, see the bibliography in the lesson for May 30. On the general subject of suffering as it is referred to in the epistles of the New Testament, see an article by William Watson, in James Hastings's *Dictionary of the Apostolic Church*, Vol. 2, 533–534; and an article, "Affliction," in the *International Standard Bible Encyclopedia*, Vol. 1, 66–68. There is a volume by H. A. Boardman, *Earthly Suffering and Heavenly Glory*, which the editor has not been able to consult. On Christ's sufferings, see an excellent chapter in J. H. Brookes: *Misery of Suffering*, 71–81; on suffering with Christ, see an excellent discussion in L. S. Chafer: *True Evangelism*, 97–110; and C. H. MacIntosh: *Leviticus*, 75–82.

For sermonic material, on 3 : 14, 15, see Alexander Maclaren: *Expositions of Holy Scripture, 1 and 2 Peter and 1 John*, 116–123; on 4 : 14, H. G. Moule: *Christ Is All*, 189–200; Abraham Kuyper: *To Be Near Unto God*, 469–475; on 4 : 15, Joseph Parker: *The People's Bible*, Vol. 27, 314–321; on 4 : 16, G. Campbell Morgan: *The Life of the Christian*, 9–26; on 5 : 5, Phillips Brooks: *The Purpose and Use of Comfort*, 334–352; Charles Hodge: *Princeton Sermons*, 226 ff.; W. G. T. Shedd: *Sermons to the Spiritual Man*, 256–271; on verse 6, Andrew Murray: *Humility*, 123–132; on verse 7, James Hastings: *Great Texts of the Bible, James to Jude*, 134–150; on verse 8, F. W. Farrar, *In the Days of Thy Youth*, 297–306; on verse 9, Charles H. Spurgeon: *Sermons*, Vol. 7, 11–27; Vol. 14, 183–203; H. C. G. Moule: *Sunday to Sunday*, 26–30; on verse 10, George H. Morrison: *The Weaving of Glory*, 69–80. There is also quite an extended discussion of the nature of the sufferings to which the Apostle refers in this Epistle, in an article on the First Epistle of Peter, by F. H. Chase, in Hastings's *Dictionary of the Bible*, Vol. 3, 784–785.

The subject of suffering is prominent both in the Gospels and in the epistles of the New Testament, but does not receive in these modern days anything like the attention which this frequency of reference in the New Testament justifies. On suffering as experienced by Christ, see Matthew 16 : 21; 17 : 12; Mark 8 : 31; 9 : 12; Luke 9 : 22; 17 : 25; 22 : 15; 24 : 26, 46; Acts 3 : 18; 17 : 3; 2 Cor. 1 : 5, 7; Phil. 3 : 10; Heb. 2 : 9, 10, 18; 5 : 8; 9 : 26; 13 : 12; 1 Peter 1 : 11; 2 : 21, 23; 3 : 18; 4 : 1, 13; 5 : 1. On the sufferings which Christians will endure see Romans 8 : 18; 2 Corinthians 1 : 6; Galatians 3 : 4; Philippians 1 : 29; 2 Thessalonians 1 : 5; 1 Peter 2 : 19, 20; 3 : 14, 17; 4 : 15, 19; 5 : 10. It will be noticed from this enumeration that there are more references to suffering in the five chapters of the First Epistle of Peter than in all the epistles Paul ever wrote, and more frequent reference to the sufferings of Christians in the First Epistle of Peter than in all the other writings of the New Testament combined. If one will examine the texts in which the sufferings of Christians are spoken of, one will discover that in many cases, the *mutual* sufferings of Christ and His followers are referred to, so that some texts may properly be said to include both Christ and Christian believers. It should also be noted, whatever be the significance of the fact, that the word *suffering*, in neither its verbal nor its noun form, appears once in either the Gospel or any of the Epistles of St. John.

1 PETER 3 : 13. And who is he that will harm you, if ye be zealous of that which is good?

14. But even if ye should suffer for righteousness' sake, blessed *are ye:* and fear not their fear, neither be troubled;

15. But sanctify in your hearts Christ as Lord: *being* ready always to give answer to every man that asketh you a reason concerning the hope that is in you, yet with meekness and fear:

I. **PRINCIPLES OF CONDUCT IN TIMES OF PERSECUTION,** 1 Peter 3 : 13–17. 13. **And who is he that will harm you, if ye be zealous of that which is good?** This verse might be compared to Romans 8 : 33–35. The word here translated *zealous* means the manifestation of zeal for the things that are good, in contrast to a life of indolence, indifference, and lethargy. The verse simply means that if we go about doing good, we need not be afraid of those who, in a civil capacity, are over us. The government cannot *rightly* punish a man who is only doing good. Of course, in the case of Christians many times throughout the ages, they have been punished in spite of the fact that they were doing no evil. 14. **But even if ye should suffer for righteousness' sake, blessed *are ye:* and fear not their fear, neither be troubled.** This verse is taken for the most part from the prophecy of Isaiah (the Septuagint text of Isaiah 8 : 12, 13; cf. Matt. 5 : 10). " In the original, the persons whose fears Isaiah and the faithful Jews are not to fear are those who were in dread of Syria and Israel. Here the persons are not named; but, of course, according to this interpretation, ' they ' cannot be the enemies who try to harm the Christians, but, if any one, those of the Christians who, for fear of man, were beginning to abandon Christianity." — *A. J. Mason.* " Blessedness is a higher thing than happiness, and is consistent with the most trying circumstances.

'This prison very sweet to me
Hath been since I came here;
And so would also hanging be,
If Thou didst then appear,'

sang Bunyan in Bedford Gaol, his eyes dazzled with frescoes painted by angel hands on the damp walls. And wherein does this blessedness consist? It comes through the enforced constraint laid upon the soul to seek its delight and rapture in the love and friendship of Christ, the Friend of the persecuted, who is always nearest to those who are most like Him in suffering, because most like in character and life. It comes through the glad consciousness of being on the path trodden already by prophets and righteous men, who have gone through flood and flame, but who have overcome, and are set down with Christ on His throne. It comes because the exceeding great reward beckons from on high." — *F. B. Meyer.* 15. **But sanctify in your hearts Christ as Lord.** " The tense of this and the two preceding imperatives shows that Peter meant this for advice to be acted upon at the moment of being called on to suffer. The passage as it stands in Isaiah, runs literally, ' Jehovah Sabaoth, him shall ye sanctify, and he (shall be) your fear, and he your dread.' It becomes, therefore, very striking when we find that, without a shadow of doubt, the right reading here is, *But sanctify the Lord the Christ in your hearts.* As to ' glorify' God means (in word and deed) to recognize His glorious perfections; as to ' magnify ' Him means to recognize His greatness; as to ' justify ' Him means to recognize His inherent justice; as to ' sanctify' Him means to recognize, in word and deed, His full holiness, and therefore to treat Him with due awe. . . . This does not mean simply ' *with* your hearts,' or ' *from* your hearts ' (*i.e.*, inwardly, or, with all sincerity and devotion), but it signifies the local habitation *where* the Christ is to be thus recognized. That is to say, Peter like Paul (Eph. 3 : 17) acknowledges an *indwelling* of Christ in the hearts of the faithful; and this indwelling not merely subjective, consisting of their constant recollection of Him, but real and objective; there He is, as in a shrine, and they must pay due reverence to His presence." — *A. J. Mason.* " Be sure that you give Him all that is His due, and in the love of your hearts, as well as in the thinkings of your hearts, recognize Him for what He is, the Lord. The one thing that delivers men from the fears that make cowards of us all is to have Christ lodged within our hearts." — *Alexander Maclaren.* ***Being* ready always to give answer to every man that asketh you a reason concerning the hope that is in you, yet with meekness and fear.** " Every

16. Having a good conscience; that, wherein ye are spoken against, they may be put to shame who revile your good manner of life in Christ.
17. For it is better, if the will of God should so will, that ye suffer for well-doing than for evil-doing.
1 PETER 4 : 12. Beloved, think it not strange concerning the fiery trial among you, which cometh upon you to prove you, as though a strange thing happened unto you:

---

cultivated, sensible man was expected by the Greeks to be prepared to discuss questions or opinions of conduct intelligently and temperately, to give and receive a reason. It is surely not fanciful to see here an allusion to St. Peter's own experience. When a critical moment came upon him, he was not ready with his answer, and so denied his Lord (Matt. 26 : 69–75). Further, it was through want of meekness and fear that he denied; of meekness because he fancied that he loved the Lord 'more than these'; and of fear because of the fear of man." — *Charles Bigg.* "This answer was to be given not in a tone of threatening defiance but in meekness as regards the interrogator, whether the questions were put officially or in private, and in fear partly because the truth should suffer through any infirmities in its defenders, partly because the spirit of reverential awe toward God was the best safeguard against such infirmities." — *E. H. Plumptre.* "Young people, the Bible has nothing to fear from the exercise of your reason! It is not possible that the God who built up your brains and endowed you with that marvelous faculty of reason will ever do violence to one of His noblest gifts. Reason was a favorite pursuit with the greatest of the apostles. But if you enthrone faith and hope, while reason waits their bidding and obeys their behest, you will be wiser than foe, or teacher, or gray-haired sage (Ps. 119 : 98–100). Let us have a reason for our faith, based on personal experience, or observation, or the study of evidence, or of fulfilled prophecy; or, above all, wrought by the Holy Spirit in our hearts; and, though we need not be ever obtruding it, let us never flinch from stating it when asked. And let us give our reasons, or conduct our arguments, in a temper which shall be the best evidence of the divine character of our faith." — *F. B. Meyer.* 16. **Having a good conscience; that, wherein ye are spoken against, they may be put to shame who revile your good manner of life in Christ.** Compare 1 Peter 2 : 18; Acts 23 : 1; 24 : 16. Plumptre's words here are excellent: "The stress is laid on this condition as warning men that no skill of speech would do the work of the apologist rightly if his life were inconsistent with his profession. Only when the two are in harmony with each other could he give his answer at once with becoming boldness and with due reverence." 17. **For it is better, if the will of God should so will, that ye suffer for well-doing than for evil-doing.** Compare 1 Peter 2 : 20. Men who are sent to a penitentiary, or who are deprived of some high political position, or are sent home from the army with a dishonorable discharge because they have committed crimes, — these men suffer, but with shame. There is no gladness or joy possible in enduring *just* punishment, but if we are sent to prison only because we are Christians, if we are tortured because we are faithful to Christ, then we can still rejoice, even though we suffer, for our hearts are at peace with God and we know we are in His will.

II. **SOME COMFORTING TRUTHS TO REMEMBER IN TIMES OF PERSECUTION,** 4 : 12–16. 12. **Beloved, think it not strange concerning the fiery trial among you.** The word here translated *fiery* is used in Revelation 18 : 9, 18, of the conflagration which devours Babylon. "Here, however, the allusion is to the fire by which gold is tested and the word is probably taken from Proverbs 27 : 21 (cf. 1 Peter 1 : 7). What Peter desires to bring out is not so much the fierceness of the heat and the pain as the refining power of fire." — *Charles Bigg.* **Which cometh upon you to prove you, as though a strange thing happened unto you.** "The word which is translated *prove* is constantly used of temptation, whether sent of God, or coming in some other way. When viewed as a process of proving, believers would be able to find some contentment under their persecutions. God was putting them to the test. The prophet Zechariah tells both of the process and the God-intended result (13 : 9). And the psalmist bears like testimony: 'Jehovah trieth the righteous; but the wicked and him that loveth violence his soul hateth' (Ps. 11 : 5), and says for those who are found faithful, the end is blessedness: 'We went through fire and through water; but thou broughtest us out into a wealthy

13. But insomuch as ye are partakers of Christ's sufferings, rejoice; that at the revelation of his glory also ye may rejoice with exceeding joy.
14. If ye are reproached for the name of Christ, blessed *are ye;* because the *Spirit* of glory and the Spirit of God resteth upon you.
15. For let none of you suffer as a murderer, or a thief, or an evil-doer, or as a meddler in other men's matters:
16. But if *a man suffer* as a Christian, let him not be ashamed; but let him glorify God in this name.

place' (Ps. 66 : 12)." — *J. R. Lumby.* "What, then, is the purpose of 'the fiery trial'? What is the meaning of this permitted ministry of suffering? Well, in the first place, it tests character. It discharges the purpose of an examination. It unfolds our strengths and our weaknesses. And so it is in the larger examination afforded by the discipline of life. The lap of luxury does not afford the elementary iron for the upbringing of strong and enduring life. Hardness hardens; antagonism solidifies; trials inure and confirm. How commonly it has happened that men who, in soft circumstances, have been weak and irresolute, were hardened into fruitful decision by the ministry of antagonism and pain." — *J. H. Jowett.* 13. **But insomuch as ye are partakers of Christ's sufferings, rejoice; that at the revelation of his glory also ye may rejoice with exceeding joy.** (Cf. 1 Peter 1 : 11; Matt. 5 : 12.) "The Greek conjunction expresses more than the ground of the joy. Men are to rejoice in proportion as they are sharers in the sufferings of Christ." — *E. H. Plumptre.* "In suffering *with* Christ the Christian may either suffer from man the reproaches of Christ, or he may come to experience with Christ a divinely wrought burden and sorrow for the lost. Beyond this it is impossible for any believer to go in the mystery of the sufferings of Christ; for what He suffered from God in becoming Himself an offering for sin could not be shared by any other, though one might greatly desire a similar ministry (see Rom. 9 : 1-3). . . . Suffering with Christ, then, in its deepest meaning, is to come to experience by the Spirit an unutterable agony for men out of Christ, and from that vision and love to be willing to offer personal sacrifice or endure physical pain, if need be, that they may be saved. This is as near to 'a cross' as the Christian can come in experience; for he can make no atonement, nor is human atonement needed. As his eyes are opened and his heart is made sensitive to the indescribable need of any soul out of Christ, he has, to that extent, experienced the divine compassion 'shed abroad in his heart.' Such suffering *with* Christ is the heritage of every regenerate soul." — *Lewis Sperry Chafer.* 14. **If ye are reproached for the name of Christ, blessed *are ye;* because the *Spirit* of glory and the Spirit of God resteth upon you.** "The outward reviling to which the disciples were exposed brought glory and not dishonor. The Spirit of glory was there — who has glory as His essential attribute — and that Spirit was none other than the very Spirit of God. The thought of the Apostle is that the humblest sufferers for the name of Christ are as truly sharers in the gift of the Eternal Spirit as were the greatest prophets. It rests on them — not coming and going, in fitful movements, or extraordinary manifestations, but dwelling with them continually. . . . Here the word for 'is evil spoken of' would rightly be rendered as *blasphemed,* and 'Christ' or 'the Spirit of God' must be taken as the subject of the sentence. In this case, that of suffering for the truth, the very blasphemies which men utter in their rage, are a witness to the effective work which has been done through the power of the Spirit, and in respect of those who suffer, are working for His glory. Appalling as is the contrast between the blasphemy of the persecutors and the doxologies of the sufferer, the one is almost the necessary complement of the other." — *E. H. Plumptre.* 15. **For let none of you suffer as a murderer, or a thief, or an evil-doer, or as a meddler in other men's matters:** 16. **but if *a man suffer* as a Christian, let him not be ashamed; but let him glorify God in this name.** Let us first look at this word Christian, and then try to understand why the word appears at the end of a list of words indicating crime. It occurs only three times in the New Testament — twice in the Acts of the Apostles (11 : 26; 26 : 28), and here. 'The disciples were called Christians first in Antioch.' They were originally described among themselves as 'the disciples,' 'the brethren,' 'the believers,' 'the elect,' or 'the saints'; by the Jews they were called 'the Nazarenes' (Acts 24 : 5), as still in Mohammedan countries. The name Christian was probably invented by the heathen, and used at first as a term

1 PETER 5 : 6. Humble yourselves therefore under the mighty hand of God, that he may exalt you in due time;
7. Casting all your anxiety upon him, because he careth for you.

of derision. It did not at once become common among the disciples of the Lord. Peter is the only sacred writer who adopts it instead of the older names. "The Hebrew origin of the word, the Greek dress, the Latin termination, seemed to point, like the threefold inscription on the cross, to the universality of Christ's religion — to its empire, first over all the civilized nations, and through them, by continually increasing triumphs, over the whole world." — *B. C. Caffin.* The words *murderer, thief, evil-doer*, are easily understood, but the word here translated "a meddler in other men's matters," has given rise to a great deal of speculation. The Greek word is one not found elsewhere, and was probably coined by Peter himself. The root of the word means "that which belongs to another," and it has been supposed to refer to other people's money or to other people's affairs generally. So the entire word used by Peter here means meddlesomeness, which "was regarded as a high social misdemeanor, and a Christian might give great offense by ill-timed protests against common social customs." — *Charles Bigg.* Sir William Ramsay, in his *The Church in the Roman Empire* quotes the great historian of the Roman Empire, Mommsen, as saying: "The persecution of the Christians was a standing matter as was that of robbers," and Ramsay himself adds: "It was inherent in the nature of the imperial constitution that it should stamp out Christianity just as it was inherent in its nature that it should stamp out brigandage." This situation confronting the Christian Church in Peter's day has been duplicated in our own time, when some nations have as severely legislated against church attendance and fidelity to Christ as they have legislated against treason against the State. "Why is it that men suffer reproach for Christ? It is the reproach of Christ that they suffer. Do not minimize that statement. It is not merely reproach *for* Christ, it is the reproach *of* Christ. That very separation from evil which stirred enmity in the hearts of men against Christ is the condition of life which creates reproach for the believer. The purity which contradicts impurity, the light which reveals darkness, the separateness to God which is a perpetual rebuke to rebellion against God; this, which in the life of Jesus issued in the Cross, being reproduced in the life of the believer, is the occasion of reproach and suffering." — *G. Campbell Morgan.*

III. **THE CHARACTERISTICS OF CHRISTIAN LIFE ESPECIALLY WHEN BESET BY SATAN,** 5 : 6–10.

1. A LIFE OF HUMILITY, v. 6. 6. **Humble yourselves therefore under the mighty hand of God, that he may exalt you in due time.** This verse should not be read apart from the one that immediately precedes it. Mr. Mason tells us that the Greek word here translated "*gird yourselves with humility* is a rare and curious one. It means properly, 'tie yourselves up in humility.' Humility is to be gathered tight round about us like a cloak, and tied up so that the wind may not blow it back, nor the rain beat inside it. But there is a still further and more delicate shade of meaning in the word. There was a peculiar kind of cape, well known by a name taken from this verb (we might call it a *tieup*), and this kind of cape was worn by slaves, and by no others. It was a badge of servitude. Thus Peter bids them all gird themselves for one another in a slave's 'tieup' of humility. . . . The humility here recommended is not merely a submissive bearing of the strokes which it pleased God to let fall upon them, but it was to be shown, as we see in the former verse, in their bearing one toward another. And 'the mighty hand of God' is not to be regarded as that which is chastising them, but as the protecting shelter which they are humbly to seek."

2. A LIFE WHOSE ANXIETIES ARE CAST UPON GOD, v. 7. 7. **Casting all your anxiety upon him, because he careth for you.** The word here translated *anxiety* comes from a verb meaning "to part," "to disunite," "to detract." Alford says: "It signifies care by which the spirit is divided, part for God and part for unbelief; which is in fact, an exalting self against God." Such a division of life destroys peace, takes away our strength, and smothers our spiritual life (Matt. 6 : 25). The verb here translated *careth* means in the original "to be of interest," "to conserve," and the phrase should literally be translated, "he has you on his heart." Moffatt translates it, "for his interest is in you." (An illustration may be found in Luke 10 : 40; cf. Psalm 68 : 19.) Huther says that the singular "unites all individual cares together into one uniform whole." "If the father is providing for tomorrow's

8. Be sober, be watchful: your adversary the devil, as a roaring lion, walketh about, seeking whom he may devour:

9. Whom withstand stedfast in your faith, knowing that the same sufferings are accomplished in your brethren who are in the world.

needs, why should his little boy leave his play, and lean pensively against the wall, wondering what had better be done? If the pilot has come on board, why should the captain also pace the deck with weary foot? If some wise, strong friend, thoroughly competent, has undertaken to adjust some difficult piece of perplexity for me, and if I have perfect confidence in him, and he assures me that he is well able to accomplish it, why should I fret longer? The thing is as good as done, since he has taken it in hand." — *F. B. Meyer.*

3. A LIFE OF SOBRIETY AND VIGILANCE, v. 8 *a*. **Be sober, be watchful.** "These are the sudden cries of warning of a shepherd who spies a lion prowling around the flock in the darkness while the guardians of the flock lie drowsy and secure." — *A. J. Mason.* These same two words are found in 1 Thessalonians 5 : 6. Professor Plumptre says that "the first word has the strict meaning of abstinence from that which inebriates." The editor can never read this line without thinking of the opening and closing of Daniel 5. The scene there described opens with an orgy of drunkenness on the part of the Babylonians. It closes with the capture of the city, that very same night, while the heads of the government and its high counsellors were reeling with intoxication. No moral needs to be drawn from this.

4. A LIFE OF RESISTANCE TO THE DEVIL, vs. 8 *b*, 9. 8 *b*. **Your adversary the devil, as a roaring lion, walketh about, seeking whom he may devour:** 9. **whom withstand stedfast in your faith, knowing that the same sufferings are accomplished in your brethren who are in the world.** Compare Psalm 22 : 14 and Job 1 : 7. "The imagery of the sentence is mixed, derived partly from the prowling lion of the psalm, partly from the accuser of Job, who walks up and down the earth to spy out the weakness of God's servants. Satan's slander is that Job 'doth not

The Christian Martyrs. Jean Leon Gerome.

fear God for naught,' and God allows him to test the truth of this charge by trying Job, first with loss of property and children, afterwards with personal suffering. So here the Devil is the author of persecution . . . in its physical sense the word here translated *steadfast* means hard or solid, and refers frequently to a strong wall or foundation (cf. Col. 2 : 5). In the present passage, its meaning appears to be solid, impenetrable, like a wall. Solidity applies to convictions which are well grounded, firmly connected, and therefore impenetrable." — *Charles Bigg.* "When the Devil also comes as a roaring lion, the sublety of the serpent is laid aside; he discards the sheen of the angel of light; he appears as sheer brutal force, an antagonist of terrific and naked violence, bearing down his victims under the heavy paws of relentless persecution. When the apostle wrote this letter, the lion was about; Nero was at work; the Christians were being hunted unto death, in the vain attempt at

10. And the God of all grace, who called you unto his eternal glory in Christ, after that ye have suffered a little while, shall himself perfect, establish, strengthen you.

stamping out their faith and devotion to the Man of Nazareth, their Saviour and their Lord." — *J. H. Jowett.* The words of Canon Farrar preached at Marlborough College, now nearly seventy years ago, are still true and eminently worth considering. " Resist the beginnings of evil; a mere remedy is all too late. If you have not resisted at the stage of thought, then summon every power of your soul to resist at the stage of the act. Fight inch by inch; fight step by step — if not at the thought, then at the act; if not at the act, then at the habit; if not even at the habit then, at least, at the frightful surrender — the utter massacre of the last defenders of all that is holy or pure within you. But bear in mind that each stage of the losing battle is more perilous, more difficult than the last. It is easier to frighten the enemy than to rout him by a charge; easier to rout than to await his onset; easier to defeat him then than to recover one lost inch of ground; easier to recover an inch than to rally finally the demoralized and broken troops. There is more hope for a boy who may have had bad thoughts than for one who has let them pass into bad words; and more hope for bad words than for bad deeds; and more hope again for him who hath sinned once than for him who has sinned twice, and for the sinner of a week than for the sinner of a month. Oh, if any of you have lost the drawbridge, in God's name drive back the enemy from the wall; if he has reached the wall, fight for the portcullis; if he has carried the portcullis, rally every shattered power and wounded energy, and die rather than admit him at the gate. And don't have any truce or any parleys; don't stop even to bury your dead. Your enemy hates you, and he is as false as he is deadly. He will say: ' Only this once. You are tired of fighting; give me the fortress only now, I promise you that I will evacuate it whenever you like; if not, at any rate you can at any time drive me out.

'Be mine and Sin's for one short hour; others
Be all thy life the happiest man of men.'

Oh, do not believe him! He is a liar from the beginning. A boy may be tempted to lie, to steal, to wrong his neighbor, to indulge some bad passion, and thinks that *once* cannot matter. Oh, pause! That one sin — is it not the trickling rill, which must become the bounding torrent, the broad river, the waste, troubled, discolored sea? You drop a stone out of your hand: is it not the very law of gravitation that, if it falls twelve feet the first second, it will fall forty-eight feet the next second, and 108 feet the third second, and 300 feet the fifth second; and that, if it falls for ten seconds — do you know how many feet of air in that last second it will have rushed through? In that last second it will have rushed through 1200 feet, till earth stops it. Even with that prodigiously increasing momentum, even with that rushing acceleration of velocity, is the increase and multiplication of unchecked sin — and too often it falls on and on, until it is dashed to shivers on the rock of death." — *F. W. Farrar.* It is a very interesting point, one which I have not seen in any commentary, that whenever Satan is introduced in the New Testament as an enemy of the followers of Christ, a victory is spoken of, and that victory is always expressed as obtained through faith.

5. A LIFE OF INCREASING STRENGTH AND STABILITY, v. 10. 10. **And the God of all grace, who called you unto his eternal glory in Christ, after that ye have suffered a little while, shall himself perfect, establish, strengthen you.** " God is the author and giver of all grace that the child of God needs. In connection with this attribute of God, there follows the fact that He had called those to whom the apostle writes to nothing less than a share in His ' eternal glory.' . . . This calling is ' in Christ,' *i.e.*, not merely by Him as the instrument through whom the call came, but as being ' in him,' *i.e.*, by virtue of our union with Him. . . . Each verb has a distinct meaning. That for ' make you perfect ' implies, as in Matthew 4 : 21; Luke 6 : 40; 1 Corinthians 1 : 10, restoring to completeness; that for ' stablish,' as 2 Thessalonians 2 : 17; 3 : 3, the fixity of Christians; that for ' strengthen ' (not found elsewhere in the New Testament) giving power to resist attack. In ' settle ' (literally, to lay a foundation), as in Matthew 7 : 25; Luke 6 : 48, which may well have been in the apostle's thoughts, we have the idea of building up the spiritual life upon Christ as the one foundation (1 Cor. 3 : 11)." — *E. H. Plumptre.*

What are some of the reasons which you can suggest why Christians should be persecuted by the world of unbelieving men? How many different reasons can you find in the passages we have just studied for a Christian's rejoicing even in a time of persecution? Do you think that joy under persecution is possible for any people except those who belong to the Lord Jesus Christ? What comfort and help do you draw from the fact that with the end of Christ's earthly life His sufferings forever are over? — He endures no suffering from the time of His death on the Cross down through all the endless ages of eternity. How can we prepare ourselves that we may be ready to give a reason for our convictions as Christians? Do you think it is much worse for the Christian to have to suffer as an evil-doer than for a non-Christian to suffer as an evil-doer? (Yes, the Christian ought not be guilty of wrong-doing, because he is a Christian.)

LESSON XI. — June 13.

GOD'S EXCEEDING GREAT PROMISES. — 2 Peter 1 : 1–11.

GOLDEN TEXT. — *He hath granted unto us his precious and exceeding great promises; that through these ye may become partakers of the divine nature.* 2 PETER 1 : 4.

Devotional Reading: Colossians 3 : 12–17.
Beginner Topic: THE CHILDREN'S FRIEND.
Lesson Material: 1 John 4; Mark 10 : 13–16.
Memory Verse: For thou, Jehovah, hast made me glad. Psalm 92 : 4.
Primary Topic: WHEN JESUS DIED FOR US.
Lesson Material: 1 John 2 : 1–6; John 19.
Memory Verse: For God so loved the world, that he gave his only begotten Son, that whosoever believeth on him should not perish, but have eternal life. John 3 : 16.
Junior Topic: JESUS OUR SAVIOUR.
Lesson Material: 1 John 2 : 1–6; John 19.
Memory Verse: For God so loved the world, that he gave his only begotten Son, that whosoever believeth on him should not perish, but have eternal life. John 3 : 16.
Intermediate and Senior Topic: GROWING IN CHRISTIAN CHARACTER.
Topic for Young People and Adults: OUR RESPONSE TO GOD'S PROMISES.

THE TEACHER AND HIS CLASS.

The Younger Classes might be asked what one thing they expect to characterize the life of a child during its first few years of life. The answer, of course, is *growth.* We expect a babe to grow physically, day by day, month by month. Toward the end of babyhood, and for years thereafter, we also expect to see mental growth. How tragic it is to see any one who has not grown physically beyond childhood! How tragic to see one who has never grown mentally, beyond a baby's mentality! So also as Christians, we are to manifest sturdy growth by the nurture and cultivation of our spiritual life. It is regarding such growth that our lesson is concerned.

The Older Classes should be reminded that wild apple trees produce no fruit fit for marketing, and in these days, unless an apple orchard is constantly sprayed, trimmed, and watched over in many ways, it will become over-ridden with insect pests, shoot out great worthless growths, its foliage will become so massed that the sunlight cannot reach the fruit. As orchards need the watchful care of men to produce good fruit, so does the heart of man need watchful care to produce the fruits that God intends it to bear. There are some things in life that come to us, as it were, by second nature; such as the instinct for work, for love, for protection, the desire in every normal person's being to be honest and fair, and to expect fairness from others. But there are many things which *ought* to characterize the life of a Christian, which do not come to us in this natural way, but need constant cultivation, aspects of character that will only grow by discipline and watchfulness. Among these virtues are those which are enumerated in our lesson; virtues that will not be found constantly adorning any of our lives unless we give diligence to cultivate them.

THE LESSON IN ITS SETTING.

Time. — The Apostle Peter wrote his Second Epistle in A.D. 66.

Place. — We do not know from what place this epistle was written, and we probably never will be able to determine it.

THE PLAN OF THE LESSON.

SUBJECT: The Necessity for Diligence in the Cultivation of the Virtues That Should Adorn Every Christian Life.

I. THE SALUTATION, 2 Peter 1 : 1, 2.

1. The writer identifies himself.
2. The writer describes those to whom he is addressing this epistle.
3. His benediction.

II. WHAT CHRISTIAN BELIEVERS POSSESS, VS. 3, 4.

1. "All things that pertain unto life and godliness."
2. A knowledge of God.
3. "His precious and exceeding great promises."
4. Participation in the divine nature.
5. Deliverance from the corruption that is in the world.

III. WHAT CHRISTIANS SHOULD BE DILIGENTLY DOING, VS. 5–7.

1. "In faith supplying virtue."
2. Adding knowledge to virtue.
3. Adding temperance to knowledge.
4. Adding patience to temperance.
5. Adding godliness to patience.
6. To godliness adding love.

IV. SOME IMMEDIATE AND ULTIMATE CONSEQUENCES THAT WILL OCCUR FOR THOSE WHO SO LIVE, VS. 8–11.

1. Deliverance from idleness and unfruitfulness.
2. Stumbling made impossible.
3. An abundant entrance into the eternal kingdom of Christ.

THE TEACHER'S LIBRARY.

For commentaries on Second Peter, see Henry Alford, in his *New Testament for English Readers;* Charles Bigg, in the *International Critical Commentary* Series (especially helpful for those who know Greek); B. C. Caffin, in the *Pulpit Commentary* Series; E. H. Plumptre, in the *Cambridge Bible for Schools and Colleges;* Alfred Plummer, in the *Bible Commentary for English Readers;* N. M. Williams in the *American Commentary on the New Testament* Series; J. R. Lumby in the *Expositor's Bible;* G. F. C. Frönmueller, in the Lange Series of Commentaries.

For expository material, see W. Graham Scroggie: *Biblical Review*, July, 1927, Vol. 12, 348–360; and Alexander Maclaren: *Expositions of Holy Scripture, First and Second Peter and First John*, on verse 1, pages 170–178; on verse 3, 178–189; on verse 4, 189–198; on verse 5, 198–206. For an excellent sermon on the entire passage, see especially James M. Gray: *Salvation from Start to Finish*, 69–84. (This small volume may be purchased for ten cents from the Bible Institute Colportage Association, Chicago.) On verse 4, see T. H. Darlow: *The Upward Calling*, 167–170; J. D. Jones: *The Hope of the Eternal*, 271 ff. On the series of virtues mentioned in verses 5–7, there is one volume devoted exclusively to this passage which the editor has never been able to secure, John Monro Gibson: *The Gamut of Graces* (London, 1926). See a series of seven wonderfully rich sermons in Henry Howard: *The Summits of the Soul*, 3–79; and James Iverach: *The Other Side of Greatness*, 102–118. On verse 9, W. L. Watkinson: *The Supreme Conquest*, 41–51; J. H. Jowett: *Apostolic Optimism*, 247–261; J. D. Jones: *Elms of Life*, 124–139; on verse 10, W. L. Watkinson: *Studies in Christian Character*, 128–133; D. J. Burrell: *A Quiver of Arrows*, 255 ff.; and, by the same author: *The Religion of the Future*, 216 ff.

Some young men, starting out with great assets, abundant gifts, winning immediate success in their work, with a most attractive personality, seem for some tragic reason, known or unknown, to grow smaller and smaller as the years come and go. In the editor's own particular field, that of preaching, he has known men who could preach upon graduation from seminary, at the age of twenty-five, with greater fervor, smoother language, and points more logically developed, than twenty years later, when they were nearing the time of greatest maturity. Other men have grown and developed — they have grown deeper in their character, broader in their sympathies, gentler in their natures and richer in their thoughts. Hardly a greater illustration of true growth can be found in the annals of the Church than is to be discovered in the life of the one who wrote the words forming the text of our lesson today. Forty years before this, the man who wrote this Epistle (and the preceding one also bearing his name) was nothing but an uncouth, rugged, boastful, loud-spoken, untutored fisherman on the sea of Galilee, and is now a man capable of setting forth ideals for life, so high, so noble, so glorious that none of us can say we have ever fully attained them; one whose fidelity to Christ can now never be questioned; one who once attempted to prevent our Lord from going to the Cross, but who now sees that the Cross is the very center of his faith. Such growth as this would never have been the experience of Simon son of Jona, except he came into contact with Christ, came to believe Christ was the Son of God, and had lived for years in the power of the indwelling of the Spirit of Christ. The growth that Peter knew is the growth which he would have all believers to know. He does not set himself up as an example, but, by the inspiration of the Holy Spirit, he sets forth ideals for himself and for all of us, in every age, to strive for until our Lord shall come.

2 PETER 1 : 1. Simon Peter, a servant and apostle of Jesus Christ, to them that have obtained a like precious faith with us in the righteousness of our God and *the* Saviour Jesus Christ:

2. Grace to you and peace be multiplied in the knowledge of God and of Jesus our Lord;

I. **THE SALUTATION,** VS. 1, 2. 1. **Simon Peter, a servant and apostle of Jesus Christ.** It makes a difference who is writing a letter, who signs a communication, whose signature appears at the end of a command. This letter of Peter's carries apostolic authority, recognized as carrying such wherever the letter was read in the Christian Church. Being a divinely-appointed apostle, Peter had a right to speak with the highest authority, under, of course, the inspiration of the Holy Spirit. Peter's authority comes not from any great achievements of his own, not by any intellectual brilliance which he himself possessed, not by any peculiar gifts of oratory, but by the fact he was nothing less than a servant and apostle of Jesus Christ. And so, for all of us, our authority, our strength, our boldness, come alone from our being united to the Lord, and being in His will. **To them that have obtained a like precious faith with us in the righteousness of our God and *the* Saviour Jesus Christ.** "In speaking of 'us' the apostle may either be asserting the full equality of blessedness between the Jews of the *Diaspora* and those of the mother Church of Jerusalem and the personal disciples of the Lord Jesus, or (addressing his epistle to a wider circle than before, and therefore purposely altering the form of address) between the Gentile and the Jewish converts. They have, he says, 'obtained' (the word carries with it the idea of obtaining by lot or by God's appointment as distinct from a man's own exertions, as in Luke 1 : 9; Acts 1 : 17) 'a faith of equal worth with ours.'" — *E. H. Plumptre.* "How much and how little it takes to make a Christian! 'Only faith?' you say. Yes, thank God, not this, or that, not rites, not anything that a priest can do to you. Not orthodoxy; not morality; these will come, but trust in Christ and His blood and righteousness. You are a Christian; are you? Are you trusting in that Christ? If you are not, no, though you be orthodox up to the eyebrows, and though seven or seven hundred sacraments may have been given to you, and though you be a clean living man — all that does not make a Christian, but *this* does — 'Like precious faith with us in the righteousness of God and our Saviour.'" — *Alexander Maclaren.* "There can be no growth at all in the physical sense, for example, unless there is physical life as the basis of it. And it is so in the spiritual sense, too. There can be no spiritual growth without spiritual life preceding. And there can be no spiritual life except through the new birth. And the new birth comes as we obtain this 'precious faith in the righteousness of our God and Saviour Jesus Christ.'" — *James M. Gray.* 2. **Grace to you and peace be multiplied in the knowledge of God and of Jesus our Lord.** This is what we call an apostolic salutation. It is the way almost all the epistles of the New Testament begin. We need to pay particular attention only to the phrase, "in the knowledge of God, etc." "It is that knowledge of truth which Paul so often commends to Timothy (1 Tim. 2 : 4; 2 Tim. 3 : 7) and speaks of as that acknowledging of the truth, allowing it to be effective on the life, which follows repentance (2 Tim. 2 : 25); it is specially the knowledge of God and of things divine; it is that knowledge which must temper religious zeal (Rom. 10 : 2) that it may be effective; it is the knowledge against which if a man sin (Heb. 10 : 26) he is verily reprobate. And this true

> **A Christian is**
>
> A MIND
> *Through which Christ Thinks*
>
> A HEART
> *Through which Christ Loves*
>
> A VOICE
> *Through which Christ Speaks*
>
> A HAND
> *Through which Christ Helps*
>
> —F. A. NOBLE

3. Seeing that his divine power hath granted unto us all things that pertain unto life and godliness, through the knowledge of him that called us by his own glory and virtue;

4. Whereby he hath granted unto us his precious and exceeding great promises; that through these ye may become partakers of the divine nature, having escaped from the corruption that is in the world by lust.

---

knowledge can only come of faithful service. He shall know the Lord who loves to do His will."

II. **WHAT CHRISTIAN BELIEVERS POSSESS,** vs. 3, 4. 3. **Seeing that his divine power hath granted unto us all things that pertain unto life and godliness.** There is probably a double meaning in this clause: on the one hand, Peter certainly wishes to remind his readers that in Christ we have everything necessary for the fullness of life in its deeper implications; that is, spiritual life, inner life, eternal life, life that issues in godliness; and, on the other hand, he means to imply that because we have all that life can ever require in Christ, we do not need to turn to any other teacher for things which Christ cannot supply, for there is nothing He cannot supply. The Christian faith is one of utter, absolute fullness of blessing, and no so-called religious teacher in the world, no extra-Christian philosophy, no antisupernaturalistic ideas, no humanly conceived schemes for the deepening of life, can ever add anything whatsoever to that life which we have in Christ Jesus. **Through the knowledge of him that called us.** " Suppose, instead of talking about calling, you were to talk about inviting, summoning, beckoning; or I might use tenderer words still — beseeching, wooing, entreating; for all that lies in the thought. God summoning and calling, in that sense, men to Himself, by the raying out of His own perfect beauty, and the might with which the beams go forth into the darkness. Ah! is not that beautiful, dear brethren; that there is nothing more, indeed, for God to do to draw us to Himself than to let us see what He is? So perfectly fair, so sweet, so tender, so strong, so absolutely corresponding to all the necessities of our beings and the hunger of our hearts, that when we see Him we cannot choose but love Him, and that He can do nothing more to call wandering hearts back to the light and sweetness of His own heart than to show them Himself." — *Alexander Maclaren.* **By his own glory and virtue.** " The attributes of God manifested by Him are the means by which He calls men to the knowledge of the truth." " Some trace the word *virtue* to the word signifying man, and it is certain that manliness or bravery in war was the principal idea which it expressed. The Latin equivalent *virtus* was used by the Romans in the same way. As Trench says: ' It is as if for them all virtues were included in warlike courage alone.' As the same writer also reminds us, the Italians of today ' degrade the word *virtuoso*, or *the virtuous*, to signify one accomplished in painting, music, and sculpture, such things as are the ornamental fringe of a nation's life, but can never be made, without loss of all manliness of character, its main texture and woof, not to say that excellence in these fine arts has been in too many cases divorced from all true virtue and worth.' Christianity took the word virtue out from the ignoble uses to which it had been consecrated, and made it the watchword of Godlike excellence." — *H. Harvey.* 4. **Whereby he hath granted unto us his precious and exceeding great promises.** " The whole Bible may be called God's charter of promises — beginning with the promise uttered when paradise was lost, and ending with the unfulfilled vision of paradise regained. It is true, of course, that not a few promises which are recorded there were made explicitly to particular persons, or limited to some definite occasion, or conditioned by some special crisis. Nevertheless, the Bible warrants us in appropriating to ourselves the broad drift and purport of each word for good which God has ever spoken concerning man. . . . God's promises are not only for the individual believer but for the universal Church. With Him there is no respect of persons. And so what He desires and intends for a single soul becomes an index of His eternal purpose for all the souls that He has made. When Dr. Judson, the pioneer of Christian missions in Burma, was asked what were the prospects of his work, he replied: ' As bright as the promises of God.' " — *T. H. Darlow.*

That through these ye may become partakers of the divine nature. " The teaching of my text is no dreamy teaching, such as an eastern mystic might proclaim, of absorption into an impersonal divine. There is no notion here of any partaking of these great though secondary attributes of the divine mind which to many men are

5. Yea, and for this very cause adding on your part all diligence, in
your faith supply virtue; and in *your* virtue knowledge;
6. And in *your* knowledge self-control; and in *your* self-control patience;
and in *your* patience godliness;

---

the most Godlike parts of His nature. But what my text mainly means is, you may, if you like, become 'holy as God is holy.' You may become loving as God is loving, and with a breath of His own life breathed into your hearts. The central divinity in the divine, if I may so say, is the amalgam of holiness and love. That is God; the rest is what belongs to God. God *has* power; God *is* love. That is the regnant attribute, the spring that sets everything agoing. And so, when my text talks about making us all, if we will, partakers of a divine nature, what it means, mainly, is this — that into every human spirit there may pass a seed of divine life which will unfold itself there in all purity of holiness, in all tenderness and gentleness of love. 'God is love; and he that dwelleth in love dwelleth in God, and God in him.' Partakers we shall be in the measure in which by our faith we have drawn from Him the pure and the hearty love of whatever things are fair and noble; the measure in which we love righteousness and hate iniquity." — *Alexander Maclaren.* **Having escaped the corruption that is in the world by lust.** The word here translated corruption " describes the moral filth of the world without Christianity. Paul uses the same word in Romans 8 : 21, contrasting it with the glorious liberty of the children of God. The fearful immorality which, with few exceptions, characterized the social life of Greece and Rome, the highest state as well as the lowest, and which has equally marked non-Christian society in all lands and all times, fully justifies the apostolic application of the term 'corruption.' The vileness of man left traces of itself in durable form on the walls of dwellings and in bronze castings, the details of which would be indecorous to relate; and in proportion as society, after being purified by Christianity, has withdrawn from the purifying influence, it has relapsed into similar pollution. *The world's corruption, which is founded in lust*, expresses the meaning." — *H. Harvey.* Just as a person almost dying with pernicious anæmia, needs a transfusion of new blood; just as one in a low climate, suffering from tuberculosis, if he is to be saved from early death, must be taken up into a high altitude; so you and I, if we would be delivered from the powerful evil forces that so feverishly are at work throughout the world, must continually breathe the atmosphere of the promises of God's Word, being, to change the figure, lifted up by them, allured and captivated by them, so that the corrupt things of this world will hold for us no allurement whatever.

III. **WHAT CHRISTIANS SHOULD BE DILIGENTLY DOING,** vs. 5-7. 5. **Yea, and for this very cause adding on your part all diligence.** " The diligence of which he speaks is that sort of endeavor which springs from a sense of duty; an earnest zeal and will to accomplish whatever it finds to do; that does not linger till some great work offers, but hastens to labor in the immediate present." — *J. R. Lumby.* " We are concerned about dress, but are content that our souls be ill-clad; we are attentive to food, while yet our inner man remains unfed; we are eager in our pursuit of material wealth, but too often despise the heavenly riches; we take every precaution to safeguard this life, but make little or no preparation for the next." — *W. Graham Scroggie.* **In your faith supply virtue.** " Virtue means the best development of such power as a man possesses. It may be little or great, but in its kind it is to be made excellent. And here it is that the Christian workers in every sphere must surpass others. They work from a higher motive. What they do is a constant attestation of their faith, is done as in God's sight, and in the confidence that in every act it is possible to give Him glory. There can be no carelessness in such lives, for they are filled with a sense of responsibility, which is the firstfruit of a living faith." — *J. R. Lumby.* **And in *your* virtue knowledge.** " The word for knowledge here is not the compound used in verses 2 and 3, but the simple substantive. It means, therefore, knowledge that still admits of growth, not yet ripe or complete. Here it probably means spiritual discernment as to what is right

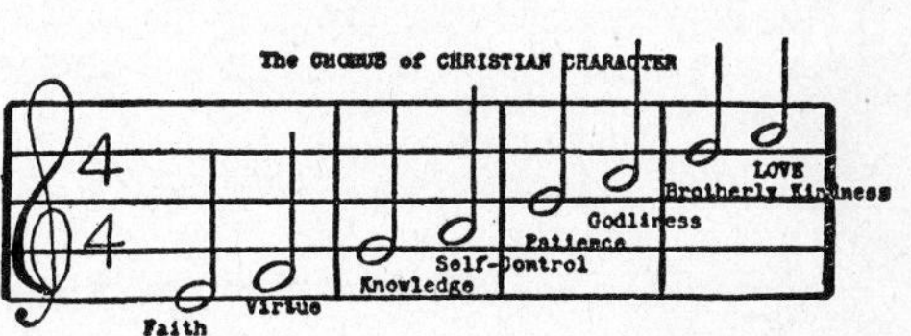

7. And in *your* godliness brotherly kindness; and in *your* brotherly kindness love.

---

and what is wrong in all things; the right object, the right way, the right time." — *Alfred Plummer*. Notice that true knowledge, spiritual knowledge, the knowledge of what is right and wrong, the knowledge of the finer, more delicately discerned things of life, does not come until we are truly living virtuously. **And in *your* knowledge self-control.** "When we think of temperance our minds naturally turn to that form of temperance which consists in refusing to have anything to do with strong drink. The battle with that form of intemperance is so close, the results of that kind of intemperance are so deadly, that one does not wonder that it has usurped the whole meaning of the word. But the word 'temperance' has a much wider meaning in Scripture. It means self-control all round. It means that we have learned to know what is the Christian ideal of life, and to know what helps and what hinders the growth of that life. It grows out of knowledge, it is using Christian knowledge for the guidance of life." — *James Iverach*. **And in *your* self-control patience.** "Patience grows out of self-control. It grows with the growth of the new nature. Such growth might be illustrated in many ways. I have known men become impatient with themselves, and bring on themselves much gratuitous misery, because they were not able all at once to overcome an inveterate fault, or to secure an ideal attainment. I have known men become impatient with other people because of some shortcomings. I have known ministers to be impatient with their congregations, and congregations with their ministers. I have known men become impatient with the arrangements of Providence, and utter impatient sayings about the weather. I have known men impatient with the government of the world, yea, I find that impatience finding expression in the prayers of the congregation, in the hymns they sing, and sometimes in the sermons which are preached. . . . Be patient with yourself in your warfare with sin and temptation, and try to remember that you can win the victory over sin only by watchful care. Be patient with the government of the world. Remember that God is working for eternity, and has eternity to work in. It takes centuries to make an oak tree, things without worth complete their life course in a day or a week or a year. As for yourself, have patience with yourself, for you are building up a character which shall have eternal worth. Have patience with God in the working out of His purpose, for He is making a kingdom which shall endure forever, and shall need no further change of principle. Be patient with other people, and out of that patient expectation try to help them, so that they may rise to the height of the ideal you have formed for them. Let us learn to be patient as the Father in heaven is patient." — *James Iverach*. **And in *your* patience godliness.** This last word strictly means, true reverence for God, and here, the state of one who is "godly" or "like God." This is the ultimate aim of our whole redemption, that we may be made conformable to the image of God's Son. While we have never seen it in any commentary, does it not seem to be a very simple statement of fact that the phrase "partakers of the divine nature" in verse 4 is paralleled by this word "godliness" of our verse? **And in *your* godliness brotherly kindness; and in *your* brotherly kindness love.** "The last-named love is that highest love, the love of God to men, which is set up as the grand ideal toward which His servants are constantly to press forward; but from this the love of the brethren cannot be severed, nay it must be made the stepping-stone unto it. For, as another apostle says, 'he that loveth not his brother, whom he hath seen, cannot love God, whom he hath not seen' (1 John 4 : 20). But love of the brethren is not to be narrowed in the verse before us or elsewhere to love of those who are already known to the churches as brethren in the Lord. We have with us, too, the acts of God Himself, who would have all men come to the knowledge of the truth, and who, with impartial love, maketh His sun to rise on the evil and on the good, and sendeth His rain upon the just and the unjust, that thus even the evil and unjust may be won to own His Fatherhood. Such divine love is the end of the commandment (1 Tim. 1 : 5), and terminates the list of those graces the steps whereto Paul has more briefly indicated when he says the love which is most like God's springs from a pure heart, a good conscience, and faith unfeigned." — *J. R. Lumby*. Children of the same parents are necessarily related to one another, and should love one another. God's elect are knit together in one communion of fellowship. Christian love must begin with "them that are of the household of faith." Our love for our fellows is to be as God's love for us, not dependent on their worthiness of it, and not

8. For if these things are yours and abound, they make you to be not idle nor unfruitful unto the knowledge of our Lord Jesus Christ.

9. For he that lacketh these things is blind, seeing only what is near, having forgotten the cleansing from his old sins.

10. Wherefore, brethren, give the more diligence to make your calling and election sure: for if ye do these things, ye shall never stumble:

11. For thus shall be richly supplied unto you the entrance into the eternal kingdom of our Lord and Saviour Jesus Christ.

---

deterred by their disregard of it. While also this has not been seen by the editor in any commentary, yet is there not a definite relationship between the characteristics of a truly growing Christian, as set forth in these verses, and the sevenfold fruit of the Holy Spirit which the Apostle Paul sets forth in Galatians 5 : 22, 23?

IV. **SOME IMMEDIATE AND ULTIMATE CONSEQUENCES THAT WILL OCCUR FOR THOSE WHO SO LIVE,** vs. 8–11. 8. **For if these things are yours and abound, they make you to be not idle nor unfruitful unto the knowledge of our Lord Jesus Christ.** The word here translated *make you* literally means, to bring a person to a place. In verses 2 and 3, Christian progress is made to begin with knowledge and is in knowledge. "Knowledge is the germ which makes progress by us and is developed by the progress but is now represented here as the goal toward which the progress tends. This knowledge, which grows with our growth, might very well be said to be the issue of all our strivings (cf. Col. 1 : 10)." — *Charles Bigg.* 9. **For he that lacketh these things is blind, seeing only what is near.** "The word *blind,* applied originally to the eyes, was applied figuratively and with great significance to the mind; and while the intellect of man is blind, it is chiefly the heart (the affections, in which blindness is seated). The blindness is alienation from spiritual things, which does indeed produce stupidity of understanding." — *N. M. Williams.* The word translated *what is near* means literally to be short-sighted. "The characteristics of a short-sighted man are that he sees things dimly or that he sees what is close at hand more distinctly than what is far off. The first gives tolerable sense, but many commentators prefer the second." — *Charles Bigg.* **Having forgotten the cleansing from his old sins.** "The man who forgets this cleansing of his soul and acts as if he were in his simply natural state with no power to resist temptation, does in fact ignore what God has done for him and treats 'the sins of long ago as though they were still the inevitable accompaniments of the present." — *E. H. Plumptre.* 10. **Wherefore, brethren, give the more diligence to make your calling and election sure: for if ye do these things, ye shall never stumble.** "Because God has bestowed such gifts on men, because the use of those gifts leads on to the full knowledge of Christ, therefore all the more give diligence. The calling and election are the act of God (1 Peter 1 : 2; 2 : 21)." — *B. C. Caffin.* "If one is walking a narrow path on a dark night, if he knows that there are stones and a ditch on either side, and yet he is never tripping over the one or slipping into the other, he must be pretty certain he is on the right road. And in the same way, if we are never failing in these things, if virtue, and knowledge, and temperance and patience, and godliness and brotherly kindness and love, are in us and abounding, we experience little anxiety about the things of greatest concern. We know that all is well, and peace that floweth as a river is our continued portion." — *James M. Gray.* 11. **For thus shall be richly supplied unto you the entrance into the eternal kingdom of our Lord and Saviour Jesus Christ.** The only really clear interpretation which the editor has seen of this last verse is in the sermon of Dr. Gray's, from which we have already frequently quoted. "There is such a thing as just an entrance into that kingdom, and then there is such another thing as an abundant entrance, a figure which suggests that of Paul in his First Epistle to the Corinthians (3 : 12), where he speaks of a building of wood, hay, stubble, and another of gold, silver, precious stones. The first shall be burned, and the man shall suffer loss, though 'he himself shall be saved.' It will be a salvation though, as of fire. And so this may be an entrance, if the man is a true believer, and regenerated, but only an entrance and nothing more if he be not diligent. The gate will close behind him and that is all. . . . And the 'everlasting kingdom of our Lord and Saviour Jesus Christ,' what is meant by that? The kingdom bequeathed to Him by His Father, and yet to be established in manifested glory throughout the earth? Yes, doubtless, for He has promised to come again and bring His reward with Him. And 'When

Christ, who is our life shall appear, then shall we also appear with him in glory' (Col. 3 : 4). There is joy in that kingdom and degrees of joy, there is honor and degrees of honor, there is power and degrees of power. There is everything to accentuate the thought of the abundant entrance. And still, I like the thought of Calvin, that Peter is here referring to supplies of present grace. In a sense the kingdom is here now. Not in its manifested state, of course, but as represented in the lives of those children of the kingdom who through faith have accepted the King and are waiting for His coming. There is an entrance into that kingdom now, and an abundant entrance. There are Christians who know what the abundant entrance means today. 'Great peace have they that love thy law,' the psalmist sings. This is the abundant entrance and the cause of it. 'These things have I spoken unto you that my joy might remain in you, and that your joy might be full' (John 15 : 11). Here we see it again. The Bible is rich in these intimations, and the experience of the saints corroborate them."

"Weeds will grow in your garden without your attention, but not flowers. Is it not time you did a bit of gardening in the soil of your soul?" — *W. Graham Scroggie.* As we close this lesson, we ought to remember one thing. This passage is a revelation of the will of God for us. This is not what some philosopher has pictured, an impossible idealistic life; this is not the dream of a monk in some monastery; this is not the mere joining of pietistic phrases, or a disconnected sequence of hypothetical virtues. This is a portrait of a true Christian, drawn by the Apostle Peter, under the inspiration of the Holy Spirit; drawn by a man who had known the sufficiency of Christ for forty years; drawn by one, remember, who had many blemishes of his own, and who knew the necessity of constant watchfulness, and daily discipline. If Peter could live this kind of life, so can the rest of us; if this is the life God would have us live, He will enable us to live it, if we so choose.

In how many ways did our Lord manifest in His earthly life the virtues that are here set forth? Why do we know that this passage is exclusively for Christian believers, and should never be applied to men outside of Christ? What do you think would be the ultimate result in a person's heart if they daily lived the life here set forth for us? Why do we want to be delivered from the corruption that is in the world? Why do you think that whereas Paul designated love as the first in the series of seven fruits of the Spirit, here the Apostle places it last? What characteristic of life set forth in these verses do you think will be continually manifested by all those who are gathered together in heaven? Do you think, spiritually speaking, you are diligent or indifferent and slovenly?

LESSON XII. — June 20.

JOHN DESCRIBES TRUE CHRISTIANS. — 1 John.

PRINTED TEXT, 1 John 2 : 1–6; 3 : 13–18; 4 : 15–17.

GOLDEN TEXT. — ***But if we walk in the light, as he is in the light, we have fellowship one with another, and the blood of Jesus his Son cleanseth us from all sin.*** 1 JOHN 1 : 7.

Devotional Reading: Psalm 15.
Beginner Topic: A SONG JESUS LIKED.
Lesson Material: Matthew 21 : 12–16.
Memory Verse: I will sing unto Jehovah. Exodus 15 : 1.
Primary Topic: JESUS' RULE OF LOVE.
Lesson Material: 2 John; Luke 10 : 25–37.
Memory Verse: This is my commandment, that ye love one another, as I have loved you. John 15 : 12.
Junior Topic: THE GOOD SAMARITAN.
Lesson Material: 2 John; 3 John; Luke 10 : 25–37.
Memory Verse: This is my commandment, that ye love one another, as I have loved you. John 15 : 12.
Intermediate and Senior Topic: MARKS OF A CHRISTIAN.
Topic for Young People and Adults: WHO IS A CHRISTIAN?

THE TEACHER AND HIS CLASS.

The Younger Classes might have their interest aroused in this lesson (which will prove quite difficult for children), if the teacher would draw on the blackboard a map, showing a rather large area of some uninhabited waste place, like one of the vast defrosted sections of Michigan, the map indicating a number of intertwining sand roads, frequently crossing each other, sometimes curving, sometimes straight, sometimes going in one direction, sometimes in another, necessitating, if one is to find one's way through the area, signs indicating to which destination each road will lead without which one would quickly become lost. Life is like this, a very complex matter, in which voices, calling us this way and that way, try to allure us to take one path or another. We need divine guidance to direct us in the way God would have us to walk, the way that will lead to eternal life, to joy, to communion with God, to victory over sin. Now, this First Epistle of John is something like a guidebook, warning us from certain roads, and definitely leading us to take other roads.

The Older Classes will discover in this book a constant reiteration of the theme of *love for others*, a subject we hear very little about, in fact, a subject we think very little about. It will be noticed that almost all the blessings spoken of in this book relate to this practice of loving one another, and, if we are to have such a life of blessing as is here depicted, we will have it only by practicing this fundamental principle of love for others. We must remember that the New Testament writings do not set forth one particular ideal of life, as though we may choose it *or* some other, set forth by another religion, but the New Testament sets forth *God's* ideal for life, and if we do not strive for this ideal, we will not have abundant life. However, contrary to the teachings of the world, and our own selfishness, this love-life must be recognized as God's definite commandment to us.

THE LESSON IN ITS SETTING.

Time. — We do not know exactly when John wrote this epistle, but probably between A.D. 85 and 95.

Place. No doubt this epistle was written from Ephesus.

THE PLAN OF THE LESSON.

SUBJECT: How a Child of God May Live in Full Communion with God the Father and His Son Jesus Christ, in Continual Victory over Sin and the Evil One, Exercising Great Power in Prayer, Knowing Abounding Joy and Fullness of Life.

I. THE PRIVILEGE AND CONDITIONS OF FELLOWSHIP WITH GOD AND WITH CHRIST, 1 John 1 : 1—2 : 2.

1. The apostolic knowledge of Christ, 1 : 1, 2.
2. The privilege of fellowship announced, 1 : 3, 4.
3. Fellowship is assured if we walk in the light, 1 : 5–7 *a*.
4. The divine way of putting away sin that fellowship may be maintained, 1 : 7 *b*—2 : 2.
   a. Christ's blood cleanses from sin.
   b. We are forgiven if we confess our sins.
   c. We are to live apart from sin.
   d. Christ is our Advocate.
   e. Christ is our propitiation.

II. THE RIGHT AND WRONG OBJECTS OF LOVE, 2 : 3–17.

1. The obligation to keep God's commandments, vs. 3–7.
2. The duty of loving our brother, vs. 8–11.
3. Three groups of Christians to whom John is writing, vs. 12–14.
4. The world we should not love, vs. 15–17.

III. WARNING AGAINST ANTICHRIST AND ERROR, 2 : 18–29.

IV. SOME REASONS WHY OUR LIVES SHOULD BE PURE, 3 : 1–10.

1. Because some day we are to be like Christ, vs. 1–3.
2. Because Christ came to take away sins, vs. 4, 5.
3. Because we abide in Christ, v. 6.
4. Because Christ came to destroy the works of the devil, vs. 7–10.

V. THE PRIMACY OF LOVING ONE ANOTHER, 3 : 11–24.

1. The obligation to love one another, vs. 11–19.
2. The privilege in prayer such a life bestows, vs. 20–22.
3. The commandment repeated, vs. 23, 24.

VI. WARNING AGAINST FALSE TEACHERS, 4 : 1–6.

VII. THE THIRD ADMONITION TO LOVE ONE ANOTHER, 4 : 7–21.

VIII. THE LIFE OF VICTORY OVER THE WORLD, 5 : 1–21.

1. The victory faith bestows, vs. 1–13.
2. The privilege of prayer, vs. 14, 15.
3. Kept by the power of God, vs. 16–21.

THE TEACHER'S LIBRARY.

On the First Epistle of John itself, see J. B. Tidwell: *John and His Five Books* (1937), 89–100; D. A. Hayes: *John and His Writings* (1917), 159–202; W. H. Griffith Thomas: *The Apostle John* (1923) 231–325; P. J. Gloag: *Introduction to the Johannine Writings* (1891), 215–263; a very excellent article, by Robert Law, "Epistles of John," in the *International Standard Bible Encyclopedia*, Vol. 3, 1711–1720; A. H. Strong: *Popular Lectures on the Books of the New Testament*, 354–368; and a brief but helpful treatment in William G. Moorehead: *Outline Studies in the New Testament — the Catholic Epistles*, 86–119; also Charles R. Erdman: *The General Epistles*, 110–152.

For commentaries and expositions of this volume, see Alfred Plummer, in the *Cambridge Bible for Schools and Colleges;* A. E. Brooke, in the *International Critical Commentary* Series; B. F. Westcott: *The Epistles of St. John* (the last two only for those who can handle the Greek). One of the greatest expository works in the English language, on any portion of the New Testament, is Robert S. Candlish's *The First Epistle of John* (Edinburgh, 1866); a very searching volume is Robert Law: *The Tests of Life* (Edinburgh, 1909); see also F. D. Maurice: *The Epistles of John;* G. G. Findlay: *Fellowship in the Life Eternal;* William Kelly: *Exposition of the Epistles of John;* J. M. Gibbon: *Eternal Life;* G. S. Barrett, in the *Devotional Commentary* Series; J. J. Massee: *Eternal Life in Action;* and a work of great practical value with many illuminating passages, H. A. Ironside: *Addresses on the Epistles of John.* All sermonic references have been purposely omitted.

SOME INTRODUCTORY MATTERS.

That this Epistle, which we are about to study, was written by the Apostle John, the disciple whom Jesus loved, and the author of the Fourth Gospel, has been acknowledged by the Church throughout all ages, even though the Epistle itself does not carry John's name, nor the name of any of the other apostles. " The epistle was not addressed to one particular church, but to the churches of pro-consular Asia. John was in intimate relationship with these churches. For many years he resided at Ephesus, the center of the district, and, as we learn from Eusebius, he was accustomed to make them pastoral visitations. He is evidently acquainted with their wants and temptations, and he writes to them not as strangers, but with all the love of a spiritual father. The dangers which threatened the churches of Asia arose not from without but from within. Heresies had sprung up within them." — *P. J. Gloag.*

PURPOSE OF THE EPISTLE.

John sets forth the purposes he had in mind in writing this letter in three different passages: that his readers might have fellowship with all other believers (1 : 4); that the Christians whom he addressed should learn how to live triumphantly over sin (2 : 1); and, finally, " that ye may know that ye have eternal life, even unto you that believe on the name of the Son of God " (5 : 13). Underneath these stated purposes is another: " The Apostle writes to warn Christians against certain erroneous views of the person of Christ which were doubtless circulated among the Asiatic churches. He cautions them against being led astray by certain prevalent opinions and exhorts them to test these opinions by their nature and tendency (4 : 1)." — *P. J. Gloag.*

THE VOCABULARY OF THIS EPISTLE.

John is here writing in a most fatherly way, and continually calls his readers by the most affectionate terms: twice they are called " children of God "; four times, " little children "; four times, " my little children "; five times he speaks to them as " beloved." The Epistle is saturated with the idea of love and all that relates to it. The word *love* as a noun occurs eighteen times in the Revised Version, and as a verb twenty-eight times. In fact, as a verb, Professor Hays says, the word occurs " twice as many times in this Epistle as in any other book of the New Testament except the Gospel according to John." We are, perhaps, at first surprised to find that in such an epistle, saturated with the idea of love, sin and all that relates to it is continually rising up for discussion. I find the word sin as a noun eighteen times, and as a verb nine times. The originator and prime instigator of all sin, Satan, is frequently referred to in this Epistle as the *devil*, *the evil one*, and "he that is in the world." Christians are often warned against Satan's agents, as antichrist, false teachers, false prophets, and liars. Yet, though the forces of evil are set forth so frequently, at the same time the Epistle unhesitatingly proclaims a life of victory over sin, over error, over darkness, and over the evil one. The idea of overcoming the world is fundamental (4 : 4; 5 : 4, 5); of overcoming the evil one (2 : 13, 14); of light overcoming darkness, of truth winning against error, of Christ within us leading us in triumph over him who is in the world.

CHRIST IN THE FIRST EPISTLE OF JOHN.

More is said about the death of Christ in this Epistle than about any other one aspect of His being and work. It is by His blood that we are cleansed (1 : 7); He is a prepitiation for sins (2 : 2; 4 : 10); He came to take away sin (3 : 5); He laid down His life for us (3 : 16); He came to be a Saviour (4 : 14); He came to destroy

1 John 2 : 1. My little children, these things write I unto you that ye may not sin. And if any man sin, we have an Advocate with the Father, Jesus Christ the righteous
2. And he is the propitiation for our sins. and not for ours only, but also for the whole world.

---

the works of the devil (3 : 8). So victory, power, fellowship, life, joy are not the consequences of a mere struggle of a human being against the forces of evil, but are possible only through the work of the Lord Jesus Christ and the indwelling of His Spirit and a knowledge of God the Father. Victory then, derives from the Triune God.

I. **THE PRIVILEGES AND CONDITIONS OF FELLOWSHIP WITH GOD AND WITH CHRIST,** 1 : 1—2 : 2. We have purposely given a somewhat extensive introduction to this Epistle because the entire five chapters are assigned for our lesson, and, inasmuch as it is utterly impossible for any teacher to cover these 104 verses in any half hour period, we have thought it best to give some general ideals of the Epistle first, even though it necessitates briefer comment on the printed portion of the lesson. The Epistle opens with a declaration on John's part, that the One of whom he is going to speak, the Word of life, is One of whom he, and the other apostles, had personal knowledge; they saw Him, they were present with Him; they heard Him. Thus the fellowship he is about to speak of is something known to him by personal experience. This fellowship, however, John says is continuing. He still has fellowship with God the Father, and with the risen Christ, and that fellowship he desires his readers to enter upon in all its fullness, for such a fellowship would make their joy to abound. At once then he begins to discuss those fundamental conditions which make such fellowship possible. Well, if God is light, and so He is here set forth to be, then a man who walks in darkness cannot have fellowship with God the Father, for only those who walk in the light as God Himself is in the light will have fellowship with Him. The light here spoken of is first the light shed by the Word of God upon our path. It is really a revelation of the will of God. God's will for us is expressed by light, because His will is pure and holy. 2 : 1. **My little children, these things write I unto you that ye may not sin. And if any man sin, we have an Advocate with the Father, Jesus Christ the righteous.** 2 : 2. **And he is the propitiation for our sins; and not for ours only, but also for the whole world.** Cleansing has to do with the condition of our own heart here on earth. Forgiveness has to do with our relationship to God. Moreover, if we sin we have an Advocate with the Father, even His Son the righteous Saviour. An advocate is one who stands at our side to plead our case. If a Christian sins, he has no case of *his own* to plead. He must confess it. What then does Christ plead? Why, He pleads His own righteousness, claiming us as His own children, and God hears that advocacy. Note, however, the phrase, "If we confess." Unconfessed sin does not mean the loss of salvation, but it certainly means the interruption of communion with God. We regret to have to pass over this passage so quickly. "It is because he is our propitiation that he can be our Advocate. Thus the One whose character is righteous is shown to be competent by reason of what

Helen Keller Reading of "The Light of the World."

3. And hereby we know that we know him, if we keep his commandments.
4. He that saith, I know him, and keepeth not his commandments, is a liar, and the truth is not in him;
5. But whoso keepeth his word, in him verily hath the love of God been perfected. Hereby we know that we are in him:
6. He that saith he abideth in him ought himself also to walk even as he walked.

---

he has done. And it is interesting to notice that the apostle does not say, 'His death was the propitiation,' but that 'He himself is the propitiation.' It is the person of Christ who gives efficacy to his work, which means, as Hooker says, 'the infinite worth of the Son of God.' It is important to bear in mind that propitiation (a word in the original found only in this epistle) means the removal of God's righteous judgment against sin by means of sacrifice, and it is obvious that man, as represented by Christ, is the subject and God the object of propitiation. We recall the publican's prayer, 'God be propitious to me a sinner' (Luke 18 : 13). . . . Propitiation can mean but one thing, the expiation of the guilt of sin, which restores the sinner to God by removing every barrier to fellowship." — *W. H. Griffith Thomas.*

II. **THE RIGHT AND WRONG OBJECTS OF LOVE,** 2 : 3–6. 3. **And hereby we know that we know him, if we keep his commandments.** 4. **He that saith, I know him, and keepeth not his commandments, is a liar, and the truth is not in him.** 5. **But whoso keepeth his word, in him verily hath the love of God been perfected. Hereby we know that we are in him.** Having assured his readers that God has made every provision for cleansing from sin, and that there is a divine way of perfectly restoring the child of God who has committed sin, the Apostle immediately proceeds to show his readers how absolutely essential it is for believers to keep God's commandments. It seems that there is something of a parallel here with Paul's words opening the sixth chapter of his epistle to the Romans after discussing justification by faith. Dr. Griffith Thomas, commenting upon the phrase, "We know that we know him," says: "The original is very striking, and may perhaps be rendered something like this: 'Hereby we are continually getting to know by experience that we have experienced and still do experience him.' Doctrine with the apostle was not intellectual knowledge only, but a real experience. We may perhaps include in his thought of knowledge the three ideas of intellectual observation, personal experience, and spiritual certainty. . . . From knowledge he proceeds to love, because of 'the emptiness of a loveless knowledge' (Findlay). The words 'love of God' may include His love to us and ours to Him, because our love is always inspired and prompted by His, and the perfection of love means its consummation in life; it has reached its goal in the one who is thus obedient to the Word of God. Findlay calls attention to the somewhat parallel idea of faith perfected by works (James 2 : 22), just as here we have love perfected by obedience."

2 : 6. **He that saith he abideth in him ought himself also to walk even as he walked.** "The life which is from God and in God must be manifested after the pattern of the divine life which has been shown upon earth (cf. John 1 : 18; 2 Tim. 2 : 13)." — *B. F. Westcott.* "Patience and diligence in petty trades, in services called menial, in waiting on the sick and old, in a hundred such works, all come within the sweep of this net, with its lines that look as thin as cobwebs, and which yet for Christian hearts are stronger than fibers of steel — 'walk even as he walked.' This too, is our only security." — *William Alexander.*

From a general admonition to obey the commandments of God, the Apostle becomes specific in telling us to particularly obey the commandment to love our brethren, which Christ Himself frequently spoke of (John 13 : 14, 34). Probably the reference here is not to all men in general, but to Christians specifically. While love is not here defined, yet perhaps a definition would not be out of place. Let us say, without pretending to formulate any complete and fully satisfying definition, which by the way we have never seen, that love is the desire on the part of the one loving to do everything possible for the good of the one loved at whatever cost or sacrifice, joyfully and voluntarily.

The next paragraph seems to be somewhat parenthetical. "He says in effect that the reason for his message is not any doubt as to their Christian standing or progress, but rather to encourage them to further achievements and to caution them against temptations from which even they cannot be free. The reasons combined in this sixfold statement are arranged in two parallel series of three each. The first in each series is addressed to the readers in general, the second to the more mature readers, and the third to the younger among them. 'Little children' is the term which the writer applies to all his readers, to whom he stands in the affectionate relation of a spiritual father." — *Charles R. Erdman.*

The Apostle now returns to the negative aspect of love. Previously he set forth the primary duty of loving our brethren, now he warns against loving the world. "When the writer speaks here of 'the world,' he, of course, does not refer to the beautiful world of nature, with its changing seasons, its sunlight, and flowers, its mountains, seas, and summer skies. Nor does he refer to the complex world of human relationships, with its duties and joys, its friendships, its struggles, its triumphs, and its tears. He refers to 'the world' of unbelieving men and women, to the society of the unspiritual and the godless. This is 'the world' we are not to love. We are not to court its favors, not to follow its customs, not to adopt its maxims, not to covet its prizes. 'If any man love the world, the love of the Father is not in him.' The Christless world has always been opposed to the will of God. It would be impossible for the heart to be set upon 'the world,' and at the same time to be filled with love for the Father." — *Charles R. Erdman.*

III. **WARNING AGAINST ANTICHRIST AND ERROR,** 2 : 18–29. By antichrist is meant all that is opposed to Christ, generally manifested in particular individuals, who are possessed with a hatred for Christ, and are attempting to do everything within their power to destroy the work of Christ on earth. Such an antichristian spirit will consummate at the end of the age in one outstanding enemy of God, known in the Scriptures as the Antichrist. Still the spirit of antichrist was present in the world even in John's day, and he now writes to warn his readers concerning such a subtle and Satanic influence as they will have to face. Note particularly that in this passage those who are called antichrists were, it seems, once within the Christian church and went out from it in apostasy. Some of the greatest enemies the Church has ever known were once ordained ministers within the Church. Now the secret for victory over the lies and deceptions of antichristian teachings and personalities is to be found in our being taught by the Holy Spirit, who communicates to us the truth and thus enables us to detect falsehood when we hear or read it. When it reads: "Ye need not that any man teach you," it should not be understood that Bible teachers do not have their place in God's program, nor that we should not read books which attempt to help us to understand the Word of God. It means that our final authority is the Word of God, and that we do not take any man as final authority because the Holy Spirit divinely instructs us in what is true and what is false.

IV. **SOME REASONS WHY OUR LIVES SHOULD BE PURE,** 3 : 1–10. Again and again the Apostle goes back to this question of living a holy life, and in this passage he sets forth four reasons why we should strive to live in purity: because some day we are truly to be like Christ when He returns; because Christ came for the specific reason of taking away our sins; because we abide in Christ and He is absolutely pure, and the life that we live ought to have the characteristics of the life that He lived; and finally, because Christ came to destroy the works of the devil, and we should have victory in that finished work. Professor Moorehead's comment on verse 6 is excellent, and because the verse may present difficulties to our readers we quote in part: "The child of God does not live in the practice of sin, he lives in the practice of righteousness. Sin is in him, but he does not live in it; holiness is the realm where he seeks to dwell. John's doctrine on this matter is summed up in 3 : 9. It is a difficult verse, but its main idea is clear: 'Whosoever is begotten of God doeth no sin, because his seed abideth in him: and he cannot sin because he is begotten of God' (Revised Version). Sinless perfection certainly is not meant, for that would contradict 1 : 8: 'If we say that we have no sin, we deceive ourselves, and the truth is not in us.' He who is begotten of God does not love sin nor live in the practice of it; he hates it, and abhors himself when he commits it; he devoutly seeks total deliverance from it. He that is not born of God loves sin and is its slave. The seed that abides in him probably is the new, the divine nature which he receives in regeneration, and which is not extirpated when even gross sin is committed. 'He cannot sin' signifies that it is impossible a believer should live in evil and make it the habit of his life. He cannot live in it, it is foreign to his new nature."

1 JOHN 3 : 13. Marvel not, brethren, if the world hateth you.

14. We know that we have passed out of death into life, because we love the brethren. He that loveth not abideth in death.

15. Whosoever hateth his brother is a murderer: and ye know that no murderer hath eternal life abiding in him.

16. Hereby know we love, because he laid down his life for us: and we ought to lay down our lives for the brethren.

17. But whoso hath the world's goods, and beholdeth his brother in need, and shutteth up his compassion from him, how doth the love of God abide in him?

18. *My* little children, let us not love in word, neither with the tongue; but in deed and truth.

V. **THE PRIMACY OF LOVING ONE ANOTHER,** 3 : 11–24. Once again the Apostle goes back to the fundamental theme of loving one another. The importance of the subject, if we are to live a truly godly life, is revealed in the frequency with which John mentions it. 13. **Marvel not, brethren, if the world hateth you.** 14. **We know that we have passed out of death into life, because we love the brethren. He that loveth not abideth in death.** 15. **Whosoever hateth his brother is a murderer: and ye know that no murderer hath eternal life abiding in him.** "Here then we have, in broad contrast, the way of the world, which is death, and the way of God, which is life. It is the way of the world to hate; and so to hate as to murder. It is the way of God to love, and so to love as to lay down life to save. And it is in virtue of this contrast that the test holds good: 'We know that we have passed from death unto life, because we love the brethren.' . . . The wicked one, in whom the world lies, hates the brethren. His hatred fastens on the godly. In his hatred he will not scruple about murdering them outright in cruelest fashion. But he is as well, or better pleased, if he succeeds in murdering them after a milder method; by getting them to listen to his wily speech. The Holy One loves. His love fastens on the lost. Whoever heard of the wicked one laying down his life to secure the accomplishment of his object? 'But hereby perceive we the love of God, because he laid down his life for us: and we ought to lay down our lives for the brethren.'" — *R. S. Candlish.*

16. **Hereby know we love, because he laid down his life for us: and we ought to lay down our lives for the brethren.** "We have obtained the knowledge of what love is in the concrete example of Christ's vicarious death. Christ is the archetype of self-sacrificing love, as Cain is of brother-sacrificing hate. Love and hate are known by their works. . . . The phrase 'to lay down one's life' is peculiar to John (10 : 11, 15, 17; 13 : 37, 38; 15 : 13). In Greek the pronoun marks more plainly than in English *who* laid down His life; but John's readers had no need to be told. In 'and we ought,' the 'we' is emphatic; this on *our* side is a Christian's duty; he 'ought himself also to walk *even as* he walked' (2 : 6). Christians must imitate Him in this; their love must be (1) practical, (2) absolutely self-sacrificing, (3) all-embracing. 'God commendeth his own love toward us, in that, *while we were yet sinners*, Christ died for us' (Rom. 5 : 8)." — *Alfred Plummer.* 17. **But whoso hath the world's goods, and beholdeth his brother in need, and shutteth up his compassion from him, how doth the love of God abide in him?** 18. ***My* little children, let us not love in word, neither with the tongue; but in deed and truth.** "Small things are the best test of love, and it is shown that if we are unwilling to help our brother in his need, it is impossible that God's love is dwelling in us. There ought to be in every believer a reality of love in the threefold expression of it; in a capacity to help, a knowledge of needs, and a self-sacrificing attitude. It is not the utterance of some great or profound truth, or the accomplishment of some wonderful deed, but the quiet, simple help of a needy brother that beyond all else demonstrates our possession of the love of God. To possess life's good things and then to gaze at a needy one, and at the same time to shut up as with a key our compassion, is to disprove our possession of the first principle of love. . . . But whatever may be the object of our affection, it is to be practical and not theoretical, in actual reality and not in mere profession. Thus love is seen to be the manward evidence of our being children of God. Not what we think, however accurately; not what we feel, however strongly; not what we say, however eloquently; but what we do

1 John 4 : 15. Whosoever shall confess that Jesus is the Son of God, God abideth in him, and he in God.

in genuine, practical, self-sacrificing activity, is the sole proof and test of our brother-love." — *W. H. Griffith Thomas.*

VI. **WARNING AGAINST FALSE TEACHERS,** 4 : 1–6. "This passage treats of false spirits and of their detection and repulsion. The right to judge teachers and to test doctrine belongs to all Christians. Our Lord Himself imposed this duty on His people (Matt. 7 : 15–19). Never perhaps has there been more need of trying the spirits than now. The Apostle furnishes two infallible tests of both teachers and teaching (vs. 2–6). The first relates to Christ's person and work. What do they say of Him? What is their doctrine concerning Him? Do they deny His mission? His deity? His virgin birth? His resurrection? If they do, then they are of the spirit of Antichrist, they are enemies of the blessed Lord Jesus, and therefore no believer in Him can hold fellowship with them. The second is their following: 'They are of the world; the world heareth them.' God's children are not of this company nor can be. 'A stranger will they not follow, but will flee from him; for they know not the voice of strangers.' These are sure tests both of profession and of character." — *William G. Moorehead.*

VII. **THE THIRD ADMONITION TO LOVE ONE ANOTHER,** 4 : 7–21. "In these verses we enter upon what is really the central part of the second half of John's epistle. As has been already noticed, two great keywords dominate the two halves of this epistle; the first 'God is light,' the second 'God is love.' Around these two truths about God all the various parts of each half, so to speak, revolve. . . . Twice before John has spoken of brotherly love, but now he reaches the climax of his exhortation by declaring that love ought to be the characteristic of all the children of God, because it is of the very nature of their Father, of God Himself. 'Beloved,' he says, 'let us love one another: for love is of God; and every one that loveth is begotten of God, and knoweth God. He that loveth not knoweth not God; for God is love.' It is evident that we cannot take John's words, 'Every one that loveth is begotten of God,' without some kind of limitation. In fact, love in itself is a purely natural emotion, and although we may believe that, howsoever adulterated it often is with baser feelings, it had its original home and origin in God — as John himself says, 'love is of God' — it is equally certain that the possession of a natural emotion can never be the proof of the possession of a supernatural grace, of being 'begotten of God.' How then can we explain the apparently unlimited character of the apostle's assertion that 'every one that loveth is begotten of God'? John is here thinking, not of love in general to all men, but of the love of which he had before been speaking, the 'new commandment' Christ had given to His own disciples to 'love one another.' In this narrow and more restricted sense it is absolutely true that the love of the brethren is an unfailing proof of having been 'begotten of God.' If I love my own relatives, or my own friends, I am indulging a purely natural and human instinct — 'do not even the publicans the same?' — but if, on the other hand, I find myself drawn out in affection toward those whose only bond between them and myself is a common faith in Christ, then that is a sure and blessed sign that I have been 'born again.' And, after John's manner, he goes on to emphasize the opposing truth to that which he had just uttered, 'he that loveth not,' he adds — and here the change of tense is remarkable — 'knew not God,' that is, referring in all probability to the time of his public profession of faith. And then, at last, we come to the culmination and crown of all John has to say, the greatest words ever spoken in human speech, the greatest words in the whole Bible, that one truth 'Well worth all languages in earth or heaven,' 'God is love.' . . . And now the apostle goes on to tell us that not only is God 'love' in Himself, in His inmost nature, but that He has 'manifested' that love to men, and in three wonderful ways. First of all, in the supreme glory of the incarnation. . . . If God had sent a Son into the world, it would have been a revelation of wonderful love, but to have sent His 'only born' Son is a surpassing manifestation of love. . . . The incarnation is not a dream, it is history. . . . Next, the love of God has been manifested, not only in the incarnation, but in its object — 'that we might live through him.' This is the only place in John's epistles in which he uses the verb 'to live,' but its use here is most impressive. The whole object of the incarnation was the bestowal of life upon those who were dead — 'I am come,' said Jesus, 'that they might have life, and have it more abundantly.'" — *G. S. Barrett.* 15. **Whosoever shall confess that**

16. And we know and have believed the love which God hath in us. God is love; and he that abideth in love abideth in God, and God abideth in him.

17. Herein is love made perfect with us, that we may have boldness in the day of judgment; because as he is, even so are we in this world.

Jesus is the Son of God, God abideth in him, and he in God. 16. **And we know and have believed the love which God hath in us. God is love ; and he that abideth in love abideth in God, and God abideth in him.** 17. **Herein is love made perfect with us, that we may have boldness in the day of judgment ; because as he is, even so are we in this world.** "Can this really mean anything else than that His love to us has become His love in us; and that we have known and believed it as such? In the gospel, it is His love manifested in us. Here, in our hearts, it is His love felt in us — not merely felt by us as the conscious objects of it, but felt by us as His love in us — in us, so as to make us the conscious depositories of it, and the dispensers of it to others who are as much its objects as we are ourselves. The love of God, having us for its objects, passes from God's outer record into our inner life. It enters into us. . . . It is the love of which we ourselves, in the first instance, are the objects; of which it was our first relief and joy, when we were convinced of sin, to find ourselves the objects. . . . Not only have we known and believed it, so as to apprehend and appropriate it, as it comes from without and from above — not only so as to take it and make it available for our own spiritual life and comfort — but also, and especially, so as to imbibe it, to drink it into the very essence of our renovated nature, our renewed selves. This love is the bond of union between Him and us. It is the meetingplace, the habitation, the home, in which we dwell together; He in us and we in Him. This love, this holy love, is that which God and we may have in common. And therefore it is that in respect of which there may be mutual indwelling of us in God and of God in us." — *Robert S. Candlish.*

VIII. **THE LIFE OF VICTORY OVER THE WORLD,** ch. 5. Previously the Apostle has told us we are not to love the world, that the world passes away, that the world will hate us. Now he concludes with a bold declaration concerning the secret of victory over the world. The world is simply humanity without God, and all that humanity does and thinks without God. We use the idea in such an expression as "She was a worldly woman," or, "He lived a worldly life." The world is given to pleasure, thoughts of self, the acquisition of wealth and power, of doing all things for one's own advancement. The world may be attractive and alluring and will appeal, certainly, to unregenerated human nature, but the world never satisfies. The world can only bring death, and, generally, disillusionment, and a sense of wasted effort. Now, says the Apostle, victory over the world is to be found in faith in Jesus Christ. Faith in Christ delivers us from the fascination and the deceptions and the false teachings of the world, centering our life in Him instead of in self, in spiritual things that abide instead of visible things that pass away. (The editor suggests that the teacher deliberately stay away from the very difficult matter found in verses 6–8. Do not allow the class to sidetrack you in discussing this complicated matter when there are so many practical things in this epistle that should be taught and can be immediately understood.)

The Apostle John brings his epistle to a close by reaffirming some of the great Christian certainties: the possession of eternal life (v. 11); the assurance of answered prayer (vs. 14, 15); the reality and the absolute necessity of righteousness (v. 17); the reality of the new birth (v. 18); the divine mission of Christ (v. 20). We tarry for a moment to bring the precious truth of verse 18 to the attention of our readers. Note carefully the change in the Revised Version which the editor believes is correct, declaring not that we keep ourselves as the children of God, but that Christ, who 'was begotten of God' keepeth us. Christ will keep us if we put ourselves in His care, as a banker keeps our bonds and valuables from fire and theft, if we turn them over to the vault official. Being thus kept, the wicked one will not touch us. The word translated *touch* does not mean a mere superficial touch, but a laying hold of, a grasping, an actual holding. Now Satan may brush against us, he may touch us, we may feel his presence, but if we are kept by Christ he will never be able to hold, or grasp us. Thus, *e.g.*, if we clasp a book firmly in our hands, another one may touch the book, but will never be able to hold it because we are holding it. When we are embraced by Christ we can never be grasped by the evil one.

How many different names of Christ do you find in this epistle, and what does each one mean to us individually? How many different things do you find in these five chapters that the Lord Jesus Christ did for us when He was on earth, and how many things do you find Christ is doing for us as our exalted Lord in heaven? What are the expressions in this epistle which indicate what Christ has done for our sins that have been committed, and what are the phrases and promises revealing what Christ now does for us to keep us from sinning? In the light of this epistle, if we do not wish to be delivered from sin, what is the conclusion which we are forced to acknowledge regarding ourselves? How do you think love for Christian brethren can be revealed in our relationship to other members of our church?

LESSON XIII. — June 27.

JOHN'S COUNSEL TO CHRISTIANS. — 2 John and 3 John.

PRINTED TEXT, 2 John 4-11; 3 John 5-12.

GOLDEN TEXT. — ***Beloved, I pray that in all things thou mayest prosper and be in health, even as thy soul prospereth.*** 3 JOHN 2.

Devotional Reading: Acts 20 : 28–35.
Beginner Topic: WHY THE LAME MAN WAS GLAD.
Lesson Material: Matthew 24 : 25–47; Acts 3 : 1–26.
Memory Verse: Be ye kind. Ephesians 4 : 32.
Primary Topic: WHY JOSEPH WAS NOT AFRAID.
Lesson Material: Matthew 24 : 45–51; Genesis 39.
Memory Verse: What time I am afraid, I will put my trust in thee. Psalm 56 : 3.
Junior Topic: A BOY AWAY FROM HOME.
Lesson Material: Matthew 24 : 45–51; Genesis 39.
Memory Verse: Commit thy way unto Jehovah; trust also in him and he will bring it to pass. Psalm 37 : 5.
Intermediate and Senior Topic: WHOM SHALL I FOLLOW?
Topic for Young People and Adults: HELPERS AND HINDERERS IN THE CHURCH.

THE TEACHER AND HIS CLASS.

The Younger Classes may be best introduced to this lesson, which seemingly does not consider subjects that normally are of interest to children, by reminding them that we have to live in the midst of other people, that there are certain homes into which we will frequently enter, there are certain people who *will* be coming into our homes; there are friends with whom we will be in close communion; and vast hosts of people with whom we will have little fellowship. Throughout the years of life we must be continually choosing some friends, and refusing close friendship to others. There will always be some people, criminals, corrupt politicians, blasphemers, sensualists, gamblers, etc., with whom we *never* want to be seen. There are other people whose friendship we would count it an honor to enjoy. In these two Epistles we have some of the principles laid down by which we are to determine what kind of people we are to have fellowship with and what people we are to shun.

The Older Classes will find here a much needed lesson in regard to the sinfulness of close association with those who repudiate the great doctrines of our faith. It is one of the most subtle temptations of our day for true believers to publicly and officially associate with those who repudiate the faith. Today in great so-called religious mass meetings, we are saddened to find men who really believe the Word of God co-operating in some ecclesiastical venture with those who deny that Jesus is the Christ. At whatever the cost, and however painful it may be, we need in these days, preeminently, to avoid official public cooperation in religious matters, with those who in their hearts and on their lips are denying the Lord whose headship alone makes the true Church of Christ.

THE LESSON IN ITS SETTING.

Time. — We do not know when these two brief Epistles of John were written, whether before his imprisonment on the Isle of Patmos, or after his release. As good a guess as any would be about A.D. 90–95.

Place. — It is presumed that these two Epistles were written from Ephesus, where John resided for the most part of his life after the ascension of Christ.

THE PLAN OF THE LESSON.

SUBJECT: Some Fundamental Principles Regarding the Refusal of Fellowship to Deceiving Teachers, and the Liberal Offering of Hospitality to True Christian Evangelists.

THE SECOND EPISTLE OF JOHN.

I. THE SALUTATION, vs. 1–3.

II. THE PRE-EMINENCE OF LOVE AND TRUTH, vs. 4–6.
1. Walking in the truth.
2. Walking in love.

III. THE DANGER OF TEACHERS OF FALSE DOCTRINE, vs. 7–11.
1. A characteristic of such men — deceivers.
2. The fundamental error taught — denying that Jesus Christ is come in the flesh.
3. The deeper tragedy of such men: they have not God.
4. The attitude of true believers toward these false teachers.

IV. THE SUPERSCRIPTION, vs. 12–13.

THE THIRD EPISTLE OF JOHN.

I. THE SALUTATION, vs. 1–4.
1. The one writing.
2. The one written to.
3. The writer's hope for and joy in the one written to.

II. THE IMPORTANCE OF CHRISTIAN HOSPITALITY, vs. 5–8.

III. THE CONDEMNATION OF DIOTREPHES, vs. 9, 10.

IV. THE COMMENDATION OF DEMETRIUS, vs. 11, 12.

V. THE SUPERSCRIPTION, vs. 13, 14.

THE TEACHER'S LIBRARY.

Many books which treat the First Epistle of John have nothing in them concerning the Second and Third Epistles: some we discover which attempt to expound all three epistles have excellent material on the First one, and very little on the Second and Third. For introductory matters, see P. J. Gloag: *Introduction to the Johannine Writings* (1891), 264–280; D. A. Hayes: *John and His Writings* (1917), 205–219. The best commentary is by Alfred Plummer, in the *Cambridge Bible for Schools and Colleges*. The editor has found the notes of A. E. Brooke, in the *International Critical Commentary*, rather dry. There are some good general remarks in Charles R. Erdman: *The General Epistles;* William Alexander expounds only portions of the two epistles in his work in the *Expositor's Bible*. The only character sketches of Gaius, Diotrephes, and Demetrius that I have seen worth reading are all found, strange to say, in one book, and are excellent examples of biographical study; see Samuel Cox: *Expositions, the Fourth Series* (1888), 239–279. For expository matter, one should certainly read that magnificent sermon on verse 7 of the Third Epistle, "For the Sake of the Name," in Alexander Maclaren: *Expositions of Holy Scripture, John, Jude, and Revelation*, 61–70; on verse 8 of the same epistle, see also the same, 70–79; on verse 12, 79–86; on the entire Second Epistle there is a good chapter, "Fellowship in the Truth," in W. B. Riley: *The Bible of the Expositor and the Evangelist, 1 John to Jude*, 143–161; and, in the same work, on the Third Epistle, a helpful chapter, "Three Typical Church Members," 185–202.

THE THREE PRIVATE LETTERS OF THE NEW TESTAMENT.

The words of the late Professor Gloag, beginning his excellent discussion of these two epistles, form a perfect introduction for the study of our lesson, and we take the liberty of quoting them. "In the canon of the New Testament, three private letters are preserved, one ascribed to Paul and two to John; but these must evidently constitute but a small fragment of the correspondence of the sacred writers. Of course, letter-writing was not so much practiced at that time as in our own day; but still, as we learn both from classical and from patristic remains, it was not uncommon. Frequent allusions are made to it in Scripture. Paul speaks of 'epistles of commendation' (2 Cor. 3 : 1) in such a manner as to intimate that such letters were not infrequent. Writing to the Corinthians relative to the general collection which he was making for the Christians at Jerusalem, he says (according to the correct rendering), 'When I come, whomsoever ye shall approve, them will I send by letters to bring your liberality to Jerusalem' (1 Cor. 16 : 3). And we have in the Third Epistle of John a reference to a letter of recommendation which that apostle sent to the Church, and which is not now extant: 'I wrote somewhat unto the Church, but Diotrephes, who loveth to have the pre-eminence among them, received us not.' Much then of the correspondence of the apostles is lost; of their private letters we have only three, or, if we include the Pastoral Epistles, at the most six; and there are also traces of letters written by Paul to Churches which must be regarded as lost epistles (1 Cor. 5 : 9; Col. 4 : 16). As Meyer observes, when adverting to Paul's letters of recommendation: 'Hence we see how common in Paul's practice was the writing of epistles. Who knows how many private letters of his, not addressed to Churches, have been lost? The only letter of the kind which remains to us (that of Philemon) owes its preservation perhaps to the mere circumstance that it is at the same time addressed to the Church in his house.'"

2 JOHN 4. I rejoice greatly that I have found *certain* of thy children walking in truth, even as we received commandment from the Father.

5. And now I beseech thee, lady, not as though I wrote to thee a new commandment, but that which we had from the beginning, that we love one another.

6. And this is love, that we should walk after his commandments. This is the commandment, even as ye heard from the beginning, that ye should walk in it.

THE SECOND EPISTLE OF JOHN.

I. **THE SALUTATION,** vs. 1–3. There has been a vast amount of discussion concerning the meaning of John's phrase, "The elect lady," which in the Greek reads *ecclecte kuria,* for it is to this person, if it is a person, that John addresses his letter. Probably the remarks of Gloag form as good a summary of the entire problem as can be found in one brief paragraph. "Some suppose that it is a metaphorical designation of the Catholic Church; an opinion which is refuted by the Apostle mentioning his intention of visiting her. Others think that some particular Church is meant; but there is no reason to assign a figurative meaning to the expression. Others, thinking that a particular lady is mentioned, suppose that her name was Electa — 'the lady Electa' — an opinion which has the support of Clemens Alexandrinus; and others think that her name was Kyria, 'the elect Kyria,' a common female name among the Greeks, being the feminine of Cyrus. It is best, however, to render the words indefinitely as in our version, 'the elect lady,' the name not being given. Along with the lady are mentioned her children. This epistle, then, was addressed to some unknown Christian lady and her family, resident probably in the neighborhood of Ephesus." Here again we find John emphasizing *the truth,* which idea occurs so frequently in his Gospel, and continually in his First Epistle. The truth here spoken of is, fundamentally, the Christian truth, the truth as it relates to and is found in and proceeds from the Lord Jesus Christ, who is *the* Truth. John purposely begins his epistle by emphasizing the virtue of abiding in the truth, and commending the one to whom he writes for knowing the truth, because shortly he is going to speak sharply concerning those who have rejected the truth. Dr. Erdman has an excellent comment on the phrase which we pass over too easily, "grace, mercy, peace," reminding us that we, "because of their familiarity are in danger of losing their deep significance. They include all the blessings known to believers, from their source in the 'unmerited favor' of God, to their ultimate issue in the peace 'which passeth all understanding.' Here the enjoyment

SANCTVM IESV CHRISTI EVANGElium ſecundum Iohannem.

¶Chriſtum ab initio cum patre fuiſſe. De Iohanne eiusq; de Chriſto elogio, ſuiq; deiectione. De Andrea, Simone, Philippo & Nathanaele uocatis. Cap. I, A

N principio erat † uerbum, & uerbũ erat apd deũ, & deus erat uerbum. Hoc erat in principio apud deũ. Oĩa per ipſum facta ſunt: & ſine ipſo factum eſt nihil, quod factũ eſt, In ipſo uita erat, & uita erat lux hominũ, & lux ĩ tenebris lucet, & tenebre eam nõ comprehenderũt. Fuit homo miſſus a deo, cui nomen erat Iohannes. Hic uenit in teſtimoniũ, ut teſtimonium perhiberet de lumine, ut omnes crederent per illũ. Non erat ille lux: ſed ut teſtimoniũ p̱hiberet de lumine. Erat lux uera, quæ illuminat oẽm homiem uenientẽ in hunc mundum. In mundo erat, & mũdus p̱ ipm factus eſt, & mũdus eũ nõ cognouit. In propria uenit, & ſui eum nõ receperunt. Quotquot autẽ receperunt eũ, dedit eis poteſtatẽ filios dei fieri, his qui credũt in nomine eius: q nõ ex ſanguinibus, neq; ex uoluntate carnis, neq; ex uoluntate uiri, ſed ex deo nati ſunt. Et uerbũ caro factum eſt, & habitauit in nobis (Et uidimus gloriam eius, gloriã quaſi † unigeniti, a patre) plenum gratiæ & ueritatis. * Iohãnes teſtimoniũ perhibet de ipſo, & clamat dicẽs: Hic erat quẽ dixi: Qui poſt me uẽturus eſt, añ me factus eſt, quia prior me erat. * Et de plenitudine eius nos oẽs accepimus, & grãm pro grã: qa lex per Moſen data eſt, grã & ueritas p̱ Ieſum Chrm̃ facta eſt. Deũ nemo uidit unq̃. Vnigenitus filius q ẽ in ſinu patris, ipẽ enarrauit. ¶ Et hoc ẽ teſtioniũ Iohãnis, qñ miſerũt Iudei ab Hieroſolymis ſacerdotes & leuitas ad eũ, ut interrogarẽt eũ: Tu qs es? Et cõfeſſus ẽ & nõ negauit, Et cõfeſſus eſt, Quia nõ ſum ego Chrũs. Et interrogauerũt eũ: Quid ergo? Elias es tu? Et dixit: Nõ ſum. Propheta es tu? Et rñdit, Nõ. Dixerũt ergo ei: Quis es, ut rñſum demus his q miſerũt nos? quid dicis de teipſo? Ait: *Ego uox clamantis in deſerto, dirigite uiam dñi, ſicut dixit Iſaias propheta. Et qui miſſi fuerant, erant ex phariſæis. Et interrogauerunt eũ, & dixerunt ei: Quid ergo baptizas, ſi tu non es Chriſtus, neq; Elias, neq; propheta? Reſpondit eis Iohannes, dicẽs: Ego baptizo in aqua medius aũt ueſtrũ ſtetit quẽ uos neſcitis, ipẽ eſt q poſt me uẽturus ẽ, q añ me factus ẽ, cuius ego nõ ſum dignus ut ſoluã eius corrigiã calciamẽti. Hec ĩ Bethabara facta

ὁ λόγος — B — De conſ. di. c. ſi quis. — unic. — C — Mat. 3. a, Mar. 1. a, 1. Tim. 6. c, 1 Joh. 4. c, 1. Tim. 6. c, Iſa. 40. a, Mat. 3. a, Mar. 1. a, Luc. 3. a

Gospel, According to St. John.

Figure Representing the Evangelist with the Apocalyptic Figure of an Eagle.

From the first compiled Protestant Bible ever printed in Latin. Now in the Public Library, Cambridge, Massachusetts.

7. For many deceivers are gone forth into the world, *even* they that confess not that Jesus Christ cometh in the flesh. This is the deceiver and the antichrist.

8. Look to yourselves, that ye lose not the things which we have wrought, but that ye receive a full reward.

9. Whosoever goeth onward and abideth not in the teaching of Christ, hath not God: he that abideth in the teaching, the same hath both the Father and the Son.

---

of these blessings is not, as usual, the substance of a prayer, but of a prediction: 'shall be with us'; it is ascribed to the Father but also to Jesus Christ, who is here designated as 'the Son of the Father'; it is conditioned upon a right state of mind and heart, 'in truth and love'; for the experience is only for those who accept Christ as the divine Son of God, and walk in love toward him and toward their fellow men."

II. **THE PRE-EMINENCE OF LOVE AND TRUTH,** vs. 4–6. 4. **I rejoice greatly that I have found *certain* of thy children walking in truth, even as we received commandment from the Father.** "Walking" in these epistles is a figure of speech, indicating simply the activity of human life: to walk in the truth is to live in conformity with Christian truth, revealed in the Gospels and through the apostles. Of one of these truths he is now about to speak, that we should love one another. 5, 6. **And now I beseech thee, lady, not as though I wrote to thee a new commandment, but that which we had from the beginning, that we love one another.** 6. **And this is love, that we should walk after his commandments. This is the commandment, even as ye heard from the beginning, that ye should walk in it.** On the commandment to love one another, see 1 John 2 : 7, 24; 3 : 11. Love for others is something that was distinctly absent in the normal life of the Roman world, in which John and his readers lived. Unregenerated humanity is fundamentally selfish, and loves itself; regenerated men and women by the Spirit forget self and love others. This is the fruit of the Spirit; this is what appeals to the unsaved; this is the foundation of sweet, helpful, joyful fellowship among Christian believers; this is that which unites the Church into one great body. In this way we are emulating the Master who bought us; thus do we manifest the love of God; so do we bear testimony to the world of that which they would never know, except they behold the life of God in us.

III. **THE DANGER OF TEACHERS OF FALSE DOCTRINES,** vs. 7–11. 7. **For many deceivers are gone forth into the world, *even* they that confess not that Jesus Christ cometh in the flesh. This is the deceiver and the antichrist.** 8. **Look to yourselves, that ye lose not the things which we have wrought, but that ye receive a full reward.** 9. **Whosoever goeth onward and abideth not in the teaching of Christ, hath not God: he that abideth in the teaching, the same hath both the Father and the Son.** John now turns to a most disagreeable subject, a subject concerning which few men, in the church today, wish to speak. As soon as a man raises his voice against such men as here John condemns, he is considered fanatical, or a crank, or contentious. All the more reason why this matter should be carefully considered. Before he even defines what this group of men is about which (or concerning whom) he wishes to speak, he frankly calls them deceivers. This word is from a root meaning, to make to wander, to lead astray, implying that these men have great influence, and furthermore, that many weak Christians will be disastrously influenced by them unless something drastic is done to terminate their influence. These men were teaching that Jesus Christ had not come in the flesh (see 1 John 4 : 2). Of course, they admitted that there was a person Jesus of Nazareth, and that He had lived and taught in their midst, but they denied that this person was the Anointed One of God, the Christ of God, the Son of God. There were many different heretical theories about the incarnation in the early Church, into which we need not enter here, except to say that some claimed that Christ the Son of God never was truly a man, but only clothed Himself with human form. Others claimed that Jesus of Nazareth was never truly God, but that He was only temporarily filled with divinely-given power for the performances of certain deeds. The Christian truth is that the Son of God truly become man, took upon Himself our flesh, became flesh (John 1 : 14), and thus was, from the time of His incarnation, and continues forever to be, both God and man, two natures in one Person forever.

10. If any one cometh unto you, and bringeth not this teaching, receive him not into *your* house, and give him no greeting:
11. For he that giveth him greeting partaketh in his evil works.

There are multitudes of people in the Christian Church today, some in theological seminaries, some in pulpits, some in editorial chairs, some in our universities, who frankly declare that while Jesus was a good man, He was never truly Very God of Very God. These are the kind of men to whom John is referring. Such deceivers, said the Apostle, are antichrist; that is, they oppose Christ; they are doing the work of Satan, and they are preparing for the final supreme Antichrist, who will attempt in every way to thwart the Saviour's work. John says that men who deny that Christ is come in the flesh do not have God, which means that that man does not possess God in his heart, to adore, and trust, and love, for God sent His only begotten Son to be believed on, and when we do not believe on Him, we do not believe God. To be without the Son is to be without the Father also.

10. **If any one cometh unto you, and bringeth not this teaching, receive him not into *your* house, and give him no greeting:** 11. **For he that giveth him greeting partaketh in his evil works.** Having warned his readers of the deeper, darker factors relating to these false teachers, who were moving in and out of the early Church, John concludes by laying down a severe but necessary rule regarding them, namely, that true believers were not to receive such teachers into their homes, nor give them any greeting. "Charity has its limits: it must not be shown to one man in such a way as to do grievous harm to others; still less must it be shown in such a way as to do more harm than good to the recipient of it. If these deceivers were treated as if they were true Christians, (1) their opportunities of doing harm would be greatly increased, (2) they might never be brought to see their own errors." — *Alfred Plummer.* For men to receive such teachers into their homes, and to be on good terms of fellowship with them, really meant that they condoned what these men taught, or at least did not think their errors were serious enough for condemnation. Frankly, the world will always believe that those with whom we frequently associate are those whom we approve, for true fellowship can only rest on a more or less complete harmony of conviction and purpose.

Professor Hayes has a very remarkable illustration of the practice of this condemnation in modern times, which we think our readers will be glad to see. "One winter night some years ago, I was seated before the blazing logs in the fireplace of a comfortable farmhouse in southern Ohio, when we were startled by a loud halloo at the garden gate outside. The farmer went out to see what was wanted. He returned a few minutes later and said that two men who had announced themselves as Mormon missionaries had asked for a night's lodging and he had turned them away. It was about ten o'clock at night, and bitter cold. There were no hotels within many miles. I wondered what the poor fellows would do. I asked my uncle about it, and he did not seem much interested. He simply remarked that they did not want men like that in their neighborhood. I learned the next day that those two Mormon missionaries had gone on down the country road, asking for entertainment at every farmhouse they found on it, and they had been turned away from every door until they had traveled about twelve miles and it was two o'clock at night. Then they found a man who allowed them to sleep on the hay in his barn until morning. There had been no collusion among those neighbors. They had not been expecting these visitors. Every man had decided for himself that he could not afford to grant them hospitality. It was no lack of the milk of human kindness. I never knew a community more generous with lodgings and meals and more unstinted in its hospitality on ordinary occasions. The only reason for that treatment of these men was that they announced themselves as Mormon propagandists, and every one of those Ohio farmers decided at once that he would not be a party to the introduction of any such despicable doctrine, even to the extent of harboring its missionaries over one night. They were all of them patriots. That neighborhood had sent its sons without hesitation into the ranks in the Civil War. They believed that Mormonism was heretical and treasonable and they would have nothing to do with it. They were largely of Puritan stock and they had the downright spirit of a Boanerges in their adherence to principle. They were literally faithful to the command of John in this epistle, although it may be doubtful if any one among them thought of it or knew about it." Then Professor Hayes, reminding us that this epistle was written to a lady in Ephesus, shows how such a warning was particularly needful, perhaps in her case. " Designing men must not be admitted within the circle of her family, for her children might be led astray by those whose only intent was to deceive. Their salvation and their security from harm was her first concern, and all else was to bend to that end. No one must be permitted under the shelter of her roof to undermine the faith of her family; and if the zealous propagators of any form of evil heresy were known to be about the town, it would be just as well for the woman, who was the head of a family, to abstain from all social intercourse with them."

IV. **THE SUPERSCRIPTION,** vs. 12, 13. What John says here, all of us have said more than once: however much we enjoy writing to our friends, and however grateful we may be for letters from them, how much more we desire to see them face to face, that our joy may be full. This is the only time in the New Testament where the word " paper " occurs. It refers here to Egyptian papyrus. Ink is also mentioned at the conclusion of the Third Epistle, and nowhere else in the New Testament (except in 2 Corinthians 3 : 3). Ink was made of lamp black and gall juice, or, more simply, of soot and water (see an interesting, brief account of ink by W. M. Sinclair, in the *Bible Commentary for English Readers, in loco*).

THE THIRD EPISTLE OF JOHN.

I. **THE SALUTATION,** vs. 1–4. This Third Epistle was addressed to a friend of John by the name of Gaius. There are four men in the New Testament by this name: (1) a member of the church at Corinth, baptized by Paul (1 Cor. 1 : 14; Rom. 16 : 23); (2) a companion of Paul seized at Ephesus (Acts 19 : 29); (3) a companion of Paul who accompanied him from Greece to Asia Minor (Acts 24), who may be the same one mentioned in Acts 19 : 29; and (4), the one mentioned

The Apostle John. Bida.

here, who generally is recognized as a person altogether different from the others in the New Testament bearing the same name. The salutation with which John introduces this brief note to Gaius is one of the most exquisite in all the Scriptures: " I pray that in all things thou mayest prosper and be in health, even as thy soul prospereth." " In the opening of no other New Testament epistle is there recorded a petition for temporal blessings and for physical health. It would appear that Gaius had been ill. What is specially remarkable, however, is the measure of prosperity which John proposes: ' even as thy soul prospereth.' The prayer is that the temporal prosperity of Gaius may be as great as his spiritual welfare and that his body may be as well as his soul. Few of us dare offer that prayer; by most

3 JOHN 5. Beloved, thou doest a faithful work in whatsoever thou doest toward them that are brethren and strangers withal;

6. Who bare witness to thy love before the church; whom thou wilt do well to set forward on their journey worthily of God:

7. Because that for the sake of the Name they went forth, taking nothing of the Gentiles.

8. We therefore ought to welcome such, that we may be fellow-workers for the truth.

Christians the terms need to be reversed. The proof of his spiritual prosperity is found in the report which has come of the generosity shown by Gaius." — *Charles R. Erdman.*

II. **THE IMPORTANCE OF CHRISTIAN HOSPITALITY,** vs. 5–8. 5. **Beloved, thou doest a faithful work in whatsoever thou doest toward them that are brethren and strangers withal;** 6. **who bare witness to thy love before the church; whom thou wilt do well to set forward on their journey worthily of God:** 7. **because that for the sake of the Name they went forth, taking nothing of the Gentiles.** " In the apostolic times it would appear that evangelists were sent forth by the apostles or by the churches, either to act as missionaries in the conversion of the heathen, or to arouse and confirm believers in the faith. Timothy and Titus appear to have been such evangelists; and so also were Epaphras, Aristarchus, Trophimus, Tychicus, and many of the disciples of Paul. These itinerant evangelists were of different characters. Some were false apostles, and introduced pernicious errors; and some were covetous men, who made gain of preaching the gospel (2 Cor. 11 : 13; 1 Tim. 6 : 5). Others were true apostles, faithful ministers of Christ. Hence great care was to be exercised in judging them; some were to be rejected, and others were to be received. And we have this difference of treatment stated in these two epistles. John exhorts the elect lady not to receive into her house those who brought not the true doctrine (2 John 10), while he exhorts Gaius to receive and entertain those sent by him, because ' for his name's sake they went forth, taking nothing of the Gentiles ' (3 John 7)." — *P. J. Gloag.* " The hotel is a comparatively modern institution. Ancient inns were not usually of good repute. Frequently these travelers were poor; in any event, they hesitated to place themselves under obligations to unbelievers. It was necessary, therefore, that Christians should open their homes and welcome as guests many strangers, especially such as came to them bearing the Name. It is evident that such hospitality was a direct and potent means of furthering the gospel and of extending the influence of the Church." — *Charles R. Erdman.* On the phrase, " taking nothing of the Gentiles," cf. Matthew 5 : 47; 6 : 7; 18 : 17.

Alexander Maclaren has a marvelous sermon on " For the Sake of the Name They Went Forth," which we wish we could reprint in its entirety, which, of course, is impossible. The following portions will have to suffice: " The ' Name ' means the whole Christ as we know Him, or as we may know Him, from the Book, in the dignity of His Messiahship, in the mystery of His divinity, in the sweetness of His life, in the depth of His words, in the gentleness of His heart, in the patience and propitiation of His sacrifice, in the might of His resurrection, in the glory of His ascension, in the energy of His present life and reigning work for us at the right hand of God. . . . There is one Name, and one alone, because in the depths of that wondrous nature, in the circumference of that mighty work, there is all that a human heart, or that all human hearts, can need for peace, for nobleness, for holiness, for the satisfaction of all desires, for the direction of efforts, for the stability of their being. The name stands alone, and it will be the only Name that, at last, shall blaze upon the page of the world's history when the ages are ended; and the chronicles of earth, with the brief ' immortality ' which they gave to other names of illustrious men, are molded into dust. ' The name is above every name,' and will outlast them all, for it is the all-sufficient and encyclopedical embodiment of everything that a single heart, or the whole race, can require, desire, conceive, or attain. . . . Oh, brother, where is there such a force to quicken, to ennoble, to lead men to higher selves than their dead past selves, as lies in the grand sweep of that historical manifestation which we understand by the name of Jesus? There is nothing else that will so strike the shackles off the prisoned will, and ban back to their caves the wild beasts that tyrannize within, and put the chain around their necks, as the name of Jesus Christ." 8. **We therefore ought to welcome such, that we may be fellow-**

9. I wrote somewhat unto the church: but Diotrephes, who loveth to have the pre-eminence among them, receiveth us not.
10. Therefore, if I come, I will bring to remembrance his works which he doeth, prating against us with wicked words: and not content therewith, neither doth he himself receive the brethren, and them that would he forbiddeth and casteth *them* out of the church.
11. Beloved, imitate not that which is evil, but that which is good. He that doeth good is of God: he that doeth evil hath not seen God.

---

workers for the truth. "No man is ever smitten with the conviction that it is his duty to go out into the world and proclaim that 'two and two make four,' or truths of that sort. But once lodge in a man's heart thoughts of a moral, religious, spiritual character, and as soon as he believes them he wakes up to feel, 'Then I must — I must proclaim them, and get somebody else to share my convictions.' It is the test of real, deep, vital possession of 'the truth' that it shall be as a fire shut up in our bones, burning its way necessarily out into the light; and that no man who has it dare wrap it in a napkin and bury it in the ground. The truth, for all its majesty and dignity and divinity, needs men for its helpers. The only way by which it can spread is through us and our fellows. There is no magic by which it can divide and impart itself, apart from the agency of the men who already possess it. Every man that is Christ's companion is thereby bound to be a worker with the incarnate truth. He needs our help. He finds all the capital, but we are His partners, His representatives and agents here on earth, as He has taught us in more than one parable." — *Alexander Maclaren.*

III. **THE CONDEMNATION OF DIOTREPHES,** vs. 9, 10. 9. **I wrote somewhat unto the church: but Diotrephes, who loveth to have the pre-eminence among them, receiveth us not.** 10. **Therefore, if I come, I will bring to remembrance his works which he doeth, prating against us with wicked words: and not content therewith, neither doth he himself receive the brethren, and them that would he forbiddeth and casteth *them* out of the church.** The Apostle John was one of the greatest of all saints, and if there was anything that characterized his life it was love for others, yet this did not mean that John did not have his troubles also, nor does it mean that the Christian Church over which he exercised apostolic authority was free from political climbers, from selfish workers, from those who would have the church turn against its legally appointed overseers, and give to them, the complainers, the offices of high authority which they were selfishly seeking. Such a man was Diotrephes, who loved to be in a place of ecclesiastical power, speaking bitterly against John with wicked words, and attempting to cast out of the church those who would not unite with him in his diabolical schemes. "There is nothing in the epistle to suggest that Diotrephes held unsound doctrinal views, or that he fell into what are called gross and open sins. Had he been unorthodox, indeed, or flagrantly immoral, he would never have gained that eminence in the church which he insisted on converting into pre-eminence. All that he is blamed for is the conceit and self-assurance which rendered him impatient of rivalry or resistance, and set him on seeking power rather than usefulness. To stand first, not to do most, was his supreme aim and desire. Any man who insists on the Church taking his way is only too certain to prove a blind guide, who will lead those who follow him into a ditch, and perhaps leave them in the ditch when he himself scrambles out of it. . . . It is his own way he wants, not the best way, not the way which will be most beneficial to others; and if he cannot get it by fair means, he will often stoop to foul or dubious means, stirring up division and discontent, prating with malicious words against those who oppose him when fair words will no longer serve his turn." — *Samuel Cox.* The rule for church membership is that we are to honor, to prefer one another, to humble ourselves, to have the same mind that was in Christ Jesus: that is, to be a servant of all. It may be all right for a man to seek political pre-eminence, intellectual pre-eminence, commercial pre-eminence, but seeking for one's own self pre-eminence in the Church where we are all one in Christ and where authority and power are bestowed in the leading of the Holy Spirit, is to go contrary to everything taught in the New Testament.

IV. **THE COMMENDATION OF DEMETRIUS,** vs. 11, 12. 11. **Beloved, imitate not that which is evil, but that which is good. He that doeth good is of God: he that doeth evil hath not seen God.** 12. **Demetrius hath the witness of**

12. Demetrius hath the witness of all *men*, and of the truth itself: yea, we also bear witness; and thou knowest that our witness is true.

all *men*, and of the truth itself: yea, we also bear witness; and thou knowest that our witness is true. There are two men by the name of Demetrius in the New Testament, one the silversmith of Ephesus (Acts 19); and the other the one referred to in these two epistles. Hardly anything more beautiful could be said about any one than is said here about this well-known believer, that he had "the witness of all men, and of the truth itself." "There is something wrong unless a Christian can put popular opinion into the witness box in his favor. Of course, there is a sense in which there is nothing more contemptible than seeking for that, and in which no heavier woe can come upon us, and no worse thing can be said about us, than that all men speak well of us. But, on the other hand, whether men speak well of us or not, there should be a distinctive characteristic plainly visible in us Christians which shall make all sorts of observers say to themselves, 'Well! that is a good man any-how. I may not like him; I may not want to resemble him; but I cannot help seeing what sort of a man he is, and that there is no mistake about his genuine goodness.' That is a testimony which Christians ought to be more ambitious of possessing than many of them are, and to lay themselves out more consciously to get, than most of them do." — *Alexander Maclaren.* "For he who daily sets his life upon the die that he may be true to his convictions, he who, moved by the grace and love of Christ, seeks not his own things but the things of others; he who devotes himself with burning zeal and all-enduring courage to the service of truth and the salvation of men — to him the truth itself, which has made him what he is, bears witness." — *Samuel Cox.* Demetrius had a threefold testimony to his character — the members of the church, the Christian truth itself, and John the Apostle.

V. THE SUPERSCRIPTION, vs. 13, 14. Here again John expresses his desire to see Gaius and his fellow Christian friends. It is the only sentence of this super-scription that needs consideration here. "The friends spoken of are probably the friends of Gaius. It is perhaps on account of the private character of the letter, as addressed to an individual and not to a Church, that John says 'the friends' rather than 'the brethren.' . . . The phrase 'by name' occurs in the New Testa-ment in only one other passage (John 10 : 3). The salutation is not to be given in a general way, but to each individual separately. John as shepherd of the churches of Asia would imitate the Good Shepherd and know all his sheep by name." — *Alfred Plummer.*

As we look back over these two epistles, we see how John vividly illustrates the practical implications of walking in the truth and walking in love. He illustrates walking in the truth, *negatively*, by warning his readers against those who were teaching false doctrines, who were denying the truth as it is in Christ; he illustrates this *positively* in the life of Demetrius, who walked according to the truth, and to whose life the truth bore testimony. He illustrates the meaning of walking in love first, *negatively*, by showing the selfishness of Diotrephes; then, *positively*, by com-mending the spirit of hospitality among Christians of that early day. We can walk in one direction only at one time. If we are walking in the truth, we will be kept from error; if we are walking in love, we will be kept from selfishness.

How many different characters appear in these two brief epistles, and how do you distinguish one from another? How do you account for the fact that in the same city during the same period of time, men can be found manifesting such con-tradictory characteristics? Why does not the same truth produce the same type of character? In how many different ways is it dangerous for true believers to have continuous fellowship with those who are denying the truth which they believe? Why is it especially important that we should not bring our children under the in-fluence of false teachers by entertaining such in our homes? Do you think that the spirit of hospitality among Christians today is generally and generously culti-vated? Is it so easy to walk in error and yet difficult to continue constantly to walk in the truth?

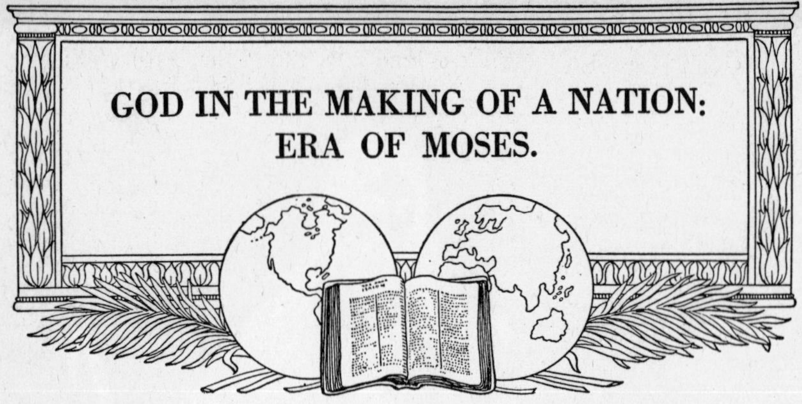

THIRD QUARTER.

JULY 4—SEPTEMBER 26, 1943.

AIM: To help the student to find and appreciate God's part in the making of a nation in the days of Moses and today.

LESSON I.—July 4.

A PEOPLE IN DISTRESS.—Exodus 1 : 1–22; 2 : 23–25.

PRINTED TEXT, Exodus 1 : 6-14; 2 : 23-25.

GOLDEN TEXT.—***They cried, and their cry came up unto God by reason of the bondage.*** EXODUS 2 : 23.

Devotional Reading: Psalm 61.
Beginner Topic: MOSES' NEW HOME.
Lesson Material: Exodus 2 : 11–22.
Memory Verse: God is love. 1 John 4 : 8.
Primary Topic: SISTER MIRIAM.
Lesson Material: Exodus 1; 2 : 1–10, 23–25.
Memory Verse: Even a child maketh himself known by his doings. Proverbs 20 : 11.
Junior Topic: THE WORLD'S GREATEST BOOK.
Lesson Material: Exodus 1; 2 : 23–25.
Memory Verse: The Lord giveth the word: the women that publish the tidings are a great host. Psalm 68 : 11.
Intermediate and Senior Topic: GOD CARES—DO WE?
Topic for Young People and Adults: CONCERN FOR THE OPPRESSED.

THE TEACHER AND HIS CLASS.

The Younger Classes will find this lesson a difficult one, as far as obtaining some practical teaching from it is concerned, and the teacher will probably prefer not to explain parts of it in great detail. Probably a good way to begin the lesson, with children, would be to ask the question, What are some of the reasons why some people do not like us, or why we do not like some people? It may be we are jealous of their good looks; it may be we are envious of their beautiful home, while we live in simple circumstances; it may be we do not like their pious pretenses; it may be they put on airs, and we do not like that; it may be they are better than we are, and we have to admit it; it may be they are proud of their superior intellect, etc., etc. In our lesson we are going to study the animosity of one great nation, Egypt, toward the people of Israel, and how they made

B. PLOCKHORST.

THE GOOD SHEPHERD.

Israel suffer, because of this attitude of suspicion, and later, of hatred.

The Older Classes will here find the first significant manifestation in history of anti-Semitism, that is, the hatred and the persecution of the Jews. It has been a disease breaking out with more or less virulence at different times for the last 3,200 years. We are in the midst of the most terrible outbreak of this disease that the world has ever known, in the determination of the Nazi powers to wipe the Jewish people off the face of the earth. In this lesson we will find that the suspicion of the Egyptians was absolutely unfounded, and, later, we will discover that all the suffering which Israel had to endure only disciplined her, and prepared her for a greater career than ever.

THE LESSON IN ITS SETTING.

Time. — The verses of our lesson cover a considerable period of time, not definitely marked off, but if the Pharaoh here who knew not Moses was Thothmes III, his reign fell between 1501 and 1447 B.C.

Place. — The land of Goshen generally, and the cities of Pithom and Rameses particularly.

THE PLAN OF THE LESSON.

SUBJECT: The Beginning of Israel's Suffering in Egypt, and the Consequent Cry on Her Part for Deliverance.

I. A RECAPITULATION, Exodus 1 : 1–7.

II. THE AFFLICTIONS OF ISRAEL IN EGYPT, 1 : 8–22.

1. The reason given by the Egyptian government for their scheme of persecution, vs. 8–10.
2. The first plan to hinder Israel's phenomenal growth and its failure, vs. 11–14.
3. The second scheme for preventing Israel's further growth and its failure, vs. 15–22.

III. ISRAEL'S PRAYER FOR DELIVERANCE, 2 : 23–25.

1. "God heard their groaning."
2. "God remembered His covenant."
3. "God saw."
4. "God had respect."

THE TEACHER'S LIBRARY.

For a list of commentaries on the book of Exodus, and for a list of books dealing with the life of Egypt, see the bibliography in the Introduction to this volume. There is a good chapter, "The House of Bondage," in J. M. Adams: *Biblical Backgrounds* (1934), 89–111; on the city of Pithom, see the article by A. H. Sayce, in James Hastings: *Dictionary of the Bible*, Vol. 3, 886, 887; and, for the city of Rameses, an article by the same author in the same work, Vol. 4, 188, 189. See also an excellent chapter, "The Oppression in Egypt," in Cunningham Geikie: *Hours with the Bible, Moses to Judges*, 77–113.

Sermonic material on this chapter is astonishingly meager. I know of only two sermons directly relating to these verses, and both of them are by Charles H. Spurgeon, in his *Metropolitan Tabernacle Pulpit*. On 1 : 10–12, he has a magnificent sermon, "Prosperity Under Persecution," in the volume for 1871, 349–360; on 2 : 23–25, see a sermon in the volume of 1899, 337–345. Dr. John A. Hutton has a sermon on 1 : 8, which he calls "The Passing Away of an Entire Life System," in his *The Victory Over Victory*, 19–29. There is a good chapter on "Israel in Egypt," in George Rawlinson: *Moses, His Life and Times*, 1–12.

Since writing these notes, a new volume has come to the editor's desk, which contains a superb though brief discussion of "Israel's Sojourn in Egypt," namely, *The Bearing of Archaeology on the Old Testament*, by Dr. Geo. L. Robinson, pp. 38–59.

THE BOOK OF EXODUS.

The title assigned, by the Hebrew people, to the second book of Moses, which is the second book in our Old Testament, was *Welleh Shemoth*, meaning "now these are the names," a title which one can immediately discover is taken from the first line of the first verse of the book. The Greek translators of the Old Testament many centuries later, called the book *Exodos*, which is the Greek word for "a going out," corresponding exactly to our word Exodus, which we find used in one way or another. It was so called because the book is primarily concerned with Israel's exodus from Egypt. This very Greek word *exodos* is found in a very interesting place in our New Testament, namely, in the account of our Lord's transfiguration, where the angel speaks to Christ "of his decease which he was about to accomplish at Jerusalem" (Luke 9 : 31). The word *decease* is a Latin form for "going out," of which *exodos* is the Greek form, and the word that Luke used, meaning "a going out from the earth into heaven." The book divides primarily into four parts. The introduction is contained in 1 : 1–7; from 1 : 8 to 7 : 7 we have an account of Israel's increasingly severe sufferings under the oppression of the Pharaohs of Egypt; from 7 : 8 to 18 : 27, we have an account of the miraculous deliverance of Israel from Egypt, known as the Exodus. The remaining twenty-two chapters are occupied with the laws and instructions given to Moses at Mount Sinai. The events recorded in Exodus are found repeated in and interwoven with all the subsequent books of both the Old and the New Testaments. The exodus from Egypt, the career of Moses, the giving of the Decalogue, the establishment of the Passover feast — all these matters exerted a tremendous influence over the life and thinking of Israel down

EXODUS 1 : 6. And Joseph died, and all his brethren, and all that generation.

7. And the children of Israel were fruitful, and increased abundantly, and multiplied, and waxed exceeding mighty; and the land was filled with them.

8. Now there arose a new king over Egypt, who knew not Joseph.

---

to the beginning of the New Testament and over the life of the apostles to the end of the apostolic age. For instance, the name Moses is found 119 times in the Old Testament in the books subsequent to the Pentateuch; and his name appears 79 times in the New Testament in 12 different books. Every commandment of the whole Decalogue reappears for consideration in the Gospels and in the epistles (except we have no new legislation concerning the Sabbath in the New Testament). It might be suggested then, that as the book of Genesis is a true foundation for understanding the history of the human race, so the book of Exodus may be considered foundationally essential for understanding the entire history of the Hebrew people.

I. **A RECAPITULATION,** 1 : 1–7. The book of Exodus opens with the migration of the family of Jacob into Egypt, which is recorded in detail in the forty-sixth chapter of Genesis. "The number is made up as follows — Jacob himself, 1; his sons, 12; his daughter, Dinah, 1; his grandsons, 51; his granddaughter, Serah, 1; his great grandsons, 4; total, 70. His daughters, except Dinah, and his sons' daughters, except Serah, spoken of in Genesis 46 : 7, are not included. If his female descendants were, at the time of his descent into Egypt, as numerous as the males, the entire number of those who 'came out of his loins' must have been 132. To form a calculation of the number of persons who entered Egypt with him, we must add the wives of his sons and grandsons, and the husbands of his daughters and granddaughters. A further liberal allowance must be also made for retainers. It is not perhaps surprising that Kurtz, taking all these classes into account, should calculate that those who entered Egypt with Jacob amounted to 'several thousands.'" — *George Rawlinson.* 6. **And Joseph died, and all his brethren, and all that generation.** This verse connects the book of Exodus with the last verse of the book of Genesis. 7. **And the children of Israel were fruitful, and increased abundantly, and multiplied, and waxed exceeding mighty; and the land was filled with them.** "A great multiplication is evidently intended. Egypt was a particularly healthy country, and both men and animals were abnormally prolific there. Grain was so plentiful that want, which is the ordinary check on population, was almost unknown. The Egyptian kings for many years would look favorably on the growth of the Hebrew people, which strengthened their eastern frontier, the quarter on which they were most open to attack. God's blessing was moreover upon the people, which He had promised to make 'as the stars of the heaven, and as the sand which is upon the seashore, for multitude.'" — *George Rawlinson.* It will be noted that in Exodus 12 : 37, it is said that Israel numbered at the time of the Exodus, 600,000 men on foot, beside women and children, which means that the nation must have embraced not far from two million souls. If the sojourn in Egypt was 430 years, and if the population doubled itself every twenty years, as many sociologists say a population does in the absence of artificial checks, it will be discovered that 3,000 persons in not more than two hundred years will increase to a number exceeding three million. But if Israel stayed in Egypt 430 years, then the population would only have to double once every forty-five years to attain the great number recorded in Exodus 12 : 37.

II. **THE AFFLICTION OF ISRAEL IN EGYPT,** 1 : 8–22. 8. **Now there arose a new king over Egypt, who knew not Joseph.** It is today generally understood that this was Thothmes III of the eighteenth dynasty. As long as the memory of Joseph remained fresh in the minds of the Egyptians, the people related to Joseph, whom the ruler of Egypt in his day had graciously allowed to settle in the land of Goshen, would be kindly cared for and left unmolested. But they were foreigners, and when the memory of Joseph, and of all he had done for Egypt, had practically vanished, it is easily conceivable how they should, waxing strong and great, arouse the animosity of the native Egyptians. How easy it is for a nation to forget those who have been its deliverers, and to neglect the families of those without whom their nation might easily have succumbed in an hour of danger and threatened misfortune. 9. **And he said unto his people, Behold, the people of the children of Israel are more**

9. And he said unto his people, Behold, the people of the children of Israel are more and mightier than we:
10. Come, let us deal wisely with them, lest they multiply, and it come to pass, that, when there falleth out any war, they also join themselves unto our enemies, and fight against us, and get them up out of the land.
11. Therefore they did set over them taskmasters to afflict them with their burdens. And they built for Pharaoh store-cities, Pithom and Raamses.
12. But the more they afflicted them, the more they multiplied and the more they spread abroad. And they were grieved because of the children of Israel.
13. And the Egyptians made the children of Israel to serve with rigor:
14. And they made their lives bitter with hard service, in mortar and in brick, and in all manner of service in the field, all their service, wherein they made them serve with rigor.

---

and mightier than we: 10. come, let us deal wisely with them, lest they multiply, and it come to pass, that, when there falleth out any war, they also join themselves unto our enemies, and fight against us, and get them up out of the land. "As they grew in numbers, Goshen became too small for them, and they were compelled to take up their abode in the great towns, or to emigrate into the neighboring districts, where they had to work as common laborers on the land of others, or else to occupy themselves in handicrafts. Egypt was very flourishing at the time, and they would have had little difficulty in finding employment. Rapid increase of numbers is, however, an advantage only under certain circumstances, *i.e.*, when a tribe or a people has a large unoccupied territory, or when commerce or manufactures offer practically unlimited employment to any multitude of applicants. But the circumstances of Egypt were not such as to afford these facilities; and the result must have been a difficulty in obtaining subsistence on the part of the Israelites, unless they consented to a low wage or to occupations which were generally distasteful. Toward the close of the second period we may be tolerably sure that a large number of them were forced to submit to both these inconveniences; that the lowest kinds of employments were eagerly accepted by thousands of Hebrews who found the struggle for existence a hard fight, and that these persons worked at wages which were barely sufficient to keep the wolf from their doors. . . . In alliance with the other Canaanite nations, with the Philistines, and even with the Arabs (Shasu), the Hittites threatened an invasion of Egypt, which, it was felt, might have the most disastrous consequences. What, if this contingency actually occurred, would be the part taken by the Israelites? Might it not be that they would 'join themselves to Egypt's enemies, and fight against the Egyptians' (Exod. 1:10), and so either help to bring them under subjection to the Hittites, or else 'get themselves up out of the land'? The Israelites occupied the portion of Egypt which the Hittites would first enter; if they joined the enemy they would deliver into his hands a large tract of most valuable territory, and put him in a position from which he would threaten the most important of the Egyptian cities — Tanis, Heliopolis, Bubastis, Memphis." — *George Rawlinson.*

11. **Therefore they did set over them taskmasters to afflict them with their burdens. And they built for Pharaoh store-cities, Pithom and Raamses.** 12. **But the more they afflicted them, the more they multiplied and the more they spread abroad. And they were grieved because of the children of Israel.** 13. **And the Egyptians made the children of Israel to serve with rigor:** 14. **and they made their lives bitter with hard service, in mortar and in brick, and in all manner of service in the field, all their service, wherein they made them serve with rigor.** Rameses II was noted for his vast building enterprises, and just at the time when he needed thousands of men to construct new public works throughout Egypt, he found it opportune and possible to force these helpless Hebrews to work practically as slaves in the making of brick and laboring on the walls of these buildings under the blistering sun of North Africa. "The city Pithom was unidentified for centuries until the excavations in Egypt of the French archeologist, Dr. Naville, who definitely established the fact that the city Tell el-maskhuta in the Wady Tumilat was the city of Pithom of our text, and

not the city of Rameses as many previously had thought." The result of his excavations on the spot "was the discovery of a temple, as well as of storehouses, private habitations, the walls of the city, and various inscriptions. The city and temple proved to have been built by Rameses II and to have lasted down to the Roman era. The city was in the form of a square, containing about 55,000 square yards. To the north was a series of brick buildings in which Dr. Naville found storehouses consisting of chambers with thick walls without communication one with another, access to them being from the top." — *A. H. Sayce.* The city of Rameses mentioned in the Egyptian text could not have been far from Pithom, somewhere in the land of Goshen, for from it the Israelites started when they fled from Egypt. "Many details of brick-making are revealed to us on the monuments of Egypt. In a tomb on the hill Abd-el-Qurnah, a picture of the time of Thothmes III, has been preserved, in which prisoners of war, set to build the temple of Amon, are seen toiling at the bitter labors of the brickfield. Some carry water in jugs from the tank hard by; others knead and cut up the loamy earth; others, again, make bricks in earthen molds, or place them carefully in long rows, to dry; and some are building walls. An accompanying inscription states that these are captives whom Thothmes III had carried away, to build the house of his father, the god Amon. The 'baking of the bricks' is for a new provision house of the god. Nor is there wanting a taskmaster for the overseer watches the works; the words, 'Don't idle, the stick is in my hand,' being painted as if coming from his lips. The monuments often, indeed, speak of brick-making by forced labor, and in the various paintings which represent this, or any other kind of 'task work,' the overseer with his stick is rarely absent. Thus, among the pictures at Beni Hassan, workmen are represented being beaten severely with short sticks, which differed from the long rods of office, and were used solely to bastinado the unfortunate laborers. Some of these are seen thrown naked on the ground, two men holding the arms and another the feet, while the taskmaster showers blows on the exposed body. There are even pictures at Beni Hassan of women and children being thus bastinadoed. The taskmasters in Exodus — literally Chiefs of the Tribute — were dignified officials, apparently over large divisions of the corvée. Inferior officers were placed over sections of these, and the *zekanim*, or elders, and the *shoterim*, or scribes, of the Hebrews themselves, seem to have been responsible for the work to be done by the men of their respective localities." —*C. Geikie.*

The Great Rock Temple of Aboo Simbel.

The "grandest ever created by Egyptian skill," constructed by Rameses II, the Pharaoh of the Oppression. It is at Wady Halfa in Egypt, about one thousand miles south of Cairo and about twenty-five miles north of the second cataract of the Nile.

Prisoners Making Brick for the Temple of Amon.

Depicted on a tomb at Thebes, Egypt. On the right hand the overseer with his staff.

The attempt to reduce the population of the Hebrews by hard work, and to bring about, apparently, the death of many from exhaustion and insufficient food, failed, so the Pharaoh of Egypt proposed a much more drastic scheme. He issued an order that when the midwives of the Hebrew women discovered that the baby born was a son, the baby should be killed. "It has been thought that they were themselves of Hebrew blood, and that their two names can be traced to Hebrew roots referring to personal comeliness. The balance of recent expert judgment inclines toward the view that they were native Egyptians, and that Shiphrah and Puah are still (through still surviving Coptic) traceable to Egyptian words having reference to childbirth. As to the sufficiency of two midwives for so great a population, (1) they may have been only in charge of the department of midwifery in Goshen. (2) The cruel edict may have referred only to the upper class of Hebrew families; as Pharaoh may have felt no interest in going beyond that class to a promiscuous 'massacre of innocents.' Mark the (perhaps contemptuous) use of the name of Hebrews coming in, as soon as we begin to look through Egyptian eyes." — *James MacGregor*. "But the midwives feared God, and did not as the king of Egypt commanded them, but saved the men children alive." This disobedience led the king of Egypt to demand of the midwives why they had not slain the male babies as soon as they were born, as he had commanded. The midwives replied: "Because the Hebrew women are not as the Egyptian women; for they are lively, and are delivered ere the midwife come unto them." "This was quite true in point of fact. Among the Bedouin to this day, and others whose bodies are well-developed by pastoral occupations and loose clothing, child-bearing is comparatively easy." — *J. G. Murphy*. The word translated in our Revised Version *birth-stool* has given rise to a great deal of discussion, and its meaning frankly can only be guessed at. "Some suggest two stone discs such as go to make a corn handmill, with some corresponding use that cannot be expounded here. Others suggest the stone bath with a stone lid or covering, reminding us that in ancient heathen lands infants doomed to die were murdered in the bath; others a sort of couch or seat adapted to the condition of the patients." — *James MacGregor*. Probably we can sum it all up by saying that it simply referred to some kind of special stool used by women in labor. Pharaoh, now discovering that his second scheme for checking the growth of the Israelitish nation was failing, "charged all his people, saying, Every son that is born ye shall cast into the river, and every daughter ye shall save alive." "The command implies that the Israelites lived near the river. The Hebrew word for 'the river' is used almost exclusively of the Nile, occurring twenty-two times in the book of Exodus." — *A. H. McNeile*. "By the Egyptians, this river was worshiped, as to them the beneficent deity. The king may have thought to propitiate this deity by sacrificing to it the born lives of the race dishonoring the gods of Egypt. The plan failed. Perhaps there was no hearty co-operation on the people's part." — *James MacGregor*. "The Egyptians had no quarrel with their Hebrew neighbors, and would not care to act as executioners; but government officials would be employed to see the king's orders carried out, and no doubt for several years many thousands of innocent lives were sacrificed. Still, however, the king's purpose was not effected. Had the edict been rigorously enforced, the people would have been extinguished before the date of the Exodus. But it had then reached to a total of above two million souls (Exod. 12 : 37). Either, therefore, the edict must have been revoked after a while, or it must gradually have sunk into oblivion. In one way or another, God's will triumphed over man's, and the people, doomed to extinction by the highest human power which existed on earth at the time, was preserved by God's providence through all the perils which threatened it, to become, according to the promise given to Jacob (Gen. 35 : 11), 'a nation and a company of nations.'" — *George Rawlinson*.

THE DEEPER MEANING OF EGYPT.

"Babylon stood on the great highway of the world. For the traffic of the old generation the valley of the Euphrates was the natural highway between east and west; but Egypt lay as it were in a nook, a corner by herself, hemmed in by mighty deserts. She could live and die to herself. She could pamper and caress her children till their nobler qualities became enervated and dwarfed; and therefore she has always stood as the symbol of the enervating influence of worldly prosperity. There were the seed-germs of noble things in Egypt, as in the rest of the human family; but they were diverted from the service of God and man to the gratification of sense; and, as we know, the prostitution of the best is always worst. The soil that would

EXODUS 2 : 23. And it came to pass in the course of those many days, that the king of Egypt died: and the children of Israel sighed by reason of the bondage, and they cried, and their cry came up unto God by reason of the bondage.

24. And God heard their groaning, and God remembered his covenant with Abraham, with Isaac, and with Jacob.

25. And God saw the children of Israel, and God took knowledge *of them.*

---

be ideal for cereals is prolific in the poppy. So that the total contribution of Egypt to the world is a race of slaves, the poor ryots, who for two thousands years at least have been the drudges of their rulers and the helots of the human family."— *F. B. Meyer.*

III. **ISRAEL'S PRAYER FOR DELIVERANCE,** 2 : 23–25. 23. **And it came to pass in the course of those many days, that the king of Egypt died: and the children of Israel sighed by reason of the bondage, and they cried, and their cry came up unto God by reason of the bondage.** 24. **And God heard their groaning, and God remembered his covenant with Abraham, with Isaac, and with Jacob.** 25. **And God saw the children of Israel, and God took knowledge** ***of them.*** Trouble, oppression, suffering, fear, led Israel to plead with God for deliverance, and four significant things are said about the prayers that were offered. God heard their prayers; God remembered His covenant; God saw His people in distress; and God had respect for them. Spurgeon well reminds us, "there are some people who seem to hear things, but the sounds pass through their ears, and there the matter ends. But if you go to visit a sick woman, and you sit down, and she tells you all about her ailments, and about her poverty, she is cheered because you listen to her kindly, and because you are willing to hear her even if you cannot help her, and it does help her even to hear her tell her sad story. Well now, God heard Israel's crying and groaning; He heard them, not merely as men hear a sound, and take no notice of it, but He seemed to stand still, and listen to the sighs, and groans, and cries of His people. Sinner, tell God your misery even now, and He will hear your story. He is willing to listen, even to that sad and wretched tale of yours about your multiplied transgressions, your hardness of heart, your rejections of Christ. Tell Him all, for He will hear it. Tell Him what it is you want — what large mercy — what great forgiveness; just lay your whole case before Him. Do not hesitate for a single moment; He will hear it, He will be attentive to the voice of your cry."

The covenant which God is said to have remembered with Abraham (Gen. 12 : 2, 3; 13 : 14–17; 15 : 4–21; 17 : 1–14; 22 : 16–18), and with Isaac (17 : 19, 20; 26 : 2–5), and with Jacob (28 : 13–15; 35 : 11, 12; 46 : 3, 4), involved the perpetuity of the Israelitish nation, the descendants of Abraham, and their being brought into Palestine for their permanent dwelling-place. When it says God remembered His covenant with Abraham, Isaac, and Jacob, it means that God is about to bring into reality that covenant which involved Israel's going back up into Palestine to dwell there in the land which the Lord God would give to her. On the phrase, *God saw*, F. B. Meyer has a precious page of comforting comment: "'The eyes of the Lord are toward the righteous, and His ears are open unto their cry'; and though Israel was not righteous for their own sake, they were beloved for their father's sake.

'And the Lord said, I have surely seen the affliction of my people which are in Egypt.' There is a remarkable succession of affirmations made of the Father by our Lord in the Sermon on the Mount: Your Father which is in heaven; thy Father which is in secret; thy Father which seeth in secret; your Father knoweth; your heavenly Father will forgive you; your heavenly Father feedeth; your Father which is in heaven shall give good things. To realize that He sees and knows, that nothing which concerns us is hidden from Him, that the darkness shines as the day, and the lowest part of the earth conceals nothing from His omniscience — this carries with it all the rest: for He cannot see without coming down in pitying help. When in after days the children of Israel were assured that Jehovah had seen their affliction, 'then they bowed their heads, and worshiped,' as though they had nothing more to ask; and the result justified their act. Every blow of the hand that buffets you, every cut of the scourge, every scorching hour under the noontide sun, every lonely hour when lovers and friends stand aloof, every step into the valley of shadow, every moment of sleep beneath the juniper tree, is watched by the eyes that never slumber nor sleep."

GOD'S OVER-RULING AT A TIME WHEN HIS PEOPLE ARE ENDURING PERSECUTION.

"Whenever there has been a great persecution raised against the Christian Church, God has overruled it, as He did in the case of Pharaoh's oppression of the Israelites, by making the aggrieved community more largely to increase. The early persecutions in Judæa promoted the spread of the gospel; hence, when after the death of Stephen the disciples were all scattered abroad throughout the regions of Judæa and Samaria, except the apostles, the result is thus given: 'Therefore they that were scattered abroad went everywhere preaching the word.' So, too, when Herod stretched forth his hands to vex certain of the church, and killed James, the brother of John, with the sword; what came of it? Why, Luke tells us in almost the same words that Moses had used: 'The word of God grew and multiplied.' Those terrible and bloody persecutions under the Roman emperor by no means stayed the progress of the gospel; but strangely enough men seemed to press forward for the crown of martyrdom. The Church probably never increased at a greater ratio than when her foes were most fierce to assail and most resolute to destroy her. It was so in after times. The Reformation in this country and throughout Europe never went on so prosperously as when it was most vigorously opposed. You shall find in any individual church, that wherever evil men have conspired together, and a storm of opposition has burst forth against the saints, the heart of the Lord has been moved with compassion, and the hand of the Lord has been raised to succour, till we have come to look upon opposition as an omen of good, and persecution for righteousness' sake as a tearful seed-time, quickly to be followed by a harvest of joy. We have looked on our adversaries, though they seemed like stormy petrels, as being the index of a favorable wind to the good barque of Christ's Church. Persecution seems to be the wave that, when it leaps up around her, speeds her course. Let the mountains be removed, and cast into the midst of the sea; but after long experience of Jehovah's faithfulness toward His people, we are confident that His Church shall not be moved: in quietude shall she possess her soul." — *Charles Spurgeon* (1871).

Was the fear of the Israelites on the part of the Egyptians just? In how many different ways did the Egyptian government attempt to prevent the continuance of the phenomenal growth of Israel, and were these measures fair? Why did God allow Israel to suffer in Egypt like this? If Israel had not been forced to endure such terrible hardships in Egypt, would she have wanted to have left Egypt to go up into a land with which they were not personally acquainted? How did the Israelites come to know that God was hearkening to their prayers? Can you name some nations today in the world which are suffering terrible persecution and hardship? What is the difference between a nation suffering great persecution and bondage that knows not God and the nation suffering the same trials but able to call upon God?

LESSON II. — July 11.

GOD CALLS A LEADER. — Exodus 2 : 1—3 : 12.

PRINTED TEXT, Exodus 3 : 1-12.

GOLDEN TEXT. — *Come now therefore, and I will send thee unto Pharaoh, that thou mayest bring forth my people the children of Israel out of Egypt.* Exodus 3 : 10.

Devotional Reading: Psalm 106 : 1–5.
Beginner Topic: Eli's Little Helper.
Lesson Material: Exodus 3 : 1, 2; 1 Samuel 3.
Memory Verse: Thou art nigh, O Jehovah. Psalm 119 : 151.

Primary Topic: The Bush Moses Saw.
Lesson Material: Exodus 3 : 1–12.
Memory Verse: Many, O Jehovah my God, are the wonderful works which thou hast done. . . . They are more than can be numbered. Psalm 40 : 5.
Junior Topic: In a Desert Place.
Lesson Material: Exodus 3 : 1–12.
Memory Verse: Thou art nigh, O Jehovah; and all thy commandments are truth. Psalm 119 : 151.
Intermediate and Senior Topic: Answering God's Call.
Topic for Young People and Adults: God's Call to Service.

THE TEACHER AND HIS CLASS.

The Younger Classes may be reminded that all men in high positions, indeed, in all important positions, have had long years of training to adequately equip them for doing the work they finally are called to do. But in the early years of their life, while experiencing this training, they did not know to what great things it would ultimately lead them. The President of the United States did not know that his years of executive labors in Albany as Governor of the State of New York would lead him to a twelve-year term in the White House. A friend of mine, who gave himself constantly day and night to the study of mathematics and chemistry in college, is now the chief chemist in one of the greatest industrial concerns in the country, earning $50,000 a year. He did not know when he was studying chemistry at the age of nineteen that he was preparing for this work. Our lesson is the record of God's preparing Moses for the great task of bringing His people out of Egypt. We, too, if we are in the will of God, should count each year as a training school for something bigger and more important in the years to follow.

The Older Classes will discover here a sudden revelation of God to a man who, for nearly forty years, had been tending sheep, exiled from Egypt. During that time he had been growing strong in his inner life; he had come to know God intimately; he had come to learn self-control. He had no doubt lived a life separate from coarse indulgences and exhausting vices. Suddenly, without warning, God calls him to his life work. Moses is ready, even though he does not think so. What we need to do is to quietly submit to God's providential leading, year by year, so that when a great task suddenly must be done, God can put his hand upon us and say, "You are the one to do this piece of work." There are great tasks awaiting men who will live in the will of God today. There are not enough ministers for the pulpits of our land; there are not enough men who can open the Word of God today; there are not enough true Christians in the great offices of our government; there are not enough who will speak prophetically to this bewildered world.

THE LESSON IN ITS SETTING.

Time. — 1526–1446 B.C.

Place. — The events identified with the birth of Moses took place, probably, near the city of Tanis, one of the royal residences in the northeast of the Delta, near the mouth of the Tanitic branch of the Nile. The call of Moses took place in Midian, near Mount Sinai.

THE PLAN OF THE LESSON.

SUBJECT: How God Overrules the Experiences of Life, Great and Small, So As to Make Them All, the Disagreeable and the Agreeable, Days of Defeat and Hours of Victory, to Prepare Men for the Specific Tasks Which He Has Determined They Are to Accomplish.

I. The Birth and Protection of Moses, Exodus 2 : 1–10.
1. The birth of Moses, vs. 1, 2.
2. He is brought up in Pharaoh's house, vs. 3–10.

II. Moses Attempts to Deliver His Brethren, Exodus 2 : 11–14.
1. What he saw.
2. What he did.
3. What he was subsequently told.

III. Moses' Forty Years' Exile in Midian, Exodus 2 : 15–25.
1. Why he fled.
2. His kindness to the priest's daughters.
3. He marries Zipporah.
4. The Lord looks upon the suffering Israelites.

IV. The Call of Moses, Exodus 3 : 1–12.
1. What he was doing, v. 1.
2. What he saw, vs. 2, 3.
3. What he heard, v. 4.
4. What he was first told to do, v. 5.
5. What was revealed to him, vs. 6–10.
   a. The One speaking, v. 6.
   b. The purpose of God to deliver Israel, vs. 7–9.
   c. The place he was to have in God's purpose, v. 10.
6. Moses' consciousness of inability for such a task, v. 11.
7. The promise of God to be with him, v. 12.

THE TEACHER'S LIBRARY.

For a list of commentaries on the book of Exodus, and for a list of biographies of Moses, see the bibliography in the Introduction to this volume. On the entire subject of Moses' preparation, see a fine sermon by G. Campbell Morgan, in the *Westminster Pulpit*, Vol. 7, 385–392; on the call of Moses, there is a very fine chapter in Henry Schaeffer: *The Call to Prophetic Service*, 41–54; for sermonic material, on verses 2 and 3, see Alexander Maclaren: *Expositions of Holy Scripture, Exodus, Leviticus, Numbers*, 19–26; James Hastings: *Great Texts of the Bible, Genesis to Numbers*, 260–273; Joseph Parker: *The City Temple Pulpit*, Vol. 2, 239–246; Hugh MacMillan: *The Gate Beautiful*, 144–154; Harris E. Kirk: *One Generation to Another*, 75–85; C. F. Wishart: *The Unwelcome Angel*, 161–187; on 3 : 4–6, Andrew Murray: *Holy in Christ*, 36–43; on verse 7, Joseph Parker, as above, Vol. 4, 270–272; on verse 11, Harris E. Kirk, as above, 86–95. The editor is informed that there is a fine sermon on 3 : 2, in a book by Mrs. Penn Lewis, *Face to Face*, but he has never been able to find a copy of it.

The following words of Professor Murphy, with which he introduces his investigation of the second chapter of Exodus, may well serve as a fitting introduction for our study today. "In the preceding chapters, is recorded the extremity of the chosen seed. This hard pressure of affliction was not unneeded. In the abundance and prosperity of Goshen they had well nigh forgotten the absolute and exclusive claim of God on their homage and obedience. Nothing but the strong hand of oppression could bring them to a sense of their dependence and their duty. But they were a chosen race. The Most High does not allow them, as He might otherwise have done, to merge into the superstition and apostasy of the surrounding nations. He has, moreover, a purpose to serve by them, an end ulterior to their own spiritual benefit. He intends through them to perpetuate the knowledge of God, to bring in the Redeemer into the world, to effect a redemption that will be sufficient for all the nations of mankind, and finally to bring all the world into reconciliation with himself and with themselves. He will not be thwarted in this sublime and benign purpose. He has therefore laid the heavy hand of chastisement on this people to bring them to repentance. He will not, however, leave them to perish by the murderous devices of Pharaoh. He will gradually prepare them to shake off the fetters of Egypt, and take their departure for the land of promise. And His providence is at work in another direction. Immediately after the issue of the bloody edict for the extermination of the people, the deliverer is born who is to head the movement of national emancipation, and is preserved from destruction by the indirect influence of the hostile monarch himself. In this chapter, accordingly, we have the parentage, birth, preservation, education, and exile of Moses, the coming deliverer of God's people."

I. **THE BIRTH AND PROTECTION OF MOSES,** Exod. 2 : 1–10. The narrative here is marked with great simplicity and beauty. The father and mother of Moses are not named in this place. It is simply said that both were of the house of Levi, and that at this time of terrible persecution a son was born to them, who, because of the severe edict of the government, had to be hidden lest he should be destroyed by the order of Pharaoh. There came a time, when the babe was two months old, when the mother could no longer hide the child, and was led to make an ark of bulrushes for him. She covered it with pitch, and placed it with its priceless treasure in the papyri plants by the river's brink, leaving the older sister, Miriam (who certainly must have been at least eight or ten years old at this time), to watch what would happen to the babe. The word here translated *bulrush* refers to the famous plant known as the *papyrus* (from whence comes our word *paper*), a reed that once was prolific along the banks of the Nile, but is now almost extinct. "It is triangular in section, growing to be rather taller than a man. The light, strong stalks were made into boats, to be seen on the monuments, for the smooth river. It was an inner rind that was made into paper." — *James MacGregor*. No doubt the mother expected, when she hid her babe by the bank of the Nile, that something like this would happen. "It is possible, that there may have been some place in the

Papyrus Basket from an Egyptian Tomb.

Probably the same kind as that in which the infant Moses was laid after his mother had covered the sides and bottom with asphalt. (From the Egyptian Exploration Fund.)

neighborhood which was known to be frequented by the members of the court, and so Jochebed selected that with the feeling half of hope and half of mysterious apprehension that something might occur similar to that which actually happened." — *W. M. Taylor.* There came down to the river to bathe this day the daughter of Pharaoh, attended by her maidens. " The providence of God, ever working through means, brought the princess to the river brink at the critical moment, accompanied by the high-born maidens who constituted her personal attendants. It was His hand that guided her eye to the ark half concealed by the rushes; and it was at His prompting that the maid was sent to fetch it. All this came forth from the Lord of hosts, who is wonderful in counsel and excellent in effectual working. With her own hands the princess opened the lid of the little basket. It is not impossible that she guessed what its contents were. She was more than willing to fall in with the shrewd suggestion of Miriam that a nurse of the Hebrew race would be the more fitting to rear it. So it befell that Moses' life was saved, that he was nourished from the breasts of his own mother, and received as his earliest impression those sacred teachings which had come down as a rich heritage from the tents of Abraham. Till he had grown, probably to the age of three years, he remained under the protection of the princess, though in his parent's home, and Jochebed's wages were duly paid till she brought him to the palace, and he became her son. 'And she called his name Moses' (' Drawn forth ')." — *F. B. Meyer.* We read in the Epistle to the Hebrews (11 : 23) that Moses was hidden three months by his parents " by faith," which means that he was born into a godly home, and that everything done for the boy was done, as far as they were aware, according to the will of God.

Papyrus of Egypt.

This remarkable deliverance from death; this preservation of the babe by members of the royal family of Egypt, assured Moses of the finest education that Egypt could afford, gave him easy access to the royal court, and surrounded him in all his early and most impressionable years with the most important personalities of the Egyptian government, with the best teachers and scientists which Egypt at that time contained.

II. **MOSES ATTEMPTS TO DELIVER HIS BRETHREN,** Exodus 2 : 11–14. The first forty years of Moses' life are passed over quickly. Now in middle life, as he was moving in and out among his brethren, who were suffering greatly from the ever-increasing burdens placed upon them by the harsh laws of a government determined upon their extermination, he saw an Egyptian taskmaster whipping one of his own Hebrew men; and in looking around, finding that no one was near, he slew the Egyptian and hid him in the sand. Before considering the consequence of this deed, which was certainly a wicked one, we should first recognize that Moses, in attempting to deliver this Hebrew from undeserved and humiliating punishment, went out of his way to identify himself with his own people. He was held in high regard in the Egyptian court. No doubt, he was being prepared for a noble career in the Egyptian government. He certainly could have enjoyed a comfortable existence all of his life and could have kept himself aloof from the sufferings of his own flesh and blood, but as the writer to the Hebrews reminds us (11 : 24–26), he " refused to be called the son of Pharaoh's daughter; choosing rather to suffer affliction with the people of God than to enjoy the pleasures of sin for a season." In the second place, this act of Moses indicated a heart capable of being moved by suffering, and a nature which was made for leadership, an individual who could take a leading part in any great movement for the emancipation of a downtrodden race.

But this hasty deed was certainly nothing less than murder, and God did not intend for Moses to free His people in such an iniquitous way as this. Some one saw him kill this Egyptian, and the next day when he attempted to settle a dispute between two Hebrew men striving together, one of them startled Moses by asking him if it was his intention to kill one of them as the day before he had killed the Egyptian. There was nothing else for Moses to do but to flee. Pharaoh, of course, heard what had happened, and nothing would have saved Moses at this time from immediate death had Pharaoh been able to apprehend him. "For the last thirty years, we may imagine him now and then stealing out of the royal precincts to look on the burdens of his people. Oft with a sore heart may the young patriot have returned to the palace, contrasted the freedom, luxury, and mental culture around him with the degradation of that race which he knew was chosen of God to hold the foremost rank and achieve the noblest ends for humanity. The hope of their deliverance was cherished. The wish to take part in it was gathering strength with his years. He was at length precipitated into action by the scenes before him." — *J. G. Murphy.* The deliverance which Moses here attempted to accomplish for this one man in his own strength, and certainly not according to the leading of the Lord, forty years later he will be privileged to accomplish for his whole nation, not by his strength, but by the miraculous intervention of God. The desire that burns in his breast now will prepare him for that time when he will be able passionately to throw himself into the tremendous task of delivering a whole nation from this galling bondage. Had Moses at the age of forty cared nothing for the sufferings of his people, he would not have been appointed by God their deliverer at the age of eighty.

Julius Schnorr.

Moses, Beholding One of His Countrymen Flogged in the Brickfields, Prepares to Slay the Egyptian Taskmaster.

III. **MOSES' FORTY YEARS' EXILE IN MIDIAN,** Exodus 2 : 15–25. Moses, no doubt, fled to Midian, the region that lay mainly beyond the Ailanitic Gulf, on the east of the Sinaitic peninsula, because here he would be among kinsfolk, for the Midianites too were sprung from Abraham. He probably now took a route through Sinai from Goshen, somewhat like the route taken forty years later by the entire Hebrew nation. There was a priest in Midian at this time by the name of Raguel (see Num. 10 : 29), also called Jethro, who was, it seems, "a worshiper of the true God, something after the stamp of that Melchizedek whom Abraham honored, and it may be also having spiritual kinship to the patriarch whose trials and triumphs are so dramatically told in the book of Job. If this were indeed the case, then Moses must have had much profitable fellowship with those among whom his lot was cast; and in their common worship of the one living and true God there would be a bond of union between them of the tenderest kind." — *W. M. Taylor.* Weary with traveling, Moses sat down at a well in a part of Midian not definitely identified, and, little dreaming of what such a casual incident would mean, he soon beheld the seven daughters of Raguel gathered around the well to draw water for their father's flocks. Before they had finished their task, rough, heartless shepherds came to the place and attempted to drive them away, "but Moses stood up and helped them, and watered their flock." "It would be a different world today, if all who claim to be 'the salt of the earth' were as eager to repress injustice in its smaller and meaner

EXODUS 3 : 1. Now Moses was keeping the flock of Jethro his father-in-law, the priest of Midian: and he led the flock to the back of the wilderness, and came to the mountain of God, unto Horeb.

2. And the angel of Jehovah appeared unto him in a flame of fire out of the midst of a bush: and he looked, and, behold, the bush burned with fire, and the bush was not consumed.

forms as to make money or influential friends." — *G. H. Chadwick.* The same spirit which led Moses to attempt to deliver the persecuted Hebrew slave some days before this, is the same spirit that compels him to save these helpless daughters of the Midianite priest from the coarse selfishness of the shepherds. Of course, as soon as the daughters returned home they told their father all that had happened, and immediately he sent them back to bring their deliverer to his tent, that he might break bread with them. So naturally did Moses find himself fitting into the home life of Raguel that it was not long before he was married to one of the seven daughters, Zipporah. We regret to say that this marriage of Moses did not turn out to be an especially happy one.

IV. **THE CALL OF MOSES,** Exodus 3 : 1–12.

1. WHAT HE WAS DOING, v. 1. 1. **Now Moses was keeping the flock of Jethro his father-in-law, the priest of Midian: and he led the flock to the back of the wilderness, and came to the mountain of God, unto Horeb.** "The pastoral life is always one that favors contemplation. In the East, the shepherd rises with the early dawn, and leads forth his flock from the rough sheepfolds in which they have passed the night, going before them, and guiding them to the pastures. When he has brought them to the spot where he intends them to graze, they scatter themselves, while he seats himself and rests on some convenient knoll, or bank, or stone, whence he can command a view of the beasts under his care, and see that they do not wander away too far. There would be long hours during each day when practically he would be by himself, face to face with nature and with God, unconsciously drinking in the influences of his surroundings, gaining mental strength and vigor from his contact with the simplicity and solemnity of nature. At the same time he would be disciplining his body by spare and simple meals, by much walking in the open air, by sleep on the ground, short nights, and early risings; while he invigorated his whole character by communing with himself and with God, by deep 'searchings of heart,' sharp questionings of conscience, reflections upon his past life, repentance of his sins, and good resolutions with respect to the future. A long spell of solitude, or comparative solitude, is of the highest value for the formation of a high, noble, and a commanding personality." — *George Rawlinson.*

Shepherd in the Field Tending Sheep.

2. WHAT HE SAW, VS. 2, 3. 2. **And the angel of Jehovah appeared unto him in a flame of fire out of the midst of a bush: and he looked, and, behold, the bush burned with fire, and the bush was not consumed.** 3. **And Moses said, I will turn**

3. And Moses said, I will turn aside now, and see this great sight, why the bush is not burnt.

4. And when Jehovah saw that he turned aside to see, God called unto him out of the midst of the bush, and said, Moses, Moses. And he said, Here am I.

5. And he said, Draw not nigh hither: put off thy shoes from off thy feet, for the place whereon thou standest is holy ground.

---

aside now, and see this great sight, why the bush is not burnt. The bush, which Moses beheld burning, was probably some species of thorn. "The fire was supernatural, and did not affect the vegetative life of the bush. This it was that arrested the attention of Moses. The mode of the divine appearance is not without design. The bush that lives unscathed by the lambent flame that winds round all its leaves and branches, is an emblem of that which is pure and holy, and therefore of the true Church of God in the furnace of affliction. The lowliness of the shrub comports well with the seeming feebleness and insignificance of the people of God. The flame of fire corresponds with the fiery trial through which they have had to pass, that the lusts of the flesh, which had grown up in Egypt, might be consumed, and faith and its kindred virtues be left behind in all their vigor and beauty." — *J. G. Murphy.* "He was called amid the common things of life, but he was called by an uncommon thing. It was only a common bush in the wilderness; but that flaming glory was not a common thing. He quietly looked at that burning bush and said: 'I will turn aside now, and see this great sight, why the bush is not consumed.' There was no hurry, no fear. The forty years had resulted in a quiet, calm, peaceful dignity, enabling him to say: 'I will turn aside and see this great sight, why the bush is not consumed.'" — *G. Campbell Morgan.*

Moses and the Burning Bush.

3. WHAT HE HEARD, v. 4. 4. **And when Jehovah saw that he turned aside to see, God called unto him out of the midst of the bush, and said, Moses, Moses. And he said, Here am I.** "God speaks to him out of the bush, calls him by name, and under the spell of that voice his whole history passed before him: his exile, his heartache, his disillusionment, his pain and his longing, and above all the feeling that had steadied him through the whole of the discipline that this simply could not be the end. Somewhere and somehow God must break in on his soul. And this is what happened to him, when the voice called him by name. Let us not miss the significance of this, for a man's name stands for the lonely mystery of individuality." — *H. E. Kirk.*

4. WHAT HE WAS FIRST TOLD TO DO, v. 5. 5. **And he said, Draw not nigh hither: put off thy shoes from off thy feet, for the place whereon thou standest is holy ground.** Literally, the word *shoes* here should read *sandals.* "Egyptians, before the time of Moses, and Orientals generally, in ancient as in modern times,

6. Moreover he said, I am the God of thy father, the God of Abraham, the God of Isaac, and the God of Jacob. And Moses hid his face; for he was afraid to look upon God.

7. And Jehovah said, I have surely seen the affliction of my people that are in Egypt, and have heard their cry by reason of their taskmasters; for I know their sorrows;

8. And I am come down to deliver them out of the hand of the Egyptians, and to bring them up out of that land unto a good land and a large, unto a land flowing with milk and honey; unto the place of the Canaanite, and the Hittite, and the Amorite, and Perizzite, and the Hivite, and the Jebusite.

9. And now, behold, the cry of the children of Israel is come unto me: moreover I have seen the oppression wherewith the Egyptians oppress them.

---

removed their sandals or their shoes from their feet on entering any place to which respect was due, as a temple, a palace, and even the private house of a great man. It is worthy of notice that God Himself orders this mark of respect to be shown to the place which His presence has hallowed." — *George Rawlinson.* The Boy Scout oath concludes with the admonition to be *reverent.* Here is a great verse for the minister to use in preaching to Boy Scouts, as they are gathered together in his church some Sunday night. Reverence is due all the sacred privileges and experiences of life. We should be reverent in the home, reverent in church, respectful toward our elders, respectful toward the flag, respectful to the name of God. Tragic and empty the life that knows no hour and no place where in a particular way a sense of awe and a consciousness of God's presence is not known.

5. WHAT WAS REVEALED TO HIM, vs. 6–10. 6. **Moreover he said, I am the God of thy father, the God of Abraham, the God of Isaac, and the God of Jacob. And Moses hid his face; for he was afraid to look upon God.** "These words are used by our Lord (Matt. 22 : 31; Luke 20 : 37) to prove to the Sadducees, who clung to the letter of the Law, the truth of the resurrection of the dead. The words, 'I am the God, etc.,' are true for all time. They imply a personal relation between God and man which carries with it the germ of eternal life. He is the God of the living, not of the dead; therefore Abraham, Isaac, and Jacob are living." — *A. H. McNeile.* 7. **And Jehovah said, I have surely seen the affliction of my people that are in Egypt, and have heard their cry by reason of their taskmasters; for I know their sorrows.** "Now for the first time, God calls Israel *My people*, adopting a phrase already twice employed by earthly rulers (Gen. 23 : 11; 41 : 40), and thus making Himself their king and the champion of their cause. Often afterwards it was used in pathetic appeal: 'Thou hast showed thy people hard things,' 'Thou sellest thy people for nought,' 'Behold, look, we beseech thee; we are all thy people' (Ps. 60 : 3; 44 : 12; Isa. 64 : 9). And often it expressed the returning favor of their king: 'Hear, O my people, and I will speak'; 'Comfort ye, comfort ye my people' (Ps. 50 : 7; Isa. 40 : 1). It is used of the nation at large, all of whom were brought into the covenant, although with many of them God was not well pleased. And since it does not belong only to saints, but speaks of a grace which might be received in vain, it is a strong appeal to all Christian people, all who are within the New Covenant. Them also the Lord claims and pities, and would gladly emancipate; their sorrows also He knows." — *G. H. Chadwick.* 8. **And I am come down to deliver them out of the hand of the Egyptians, and to bring them up out of that land unto a good land and a large, unto a land flowing with milk and honey; unto the place of the Canaanite, and the Hittite, and the Amorite, and the Perizzite, and the Hivite, and the Jebusite.** 9. **And now, behold, the cry of the children of Israel is come unto me: moreover I have seen the oppression wherewith the Egyptians oppress them.** "The main original Egypt (Upper Egypt, above the Delta) was only an oasis in the desert, seldom ten miles broad, and on the average about half of that, an extremely narrow green ribbon stretched across a surface of sand and rock, with a silver thread (of Nile) running along the middle of its length. That, in a boundless desert! In fertile Goshen the great population must have been close packed. Palestine, though not much larger than Wales, was in David's time capable of accommodating some five millions, in great happiness of plenty (1 Kings 4 : 20, 25).

10. Come now therefore, and I will send thee unto Pharaoh, that thou mayest bring forth my people the children of Israel out of Egypt.
11. And Moses said unto God, Who am I, that I should go unto Pharaoh, and that I should bring forth the children of Israel out of Egypt?
12. And he said, Certainly I will be with thee; and this shall be the token unto thee, that I have sent thee: when thou hast brought forth the people out of Egypt, ye shall serve God upon this mountain.

The *ideal* Canaan, the land of promise (Gen. 15 : 18–20), appears to have extended (Ps. 72) far beyond to the Euphrates. And in Israel's realization, the failure was in respect of moral conditions on their part. It was ungodliness that made Canaan, not too narrow for them, but too hot. . . . As to those mentioned here we note: (1) *Canaanites* may be a general description, as we would say ' Palestinians '; specifically, *the* Canaanites were situated in the lowlands of the Jordan valley and the Mediterranean coast. (2) *Hittites* (of Heth), toward the north. In the monumental history of Egypt, there appears before this time a strong Hittite power (empire or confederation), in that North Syria, with which Pharaoh goes to war. (3) *Amorites*, mountaineers on both sides of the Jordan. (4) *Perizzites*, scattered up and down, in little detached settlements, perhaps more or less nomadic (such is the condition of Maoris in the Middle Island of New Zealand). (5) *Hivites*, to the north-east, wealthy and unwarlike. (6) *Jebusites* retained their stronghold (which became Jerusalem) till it was taken by storm in David's time: as long after the exodus as we are from Bannockburn! That first wrestling (Eph. 6 : 10, etc.) with heathenism for the good land was thus arduously protracted." — *James MacGregor*. 10. **Come now therefore, and I will send thee unto Pharaoh, that thou mayest bring forth my people the children of Israel out of Egypt.** " If God has Himself come down to do the work of redemption, what need of Moses? Would not a word from those Almighty lips be enough? Why summon a shepherd, a lonely and unbefriended man, a man who has already failed once, and from whom the passing years have stolen his manhood's prime, to work out with painful elaboration, and through a series of bewildering disappointments, the purposed emancipation? But this is not an isolated case. Throughout the entire scheme of divine government, we meet with the principle of mediation. God ever speaks to men, and works for them, through the instrumentality of men." — *F. B. Meyer*.

6. Moses' Consciousness of Inability for Such a Task, v. 11. 11. **And Moses said unto God, Who am I, that I should go unto Pharaoh, and that I should bring forth the children of Israel out of Egypt?** " The men most fit for great missions are apt to deem themselves unfit. When God called Jeremiah to be a prophet, his reply was ' O Lord! behold, I cannot speak, for I am a child ' (Jer. 1 : 6). St. Ambrose fought hard to escape being made Archbishop of Milan. Augustine was loathe to undertake the mission to England. Anselm was with difficulty persuaded to accept the headship of our Church in the evil days of Rufus. The first impression of the fit man selected for a high post generally is, ' Who am I? ' In Moses' case, though there were some manifest grounds of fitness, *e.g.*, his Egyptian training and learning, his familiarity with the court, his knowledge of both nations and both languages — yet on the other hand, there were certain very marked (apparent) disqualifications. Forty years of exile and of a shepherd's life had at once unfitted him for dealing with a court and made him a stranger to his brethren. Want of eloquence seemed to be a fatal defect in one who must work mainly by persuasion. Even his age of eighty might well have seemed to him unsuitable." — *George Rawlinson*. " Preachers, teachers, emancipators, and all ministers of good, should see their work to be infinitely greater than themselves, if they would work at the highest point of energy. Let a man suppose his work to be easy, to be beneath him, to be unworthy of his talents, and he will work flippantly, without taxing his strength or making any drain upon the life of his heart. He will not be a worker; at best he will be but a fussy idler in the great field overgrown with the weeds and tares sown by the power of evil." — *Joseph Parker*.

7. The Promise of God to Be with Him, v. 12. 12. **And he said, Certainly I will be with thee; and this shall be the token unto thee, that I have sent thee: when thou hast brought forth the people out of Egypt, ye shall serve God upon this mountain.** " On one occasion, when a crowded audience had assembled to hear Paganini play, the great violinist, to the dismay of those who had paid great prices for their

seats, deliberately broke all the strings of his instrument save one; and then triumphantly holding up the violin before the people, cried, 'One string and Paganini!' Ah, what cannot God do, when He obtains entire possession and control of one nature, wholly yielded to Him? There are no limits, except those imposed by our unbelief." — *F. B. Meyer.* "The word here for *I will be* (*ehyeh*) is that from which the great Name in verse 14 is formed. . . . At the outset, the fixing of that future meeting place would serve to give confidence to Moses, by showing a resolute clear purpose on the part of God, His trumpet blowing no uncertain sound. And especially, in the end, the actual meeting is predicted, evincing a miracle of foresight (cf. John 2 : 6), which would be a definitive evidence of the divinity of this revelation." — *James Macgregor.* God never asks any of us to undertake a great task until He Himself has first determined that this work must be done, that the hour is ripe for its accomplishment, and at the same time, that He will supply the strength, the wisdom, the guidance, and if need be, the miraculous intervention for the glorious achievement of that which He undertakes. Moses wanted to do this kind of work forty years before, but the hour had not come for such a deliverance. We often may want to do that which God wishes to be done before the hour that God has appointed for the doing of it. In the desire we are at one with God; we must watch that the execution of the desire is also at the time God has set. "It is a most pitiful thing that a man should read of Moses being divinely called to certain service, and forget that he himself is also a subject of the divine government. If God called one man to special work, we are entitled to reason upon the basis of that fact that God has a special work for every man to do. It is in our power to turn such miracles into gracious commonplaces by seeking for their repetition in our own lives. It is impossible that God has called us into existence without having some purpose for us to work at within the limit of time. To be here at all is to be in possession of a destiny." — *Joseph Parker.*

NOTE. We are now brought to the hour when Moses will begin his great life work, the mighty deliverance by the power of God of an entire nation from the oppression of the Egyptian bondage. Moses was divinely prepared for such an undertaking in the following ways: (1) By being born in a home of faith, where no doubt he was taught the covenant God had made with his ancestors, Abraham, Isaac, and Jacob; (2) by being educated in all the learning of the Egyptians, and made intimately acquainted with the court life of this great empire; (3) by having within him a burning passion to see his people delivered from the brutal bondage which was making their lives such a curse; (4) by forty years of quiet life away from the noise, the tumult, the pettiness of official life, the temptations of the Egyptian court, where he could grow strong in body, with outdoor occupations, and strong in mind and soul in long periods of communion with God; (5) by a miraculous, divine call to a specific work, a call, the reality of which he could not deny; (6) by a promise of God's abiding presence and strength.

How many different manifestations of God's overruling do you discover in this lesson as related to the life of Moses? What do you think are some of the leading characteristics of Moses as a man as revealed in this lesson? What was a dangerous characteristic which God, during long years of training, had to subdue in Moses' life? (We refer to his natural instinct for hasty action.) In how many ways is the wisdom and the grace and the knowledge of God revealed in our lesson? What would have happened if Moses had not turned aside to see the burning bush that was not consumed? In what way would you say that this hour was not only the one hour when God was ready to begin a great movement, but was simultaneously the perfect hour in Moses' life when he was equipped for beginning such a task?

LESSON III. — July 18.

GOD ENCOURAGES MOSES. — Exodus 3 : 13—4 : 31.

PRINTED TEXT, Exodus 3 : 13-16; 4 : 10-17.

GOLDEN TEXT. — ***Certainly I will be with thee.*** EXODUS 3 : 12.

Devotional Reading: Psalm 121.
Beginner Topic: BROTHER AARON.
Lesson Material: Exodus 4.
Memory Verse: The Lord is my helper. Hebrews 13 : 6.

Primary Topic: MOSES' HELPER.
Lesson Material: Exodus 3 : 13—4 : 31.
Memory Verse: The Lord is my helper; I will not fear. Hebrews 13 : 6.
Junior Topic: THE HELPER GOD GAVE MOSES.
Lesson Material: Exodus 3 : 13—4 : 31.
Memory Verse: I will trust, and will not be afraid: for Jehovah, even Jehovah, is my strength and song. Isaiah 12 : 2.
Intermediate and Senior Topic: OUR EXCUSES.
Topic for Young People and Adults: OUR CHIEF SOURCE OF ENCOURAGEMENT.

THE TEACHER AND HIS CLASS.

The Younger Classes may be introduced to this lesson by the following illustration. Two men in talking arrange for a certain future hour, when one man will send to the other man, by a trusted messenger, for a very large sum of money. Unknown to anyone else, they cut in two a strip of linen, with a peculiar zigzag edge. One keeps one piece, and the other the other. When the hour comes for this messenger to go for the large sum of money, he carries one piece of linen with him, and when he arrives at his destination, the man, before turning over the money, asks to see his credentials. He takes out of his pocket this strip of linen. The man with the money takes out his, and if they match perfectly, he knows this man comes with authority. So in a much greater way, in a way involving miracles, God gives to Moses adequate credentials for proving to Israel that he is sent of God.

The Older Classes will find here a lesson in divine equipment. God has many tasks for us to do. God commissions many men to do different things in His name, but as He did not send Moses without sufficient promise of His help, without equipment, and without credentials, so He will never send us on *any* errand, but, at the same time, He will provide fully for all those things which we will need in the execution of this commission.

THE PLAN OF THE LESSON.

SUBJECT: God's Perfect Equipment of His Servant on the Threshold of the Servant's Undertaking a Great and Divinely-Designated Task.

I. GOD PREPARES AND STRENGTHENS MOSES FOR HIS GREAT TASK, Exodus 3 : 13–22.

1. By a new revelation of His name, vs. 13, 14.
2. By a definite, comprehensive commission, vs. 15–17.
3. By forewarning him of the opposition he must expect from Pharaoh, vs. 18–22.

II. MOSES IS PROVIDED WITH CREDENTIALS TO CONVINCE UNBELIEVING ISRAEL GOD HAS SENT HIM, Exodus 4 : 1–9.

1. The rod that became a serpent, vs. 1–5.
2. The leprous hand, vs. 6–8.
3. The water turned to blood, v. 9.

III. GOD'S TWOFOLD ANSWER TO MOSES' PLEAS THAT HE IS NOT ELOQUENT, Exodus 4 : 10–17.

1. God assures him He will teach him what to say, vs. 10–12.
2. Aaron is appointed spokesman for Moses, vs. 13–17.

IV. MOSES RETURNS TO EGYPT, Exodus 4 : 18–31.

1. He obtains permission from Jethro, v. 18.
2. God reaffirms His commission to Moses, vs. 19–23.
3. Moses is circumcised, vs. 24–26.
4. He is met by Aaron, vs. 27, 28.
5. The elders of Israel are brought together, vs. 29–31.

THE LESSON IN ITS SETTING.

Time. — 1446–1445 B.C.

Place. — The call to Moses occurred near Mount Sinai (or Mount Horeb).

THE TEACHER'S LIBRARY.

In addition to commentaries on the book of Exodus, and the standard lives of Moses, lists of which will be found in the bibliography in the Introduction to this volume, there really is not much valuable material. On 3 : 13, 14, see Charles Kingsley: *The Gospel of the Pentateuch*, 118–131; James Hastings: *Great Texts of the Bible, Genesis to Numbers*, 276–288; and a long article on the name of God here revealed, by Samuel Cox in *The Expositor*, Vol. 1, 12–24; on "I Am That I Am," Andrew Jukes: *The Names of God in Holy Scripture*, 40–58; A. C. Gaebelein: *The Lord of Glory*, 8–12; Abraham Kuyper: *"Keep Thy Solemn Feasts,"* 261–271; on 4 : 10–12, W. L. Watkinson: *The Conditions of Conversion*, 28–42; and the same: *The Furnace of Trial*, 22–38.

INTRODUCTORY.

As far as the editor remembers, the call of Moses is recorded with greater detail than the call of any other one character in either the Old or the New Testaments. The call of Abraham was recorded with brevity; the call of most of the prophets is given with extreme brevity; the call of David, of course, is given with some detail,

EXODUS 3 : 13. And Moses said unto God, Behold, when I come unto the children of Israel, and shall say unto them, The God of your fathers hath sent me unto you; and they shall say to me, What is his name? what shall I say unto them?

14. And God said unto Moses, I AM THAT I AM: and he said, Thus shalt thou say unto the children of Israel, I AM hath sent me unto you.

---

but there were not many, what we would call *momentous* things, involved in the call of the shepherd boy. Much more space is given to the call of Moses than, say, to the call of the Apostle Paul. The reason for this extended account, and for the long dialogue between Moses and God is no doubt the tremendous importance of the work which Moses was about to do. A brief word from God would be sufficient for directing a man to a small task, but when a man must face the difficulties, problems, and antagonisms that Moses would be compelled to face, when he must endure the murmuring of this vast multitude of people for forty years, when the welfare of two or three million people are involved in what he does, when he must contend against the power of the whole Egyptian empire (and, no doubt, demon powers besides), then it is very necessary for him to come to profound convictions, from which he will never be moved, to have an experience with God which he can never forget, and to receive an assurance from God that will stand him in stead for the weary days of trial that lie ahead.

I. **GOD PREPARES AND STRENGTHENS MOSES FOR HIS GREAT TASK,** 3 : 13–22.

1. BY A NEW REVELATION OF HIS NAME, VS. 13, 14. 13. **And Moses said unto God, Behold, when I come unto the children of Israel, and shall say unto them, The God of your fathers hath sent me unto you; and they shall say to me, What is his name? what shall I say unto them?** 14. **And God said unto Moses, I AM THAT I AM: and he said, Thus shalt thou say unto the children of Israel, I AM hath sent me unto you.** By one's *name* the Scriptures generally mean, when a name is emphasized, one's character, one's person. When we are told to pray to God in the name of Christ, it means the person of Christ, the character of Christ, for which His name stands. Thus, for instance, Christ is the Lamb of God, but that is more than a name, it is an indication of His sacrificial work. So when Moses asks God for a special revelation of His name, that he might assure the Israelites he had come to them under a divine commission, God told him that His name was I AM THAT I AM. "Now the word here translated "I AM" is in Hebrew the word EHJEH, and forms one of the most important titles for God in the entire Bible. The word here is only in consonants, the vowels have to be added. What those vowels were no one really knows. It is, however, suggested that the word should be pronounced *Jehovah.* The Hebrew people never pronounced this word, but when they came to it they used another word, *Adonai,* meaning, *Lord.* The verb when applied to the Eternal means no absolute beginning, or essential change of being. "The use of the first person is a plain indication that the name is intended not merely to distinguish an individual, but to express a sentiment that will animate the people with hope and resolution. Such a form is strictly appropriate only in the mouth of the speaker: and, accordingly, it is not afterwards employed as a name of God. Moses was now, therefore, armed with a name of potent significance by which to designate Him by whose authority he was to approach the people. He could say, He in whose name I come is about to realize the promise of the land of Canaan made to the seed of Abraham; and He has deigned to embody this fact in a significant name, indicating His present adherence to His covenant with your fathers." — *James G. Murphy.* Dr. F. B. Meyer has a most wonderful chapter on this name, from which we take the following sentences: "The significance of this word is so deep, that as the margin indicates, no one rendering can convey all its connotation. The first element in it is *the personality of God.* Mark that sublime egoism, 'I am.' There cannot be less in the Creator than we discover in the creature. . . . The next element in this sublime name is THE ETERNITY OR UNCHANGEABLENESS OF GOD. 'I AM.' The Eternal is not primarily the ever-enduring or everlasting; but that which is independent of time, which is not measured by the flight of years, which is unregistered by the revolutions of the earth, or unaffected by the sweep of systems through vast cycles around some central sun. There is no *was* or *will be* with Him, but always the present tense. All that He was to the fathers, He is today; and all

15. And God said moreover unto Moses, Thus shalt thou say unto the children of Israel, Jehovah, the God of your fathers, the God of Abraham, the God of Isaac, and the God of Jacob, hath sent me unto you: this is my name for ever, and this is my memorial unto all generations.

16. Go, and gather the elders of Israel together, and say unto them, Jehovah, the God of your fathers, the God of Abraham, of Isaac, and of Jacob, hath appeared unto me, saying, I have surely visited you, and *seen* that which is done to you in Egypt:

---

that He will be to their children, He is now. Nothing to learn; nothing to acquire; nothing to become. He alone is Reality, as contrasted with the vanities of heathen deities."

2. BY A DEFINITE, COMPREHENSIVE COMMISSION, VS. 15–17. 15. **And God said moreover unto Moses, Thus shalt thou say unto the children of Israel, Jehovah, the God of your fathers, the God of Abraham, the God of Isaac, and the God of Jacob, hath sent me unto you: this is my name for ever, and this is my memorial unto all generations.** "This statement contains a very important truth — a truth which many professing Christians seem to forget, namely, that God's relationship with Israel is an eternal one. He does not say, 'This is my name for a time, so long as they continue what they ought to be.' No; 'this is my name *forever*, and this is my memorial unto *all generations*.' Let my reader ponder this. 'God hath not cast away his people which he foreknew' (Rom. 11 : 2). They are His people still, whether obedient or disobedient, united together, or scattered abroad; manifested to the nations, or hidden from their view. They are His people still, and He is their God. Exodus 3 : 15 is unanswerable. Let us beware how we tamper with this weighty word *forever*. If we say it does not mean forever when applied to Israel, what proof have we that it means forever when applied to us? God means what He says; and He will ere long make manifest to all the nations of the earth, that His connection with Israel is one which shall outlive all the revolutions of time." — *C. H. Mackintosh.* 16. **Go, and gather the elders of Israel together, and say unto them, Jehovah, the God of your fathers, the God of Abraham, of Isaac, and of Jacob, hath appeared unto me, saying, I have surely visited you, and *seen* that which is done to you in Egypt.** "Officers of this class were common to all mankind in primeval times. We have already met with them in Egypt (Gen. 50 : 7). We here find them established in Israel antecedent to the legislation of Moses. Their name is derived from the quality of age, which confers experience and claims authority. They were perpetuated through all the variations of the commonwealth of Israel, and descended from them to the Christian Church, in which they still maintain their place." — *James G. Murphy.* Here is a definite promise on the part of God that He will surely deliver His people out of the affliction of Egypt, and will bring them "into a land flowing with milk and honey." God never takes us out of the place which He has told us to leave but that He brings us into a place of greater beauty, and blessing, and fullness, than that which we are to part with. Satan leads us out of a garden into a wilderness; out of plenty into want; out of liberty into bondage. God brings us back from the wilderness into a garden; out of the dark into the light; out of bondage into liberty.

3. BY FOREWARNING HIM OF THE OPPOSITION HE MUST EXPECT FROM PHARAOH, VS. 18–22. God is omniscient; He foresees all events, He knows all forces, even the most secret and inner forces that bring events to pass. So He forewarns Moses that, when he shall ask Pharaoh to allow the Israelites to go for three days' journeying into the wilderness to sacrifice to the Lord, Pharaoh would not let them go, until God had smitten Egypt in such a way that they would recognize Him to be omnipotent, and would be glad to release the Hebrew people from their midst. We should remember, as Chadwick points out, that this demand for a furlough of three days was not an insincere or tricky demand, by which they planned to permanently depart from Egypt under the subterfuge of getting away for a brief period simply to sacrifice. "It only would have been insincere if consent were expected and if the intention were thereupon to abuse the permission and refuse to return. There is not the slightest hint of any duplicity of the kind. The real motives for the demand are very plain." — *G. H. Chadwick.* The closing verse of this chapter has been a stumblingblock to many, and it needs our careful attention. In the Authorized

Version, it reads, " Every woman shall borrow of her neighbor," but in the Version which we are using the passage reads, " Every woman shall ask of her neighbor, etc." Professor Macgregor's remarks here are excellent: " The Hebrew word (*shaal*) is elsewhere (*e.g.* Ps. 2 : 8) rendered simply *ask*, or request. It is nowhere else made *borrow*. One can ask a loan, or he can ask a free gift. But in this text there is nothing about either loan or gift. What is here is simply the asking. The word for *spoil* here (*natzal*) has not the meaning of purloining or thieving. Its ordinary meaning is robbing, taking another's property by violence. Such a word is sometimes employed to describe the *effect* of robbery, in leaving bareness or emptiness behind. One who fears he is accepting too much of what is pressed upon him says, ' I am robbing you.' The Israelites were to obtain the Egyptian wealth for the asking. The meaning is, what had been promised to Abraham, that they would leave Egypt ' with great substance ' (Gen. 15 : 14); also that as to the style or manner of thus leaving, not poverty-stricken but wealthy, it was not to be that of men stealing with booty, but that of an army, victorious and glorious. That they were fairly entitled to what they carried away, having worked for it in Egypt, is not to the point. Their having wrought for it did not entitle them to take it dishonestly."

II. **MOSES IS PROVIDED WITH CREDENTIALS TO CONVINCE UNBELIEVING ISRAEL THAT GOD HAS SENT HIM,** 4 : 1–9. First, Moses asked God for a revelation of His name, by which he could assure the stubborn, hard-hearted Israelites that he had been divinely commissioned to undertake bringing them out of Egypt. After this extended, and, no doubt, strengthening commission from God, Moses was not yet fully persuaded in his own heart that his mission would be successful, so he asks God what he should do when the people would say that the Lord had not appeared to him. The credentials which God put in his hand were three, and all of a miraculous nature. They were specifically given to Moses. We are not to assume that they should be expected by any one else, unless also specifically given by God to some one else. They belong to Moses, and they do not belong to us. Nevertheless, they are worthy of careful study.

1. The Rod That Became a Serpent, vs. 1–5. The Lord asked Moses what he had in his hand, and, being told a rod, He told him to cast it down on the ground and let it become a serpent. Then the Lord told him to put forth his hand and take it by the tail, and it became a rod again in his hand. " The etymology of the word *rod* employed seems to point to an ordinary staff, or walking-stick. Egyptians of rank usually carried long batons. Probably the rod was a common staff, such as a shepherd of eighty years old might need for a support." — *George Rawlinson.* F. B. Meyer's words here are, as usual, so appropriate. " Every life has some capacity. God says to each of us, ' What is that in thine hand? ' He takes it for granted that there is something there. To every one of us is given grace, according to the measure of the gift of God; and perhaps the hardest lesson that any one can learn, is to believe that every gift from heaven is of equal intrinsic worth. Our success is to be measured, not by the character of the capacity, but by its realization and full use. God always begins by using what we have in hand. Page after page of God's Word reveals that there is a chance for true usefulness, in the consecrated employment of whatever we have already in possession."

2. The Leprous Hand, vs. 6–8. Again, the Lord told Moses to put his hand into his bosom, and when he did, behold, it came out leprous, white as snow. Then, at God's command, putting his hand back into his bosom again, and taking it out, he found it completely healed of this awful disease. " Here, as in the series of plagues, there is a progression in the greatness of the work. Leprosy was the most terrible disease known to Israel. The first miracle shows the chastening hand of God; the second shows His restoring mercy." — *James Macgregor.* Note especially the word *sign*, in verse 8. " The Hebrew word thus translated is entirely different from that rendered *wonder*. A *wonder* is marvellous and terrific. It represents the startling and awful (see 34 : 10). But ' a sign ' is rather the revelation in our ordinary life of some characteristic of the divine nature or work. It is a symbol of the Unseen. In the *wonder* there is a predominance of the divine power and majesty; in the *sign*, of the divine truth and grace. The one is terrible, the other tender." — *F. B. Meyer.*

3. The Water Turned to Blood, v. 9. Finally, the Lord said if they would not believe these two signs, nor hearken unto the voice of Moses, he should take some of the water of the river and pour it out upon the dry land, and the water on that particular occasion would become blood. " The Nile was venerated as a divinity, under the name of Hapi — cognate, if not identical, with Apis. Its waters were therefore regarded as sacred, and highly esteemed as salubrious to the drinker and

EXODUS 4 : 10. And Moses said unto Jehovah, Oh, Lord, I am not eloquent, neither heretofore, nor since thou hast spoken unto thy servant; for
I am slow of speech, and of a slow tongue.
11. And Jehovah said unto him, Who hath made man's mouth? or
who maketh *a man* dumb, or deaf, or seeing, or blind? is it not I,
Jehovah?
12. Now therefore go, and I will be with thy mouth, and teach thee what
thou shalt speak.
13. And he said, Oh, Lord, send, I pray thee, by the hand of him whom
thou wilt send.

---

fertilizing to the soil. To change these waters into blood shed on the ground is to turn the stream of life into a pool of death. It speaks of disaster and death to Egypt and its gods. He that has power over the deified Nile may defy all the might of Pharaoh. He is accredited as the minister of God, called to his office, qualified for his holy task, and armed with miraculous powers for the discomfiture of Egypt by the Lord, the most high God, founder of heaven and earth." — *James G. Murphy.*

III. **GOD'S TWOFOLD ANSWER TO MOSES' PLEA THAT HE IS NOT ELOQUENT,** 4 : 10–17. Even yet Moses is not fully convinced he is the one to undertake this task. In fact, he seems to increasingly shrink from it. So this time he brings up as an obstacle, not the stubbornness of Israel, but his own poor, personal equipment, especially emphasizing the fact that he was not eloquent of speech. 10. **And Moses said unto Jehovah, Oh, Lord, I am not eloquent, neither heretofore, nor since thou hast spoken unto thy servant; for I am slow of speech, and of a slow tongue.** 11. **And Jehovah said unto him, Who hath made man's mouth? or who maketh *a man* dumb, or deaf, or seeing, or blind? is it not I, Jehovah?** 12. **Now therefore go, and I will be with thy mouth, and teach thee what thou shalt speak.** " The expressions used by Moses himself — 'not a man of words,' 'slow of speech,' 'of a slow tongue,' 'of uncircumcised lips' — seem rather to indicate mere unreadiness, want of an easy flow of words; an inability like that of Cromwell rather than like that of Demosthenes — not a stammer, or a stutter, or a lisp, or a difficulty in the pronunciation of any letter, but a slowness to find appropriate words for the expression of his thoughts, a want of facility in the use of the weapon of speech. Such a defect is not unusual in those who ultimately become great speakers; it belonged to Luther, to John Knox, perhaps even to Paul, whose early efforts at preaching were, according to his detractors (2 Cor. 10 : 10), 'contemptible.' " — *George Rawlinson.* Joseph Parker's words here are for all of us. " The work had nothing whatever to do with the eloquence or ineloquence of Moses. It was not to be measured or determined by his personal gifts. The moment, therefore, that he turned to his individual talents, he lost sight of the great end which he was called instrumentally to accomplish. How sublime is the rebuke of God! Cannot the Maker of man's mouth touch with eloquence the lips which He has fashioned? . . . How inventive we are in finding excuses for not doing the will of God! . . . It should be our supreme delight to find reasons for co-operating with God, and to fortify ourselves by such interpretations of circumstances as will plainly show us that we are in the right battle, fighting on the right side, and wielding the right weapon." 13. **And he said, Oh, Lord, send, I pray thee, by the hand of him whom thou wilt send.** " This," says Professor Rawlinson, " is a curt, impatient, and scarcely reverent speech. Moses means that he will undertake the task if God

The Nile God.

Egypt was the gift of the Nile, the life-giving and fertilizing river.

14. And the anger of Jehovah was kindled against Moses, and he said, Is there not Aaron thy brother the Levite? I know that he can speak well. And also, behold, he cometh forth to meet thee: and when he seeth thee, he will be glad in his heart.

15. And thou shalt speak unto him, and put the words in his mouth: and I will be with thy mouth, and with his mouth, and will teach you what ye shall do.

16. And he shall be thy spokesman unto the people; and it shall come to pass, that he shall be to thee a mouth, and thou shalt be to him as God.

17. And thou shalt take in thy hand this rod, wherewith thou shalt do the signs.

---

insists; but that God would do far better to send another. Hence the 'anger of the Lord' against him which led to Aaron's association with him as joint leader of the people." 14. **And the anger of Jehovah was kindled against Moses, and he said, Is there not Aaron thy brother the Levite? I know that he can speak well. And also, behold, he cometh forth to meet thee: and when he seeth thee, he will be glad in his heart.** 15. **And thou shalt speak unto him, and put the words in his mouth: and I will be with thy mouth, and with his mouth, and will teach you what ye shall do.** 16. **And he shall be thy spokesman unto the people; and it shall come to pass, that he shall be to thee a mouth, and thou shalt be to him as God.** 17. **And thou shalt take in thy hand this rod, wherewith thou shalt do the signs.** "The word here translated *anger* is the Scripture phrase appropriate for description of God's feeling toward idolatry (Exod. 25). Perhaps Moses here betrays an inward fear of Egypt's heathenism, as well as lack of frank ardor or readiness for battle with it. Aaron is here mentioned for the first time. Three years older than Moses (Exod. 7 : 7), he seems to have been all this time in good standing in Egypt. In Aaron we never see real greatness; in Moses when once he is under way, we never see littleness." — *James Macgregor.* No one has written quite so refreshingly on this portion of Scripture as Dr. F. B. Meyer. "Well indeed is it when the soul cries with the great apostle: 'We are not sufficient of ourselves to think anything as of ourselves.' But we must beware, for there is a hidden line over which self-distrust may not pass, lest it become unbelief. Cherish the lowliest thought you choose of yourself, but unite it with the loftiest conception of God's all-sufficiency. Self-depreciation may lead to the marring of a useful life. We must think soberly of ourselves, not too lowly, as not too extravagantly. The one talent must not be buried in the earth."

IV. MOSES RETURNS TO EGYPT, 4 : 18–31.

1. HE OBTAINS PERMISSION FROM JETHRO, v. 18. "When Moses married Zipporah, he was probably adopted into the tribe of which Reuel, and after him, Jethro, was the head. . . . Jethro's character is altogether one of which kindness and peacefulness are the main elements. If he be identified with Reuel, the pleasing picture drawn in 2 : 18–21 will furnish traits towards his portraiture. Even without this, the present passage and the notice in chapter 18 sufficiently delineate him. He is a sort of second Melchizedek, both priest and king, a worshiper of the true God, and one in whose presence both Moses and Aaron are content to play a secondary part (18 : 9, 12). But he never asserts himself; he is always kind, gentle, acquiescent, helpful. His words are simply, 'Go in peace.' He consents, and does not mar the grace of his act by any show of reluctance. He lets Moses take his wife and children. He afterwards receives them back, and protects them (18 : 2); and finally, when his protection is no more needed, he restores them to their natural guardian, by a spontaneous act, as it would seem." — *George Rawlinson.*

2. GOD REAFFIRMS HIS COMMISSION TO MOSES, vs. 19–23. It would seem as though in every step of the way at this time in Moses' life, he needed reassurance from God that he *cannot* turn back and fail to achieve the great task which God now was ready to have accomplished. So the Lord spoke to him once again, telling him not to hesitate to go back to Egypt, for all the men were dead who had sought his life. Moses, when he went down to Egypt, should do all those things which the Lord had told him to do and not just simply to arrive there as the place to which God had sent him, but also to do that for which he was sent. There is in verse 21

here, a phrase which has greatly troubled many people: " I will harden his heart." " It is somewhat remarkable that the hardening of Pharaoh's heart is ascribed in this history ten times to God, and that in an equal number of passages it is affirmed that Pharaoh hardened his own heart. It is to be noted, also, that up till the sixth plague it is always said that Pharaoh hardened his own heart, and that it is only after that we read, as a matter of history, that the Lord hardened it. In the outset of this contest, and on till the fifth plague, Pharaoh, in the exercise of his free agency, resisted God's demand. This repeated resistance had in itself a hardening influence, so that each time he rejected the demand of Jehovah his heart was left more indurated than it had been before. But at length he passed the boundary of God's forbearance, and, as a judicial punishment upon him, that which had been, up till this point, the natural consequence of his conduct, was confirmed by the decree of God, who gave him over ' to a reprobate mind to do those things which are not convenient.' At first, the hardening was Pharaoh's own act; later, its increase was the fruit of his repeated resistance; and then, last of all, it was the punitive infliction of Jehovah." — *William M. Taylor.* Though Aaron was appointed to be the spokesman of Moses, God does not turn to Aaron, setting him in Moses' place, but he actually gives to Moses in this place the very words he should say to Pharaoh. It was Moses who was always the leader.

3. Moses Is Circumcised, vs. 24–26. This is, indeed, a very strange portion of Scripture. " It appears that his youngest son had not been circumcised through some unexplained fault of Moses. The neglect of the divinely appointed sign of the covenant of peace with God was a serious delinquency, especially in him who was to be the leader and lawgiver of the holy people. It was meet that the austere perfection of the divine holiness should be made known to Moses. It was necessary at this stage of his experience that he should learn that God is in earnest when He speaks, and will assuredly perform all that He has threatened. Hence the Lord sought to kill him, probably by some disease or sudden stroke, which threatened immediate death. It is probable from her spontaneous promptitude that Zipporah was in some way the cause of the delay in circumcising the child. The *sharp stone* was a stone or flint knife, such as was used afterwards by Joshua in circumcising the children of Israel on their entrance into the land of Canaan (Josh. 5 : 2). . . . The Lord, who sought to put him to death, remitted the penalty now that the neglected duty was performed. *Because of the circumcision* explains her accosting Moses as a spouse of blood, as it was to save him from death that she was constrained to do herself the masculine part of circumcising her child. This was a salutary and seasonable lesson to Zipporah as well as to Moses. The occurrence probably took place on the first night of their journey, as they had not reached the mount of God (v. 27). The child was now unfit for travel, and it was easy for the mother to return with the two children to her father. It is most likely, therefore, that this was the point from which she was sent home by her husband (18 : 2), in order to avoid the dangers and inconveniences which she was willing to brave on his account, had not this providential interposition ordered it otherwise." — *J. G. Murphy.*

4. He Is Met by Aaron, vs. 27, 28. " The third incident of his journey was his meeting with his brother Aaron, whom God had directed where to find him. No doubt, after their affectionate salutation, they asked each other of their welfare, and each would have much to say to the other of the incidents of those forty years in Egypt and in Midian. But the hearts of both were heavy for their enslaved kinsmen, and the younger brother did not care to record anything of their interview but this: ' Moses told Aaron all the words of the Lord who had sent him, and all the signs which he had commanded him.' That was enough for Aaron. He makes no objection and interposes no delay. So, together, they go to Goshen and there assemble the elders of Israel." — *William M. Taylor.*

5. The Elders of Israel Are Brought Together, vs. 29–31. " The Israelites in Egypt, though suffering under severe oppression, had an organization of their own, jurisdiction attaching probably to the heads of tribes, or of chief families (cf. Num. 1 : 4–16). These persons are here called ' elders,' which the Septuagint renders ' the senate.' Moses and Aaron could have no power to convoke them; but they invited them to a conference, and the elders came. . . . The narrative is very much compressed. The elders heard the words, and saw the signs first. Then they must have summoned an assembly of the people, after working hours, and the people must have been addressed and shown the signs. The effect was to convince them also, and to induce them to accept Moses and Aaron for the national leaders." — *George Rawlinson.*

OUR FELLOWSHIP WITH GOD IN HIS GREAT PURPOSES FOR MEN.

" There was a sense in which God was alone responsible for the redemption of His people and their creation into a nation; but it was also certain that He could not do it apart from Moses. Browning says: ' If any two hearts shall grow into one, they will do more than the world has done.' If this is true as between man and man, how much more between man and God; and how truly the might of that union was manifested in the life work of the man of God! To such a fellowship we are called. It may be that at the beginning of our life we made some egregious blunder, which has cast its shadow on our whole after-career. We also slew our Egyptian and hid him in the sand, but the slow-moving years which have succeeded have altered a great many things in us. We are less confident and boastful, more humble and dependent. The desert solitudes and silences have wrought their last effect on your character. Reluctant you may be, but you are not rebellious, neither do you turn yourself backward. Faithful in a few things, you are now to rule over many, and to enter into the joy of your Lord, which is surely found in the inner secrets of fellowship." — *F. B. Meyer.*

Dr. F. B. Meyer mentions seven different disqualifications which Moses at different times in this lesson suggested — can you discover these seven? How do you account for the fact that forty years before this Moses was so confident of his own ability to redeem the afflicted Israelites from their bondage in Egypt, whereas now, he manifests a very marked timidity? In how many different ways in this lesson do we find God equipping Moses for the work of bringing Israel out of Egypt? What natural qualifications did Moses have for this work, which led God to specifically designate him as the leader in this vast undertaking? What does God here say about Himself that is as true for us in our service to God as for Moses in his service to God? What was the fundamental reason for God telling Moses beforehand of the strong opposition which he would have from Pharaoh?

LESSON IV. — July 25.

BIBLE TEACHINGS ON THE COST OF DRINKING. — Deuteronomy 21 : 18–21; Proverbs 23 : 20, 21; 1 Corinthians 6 : 9–11.

GOLDEN TEXT. — ***Know ye not that the unrighteous shall not inherit the kingdom of God?*** 1 CORINTHIANS 6 : 9.

Devotional Reading: Psalm 37 : 1–11.
Beginner Topic: FOUR BOYS AWAY FROM HOME.
  Lesson Material: Deuteronomy 21 : 18–21; Daniel 1.
  Memory Verse: Children, obey your parents. Colossians 3 : 20.
Primary Topic: PAUL'S HAPPY DAY.
  Lesson Material: 1 Corinthians 6 : 9–11; Acts 9 : 1–9.
  Memory Verse: For Thou, Lord, art good, and ready to forgive. Psalm 86 : 5.
Junior Topic: THE CHANGE IN SAUL.
  Lesson Material: 1 Corinthians 6 : 9–11; Acts 9 : 1–9.
  Memory Verse: Believe on the Lord Jesus, and thou shalt be saved. Acts 16 : 31.
Intermediate and Senior Topic: WHAT THE DRINK HABIT COSTS.
Topic for Young People and Adults: WHAT THE DRINK HABIT COSTS.

THE TEACHER AND HIS CLASS.

The Younger Classes may be reminded that on every railroad there are, along the track, suspended over it, or lifted high along the side, signal lights, controlled by those who know where each train is, and the condition of the track in the particular area where the lights which he controls are stationed. These lights may be red or green, and it is the absolute duty of the engineer to stop his train before he passes a red light, just as he knows he is allowed to continue his flying journey when the signal lights are green. He does not have to know *why* a red light is before him, but he does know that that red light means to *stop*. The Word of God has many passages that may be called red signal lights, warnings about proceeding along some road over which one may be swiftly traveling. Sometimes the Word of God explains why the light is red; sometimes a mere commandment is given. Whether the explanation is offered to us or not, we ignorant mortals will act wisely if we strictly heed the warning signals of an omniscient God, who created us in His image.

The Older Classes recognize that the Word of God is the word of life, and is concerned for man's welfare. The God who inspired the prophets, whose Son Christ is, whose Spirit was sent to the apostles to give us this Book, is a God of love, and a God of wisdom, who desires men to have the fullest, richest, most abounding life possible. The laws of the Word of God are not to shrivel man's life, and confine him, as it were, to a moral prison, but to enlarge and enrich his life, to give him true liberty in the years when he is on earth. So let us take the warnings of our lesson as those which proceed from the heart of God in love for us.

THE LESSON IN ITS SETTING.

Time. — The final instructions of Moses were given in 1405 B.C.; the Book of Proverbs was written probably about 1000 B.C.; the First Epistle to the Corinthians was penned by Paul A.D. 58 or 59.

Place. — We do not know exactly where the Book of Deuteronomy was written, but it may have been not far from Mount Nebo, east of the Jordan; the Book of Proverbs was probably written in Jerusalem; Paul wrote this Epistle from Ephesus.

THE PLAN OF THE LESSON.

SUBJECT: Some Warning Signals of Heaven to Keep Man from Destroying Himself by Unrestrained Appetites for Destructive Liquids.

I. THE PUNISHMENT OF THE SON WHO IS A DRUNKARD UNDER ISRAEL'S LAW, Deut. 21 : 18–21.
   1. The charge, vs. 18–20.
   2. The punishment, v. 21.

II. THE POVERTY THAT ACCOMPANIES HABITUAL DRUNKENNESS, Prov. 23 : 20, 21.

III. THE SINS THAT KEEP MEN OUT OF THE KINGDOM OF GOD — AND HOW CHRIST CLEANSES AND JUSTIFIES MEN SO GUILTY, 1 Cor. 6 : 9–11.
   1. The sins enumerated, vs. 9, 10.
      a. In general — unrighteousness.
      b. In particular — fornication, idolatry, etc.
   2. What Christ and the Spirit of God can do for such sinners, v. 11.
      a. We are washed.
      b. We are sanctified.
      c. We are justified.

THE TEACHER'S LIBRARY.

On Deuteronomy 21 : 18–21, the best comments by far are those by Matthew Henry. In addition, one may consult the relevant pages in C. H. Mackintosh's *Notes on the Book of Deuteronomy*, Vol. 2. There is no sermonic material, as far as the editor knows, worth looking at on the verses of our lesson taken from Deuteronomy and Proverbs. On the passage from Proverbs, the editor does not even know of a commentary which is worth reading. On the passage from 1 Corinthians, the best commentaries to consult are those by Charles Hodge, F. Godet, T. C. Edwards, and A. Robertson, in the *International Critical Commentary* series. On these verses, see also W. B. Riley: *The Bible of the Expositor and the Evangelist: New Testament*, Vol. 10, 55–58; also, if one is able to secure a copy, an excellent sermon by Dr. James M. Gray, in pamphlet form, published by the Bible Institute Colportage Association, called, "*And Such Were Some of You.*" Some of the more recent literature on temperance matters will be found listed in the bibliography in the Introduction to this volume.

DEUTERONOMY 21 : 18. If a man have a stubborn and rebellious son, that will not obey the voice of his father, or the voice of his mother, and, though they chasten him, will not hearken unto them;

19. Then shall his father and his mother lay hold on him, and bring him out unto the elders of his city, and unto the gate of his place;

20. And they shall say unto the elders of his city, This our son is stubborn and rebellious, he will not obey our voice; he is a glutton, and a drunkard.

I. THE PUNISHMENT OF THE SON WHO IS A DRUNKARD UNDER ISRAEL'S LAW, Deut. 21 : 18–21. 18. **If a man have a stubborn and rebellious son, that will not obey the voice of his father, or the voice of his mother, and, though they chasten him, will not hearken unto them;** 19. **then shall his father and his mother lay hold on him, and bring him out unto the elders of his city, and unto the gate of his place;** 20. **and they shall say unto the elders of his city, This our son is stubborn and rebellious, he will not obey our voice; he is a glutton, and a drunkard.**

21. And all the men of his city shall stone him to death with stones: so shalt thou put away the evil from the midst of thee; and all Israel shall hear, and fear.

21. **And all the men of his city shall stone him to death with stones: so shalt thou put away the evil from the midst of thee; and all Israel shall hear, and fear.** This is a very difficult passage to teach to young people, and one should be careful to properly interpret it. In the first place, it should be clearly recognized that "the power of parents over their children (Exod. 21 : 7; Gen. 31 : 15), even to putting them to death, which prevailed in early Israel also to this degree (Gen. 38 : 24), is here enforced and controlled by public authority. (Cf. Deut. 27 : 16; Lev. 20 : 9; Prov. 30 : 17.)" — *George Adam Smith.* The editor has given considerable thought to this passage during the week before writing the lesson, and he believes that in looking at this severe law, one should be reminded of God's purpose for Israel among the nations, which demanded severe legislation. Laws may greatly vary, for the same crime or misdemeanor, from day to day, and under varying circumstances. Thus, *e.g.*, it is not a crime for a man to fall asleep over his work, though it is very bad form, and he may get dismissed for it; — but he cannot be sent to prison. However, it *is* a crime, punishable by death, for a man to fall asleep while on sentry duty in war. The circumstances determine the severity of the penalty. Israel was to be kept a clean, pure, priestly nation, to bear witness to the holiness of God among the nations of the earth, and this holy calling greatly enhanced the seriousness of transgressions and iniquities. The words of Matthew Henry here are exceptionally good. "No child was to fare the worst for the weakness of his capacity, the slowness or dullness of his understanding, but for his wilfulness and obstinacy. If he carry himself proudly and insolently toward his parents, condemn their authority, slight their reproofs and admonitions, disobey the express commands they give him for his own good, hate to be reformed by the correction they give him, shame their family, grieve their hearts, waste their substance, and threaten to ruin their estate by riotous living — this is a stubborn and rebellious son. He is particularly supposed to be a glutton or a drunkard. This intimates either (1) that these were sins which his parents did in a particular manner warn him against, and therefore that in these instances there was a plain evidence that he did not obey their voice. Lemuel had this charge from his mother (Prov. 31 : 4). Or, (2) that his being a glutton and a drunkard was the cause of his insolence and obstinacy toward his parents. There is nothing that draws men into all manner of wickedness, and hardens them in it, more certainly and fatally than drunkenness does. When men take to drink they forget the law, they forget all law (Prov. 31 : 5), even that fundamental law of honoring parents. . . . Those that give up themselves to vice and wickedness, and will not be reclaimed, forfeit their interest in the natural affections of their nearest relations; the instruments of their being justly become the instruments of their destruction. The children that forget their duty must thank themselves, and not blame their parents if they are regarded with less and less affection. And, how difficult tender parents find it to reconcile themselves to the just punishment of their rebellious children. In the day of the revelation of the righteous judgment of God all natural affection will be entirely swallowed up in divine love that will acquiesce even in the condemnation of those children, because God will be therein forever glorified. The paternal authority was supported, and God, our common Father, showed Himself jealous for it, it being one of the first and most ancient streams derived from him that is the fountain of all power. This law, if duly executed, would early destroy the wicked of the land (Ps. 101 : 8), and prevent the spreading of the gangrene, by cutting off the corrupt parts betimes; for those that were bad members of families would never make good families of the commonwealth. It would strike an awe upon children, and frighten them into obedience to their parents, if they would not otherwise be brought to their duty and kept in it: 'All Israel shall hear.' The Jews say: 'The elders that condemned him were to send notice of it in writing all the nation over, *In such a court, such a day, we stoned such a one, because he was a stubborn and rebellious son.* And I have sometimes wished that as in all our courts there is an exact record kept of the condemnation of criminals, that the memorial may never be lost, so there might be public and authentic notice given in print to the kingdom of such condemnations, and the executions upon them, by the elders themselves — *that all may hear and fear.*" "It is marvelous to think that it is the same God who speaks and acts in Deuteronomy 21 and in

PROVERBS 23 : 20. Be not among winebibbers,
Among gluttonous eaters of flesh:
21. For the drunkard and the glutton shall come to poverty;
And drowsiness will clothe *a man* with rags.

Luke 15; but oh, how different the action! How different the style! Under the law, the father is called upon to lay hold of his son and bring him forth to be stoned. Under grace, the father runs to meet the returning son, falls on his neck and kisses him; clothes him in the best robe, puts a ring on his hand, and shoes on his feet, has the fatted calf killed for him, seats him at the table with himself, and makes the house ring with the joy that fills his own heart at getting back the poor wandering spendthrift. Striking contrast! In Deuteronomy we see the *hand* of God, in righteous government, executing judgment upon the rebellious; in Luke we see the *heart* of God pouring itself out, in soul-subduing tenderness, upon the poor repentant one, giving him the sweet assurance that it is His own deep joy to get back His lost ones. The persistent rebel meets the stone of judgment; the returning penitent meets the kiss of love." — *C. H. Mackintosh.*

II. **THE POVERTY THAT ACCOMPANIES HABITUAL DRUNKENNESS,** Prov. 23 : 20, 21. 20. **Be not among winebibbers, among gluttonous eaters of flesh: 21. For the drunkard and the glutton shall come to poverty; and drowsiness will clothe *a man* with rags.** It is quite significant, to begin with, that the word here translated *glutton* is exactly the same as that found in the passage taken from Deuteronomy which we have just considered. Let us note something here, normally passed over in temperance lessons and by temperance speakers, namely that gluttonous eating is put in the same category with drunkenness. There are people in our country who fearlessly and constantly denounce any kind of intoxicating drinking, who at the same time are really gluttonous in their eating. One is as bad as the other; in fact, the glutton can be so easily condoned, because intoxication does not follow, that many forget gluttony is an actual sin. Two reasons are given why we should even avoid the company of those indulging in this manner. In the first place, such men are swiftly running toward a state of poverty, and secondly, because they must, by the very laws of human nature be frequently overcome with a spirit of drowsiness, which prevents them from enthusiastically entering into their daily work. In some strange way, God has established certain economic laws on earth which, if war, or famine, or a terrible depression are not making for abnormality, allow the people of the earth, especially in civilized countries, to make a decent living, whereby the necessities of life can be provided. With the great mass of men and women, the day's labor does not provide the means for continuous indulgence in extravagant tastes. In other words, if a normal man, in normal times, can make enough to support himself and family, with a little left over for insurance, some savings, and a few pleasures, he is getting out of life about all, materially speaking, that can be expected, — unless he has an unusual gift in business which allows him to pile up a fortune or demand a large salary. We are not speaking about the few wealthy people of the world. However, if this man begins to spend as much money, or even more, on alcoholic beverages, as he does on food, and then, as the habit grips him, as much for liquor as for food and clothes and rent combined, the rotten stuff, taking away his common sense, drives him to the place where the family is not provided with food, where he would rather have whiskey than decent clothes. Subsequently, the rent is in arrears, he even begins to sell some of his furniture, and soon he finds he is with practically nothing in life but a burning appetite for this destructive stuff. Millions of people who have had a decent income, and could have been comfortable, have found themselves, finally, in abject poverty, because of the drain that a thirst for liquor makes upon their income. Most of us are " laboring " people, and we do not have the income to pour into the coffers of selfish monsters who manufacture and sell this vile stuff. Ultimately, continuous indulgence in alcoholic liquors, and heavy eating, will make a man lazy, indifferent, and weary, because of which he will have to have long periods of sleep. A man's wife will not have to call his employer many mornings in a year to tell him that her husband will not be able to work, until the employer, knowing the reason, without even asking, will dismiss him, and that too will bring him to rags. Business conditions being what they are, we need all the wisdom, strength, and common sense, that we can muster, and woe be to the man who is stupefying his mind and weakening his body with intemperate living. He will soon be on the side lines, then a care to the state, and a grief to himself and loved ones.

1 CORINTHIANS 6 : 9. Or know ye not that the unrighteous shall not inherit the kingdom of God? Be not deceived: neither fornicators, nor idolaters, nor adulterers, nor effeminate, nor abusers of themselves with men,

10. Nor thieves, nor covetous, nor drunkards, nor revilers, nor extortioners, shall inherit the kingdom of God.

11. And such were some of you: but ye were washed, but ye were sanctified, but ye were justified in the name of the Lord Jesus Christ, and in the Spirit of our God.

III. **THE SINS THAT KEEP MEN OUT OF THE KINGDOM OF GOD — AND HOW CHRIST CLEANSES AND JUSTIFIES MEN SO GUILTY,** 1 Cor. 6 : 9–11. 9. **Or know ye not that the unrighteous shall not inherit the kingdom of God? Be not deceived: neither fornicators, nor idolaters, nor adulterers, nor effeminate, nor abusers of themselves with men,** 10. **nor thieves, nor covetous, nor drunkards, nor revilers, nor extortioners, shall inherit the kingdom of God.** First in this terrible catalogue of iniquities we have a general phrase, covering all who are here enumerated — "the unrighteous." Righteousness is that which is *right* in the sight of God; unrighteousness is that which is wrong in the sight of God. An unrighteous man is a man who is not living right, and that includes all those whom Paul now begins specifically to designate. It is not necessary in this particular lesson to give definitions of all of these words. Notice, however, that sexual sins are named first, probably because they were the most prevalent, and continually indulged in, everywhere in the empire at the time Paul was writing, as contemporary Roman literature informs us. Many of the sins here named one will find set forth with terrible reality in the last half of the first chapter of Paul's Epistle to the Romans. Idolatry is placed between fornication and adultery, no doubt because the worship of idols in Paul's day was so definitely connected with rites of impurity. There does not seem to be any particular order in which Paul has arranged these words. In the midst of this dreadful catalogue, is the one word which concerns our lesson — drunkards. There seems to be today a sort of feeling that there is something just a little smart about getting drunk, and that we must not be too harsh on those who, by their constant indulgence in alcoholic liquors, find themselves in such a revolting condition. It is true, we ought to be willing to do everything for our soldiers, but that does not mean we should condone their drunkenness. It is no more excusable in the army and navy than it is in civilian life; in fact, it is the curse of many armies. People are working and living at high tension these days, which will mean they will often be tempted to find release from this tension with artificial stimulants, but this is not the safe way of being delivered from the strain of our contemporary life. Drunkenness is drunkenness — inexcusable, hideous, vulgar, resulting in coarseness, often in terrible crimes, and always in the ultimate weakening of the mind and body of the one drunk. Our text says that such men will not enter into the kingdom of God, and it says we ought not to be deceived in thinking they will. Is not this our danger today, in this very point, that we are being deceived into thinking that after all drunkenness is just a weakness which we must not too severely criticize? The Apostle Paul, by the inspiration of the Holy Spirit, says it will shut men out of the kingdom of heaven. We cannot get around this verse. (Cf. Rev. 21 : 8; 22 : 15.) 11. **And such were some of you: but ye were washed, but ye were sanctified, but ye were justified in the name of the Lord Jesus Christ, and in the Spirit of our God.** The Corinthians, living in a city famous for its immorality, had, before their conversion, been guilty of these very things, but now, Paul says, everything was changed. In the name of the Lord Jesus Christ, who became their Saviour, and in the Spirit of God, that is, in the power of the Holy Spirit, they had come into a threefold experience. "With regard to the three terms — washed, sanctified, justified — they may be taken, as by Calvin and others, to express the same idea under different aspects. That idea is, that they had been converted, or completely changed. They had put off the old man, and put on the new man. Their sins, considered as filth, had been washed away; considered as pollution, they had been purged or purified; considered as guilt, they had been covered with the righteousness of God (Rom. 1 : 17). The majority of commentators take the several terms separately, each expressing a distinct idea. In what precise sense each of these words is to be understood, becomes, then, somewhat doubtful." — *Charles Hodge.* Some take the first verb, *washed*, as referring to our being cleansed by the shed blood of Christ, but Godet is right when he says practically all commentators " are at one in applying the first of the three verbs to baptism. In fact, outwardly speaking, it was the act which had transferred them from the state of heathens to that of Christians, from the condition of beings polluted and condemned, to that of beings pardoned and purified. The middle form of the verb, *ye washed yourselves*, expresses the freedom and spontaneity with which they had done the deed. The term *bathe, wash,* is explained by the two following terms. Baptism, when it is done in faith, is not a pure symbol; two purifying graces are connected with it, *sanctification* and *justification.* The verbs which express these two facts are in the passive; for they signify two divine acts, of which the baptized are the subjects. The two verbs in the aorist can only refer both of them to a deed done once for all, and not to a continuous state. That is what prevents us from applying the term *sanctify* to the growing work of Christian sanctification. This word here can only designate the initial act whereby the believer passed from his previous state of corruption to that of holiness, that is to say, the believer's consecration to God in consequence of the gift of the Spirit bestowed on him in baptism (cf. Acts 2:38; 2 Cor. 1:21, 22; Eph. 1:13). The verb *sanctify* is placed before *justify*, because, as Edwards says: ' Paul, wishing to contrast the present moral condition of believers with their former state, lays special emphasis on the characteristic of sanctification.' . . . By closing with the idea of the justification bestowed on believers, he points to them as the true possessors of righteousness, first in their relation to God, and thereby in all the relations of life." — *F. Godet.*

No matter what the past has been, there is a way open for forgiveness and cleansing, for deliverance and redemption, through the Lord Jesus Christ. Whatever we have been, we need no longer be; whatever be the chains of the past, Christ can break them today; whatever the shame and stain of the years gone by, purity and holiness may mark our life beginning with this very hour, and there is no man so sunk in sin, no man so long in sin, but that he cannot be washed, and sanctified, and justified this very day.

ALCOHOL AND WAR.

It is sometimes argued that Abraham Lincoln sold alcoholic beverages when a young man, and, so it is said, if he could grow up into so great a president, and still traffic in this stuff at an early time of life, what right have we to condemn it if his high moral principles tolerated it? But this is what Abraham Lincoln said about the whole vile business, in a speech which he made on Washington's birthday in 1842, words which the liquor interests are afraid to quote, and words which we do not see referred to in any of our ordinary books on Lincoln. In speaking of prohibition, he declared that " In it we shall find a stronger bondage broken, a viler slavery manumitted, a greater tyrant deposed; in it, more of want supplied, more of disease healed, more of sorrow assuaged. By it, no orphans starving, no widows weeping. By it, none wounded in feeling, none injured in interest. . . . If the relative grandeur of revolutions shall be estimated by the great amount of human misery they alleviate and the small amount they inflict, then, indeed, will this be the grandest the world shall ever have seen. . . . And when victory shall be complete — when there shall be neither a slave nor a drunkard on the earth — how proud the title of that land which may truly claim to be the birthplace of both these revolutions that shall have ended in that victory. How nobly distinguished that people who shall have planted and nurtured to maturity both the political and moral freedom of their species."

General Pershing, the outstanding soldier among the American forces in the first World War, who certainly knew, by a lifetime of military service, the conditions which favor victory and those which lead to defeat, has given us his opinion about this matter of liquor in relation to war, in the following words: " Banish the entire liquor industry from the United States; close every saloon and brewery; suppress drinking by severe punishment to the drunkards . . . and the nation will suddenly find itself amazed at its efficiency and startled at the increase in its labor supply. . . . I know what is the greatest foe of my men, greater even than the bullets of the enemy."

Every one admits that one of the reasons for the debacle of the French army in this present war was their habit of heavy, constant drinking.

A remarkable statement of Col. George Skinner, recently retired, for many years a ranking officer in the Medical Corps of the United States Army, should be carefully considered by every one of us, in this day when we are thinking of nothing but victory in this terrible war. " Today our development is so largely mechanical and our equipment moves at such speed that even the most ordinary routine of daily life requires the clearest brain and the most accurate and rapid muscular action possible. This is demonstrated daily by the number of traffic injuries, and as traffic is now mostly automobile, the injuries and deaths from this cause are appalling. A large percentage of them are the direct result of the use of alcoholic drinks. Why? We depend largely upon the quick action of the mind and the rapid response of the muscles to the needs of the body. The first action of alcohol is to break up the connection between the mind and body, to confuse the mind, and to slow the muscular action. Hence, even if the mind notes that the body is in danger and orders the muscles to act, the order is badly mixed up in reaching the muscles, and the response may be directly opposite from what it should be. The worst of it is that the owner of the mind does not realize the difficulty and proceeds serenely on his destructive way until he is either killed, injured, or taken out of circulation some other way. These reactions to alcohol operate as surely in the army as in civil life. In our present defense needs, the protective armament is very largely mechanical and often exceedingly complicated, requiring the finest training and muscular response (co-ordination) possible. As a man's life — and the lives of others — in an airplane depends upon the accurate judgment and co-ordination of the pilot — and both judgment and co-ordination are badly disturbed by alcohol — it stands to reason that a man who indulges in alcohol is not going to be trusted with such an important assignment. The same is true in practically every other part of the modern army and if our country is to survive in a crisis depending upon defense, we must have trained defense forces relatively free from the disturbances of alcohol. An air pilot who has alcoholic inclinations is not going to last long on his job, for not only is there danger to the lives of others besides himself, but he is in charge of a very expensive machine which takes months to replace if damaged or destroyed, and by which the safety of our country may largely and radically be altered; and he would be removed entirely from his assignment. Not only does he not have to drink to be a soldier, but if he does drink he cannot occupy any responsible position."

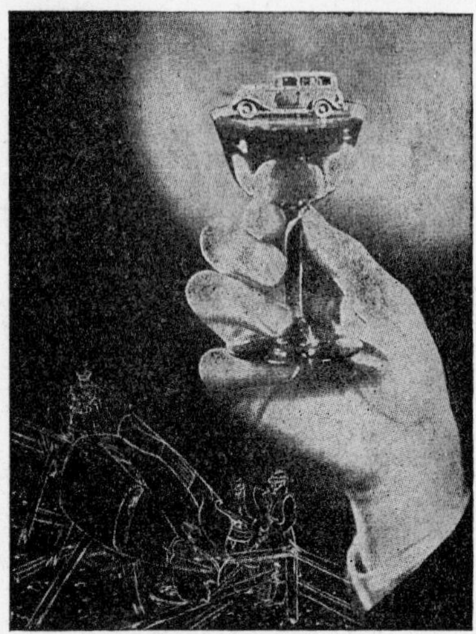

Courtesy of The United Presbyterian.

Automobile and Alcohol.

How many different reasons do you find in this lesson why men should not give way to this vice of drinking? What is the difference between the penalty for drunkenness in the Old Testament, and the penalty pronounced for the same thing in the New Testament? When once sins of the flesh get hold of us, does their power over us decrease or increase? If we continue very long to indulge in any of the sins set forth by the Apostle Paul, and especially this sin of heavy drinking, does our power to resist the demands of these fleshly appetites increase or decrease?

LESSON V. — August 1.

GOD DELIVERS HIS PEOPLE. — Exodus 5—12.

PRINTED TEXT, Exodus 5 : 22, 23; 6 : 1-7; 12 : 51.

GOLDEN TEXT. — *Call upon me in the day of trouble: I will deliver thee, and thou shalt glorify me.* PSALM 50 : 15.

Devotional Reading: Psalm 81 : 8–16.
Beginner Topic: ON A LONG TRIP.
Lesson Material: Exodus 6 : 1–7; 12 : 37–42, 51.
Memory Verse: Thou art nigh, O Jehovah. Psalm 119 : 151.

Primary Topic: WHEN PEOPLE PRAY.
Lesson Material: Exodus 5—12.
Memory Verse: Every day will I bless thee; and I will praise thy name for ever and ever. Psalm 145 : 2.
Junior Topic: A PRAYING LEADER.
Lesson Material: Exodus 5—12.
Memory Verse: O Jehovah, in the morning shalt thou hear my voice; in the morning will I order my prayer unto thee, and will keep watch. Psalm 5 : 3.
Intermediate and Senior Topic: GOD'S HELP IN TIMES OF NEED.
Topic for Young People and Adults: MAN'S EXTREMITY, GOD'S DELIVERANCE.

THE TEACHER AND HIS CLASS.

The Younger Classes might be reminded that whenever any man undertakes to deliver people, either a small group or a whole nation, from some evil or bondage, from a corrupt government which declares that certain groups remain in servility and poverty, or a corrupt enterprise like the liquor traffic, which prefers men to remain drunkards, so long as they have their undeserved income — whenever such a deliverance is undertaken, it must be expected that these evil powers will fight any who undertake to break their hold on these helpless people. So in our lesson, the record of Moses pleading with Pharaoh to let the people of Israel go out of Egypt, we find the fiercest antagonism on Pharaoh's part against such a deliverance. In fact, in *this* lesson there is actually a conflict between supernatural evil powers, the satanically-possessed magicians of Egypt, and the omnipotence of God Himself.

The Older Classes will find in this lesson a glorious illustration of the overruling purpose of God in great historic events. There are a number of miracles in this lesson, it is true, but the miracles are not here for the sake of a mere demonstration of miraculous power. They all occur with a definite end in view, the breaking of the power of Pharaoh, and the ultimate liberation of the people of Israel. In bringing about His great purposes, God will use men, good and evil, will use the circumstances prevailing at a certain time, will use every human experience He chooses to use, and then, when necessary, He will manifest His own omnipotence in miraculous events. God's purposes will be accomplished. They have been in the past; they will continue to be in the future. No power in the world can prevent God from fulfilling the counsel of His will.

THE TEACHER'S LIBRARY.

All lives of Moses, and all commentaries on the Book of Exodus, will be found helpful for the study of this lesson. There is such a vast amount of Scripture material included in the assignment that probably most teachers will not have time for more than the reading of one book. If one intends to read concerning all the events described in these eight chapters, see especially the volume on Exodus by Chadwick, in the *Expositor's Bible*, pp. 89–198; see also George Rawlinson's excellent *Life of Moses*, 85–118. For extended expository material one should consult George F. Pentecost: *Out of Egypt*, 94–163. Then by all means one should consult the superb article, "Plagues," by Dr. Melvin E. Kyle, in the *International Bible Encyclopedia*, 2403–2406. If there is any worth-while sermonic material on the printed passage, the editor is not acquainted with it.

THE PLAN OF THE LESSON.

SUBJECT: How a Great, Critical Event in God's Program Involves Suffering and Tragedy for Those Who Contend Against Him, and Spiritual Blessing and Freedom for Those Whom He Has Chosen to Bless.

I. THE FIRST DEMAND OF PHARAOH AND ITS CONSEQUENCES, Exodus 5 : 1—7 : 9.
1. The demand itself, 5 : 1–4.
2. The increased burdens placed on the Israelites, 5 : 5–19.
3. The Israelites denounce Moses, 5 : 20, 21.
4. Moses' prayer, 5 : 22, 23.
5. God reassures Moses, 6 : 1–13.
6. Parenthetical — the families of Israel, 6 : 14–27.
7. Moses is commissioned anew, 6 : 28 — 7 : 9.

II. THE SUBSEQUENT DEMANDS MADE OF PHARAOH AND THE ACCOMPANYING MIRACLES, Exodus 7 : 10—10 : 29.
1. The second demand made of Pharaoh and the first miracle, 7 : 10–13.
2. The third demand and the turning of water into blood, 7 : 14–25.
3. The fourth demand and the plagues of frogs and lice, 8 : 1–19.
4. The fifth demand and the plague of flies, 8 : 20–32.
5. The sixth demand and the plagues of murrain and boils, 9 : 1–12.
6. The seventh demand and the plague of hail, 9 : 13–35.
7. The eighth demand, the plague of locusts, and the judgment of darkness, 10 : 1–29.

III. EVENTS IMMEDIATELY PRECEDING THE EXODUS, Exodus 11 : 1—12 : 36.

IV. THE EXODUS FROM EGYPT BEGINS, Exodus 12 : 37–51.

THE LESSON IN ITS SETTING.

Time. — 1445 B.C.

Place. — The Passover feast itself was observed only in the land of Goshen where the Jews were then living, but the plagues recorded here, of course, occurred throughout the whole land of Egypt, and the conversations that are recorded here probably took place in the city of Zoan, known also as Tanis, where was located Pharaoh's palace.

SOME INTRODUCTORY MATTERS.

As Joseph was dying, he said to those gathered about him, that God would surely visit them and bring them up out of the land of Egypt into the land which He had promised to Abraham, and Isaac, and Jacob (Gen. 50 : 24, 25). A long intervening period of suffering, disappointment, and hardship followed Joseph's death, until the hour came when God was ready to fulfill His promise, to bring them at last into the land flowing with milk and honey. In the third chapter, God declares such a purpose to Moses; at the end of the fourth chapter, Moses reiterates this promise of God to the elders of Israel. Our lesson is an account of those tremendous events which convulsed Egypt at this time, sent by God to break the fetters of Israel's bondage, and to throw open a door through which they could make their exit from this land of fleshpots and garlic, of bondage, and idolatry. The entire narrative is a revelation of a fierceness of antagonism on the part of Pharaoh, a wrestling of the powers of darkness with the omnipotent God Himself. Murphy's words on this point are excellent. "To understand the deep import of the conflict before us, let us bear in mind that now for the first time since the dispersion of mankind the opposition between the children of God and the children of disobedience is coming out into broad daylight. Egypt, that was the kind fosterer of the chosen family, has now become the persecutor of Israel, and the avowed antagonist of God. The present struggle is therefore no raid for the gathering of booty, nor encounter between two rival nations, nor expedition for the selfish ends of an earthly ambition. It is the controversy between light and darkness, in which the God of heaven and earth manifests His presence and power on behalf of His people and against the defiant nation. This nation is for the time being the representative of all heathendom, which is the kingdom of the prince of darkness; and the battle now fought is the model and type of all future warfare between the seed of the woman and the seed of the serpent. Hence it rises to a transcendent importance in the ways of God with man, and fitly holds a place even in the preface to the ten commandments (20 : 2)."

I. THE FIRST DEMAND OF PHARAOH AND ITS CONSEQUENCES, 5 : 1—7 : 9.

1. THE DEMAND ITSELF, 5 : 1–4. At last the hour had come when Moses and Aaron, the two appointed servants of God for this particular task, are found standing in the presence of Pharaoh, at that time the mightiest ruler on earth; two servants of the living God announcing to the head of that great empire of idolatry, that the Lord God of Israel had said, "Let my people go." The answer of Pharaoh is tremendously significant, one I think that could easily serve as the basis for a great sermon. "Who is the Lord that I should hearken unto his voice to let Israel go? I know not the Lord, and moreover, I will not let Israel go." That is what a great many people are saying today. "Who is the Lord God of the Bible that I should obey His commandments? I do not recognize Him as God, and therefore I will not obey what some choose to call His statutes." What we need in our generation is a knowledge of the character, the power, the eternity, the righteousness, and the wrath of God. It is ignorance of God that makes people so bold in their iniquity and lawlessness.

2. THE INCREASED BURDENS PLACED ON THE ISRAELITES, 5 : 5–19. "Pharaoh does not dispute Moses' facts, or the reasonableness of the claim that he had made. He simply acts upon his own rights. Jehovah is nothing to him and he will do with the Israelites as he pleases. . . . The order went forth that no straw should henceforth be given to the Hebrew brickmakers, but that they should themselves find the straw needed for binding the bricks together. Nevertheless, the tale of bricks was not to be diminished, imposing a burden to which human strength was unequal. Labor as hard as they might, the brickmakers could not produce the full tale of bricks required of them; and the result was that their headmen were bastinadoed for giving in a short quantity." — *George Rawlinson.*

3. THE ISRAELITES DENOUNCE MOSES, 5 : 20, 21. The inevitable happened. Instead of finding themselves near to the hour of redemption, with a little lessening

Exodus 5 : 22. And Moses returned unto Jehovah, and said, Lord, wherefore hast thou dealt ill with this people? why is it that thou has sent me?

23. For since I came to Pharaoh to speak in thy name, he hath dealt ill with this people; neither hast thou delivered thy people at all.

Exodus 6 : 1. And Jehovah said unto Moses, Now shalt thou see what I will do to Pharaoh: for by a strong hand shall he let them go, and by a strong hand shall he drive them out of his land.

2. And God spake unto Moses, and said unto him, I am Jehovah:

3. And I appeared unto Abraham, unto Isaac, and unto Jacob, as God Almighty; but by my name Jehovah I was not known to them.

---

of their already too-heavy burdens, they find themselves more terribly treated than ever before, and they simply blame Moses for it. It is easy to blame great leaders when things go wrong. I think this is a lesson we need to learn in the present war. We must not expect a great and glorious deliverance from a vicious and powerful enemy instantly. In fact, we may well expect an increase of suffering before the final destruction of diabolical forces.

4. Moses' Prayer, 5 : 22, 23. 22. **And Moses returned unto Jehovah, and said, Lord, wherefore hast thou dealt ill with this people? why is it that thou hast sent me?** 23. **For since I came to Pharaoh to speak in thy name, he hath dealt ill with this people; neither hast thou delivered thy people at all.** "Moses himself was not prepared for this turn of affairs. Like many young ministers new to their work, he was discouraged with the want of immediate success. He could not brook the appearance of failure, and was led himself into a bold complaint against God: first for sending him; and then for failing, as it seemed to him, to keep His word in the deliverance of the people. It was a good thing for Moses to have gone with his discouragement and complaint to the Lord. He could not have done better. I think it is not wresting the Scriptures to say 'in everything by prayer and supplications make your *complaints* known unto God.' God does not get angry even with the complaints of His people; especially when there is a half inquiry in them, as in this case. Jesus knows how to be touched with *this* feeling of our infirmity. He knows what it is to have suffered and wept over a hard-hearted and stiff-necked people, who would not come unto Him when He called and entreated. He knows our weaknesses, and is ready to help." — *G. F. Pentecost.*

5. God Reassures Moses, 6 : 1–13. 1. **And Jehovah said unto Moses, Now shalt thou see what I will do to Pharaoh: for by a strong hand shall he let them go, and by a strong hand shall he drive them out of his land.** 2. **And God spake unto Moses, and said unto him, I am Jehovah:** 3. **and I appeared unto Abraham, unto Isaac, and unto Jacob, as God Almighty; but by my name Jehovah I was not known to them.** "The direction which Moses now received from God applies, in principle, to all similar cases. It conveyed a fresh assurance that God would certainly accomplish His purpose; it gave a fuller revelation of His character as Jehovah, with the special promises which this implied (6 : 2–8); and it renewed the commission to Moses to undertake the work, accompanied by encouragement and assurance suitable in the circumstances. . . . When, on the occasion just referred to, God said to Moses (Exod. 6 : 2, 3): 'I am Jehovah: and I appeared unto Abraham, unto Isaac, and unto Jacob in *El Shaddai* (God Almighty), but as to my name *Jehovah* was it not known to them,' it cannot, of course, mean that the patriarchs were ignorant of the special designation *Jehovah*, since it frequently occurs in their history. By the 'name of God' we are of course to understand not a mere appellation of God, but that by which He makes Himself known to man. Now Scripture teaches us that we only *know* God in so far as He manifests, or reveals Himself. Hence the peculiar name of God indicates the peculiar manner in which He had manifested Himself, or, in other words, the character of His dealings at the time. Now the character of God's dealings — and therefore His name — was in patriarchal times unquestionably *El Shaddai* (Gen. 17 : 1; 35 : 11; 48 : 3). But His manifestation as *Jehovah* — the dealings by which, in the sight of all men, He made Himself known as such — belonged not to that, but to a later period. For the term 'Jehovah' literally means, 'He who is,' which agrees with the explanation given by God Himself: 'He who is that He is.' As here used, the word 'to be' refers not to the essential nature of

4. And I have also established my covenant with them, to give them the land of Canaan, the land of their sojournings, wherein they sojourned.

5. And moreover I have heard the groaning of the children of Israel, whom the Egyptians keep in bondage; and I have remembered my covenant.

6. Wherefore say unto the children of Israel, I am Jehovah, and I will bring you out from under the burdens of the Egyptians, and I will rid you out of their bondage, and I will redeem you with an outstretched arm, and with great judgments:

7. And I will take you to me for a people, and I will be to you a God; and ye shall know that I am Jehovah your God, who bringeth you out from under the burdens of the Egyptians.

God, but to His relationship towards man. In that relationship God manifested Himself, and He was known as Jehovah — as 'He who is that He is,' in other words, as unchangeable, when after centuries of silence, and after the condition of Israel in Egypt had become almost hopeless, He showed that He had not forgotten His promise given to the fathers, that He had all along been preparing its fulfillment; and that neither the resistance of Pharaoh, nor the might of Egypt, could stay His hand." — *Alfred Edersheim.*
4. **And I have also established my covenant with them, to give them the land of Canaan, the land of their sojournings, wherein they sojourned.**
5. **And moreover I have heard the groaning of the children of Israel, whom the Egyptians keep in bondage; and I have remembered my covenant.**
6. **Wherefore say unto the children of Israel, I am Jehovah, and I will bring you out from under the burdens of the Egyptians, and I will rid you out of their bondage, and I will redeem you with an outstretched arm, and with great judgments:**
7. **and I will take you to me for a people, and I will be to you a God; and ye shall know that I am Jehovah your God, who bringeth you out from under the burdens of the Egyptians.** "This is henceforth to be the word of encouragement, of authority, and of fellowship to Israel. It reminds them that God is now active in their behalf; that it is God who is thus active, and that He is present to dwell in the midst of them as a father among his adopted children. . . . They shall know by actual experience that He is all that is implied in the name Jehovah, an actual, and therefore tried, deliverer. . . . *I am the Lord.* This sentence is here repeated for the third time in this message, enhanced by all the emphasis which the distinction made between the divine names (v. 3) has added to its meaning. It is the seal of God thrice stamped upon His promise." — *J. G. Murphy.*

"As I glance down the seven 'I wills' of this paragraph, they become very remarkable, as contrasted with the condition of Israel at that time: 'I will bring you out'; 'I will rid you out of their bondage'; 'I will redeem you'; 'I will take you to me for a people'; 'I will be to you a God'; "I will bring you in unto the land'; 'I will give it you for an heritage.'" — *F. B. Meyer.*

6. PARENTHETICAL — THE FAMILIES OF ISRAEL, 6 : 14–27. "At the beginning of the grand historical work, of which all this has been the prelude, there is set the pedigree of Moses and Aaron, according to 'the heads of their father's houses,' — an epithet which indicates a subdivision of the 'family,' as the family is a subdivision of the tribe. Of the sons of Jacob, Reuben and Simeon are mentioned, to put Levi in his natural third place. And from Levi to Moses only four generations are mentioned, favoring somewhat the briefer scheme of chronology which makes four generations cover all the time from Abraham, and not the captivity alone. But it is certain that this is a mere recapitulation of the more important links in the genealogy. In Numbers 26 : 58, 59, six generations are reckoned instead of four; in 1 Chronicles 6 : 1 there are seven generations; and elsewhere in the same book (6 : 22) there are ten." — *J. H. Chadwick.*

7. MOSES IS COMMISSIONED ANEW, 6 : 28—7 : 9. The time for Moses to stand once again before Pharaoh has arrived, and Moses, no doubt disturbed by the apparently tragic consequences of his last interview with Pharaoh, appears here, as it were, to beg to be excused from going on with the task which God had assigned to him. The Lord informs him that Pharaoh will not in the days to come hearken unto him, but that the ultimate end of it all will be that the Egyptians, because of the plagues He is about to send, will know that the Lord is Lord, and that Israel

will be delivered. He even gave to Moses for this period of time, the assurance that when a miracle would be demanded, he had only to cast his rod to the ground and it would be changed to a serpent.

II. **THE SUBSEQUENT DEMANDS MADE OF PHARAOH AND THE ACCOMPANYING MIRACLES,** 7 : 10—10 : 29.

1. The Second Demand Made of Pharaoh and the First Miracle, 7 : 10–13. " On this occasion Aaron, when challenged by Pharaoh, proved his right to speak in the name of God. He cast down his rod, and it became a serpent, and although the magicians of Egypt 'did in like manner with their enchantments,' the superiority of Aaron appeared when his 'rod swallowed up their rods.' Without here entering into the general question of magic before the coming of our Lord, or of the power which the devil and his agents may have wielded on earth before our Saviour subdued his might, and led captivity captive, there was really nothing in what the Egyptian magicians did that Eastern jugglers do not profess to this day. To make a serpent stiff and to look like a rod, and then again suddenly to restore it to life, are among the commonest tricks witnessed by travelers. . . . It is also important to notice, that the Hebrew term for 'the serpent,' into which Aaron's rod was changed, is not that commonly used, but bears a more specific meaning. It is not the same term as that for the serpent (nachash) by which Moses was to accredit his mission before his own people, but it indicated the kind of serpent (*tannin*) specially used by Egyptian conjurers, and bore pointed reference to the serpent as the great symbol of Egypt. Accordingly Pharaoh should have understood that, when Aaron's rod swallowed up the others, it pointed to the vanquishment of Egypt, and the executing of judgment 'against all the gods of Egypt." — *Alfred Edersheim.*

Moses and Aaron before Pharaoh.

2. The Third Demand and the Turning of Water into Blood, 7 : 14–25. Here begins the account of the great series of plagues with which God afflicted Egypt until that awful night when, under the final stroke of His wrath, the firstborn child of every house was overcome by death. Before we consider these plagues separately, it might be best to say a few words generally about the plagues. " The Hebrew words are so used as to give the name 'plagues' to all the wonders God did against Pharaoh. The account of the plagues is found in Exodus 7 : 8—12 : 31; Psalm 78 : 42–51; 105 : 27–36. . . . Probably all were based upon natural phenomena which still exist in Egypt in the same order, and, when they do occur, find place somewhere during the course of one year. The miraculous elements in the plagues are no less distinctly manifest than the natural phenomena themselves. There was an intensification of the effect of the various plagues so much beyond all precedent as to impress every one as being a special divine manifestation, and it was so. . . . All these calamities may be found in Egypt to the present day, but never any of them, not to say all of them, in such overwhelming severity. That all of them should come in one year and all with such devastation was plainly a divine arrangement. Merely natural events do not arrange themselves so systematically. In this systematic severity were seen *miracles of power*. . . . The orderliness and gradually increasing severity of the plagues with such arrangement as brought 'judgment upon the gods of Egypt,' vindicating Jehovah as Ruler over all, and

educating the people to know Jehovah as Lord of all the earth, present an aspect of events distinctly non-natural. Such method reveals also a divine mind at work. . . . The discrediting of the gods of Egypt is marked at every step of the progress of the plagues. They did 'execute judgment against the gods of Egypt' (Exod. 12 : 12), and the people and the princes brought great pressure to bear upon Pharaoh to let the people go (Exod. 10 : 7). The magicians who claimed to represent the gods of Egypt were defeated, Pharaoh himself, who was accounted divine, was humbled; the great god, the Nile, was polluted; frogs defiled the temples and at last, the sun, the greatest god of Egypt, was blotted out in darkness." — *Melvin G. Kyle.*

The first plague, after Pharaoh's third refusal, was the miraculous changing of the waters of the Nile River into blood. "The Nile begins to rise about the end of June, and attains its highest point at the end of September. About the commencement of the rise it assumes a greenish hue, is disagreeable to the taste, unwholesome, and often totally unfit for drinking. It soon, however, becomes red and turbid, and continues in this state for three or more weeks. In this condition it is again healthy and fit for use. The miracle now performed was totally different from this annual change; for (1) it occurred after the winter, not the summer, solstice; (2) the water was turned into blood, and not merely reddened by an admixture of red clay or animalcula; (3) the fish died, a result which did not follow from the periodical change of color; (4) the river stank, and became offensive, which it ceased to be when the ordinary redness made its appearance; (5) the stroke was arrested at the end of seven days, whereas the natural redness continued for at least three weeks; and (6) the change was brought on instantly at the word of command before the eyes of Pharaoh. . . . This miracle was not merely a judicial, but a significant act. It marks the retribution of heaven. Pharaoh orders the male infants of the Hebrews to be cast into the river, that they might perish there, and become food for its fish. That very river is changed into a stream of death. The God of nature transforms the running water into a river of death before his eyes. It demonstrates, in the way that was most striking to the Hebrews and Egyptians, that the God of Israel was the true and only God of heaven and earth, and that all other objects of worship were but the creatures of God or the works of men's hands." — *J. G. Murphy.*

The Nile, Showing Rushes and Palace Ruins.

3. THE FOURTH DEMAND AND THE PLAGUES OF FROGS AND LICE, 8 : 1–19. We cannot tarry with a minute account of each one of these plagues, which we regret, and our comments of necessity will have to be brief. "The frog had a certain significance to Egypt. It was the symbol of human life in embryo. In the hieroglyphics it sat on a ring, one of the emblems of life, and from its back rose a palm branch, the symbol of the month, or of time. The frog-headed god is a form of Pthah, the creative or formative principle. Whatever mysterious connection the frog had with life in the mind of an Egyptian, it is evident that the reptile lives and dies at the will of the God of Moses. . . . Herodotus tells us that the priests shave their whole body every other day, that no lice or other impure thing may adhere to them when they are engaged in the service of the gods. It is manifest that this species of vermin was particularly disgusting to the Egyptians; and it is said that in the space of a year one of these creatures will produce five thousand eggs or nits. . . . The stream of blood was a distant object, which could be alleviated by digging for water. The frogs were a loathsome and disgusting nuisance in the houses and on the furniture of the people. The lice, on the other hand, inhabited the skin, sucked

the blood, caused a disagreeable itching, created a feeling of uncleanness, and threatened to become a disease of the most frightful description."

4. THE FIFTH DEMAND AND THE PLAGUE OF FLIES, 8 : 20–32. "In the second series of plagues commenced the distinction between the Egyptians and Israel, the latter being exempted from 'the strokes,' to show that it was not the 'finger of Elohim merely,' but that He was 'Jehovah in the midst of the land' of Egypt (8 : 22). The fourth stroke consisted of swarms of so-called dog flies, which not only infested the houses, but 'corrupted the land' by depositing everywhere their eggs. This plague is to this day most troublesome, painful, and even dangerous, as these animals fasten upon every uncovered surface, especially the eyelids and corners of the eyes, and their bites cause severe inflammation." — *Alfred Edersheim.*

5. THE SIXTH DEMAND AND THE PLAGUES OF MURRAIN AND BOILS, 9 : 1–12. "The fifth stroke was a very grievous murrain (not uncommon in Egypt), which has been supposed to have been of the same kind as the cattle plague in our own country, only far more extensive. But although Pharaoh ascertained, by special inquiry, that Israel had been exempted from this plague, his heart was hardened. Moses and Aaron were directed to take 'ashes of the furnace' — probably in reference to the great buildings and pyramids in which Egypt took such pride — and to 'sprinkle it up towards heaven; and it became a boil breaking forth with blains upon man and beast.' Such 'burning tumors breaking into pustulous ulcers,' but exclusively confined to man, are not uncommon in the valley of the Nile. Even the magicians seem now to have yielded, but the judgment of hardening had already come upon Pharaoh." — *Alfred Edersheim.*

6. THE SEVENTH DEMAND AND THE PLAGUE OF HAIL, 9 : 13–35. We need not enter into details regarding this plague of hail, which is not difficult to understand, but I think it will be worthwhile if we consider for a moment Murphy's comment on verses 15 and 16, where God says He might have smitten the people of Egypt with pestilence as easily as He had smitten the cattle, and that they would have been annihilated and the opposition of Egypt to God's program would have been destroyed. "The Lord here gives us some insight into the theory of His administration. It is instructive, corrective, and in the last resort punitive; but in no case merely destructive of moral agents. He that would sweep into instant annihilation all the opponents of his will has no idea of God's principle of action or mode of dealing with His rational creatures. . . . He will approach moral creatures with love, reason, and justice. Only when such methods fail, will He have recourse to a patient and duly tempered correction. And Pharaoh will be an example to all contemporary nations, and, through the books of Moses, to all succeeding generations, of the mercy, patience, forbearance, justice, and holiness of God."

7. THE EIGHTH DEMAND, THE PLAGUE OF LOCUSTS, AND THE JUDGMENT OF DARKNESS, 10 : 1–29. On this terrible plague of locusts, F. B. Meyer's words are excellent. "An invasion of locusts is probably the most terrible pest that a land can suffer. When the king's advisers heard the brothers say that this visitation would exceed anything their fathers, or fathers' fathers had heard of or seen, from the earliest days of man's history, they were profoundly moved. . . . Pharaoh was so far affected by their representations that he sent for the two brethren, and for a second time tried to enter into an arrangement. On the former occasion he stipulated that they should not go very far away; but on this he endeavored to limit the numbers of those who should participate in the proposed feast to the men. Their little ones should remain as hostages! 'No,' said Moses; 'we will go with our young and with our old, with our sons and with our daughters, with our flocks and with our herds; for we must hold a feast unto the Lord.' This so far exasperated Pharaoh that they were driven from his presence, and then the plague fell. Again he professed to repent. This time he confessed that he had sinned, not only against Jehovah, but against the two brethren. He asked them to forgive, and intercede on his behalf. But as soon as the stroke was removed he returned to his former hardness of heart."

Following the plague of locusts came the awful punishment of total darkness throughout the land of Egypt. "It was equivalent to a universal blindness, which would unfit the nation for making any effort to attend to the business of life or provide for its continuance. In case of its perpetuation, they could only await in despair the slow approach of death by starvation. Pharaoh quails before the appalling darkness. He yields another point. The women and children may go with the men, but not the flocks and the herds. Moses, however, cannot go to hold a national festival unto the Lord without sacrifices. Not a hoof of their cattle must be left behind. Pharaoh is again exasperated. His proud heart becomes hard as the nether millstone. A reckless madness takes possession of him. He forbids Moses to appear before him again on pain of death. There is something ominous in the reply of Moses. 'Well hast thou spoken; I will see thy face no more.' The sun was a leading object of adoration among the Egyptians under the name of Osiris. The very name Pharaoh means not only the king, but also the sun, and entitled in some sort to divine honors. But now the very light of the sun has disappeared, and primeval chaos seems to have returned. Thus all the forms of Egyptian will-worship have been covered with shame and confusion in those nine plagues." — *J. G. Murphy.*

III. **EVENTS IMMEDIATELY PRECEDING THE EXODUS,** 11 : 1—12 : 36. " The eleventh chapter is, strictly speaking, a supplement to the tenth: the first verses speak, as if in parenthesis, of a revelation made before the ninth plague, but held over to be mentioned in connection with the last, which it now announces; and the conversation with Pharaoh is a continuation of the same in which they mutually resolved to see each other's face no more. To account for the confidence of Moses, we are now told that God had revealed to him the close approach of the final blow, so long foreseen. In spite of seeming delays, the hour of the promise had arrived." — *G. H. Chadwick.*

From Trumbull's "Pilgrimage to Jerusalem" by permission of The Sunday School Times Company.

Symbols of the Passover.

Marks of fresh blood over the doorway of a house in imitation of the original rite.

After God had clearly foretold to Moses the details of this last and awful judgment, He at the same time revealed to Moses what that night of judgment would mean to Israel. It would be a time when a new feast in Israel's history was to be established, the Passover feast, so called because on that night the angel of death passed over all those houses on the doorposts or lintels of which there was the sprinkled blood of a fresh slain lamb. God's clear command to the Israelites was that in every household, a lamb was to be taken, without blemish, kept till the fourteenth day of the month, and then killed in the evening, its blood to be stricken on the two sideposts and the upper doorpost of the house. The lamb itself should then be eaten, nothing being allowed to remain until the morning. All Israel, at the same time, should be girded, prepared to make their exodus from Egypt.

At the end of these specific instructions, we read: " And the children of Israel went away and did as the Lord had commanded Moses and Aaron, so did they."

At the stroke of midnight, the night of the passover, the night of God's appointment, " The Lord smote all the firstborn in the land of Egypt, from the firstborn of Pharaoh that sat on his throne unto the firstborn of the captive that was in the dungeon, and all the firstborn of cattle." " All was still with an almost preternatural silence; ' broken only by the hoot of the owl, the scream of the bittern, the plunge of the monster in the water, or the cry of the jackal on the plains.' But suddenly the stillness was interrupted by a scream of anguish, as a mother rushed out into the night to tell that the Angel of Death had begun his work, and she was presently answered by the wail of a mother in agony for her firstborn; and this by another, and yet another. It was useless to summon priest or physician, magician or courtier; how could they help others who had not been able to ward off death from their own? The maid grinding at the mill and her lady sleeping under curtains of silk were in-

EXODUS 12 : 51. And it came to pass the selfsame day, that Jehovah did bring the children of Israel out of the land of Egypt by their hosts.

volved in a common sorrow, which obliterated all social distinctions, and made all one. There was not a house where there was not one dead — even Pharaoh's palace was not exempt. The news spread like wildfire that the heir to the throne was dead. 'And there was a great cry in Egypt.'" — *F. B. Meyer.*

In the midst of this awful judgment, Pharaoh called for Moses and Aaron and told them to rise up and to take the children of Israel at once, and to go and serve the Lord, to take their flocks and their herds and be gone. In this command the Egyptians themselves joined, urging the Israelites to hasten to make their exodus. Asking of the Egyptians jewels of silver and jewels of gold, and raiment, finding favor in the sight of the Egyptians, they left laden with the spoils of Egypt. We have discussed the meaning of this asking, which is wrongly translated, appearing in the Authorized Version, in our previous lesson and need not dwell on it here.

Pharaoh Urging Moses to Take the Israelites Away from Egypt.

IV. **THE EXODUS FROM EGYPT BEGINS,** 12 : 37–51. There is no time to discuss the geographical problems raised by this final paragraph, for geographical material is not the essential thing in the study of this particular lesson. There is here a reiteration of the importance of the Passover Feast, with the insistence that it be kept, not only by the Israelites, but that it might also be kept by the strangers who dwell within their land in the days to come.

51. **And it came to pass the selfsame day, that Jehovah did bring the children of Israel out of the land of Egypt by their hosts.** Here we read that the number of males departing at this time was 600,000. Often this has been considered an error. Professor Rawlinson's words are worth careful consideration here, and reassure us of the accuracy of the text which is before us. This statement "is confirmed and even enlarged, by the more accurate estimate of Numbers 1 and 2, which goes into particulars with respect to the several tribes, and makes the exact amount of the adult male population, exclusive of the Levites, to be 625,540 (2 : 32). It would follow that the nation, at the time of its departure, was one of above two millions of souls. The difficulty of handling so vast a body, and marching them from Goshen to the Red Sea, and from the Red Sea to Sinai, remains, and is no doubt considerable. . . . The plain Er-Rahah, according to the calculations of the best engineers, would have contained the entire multitude; but it is unnecessary to suppose that all were at any one time present in it. The whole Sinaitic district was probably occupied by the flocks and herds, and the herdsmen who tended them. Many of the tents may have been pitched in the Wady-el-Deir and the Seil Leja. All that the narrative requires is that the *main body* of the people should have been encamped in front of Sinai, have heard the Decalogue delivered, and consented to the covenant."

ARCHÆOLOGICAL CONFIRMATION.

Our readers will be glad for the following words, concerning the historical trustworthiness of this narrative, from a book published not long ago by the Oxford

University Press, *Bible and Spade*, by Stephen L. Caiger, recognized on every hand as authoritative. " The biblical story implies that Moses waited for the death of the great oppressor (Thothmes III) before returning to Egypt from his refuge in Midian; and that the exodus took place almost immediately in the reign of Thothmes' successor, that is, of Amenhotep II (1448–1420). Amenhotep, therefore, was probably the ' Pharaoh of the Exodus' who hardened his heart and ' would not let them go.' He followed Thothmes in 1448 B.C. The tenth plague — which smote all the firstborn in the land of Egypt, from the firstborn of Pharaoh that sat on his throne — ought, however, to be capable of archæological verification. Is there any record on the monuments that the eldest son of Amenhotep II came to an untimely end? That he did so certainly seems to be implied by the curious Dream Inscriptions of Thothmes IV, Amenhotep's immediate successor, showing that Thothmes was not that sovereign's eldest son. On an immense slab of red granite near the Sphinx at Gizeh it is recorded that Thothmes IV, while yet a youth, had fallen asleep under the famous monument, and dreamed a dream. In this the Sphinx appeared to him, startling him with a prophecy that one day he would live to be king of Egypt, and bidding him clear the sand away from her feet in token of his gratitude: which, on his accession, he did. It is clear from this inscription that Thothmes' hopes of succession had been remote, which proves — since the law of primogeniture obtained in Egypt at the time — that he could not have been Amenhotep's eldest son. In other words, there is room for the explanation that the heir apparent died in the manner related in the Bible."

In how many different ways does Jehovah, the God of the Israelites, here reveal Himself to be infinitely superior to the false gods of Egypt? In what ways do you find Moses at this time an infinitely stronger, more dependable man than he was at the time when God first commissioned him to this great task when He appeared to him in the miracle of the burning bush? Why do you think Pharaoh waited so long, necessitating Egypt to suffer so dreadfully under these successive plagues, before he set the children of Israel free? How would you say that these terrific judgments upon Egypt were sent for moral purposes; that is, to accomplish moral ends? Why did God at this time establish the Passover instead of just allowing the children of Israel to be delivered from Egypt without any such memorial observance? If an Israelitish family had not sprinkled the doorpost of their home with sacrificial blood, would there have been a death in their home also? (The answer is, Yes.) What was it, after all then, that led the Israelite to obey this command regarding blood? (It was faith in God's words.) In what ways is Christ our Passover? What parallels do you find between the deliverance of the Israelite from the bondage of Egypt and deliverance of men from the slavery of sin and the thralldom of Satan?

LESSON VI. — August 8.

GOD SHOWS HIS PEOPLE THE WAY. — Exodus 13—15.

PRINTED TEXT, Exodus 13 : 17-22; 15 : 17-22*a*.

GOLDEN TEXT. — *Jehovah is my strength and song, and he is become my salvation.* Exodus 15 : 2.

Devotional Reading: Psalm 77 : 11–20.
Beginner Topic: Twelve Springs of Cool Water.
Lesson Material: Exodus 15 : 22–27.
Memory Verse: He careth for you. 1 Peter 5 : 7.
Primary Topic: Miriam's Song.
Lesson Material: Exodus 15.
Memory Verse: Jehovah is good: sing praises unto his name; for it is pleasant. Psalm 135 : 3.
Junior Topic: Beyond the Red Sea.
Lesson Material: Exodus 15.
Memory Verse: Jehovah our God will we serve, and unto his voice will we hearken. Joshua 24 : 24.
Intermediate and Senior Topic: Following God's Leading.
Topic for Young People and Adults: God's Leadership Today.

THE TEACHER AND HIS CLASS.

The Younger Classes might be introduced to this lesson by being asked on what occasions a boy or a girl, a man or a woman, would spontaneously burst into song, either while walking through the woods, or going about doing housework, or laboring in the field. Of course, the answer to this is that people, apart from professional singing, and congregational singing (in which we all participate no matter what our mood), sing of their own volition when they are happy. This is why the Christian Church has thousands and thousands of hymns, because the members of the church are happy in Christ; they know the joy of being delivered from the power of sin, from enslavement to some terrible habit, from the fear of death, from the power of darkness. In our lesson we have the first great song to be found in the Bible, and also the reason why this song burst forth — because the children of Israel at this hour were finally delivered from their terrible enemies, the Egyptians.

The Older Classes will find in this passage words which come with especial appropriateness just at this time, when our own nation is struggling with the forces of darkness and powers bent on ruthlessly oppressing other nations. Now, while God is not today generally delivering nations by *miracles*, yet He is the same today as He was then, and if, by our love for God, our worship of God, our obedience to His laws, through His grace, we may count ourselves as God's children, He *will* deliver us ultimately from every evil thing. Only we must be careful that at the end of this war we do not simply boast of our military and economic power, but give thanks *to God*, who has given us the strength and resources for victory.

THE PLAN OF THE LESSON.

SUBJECT: The Perfect Wisdom and Omnipotence of God as Revealed in His Deliverance of Israel from Her Enemies.

I. SOME RULES FOR ISRAEL WHEN SHE SHOULD COME INTO PALESTINE, Exodus 13 : 1–16.

1. The firstborn to be set apart for the Lord, vs. 1, 2.
2. The feast of unleavened bread to be kept, vs. 3–10.
3. The law of the firstborn, vs. 11–16.

II. SOME PRINCIPLES REGARDING GOD'S LEADING OF THE ISRAELITES, Exodus 13 : 17–22.

1. Why God led them by way of the wilderness, vs. 17, 18.
2. The bones of Joseph carried with them, vs. 19, 20.
3. The pillar of cloud and the pillar of fire, vs. 21, 22.

III. THE FINAL VICTORY OVER THE EGYPTIANS, Exodus 14 : 1–31.

1. The command to encamp at Pi-hahiroth, vs. 1–4.
2. The pursuit of the Egyptians, vs. 5–9.
3. The complaint of the Israelites, vs. 10–12.
4. The encouraging words of Moses, vs. 13, 14.
5. The command of God to go forward, vs. 15–18.
6. The divine protection, vs. 19, 20.
7. The miracle at the Red Sea, vs. 21, 22.
8. The destruction of the Egyptian host, vs. 23–31.

IV. THE SONG OF REDEMPTION, Exodus 15 : 1–21.

1. The redemption God *had* accomplished, vs. 1–13.
2. The redemption God *would* accomplish, vs. 14–19.
3. The song of Miriam, vs. 20, 21.

V. AT THE WATERS OF MARAH, Exodus 15 : 22–27.

THE LESSON IN ITS SETTING.

Time. — 1445 B.C.

Place. — The Israelites as they went out of Egypt gathered together at Succoth, in the northeast of the land of Egypt. Other places in our lesson are to be found between Succoth and the northern end of the Red Sea and on the eastern shore of the Red Sea.

THE TEACHER'S LIBRARY.

One should first consult the better commentaries on Exodus and the more important lives of Moses, lists of which will be found in the bibliography in the Introduction to this volume. On the geographical aspects of the exodus, a very difficult subject, see O. T. Toffteen: *The Historical Exodus* (Chicago, 1909); J. M. Adams: *Biblical Back-Grounds* (1934), 113–136; E. H. Palmer: *The Desert of the Exodus* (New York, 1872); and G. A. F. Knight: *The Nile and Jordan* (1921). Sermonic material is not as abundant on this passage as one at first expects. On 13 : 21, see W. L. Watkinson: *The Fatal Barrier*, 110–124; on 13 : 19, a great sermon, in Dinsdale T. Young's *Unfamiliar Texts*, 102–116; on 13 : 17, 18, W. L. Watkinson: *The Duty of Imperial Thinking*, 174–180; on 13 : 21, the same, *Fatal Barter*, 110–124; on 13 : 17, G. H. Morrison: *Sunrise*, 64–73; and Hugh Black: *According to My Gospel*, 37–48; on 15 : 11–17, Andrew Murray: *Holy in Christ*, 55–63. While the specific verses do not come within the printed text of our lesson, the editor must refer to two great sermons that every one ought to read on 14 : 10, a sermon by Joseph Parker, called "Old Enemies Pursuing," in the *People's Bible*, Vol. 2, 92–99; and, on 14 : 30, Phillips Brooks: *The Battle of Life*, 55–70.

The following words of Professor George Rawlinson will serve to connect this lesson with the one which brought us down to the night of the beginning of the exodus from Egypt. "The Israelites set out at early dawn on the fifteenth of Nisan. By fixing the Passover feast for a definite day, and requiring that after eating it none should go forth 'until the morning' Moses had made all acquainted with the day and hour of departure; he had also caused all to be prepared for setting forth; and, if any had been inclined to linger, the Egyptians themselves would not have allowed it; for they 'were urgent upon the people, that they might send them out of the land in haste; for they said, We be all dead men.' Thus an almost simultaneous departure was secured. From the various points at which the Israelites were settled, extending, we conceive, from Memphis towards the south to Tanis and Pelusium on the north, columns went forth in orderly array, all streaming in converging lines towards one point, the place fixed for the rendezvous — the land of Thukot or Succoth. The largest company took its departure from Rameses-Tanis, under the conduct of Moses and Aaron. This company proceeded southeastward, and would reach Succoth, to the northwest of Lake Timseh, in about three marches. Other companies flowed in from the north, the west, and the south, till the whole people was gathered together in one — six hundred thousand men, according to the existing text, together with their families."

I. SOME RULES FOR ISRAEL WHEN SHE SHOULD COME INTO PALESTINE, 13 : 1–16.

1. THE FIRSTBORN TO BE SET APART FOR THE LORD, VS. 1, 2. The setting apart of the firstborn of man and beast for God is resumed again and expounded with much greater detail in verses 11–16 of this chapter, but perhaps it may well be considered here. "All things by nature belong to Jehovah as God. They consequently ought on man's part, as the subject lord of earth, to be devoted to that king of heaven, by a free continuous act of will, like that Life (1 Cor. 10 : 5) from the smitten Rock which followed Israel all the way. There thus ought to be consecration of the man himself for service, as well as of the lower creatures he owns for sacrifice. The firstborn, here as elsewhere, represents the whole family and estate. In this case the sanctification prescribed is in form peculiar to Israel; because it has reference to what happened only in Egypt to the firstborn. It is a monumental evidence of the tenth plague. But the spirit of the thing is in all true redemption life. . . . Clean animals were sanctified by being sacrificed; unclean, of which only the ass is specified here, by being redeemed, v. 15; where as the principle of the sacrifice there again comes into view, *substitution* of life for life and death for death." — *James Macgregor.*

2. THE FEAST OF UNLEAVENED BREAD TO BE KEPT, VS. 3–10. "The Feast of Unleavened Bread was a continuation of the Passover, and followed it on the next day, and continued for a week. From the beginning of Passover all leaven was rigorously banished from the houses of the Hebrews. So strict was the law that the Jews made search for leaven with lighted lamp, that no particle of it might remain concealed." — *W. G. Moorehead.* "*Abib*, here first named, is peculiar to the Pentateuch, so as to be incidental evidence of its Mosaic antiquity. It perhaps was not intended for an abiding proper name. It may have been employed simply, according to its meaning, an ear of corn, a green ear, as descriptive of the season (cf. midsummer as descriptive of a term, or sundown for evening time). The season which it represents or describes, of opening the ear of corn in Palestine, fixes the month as nearly coincident with our April." — *James Macgregor.* "The celebration of the Passover, being thus expounded and observed from generation to generation, will be for a sign upon the hand, and a frontlet between the eyes. There is a beautiful consecration of personal ornament in this injunction. These ornaments, being embellishments of the person, came often before the eye and the mind as pleasing objects of contemplation. . . . These phylacteries or Tephillin (prayer bands) were strips of parchment, on which were written Exod. 13 : 1–10; 11–16; Deut. 6 : 4–9; 11 : 13–21. These were enclosed in little boxes or cases of leather attached to leather straps, by which they were fastened to the places where they were worn. Thus custom was not prescribed by the present passage, and can only be regarded as an indication of a feeble and declining piety. . . . The sacraments of the divine appointment, and not the phylacteries of our own invention, are to be the signs upon our hands and the frontlets between our eyes, telling of our faith in God; our reconciliation to Him; our entrance into the glorious liberty of the sons of God." — *J. G. Murphy.*

3. THE LAW OF THE FIRSTBORN, VS. 11–16. Of course, this passage has to do with the Israelitish law, which is not the law for Christian believers today, as we recognize. Nevertheless, many things which the Israelites were commanded to do we might well do. The editor almost never makes a definitely personal statement concerning himself in these notes, but right here he would like to thank God, once again, for the fact that before he was born, the first child in his parent's family, his

Exodus 13 : 17. And it came to pass, when Pharaoh had let the people go,
that God led them not by the way of the land of the Philistines, although
that was near; for God said, Lest peradventure the people repent when they
see war, and they return to Egypt:
18. But God led the people about, by the way of the wilderness by the
Red Sea: and the children of Israel went up armed out of the land of Egypt.
19. And Moses took the bones of Joseph with him: for he had straitly
sworn the children of Israel, saying, God will surely visit you; and ye shall
carry up my bones away hence with you.

---

precious mother, now in glory, told the Lord that if her first child should be a son, she wanted him to be a minister of the gospel. This he was never told until, when nineteen years old, he heard God's call into the ministry.

II. **SOME PRINCIPLES REGARDING GOD'S LEADING OF THE ISRAELITES,** 13 : 17–22.

1. Why God Led Them by Way of the Wilderness, vs. 17, 18. 17. **And it came to pass, when Pharaoh had let the people go, that God led them not by the way of the land of the Philistines, although that was near; for God said, Lest peradventure the people repent when they see war, and they return to Egypt:** 18. **but God led the people about, by the way of the wilderness by the Red Sea: and the children of Israel went up armed out of the land of Egypt.** "The starting point of the journey being Tanis, or Rameses, in the eastern Delta, not far from the sea, he sees that the shortest, and apparently the easiest, route for the Israelites to have pursued would have been that which led along the coast, from Tanis, to Pelusium, thence to Rhinocolura, and from thence to Gaza, Ascalon, and Ashdod, the chief towns of the Philistines. The distance along this line was not more than about two hundred miles, and might have been accomplished in a fortnight. He anticipates an inquiry. Why did they not pursue this route? The reply is that such was not the will of God; and the reason why it was not His will is further given. . . . It is implied that the Philistines were already a strong and warlike people, which they may well have been, though not mentioned in the contemporary Egyptian monuments. The Egyptians mentioned by name very few of the nations of Syria, and the few names which they put on record can seldom be identified. . . . God took them, not by the direct route, through Pelusium, past Lake Serbonis, to Rhinocolura and Gaza, but led them by the most circuitous route possible — the way of the Red Sea and the wilderness of Sinai to the Transjordanic region, the land of the Amorites, and so across Jordan to Canaan proper." — *George Rawlinson.* "The barriers of life may be ranked among its greatest benedictions." — *F. B. Meyer.*

2. The Bones of Joseph Carried with Them, vs. 19, 20. 19. **And Moses took the bones of Joseph with him: for he had straitly sworn the children of Israel, saying, God will surely visit you; and ye shall carry up my bones away hence with you.** "Joseph had bound their fathers by an oath to carry his bones with them to the land

Tomb of Joseph. Shechem.

20. And they took their journey from Succoth, and encamped in Etham, in the edge of the wilderness.

21. And Jehovah went before them by day in a pillar of cloud, to lead them the way, and by night in a pillar of fire, to give them light; that they might go by day and by night:

22. The pillar of cloud by day, and the pillar of fire by night, departed not from before the people.

---

of promise (Gen. 50 : 24, 25). This oath and the hopes inseparably connected with it were often talked over in the family gatherings of the evening, and the memory of it faithfully handed down from father to son. This little incident warrants us to imagine the frequent and earnest conferences which took place in the homes and social meetings of Israel concerning the promise made to Abraham, Isaac, and Jacob; the land to which they were to return when the iniquity of the Amorite was full; the privileges and blessings that were in store for the seed of Abraham, and in that seed for all the families of the earth." — *J. G. Murphy.* Space forbids quoting from Dr. Dinsdale T. Young's most suggestive sermon on this text, but we cannot refrain from at least giving his major points: (1) We cannot disassociate ourselves from the past; (2) mortality marks the noblest; (3) the great and good departed should not be forgotten; (4) we should fulfill the injunctions of the sainted ones; (5) the past gives inspiration for future experiences; (6) the good succession does not perish. (Joseph was dead but there was a Moses to carry his bones to the promised land.) (7) we may inspire future generations. 20. **And they took their journey from Succoth, and encamped in Etham, in the edge of the wilderness.** "The exact positions of both Succoth and Etham are uncertain, and can only be conjectured; but they probably lay to the southeast of Tanis, between that city and the Bitter Lakes. Succoth may have been at or near Tel Dafneh, about fifteen miles from Tanis, and Etham near the modern Ismailia, on the verge of the desert." — *George Rawlinson.*

3. THE PILLAR OF CLOUD AND THE PILLAR OF FIRE, VS. 21, 22. 21. **And Jehovah went before them by day in a pillar of cloud, to lead them the way, and by night in a pillar of fire, to give them light; that they might go by day and by night:** 22. **the pillar of cloud by day, and the pillar of fire by night, departed not from before the people.** "In verses 17 and 18, the writer has declared that 'God led the people'; he now explains how. From Succoth certainly, probably from Rameses, He moved in front of the host in the form of a pillar, which had the appearance of smoke by day and of fire by night. The Israelites marched, it is implied, some part of each day and some part of each night, which would be in accordance with modern practice, and is an arrangement introduced to get the march accomplished before the sun attains his full power. The pillar was at once a signal and a guide. When it moved, the people moved; when it stopped, they encamped (40 : 36–38); where it went, they followed." — *George Rawlinson.*

III. THE FINAL VICTORY OVER THE EGYPTIANS, 14 : 1–31.

1. THE COMMAND TO ENCAMP AT PI-HAHIROTH, VS. 1–4. "Not far from Suez, south and eastward on the Egyptian side of the Red Sea, there is a plain, which reaches inland some twelve miles from that sea. At the upper extremity of that plain there is a height, on which is an ancient fort named Ajrud. This Ajrud we shall take as the site of Pi-hahiroth. *Pi* means town, so that Pi-hahiroth is Hahiroth town. And Hahiroth *may* have dwindled into Ajrud. From this Pi-hahiroth, at the head of the plain, facing toward the Red Sea at the foot of it, we look beyond the narrow sea, on the east side of it, for Baal-zephon, which the Israelites saw, if they looked across the sea from this plain between it and our Ajrud." — *James Macgregor.*

2. THE PURSUIT OF THE EGYPTIANS, VS. 5–9. It is strange how those who are determined to resist God, even though God has terribly punished them and brought them to shame with crushing defeat, break forth again at the first opportunity in a new manifestation of their foolish determination to contend against God. I think, though I have never seen it referred to in any expositions of this particular event, that a remarkable parallel to this is what is found in Revelation 19 : 11–19; 20 : 7–10. One would have thought that Satan would have ceased rebelling against God, with his first terrible defeat, and imprisonment for a thousand years. But, no. Armageddon is followed, a thousand years later, by one more gigantic attempt on his part to destroy the people of God. So here, even though there had only been a few days since Egypt had suffered the terrible divine judgment of the death of the firstborn

in every home, the Pharaoh of Egypt, numbed to his recent experiences by the hardness of his heart, is still determined to destroy the children of Israel who are now at the border of his country, and pursues them with horsemen and chariots, overtaking them at Pi-hahiroth. The Israelites, in their present position, were indeed, humanly speaking, in a *cul-de-sac.* "On their left hand the gulf extended much farther toward the Mediterranean than it does at present; and the land was much under water, of marsh, lagoon, or lake; while they have further been turned from that direction by the formidableness of the Philistines beyond the head of the gulf. On the right side of the plain they have reached there is broken if not mountainous ground, which practically barricades their way in that direction. The Egyptians behind them, plainly, with no outgate but the sea, they are, as the history says, *entangled* — caught as in a trap which they have entered, and which the Egyptians have now closed behind them." — *James Macgregor.*

Egyptian Chariots.

3. THE COMPLAINT OF THE ISRAELITES, VS. 10–12. The Israelitish host was many times greater than the Egyptian host, but the Egyptians were fully armed, ready for battle, while the Israelites did not make their exodus from Egypt with any adequate military equipment. You cannot expect men who have been slaves for generations to become, overnight, trained soldiers, ready to meet such a host as the Egyptians sent after them. True to nature, the Israelites are no more at ease under the bondage of the Egyptians than face to face with difficulty and threatened with annihilation. Instead of calling upon God, they began to complain to Moses that he had no business to bring them out of Egypt. One day they cry to be delivered from this land of brutality and slavery. Now forgetting the beatings and the stripes, they think it would be better had they never left. How good it is that we do not always have our way! God is determined to lead them out.

4. THE ENCOURAGING WORDS OF MOSES, VS. 13, 14. "The one man who seemed unmoved amid the panic of the people was their heroic leader, whose faith was the organ of their deliverance. And therefore it is that in all after-allusions to this great event his hand is always referred to as the instrument through which the might of Jehovah wrought. 'Thou leddest,' says the psalmist, 'Thy people like a flock, by the hand of Moses and Aaron' (Ps. 77 : 20). 'He caused,' says Isaiah, 'his glorious arm to go at the right hand of Moses' (Isa. 63 : 12, Revised Version). The people, therefore, had good reason to remember the ancient days of Moses; for they were made famous by Moses' mighty faith. By his faith they passed through the Red Sea as by dry land." — *F. B. Meyer.*

5. THE COMMAND OF GOD TO GO FORWARD, VS. 15–18. The divine command to Moses that he should lead this great army of Israelites forward at an hour when it seemed they were about to be annihilated, means, on the one hand, that God is never disturbed, as men are, by "adverse" circumstances, for He has foreseen them long before they arise. The sovereignty of God involves His perfect knowledge of all circumstances that will ever have to be faced, at any particular time, by any servant of His, and implies absolute omnipotence in the ordering of those circumstances, so that they will never prevent the ultimate accomplishment of His eternal counsel and the fulfillment of His holy promises. It is a good thing sometimes to get to the place where, humanly speaking, we are helpless, doomed to defeat, only that we might know the delivering power of God Himself.

6. THE DIVINE PROTECTION, VS. 19, 20. "The angel spoken of in Exodus is one person. He apparently is equivalent to God; and yet so that in a real sense his

presence is different from a presence of God; it is beneficent where that might be destructive. In short, it is a manifested presence and power of God in redeeming mercy; as compared with the manifestation of God in His essential nature, or, with His glory simply of holiness as appearing in law. Correspondingly, there is the doctrine of the person of Christ: that He is God, the Son who is the outshining of the Father's glory; the Word, the person who was tempted (1 Cor. 10 : 9) by Israel in the wilderness; the Redeemer whose reproach was preferred by Moses to the treasures of Egypt; the seed of Abraham who says, 'Before Abraham was, I am.' Those who believe what the Bible says about the Triune constitution of the Godhead, and about Immanuel Jesus Christ the Lord, will ordinarily see that the Exodus angel must have been Christ; whose glory (2 Cor. 3 : 18) was reflected on the shining face of Moses. How far that may have been comprehended by Moses himself (1 Pet. 1 : 10–12), who wist not even that his face shone, or by the Old Testament Church, we will not inquire. We can see that the presence and the promises represented by the angel in Exodus always had the effect of salvation as a realized fact, or in the assured hope." — *James Macgregor.*

7. The Miracle at the Red Sea, vs. 21, 22. "The orders which Moses gave were easily executed. Divinely instructed, he commanded the Israelites to form in column, facing a particular portion of the shore, to load their beasts, bring together their cattle, and have everything in readiness for a start. Then he stood at the head of the column, and stretched out his hand over the sea. At once an east, or southeast, wind arose, and drove the upper water of the shallow bay that lay before him towards the northwest, while probably a strong ebb-tide set in at the same time, and drew the lower water southwards, so that the bed of the sea was for a considerable space laid bare. A sort of broad causeway, guarded by water upon either side, was formed, and upon this the column advanced, the pillar of the cloud still lending them its brilliant light and clearly showing them their path. The distance to be traversed may not have been more than a mile, and the entire column may easily have accomplished the passage in five or six hours. As the last Israelites entered the sea-bed, the pillar of the cloud withdrew itself from the shore and followed up the retiring column, protecting it like a rearguard. Then the Egyptians began to see what had happened. Israel had quitted its camping ground, had entered the sea-bed, and was traversing it — their prey was on the point of escaping them. The sight woke in them a burning anger, and an intense longing for revenge. . . . Without waiting for orders, as far as appears, they rushed to satiate their lust of carnage and of spoil. The soft sand and ooze of the sea-bed was unsuited for the passage of chariots; the wheels sank into it up to their axles, and were in consequence clogged, and 'made to go heavily.' The result was that the Egyptian host never came in contact with the Israelites." — *George Rawlinson.*

The Destruction of Pharaoh's Host.

8. The Destruction of the Egyptian Host, vs. 23–31. "The gray morning light was breaking on the other side of the waters, when a fiercer sun than that about to rise on the horizon cast its glare upon the Egyptians. 'Jehovah looked unto' them 'through the pillar of fire and of the cloud, and troubled the host of the Egyptians.' It was the fire of His divine presence, bursting suddenly through the pillar of the cloud, which threw them into confusion and panic. The wheels of their chariots became clogged, the sand beneath them seemed to soften under the fiery glow, and they drave heavily. With that light from the fiery cloud, the conviction flashed upon them that it was Jehovah who fought for Israel and against

them. They essayed immediate flight. But already Moses had, at God's command, once more stretched his hand over the sea. In that morning watch, the wind veered round; the waters returned, and Pharaoh, with the flower of his host, sank buried beneath the waves. Thus, in the language of Scripture, 'Jehovah shook off the Egyptians in the midst of the sea.'" — *Alfred Edersheim.* The Hebrew word translated *save* in verse 30 is the first occurrence in Scripture of the verb *yasha*, which is the root of the word *Joshua*, which means, *Jehovah saves.* This is especially precious to us because the Greek word *Jesus*, in the New Testament, is the equivalent of the Hebrew word *Joshua* in the Old Testament. Thus this verse in Exodus finds its perfect fulfillment, if we may say, in Matthew 1 : 21, when an angel from heaven announces to Joseph that the son born of Mary should be called Jesus, "for he shall save his people from their sins." God begins to save His people in the lesson we are studying.

There is here a most significant phrase, "Israel saw the Egyptians dead upon the seashore." Rightly, as Dr. F. B. Meyer has written: "The sands of time are strewn with dead Egyptians, who once held the hearts and minds of men in thrall. The dominion of the priest over the human conscience, the ownership of man by man, the use of torture to extort the needed lie, the praise of ignorance as the safeguard of order, the habitual degradation of womanhood, the massacre of child-life. But they have lost their power. They are dead Egyptians. . . . What is your Egyptian? Some besetting sin that has been your taskmaster for years? Long ago it made you its slave, or perhaps it enslaved your father before you. In former days you struggled valiantly for freedom; but all your efforts were in vain. Of late you have renounced the conflict, and have allowed yourself to yield at your tyrants' imperious behests. Perhaps you cherish the hope that some day the ebbing forces of your life, or even satiety, will emancipate you from your servitude. But it is a weary prospect. . . . Now, from this hour, will you not begin to cherish the anticipation of complete deliverance, not hereafter, in old age and in heaven, but now and here? Not because of your resolutions, or strivings, or agonies, but because you will stand still and see the salvation of God, because the Lord shall fight for you, and you will hold your peace."

IV. **THE SONG OF REDEMPTION,** 15 : 1–21. While the word "song" does occur on one occasion before this (Gen. 31 : 27), yet this is the first time in which the verb *sing* occurs, and here we find an elaborate development of the idea of singing. Singing is the result of joy, and there is no joy in the world compared to that which results from a consciousness of being redeemed from an impending danger, from a bitter enemy, from a terrible physical affliction, and most of all, from the power of sin, the dominion of Satan and eternal death. This first great song in the Bible then properly comes before us at the conclusion of the first great redemptive act of God exercised toward His own people as a *nation.* (We are not thinking of Noah being delivered from the Flood here.) "Like all great poetry, this song is best enjoyed when it is neither commented upon nor paraphrased, but carefully read and warmly felt. . . . It is unquestionably archaic. The parallelism of Hebrew verse is already here, but the structure is more free and unartificial than that of later poetry; and many ancient words, and words of Egyptian derivation, authenticate its origin. . . . The song is divided into two parts. Up to the end of the twelfth verse it is historical: the remainder expresses the high hopes inspired by this great experience. Nothing now seems impossible: the fiercest tribes of Palestine and the desert may be despised, for their own terror will suffice to 'melt' them; and Israel may already reckon itself to be guided into the holy habitation (v. 13)." — *G. H. Chadwick.* It is impossible for us to enter into details of this marvelous pean of praise, but we cannot pass over the great declaration of verse 11: "Who is like unto thee, O Jehovah, among the gods? Who is like thee, glorious in holiness, fearful in praises, doing wonders?" "It had been a main object of the entire series of miraculous visitations to show that Jehovah was 'exalted far above all other gods.' Moses now emphasizes the contrast by adducing three points on which Jehovah is unapproachable — holiness, awfulness, and miraculous power. God is (1) 'glorious in holiness,' exalted in this respect far, far above all other beings; (2) 'fearful in praises' — the proper object of the profoundest awe, even to those who approach Him with praise and thanksgiving; (3) and one who 'doeth wonders,' who both through nature, and on occasions overruling nature, accomplishes the most astonishing results, causing all men to marvel at His almighty power. The gods of the heathen were, in fact, either nonentities or evil spirits. Of holiness they possessed no remnant; in awfulness they were immeasurably inferior; in the ability to work wonders

EXODUS 15 : 17. Thou wilt bring them in, and plant them in the mountain of thine inheritance,
The place, O Jehovah, which thou hast made for thee to dwell in,
The sanctuary, O Lord, which thy hands have established.
18. Jehovah shall reign for ever and ever.
19. For the horses of Pharaoh went in with his chariots and with his
horsemen into the sea, and Jehovah brought back the waters of the sea upon
them; but the children of Israel walked on dry land in the midst of the sea.
20. And Miriam the prophetess, the sister of Aaron, took a timbrel in
her hand; and all the women went out after her with timbrels and with
dances.
21. And Miriam answered them,
Sing ye to Jehovah, for he hath triumphed gloriously;
The horse and his rider hath he thrown into the sea.

---

they did not deserve to be mentioned in the same breath. 'Among the gods,' as the psalmist says, 'there is none like unto thee, O Lord; there is none that can do as thou doest' (Ps. 86 : 8)." — *George Rawlinson.*

17. **Thou wilt bring them in, and plant them in the mountain of thine inheritance, the place, O Jehovah, which thou hast made for thee to dwell in, the sanctuary, O Lord, which thy hands have established.** 18. **Jehovah shall reign for ever and ever.**
19. **For the horses of Pharaoh went in with his chariots and with his horsemen into the sea, and Jehovah brought back the waters of the sea upon them; but the children of Israel walked on dry land in the midst of the sea.** These verses, even though they are assigned to the printed text, do not contain a great deal of matter to be taught, and so the teacher should bring to the class, as far as time allows, the truths set forth principally in the preceding verses. "The bard of emancipated Israel now turns to the future. The further doings of the Lord for His people are sketched in a few master touches. First, a sudden and overwhelming trepidation unmans the adversary, and the people of the Lord are unopposed in their progress. This was the natural result of the divine interposition, and would have been the actual and uniform consequence, but for the unbelief and disobedience of the chosen people. . . . The tree is the holy people (Ps. 1 : 3); the hill is the land of promise, which was not a river valley, like Egypt, but a high land lying between the Jordan and the Mediterranean. To the hill of Zion there may be a distant allusion." — *J. G. Murphy.* 20. **And Miriam the prophetess, the sister of Aaron, took a timbrel in her hand; and all the women went out after her with timbrels and with dances.** 21. **And Miriam answered them, Sing ye to Jehovah, for he hath triumphed gloriously; the horse and his rider hath he thrown into the sea.** "Miriam and her maidens at the close of each portion of the song — *i.e.*, at the end of verses 5, 10, 12, 18 — sang the refrain which is here given — a

The Song of Miriam.

22. And Moses led Israel onward from the Red Sea, and they went out into the wilderness of Shur;

refrain very slightly altered from the opening verses of the song itself, marking, no doubt, the time with their timbrels, and moving gracefully through a stately and solemn dance. . . . By timbrels are meant tambours, or tambourines, favorite instruments in Egypt, and usually played by women there." — *George Rawlinson.*

V. **AT THE WATERS OF MARAH,** 15 : 22–27. 22. **And Moses led Israel onward from the Red Sea, and they went out into the wilderness of Shur.** " In the Biblical narrative there are several general references to the Wilderness of Shur, though none of them provides us with definite information concerning either its boundaries or its extent. It is probable, however, that the wilderness covered a considerably larger area than is usually assigned to it, certainly more than the little strip of seaboard at the northeastern corner of the Gulf of Suez. . . . The southern extension of Shur would include Marah and Elim, and on the basis of Numbers 33 : 10, 11, perhaps the camp by the sea also. In general, then, we may regard the wilderness of Shur, at least in its middle and southern portions, as including the area in the vicinity of the eastern coasts of Lake Timsah and the Gulf of Suez as far as the traditional site of the camp by the sea. . . . Its eastern extension is merely hinted at in passages describing the journeys of Abraham and Hagar from Hebron, when both travelers are represented as being in the wilderness in the way of Shur, between Kadesh (Ain Kadis) and Egypt. It is likely that other portions of its eastern borders merged with the wilderness of Paran." — *J. McKee Adams.* When the people came to Marah they found the waters here so bitter that they could not drink of them, and at once they began their customary murmuring against Moses. When Moses turned to the Lord to ask Him what to do, he was divinely directed to a tree, which, when he had cut it down, he cast into the waters, with the result that the waters were made sweet.

Woman Beating Tambourines (timbrels) and a Darabooka Drum.

The chapter closes with the Israelites resting at Elim where there was an abundance of water and welcome shade. " There are more Elims in life than Marahs; and we *encamp* by them. We are not bidden to tarry at the one, but we may spend long blessed days at the other. How refreshing the shadow of those seventy palm trees! How sweet the water of those twelve wells! How delightful those long restful days! You say that they will never come to you? Yes, but they will! They come to all tired souls. There is no desert march without an Elim at last." — *F. B. Meyer.*

THE GREAT SIGNIFICANCE OF THE EXODUS FROM EGYPT.

A. P. Stanley, in his famous *History of the Jewish Church*, with his customary brilliance, makes the following profound remarks concerning the exodus of Israel out of Egypt and her relocation in Asia. " They had passed in that night from Africa to Asia; they have crossed one of the great boundaries which divide the quarters of the world; a thought always thrilling, how much more when we reflect on what a transition it involved to them. . . . Further, this change of local situation was at once a change of moral condition. From slaves they had become free; from an oppressed tribe they had become an independent nation. It is their deliverance from slavery. It is the earliest recorded instance of a great national emancipation. In later times religion has been so often and so exclusively associated with ideas of order, of obedience, of submission to authority, that it is well to be occasionally reminded that it has had other aspects also. Thus, the first epoch of our religious history is in its original historical significance, the sanctification, the glorification of national independence and freedom. Whatever else was to succeed to it, this was the first stage of the progress of the chosen people. And when in the Christian Scriptures and in the Christian Church we find the passage of the Red Sea taken as the likeness of the moral deliverance from sin and death — when we read in the Apocalypse of the vision of those who stand victorious on the shores of 'the glassy sea, mingled with fire, having the harps of God, and singing the song of Moses the servant of God, and the song of the Lamb' — these are so many sacred testimonies to the importance, to the sanctity of freedom, to the wrong and the misery of injustice, oppression, and tyranny. . . . There are moments in the life of both men and nations, both of the world and of the Church, when vast blessings are gained, vast dangers averted, through our own exertions — by the sword of the conqueror, by the genius of the statesman, by the holiness of the saint. . . . But there are moments of still higher interest, of still more solemn feeling, when deliverance is brought about not by any human energy, but by causes beyond our own control. Such in Christian history, are the raising of the siege of Leyden, and the overthrow of the Armada; and such, above all, was the passage of the Red Sea."

In what ways in this lesson does God manifest His wisdom, His power, His mercy, His goodness? How does this lesson prove that Moses was the right leader in this critical period of Israel's history? What would you say was the difference between the influence of the dead Joseph over the Israelites and the influence of the Pharaoh then living, over the Israelites? Why does God so frequently give men tokens and various feasts and fasts and other devices for remembering great deliverances? What one great sacrament in the Christian Church is given to us to assist us in remembering our great redemption accomplished for us on the Cross? Why did not God simply lift up these millions of people in a miraculous way and plant them in some pleasant land instead of allowing them to endure so many difficult and trying experiences? Is trouble worth-while if it leads us to cry to God? How do some people in the Church remind you of these Israelites, always complaining that things are wrong instead of looking to God for help and for deliverance as God has promised? Inasmuch as God does not now lead us by a pillar of cloud or a pillar of fire, how does He lead us?

LESSON VII. — August 15.

GOD PROVIDES FOR HIS PEOPLE. — Exodus 16, 17.

PRINTED TEXT, Exodus 16 : 11-18; 17 : 3-6.

GOLDEN TEXT. — ***Give us this day our daily bread.*** MATTHEW 6 : 11.

Devotional Reading: Psalm 57 : 6-11.
Beginner Topic: GOD'S GIFT OF FOOD.
Lesson Material: Exodus 16.
Memory Verse: O give thanks unto Jehovah; for he is good. Psalm 136 : 1.
Primary Topic: OUR DAILY BREAD.
Lesson Material: Exodus 16 : 11-36.
Memory Verse: Every good gift and every perfect gift is from above, coming down from the Father. James 1 : 17.
Junior Topic: THE BREAD CALLED MANNA.
Lesson Material: Exodus 16 : 11-36.
Memory Verse: Every good gift and every perfect gift is from above, coming down from the Father. James 1 : 17.
Intermediate and Senior Topic: HOW GOD GIVES DAILY BREAD.
Topic for Young People and Adults: GOD'S PROVISION FOR OUR MATERIAL NEEDS.

THE TEACHER AND HIS CLASS.

The Younger Classes might be asked, what are the absolute necessities for the maintenance of life? Well, there is food, water, air, sleep, protection from the violence of the elements (*i.e.*, shelter and clothing). Then, of course, if we are going to live more than a mere physical life, there will be loved ones in whom our affection centers. There will be books to occupy our minds, etc. Our lesson concerns two of the absolute essentials of life, without which the human race could not live — food, and water; in this case, bread, meat, and water. How God provided for these things this interesting lesson reveals.

The Older Classes will here find a remarkable illustration of how God Himself, having called His servant to undertake a great task, faithfully abides with that servant to supply all that he needs for the execution of his task, and for the support of those whom he is called upon to lead. When we are in the will of God, then we may expect the continual provision of life's necessities. There are times, indeed, as here, when even though we are unworthy of God's mercies and care, He lavishes them upon us.

THE LESSON IN ITS SETTING.

Time. — 1445 B.C.

Place. — The Wilderness of Sin, on the eastern side of the Red Sea, on the way to Mount Sinai. Some of the places mentioned in our lesson have not yet been definitely identified.

THE PLAN OF THE LESSON.

SUBJECT: How God Miraculously Provides for the Needs of His Servants When They Are Carrying Out His Purpose for Them.

I. THE MIRACULOUS PROVISION OF FOOD, Exodus 16 : 1–36.

1. The murmuring Israelites, vs. 1–3.
2. God's promise to Moses, vs. 4–7.
3. The promise of God is reported to Israel, vs. 8–12.
4. The appearance of quail, v. 13.
5. The appearance and gathering of manna, vs. 14–21.
6. The special arrangement for a supply of manna for the sabbath day, vs. 22–31.
7. The preservation of an omer of manna for succeeding ages, vs. 32–36.

II. THE MIRACULOUS SUPPLY OF WATER FROM THE ROCK IN HOREB, Exodus 17 : 1–7.

1. The Israelites murmur because of a lack of water, vs. 1–3.
2. The prayer of Moses, v. 4.
3. The command of God, vs. 5, 6 *a*.
4. The water is supplied, vs. 6 *b*, 7.

III. THE DEFEAT OF THE AMALEKITES, Exodus 17 : 8–16.

THE TEACHER'S LIBRARY.

All commentaries on Exodus, and most lives of Moses, will be found helpful in the study of this lesson. On the subject of manna, one should especially read the article, "Manna," by C. E. Stowe, in William Smith's *Dictionary of the Bible*, Vol. 2, 229, 230; and the long article in C. Geikie: *Hours with the Bible, Moses to Judges*, 245–256. On the deeper spiritual significance of manna, see the sermon by Alexander Maclaren, "The Bread of God," in his *Expositions of Holy Scripture, Exodus, Leviticus, Numbers*, 66–72; and J. H. Todd: *Prophetic Pictures of Christ*, 78–83. On the spiritual significance of the smiting of the rock, see the same work by Todd, 84–90. All Bible dictionaries may be consulted for such subjects as Amalekites, Wilderness of Sin, and Rephidim.

There is very little sermonic material for these passages, but see, on almost the entire lesson, Joseph Parker: *The People's Bible*, Vol. 2, 121–140; and, on 16 : 15, George H. Morrison: *The Ever Open Door*, 47–51. There is an interesting article on quail, by Gene Stratton Porter, in the *International Standard Bible Encyclopedia*, Vol. 4, 2512; and, in the same author's rarely seen volume: *The Birds of the Bible.*

I. THE MIRACULOUS PROVISION OF FOOD, 16 : 1–36.

1. THE MURMURING ISRAELITES, VS. 1–3. Perhaps before we enter into the discussion of the lesson proper, we should have in our minds some conception of this great Wilderness of Sin (the word here has, of course, no reference to sin as an ethical term) through which the Israelites were traveling at this time. "The Wilderness of Sin lay along the western borders of the peninsula, exactly opposite Mt. Sinai, and extended north and south, probably a little lower than Elim, down to the tip end of the Sinaitic region. For the most part, it consisted of sandy wastes thrown broadside to the Gulf of Suez, with a few hills of inconsiderable elevation scattered through the plains. Toward the east, however, begins the piedmont section which gradually ascends to the mountain range heading up in the splendid peaks of the Sinaitic Jebel et-Tor, sixty miles to the southeast. The Hebrews reached this wilderness one month after their departure from Egypt. It is likely that the Camp by the Sea was located in this section, near to the present Wady Taiyibeh (the goodly valley), where the foothills creep close to the coast and form such an attractive camping place that nomads, through the centuries, have continued to use it as one of the chief watering places between Egypt and Sinai. In the immediate vicinity of the Wilderness of Sin toward the northeast were the ancient mining sites of the Egyptians, especially the mines at Serabit el-Khadim where many Semitic inscriptions have been found, some of which are dated as early as 1850 B.C." — *J. McKee Adams.* As our lesson opens we find the Israelites for the third time since leaving Egypt, murmuring against Moses, and really murmuring against God (see 14 : 11, 12; 15 : 24). "The Israelites had been well fed in Egypt. They had been nourished upon flesh, fish, bread, and abundant vegetables, especially cucumbers, melons, leeks, onions, and garlic (Num. 11 : 5). It was the habit of the Egyptians to feed well those whom they employed in forced labors, just as slave-owners commonly do their slaves. The remembrance of

EXODUS 16 : 11. And Jehovah spake unto Moses, saying,
12. I have heard the murmurings of the children of Israel: speak unto them, saying, At even ye shall eat flesh, and in the morning ye shall be filled with bread; and ye shall know that I am Jehovah your God.

the past abundance intensified the pain felt at the present want. It is difficult to imagine that there could have been as yet any real danger of starvation. The cattle may have suffered considerably in the passage through the wilderness of Shur, but the bulk of it survived (17 : 3), and there were lambs enough for the whole nation to observe a Passover a few months later at Sinai (Num. 9 : 1–5). But it may well be that a considerable number of the Israelites had had no cattle; others may have lost what they had, or have consumed them. Want may have stared some of them in the face, and the nation generally may have come to see that the prospect before them was a dismal one. Even supposing that the desert was anciently four or five times as productive as it is now, it could not possibly have afforded sufficient pasturage to maintain such flocks and herds as would have been requisite to support on their milk and flesh a population of two millions." — *George Rawlinson.* "When God visited and redeemed His people, and brought them forth out of the land of Egypt, it assuredly was not for the purpose of suffering them to die of hunger and thirst in the wilderness. They ought to have trusted Him, and walked in the confidence of that love which had so gloriously delivered them from the horrors of Egyptian bondage. They should have remembered that it was infinitely better to be in the desert with God, than in the brick kilns with Pharaoh. But no; the human heart finds it immensely difficult to give God credit for pure and perfect love. It has far more confidence in Satan than in God. Look for a moment at all the sorrow and suffering, the misery and degradation which man has endured by reason of his having hearkened to the voice of Satan, and yet he never gives utterance to a word of complaint of his service, or of desire to escape from under his hand. He is not discontented with Satan, or weary of serving him. . . . How different it is in reference to God! Ten thousand mercies are forgotten in the presence of a single trifling privation. Let but a cloud the size of a man's hand appear on the horizon, and we at once forget the rich mercies of the past in view of this single cloud, which, after all, may only 'break in blessings on our head.'" — *C. H. Mackintosh.*

2. GOD'S PROMISE TO MOSES, vs. 4–7. We are not told here that Moses even prayed to God concerning the murmuring of the people, but God was fully aware of every bitter word they were saying, and apparently before Moses even came to Him in this hour of trouble, He made the promise that He would rain bread from heaven upon them and gave them directions how they were to gather this bountiful supply of food. There is one particular phrase here that we should not quickly pass over: "That I may prove them, whether they will walk in my law or not." "God proves and tries those most whom He takes to Himself for His peculiar people, and the trial is often by means of positive precepts, which are especially calculated to test the presence or absence of a spirit of humble and unquestioning obedience. The Israelites were tested, both in the wilderness and afterwards throughout their career as a nation, by a number of positive precepts, whereof this concerning the manna was one. Christians are tested by positive precepts with respect to common worship and prayer, — the object being in all cases to see whether men 'will walk in God's law or no.' Men are very apt to prefer their own inventions to the simple rule of following at once the letter and the spirit of God's commandments." — *George Rawlinson.*

3. THE PROMISE OF GOD IS REPORTED TO ISRAEL, vs. 8–12. 11. **And Jehovah spake unto Moses, saying,** 12. **I have heard the murmurings of the children of Israel: speak unto them, saying, At even ye shall eat flesh, and in the morning ye shall be filled with bread; and ye shall know that I am Jehovah your God.** At once Moses went to the people and reported what God had promised to him, glad, of course, for something to say to them which would put an end to their murmuring and restore confidence and contentment in the camp. Once again the Lord speaks to Moses, telling him that through this experience of enjoying God's bounty the Israelites should know that God was the Lord their God. "The instruction of His people is a primary object with God. He has gifted them with reason, and He expects to be served with the understanding and the will. It is manifest that every event in His gracious dealings with them is a step in the process of their spiritual training. He first allows the people to feel their need (16 : 3); then He intimates His intention to Moses; then Moses and Aaron admonish the people; then Moses announces the promise of food;

13. And it came to pass at even, that the quails came up, and covered the camp: and in the morning the dew lay round about the camp.
14. And when the dew that lay was gone up, behold, upon the face of the wilderness a small round thing, small as the hoar-frost on the ground.
15. And when the children of Israel saw it, they said one to another, What is it? for they knew not what it was. And Moses said unto them, It is the bread which Jehovah hath given you to eat.

---

then Moses directs Aaron to call the people before the Lord; then the Lord, manifesting His presence, recapitulates His message to Moses, and lastly performs His promise." — *J. G. Murphy.*

4. THE APPEARANCE OF QUAIL, V. 13. 13. **And it came to pass at even, that the quails came up, and covered the camp: and in the morning the dew lay round about the camp.** The appearance of quail is mentioned historically here, in Numbers 11 : 31, 32, and in the devotional literature of the Israelites, in Psalm 105 : 40. "As evening gathered around the camp, the air became darkened. An extraordinary flight of quails, such as at that season of the year passes northward from the warmer regions of the interior, was over the camp. It is a not uncommon occurrence that, when wearied, these birds droop and settle down for rest, so as to be easily clubbed with sticks, and even caught by the hand. The miraculous provision chiefly lay in the extraordinary number, the seasonable arrival, and the peculiar circumstances under which these quails came." — *Alfred Edersheim.* "The common quail is very abundant in the East, and regularly migrates from Syria and Arabia in the autumn of the year for the purpose of wintering in Central Africa, whence it returns in immense masses in the spring. . . . The flesh of the quail is regarded as a delicacy throughout the East, though if too many are eaten it is said to be unwholesome." — *George Rawlinson.*

Gathering the Manna.

5. THE APPEARANCE AND GATHERING OF MANNA, VS. 14–21. 14. **And when the dew that lay was gone up, behold, upon the face of the wilderness a small round thing, small as the hoar-frost on the ground.** 15. **And when the children of Israel saw it, they said one to another, What is it? for they knew not what it was. And Moses said unto them, It is the bread which Jehovah hath given you to eat.** It is most important for us to consider exactly what this manna was, as far as it is possible, after all these hundreds of years have passed. "There are two natural substances, quite distinct, with which it has been compared, and by some persons identified. One is a deposit from the air, which falls indifferently on trees, stones, grass, etc., and is generally thick and sticky, like honey, but under certain circumstances is 'concreted into small granular masses.' . . . It is collected by the Arabs and eaten with their unleavened cakes as condiment. It so far resembles the manna that it comes with the dew, is spread upon the ground generally, and melts when the sun's rays attain a certain power. But it is never found in large quantities; it does not fall for more than two months in the year; and it is wholly unfit to serve as man's principal food, being more like honey than anything else. The other substance is a gum which exudes from certain trees at certain seasons of the year, in consequence of the punctures made in their leaves by a small insect, the *Coccus manniparus.* It is comparatively

16. This is the thing which Jehovah hath commanded. Gather ye of it every man according to his eating; an omer a head, according to the number of your persons, shall ye take it, every man for them that are in his tent.

17. And the children of Israel did so, and gathered some more, some less.

18. And when they measured it with an omer, he that gathered much had nothing over, and he that gathered little had no lack; they gathered every man according to his eating.

---

a dry substance, is readily shaken from the leaves, and consists of small yellowish-white grains, which are hard and have been compared to coriander seed by moderns. The name ' manna ' attaches in the East to this latter substance, which is employed both as a condiment, like the ' air-honey ' and also as a laxative. The special points in which it differs from the manna of Scripture are its confinement to certain trees or bushes, its comparative permanency, for it ' accumulates on the leaves '; and its unfitness for food. It has also, like the ' air-honey,' only a short season — the months of July and August. The manna of Scripture in certain respects resembles the one, and in certain other respects the other of these substances, but in its most important characteristics resembles neither, and is altogether *sui generis*. For (1) it was adapted to be men's principal nourishment, and served the Israelites as such for forty years; (2) it was supplied in quantities far exceeding anything that is recorded of the natural substances compared with it; (3) it continued through the whole of the year; (4) for forty years it fell regularly for six nights following, and ceased upon the seventh night; (5) it ' bred worms ' if kept to a second day, when gathered on five days out of the six, but when gathered on the sixth day continued good throughout the seventh, and bred no worms. The manna of Scripture must therefore be regarded as a miraculous substance, and not a natural product. It pleased the Creator, however, to proceed on the lines of Nature, so to speak, and to assimilate His new to certain of His old creations." — *George Rawlinson*. 16. **This is the thing which Jehovah hath commanded. Gather ye of it every man according to his eating; an omer a head, according to the number of your persons, shall ye take it, every man for them that are in his tent.** 17. **And the children of Israel did so, and gathered some more, some less.** 18. **And when they measured it with an omer, he that gathered much had nothing over, and he that gathered little had no lack; they gathered every man according to his eating.** " The manner of gathering the manna is here prescribed. . . . The tent (Gen. 4 : 20) is an awning or outside covering of any kind over the wooden poles or framework which formed the principal feature of the booth. The phrase, ' them that are in his tent,' indicates a man's family or company, whatever might be the covert under which they took shelter in the desert. In general, each had a family or company with which he tabernacled as best he could in this temporary mode of life. Every man endeavored to gather at least as much as would serve his need, but some were more successful than others in the unmeasured result. If the grasping hand of covetousness or a more favorable ground occasioned a greater gathering by some than by others, yet was the omer filled for each, and neither more nor less, a potent argument to teach them if they would learn, that all men are equal in the sight of our heavenly Father. There was a miracle here, take it how we will. He that distributed his bounty here could equalize each single gathering as easily as the collected whole with the ration allotted to each. No store is to be accumulated. It was in vain that any one disobeyed this command. That which was reserved till the second day became putrid. This in itself was miraculous, as the natural manna kept for a considerable time." — *J. G. Murphy*. " If a man trusted God for tomorrow, he would be content to stop collecting when he had filled his omer, tempting as the easily gathered abundance would be. Greed and unbelief would masquerade then as now, under the guise of prudent foresight. Only he who absolutely trusted God to provide for him would eat up his portion, and lie down at night with a quiet heart, knowing that He who had fed him would feed. When experience had taught that what was saved rotted, then laziness would come in and say, ' What is the use of gathering twice as much on the sixth day? Don't we know that it will not keep? So the whole gift was a continual training of, and therefore a continual test for, faith. God willed to let His gifts come in this hand-to-mouth fashion, though He could have provided at once what would have obviously lasted them all their wilderness life, in order that they might be habituated to cling to Him, and that their daily bread might be doubly for their nourishment, feeding their bodies and strengthening that faith which, to them as to us, is the condition of all blessedness." — *Alexander Maclaren.* There has been a great deal of discussion as to the exact meaning of the measure here called an *omer*, but it is generally recognized that it was equivalent to something between a pint and a half and two pints of our measure. It is a strange thing that we come upon in verse 20: " Notwithstanding they hearkened not unto Moses; but some of them left of it until the morning, and it bred worms, and became foul: and Moses was wroth with them." " You cannot convince some men, nor can you bind them by authority, nor can you bring them under a common discipline. Every society out of heaven is probably disturbed by some kind of eccentricity. Though the people were told in the distinctest manner that there would be no manna on the seventh day, yet they went out to gather it just as if they had never been warned! Such men are the vexation of the world." — *Joseph Parker.*

6. THE SPECIAL ARRANGEMENT FOR A SUPPLY OF MANNA FOR THE SABBATH DAY, vs. 22–31. Professor Rawlinson translates the opening phrase of God's announcement reported in verse 23 as, " Tomorrow is a rest of a holy sabbath to Jehovah." " During the Egyptian oppression the continued observance of the Sabbath would have been impossible, and the surprise of the elders, as well as the words of Moses, show that at that time the idea was, to the Israelites, practically a novelty. . . . Its essential character of a weekly ' rest ' was at once assigned to it: (1) by its name; (2) by God's resting on it from His self-imposed task of giving the manna; and (3) by the rest which the absence of manna on the seventh day imposed on the people. Thus the way was prepared for the stringent law of Sabbath observance laid down in the fourth commandment." — *George Rawlinson.*

The late Dr. William Taylor has drawn two or three excellent lessons from this particular passage. " We are not done with hardship when we have left Egypt. This may be regarded as a universal law so long as we are in the present life, and may be illustrated as really in common and secular matters as in spiritual things. . . . We have come through the fiery flood of war, and we have sung our song of gratitude to Him who, by that bloody baptism, committed us to follow on in the course of justice, of integrity, of true national union, and of hearty brotherhood throughout the land; and if now we are made to drink of the bitter waters of disappointment, it is not that we should murmur against Him whose cloud-pillar had led us to our Marah, but rather that we should, in trustful prayer, cry to Him for the healing wood which alone can make the fountain sweet."

MANNA A TYPE OF CHRIST

No one should read this lesson in the Old Testament without turning to our Lord's own exposition of it, making this material manna to be a symbol of the spiritual manna which God has given to us in the very person of the Lord Jesus Christ (John 6 : 31, 33). " Christ Himself is for all men's souls, all and more than all which the manna has been to the bodies of that dead generation. Like it, He came — but in how much more profound sense — from heaven. Like it, He was food. But unlike it, He could still forever the craving of the else famishing soul; unlike it, He not only nourished a bodily life already possessed, but communicated a spiritual life which never dies; and, unlike it, He was meant to be the food of the whole world. . . . The manna does not typically teach Christ's atonement, but it does set Him forth as the true sustenance and life-giver, sweet as honey to the soul, sent from heaven for us each, but needing to be made ours by the act of our faith. An Israelite would have starved, though the manna lay all round the camp, if he did not go forth and secure his portion; and he might no less have starved, if he did not eat what heaven had sent. The personal appropriating act of faith is essential to our having Christ for the food of our souls. The bread that nourishes our bodies is assimilated to their substance, and so becomes sustenance. This bread of God, entering into our souls by faith, transforms them into its substance, and so gives and feeds an immortal life. The manna was for a generation; this bread is ' the same yesterday, and today, and forever.' " — *Alexander Maclaren.*

7. THE PRESERVATION OF AN OMER OF MANNA FOR SUCCEEDING AGES, vs. 32–36. Finally, Moses is instructed by the Lord to fill a pot with an omerful of manna, and to lay it up before the Lord for a perpetual memorial. " The word here translated *pot* occurs in no other passage. It corresponds in form and use to the Egyptian word for a casket or vase in which oblations were presented." — *F. C. Cook.* That the Lord's command in this place was obeyed is clear from later references to this particular object in the tabernacle and in the Temple (Heb. 9 : 4).

EXODUS 17 : 3. And the people thirsted there for water; and the people murmured against Moses, and said, Wherefore hast thou brought us up out of Egypt, to kill us and our children and our cattle with thirst?

4. And Moses cried unto Jehovah, saying, What shall I do unto this people? they are almost ready to stone me.

5. And Jehovah said unto Moses, Pass on before the people, and take with thee of the elders of Israel; and thy rod, wherewith thou smotest the river, take in thy hand, and go.

6. Behold, I will stand before thee there upon the rock in Horeb; and thou shalt smite the rock, and there shall come water out of it, that the people may drink. And Moses did so in the sight of the elders of Israel.

II. **THE MIRACULOUS SUPPLY OF WATER FROM THE ROCK IN HOREB,** 17 : 1–7. 3. **And the people thirsted there for water; and the people murmured against Moses, and said, Wherefore hast thou brought us up out of Egypt, to kill us and our children and our cattle with thirst?** From the Wilderness of Sin the Israelites journeyed to Rephidim, the most fertile spot in the whole peninsula of Sinai, possibly to be identified with Paran, where, though abundantly supplied with food, they found no water. Instead of asking Moses to pray to God for relief, they began to murmur and complain again, as they had previously done, naturally provoking Moses. This time Moses is driven to ask the Lord what he is to do. "Water is scanty along the route by which we have supposed Rephidim to have been reached. Such a supply as the people may have brought with them from Elim would have been exhausted. They would have looked forward to Rephidim both for their immediate necessity and for replenishing their water-skins. They would be suffering both from thirst and disappointment. The needs of their children and their cattle would be an aggravation of their pain. They would see no hope in the future. Under the circumstances we cannot be surprised at their chiding. Nothing but a very lively faith, or an utter resignation to the will of God, could have made a people patient and submissive in such an extremity." — *George Rawlinson.* 4. **And Moses cried unto Jehovah, saying, What shall I do unto this people? they are almost ready to stone me.** 5. **And Jehovah said unto Moses, Pass on before the people, and take with thee of the elders of Israel; and thy rod, wherewith thou smotest the river, take in thy hand, and go.** 6. **Behold, I will stand before thee there upon the rock in Horeb; and thou shalt smite the rock, and there shall come water out of it, that the people may drink. And Moses did so in the sight of the elders of Israel.** In the divine provision of manna each person was commanded to co-operate, that is, while it was the Lord who sent the manna, the people were to gather it in. In the giving of the water, Moses himself was to be the agent by which the miracle was to be accomplished for these people. He was commanded to strike some large rock of Mount Horeb, which we cannot identify today, of course, with the rod which he had previously used so effectively in working miracles in the court of Pharaoh, being promised by God that when the rock was smitten water would come forth in sufficient abundance for the supply of the feverish thirst of this vast multitude. Immediately obeying the command of the Lord, no doubt grateful in his own heart for such divine intervention, and such a miraculous supply, Moses struck the rock, and at once there came forth water for all the people. "The tradition about water following Israel through the wilderness from this rock has no foundation, and is in effect contradicted by Numbers 20 : 11. What is said in 1 Corinthians 10 : 4 to have followed them is not the water, but 'a spiritual rock' (Revised Version), which 'was Christ.'" — *James Macgregor.* The words of Professor Todd on the spiritual significance of this event are exceptionally helpful: "The very name 'Horeb' means dry, or desolate, and the grace of God is, therefore, all the more seen in that He turned the dry place into a standing water. At the very beginning of the wilderness wanderings we have this example of the truth uttered by Jeremiah (31 : 2), 'the people that were left of the sword found *grace* in the wilderness.' And an instance is given in which God once more proves Himself to be Jehovah-Jireh. . . . The abundant provision of water for a thirsty people, and the bringing of it near to them, speaks of God's supply of the water of life in Christ. It is the bringing of salvation near to sinful men and women in Christ through His atoning death for them. This is the water Christ spoke of to the woman of Samaria in John 4, when He said: 'Whosoever drinketh of the water that I shall give him shall never thirst.' He spoke of it as the gift of God (cf. Rev. 21 : 6; 22 : 17). . . . As from the smitten rock the water flowed abundantly and satisfied the cravings of the people, even so from Christ, smitten at the cross, the water of life, as salvation flows abundantly to satisfy the cravings and thirst of hearts. 'Whosoever drinketh of this water shall never thirst.'" — *J. H. Todd.*

"Has not something of that spirit infected our own peace? We have served Him from our youth, have even kept His glory and kingdom before our eyes, have denied ourselves for His sake, have had many an answer to prayer, have reckoned that there was a very special alliance, and friendship between Him and us. Then suddenly we have been brought to our Rephidim, in which there has been no drop of water. We have come into some bitter situation of personal or relative suffering, we have cried out for help, but the heavens have seemed as brass, and we have been inclined to doubt whether our religious life has not been one long deception. Does God care for me? Does He hear prayer? Is He with me, as I thought? Instead of saying, God is with me, He is steering the boat, He is leading the pilgrimage, He is adequate for this emergency, He has borne me on eagles' wings from Egypt, and cannot desert me now — we say, Is He among us or not? It becomes then a debatable question, Aye or Nay; and when once faith has relaxed its unswerving affirmation, we are on an ocean without chart or compass, or trying to cross a quaking quagmire." — *F. B. Meyer.*

III. **THE DEFEAT OF THE AMALEKITES,** 17 : 8–16. No paragraph could more succinctly summarize this entire episode in Israel's history than the words of the late Professor Macgregor: "The Amalekites, their own kinsmen through Esau the brother of Jacob, appear to have been in commanding occupation of that region of the peninsula extending from the Egyptian settlements on the northwest to the southern border (Gen. 14 : 7) of Canaan. They, with Abrahamic governing faculty, may have organized many loose fragments of humankind into unity. It was (and is) the (Bedouin) habit in the region, at this spring season of the year, to migrate their flocks from the plains to the mountains, for pasture in the approaching summer droughts. The Amalekites appear to have been awakened to jealousy by the invasion of Israel's millions, formidable as locusts. The most recent describer (1888) says that on the very field of battle there is what seems a perennial stream. There was a deliberate mustering concentration, and (Deut. 25 : 17, 18) a tactic of assailing Israel in the rear, where his laggard men were faint and weary. The battle was fiercely contested, extending through the day. It brought to the front Joshua, apparently always the stainless hero, then in his prime of life, the great future leader in Jehovah's war of conquest. And it gave occasion for the memorable illustration, through the prayer of Moses visibly prevailing, of the sovereignty of Jehovah as the Lord of hosts. As for Amalek, the first of the nations to set themselves in open antagonism to His people and His cause, they were placed under doom of extirpation as a people — a doom which, visibly descending in the times of Saul and David, was finally executed (1 Chron. 4 : 43) by a party of Simeonites in the reign of Hezekiah."

From an old print.

Holding up the Hands of Moses.

The following words of Professor Rawlinson, in his excellent *Life of Moses*, vividly describe the famous incident of the elders of Israel lifting up the weary arms of the great law-giver. "The battle rages in the valley beneath; now one side, now the other, has the better of it. Moses observes that, while he can hold his hands aloft, success attends his own countrymen, but when through faintness and weariness he lets them drop, Amalek recovers itself and begins to have the upper hand. He has with him his two most natural supports, Aaron, his elder brother, and Hur, who, according to Josephus, was the husband of Miriam, his sister, and these chieftains come to his relief. Setting him on a stone seat, and standing one at either side of him, they prop up the weary arms, and hold them steady in an erect position through the long hours of that eventful day, until the sun goes down."

"Amalek is a type of the flesh. Israel's conflict began when they stood in the full power of redemption, and had tasted 'that spiritual meat and drunk of that spiritual Rock.' Until they met Amalek they had nothing to do. They did not cope with Pharaoh. They did not break the power of Egypt nor snap asunder the chains of its thraldom. They did not divide the sea nor submerge Pharaoh's hosts beneath its waves. They did not bring down bread from heaven, nor draw forth water out of the flinty rock. They neither had done, nor could they do, any of these things; but now they are called to fight with Amalek. All the previous conflict had been between Jehovah and the enemy. They had but to stand still and gaze upon the mighty triumphs of Jehovah's outstretched arm and enjoy the fruits of victory. The Lord had fought *for* them; but now He fights *in* or *by* them." — *C. H. MacIntosh.*

In how many ways, in this lesson, is the power of God manifested? How is the patience of God in His dealings with Israel revealed in these two chapters? How does Moses here reveal himself to be a true leader of Israel? How would you say that the Lord is still the divine Provider for " our daily bread " (Matt. 6: 11)? Why did not the Lord send the manna before the Israelites got hungry, and make the water to appear before they experienced thirst? Do you think that there were some in this great company who did not believe in God at all, who were not inclined to leave Egypt, who never prayed to God, and yet who received all the blessings that the others had bestowed upon them? Do you think there are a great number of people in America who enjoy the blessings of a Christian nation, without believing in Christ? In how many different ways is the Lord Jesus Christ symbolically set forth in the manna which was supplied in this lesson?

LESSON VIII. — August 22.

GOD GIVES LAWS FOR HIS PEOPLE. — Exodus 19—24; Deuteronomy 11 : 18–21; Galatians 3 : 23–28; 5 : 13, 14.

PRINTED TEXT, Exodus 23 : 1–9; Galatians 3 : 23–28; 5 : 13, 14.

GOLDEN TEXT. — ***Thou shalt love the Lord thy God with all thy heart, and with all thy soul, and with all thy strength, and with all thy mind; and thy neighbor as thyself.*** LUKE 10 : 27.

Devotional Reading: Psalm 19 : 7–14.
Beginner Topic: GOD'S BEAUTIFUL WORLD.
Lesson Material: Genesis 1.
Memory Verse: He hath made everything beautiful in its time. Ecclesiastes 3 : 11.
Primary Topic: GOD'S FRIENDLY RULES.
Lesson Material: Exodus 23 : 1–9.
Memory Verse: He that keepeth the law, happy is he. Proverbs 29 : 18.
Junior Topic: RULES FOR EVERY DAY.
Lesson Material: Exodus 23 : 1–9.
Memory Verse: All that Jehovah hath spoken will we do, and be obedient. Exodus 24 : 7.
Intermediate and Senior Topic: GOD'S LAWS FOR LIVING.
Topic for Young People and Adults: ORIGIN AND PURPOSE OF LAW.

THE TEACHER AND HIS CLASS.

The Younger Classes may be asked what are some of the laws of the community in which they live which help to preserve their own life and their property, *e.g.*, the laws that prohibit one man from stealing another man's possessions; or the law that prohibits one man from telling a lie about another person in court; or the law that prohibits some one from taking a club and hitting another person over the head and killing him. We are protected from all these things, and many others, by the laws of our land. These laws are necessary, because men are selfish, and unless they were restrained by law many would rush ahead for their own selfish purposes and make peace, liberty, and the pursuit of happiness impossible for every one else. Our lesson is about some of the great laws which came from God to Israel, laws just as fundamental today as when they were given.

The Older Classes will find here a remarkable series of fundamental commandments relating on the one hand to man's relationship to God, and on the other hand, to man's relationship to men. When one of these is wrong, both are wrong, and when they are wrong then a man is a curse to himself and to others. When men disobey law then the state has to shut them up where they cannot do their fellow men harm. God's laws are right and good, and when we obey them our life will be the stronger, the more satisfying, the more blessed to others, and approved by God. When a man rebels against God's laws it is not because the law is wrong, but he is wrong. One might just as well rebel against the law of gravitation as to think he will succeed in living a life contrary to the laws of God.

THE LESSON IN ITS SETTING.

Time. — 1445 B.C.
Place. — At the foot of Sinai.

THE PLAN OF THE LESSON.

SUBJECT: God's Concern and Love for His Own People as Manifested in the Laws Which He Gave Them for Their Own Welfare and Protection.

I. PREPARATION FOR THE DIVINE DELIVERANCE OF THE LAW, Exodus 19 : 1–25.
1. The place — Mount Sinai, vs. 1, 2.
2. God's purpose that Israel should be a holy nation, vs. 3–6.
3. The covenant of obedience, vs. 7, 8.
4. The sanctification of the people, vs. 9–25.

II. THE TEN GREAT COMMANDMENTS, Exod. 20 : 1–17.

III. LAWS CONCERNING MAN'S RELATIONSHIP TO GOD AND TO HIS FELLOW MEN, Exod. 20 : 18—23 : 33.
1. The erection of altars, 20 : 18–26.
2. Relationship of master and servant, 21 : 1–11.
3. Injuries inflicted upon others, 21 : 12–36.
4. Rights of property, 22 : 1–15.
5. Sex crimes, 22 : 16–19.
6. The prohibition of all forms of oppression, 22 : 20–27.
7. The offering of the firstfruits and the firstborn, 22 : 28–31.
8. Laws prohibiting falsity, 23 : 1–9.
9. The Sabbath, 23 : 10–13.
10. Israel's three great feasts, 23 : 14–19.

IV. INSTRUCTIONS FOR THEIR CONDUCT WHEN ENGAGED IN CONQUERING PALESTINE, Exod. 23 : 20–33.

V. ISRAEL'S WORSHIP, Exod. 24 : 1–18.

VI. HOW THE ISRAELITES WERE TO KEEP THE LAW EVER BEFORE THEM, Deut. 11 : 18–21.

VII. THE OLD DISPENSATION AND THE NEW.
1. The law a schoolmaster to lead to Christ, Gal. 3 : 23–28.
2. Love the fulfilling of the law, Gal. 5 : 13, 14.

THE TEACHER'S LIBRARY.

For the long passage taken from the Book of Exodus, one may consult any of the more important commentaries on Exodus, a list of which will be found in the Introduction to this volume. On the two passages taken from Galatians, which probably the teacher will not find a great deal of time to expound, see the *Expositor's Bible*, by G. G. Findlay; the volume on this Epistle in the *Cambridge Bible for Schools and Colleges*, by E. H. Perowne; the very valuable handbook, by Charles R. Erdman: *The Epistle of Paul to the Galatians;* and, for those who wish for extended comments, the large commentaries on the Greek text, by J. B. Lightfoot and John Eadie. As far as the editor knows, there is no valuable sermonic material on Exodus 23 : 1–9. On the Galatian passages there is also little. However, on 3 : 23, one may consult D. T. Young: *Travels of the Heart*, 101–113; on 3 : 24, H. P. Liddon's two great sermons, in his *Sermons on Some Words of St. Paul*, 170–198; and, on 3 : 28, F. E. Shannon: *The Enchanted Universe*, 75–90. Speaking of commentaries on Exodus, by far the two most helpful for this lesson will be found to be the chapters in F. B. Meyer's *Devotional Commentary* on *Exodus*, and the invaluable work by Chadwick, in the *Expositor's Bible.*

I. PREPARATION FOR THE DIVINE DELIVERANCE OF THE LAW, Exod. 19 : 1–25.

1. THE PLACE — MOUNT SINAI, vs. 1, 2. Because our lesson is so very long, we will not be able to comment upon many interesting things, but we must, as far as possible, get into our minds an idea of the grandeur of the place where Israel received the law. "Leaving Rephidim, the pilgrim-host, led by the cloud, traveled slowly along the Wady-es-Sheykh, which still forms the great highway of the desert, running due east and west, from the Red Sea to the Gulf of Suez, until they came on the plain *Er Raheh*, which means 'the palm of the hand.' It lies outspread from

north to south two miles long and half a mile wide, nearly flat, and dotted over with tiny shrubs. On either side are mountains far higher than the loftiest mountain in Britain, composed of black and yellow granite, and at the end, blocking the southern extremity of the plain, rises the sheer precipice of Sinai, 1200 to 1500 feet in height — the Mount of God. The peculiarity about this huge cliff is that it resembles, as nearly as possible, a colossal pulpit. It springs perpendicularly from the level of the plain, and might easily be touched, as though it were a wall, and in front are some slight alluvial mounds, on which the artificial railing was probably placed. From this pulpit on which the cloud brooded, the Almighty spake, in words that linger still upon the trembling air. Clouds and darkness were round about Him, and justice and righteousness were the habitation of His throne. No spot on earth, it has been affirmed, combines in a more remarkable manner the conditions of commanding height and of a plain in which the sights and sounds described here could reach the assemblage of two million souls. 'That such a plain should exist at all in such a place,' says Dean Stanley, 'is so remarkable a coincidence with the sacred narrative as to furnish a strong internal argument, not merely of this being the actual scene of the giving of the law, but of it having been described by an eye-witness. All the surroundings suit the narrative. The awful and lengthened approach, as to some natural sanctuary, the long retiring sweep of the plain enabling the people to remove and stand afar off, the cliff rising like a huge altar, and visible against the sky in lonely grandeur from end to end of the whole plain.' " — *F. B. Meyer.*

Mount Sinai.

2. GOD'S PURPOSE THAT ISRAEL SHOULD BE A HOLY NATION, vs. 3–6. In our lesson Moses ascends into the mount for communion with and instructions from God, three different times. This section records the first, which we may speak of as fundamental for an understanding of all that follows. God here reminds Moses, and through him the Israelites, of His grace toward them in bringing them out of Egypt, and bringing them to Himself. This leads Him to announce to Moses that He desires all of Israel in the centuries to come from that time on to be a peculiar treasure unto him, a kingdom of priests and a holy nation. " But while all the earth was the Lord's, Israel was to be His 'precious possession from among all nations,' His choice treasure — for this the Hebrew expression implies — or, as Paul and Peter explain it, 'a peculiar people.' The expression 'kingdom of priests' means a kingdom whose citizens are priests, and as such possess royal dignity and power, or, in the language of Peter, 'a royal priesthood.' So far as Israel was concerned, the outward and visible theocracy, which God established among them, was only the *means* by which this end was to be obtained, just as their observing the covenant was the *condition* of it. . . . The final object of the royal priesthood of Israel were those nations, from among whom God had chosen His people for a precious possession. Toward them Israel was to act as priests. For, just as the priest is the intermediary between God and man, so Israel was to be the intermediary of the knowledge and salvation of God to all nations. . . . It was not the selection of Israel from all other nations that made them holy, but the relationship to God into which it brought the people." — *Alfred Edersheim.*

The law itself was given that Israel might conform to this high ideal. All the laws that related to worship, to social life together, the laws pertaining to hygienic matters, to marriage, to property, to conduct in Canaan, the large laws and the small ones, all had for one object that Israel should be a holy nation.

3. THE COVENANT OF OBEDIENCE, vs. 7, 8. When Moses came down from this first interview with God, and laid before the elders of the people the words which God had commanded him, " All the people answered together, and said all that

the Lord hath spoken we will do." It has been suggested by some that this was a foolish statement on Israel's part, that up to this time she had lived before God in grace, and now she must live before God under the law, which because of her constant disobedience ever condemned her. This hardly seems to the editor a fair thing to say. It was God who called Moses up into the mount and gave him the commandments. Israel could hardly say, "We are not going to live by your commandments, but we will live by your grace." There was nothing else for Israel to do than to say she would obey the Lord, *if she meant it.* It seems that the real transgression here is a light, superficial acceptance of God's law without a deep heart determination to obey it.

4. THE SANCTIFICATION OF THE PEOPLE, vs. 9–25. Once again Moses goes up to the mount to hear the mind of God, and this time we find the commands explicitly relating to the immediate occasion which Israel was confronting, though she knew it not; that is, the full revelation of God's law for His people through His servant Moses. It is an inevitable tendency in fallen human nature to lose a clear conception of the holiness, the awefulness, the infinite transcendence of God, and, as it were, to fall into habits of irreverent carelessness in approaching God and listening to His Word. To bring the people of Israel into a proper frame of mind that they might more accurately apprehend what was now about to take place, that they might have a new conception of the majesty and holiness of God, Moses was instructed to tell the people to wash their clothes and to sanctify themselves for a period of three days. They were to be kept back from the mountain on which God would appear to Moses, by a fence, so that the great mass of people could not push the Israelites nearest the front on to ground which was now made holy by this awful transaction about to take place. Mount Sinai was enveloped in a great smoke because the Lord descended upon it in fire and smoke, and the whole mountain quaked as though shaken with an earthquake. Even when all these preparations had been carefully carried out, God sent Moses down the mountain once more to warn the people that they must not, even the priests, break through "to go up unto the Lord, lest he break forth upon them." All of our lives would be the purer, richer, and more meaningful if we sacredly observed certain times of preparation; *e.g.*, the Presbyterian Church has for centuries preceded the day of the Sunday of sacrament by what is called a "preparatory service," generally held on Friday or Saturday night. The whole season of Lent is a preparation for the more proper observance of the death and resurrection of our Lord. Would not every Sunday be a holier, more spiritually profitable day, for all of us who are believers, if Saturday night were spent quietly at home, reading, praying, preparing our hearts and minds for congregational worship on the Lord's Day?

Moses and the Commandments.

From Sargent's Frieze of the Prophets in the Boston Public Library.

II. **THE TEN GREAT COMMANDMENTS,** Exod. 20 : 1–17. This well-known, famous passage, which has often been assigned in the cycle of the International Sunday School Lessons, need not occupy us here for long, allowing us to discuss more fully the less familiar sections. These things, however, ought at least to be noticed. The laws here given are not for any one people. There are laws which relate to the very foundations of human life everywhere. These are not ritual laws, as the Levitical code is, laws that are exclusively for one nation or for one period of time, but laws that demand our obedience in every age everywhere on earth. In the second place, it should be noted that the table of ten words divides into two parts the first section considering man's relationship to God, the second section man's relationship to his fellow men. The first and most important relationship is that to God, and when that is not rightly maintained, man will not be in right relationship to his fellow men. All one needs to do is look at the first chapter of Romans to realize that, when men have forsaken God and have false gods whom they worship, they sink to every unspeakable crime. There is no great *fundamental* problem of life that does not come under one of these ten commandments. Some in dividing the Decalogue make the first table to consist of four laws, and the second, of the remaining six, but possibly Professor Chadwick is right, following many great branches of the Christian Church, in making each division of the Decalogue to consist of five laws. " There seems to be something more sacred and divine about my relationship with my father and mother than those which connect me with my neighbor. The first table begins with the gravest offense, and steadily declines to the lowest; sin against the unique personality of God being followed by sin against His spirituality of nature, His name, and His holy day. If now the sin against His earthly representative, the very fountain and sanction of all law to childhood, be added to the first table, the same order will pervade those of the second — namely, sin against my neighbor's life, his family, his property, his reputation, and lastly, his interest in my inner self, in the wishes that are unspoken, the thoughts and feelings which ' I wad nae tell to nae man.' We thus obtain both the simplest division and the clearest arrangement. The first table forbids sin against God in thought, word, and deed; and the second table forbids sin against man in deed, word, and thought." — *G. A. Chadwick.*

III. **LAWS CONCERNING MAN'S RELATIONSHIP TO GOD AND TO HIS FELLOW MEN,** Exod. 20 : 18—23 : 33.

1. The Erection of Altars, 20 : 18–26. At first sight, it seems quite strange that the first instruction God should give after the promulgation of these series of fundamental laws concerns the building of an altar and the prohibition to make any image of God. " The propitiation which makes way for His mercy to the penitent sinner by satisfying His justice, has its type in the altar and the sacrifice thereon. This special provision for the salvation of sinners, though it would be out of place in the ten words, yet forms the main substance of all that is shadowed forth in the whole ceremonial law. It therefore comes in here as the necessary antecedent of all acceptable approaching to God and walking with Him. The word *altar* connects Moses and the people of Israel with Noah and his rescued family (Gen. 8 : 20). Earth was the scene of man's sin; it is also to be the scene of the sacrifice for sin. The altar of earth is merely the definite spot of this earth set apart for sacrifice, and elevated to raise the offering towards God, who is in heaven. . . . The altar may be of stones, if unhewn. It is thus entirely a work of God, and so in keeping with that propitiation which comes entirely from God. . . . The altar of rude stone was common among the ancient nations. Motives of decency dictated that the altar was not to be approached by steps. The prescription here concerning the altar appears in the most general form. The details of legislation on this subject will appear in their proper place." — *J. G. Murphy.*

2. Relationship of Master and Servant, 21 : 1–11. Here begins what is commonly called " the Book of the Covenant." Professor Macgregor is probably right when he says: " These laws apparently are more or less a reproduction of what had been in some way known before. Probably they include a sort of simple codification of what had grown into the possession of Israel as traditionary consuetudinary law, both during the Egyptian sojourning and back to the first beginning of their history in the Patriarchal Age. Now they are completed and adjusted to the existing and prospective condition of Israel by authority of God, and solemnly accepted from Him by the infant nation as at the foundation of their national covenant with Jehovah." Is it not significant, and indeed, an evidence of God's loving concern for those whom men would be prone so often to forget, that the first law concerns the very lowest order (speaking now only by *human* classification), of all the people, *i.e.*, the servants. They, of course, are just as noble as any one else, but they could be so easily neglected and mistreated. The law was that the servant should be released of his servitude after six years, and if he brought his wife with him, his wife should go out with him; but if his master gave him his wife and she had borne sons and daughters, the wife and children were to remain with the master. If the servant said he loved his master and wife and children, he could enter then into a permanent relationship by which he served his master for the rest of his life. The daughter who became a maidservant should not go out at the end of the six years, but if she was not pleasing to her master, and took, as it were, the place of a

second or third wife, the master was never to be allowed to sell her to a strange nation, but he should deal with her after the manner of his daughters, should not diminish her food or raiment, and if he disobeyed any of these laws she was to go out absolutely free. While we thank God we do not have such a type of servitude today, yet at that time surely these laws were needed.

3. INJURIES INFLICTED UPON OTHERS, 21 : 12–36. This series of laws, the largest individual section in our lesson, had to do with those occasions when one man should slay another innocently or deliberately, and then from this there proceeded the condemnation of a man stealing, cursing his father or mother, or in any way injuring the body of a servant, the law being an eye for an eye, and a tooth for a tooth, hand for a hand, foot for a foot. Whatever some one else suffered because of his brutality, or hatred, or anger, he likewise was to suffer. It is impossible to go into the details of these laws in our lesson.

4. RIGHTS OF PROPERTY, 22 : 1–15. There is a threefold protection in this part of the Israelitish code. First, a man is protected from definite theft or robbery (vs. 1–4); from trespassers (vs. 5, 6); from betrayal of trust (vs. 7–13). "There were no banks; and a man sometimes — say, going on a journey — had to place his property for keeping — *e.g.*, in a neighbor's hand. *Stuff* here has this general meaning: it is *vessels — that sort of property — e.g.* the Egyptian 'spoils.' This would include fine cloths, from needle and loom, as well as jewelry of gold and silver. In any case, his neighbor has accepted the trust. If the goods be stolen, and the thief be found, there shall be double restitution out of his purse (or his bones, v. 3). Otherwise, the trustee has to clear himself before the judges (here again, lit. *the gods*, under 22 : 28) of the suspicion of a pretended robbery; as when a man burns his house in order to get compensation from the insurance office for his goods (which perhaps were not in it)." — *James Macgregor.*

5. SEX CRIMES, 22 : 16–19. "It is enacted that a seducer must marry the woman he has betrayed, and if her father refuse to give her to him, then he must pay the same dower as a bridegroom would have done (22 : 16, 17). And presently the sentence of death is launched against a blacker sensual crime (v. 19). But between the two is interposed the celebrated mandate which doomed the sorceress to death, remarkable as the first mention of witchcraft in Scripture, and the only passage in all the Bible where the word is in the feminine form — a witch, or sorceress; remarkable also for a far graver reason, which makes it necessary to linger over the subject at some length. . . . Sorcery in all its forms will die when men realize indeed that the world is His, that there is no short or crooked way to the prizes which He offers to wisdom and to labor, that these rewards are infinitely richer and more splendid than the wildest dreams of magic, and that it is literally true that all power, in earth as well as heaven, is committed into the hands which were pierced for us." — *G. A. Chadwick.*

6. THE PROHIBITION OF ALL FORMS OF OPPRESSION, 22 : 20–27. Here God shows His tender regard for strangers, for widows, for the fatherless, for those who because of strained circumstances had to borrow money on their raiment or whatever goods they possessed. "In itself (cf. Matt. 25 : 27), payment of interest for the use of money is like payment of rent for the use of land, a business transaction which may be profitable and convenient for both parties, and an advantage to the community through facilitating business ('circulation'). In the text the case contemplated (as also *e.g.* Lev. 25 : 35; Deut. 15 : 7) appears to be that, not of ordinary business, but of a neighbor in real distress of straitened circumstances, helped 'at a pinch.' Now the Israelites all were brethren by law and covenant; and it seems to have become a recognized custom among them, if not a law, that no interest should be taken for loan of money to an Israelite (cf. Ps. 15 : 5). . . . In this very simple case the 'humane' comes out with great force: God, from His tender heart, speaking to the very heart of selfish man (pointing to *the sore place* — that 'finger,' cf. 8 : 19). The raiment is the large loose plaid blanket, or *bournous*, which can serve as outer garment during the day, and is indispensable as a covering and wrap through the night, in a country where the biting cold of night is sharpened by abrupt transition from the hard brilliant heat of day. The present writer has known cases in which factory girls placed their Sunday clothes in pledge during the week, on condition of having the use of them for the Lord's Day. The poor Israelite had secured to him by the merciful Redeemer and King, inalienably, the use of his covering for the night. Beyond that, it remained in pledge till the loan was repaid." — *James Macgregor.*

Thus the social implications of the Word are marked and evident.

EXODUS 23 : 1. Thou shalt not take up a false report: put not thy hand with the wicked to be an unrighteous witness.
2. Thou shalt not follow a multitude to do evil; neither shalt thou speak in a cause to turn aside after a multitude to wrest *justice:*
3. Neither shalt thou favor a poor man in his cause.
4. If thou meet thine enemy's ox or his ass going astray, thou shalt surely bring it back to him again.
5. If thou see the ass of him that hateth thee lying under his burden, thou shalt forbear to leave him, thou shalt surely release *it* with him.
6. Thou shalt not wrest the justice *due* to thy poor in his cause.

---

7. THE OFFERING OF THE FIRSTFRUITS AND THE FIRSTBORN, 22 : 28–31. We must carefully note one thing here; otherwise we are faced with an insolvable problem. In the phrase, "Thou shalt not revile the gods," the Hebrew word is *Elohim*, without the definite article, and almost all scholars agree that the better translation here would simply be God. Elohim is a word used hundreds of times in the Old Testament for the only true God Jehovah. Here we have simply a command to the Israelites warning them not to postpone the offering to God of the firstfruits of the field and their firstborn sons, as well as the first to be born of all the cattle. It is so easy to use for ourselves what we know belongs to God, with the intention of later repaying it, only we seldom keep our private vows, and then we become careless in these matters.

8. LAWS PROHIBITING FALSITY, 23 : 1–9. 1. **Thou shalt not take up a false report: put not thy hand with the wicked to be an unrighteous witness.** "How many heedless whispers, conjectures lightly spoken because they are amusing, yet influencing the course of lives, and inferences uncharitably drawn, would have been stillborn if this had been remembered! But when the scandal is already abroad, the temptation to aid its progress is still greater. Therefore it is added, 'Put not thine hand with the wicked to be an unrighteous witness.' Whatever be the menace or the bribe, however the course of opinion seem to be decided, and the assent of an individual to be harmless because the result is sure, or blameless because the responsibility lies elsewhere, still each man is a unit, not an 'item,' and must act for himself, as hereafter he must give account." — *G. A. Chadwick.* 2. **Thou shalt not follow a multitude to do evil; neither shalt thou speak in a cause to turn aside after a multitude to wrest *justice*.** "The blind impulses of a multitude are often as misleading as the solicitations of the bad, and to aspiring temperaments much more seductive. There is indeed a strange magnetism in the voice of the public. Every orator knows that a great assembly acts upon the speaker as really as he acts upon it. Its emotions are like a rush of waters to sweep him away, beyond his intentions or his ordinary powers. Yet he is the strongest individual there; no other has at all the same opportunity for self-assertion, and therefore its power over others must be more complete than over him." — *G. A. Chadwick.* 3. **Neither shalt thou favor a poor man in his cause.** "To countenance or honor the poor man in his cause is to connive at his criminality from a mistaken compassion for his poverty. This rule is extended to the rich as well as the poor in Leviticus 19 : 15." — *James G. Murphy.* 4. **If thou meet thine enemy's ox or his ass going astray, thou shalt surely bring it back to him again.** "The fifth injunction transcends the obligation to speak the truth. He that meets his enemy's beast going astray is not only not to be silent on the subject, but not to refrain from interfering. He is to beat down the exasperated feeling of his heart, and bring back the straying animal to his enemy, as if he were a friendly brother. This would be a happy means of softening many asperities." — *James G. Murphy.* 5. **If thou see the ass of him that hateth thee lying under his burden, thou shalt forbear to leave him, thou shalt surely release *it* with him.** "In this verse there is a climax: the enemy (one hated) is actively hostile. The beast is in sore distress; and the help extends to peaceful contact of the foes. *Forbear — surely:* see the same struggle (of old Adam with new) in Romans 7 : 23; but here the new Adam comes from Sinai (Exod. 20 : 2; cf. 1 John 2 : 7, 8). *With him*: 'lend us a hand' — in neighborliness — touch the enemy! The suggestion is, that hands would have to meet in jointly raising the fallen ass." — *James Macgregor.* 6. **Thou shalt not wrest the justice *due* to thy poor in his cause.** 7. **Keep thee far from a false matter; and the innocent and righteous slay**

7. Keep thee far from a false matter; and the innocent and righteous slay thou not: for I will not justify the wicked.
8. And thou shalt take no bribe: for a bribe blindeth them that have sight, and perverteth the words of the righteous.
9. And a sojourner shalt thou not oppress: for ye know the heart of a sojourner, seeing ye were sojourners in the land of Egypt.

---

thou not: for I will not justify the wicked. "We return again to truthfulness of speech. The needy and dependent are exposed to oppression and injustice in a selfish world. But the man of God is not to wrest the judgment of the needy. *Thy needy*, thy brother who is needy. This touches the feelings of a common humanity. The eighth precept inculcates the avoidance of all connection with a false matter, particularly in lawsuits, where it may involve the judicial slaying of the innocent and the righteous." — *James G. Murphy.* 8. **And thou shalt take no bribe: for a bribe blindeth them that have sight, and perverteth the words of the righteous.** This passage refers to bribery, and how true it is! Gifts have been the cause for false decisions in court, for favors in universities, for unfairness in business relationships, and for many other unjust acts on the part of men — giving favors to those who deserve not, and keeping back honors from those who are entitled to them. 9. **And a sojourner shalt thou not oppress: for ye know the heart of a sojourner, seeing ye were sojourners in the land of Egypt.** "This verse is a repetition of 22 : 21, but the precept is there addressed to the people at large, while it is here addressed to the judges in reference to their official duties. This is Knobel's explanation; but Bleek and others, overlooking the very distinct contexts, take the repetition as merely redundant." — *Samuel Clark.*

9. THE SABBATH, 23 : 10–13. As a man was to work six days and then rest, so was he to sow his field six years, and the seventh year he should let it rest and whatever grew during that year without effort in the field should be left for the poor to eat; and what they left the beasts should be allowed to enjoy. The Sabbath day has been so frequently the subject of our study that we need not dwell on it further here.

10. ISRAEL'S THREE GREAT FEASTS, 23 : 14–19. "The Code closes with a specification of the religious festivals which were to be observed by the people. . . . Thrice each year the males were required to appear before God, and none was to appear before Him empty. All ancient religions had their festivals; and it is well that the children of God should maintain great convocations and conventions, when they feel the pulse of a great multitude engaged in praise, and prayer, and consecration. Heaven itself owes much of its delight to the great multitude, which no man can number, and to the vast orchestra of ten thousand times ten thousand voices. The feast of unleavened bread fell in the early spring and commemorated the exodus. The feast of harvest (or weeks) followed fifty days afterwards and commemorated the giving of the law; it was a peculiarly joyful occasion (Deut. 16 : 9–11), and for us is associated with the marvels of Acts 2. The feast of ingathering (or tabernacles) began in the early part of October, when the olives had been gathered and the vintage was completed. The demand for this thrice-repeated visit to a common meeting-place was not tiresome, because Palestine was not bigger than Wales; and there was no better way of maintaining the unity of the nation in an age when there were no posts, telegraphs, telephones, or daily press." — *F. B. Meyer.*

IV. INSTRUCTIONS FOR THEIR CONDUCT WHEN ENGAGED IN CONQUERING PALESTINE, Exod. 23 : 20–33. "The 'judgments' which the Lord enjoins upon His people are appropriately followed by promises, in which, as their King and Lord, He undertakes their guidance and protection, and their possession of the land He had assigned to them. First and foremost, assurance is given them of the personal presence of Jehovah in that Angel, in whom is the name of the Lord (v. 20). This was no common angel, however exalted, but a manifestation of Jehovah Himself, prefigurative of, and preparatory to His manifestation in the flesh in the person of our Lord and Saviour Jesus Christ. For all that is here said of Him is attributed to the Lord Himself in Exodus 13 : 21; while in Exodus 33 : 14, 15, He is expressly designated as 'the face' of Jehovah ('My face' — in the Authorized Version 'my presence'). Accordingly, all obedience is to be shown to His guidance, and every contact with idolatry and idolaters avoided. In that case, the Lord would fulfill every good and gracious promise to His people, and cause them to possess the land in all its extent." — *Alfred Edersheim.*

GALATIANS 3 : 23. But before faith came, we were kept in ward under the law, shut up unto the faith which should afterwards be revealed.
24. So that the law is become our tutor *to bring us* unto Christ, that we might be justified by faith.
25. But now that faith is come, we are no longer under a tutor.
26. For ye are all sons of God, through faith, in Christ Jesus.
27. For as many of you as were baptized into Christ did put on Christ.
28. There can be neither Jew nor Greek, there can be neither bond nor free, there can be no male and female; for ye all are one *man* in Christ Jesus.

V. **ISRAEL'S WORSHIP,** Exod. 24 : 1–18. All of this chapter is worthy of careful consideration, but we can only spend a moment with it. Note especially the words, " And Moses wrote all the words of Jehovah " (v. 4). Chadwick says: " It is a memorable statement, recording the origin of the first portion of Holy Scripture that ever existed as such, whatever earlier writings may now or afterwards have been incorporated in the Pentateuch. He then built an altar for God, and twelve pillars for the tribes, and sacrificed burnt-offerings and peace-offerings unto the Lord." Verse 10 is very difficult, but perhaps the words of Professor Murphy will be found helpful: " We take these words in their simple sense. Whatever were the sensible circumstances of the divine presence, they were permitted to see with the eye of sense. Whatever aspect of God Himself with face averted from them was presented to them, they discerned, we may venture to presume, with the eye of the spirit. Hence they do not say a word of the ' similitude of any figure ' of the divine Being, because they had not seen any such (33 : 20–23; Deut. 4 : 15–19)."

VI. **HOW THE ISRAELITES WERE TO KEEP THE LAW EVER BEFORE THEM,** Deut. 11 : 18–21. Obedience to the law of God does not come *naturally* to fallen man. Man's tendency is downward, not upward; away from God, not toward God. Man does not have to be reminded to eat or to sleep or to read. Man does not have to be urged to fall in love with some one. This passage is fully commented upon in the lesson for September 26, and we believe it unnecessary to add additional material here. In verse 21, there is one of the most beautiful phrases to be found in all the Bible, something we never hear any one refer to and no one ever preaches about. Obedience to these laws was that the days of the Israelites, yes, and our days, might be " as the days of heaven upon the earth."

VII. **THE OLD DISPENSATION AND THE NEW,** Gal. 3 : 23–28; 5 : 13, 14.

1. THE LAW A SCHOOLMASTER TO LEAD TO CHRIST, 3 : 23–28. 23. **But before faith came, we were kept in ward under the law, shut up unto the faith which should afterwards be revealed.** 24. **So that the law is become our tutor *to bring us* unto Christ, that we might be justified by faith.** 25. **But now that faith is come, we are no longer under a tutor.** 26. **For ye are all sons of God, through faith, in Christ Jesus.** 27. **For as many of you as were baptized into Christ did put on Christ.** 28. **There can be neither Jew nor Greek, there can be neither bond nor free, there can be no male and female ; for ye all are one *man* in Christ Jesus.** " Paul insists that the law had kept the Jews in the state of children under age, or at best had served as a tutor to prepare them for the acceptance of Christ. On the other hand, faith in Christ had brought them into the position of full-grown sons, to whom belonged the privilege of free access to the Father, into whose hearts God had sent the Spirit of His Son, and who had indeed entered upon their rightful heritage. How foolish and senseless, then, for these Galatians to seek for superior sanctity by submitting to the law! Instead of making an advance, this would be turning back to a state of spiritual immaturity and bondage. The law revealed the need of righteousness and prepared for the acceptance of Christ. All who came under its influence were made prisoners of sin that they might long for the gracious deliverance which Christ freely offers to those who trust in Him. . . . Its function is that of a tutor. Probably this is the best translation of the Greek word *paidagogos* which Paul here employs. The pedagogue, in the days of Paul, was a trusted servant, usually a slave, whose duty was not merely to lead his young master to school but in some measure to supervise his manners and morals. He was not qualified to instruct, nor was he given authority to control, but he was appointed to attend and to safeguard the child until his charge attained maturity and was no longer in need of guidance and discipline. Such, according to Paul, was the place and

GALATIANS 5 : 13. For ye, brethren, were called for freedom; only *use* not your freedom for an occasion to the flesh, but through love be servants one to another.

14. For the whole law is fulfilled in one word, *even* in this: Thou shalt love thy neighbor as thyself.

---

function of the Mosaic law. It was a stern tutor intended for the guidance of the Jewish race. It regulated outward actions. It prescribed right conduct. It imposed certain checks upon evil until those under its guidance were ready for the spiritual freedom to be found in Christ." — *Charles R. Erdman.* In the old covenant there was only one nation primarily in favor with God, with a true knowledge of God, and this nation was the nation of Israel into which a man came by natural birth. Now, however, all may become the children of God through Christ, whether they be Jew or Gentile, bond or free, male or female. If we are in Christ we are all one, standing on the same plane of equality before God.

2. LOVE THE FULFILLING OF THE LAW, 5 : 13, 14. 13. **For ye, brethren, were called for freedom; only *use* not your freedom for an occasion to the flesh, but through love be servants one to another.** 14. **For the whole law is fulfilled in one word, *even* in this: Thou shalt love thy neighbor as thyself.** The Apostle here means to say that just because we are not under the law but under grace, we are not to live as we please, to satisfy our own selfish instincts and desires, but we are to live in love for one another, for all the law — all the law, is fulfilled in this one word, taken from Leviticus 19 : 18, "Thou shalt love thy neighbor as thyself." "If a man should love God perfectly, but have never seen the Decalogue, and if after years of holy communion with God, he should suddenly meet with this enumeration of the divine code, there would be no new feature that he would have to introduce into his behaviour, and no newly discovered wrong that he would have to avoid. On the other hand, it is certain that, apart from love, obedience to the law of God is impossible. It is in proportion as we love Him, that we can obey Him! Whatever of outward service or obedience we render to God or man, if love is withheld, the law is not fulfilled. 'If I bestow all my goods to feed the poor, and if I give my body to be burned, but have not love, it profiteth nothing.' It is impossible to worship God in spirit and in truth, to reverence His name, or delight in His day, unless we love Him. It is impossible to keep the heart free from malice, hate, covetousness, and passion, except as it is possessed and filled by the opposite principle of love. Therefore when in answer to the challenge of His critics, our Lord refused to particularize any one of the ten words, but summed up the first table of the law by saying: 'Thou shalt love the Lord thy God with all thy heart, and with all thy soul, and with all thy mind, and with all thy strength'; and summed up the second by saying: 'Thou shalt love thy neighbor as thyself,' we can repeat the comment of His interlocutor, and say: 'Master, thou hast well said! There is none other commandment greater than these!'" — *F. B. Meyer.*

In how many different ways is the mercy of God revealed in the laws which we have studied in this lesson? What laws would you say, of all those here enumerated, refer primarily to Israel and not directly to other nations of the world, nor to our time? (As i.e., the laws regarding the three great feasts, and those pertaining to the conquest of Palestine.) What characteristics of Moses stand forth most prominently in this lesson? In how many different ways is the holiness of God revealed in the six chapters of Exodus here assigned to us? How does the law lead men to Christ? Do you think that America's tragic neglect of the Lord's Day, and increasing absence from the house of God, have any direct bearing upon the recognized fact that America has the worst crime record of all civilized nations today? What do you think will ever bring our nation back again to a sincere and fervent worship of God?

LESSON IX. — August 29.

ISRAEL'S SIN AND RESTORATION. — Exodus 32—34.

PRINTED TEXT, Exodus 32 : 7-10; 34 : 4-9, 27, 28.

GOLDEN TEXT. — ***Jehovah is slow to anger, and abundant in lovingkindness, forgiving iniquity and transgression.*** NUMBERS 14 : 18.

Devotional Reading: Jeremiah 31 : 31–34.
Beginner Topic: IN GOD'S HOUSE.
Lesson Material: Exodus 33 : 7–17.
Memory Verse: I was glad when they said unto me, Let us go into the house of Jehovah. Psalm 122 : 1.
Primary Topic: GOD'S TENT HOUSE.
Lesson Material: Exodus 33 : 7–19.
Memory Verse: I was glad when they said unto me, Let us go into the house of Jehovah. Psalm 122 : 1.
Junior Topic: EVERY MAN AT HIS TENT DOOR.
Lesson Material: Exodus 33 : 7–19.
Memory Verse: Let the words of my mouth and the meditation of my heart be acceptable in thy sight, O Jehovah, my rock, and my redeemer. Psalm 19 : 14.
Intermediate and Senior Topic: IF WE SIN — WHAT?
Topic for Young People and Adults: THE WAY TO RESTORATION.

THE TEACHER AND HIS CLASS.

The Younger Classes may be reminded that it is not until the teacher goes out of the schoolroom that the children are tempted to suddenly burst forth in wild confusion and unrestraint, throwing chalk and erasers at one another, and, maybe, writing comical things about the teacher on the board. But as soon as the teacher is in the room, order, quiet, and discipline prevail. In our lesson, it is not until Moses is absent from the camp that the children of Israel led by Aaron even dare to make an idolatrous image for worship directly contrary to God's explicit and repeated commands.

The Older Classes will find here a most remarkable illustration of a life of *intercession*, as manifested in the prayers of Moses that are here recorded. An intercessor is one who stands between two parties who have been alienated. An intercessor in prayer is one who stands between man and God, and here between a disobedient nation deserving punishment, and a holy, just, and righteous God. The character of Moses is not revealed in any part of the Scriptures more magnificently than in the three chapters assigned for our lesson.

THE PLAN OF THE LESSON.

SUBJECT: How a People Continually Favored with God's Mercy and Grace Nevertheless Rebel Against Him, and How Both the Justice and Love of God Are Revealed in Righteously Dealing with His People in Such an Hour.

I. ISRAEL'S GROSS IDOLATRY, Exodus 32 : 1–35.
1. The making and worshiping of the golden calf, vs. 1–6.
2. God declares His intention to judge Israel, vs. 7–10.
3. Moses pleads with God for mercy, vs. 11–14.
4. Moses' anger upon coming down from the mount, vs. 15–25.
5. Punishment for sin, vs. 26–29.
6. Confession and intercession, vs. 30–35.

II. THE COMMAND TO RESUME THE JOURNEY, Exodus 33 : 1–6.

III. MOSES THE FRIEND OF GOD, Exodus 33 : 7—34 : 28.
1. "The Lord spake unto Moses face to face," 33 : 8–11.
2. Moses pleads for a new revelation of God, 33 : 12–18.
3. The prayer is answered, 33 : 19—34 : 9.
   a. The promise, 33 : 19–23.
   b. The command, 34 : 1–4.
   c. The revelation, 34 : 5–9.
4. The renewed commission, 34 : 10–27.
   a. Israel warned against being contaminated by the Canaanites, vs. 10–17.
   b. A brief summary of some cardinal laws to be obeyed, vs. 18–27.
5. A final word, 34 : 28.

IV. THE EFFECT UPON MOSES OF HIS FORTY DAYS IN THE MOUNT AND THE CONSEQUENT FEAR AMONG THE ISRAELITES, Exodus 34 : 29–35.

THE LESSON IN ITS SETTING.

Time. — 1445–1444 B.C.
Place. — At the foot of Sinai.

THE TEACHER'S LIBRARY.

Most commentaries on the book of Exodus and most of the lives of Moses, lists of which will be found in the bibliography in the Introduction to this volume, will be found helpful for the study of this lesson. We regret to say that Chadwick in the Expositor's Bible on these three chapters is worthless, probably because the publishers told him his book was already too long. Sermonic and expository material on these chapters is not abundant. On chapter 32, Joseph Parker: *The People's Bible*, Vol. 2, 265–272; on 32 : 9, Joseph Parker: *The City Temple Pulpit*, Vol. 4, 272–274. But, most of all, one should read on 34 : 7, the magnificent sermon, "The Dark Line in God's Face," in W. M. Clow: *The Cross in Christian Experience*, 28–40; on 34 : 6, 7, see Alexander Maclaren: *Expositions of Holy Scripture, Exodus, Leviticus, and Numbers*, 195–204.

EXODUS 32 : 7. And Jehovah spake unto Moses, Go, get thee down; for thy people, that thou broughtest up out of the land of Egypt, have corrupted themselves:

8. They have turned aside quickly out of the way which I commanded them: they have made them a molten calf, and have worshipped it, and have sacrificed unto it, and said, These are thy gods, O Israel, which brought thee up out of the land of Egypt.

I. ISRAEL'S GROSS IDOLATRY, 32 : 1–35.

1. THE MAKING AND WORSHIPING OF THE GOLDEN CALF, VS. 1–6. To the editor this passage has always seemed one of the most amazing of all the remarkable records of the wonderful Word of God, remarkable not because of the sublimity of what is here recorded, but because of the depravity that it reveals as present in the hearts of these people so remarkably favored by God. With Moses away, not knowing when he would come back, and really not caring much, they asked Aaron to make some gods for them, who might "go before them," by which they meant some images that might guide them through and protect them in the wilderness. And all this after God had graciously promised to help them! That they went to Aaron reveals his place of high honor and leadership among the Israelites, but the fact that he condescended to co-operate with them in this wicked scheme, reveals him to be a man of provokingly weak character, not at all such a leader as Israel needed, and as Israel had in Moses. At his suggestion, they threw their golden earrings into the fire, and, when the gold came out, Aaron fashioned the huge lump into the form of a golden calf, making, as no one can deny, an actual idol. "The word calf may mean a yearling ox. The Israelites must have been familiar with the ox-worship of the Egyptians; perhaps many of them had witnessed the rites of Mnevis at Heliopolis, almost on the borders of the land of Goshen, and they could not have been unacquainted with the more famous rites of Apis at Memphis. It is expressly said that they yielded to the idolatry of Egypt while they were in bondage (Josh. 24 : 14; Ezek. 20 : 8; 23 : 3, 8). The earliest Jewish tradition derives the golden calf from an Egyptian origin. Their sin lay, not (only) in their adopting another god, but in their pretending to worship a visible symbol of Him whom no symbol could represent. The close connection between the calves of Jeroboam and this calf is shown by the repetition of the formula, 'which brought thee up out of the land of Egypt' (1 Kings 12 : 28)." — *T. E. Espin.*

"We are dependent upon our elder brother, our strongest man, our noblest suppliant, our wisest leader, in many of the crises and agonies of life. For a long time we are as good as he is; we know no difference between him and us; we wonder sometimes at apparent tokens of superiority — but suddenly we are confronted with circumstances which classify men: we come in face of great claims and demands which search us, and try us, and see what our quality really is — then we know which is Moses, which is Aaron, which is the man of prayer, and which is the man of mighty tact." — *Joseph Parker.*

2. GOD DECLARES HIS INTENTION TO JUDGE ISRAEL, VS. 7–10. 7. **And Jehovah spake unto Moses, Go, get thee down; for thy people, that thou broughtest up out of the land of Egypt, have corrupted themselves:** 8. **they have turned aside quickly out of the way which I commanded them: they have made them a molten calf, and have worshipped it, and have sacrificed unto it, and said, These are thy gods, O Israel, which brought thee up out of the land of Egypt.** No matter what excuse some might offer for this heinous crime, the sinfulness of the act is clearly revealed in what God says about it. The psalmist said: "In thy light shall we see light" (Ps. 36 : 9). Our acts must be judged not by custom, nor by mere external circumstances, nor by what great men say is right and wrong, but by the law of God, as it is revealed in His Word to us. Parker, with his customary brilliance, emphasizes the word *quickly* in this verse. "We go with eagerness in the wrong direction, and

9. And Jehovah said unto Moses, I have seen this people, and, behold, it is a stiffnecked people:

10. Now therefore let me alone, that my wrath may wax hot against them, and that I may consume them: and I will make of thee a great nation.

---

with leaden feet we climb the steep which leads us away to the upper places."
9. **And Jehovah said unto Moses, I have seen this people, and, behold, it is a stiffnecked people.** "This word 'stiffnecked,' afterwards so common (33 : 3, 5; 34 : 9; Deut. 9 : 6, 13; 10 : 16; 2 Chron. 30 : 8; 36 : 13; Ps. 75 : 5; Jer. 17 : 23; Acts 7 : 51), occurs here for the first time. It is generally explained as 'obstinate,' but rather means 'perverse,' the metaphor being taken from the horse that stiffens his neck against the pull of the rein, and will not be guided by the rider." — *George Rawlinson.* 10. **Now therefore let me alone, that my wrath may wax hot against them, and that I may consume them: and I will make of thee a great nation.** What the Lord told Moses to do Moses did not do; the Lord told him to let Him alone that He might destroy these people, though he would preserve Moses and make of him a great nation. It is in an hour like this that Moses' undying love, true compassionate love for Israel, bursts forth in one of the greatest intercessory episodes to be found anywhere in the Word of God.

Aaron's Hill or the Hill of the Golden Calf.

A cone-shaped mountain of red and brown colored sandstone.

3. MOSES PLEADS WITH GOD FOR MERCY, VS. 11–14. The offer to make of Moses a great nation was immediately, without hesitation, put aside by the great lawgiver; instead, he pleads in a threefold way that God might refrain from destroying these people in His wrath. In the first place, he reminds God, though God needs no such reminding, that these are the people whom He had brought out of Egypt with a mighty hand; then he says that, if they should now be destroyed, the Egyptians would say that God had only brought them up to slay them in the mountains. In the third place, he reminds God of the covenant which had been made with the patriarchs Abraham, Isaac, and Jacob, that He would multiply their seed as the stars of the heaven, and that He would give them the land toward which they were marching. The clause, "The Lord repenteth of the evil which he thought to do unto his people," needs careful consideration. "He 'is not a man that he should repent'; but He does repent (Gen. 6 : 6; Ps. 90 : 13). He repents divinely: not abandoning a purpose; but (1) changing His manner of action, (2) being grieved by sin of creatures, (3) mourning over the ruinous misery of sinners (Luke 19 : 41–44). Here the speciality is, the trial to which He subjects the mediator (cf. Gen. 22 : 1, case of Job). This trial, too, came at the close of forty days' seclusion (presumably, of fasting, cf. 34 : 28) in the case of Moses as in that of Christ. The people *do* belong to Moses (mediatorially); so that their lot is dependent on his choice. How an offer could be made by a holy God, which it would be disloyal for Moses the mediator to accept, we cannot comprehend; nor can we comprehend how the Almighty *permits* temptation by Satan or by man. We will not inquire beyond *our* 'depth' (Rom. 11 : 33), remembering what happened to 'the Egyptians essaying to do so.'" — *James Macgregor.*

4. MOSES' ANGER UPON COMING DOWN FROM THE MOUNT, VS. 15–25. Assured now that God would not totally destroy Israel because of its sin, Moses turned and went down the mount with the two tables of the law in his hand, "the work of God." The noise of the shouting and revelry of the Israelites, as they wantonly danced around this prohibited fruit of their own unfaithfulness and unbelief, reached Joshua and Moses long before they saw the calf itself. But as soon as they came

nigh to the camp and actually saw this image of a beast worshiped by the children of Jehovah, Moses cast the tables of the law out of his hands, smashing them on the rocks under his feet. Then he took the golden calf, ground it to powder, and threw the resulting gold dust on the water, making the children of Israel to drink of it. " He had it submitted to the action of fire, whereby its form was destroyed, and the material, as it would seem, calcined. This calcined material he reduced to a fine powder by rubbing or pounding, and then had the powder sprinkled on the surface of the stream which supplied the camp with water, so that the people might *seem*, at any rate, to swallow their own sin." — *George Rawlinson.* Such a righteous indignation as now burst forth from Moses' heart is the other side of a nature which could also plead with God to be merciful to these rebellious people. Wrath against sin and love for the sinner are here wonderfully blended in the conduct of Moses in this hour of crisis.

Image of the Egyptian Goddess, Hathor, in the Boulak Museum.

The Golden Calf was probably similar.

Having destroyed the idol, Moses now turns to Aaron and asks for an explanation of what had happened, in reply to which Aaron makes one of the weakest, silliest excuses, utterly false, that was ever uttered by any man in the whole narrative of the Old and New Testaments. He acknowledged that he had asked for the gold, and had thrown it into the fire, but, he said, when he cast it in the fire, " there came out this calf." Impossible! The fire did not make the calf. The fire only melted the gold. Aaron made the calf. So many people want to blame their own sins on impersonal forces, which can never be blamed for deliberate sinful acts that reveal a determined purpose on the part of men. Strange that we should read here that the people were naked. Some commentators translate: " The people were licentious," but probably the Authorized Version is correct. " In the lewd and excited dancing of idolatrous orgies, garments were frequently cast aside, and the person exposed indecently. Egyptian dancers are represented on the monuments with scarcely any clothing." — *George Rawlinson.*

5. PUNISHMENT FOR SIN, vs. 26–29. Moses is not through with this awful rebellion against God. Israel must learn, by suffering, of the heinousness of her crime. So he called together all those who were on the Lord's side, for the most part the sons of Levi, and commanded them to take their swords and go in and out, from gate to gate, throughout the camp, slaying right and left. On the first day this resulted in the destruction of three thousand men. " The seeming indiscriminateness of the slaughter may mean, where all alike are guilty, ' decimation ' as by lot; or perhaps there were some who ' stood out,' contumacious in mutineering, though not actively resisting ' Moses in the law.' It was terrible, and was *meant* to be so *in terrorem* for all time." — *James Macgregor.* " Is not this clarion call still ringing: ' Who is on the Lord's side? ' Was there ever a time when stalwarts like these were in greater demand? We have to hold God's truth against many idols which are placed in competition with it. Idols of the tribe, of the forum, and of the heart. But before we can hope to cope with the heresies and superstitions of our age, we must turn the sword in against ourselves. And ' little children, keep yourselves from idols,' is very pertinent advice." — *F. B. Meyer.*

6. CONFESSION AND INTERCESSION, vs. 30–35. Again Moses comes before the Lord to stay God's wrath. This time, with his whole heart so full of love for Israel, so grieved for Israel's suffering he actually went so far as to tell the Lord that if he would not forgive Israel's sin he wanted to be blotted out himself from the book of the Lord. (Cf. Romans 9 : 1–3.) " Moses seems to have risen to the same height of self-abnegation as Paul, and to have willed to be ' accursed from God for his brethren, his kinsmen according to the flesh.' "

One precious promise resulted from Moses' intercession: " Behold, mine angel shall go before thee." Compare 23 : 20; 33 : 3, and see comment on the latter occurring in the next paragraph.

THE NATURE OF IDOLATRY.

" Men sometimes speak of idolaters bowing down before material forms, whether of gold, stone, or wood, as if they supposed that these were divine, and possessed divine attributes — and such may be the case with the more degraded and debased; but in the beginning it was not so. And if we carefully study the question in all its bearings, we shall discover that the idolater does not — in the first instance, at least — look upon his image as God, but as a representation or manifestation of God. It is an attempt on the part of the human spirit, which shrinks from the effort of communion with the unseen and spiritual, to associate God with what it can own and handle; so as to have a constant and evident token of the presence and favor of God." — *F. B. Meyer.*

II. **THE COMMAND TO RESUME THE JOURNEY,** 33 : 1–6. After this second intercessory act, God commands Moses to proceed toward Palestine, promising to send His angel before him to drive out the pagan tribes that were then inhabiting this divinely designated territory, a land flowing with milk and honey, adding the strange phrase: " For I will not go up in the midst of thee for thou art a stiffnecked people." " This is the awful qualification with which the possession of the promised land might have been granted. Jehovah Himself was not to go before the people. The angel here mentioned is expressly spoken of as the angel of Jehovah in 32 : 34. In whatever way we understand the mention of the angel in this passage as compared with 23 : 20, the meaning of the threat appears to be that the nation should be put on a level with other nations, to lose its character as the people in special covenant with Jehovah." — *T. E. Espin.*

III. **MOSES THE FRIEND OF GOD,** 33 : 7—34 : 28.

1. " THE LORD SPAKE UNTO MOSES FACE TO FACE," 33 : 8–11. When we are here told that Moses pitched a tent, and called it " the tent of meeting," that all those who sought the Lord went out to this tent of meeting which was without the camp, and that into this tent Moses entered to speak with the Lord, we are not to understand that this is the famous tabernacle, for that tabernacle, which was later carried up into the Temple of Jerusalem, had not yet been erected. " It was simply the tent or pavilion of Moses, in which he officially abode. This he now pitched outside the camp at some distance, and called it the tent of meeting, because, like the tabernacle, it was the place where God met with him. The object of this removal was to maintain intercourse with the Lord, when He would no longer manifest Himself amidst the people who had broken the covenant. Moses had not transgressed, and was still in fellowship with God. He will avail himself of this privilege to bring about a renewal of friendly relations between God and the people. The separation had also the effect of setting before the eyes of the people not only the continued fellowship of Moses with God, but also their own present estrangement from Him. And now any one who sought the Lord for counsel, judgment, or aid, went out to the tent of meeting. The wondering people bowed down with devout reverence when they beheld the supernatural signs of the divine presence. The Lord spake with Moses, not by a voice from heaven but in the pillar standing at his door, *face to face, as a man speaketh with his friend.* He beheld not the divine essence (v. 20), but such a vision of his face as is possible for a man to behold and live. When Moses was absent from the tent, Joshua his minister took his place." — *James G. Murphy.*

2. MOSES PLEADS FOR A NEW REVELATION OF GOD, 33 : 12–18. Undoubtedly, Moses is weary with all the heavy responsibilities and sad duties that rested upon him because of the transgression of these people, wearied in his own soul with pleading fervently for their forgiveness, and no doubt discouraged with these people, utterly unable to understand how they, the recipients of God's grace, could so very quickly depart from the clear instructions which they had received from God Himself. In this weariness, Moses now asks for a new revelation of God and a new assurance of God's presence. The Lord immediately assures him that His own divine presence will go with him and that He will give Moses rest. " There is no ' with thee ' in the original, and consequently the phrase is ambiguous. Moses could not tell whether it was a personal promise to himself, or a renewal of the old engagement to go with the people. He consequently requires something more explicit. Will God go, not merely with him, but with the people? " — *George Rawlinson.* And not until he is assured that God personally will go with him, does Moses make a request for himself. " It is not a mere angel, but Jehovah, the angel of the covenant (Mal. 3 : 1), whom he desires to have with him. This is the only incontestable

EXODUS 34 : 4. And he hewed two tables of stone like unto the first; and Moses rose up early in the morning, and went up unto mount Sinai, as Jehovah had commanded him, and took in his hand two tables of stone.
5. And Jehovah descended in the cloud, and stood with him there, and proclaimed the name of Jehovah.
6. And Jehovah passed by before him, and proclaimed, Jehovah, Jehovah, a God merciful and gracious, slow to anger, and abundant in lovingkindness and truth;
7. Keeping lovingkindness for thousands, forgiving iniquity and transgression and sin; and that will by no means clear *the guilty*, visiting the iniquity of the fathers upon the children, and upon the children's children, upon the third and upon the fourth generation.

---

evidence that they had found favor with God. ' I and thy people.' He now associates himself with the people, and the people with God. The presence of the Lord distinguishes them from all the people on the whole earth." — *James G. Murphy.* Now Moses makes a request for himself. " I beseech thee, show me thy glory." " The faithful servant of Jehovah, now assured by the success of his mediation, yearns, with the proper tendency of a devout spirit, for a more intimate communion with the divine Master than he had yet enjoyed. He seeks for something surpassing all former revelations. He had talked with the Lord ' face to face, as a man speaketh unto his friend ' (v. 11; cf. Deut. 34 : 10), but it was in the cloudy pillar: and he, and the people with him, had seen ' the glory of the Lord,' but it was in the form of ' devouring fire ' (16 : 7, 10; 24 : 16, 17); he had even beheld the similitude of the Lord in a mystical sense (Num. 12 : 8). But he asks now to behold the face of Jehovah in all its essential glory, neither veiled by a cloud nor represented by an angel." — *T. E. Espin.*

3. THE PRAYER IS ANSWERED, 33 : 19—34 : 9. The Lord does more than grant Moses the specific request to behold His glory, but first He does give him, as far as possible, what he specifically asked for. Though he told Moses no man could actually see the face of God and live, yet He would put him in a cleft of the rock, and cover him there with His hand, and when His glory passed by, He would take away His hand and Moses would see God's back, but not His face. Now what does all this mean? It is in the Word of God, and is thus not to be carelessly or irreverently considered. " It is a *kind* of view of that glory of grace which perhaps no creature has received before, and no creature shall afterwards receive, until (Luke 9 : 30, 31) Moses and Elias appear in glory on the mount of transfiguration, and converse with Jesus about His *exodus* — ' decease.' " — *James Macgregor.* " All that we can legitimately gather is that Moses was directed to a certain retired position, where God miraculously both protected him and shrouded him, while a manifestation of His glory passed by of a transcendent character, and that Moses was allowed to see, not the full manifestation, but the sort of afterglow which it left behind, which was as much as human nature could endure." — *George Rawlinson.*

After this mysterious, never-to-be-forgotten experience of beholding the glory of the Lord, Moses was commanded to hew two tables of stone that God might write again on them " the words that were in the first tables which thou brakest." 4. **And he hewed two tables of stone like unto the first; and Moses rose up early in the morning, and went up unto mount Sinai, as Jehovah had commanded him, and took in his hand two tables of stone.** 5. **And Jehovah descended in the cloud, and stood with him there, and proclaimed the name of Jehovah.** 6. **And Jehovah passed by before him, and proclaimed, Jehovah, Jehovah, a God merciful and gracious, slow to anger, and abundant in lovingkindness and truth;** 7. **keeping lovingkindness for thousands, forgiving iniquity and transgression and sin; and that will by no means clear *the guilty*, visiting the iniquity of the fathers upon the children, and upon the children's children, upon the third and upon the fourth generation.** " In this brief phrase we have the entire historical narrative of the manifestation to Moses of God's glory. For details we must refer to the terms of the promise (33 : 21–23), which are also characterized by brevity, but still add something to the bare statements of the present passage. Moses was, no doubt, hidden and protected by God's hand in a ' cleft of the rock ' while God's glory passed by. He was only allowed to look out from his hiding-place after the glory had passed, when he

8. And Moses made haste, and bowed his head toward the earth, and worshipped.
9. And he said, If now I have found favor in thy sight, O Lord, let the Lord, I pray thee, go in the midst of us; for it is a stiffnecked people; and pardon our iniquity and our sin, and take us for thine inheritance.

saw the remains of it — the 'back parts'; even this was, however, so brilliant a vision that it left a permanent light upon his countenance, which he was fain ordinarily to conceal from the people by means of a veil (vs. 29–35). 'The Lord, The Lord God. . . . The new name of God is not a name, as we understand the expression; it is rather a description of His nature by means of a series of epithets. At the bush He had revealed His eternal, self-existent character; in the descent on Sinai (19 : 16–19; 20 : 18–21) He had shown His terribleness; now, in the act of pardoning His people and taking them once more into favor, He made known His attribute of mercy. The more to impress this feature of His character on Israel, He accumulated epithet on epithet, calling Himself *Rakhum*, 'the tender or pitiful one'; *Khannun*, 'the kind or gracious one,' who bestows His benefits out of mere favor; *Erek appayim*, 'the long-suffering one'; *Rab khesed*, 'the great in mercy'; *Notser khesed*, 'the keeper of mercy'; and *Nose 'avon*, 'the forgiver of iniquity.' Still, to prevent the fatal misapprehension that He is a Being of pure and mere benevolence He added, to complete the description, a reference to His justice. He 'will by no means clear the guilty' (cf. Nahum 1 : 3), and will 'visit iniquity to the third and fourth generation.'" — *George Rawlinson.* "Mark, at the outset, how clear is the testimony of Scripture. In the first story of God's dealing with man, that story of the garden which foreshadows all His love and grace, we see it in the face of God. Adam and Eve are driven out of Eden, and the angel with the flaming sword which turned every way keeps the way of the tree of life. That is the first declaration that God will by no means clear the guilty. Again, when the flood desolates the earth we see the first visitation of vengeance on the hopelessly corrupt and the wilfully impenitent. Or when we stand where Abraham stood on the hillside overlooking the cities of the plain, and listen to his pleading with God, we see how he shrank from believing that the face of God could be so set against them that do evil. The one truth of which all secular historians are sure is that the Nemesis of judgment forgets nothing and forgives nothing. As they visit the ruins of the perished kingdoms of the East, as they tell the story of the decline and fall of the proud empires of the West, the vanished splendor of Greece, the lost grandeur of Rome, the despoiling of the glory of France, they emphasize the truth that there is no clearing of the guilty." — *W. M. Clow.*

8. **And Moses made haste, and bowed his head toward the earth, and worshipped.**
9. **And he said, If now I have found favor in thy sight, O Lord, let the Lord, I pray thee, go in the midst of us; for it is a stiffnecked people; and pardon our iniquity and our sin, and take us for thine inheritance.** Once again Moses pleads for the presence and mercy of God, a prayer which God does not at this time directly answer in so many words or promises, but indirectly answers by His renewal of His covenant with Israel.

4. The Renewed Commission, 34 : 10–27. Upon renewing His promise that He would drive out the various nations at that time inhabiting the land He had promised to Israel, God now warns Moses, and through him all of Israel, not to so act when the land of Palestine was reached, that they would become contaminated by the Canaanites and ensnared in their idolatrous practices, nor should they intermarry with these idolatrous people. Jehovah, the God of Israel, was and is the only true and living God; all other gods were false, man-made, impotent, and their worship resulted in vileness of character. These Israelites were God's own chosen people. He loved them, and, as a husband cannot, will not, must not, countenance unfaithfulness on the part of his wife whom he loves and whom he desires for himself, so will not God in His infinite holiness and perfect love, look with anything but holy wrath and anger upon His people when they worship some false, wicked, prohibited, pagan deity. This warning was well needed, for this is just the sin into which Israel later fell and because of which she was taken into captivity.

There follows now a brief mention of some of the fundamental laws regarding feasts and the Sabbath, which Israel was to faithfully observe. "Here, as before, the two great matters of warning and of direction to the nation seeking to be blessed of God are what regards the heathen world around them, and what regards their own ob

27. And Jehovah said unto Moses, Write thou these words: for after the tenor of these words I have made a covenant with thee and with Israel.
28. And he was there with Jehovah forty days and forty nights; he did neither eat bread, nor drink water. And he wrote upon the tables the words of the covenant, the ten commandments.

servance of the religious ordinances which God has given them (cf. 23 : 16–31). Relatively to the outside populations we observe now that in their sight God is to work miracles, distinctly with a view to the subduing terror of those wonders which was seen and felt in Egypt. Groves, mentioned here, are supposed to have really consisted in some sort of statuary, perhaps of stone, probably of wood; in some way connected with (lascivious) worship of Astarte (*Asheroth*, plur. of *Asherah*, is the word for groves). The introduction here and now, along with the expression about a jealous God, of 'go a whoring,' in prohibition of such practices, may be historically connected with impure indecencies at the recent calf worship; but it had a similar appropriateness in connection with idolatrous worship very generally. Molten gods, a peculiar expression, is accounted for in like manner by connection with the calf worship. In the direction as to ordinances, Sabbatism now, as before, has a great place. The holy nation is expressly warned against the temptation of an agricultural people, to tamper with the Lord's day, on account of urgencies of seed-time and reaping time (*earing* is Old English for ploughing; from the same root as the Latin *ar*—are)." — *James Macgregor*. 27. **And Jehovah said unto Moses, Write thou these words: for after the tenor of these words I have made a covenant with thee and with Israel.** "This express command accounts for the assignment of so much space to what is mainly repetition. The requirement of the repetition can only be explained by the importance of the laws laid down under the circumstances of the Hebrew nation, and the power of repetition to enforce upon the conscience what is pressed upon it by reiteration. 'After the tenor of these words,' means after their general aspect or bearing." — *George Rawlinson*.

5. A FINAL WORD, 34 : 28. 28. **And he was there with Jehovah forty days and forty nights; he did neither eat bread, nor drink water. And he wrote upon the tables the words of the covenant, the ten commandments.** "On this second occasion of going forty days into seclusion with God it is said that Moses fasted; and it may perhaps be presumed that he fasted on the first occasion. The writer of the ten words is shown to have been the Lord by Exodus 34 verse 1. The 'words' (in Heb. 'words' has the meaning of 'matter') which Moses has to write are, the matters connected with this renewing of the covenant — a record of the proceedings." — *James Macgregor*. Cf. Matt. 4 : 2.

IV. **THE EFFECT UPON MOSES OF HIS FORTY DAYS IN THE MOUNT AND THE CONSEQUENT FEAR AMONG THE ISRAELITES,** 34 : 29–35. Sometimes a human face is illuminated with joy because of an experience that arises from nothing more than some exalted human relationship, *e.g.*, the glow that is seen in a mother's face when she holds her first babe in her arms; or the radiance that surrounds the face of a bride as she approaches the altar. How much more glorious must have been the light shining in Moses' face, as he came down from the mountain, after being in the actual presence of God for forty days. Wholly unconscious that his face shone, yet (no doubt at the request of Aaron and the Israelites) he found it necessary when talking to them to put a veil over his face until he went in to the tent of meeting to talk again to the Lord, when he took off the veil. "The veil on the face of Moses, like the veil before the mercy seat, taught them that the present economy was adapted to the weakness of their spiritual vision; while so much of the brightness shone through as to satisfy their present needs and capacities, and give them a foreglance and earnest of what awaited them in the advancing stages of their spiritual training (2 Cor. 3 : 7–18)." — *J. G. Murphy*. "True Christian excellence is as unconscious of its beauty as Moses was; whenever it becomes self-conscious it loses its charm. Beware of the man who talks about his graces. There is such a thing as being proud of humility, and making capital out of our nothingness. The man who boasts of a shining face is a counterfeit and a cheat. The possessor of the genuine article never talks about it, never thinks about it; and would be almost overwhelmed to hear of any such thing being ascribed to him." — *F. B. Meyer*.

Do you think that the Israelitish host had not been contemplating some kind of an idolatrous image before they actually asked Aaron to do this wicked thing? Why is Aaron more guilty in this act than any other Israelite of the entire multitude?

In how many ways in this lesson is Moses strong where Aaron is weak? What spiritual benefits did Moses himself reveal, as far as this lesson is concerned, from his faithfulness to God, his long hours of intercession, and his love for his people Israel? How does Moses here in a way typify the high-priestly work of the Lord Jesus Christ? How does this entire episode reveal God's perfect wisdom and foresight in choosing Moses in the first place to be the leader and law giver of His people Israel?

LESSON X. — September 5.

ISRAEL CALLED TO BE A HOLY PEOPLE. — Book of Leviticus.

PRINTED TEXT, Leviticus 19 : 1-4, 11-18, 32-34.

GOLDEN TEXT. — *Ye shall be holy; for I am holy.* 1 PETER 1 : 16.

Devotional Reading: Leviticus 26 : 3–12.
Beginner Topic: RUTH'S KIND FRIEND.
Lesson Material: Leviticus 19 : 9, 10; Ruth 2.
Memory Verse: Be ye kind. Ephesians 4 : 32.
Primary Topic: IN THE FIELD OF BOAZ.
Lesson Material: Leviticus 19 : 1–10, 33, 34; Ruth 2.
Memory Verse: The earth is full of the lovingkindness of Jehovah. Psalm 33 : 5.
Junior Topic: AT HARVEST TIME.
Lesson Material: Leviticus 19 : 1–10, 33, 34; Ruth 2.
Memory Verse: If ye fulfill the royal law, according to the scripture, Thou shalt love thy neighbor as thyself, ye do well. James 2 : 8.
Intermediate and Senior Topic: WHAT GOD EXPECTS OF US.
Topic for Young People and Adults: WHAT GOD EXPECTS OF US.

THE TEACHER AND HIS CLASS.

The Younger Classes will enter into the meaning of this lesson most easily if they are instructed, in a simple way, in the meaning of the word *law*, and are shown something of the different kinds of law which exist. A law, fundamentally, expresses what ought to be. Thus, a law in physics tells us how certain forces should and will act under normal conditions. Laws issued by governments are for the control of the conduct of the people, guiding them in their daily actions. Laws are given for the greatest benefit of the greatest number. In this chapter we have some laws announced by God for our obeying, which, if we do obey them, will work for the greatest happiness in our own lives, and in the lives of all those with whom we mingle. All God's laws are for our good.

The Older Classes will, of course, be aware that there are many instructions in the Old Testament which do not apply to Christian believers today, *e.g.*, the entire Levitical system of offerings, which, though it still has its typical meanings for us, is *not* to be "obeyed." We are not to offer sacrifices, but to believe in Christ who is the last and supreme and perfect Sacrifice. On the other hand, the Old Testament does contain many fundamental laws which all of God's people should obey, and, in fact, which all people should obey, though we cannot expect those who have not acknowledged God to willingly submit themselves to God's laws. In this lesson, then, we have not commandments for Jews, not ancient laws which are now antiquated, but commandments from God which reach into the very fundamental conditions of life, and are just as important today as when they were declared.

THE LESSON IN ITS SETTING.

Time. — 1444 B.C.
Place. — At Sinai.

THE PLAN OF THE LESSON.

SUBJECT: Holiness, the Supreme Ideal for the People of God and Some of the Characteristics That Will Always Mark the Life of People Living in Such Holiness.

I. GOD'S FUNDAMENTAL PURPOSE FOR ISRAEL — THAT SHE SHOULD BE A HOLY PEOPLE, Leviticus 19 : 1, 2.

II. THE OBLIGATION OF MEN TOWARD THEIR PARENTS, 19 : 3 *a*.

III. TWO COMMANDMENTS RELATING TO THE WORSHIP OF GOD, 19 : 3 *b*, 4.

1. The sanctity of the Sabbath.
2. The prohibition of idolatry.

IV. LAWS REGULATING THE SOCIAL RELATIONSHIPS OF MEN, 19 : 11–18.

1. The condemnation of
   stealing
   lying
   swearing
   defrauding others of their wages, vs. 11–13.
2. Laws protecting the deaf and blind, v. 14.
3. The necessity of righteous judgment, v. 15.
4. The sin of talebearing, v. 16 *a*.
5. The sin of hiding others' crimes, v. 16 *b*.
6. Love for neighbors, vs. 17, 18.

V. THE RESPECT DUE OLD AGE, 19 : 32.

VI. THE LAW OF LOVE FOR THE STRANGER, 19 : 33, 34.

THE TEACHER'S LIBRARY.

On the Book of Leviticus, one should first of all consult the remarkable volume by Samuel H. Kellogg, in the *Expositor's Bible* series, full of rich things; for detailed exposition of verses, see the work by C. D. Ginsburg, in the *Bible Commentary for English Readers*, and, for exegetical material, the work by Samuel Clark, in the *Bible Commentary* series; and by Frederick Gardiner, in the Lange series of commentaries. Also, among the older commentaries, one will find helpful material in the commentary by George Bush, and in the very rich work by Andrew A. Bonar, *A Commentary on the Book of Leviticus*, first published in 1846, and still of great value. For brief studies of the book itself, one should consult the very scholarly article by Wilhelm Moeller, in the *International Bible Encyclopedia*, Vol. 3, 1870–1880; and then the chapters in W. G. Moorehead's *Outline Studies in the Books of the Old Testament*, 37–48; and G. Campbell Morgan: *Living Messages of the Books of the Bible, Genesis to Esther*, 46–62 (who here makes the very strange error, rare for him, of saying that the word *love* never occurs in the Book of Leviticus, for we find it in our lesson today). The editor knows of no homiletical material of any value on the verses assigned for our lesson.

THE BOOK OF LEVITICUS.

I. THE NAME OF THE BOOK. In the Hebrew Bible, this third book is called *Wayyikra*, which is the first Hebrew word occurring in the book, meaning, "He called." In the Septuagint, the book is called *Leueitikon*, and in the Vulgate it is called, as in all our Bibles, *Leviticus*, that is, the Levitical book, the book that deals with the Levitical laws, the laws of sacrifice, offerings, and holiness.

From a photograph by Wilson.
The Sinai Valley Toward the Plain of Er-Rahah.

II. THE PLACE OF LEVITICUS IN THE CANON. Every one knows that Leviticus follows the Book of Exodus, but not every one is aware of the reason for this order. Now Exodus is the book of redemption, narrating for us God's marvelous deliverance of the children of Israel from the bondage of Egypt. Redemption from Egypt, a type of redemption from sin, should lead into a new life of liberty and obedience to God, as the experience of redemption ought to lead us into a new life of true holiness. Thus, while in Exodus the great acts of redemption are recorded, in Leviticus we have the way in which redeemed people ought to walk.

III. THE PURPOSE OF THE BOOK OF LEVITICUS. The following words by Dr. Samuel H. Kellogg are so illuminating, and express so many things compactly, that we believe all of our readers will find his sentences more profitable than anything which the editor himself could write (at least in the same space). "What now was the purpose of Leviticus? In general, as regards Israel, it was given to direct them how they might live as a holy nation in fellowship with God. The keynote of the book is 'Holiness to Jehovah.' More particularly, the object of the book was to furnish for the theocracy set up in Israel a code of law which should secure their physical, moral, and spiritual well-being. But the establishment of the theocracy in Israel was itself only a means to an end; namely, to make Israel a blessing to all nations, in mediating to the Gentiles the redemption of God. Hence, the Levitical laws were all intended and adapted to train and prepare the nation for this special historic mission for which God had chosen them. To this end, it was absolutely necessary, first of all, that Israel should be kept separate from the heathen nations. To effect and maintain this separation, these laws of Leviticus were admirably adapted. They are of such a character, that obedience to them, even in a very imperfect way, has made the nation to this day to be, in a manner and degree perfectly unique, isolated and separate from all the peoples in the midst of whom they dwell. The law of Leviticus was intended to effect this preparation of Israel for its world mission, not only in an external manner, but also in an internal way; namely, by revealing in and to Israel the real character of God, and in particular His unapproachable holiness. For if Israel is to teach the nations the way of holiness, in which alone they can be blessed, the chosen nation must itself first be taught holiness by the Holy One. A lesson here for every one of us! The revelation of the holiness of God was made, first of all, in the sacrificial system. The great lesson which it must have kept before the most obtuse conscience was this, that 'without shedding of blood there is no remission of sin'; that God therefore must be the Most Holy, and sin against Him no trifle. But the law of Leviticus was not only intended to prepare Israel for the Messiah by thus awakening a sense of sin and need, it was so ordered as to be in many ways directly typical and prophetic of Christ and His great redemption, in its future historical development. . . . Leviticus speaks forevermore of the awfulness of sin in the light of the holiness of God, of the plenteous redemption springing from the love of God, and of the possibility of holiness of life, created by communion with God."

IV. SOME OF THE MORE FREQUENTLY USED WORDS AND PHRASES OF THIS BOOK. In the light of Professor Kellogg's statement regarding the purpose of this book, it is interesting to note that the English word *holiness* occurs 87 times, more, I believe, than in all the other books of the Old Testament put together. The word *blood* occurs 86 times; *kaphar*, meaning *atonement*, occurs 45 times, which is more than in all the rest of the Old Testament books combined. The word *priest* occurs 189 times, while the word *sacrifice* is found 42 times. There are four different Hebrew words translated *offering;* the word *ishel* occurring 41 times, more frequently than in any other book of the Bible; *qorban* occurs 28 times; *zebach* and *terunah*, each occur once. The word *sin*, in its noun and verbal forms, occurs 42 times, more than in any other one book in the Old Testament. The frequency of these words emphasizes the fact that this book deals fundamentally with the removal of sin and the life of holiness.

V. AN OUTLINE OF THE BOOK. The following outline is only suggestive, for it is recognized by all that the book is not easily divided into clearly circumscribed sections.

1. The Law of the Offerings, vs. 1–7.
2. The Consecration of Aaron and His Sins, vs. 8–10.
3. Laws Regarding Cleanness and Holiness, vs. 11–15, 17–22.
4. The Day of Atonement, v. 16.
5. The Sacred Calendar, v. 23.
6. Sundry Laws, vs. 24, 25.
7. Promises and Warnings, v. 26.
8. Regarding Vows, v. 27.

It is worth noting that the events recorded in Genesis cover 370 years; those in Exodus, 140 years; but all the events occurring in Leviticus can be included within one month of time. (There are only three definite historical events in the entire book: 8 : 1–13; 10 : 1–7; 24 : 10–16.)

VI. THE FUNDAMENTAL LAWS OF THE BOOK OF LEVITICUS. "The thought running throughout the whole economy is that of man, who has sinned, and so been excluded from God, being brought back to Him. . . . A general survey of the book with that unifying truth in mind will reveal the nature of that redemption by which sinning man is brought back to God. Three words indicate the consistent method. They are, substitution, imputation, death. . . . Every sacrifice was that of a life standing in the place of another. In order to the restoration of a sinning man to

Leviticus 19 : 1. And Jehovah spake unto Moses, saying,
2. Speak unto all the congregation of the children of Israel, and say unto them, Ye shall be holy; for I Jehovah your God am holy.
3. Ye shall fear every man his mother, and his father; and ye shall keep my sabbaths: I am Jehovah your God.

God, some one must take his place as a sinning man. This substitution is closely associated with imputation. In the ceremonies of this ancient ritual there were constantly included acts which suggested the transference of the guilt of man to the life which stood in his place. Finally, the one substituted, and to whom the guilt was imputed, must die. That was the one and only law of redemption suggested by all the economy of the Hebrew worship. . . . The final explanation of the divine provision of redemption is to be found in the all-inclusive statement of the New Testament, 'God is love.' The holiness of God might have been vindicated, and the last demand of His righteousness satisfied, by the absolute annihilation of everything that had failed. . . . I know the Book of Leviticus is terrible reading; it is a tragic story of blood and fire. It is time that this living message was heard anew, that sin smites God in the face, and wounds Him in the heart; and that redemption is the outcome of the tender compassion, which receives the wounding, and bends over the sinner, pardoning him by virtue of that infinite and unfathomable mystery of which the shedding of blood is the only equivalent symbolism. Redemption is in order to holiness. The final note of the message of Leviticus is that redemption does not excuse man from holiness, but that it is the method by which man is made holy. To fulfill all the requirements of the external ritual, and yet continue in sin, would be to commit the most heinous of all." — *G. Campbell Morgan.*

I. GOD'S FUNDAMENTAL PURPOSE FOR ISRAEL — THAT SHE SHOULD BE A HOLY PEOPLE, vs. 1, 2. 1. **And Jehovah spake unto Moses, saying,** 2. **Speak unto all the congregation of the children of Israel, and say unto them, Ye shall be holy; for I Jehovah your God am holy.** This command "Be ye holy, for I am holy," is found continually reiterated in this book, and repeated again in the New Testament (see Lev. 11 : 44, 45; 19 : 2; 20 : 7, 26; 21 : 8; 1 Pet. 1 : 16).

"The position of this command at the head of the long list of precepts which follows, is most significant and instructive. It sets before us the object of the whole ceremonial and moral law, and, we may add, the supreme object of the gospel also, namely, to produce a certain type of moral and spiritual character, a holy manhood; it, moreover, precisely interprets this term, so universally misunderstood and misapplied among all nations, as essentially consisting in a spiritual likeness to God: 'Ye shall be holy: for I the Lord your God am holy.' These words evidently at once define holiness and declare the supreme motive to the attainment and maintenance of a holy character. This then is brought before us as the central thought in which all the diverse precepts and prohibitions which follow find their unity; and, accordingly, we find this keynote of the whole law echoing, as it were, all through this chapter, in the constant refrain, repeated herein no less than fourteen — twice seven — times: 'I am the Lord (Heb. Jehovah)!' 'I am the Lord your God!'"

II. THE OBLIGATION OF MEN TOWARD THEIR PARENTS, 3 *a.* 3 *a.* **Ye shall fear every man his mother, and his father.** The first division of the law of holiness which follows (vs. 3–8), deals with two duties of fundamental importance in the social and the religious life; the one, honor to parents; the other, reverence to God. If we are surprised, at first, to see this place of honor in the law of holiness given to the fifth commandment (v. 3), our surprise will lessen when we remember how, taking the individual in the development of his personal life, he learns to fear God, first of all, through fearing and honoring his parents. In the earliest beginnings of life, the parent — to speak with reverence — stands to his child, in a very peculiar sense, for and in the place of God. We gain the conception of the Father in heaven first from our experience of fatherhood on earth; and so it may be said of this commandment, in a sense in which it cannot be said of any other, that it is the foundation of all religion. Alas, for the child who contemns the instruction of his father and the command of his mother, for by so doing he puts himself out of the possibility of coming into the knowledge and experience of the Fatherhood of God." — *Samuel H. Kellogg.* (Cf. Exod. 20 : 12; Eph. 6 : 2.) "The expression 'fear,' however, they take to include the following: (1) Not to stand or sit in the place set apart for the parents; (2) not to carp at or oppose their statements; and (3) not to

4. Turn ye not unto idols, nor make to yourselves molten gods: I am Jehovah your God.
11. Ye shall not steal; neither shall ye deal falsely, nor lie one to another.
12. And ye shall not swear by my name falsely, and profane the name of thy God: I am Jehovah.

---

call them by their proper names, but either to call them father or mother, or my master, or my lady." — *C. D. Ginsburg.*

III. **TWO COMMANDMENTS RELATING TO THE WORSHIP OF GOD,** 19 : 3 *b*, 4. 3 *b*. **And ye shall keep my sabbaths: I am Jehovah your God.** "Joined with this fifth commandment is the fourth of the Decalogue. The education of the children, which at the early stages of the Hebrew commonwealth devolved upon the parents, was more especially carried on by them on Sabbath days. In these leisure hours when the Israelites were strictly forbidden to engage in any secular work, they found it a pleasant task and a welcome occupation to instruct their children in the many symbols, rites, and ceremonies which formed part of the service of the Sabbaths. Hence the observance of the day implied the instruction of the people in the fear and admonition of the Lord, and in acquiring the holiness which is the keynote of this chapter. Hence, too, the violation of the sanctity of the Sabbath is denounced as the greatest sin which the Israelites committed (Ezek. 20 : 12; 22 : 8; 23 : 38, etc.)." — *C. D. Ginsburg.* Right here the editor feels compelled to insert something that is increasingly pressed upon his mind, and that is the great danger at this present time, due to the vast acceleration of our manufacturing program because of the necessities of war, of multitudes of men, compelled to work seven days a week, being forced to neglect the house of God and to neglect their own spiritual life. Christians should carefully plan their lives that even if they have to work seven days a week they will be able to regularly apportion some time of the week for definite worship, and especially for private devotional exercises. We need it these days. 4. **Turn ye not unto idols, nor make to yourselves molten gods: I am Jehovah your God.** To turn to an idol means to turn away from the true God, for God can never be represented by any man-made idol. When one turns to an idol, one turns not necessarily physically, but intellectually and emotionally. The mind turns to a recognition of an idol as God, and therefore one is following a satanic error and wicked delusion. One's affections turn to the idol, and, instead of offering praises and sacrifices to the true God in recognition of His holiness and their sinfulness, one presents gifts to a dumb statue of wood, or stone, or some precious metal. Anything that is put first in our life before God is God to us. How different the history of Israel would have been if she had hearkened to this warning, and obeyed this command, for idolatry was her downfall.

Instructing the Children.

IV. **LAWS REGULATING THE SOCIAL RELATIONSHIPS OF MEN,** 19 : 11–18. 11. **Ye shall not steal; neither shall ye deal falsely, nor lie one to another.** Stealing is condemned in the eighth commandment of the Decalogue (Exod. 20 : 15); lying is condemned in the ninth commandment (Exod. 20 : 16). Stealing and lying generally go together. A man who will steal will lie; stealing generally necessitates lying, in an attempt to cover up the evil deed. 12. **And ye shall not swear by my name falsely, and profane the name of thy God: I am Jehovah.** This admonition corresponds to the third commandment of the Decalogue

13. Thou shalt not oppress thy neighbor, nor rob him: the wages of a hired servant shall not abide with thee all night until the morning.

14. Thou shalt not curse the deaf, nor put a stumblingblock before the blind; but thou shalt fear thy God: I am Jehovah.

15. Ye shall do no unrighteousness in judgment: thou shalt not respect the person of the poor, nor honor the person of the mighty; but in righteousness shalt thou judge thy neighbor.

16. Thou shalt not go up and down as a talebearer among thy people: neither shalt thou stand against the blood of thy neighbor: I am Jehovah.

(Exod. 20 : 7), and is a warning against that sin into which men seem so prone to fall, *i.e.*, the careless, profane, and blasphemous use of the name of God. If one uses God's name in some blasphemous way, or calls upon God to witness that he is telling the truth when really he is lying, then the fear of God goes out of his life; respect for God is diminished; the sense of sin itself is almost obliterated, and, when it comes time for this man to pray, the name of God, and thus the Person of God, really comes to mean nothing to him. When one blasphemously uses God's name in the morning in speaking to men, one can hardly expect to have a true conception of God in the evening, when he kneels down to pray. 13. **Thou shalt not oppress thy neighbor, nor rob him: the wages of a hired servant shall not abide with thee all night until the morning.** " Inasmuch as the wages of a hireling, a day laborer, were the support of himself and family, they would necessarily be forced to expend it as fast as it could be earned. There are few sins marked in the Scriptures more with the emphatic reprobation of heaven than the withholding of wages from those to whom they are due." — *George Bush.* " From the declaration in the next clause, which forbids the retention of the wages over night, it is evident that the day laborer is here spoken of. As he is dependent upon his wages for the support of himself and family, the law protects him by enjoining that the earnings of the hireling should be promptly paid. This benign care for the laborer, and the denunciation against any attempt to defraud him, are again and again repeated in the Scriptures (Deut. 24 : 14, 15; Jer. 22 : 13; Mal. 3 : 5; James 5 : 4)." — *C. D. Ginsburg.* 14. **Thou shalt not curse the deaf, nor put a stumblingblock before the blind; but thou shalt fear thy God: I am Jehovah.** " To revile one who cannot hear, and is therefore unable to vindicate himself, is both inexpressibly mean and wicked. The term deaf also includes the absent, and hence out of hearing (Ps. 38 : 14, 15). . . . In Deuteronomy 27 : 18 a curse is pronounced upon those who lead the blind astray. To help those who were thus afflicted was always regarded as a meritorious act. Hence among the benevolent services which Job rendered to his neighbors, he says, ' I was eyes to the blind ' (Job 29 : 15). Similar tenderness to the weak is enjoined by the apostles: ' That no man put a stumblingblock or an occasion to fall in his brother's way ' (Rom. 14 : 13). Deafness and blindness may prevent the sufferers from detecting the offender, and bringing him to justice before an earthly tribunal, but God on high hears it when the human ear is stopped up, and sees it when the human eye is extinct. Hence the prohibition against injustice to the infirm and the poor is enforced by an appeal to fear the Lord (see v. 32)." — *C. D. Ginsburg.* 15. **Ye shall do no unrighteousness in judgment: thou shalt not respect the person of the poor, nor honor the person of the mighty; but in righteousness shalt thou judge thy neighbor.** " ' *Causes* must be heard, not persons,' says Trappe. There must be no affectation of kindness to the poor, even as there must be no fawning flattery of the great. Especially in matters of judgment, the judge must be impartial. The eye of God is on him; and as He is a just God, and without iniquity, He delights to see His own attributes shadowed forth in the strict integrity of an earthly judge. If these are God's holy principles, it follows that the misery and oppression and suffering of the lower classes will furnish no reason for their acquittal at His bar, if they be found guilty. Suffering in this world is no blotting out of sin. Hence we find at Christ's appearing, ' the great men and the mighty men, and every bondman,' cry to the rocks, ' Fall on us, and hide us from the face of him that sitteth on the throne ' (Rev. 6 : 16)." — *Andrew Bonar.* For the perfect and abiding fulfilment of this glorious ideal, in the future reign of the Lord Jesus Christ, see Isaiah 11 : 3–5. 16. **Thou shalt not go up and down as a talebearer among thy people.** " While

17. Thou shalt not hate thy brother in thy heart: thou shalt surely rebuke thy neighbor, and not bear sin because of him.

18. Thou shalt not take vengeance, nor bear any grudge against the children of thy people; but thou shalt love thy neighbor as thyself: I am Jehovah.

32. Thou shalt rise up before the hoary head, and honor the face of the old man, and thou shalt fear thy God: I am Jehovah.

---

giving just evidence in a court of justice is demanded by the law, it prohibits the circulation of slanderous reports about our neighbors. This dangerous habit, which has ruined the character and destroyed the life of many an innocent person (1 Sam. 22 : 9, 18; Ezek. 22 : 9, etc.), was denounced by the spiritual authorities in the time of Christ as the greatest sin. Three things they declared remove a man from this world, and deprive him of happiness in the world to come — idolatry, incest, and murder, but slander surpasses them all. It kills three persons with one act, the person who slanders, the person who is slandered, and the person who listens to the slander." — *C. D. Ginsburg.* **Neither shalt thou stand against the blood of thy neighbor: I am Jehovah.** "Thou shalt neither be a false witness to the endangering of a man's life, nor shalt thou stand by and see thy neighbor injured, crushed, ruined, and perhaps his life taken, without an effort to save him. This precept is joined with the preceding, because talebearing, by sowing discord and breeding broils in society often led to the shedding of blood." — *George Bush.*
17. **Thou shalt not hate thy brother in thy heart: thou shalt surely rebuke thy neighbor, and not bear sin because of him.** 18. **Thou shalt not take vengeance, nor bear any grudge against the children of thy people; but thou shalt love thy neighbor as thyself: I am Jehovah.** The words of Professor Ginsburg here are better than we have seen in any other commentary, and we take the liberty of quoting him. "As the preceding verse enjoins upon us to reprove the offender, this verse forbids us to avenge the wrong even when the rebuke has proved ineffectual, thus demanding the greatest sacrifice on the part of the injured person. When Hillel was asked by one who wished to learn the sum and substance of the divine law in the shortest possible time, this sage replied by giving a paraphrase of the precept before us in a negative form, 'What thou dost not wish that others should do to thee, that do not thou to others; this is the whole law, the rest is only its interpretation. Now go and learn.' Christ gives it in the positive form (Matt. 7 : 12; Luke 6 : 31; Rom. 13 : 8–10)."

V. **THE RESPECT DUE OLD AGE,** 19 : 32. 32. **Thou shalt rise up before the hoary head, and honor the face of the old man, and thou shalt fear thy God: I am Jehovah.** "How much praise have the Spartan institutions justly obtained for cherishing this principle, yet how much more energetic and authoritative is the language of the Jewish code, coming as it does directly from Jehovah himself! In commanding reverence to be paid to the aged, he in fact ordains it to that which is a feeble image of his own eternity. He is denominated the 'Ancient of days' (Dan. 7 : 9, 13, 22), and when he is represented as having 'the hair of his head like the pure wool' (Rev. 1 : 14), he is pleased to represent himself as having the distinguishing characteristic of old age. There is probably no object in creation so fitted to inspire reverence as the sight of the snowy locks of the old man, and consequently the duty here enjoined has been recognized in all civilized nations, as one the violation of which is deserving of the severest punishment." — *George Bush.* The words of Dr. Bonar have often been referred to as words of great beauty. "When we meet them in public places, or they come to where you are, show them reverence. Both the infirmity and the wisdom of the aged have a claim on us; and, besides, *age* has in it solemnity. By the side of it, the Lord would solemnize us in the midst of our pursuits. 'Lo! the shadow of eternity! for one cometh who is almost already in eternity. His head and beard white as snow, indicate his speedy appearance before the Ancient of Days, the hair of whose head is as pure wool.' Every object, too, that is feeble seems to be recommended to our care by God; for these are types of the condition wherein he finds us when His grace comes to save. It is therefore accepting His grace in a shadow, when the helpless are relieved, 'the fatherless find mercy' (Hos. 14 : 3), 'the orphans relieved, and the widow' (Ps. 146 : 9), and the 'stranger preserved.'"

33. And if a stranger sojourn with thee in your land, ye shall not do him wrong.

34. The stranger that sojourneth with you shall be unto you as the home-born among you, and thou shalt love him as thyself; for ye were sojourners in the land of Egypt: I am Jehovah your God.

VI. **THE LAW OF LOVE FOR THE STRANGER,** 19:33, 34. 33. **And if a stranger sojourn with thee in your land, ye shall not do him wrong.** 34. **The stranger that sojourneth with you shall be unto you as the home-born among you, and thou shalt love him as thyself; for ye were sojourners in the land of Egypt: I am Jehovah your God.** "The stranger for whose benefit the legislators enacted so many humane and benign laws, and with regard to whom the Book of Leviticus has laid down so many precepts, is one of non-Jewish origin, but who had joined the Jewish faith. He had, therefore, to undergo the rite of circumcision; he had to fast on the great Day of Atonement (16:29); he had to submit to the regulations about sacrifices (17:8, 9; 22:18); he had to abstain from eating blood and the flesh of animals torn by wild beasts (*ibid.*, vs. 10, 15); he had to practice the laws of chastity (18:26); like the Israelite by birth, he had to refrain from blasphemy, and obey the moral precepts (24:16–22). These were some of the conditions of his sojourning in the land. . . . Having once been admitted into the community, the Israelites were forbidden to upbraid him with his nationality or throw at him the fact that he was originally an idolater. He is not simply to be treated with consideration and courtesy because he is a foreigner, and enjoy the rights and receive the justice due to every human being, but he is to be put on a perfect equality with the ordinary Israelite. Hence the precept laid down, 'Thou shalt love thy neighbor as thyself' (v. 18), is here enacted with regard to the stranger. It was this humane law which attracted so many strangers to Palestine. Hence we find that in the days of Solomon there were 153,600 strangers in the Holy Land. To enforce these kindly sentiments towards strangers, which was so contrary to the practice of the surrounding nations, who had an inveterate hatred of all foreigners, the lawgiver appeals to their own bitter experience. They knew with what inhumanity they were treated in Egypt because they were strangers, how they had been humiliated and reduced to slavery. The very thought of this will not only soften their hearts, but will enable them to see that the safety of all classes consists in basing our legislation upon the principle of equal rights to all inhabitants. This pathetic appeal is to be found three times more in the Pentateuch to enforce this precept (Exod. 22:20; 23:9; Deut. 10:19)." — *C. D. Ginsburg.*

From a study of this lesson, do you think that our right relationship to God is the root out of which springs righteous acts toward men, or will our righteous conduct toward men lead us to the worship of God? In how many different ways is God's love for mankind and his desire for the welfare of men expressed in the verses we have studied in this chapter? Has it been true through history that those who are true to God, who are faithful in worship, who keep the Lord's day, are more consistent in their kindness and love for others and in the righteousness of their lives? What happens when men set themselves to break the laws that are here inculcated? (Their hearts become hard and they themselves a menace to their fellowmen.) Do you think that obedience to these laws would make for the greatest sense of security and for prosperity in any land that consistently practiced them, and why do you think so?

LESSON XI. — September 12.

ISRAEL MARCHES TOWARD CANAAN.
Numbers 10:11—12:16.

PRINTED TEXT, Numbers 10:11, 12, 29–36.

GOLDEN TEXT. — ***Come thou with us, and we will do thee good.*** NUMBERS 10:29.

Devotional Reading: Psalm 122.
Beginner Topic: WHEN MOSES NEEDED HELP.
  Lesson Material: Exodus 15:22–27.
  Memory Verse: The Lord is my helper. Hebrews 13:6.

Primary Topic: MOSES' INVITATION TO HOBAB.
Lesson Material: Numbers 10 : 29–36.
Memory Verse: What good soever Jehovah shall do unto us, the same will we do unto thee. Numbers 10 : 32.
Junior Topic: MOSES AND HOBAB.
Lesson Material: Numbers 10 : 29–36.
Memory Verse: Thou shalt rise up before the hoary head, and honor the face of the old man. Leviticus 19 : 32.
Intermediate and Senior Topic: WHAT GOD WANTS OUR NATION TO BE.
Topic for Young People and Adults: GOD'S PURPOSE FOR OUR NATION.

THE TEACHER AND HIS CLASS.

The Younger Classes might be asked: what are the two principal motives lying behind an invitation we extend to some person, or people, to come with us on a venture we are undertaking, or a trip we are planning? One motive would be that they might enjoy with us the pleasures we are anticipating; the other motive would be that they might help us either with their labor, their wisdom, or influence, or other resources, of one kind or another in the task we are about to undertake. We will find one of these motives prompting Moses to invite the neighboring tribe to join with the Israelites in their wilderness journeys, and what came of this invitation.

The Older Classes will find in this lesson a number of incidents which reveal, as by an X-ray, the disagreeable and really contemptible characteristics of some of the Israelites (though they are being divinely guided), and, on the other hand, some of the sterling qualities of the great leader, Moses. These contrasts are continually arising in our normal experiences, but especially are discernible in hours of danger, of great crisis, or of unusual opportunity. As this lesson is being written, America has discovered the sterling qualities of one of its great soldiers, General MacArthur, in his fearless and stubborn defense of the Philippines. It has also discovered the weakness of some other officers who were at Pearl Harbor.

THE LESSON IN ITS SETTING.

Time. — The spring of 1444 B.C.
Place. — The wilderness of Paran, south of Sinai.

THE PLAN OF THE LESSON.

SUBJECT: Manifestations of Divine Guidance and Mercy, and of Divine Displeasure and Wrath, in the Wilderness Experiences of Israel.

I. THE ORDER OF THE HOST, Numbers 10 : 11–28.

II. THE MIDIANITES ARE INVITED TO JOIN THE ISRAELITES, 10 : 29–32.

III. THE EXPERIENCE OF DIVINE GUIDANCE, 10 : 33–36.

IV. THE CONTINUOUS MURMURING OF ISRAEL ON THE WAY TO KADESH-BARNEA, 11 : 1—12 : 16.

1. The judgment of God by fire, vs. 1–3.
2. The murmuring about food and some of its consequences, vs. 4–35.
   a. The complaint itself, vs. 4–9.
   b. Moses bitterly complains to God, vs. 10–15.
   c. The command to appoint seventy elders, vs. 16, 17.
   d. The Lord announces His determination to satisfy the Israelites' cry for meat, vs. 18–23.
   e. The appointment of the seventy elders, vs. 24, 25.
   f. The prophets Eldad and Medad, vs. 26–30.
   g. The judgment of a plague, vs. 31–35.

V. THE MURMURING OF MIRIAM AND AARON, 12 : 1–16.

THE TEACHER'S LIBRARY.

Among the better commentaries on Numbers, one should consult C. J. Ellicott, in the *Bible Commentary for English Readers;* Thomas Whitelaw (unusually good), in the *Pulpit Commentary* series; George Bush: *Notes on the Book of Numbers;* (only occasionally helpful for the Sunday school teacher) A. H. McNeile, in the *Cambridge Bible for Schools and Colleges;* J. P. Lange, in the Lange series of commentaries; T. E. Espin, in the so-called *Bible Commentary* series; R. A. Watson, in the *Expositor's Bible.* For devotional material there is nothing better than C. H. Mackintosh: *Notes on the Book of Numbers.* Most lives of Moses, for this particular lesson, are not very helpful, but one should certainly consult the volumes by William M. Taylor and F. B. Meyer.

For expository material, on 10 : 29–36, see Joseph Parker: *The People's Bible,* Vol. 7, 183–189; on 10 : 29, Alexander Maclaren: *Expositions of Holy Scripture, Exodus, Leviticus, and Numbers,* 314–321; on 10 : 29–31, James Hastings: *Great Texts of the Bible, Genesis to Numbers,* 368–385; D. J. Burrell: *A Quiver of Arrows,* 42 ff.; also *The Religion of the Future,* 66 ff.; Hugh Black: *The Gift of Influence,* 356–365; on 10 : 33, Phillips Brooks: *The Law of Growth,* 328–345; on 10 : 35, 36, Alexander Maclaren, as above, 321–329. The editor would remark in passing that no lesson in the International Series has included Numbers 11 and 12 since 1913; much of this lesson will thus be new to most pupils.

NUMBERS 10 : 11. And it came to pass in the second year, in the second month, on the twentieth day of the month, that the cloud was taken up from over the tabernacle of the testimony.

12. And the children of Israel set forward according to their journeys out of the wilderness of Sinai; and the cloud abode in the wilderness of Paran.

29. And Moses said unto Hobab, the son of Reuel the Midianite, Moses' father-in-law, We are journeying unto the place of which Jehovah said, I will give it you: come thou with us, and we will do thee good; for Jehovah hath spoken good concerning Israel.

I. **THE ORDER OF THE HOST,** 10 : 11–28. This lesson brings us into the second year of Israel's forty years of wanderings. The problems of chronology and the difficulties of geographical identification should not so absorb the teacher that there is no time for an unfolding and application of the spiritual truths found in these lessons. 11. **And it came to pass in the second year, in the second month, on the twentieth day of the month, that the cloud was taken up from over the tabernacle of the testimony.** "It appears from Exodus 19 : 1 that the Israelites encamped before Mount Sinai in the third month of the preceding year, and, as is generally supposed, on the first day of the month. In this case the encampment at the foot of Mount Sinai had lasted eleven months and nineteen days. No day of the month, however, is specified in Exodus 19 : 1, and no *certain* reliance can be placed upon the Jewish tradition that the law was delivered fifty days after the Exodus. There is the same omission of the day of the month in Numbers 9 : 1 and 20 : 1." — *C. J. Ellicott.* The remaining portion of this chapter narrates the actual breaking up of the camp at Sinai, and the order of the march. 12. **And the children of Israel set forward according to their journeys out of the wilderness of Sinai; and the cloud abode in the wilderness of Paran.** "The fact is here mentioned by way of anticipation (see v. 33). The spot referred to is probably Kibroth-hattaavah, which may have been at the southernmost extremity of the wilderness of Paran. In Deuteronomy 1 : 19 it is called 'that great and terrible wilderness.' This wilderness is supposed to have been bounded by the land of Canaan on the north, by the valley of Arabah on the east, and by the desert of Sinai on the south. Its western boundary appears to have been the wilderness of Shur, or rather the river, or brook, of Egypt (Wady-el-Arish), which divides the wilderness into two parts, of which the western part is sometimes known as the wilderness of Shur. The sojourn of the Israelites was confined to the eastern part." — *C. J. Ellicott.* While detailed instructions in regard to the ordering of the camp for these years of wandering through the wilderness were absolutely essential for discipline and efficiency, the details do not carry great spiritual truths and we need not dwell on them. It will be noticed that the tribe of Judah, which was always the most important of all of the twelve tribes, from which David and all of the kings of Judah arose, and from which the Lord Jesus Christ ultimately came, is placed first. The precise order in which the twelve tribes were to be arranged, on the four sides of the tabernacle, is set forth in chapter 2 of the Book of Numbers.

II. **THE MIDIANITES ARE INVITED TO JOIN THE ISRAELITES,** 10 : 29–32. 29. **And Moses said unto Hobab, the son of Reuel the Midianite, Moses' father-in-law, We are journeying unto the place of which Jehovah said, I will give it you: come thou with us, and we will do thee good; for Jehovah hath spoken good concerning Israel.** "Reuel was probably not identical with Jethro (Exod. 2 : 18). It seems evident too that Hobab was in fact the brother-in-law, not the father-in-law, of Moses, and the Hebrew word translated in the Authorized Version *father-in-law,* 'signifies simply any relation by marriage.' Hobab is described as the 'son of Reuel'; and the desire of Moses to obtain his services as guide through the wilderness indicates that he was younger than Moses' father-in-law could now have been. It is stated in Exodus 18 : 27 that Jethro quitted the Israelites, before they reached Sinai, to return to his own land; while it appears from the passage now before us compared with Judges 1 : 16 and 4 : 11, that Hobab eventually accompanied them and obtained a settlement with them in the land of Canaan. Hobab and Jethro may have been brethren and sons of Reuel." — *T. E. Espin.* 30. **And he said unto**

30. And he said unto him, I will not go; but I will depart to mine own land, and to my kindred.

31. And he said, Leave us not, I pray thee; forasmuch as thou knowest how we are to encamp in the wilderness, and thou shalt be to us instead of eyes.

32. And it shall be, if thou go with us, yea, it shall be, that what good soever Jehovah shall do unto us, the same will we do unto thee.

33. And they set forward from the mount of Jehovah three days' journey; and the ark of the covenant of Jehovah went before them three days' journey, to seek out a resting-place for them.

34. And the cloud of Jehovah was over them by day, when they set forward from the camp.

---

him, I will not go; but I will depart to mine own land, and to my kindred. 31. **And
he said, Leave us not, I pray thee; forasmuch as thou knowest how we are to encamp in the wilderness, and thou shalt be to us instead of eyes.** 32. **And it shall
be, if thou go with us, yea, it shall be, that what good soever Jehovah shall do unto us, the same will we do unto thee.** These few verses set before us a most interesting problem. Why, with the assurance of the guidance of God, manifested in the pillar of cloud by day and the pillar of fire by night, did Moses think he also needed these Midianites to guide him through the desert? The words of Professor Thomas Whitelaw, one of the best of all modern commentators, will be found exceedingly helpful in this place. "It is an obvious conclusion, from the reasons here urged by Moses, that the many and wonderful promises of divine guidance and divine direction did not supersede in his eyes the use of all available human aids. . . . If we recall to mind that the host is calculated at more than two millions of people, it is quite evident that even during the march to Kadesh (and much more in the long wanderings which followed) it must have been extremely difficult to keep the various divisions together. In the broken and difficult country which they were to traverse, which had been familiar to Hobab from his youth, there would be scope enough for all his ability as a guide. And it would seem that it was just this prospect of being really useful to the people of Israel that prevailed with Hobab. He must indeed have felt assured that a wonderful future awaited a nation whose past and present were, even within his own knowledge, so wonderful. . . . Hobab does indeed seem to have gone with the people, but his descendants were not incorporated into Israel; they were with them, but not of them." "We seek our Hobabs in the advice of sage, gray-haired counsellors; in the formation of strong, intelligent, and wealthy committees; in a careful observance of precedent. Anything seems better than a simple reliance on an unseen guide. Now, in one sense, there is no harm in this. We have neither right nor need to cut ourselves adrift from others, who have had special experience in some new ground on which we are venturing. It is a mistake to live a hermit life, thinking out all our own problems, and meeting all our own questions as best we may. Those who do so are apt to become self-opinionated and full of crotchets. God often speaks to us through our fellows; they are his ministers to us for good, and we do well to listen to our Samuels, our Isaiahs, our Johns." — *F. B. Meyer.*

III. **THE EXPERIENCE OF DIVINE GUIDANCE,** 10 : 33–36. 33. **And they
set forward from the mount of Jehovah three days' journey; and the ark of the covenant of Jehovah went before them three days' journey, to seek out a resting-place for them.** 34. **And the cloud of Jehovah was over them by day, when they
set forward from the camp.** "The place at which the first protracted halt was made appears to have been either at Taberah, which means *burning*, or at Kibroth-hattaavah, *the graves of lust.* (Cf. chaps. 11 : 3; 33 : 16.) . . . It has been inferred from the fact that the Kohathites had the charge of the ark (3 : 31), and that they were to set forward, 'bearing the sanctuary,' after the second or southern camp, *i.e.*, in the midst of the host, that the position of the ark during the journeys was in that place, and not in front. The natural interpretation of this verse is that the ark was borne in front of the host, and did not merely serve to direct its line of march as a general, whose station might be in any part of an army. This interpretation is confirmed by Exodus 13 : 21; Deuteronomy 1 : 33, and also by the position which the ark occupied at the passage of the Jordan. In the latter case the people were

35. And it came to pass, when the ark set forward, that Moses said, Rise up, O Jehovah, and let thine enemies be scattered; and let them that hate thee flee before thee.

36. And when it rested, he said, Return, O Jehovah, unto the ten thousands of the thousands of Israel.

---

expressly directed to go after the ark (Josh. 3 : 3); and in verse 11 the same word is used which occurs in this verse: 'the ark of the covenant of the Lord of all the earth passeth over *before* you into Jordan.' It will not follow, however, as a necessary inference, that the ark uniformly occupied the same position in all the journeys, and it cannot be denied that verse 21 presents a difficulty, partly arising from the ambiguity of meaning which is to be attached to the word *mikdash*, *sanctuary*, and partly from the omission of any word in the Hebrew corresponding to the words in italics, *the other*." — *C. J. Ellicott*. 35. **And it came to pass, when the ark set forward, that Moses said, Rise up, O Jehovah, and let thine enemies be scattered; and let them that hate thee flee before thee.** 36. **And when it rested, he said, Return, O Jehovah, unto the ten thousands of the thousands of Israel.** Compare Psalm 10 : 12; 17 : 13; 44 : 26; 68 : 1. "The Lord's apparently *taking vengeance* upon His adversaries is elsewhere expressed by his *rising up;* as Job 31 : 14: 'What shall I do when God *riseth up?*' 'Arise, O Lord, in thine anger, lift up thyself because of the rage of mine enemies' (Ps. 7 : 6). A striking parallel to this occurs in Psalm 68 : 1, where the resurrection and ascension of the Lord are mystically set forth, showing that the words before us receive an ultimate fulfillment in Him. . . . Rosenmuller remarks in regard to the original word here rendered 'scattered' that it properly denotes the action of waters in overflowing their banks, and is thence figuratively applied to bodies of men rushing in impetuous crowds and pressing out of the pathway on either side like a raging stream that bursts over its banks. When spoken of the dispersion of enemies it implies a routing and discomfiture that shall drive them one way and another like the foundations of a flood. So, when typically viewed, the language suggests that the death and resurrection of the Saviour is the breaking and dissipation of the combined forces of His enemies (Ps. 68 : 2, 3, 13, 15), while on the other hand it is a 'gathering together in one of the children of God that were scattered abroad' (John 11 : 51, 52; Isa. 11 : 10, 11)." — *George Bush*. Alexander Maclaren's words on verse 36 are especially precious. "Ah, brother, we have more need of God in times of peace than in times of effort. It is harder to realize His presence in the brief hours of relaxation than even in the many hours of strenuous toil. Every one who goes for a holiday knows that. You have only to look at the sort of amusements that most people fly to when they have not anything to do, to see that there is quite as much, if not more, peril to communion of soul with God in times when the whole nature is somewhat relaxed, and the strings are loosened, like those of a violin screwed down a turn or two of the peg, than there is in times of work. So let us take special care of our hours of repose, and be quite sure that they are so spent as that we can ask when the day's work is done, and we have come to slippered ease, in preparation for nightly rest, 'Return, O Lord, unto Thy waiting servant.' Work without God unfits for rest with Him. Rest without God unfits for work for Him."

IV. **THE CONTINUOUS MURMURING OF ISRAEL ON THE WAY TO KADESH-BARNEA,** 11 : 1—12 : 16. The eleventh chapter of Numbers seems in violent contrast to the tenth chapter. In chapter 10, all appears to be according to divine order, and Israel seems to be perfectly provided with all the divine guidance and assurance of God's presence she would need. But in chapter 11, we find that even all these manifestations of divine wisdom and mercy do not suffice to keep great multitudes of the Israelites from bitterly rebelling against their present circumstances, and complaining against Moses and against God regarding the inconveniences of the wilderness journey.

1. THE JUDGMENT OF GOD BY FIRE, vs. 1–3. It is not specified in this passage exactly what the object of complaint here was, as later it is specified. We are simply told that when the people complained God was so displeased with their attitude that He sent fire into their midst and consumed a number of those in the camp. "Any fire sent by the Lord, is a fire of the Lord; some think it was a fire wholly supernatural; others that it was lightning; others that it was the simoom, or hot wind of the desert. . . . In what particular form this was manifested it is now impossible to say, but it was such as to carry with it a conviction of its origin, and to lead Moses to

implore earnestly its abatement. The psalmist, in allusion to this judgment, says: 'So a fire was kindled against Jacob' (Ps. 78 : 21)." — *George Bush.* Here again Moses is found to be the faithful mediator between God and His people. If Moses had been any less a man than he was, he would have let the fire consume the multitude until God was pleased to stop it, but Moses left his people and offered to intercede for them even when they had grossly sinned and were altogether at fault. This is a picture of our own perfect Mediator, the Lord Jesus Christ.

2. THE MURMURING ABOUT FOOD AND SOME OF ITS CONSEQUENCES, 11 : 4–35. THE COMPLAINT ITSELF, VS. 4–9. The murmuring of Israel now became specific, and at last it is discovered what they want — the food they once enjoyed in Egypt, even though it was a condition of slavery in which they enjoyed it. In the first place, we should carefully notice the phrase, "the mixed multitude," which Whitelaw says meant, "the riff-raff, or rabble, which had followed the fortunes of Israel out of Egypt, where they had probably been strangers and slaves themselves." The items of food here enumerated "are exactly the luxuries which an Egyptian laborer of that day would have cried out for, if deprived of them; they are *not* the luxuries which a Jew of Palestine would covet, or would even think of. The very words used here for the cucumber, the melon, and the garlic were probably Egyptian, for they may still be recognized in the common names of those vegetables in Egypt. . . . There is a physical craving in man for variety of diet, and especially for such condiments and flavors as he has been used to all his life, which makes the lack of them a real hardship. It was very ungrateful of them to speak disparagingly of the manna, which was good and wholesome food, and sufficient to keep them in health and strength; but it is useless to deny that manna only for people who had been accustomed to a rich and varied diet must have been exceedingly trying both to the palate and the stomach (cf. 21 : 5)." — *Thomas Whitelaw.* Inasmuch as manna is discussed fully in an earlier lesson, we do not go into details concerning this divinely provided food here. "The people sigh after the land of Egypt, and cast back wistful looks after its fruits and its fleshpots. They do not say aught about the lash of the taskmaster, and the toil of the brick-kilns. There is total silence as to these things. Nothing is remembered now, save those resources by which Egypt had ministered to the lusts of nature. How often this is the case with us! When once the heart loses its freshness in the divine life — when heavenly things begin to lose their savor — when first love declines — when Christ ceases to be a satisfying and altogether precious portion for the soul — when the word of God and prayer lose their charm and become heavy, dull, and mechanical; then the eye wanders back toward the world, the heart follows the eye, and the feet follow the heart. We forget, at such moments, what the world was to us when we were in it and of it. We forget what toil and slavery, what misery and degradation, we found in the service of sin and Satan, and think only of the gratification and ease, the freedom from those painful exercises, conflicts, and anxieties, which attend upon the wilderness path of God's people." — *C. H. Mackintosh.*

Flesh Pots of Egypt. From an old temple.

MOSES BITTERLY COMPLAINS TO GOD, VS. 10–15. "The complaint and remonstrance of Moses may be compared with Genesis 18 : 23, and more appositely with 1 Kings 19 : 4; Jonah 4 : 1–3. The meekness of Moses (cf. 12 : 3) sank under vexation into despair. The language shows us how imperfect and prone to degeneracy are the graces of the best saints on earth, as the answer of God manifests His readiness to meet and answer the sincere pouring out of the heart unto Him, even though its utterance be passionate and unmeasured. For certainly Moses could not justly say that God had laid 'the burden of all this people' upon him. Moses had ample direction and help from God. Such a trait as that exhibited in this passage would not have been attributed to Moses by tradition." — *T. E. Espin.* "This surely was a dark moment in the history of this illustrious servant of God. It reminds us somewhat of the prophet Elijah, when he flung himself at the base of the juniper tree and entreated the Lord to take away his life. How wonderful to see those two men together on the mount of transfiguration!" — *C. H. Mackintosh.*

THE COMMAND TO APPOINT SEVENTY ELDERS, VS. 16, 17. "Elders" of the people are referred to in Exodus 3 : 16, and " officers " are referred to in Exodus 5 : 16. " The seventy who were chosen on the present occasion may have consisted of some of those who were appointed as judges at the suggestion of Jethro, but there is no evidence of their identity with any persons previously selected (as in Exod. 24 : 1, 9)." — *C. J. Ellicott.* To this appointment of seventy the Jews traced the origin of their Sanhedrin, and probably correctly. " The council of the elders would seem to have soon fallen in desuetude. We find no traces of it in the days of the judges and the kings; nor is it easy to see how such an institution would have worked along with the forms and modes of monarchical government." — *T. E. Espin.* For some strange reason, commentators on this passage say nothing about the occasion when our Lord sent forth *seventy* to proclaim the gospel (Luke 10 : 1–17). " God is always considerate of His faithful servants. See how tender He was to Moses here. He has had a tremendous strain on him for the last eighteen months. All the conflict with Pharaoh; all the excitement of the Exodus; all the arrangement of the journeyings to Sinai, had told upon him. Jethro saw the difference in his appearance when he came to Sinai to visit him, and perhaps that was one reason for his suggesting to him to divide his judicial labors among colleagues. But the spiritual elevation of Sinai must also have produced its own effect upon his frame. His double sojourn of forty days each time upon the mount must have worn down his system; and so we cannot wonder that this new epidemic of discontent should have so distressed him. But God knew it all; and, therefore, there is no word of upbraiding addressed by Him to His servant." — *William M. Taylor.*

Quail. (Coturnix Communis.)

THE LORD ANNOUNCES HIS DETERMINATION TO SATISFY THE ISRAELITES' CRY FOR MEAT, vs. 18–23. Although Israel distinctly sinned in complaining of the diet which God had provided, instead of being grateful for His daily provision for their needs, yet He announces His determination to give Israel a bountiful supply of flesh to eat, namely, the flesh of quails. At the same time, the Lord reveals that out of this miraculous provision of food He wants Israel to learn that His arm is not shortened and that the God who led them into the wilderness is able at any time to do anything He determines to do.

THE APPOINTMENT OF THE SEVENTY ELDERS, vs. 24, 25. Previously God instructs Moses regarding the appointment of this body of seventy men; now the actual designation of these men occurs. There is only one phrase we need to look at carefully — " and took of the spirit that was upon him, and put it upon the seventy elders." This was done " not in anger, or by way of diminishing the fullness of the spirit which was in Moses, but in order that the seventy might participate, and be known to participate, in a gift originally and specially given to Moses. The whole intention of the ceremonial was to declare in the most unmistakable way that the gifts of the seventy were to be exercised only in union with and in subordination to the mediator of Israel. . . . The phenomenon of prophecy here mentioned for the first time was no doubt an ecstatic utterance beyond the origination of those who prophesied. The fundamental idea is that those affected became for the time being vents for the audible utterance of thoughts and expressions which were not theirs, but the Holy Ghost's." — *Thomas M. Whitelaw.*

THE PROPHETS ELDAD AND MEDAD, vs. 26–30. Two of the seventy are especially set forth in our text as being, it would seem, more than usually endowed with the spirit of prophecy, Eldad and Medad. " The seventy received ' of the spirit that was upon him,' and exercised their office visibly through and for him. Eldad and Medad prophesied in the camp similar to Joshua, acting independently, and so establishing a special center of authority." — *T. E. Espin.* Hardly on any other occasion is the broad sympathetic spirit of Moses so manifest as here. When Joshua complained about the prophesying of these two men, Moses cried out: " Art thou jealous for my sake? would that all of Jehovah's people were prophets," in a phrase often repeated by great leaders of God down through the ages. "Whenever the eye is single for the glory of God, and position is looked upon only as His gift to be used for His glory, and when the spirit is concentered in one eager and intense desire to see His will done, the glory of that light extinguishes the fires of ambition, and the faithful servant is willing to be anything or nothing, if only the divine purpose is accomplished. . . . There is no test more searching than this. Can I see with equanimity other and younger men coming to the front, and showing themselves possessed of gifts which I always considered to be my special province? Am I conscious of the rising of jealousy or envy when my leadership is subordinated to the claims of rivals?" — *F. B. Meyer.*

THE JUDGMENT OF A PLAGUE, vs. 31–35. As first we had a record of God's announcement concerning the seventy elders, and then a record of their actual appointment, so, in this chapter, we have first an announcement of God's intention to send an abundance of flesh for the people, and now we have the actual event itself. A great wind came up from the Red Sea, bringing vast quantities of quail which fell all over the camp, and its immediate neighborhood, in such great abundance that in places the quail were piled up two cubits high, that is, approximately three feet. It cannot mean that the entire camp was covered with quail three feet deep, as Professor Whitelaw says. "If we suppose that they were drifted by the wind which in places piled them up two cubits high, that will satisfy the exigencies of the text." At once the people, famished for such food as this, rushed out to gather as much as they could possibly carry away, no one gathering less than ten homers. The homer in Ezekiel 45 : 11, is said to contain ten ephahs, and if the ephah held nearly four and a half gallons of liquid measure, "then half a million men must have collected more quails apiece than would have filled a 450 gallon tun. No doubt the total number was something enormous and far above anything that could have been supplied by natural agencies." — *Thomas Whitelaw.* While they were yet eating this flesh, the Lord sent a great plague upon the people and many died, leading Moses to give to the place the name Kibroth-hattaavah, meaning "the graves of lust." "It would appear indeed as if they had with one consent postponed the enjoyment of eating the quails until they had gathered as huge a quantity for future use as possible; as if in defiance and contempt of the divine warning that their greed would turn to satiety and loathing. If this were so, then the feast to which they so eagerly looked forward would begin throughout the camps on the second night, and the visitation of God might well have had the sudden and simultaneous character attributed to it here and in Psalm 78 : 30, 31." — *Thomas Whitelaw.*

V. **THE MURMURING OF MIRIAM AND AARON,** 12 : 1–16. Moses' troubles are not at an end. One cause for discouragement follows another. When people are given over to murmuring and complaining and finding fault, when the reason for one complaint is removed they look around for other things to cry about. The multitude being satisfied with food for the time being, we find Moses' own sister and his brother complaining against Moses, "because of the Ethiopian woman whom he had married." There is no question about it that back of this complaint against Moses was not so much their dislike of his wife as their jealousy of Moses' prominence. "Miriam seems to have been the prime mover in the matter; and, from the words that passed between her and Aaron to this effect, 'Hath the Lord, indeed, spoken only by Moses? hath he not spoken also by us?' it is evident that envy was at the root of their estrangement. They belonged to the same family as he did; they were both older than he; they had both been chosen as the vehicles of divine instruction, as well as he; and they could not brook that he should stand at such a height above them. They thought themselves as good as he, and they wanted to have public recognition of their equality. Now, Moses had not courted pre-eminence. The leadership with which he had been invested was not of his own seeking. They grudged him his greatness, and showed that they did so by putting a slight upon his wife. But who was this wife, whom Moses, after Zipporah's death, had married, perhaps without waiting for the elapsing of a decent interval, and certainly without consulting his near relatives about the wisdom of the step which he was about to take. Much may be said in favor of that opinion. But, in the absence of any mention of the death of Zipporah, I prefer to believe that the allusion is to Zipporah herself, who is called a Cushite, 'not as being of the children of Cush, but as belonging to a country which had received from them its name.' Miriam, taking occasion from female jealousy, won Aaron over to her side, and they united in their desire to humiliate and annoy their brother. . . . This spirit in his sister ought at once to have been rebuked by Aaron, but instead of reproving it, he encouraged it. . . . Oh, ye public servants! whether in the Church or in the State, who are discharging your duties as before God, and have within you the consciousness of rectitude and entire unselfishness, take heart again when you see how Moses was assailed. And you, ye mischief-makers and self-seekers, who, because you cannot get your axes ground for nothing at the public whetstone, keep forever yelping like curs at the heels of those whose nobleness you cannot comprehend, beware lest ere long the plague of Kibroth or the leprosy of Miriam come upon you; for you are companions in the guilt of their ingratitude." — *W. M. Taylor.* It is not said that Moses even took this matter to the Lord. God Himself suddenly intervened, commanding in strong, forceful tones, " Come out ye three unto the tent of meeting." And then He told Miriam and Aaron that Moses was His own servant, that he was faithful in his house, that with him He would continue to speak mouth to mouth, and asked them why, knowing Moses' divine appointment, they were really not afraid to speak against God's servant. When the cloud through which the Lord spoke had departed, behold, Miriam was found to be leprous, and Aaron smitten at once with a sense of guilt, confessing his foolishness, pleaded that his sister might be restored. Moses, instead of telling Aaron that all these things were in the Lord's hands, and that he was not going to interfere with such a deserved punishment, cried unto the Lord: " Heal her, O God, I beseech thee." The Lord heard the prayer. After being separated from the camp according to the regulations in Israel for the treatment of such a case for a period of seven days (Lev. 13 : 4, 21; 14 : 8, 10), she was brought back completely healed. " When we pray for those who have despitefully used and persecuted us, it is marvelous how soon the soul gets calm and tender. We may begin to do it as a duty, in obedience to the command; we soon discover it to be as snow on a fevered forehead, cooling and soothing the soul." — *F. B. Meyer.*

Hazeroth, a Beautiful Oasis.

Where the Children of Israel tarried seven days, and where Miriam, the sister of Moses, was smitten with leprosy.

How many different characters do you find in this lesson, and what would you say, as far as this lesson is concerned, was the outstanding characteristic of each one in these particular events? How many different characteristics of Moses are revealed in these three chapters? What great attributes of God do you find here revealed? In what ways is it true that in our own churches it is " the mixed multitude " that gives us the most trouble? Do you find anywhere in this passage an expression of thanks to God for all of His mercies? If not, do you not think that here is a remarkable illustration of that profound summary of human history in Romans 1: 21–23 where Paul says that unthankfulness leads men into ungodliness and idolatry? Why was Miriam punished with leprosy and not Aaron?

LESSON XII. — September 19.

THE SIN OF MOSES AND AARON. — Numbers 20.

PRINTED TEXT, Numbers 20 : 1-13, 27, 28.

GOLDEN TEXT. — ***Be ye angry, and sin not.*** EPHESIANS 4 : 26.

Devotional Reading: Psalm 66 : 1–4, 16–20.
Beginner Topic: AT SCHOOL.
Lesson Material: Numbers 20 : 1–12; Daniel 1.
Memory Verse: Children, obey your parents. Colossians 3 : 20.

Primary Topic: WHEN THE PEOPLE WANTED WATER.
Lesson Material: Numbers 20.
Memory Verse: Jehovah will hear when I call unto him. Psalm 4 : 3.
Junior Topic: WHAT TO DO NEXT.
Lesson Material: Numbers 20.
Memory Verse: I will call upon God. . . . Evening, and morning, and at noonday, will I complain. Psalm 55 : 16, 17.
Intermediate and Senior Topic: SINFUL ANGER.
Topic for Young People and Adults: WHEN GOOD MEN SIN.

THE TEACHER AND HIS CLASS.

The Younger Classes may be asked what is the difference between a boy doing as his father asks him to do, gladly, and in the way in which his father told him to do it, and a boy who does a certain task assigned to him by his father, churlishly, grumblingly, with anger, and not exactly according to the instructions laid down by his father. In both cases, the father is obeyed, but in one case the boy is in fellowship with the father, while in the other the boy's heart is in rebellion against the father, and that makes a great deal of difference, even though the work is done. So in this lesson, Moses did, in part, what God told him to do, but he did it in the wrong spirit, and thus he sinned against God.

The Older Classes will find here a solemn illustration of the need of constant watchfulness in a Christian's life. Moses had now known the power and presence and guidance of God for forty years. He had come forth triumphant through these years over many temptations which had assailed him, but now, at the end of this forty-year period, we find him giving way to temper, and, in his wrath, disobeying God, an episode that must have been preceded by a lack of real communion with God. We need to be watchful down to the very end of life, ever holding up the shield of faith, lest the fiery darts of the wicked one enflame our hearts, and damage the delicate tissues of our inner life.

THE LESSON IN ITS SETTING.

Time. — About 1413–1412 B.C.

Place. — The early part of our lesson opens in Kadesh, which is really Kadesh-barnea, a most important place in the wanderings of Israel, located in the extreme southeast of Palestine. The location of Mount Hor is not exactly known, though it was, of course, somewhere in the Sinaitic desert.

THE PLAN OF THE LESSON.

SUBJECT: How in the Lives of Those Whom God Has Appointed to High Leadership and Great Responsibility, Disobedience and Unbelief Are Especially Heinous.

I. ISRAEL'S THIRST AT MERIBAH AND THE SIN WHICH IT OCCASIONED, 20 : 1–13.

1. The death of Miriam, v. 1.
2. The Israelites bitterly complain of their lot to Moses, vs. 2–5.
3. Moses and Aaron turn to God, v. 6.
4. The divine command, vs. 7, 8.
5. The incomplete obedience of Moses, vs. 9–11.
6. The punishment of Moses for his unbelief, vs. 12, 13.

II. THE EDOMITES REFUSE TO ALLOW THE ISRAELITES TO PASS THROUGH THEIR BORDER, 20 : 14–22.

III. THE DEATH OF AARON, 20 : 23–29.

THE TEACHER'S LIBRARY.

All lives of Moses, a list of which will be found in the Introduction to this volume, will be found helpful for the study of this lesson. A list of good commentaries on the book of Numbers will be found in the bibliography for the lesson of September 12. On the deeper significance of Moses smiting the rock, see J. H. Todd: *Prophetic Pictures of Christ*, 91–96; on the burial of Aaron, one should especially consult John MacBeath: *The Hills of God*, 156–166; and a very good sermon in H. P. Liddon: *Sermons on Old Testament Subjects*, 51–65. On verses 1–13, see Alexander Maclaren: *Expositions of Holy Scripture, Exodus, Leviticus, and Numbers*, 353–362.

I. **ISRAEL'S THIRST AT MERIBAH AND THE SIN WHICH IT OCCASIONED,** 20 : 1–13. We must understand that the events of this lesson occurred at the very end of Israel's forty years' wandering in the wilderness, because we read in Numbers 33 : 38, that Aaron died on Mount Hor, " in the fortieth year after the children of Israel were come out of the land of Egypt." For reasons which are not given to us, only the earlier episodes and the last events of these forty years of wandering are recorded for us in the Pentateuch.

NUMBERS 20 : 1. And the children of Israel, even the whole congregation, came into the wilderness of Zin in the first month: and the people abode in Kadesh; and Miriam died there, and was buried there.

2. And there was no water for the congregation: and they assembled themselves together against Moses and against Aaron.

3. And the people strove with Moses, and spake, saying, Would that we had died when our brethren died before Jehovah!

4. And why have ye brought the assembly of Jehovah into this wilderness, that we should die there, we and our beasts?

5. And wherefore have ye made us to come up out of Egypt, to bring us in unto this evil place? it is no place of seed, or of figs, or of vines, or of pomegranates; neither is there any water to drink.

---

1. THE DEATH OF MIRIAM, V. 1. 1. **And the children of Israel, even the whole congregation, came into the wilderness of Zin in the first month: and the people abode in Kadesh; and Miriam died there, and was buried there.** The wilderness of Zin was, it is thought, located north of the Red Sea, immediately below the Dead Sea, on the extreme western end of the peninsula of Sinai. Kadesh-barnea was located on the eastern side of this wilderness in the extreme southern end of Palestine, and it was here that Israel spent almost thirty-eight of the forty years of her wanderings. Miriam was the sister of Moses, and may be said to have been the most frequently mentioned and the most prominent woman of all those who came up out of Egypt, at least as far as the divine record reveals. Professor Thomas Whitelaw is probably right when he says: "It can scarcely be doubted that her death in the unlovely wilderness, was a punishment like the death of her brother. There is no reason whatever to suppose that she had any part in the rebellion of Kadesh, or that the sentence of death there pronounced included her; she was indeed at this time advanced in years, but that would not in itself account for the fact that she died in exile; it is no doubt to the arrogance and rebellion recorded in chapter 12 that we must look for the true explanation of her untimely end."

From a photograph by Wilson.

Kadesh-barnea, as located by Trumbull.

2. THE ISRAELITES BITTERLY COMPLAIN OF THEIR LOT TO MOSES, VS. 2–5. 2. **And there was no water for the congregation: and they assembled themselves together against Moses and against Aaron.** 3. **And the people strove with Moses, and spake, saying, Would that we had died when our brethren died before Jehovah!** 4. **And why have ye brought the assembly of Jehovah into this wilderness, that we should die there, we and our beasts?** 5. **And wherefore have ye made us to come up out of Egypt, to bring us in unto this evil place? it is no place of seed, or of figs, or of vines, or of pomegranates; neither is there any water to drink.** In reading these verses, our minds go back to a somewhat similar occasion (recorded in Exodus 17 : 1–7), when, at the very beginning of her forty years of wanderings, soon after leaving Egypt, Israel, suffering from thirst, complained to Moses, and even

6. And Moses and Aaron went from the presence of the assembly unto the door of the tent of meeting, and fell upon their faces: and the glory of Jehovah appeared unto them.
7. And Jehovah spake unto Moses, saying,
8. Take the rod, and assemble the congregation, thou, and Aaron thy brother, and speak ye unto the rock before their eyes, that it give forth its water; and thou shalt bring forth to them water out of the rock; so thou shalt give the congregation and their cattle drink.

---

went so far as to tell him that it would have been better had they never come out of Egypt, than to suffer as they were suffering. "The congregation were no doubt supplied with water from such springs as they met with in their journeyings. At the present day, water, though not plentiful in the Arabian desert, still is by no means utterly wanting, and the inhabitants, with their cattle and flocks, are continually passing over it from place to place. We have no intimation that water, like their food, was usually furnished to the Israelites miraculously. At the spot where they were now encamped there was, for some reason, a scarcity, although we read of nothing of the kind on the former occasion, when they were there. But the wells and fountains of the East have not always a constant supply of water. . . . The present was a new outbreak of that characteristic perversity, which though occasionally suppressed by severe judgments, seems never to have been effectually subdued. But while they thus proved themselves the children of their fathers, we should not forget that our waywardness proves equally that we are their children in moral relationship, and that the deeds of our fathers we continue to do." — *George Bush.* Is it not strange that, after experiencing for these many years so many tokens of the grace and mercy of God, these people should not have turned in prayer to God, instead of complaining to Moses? Well, that is one of the prices one must pay for leadership and fame — exposure to criticism, to the insults, the rebukes of the multitude, who themselves would have no capacity for such leadership as possessed by those whom they so severely condemn.

3. MOSES AND AARON TURN TO GOD, v. 6. 6. **And Moses and Aaron went from the presence of the assembly unto the door of the tent of meeting, and fell upon their faces: and the glory of Jehovah appeared unto them.** "It is deeply touching to find Moses, again and again, on his face before God. It was a sweet relief, to make his escape from a tumultuous host, and betake himself to the only One whose resources were adequate to meet such an occasion. 'They fell upon their faces: and the glory of the Lord appeared unto them.' They do not appear, on this occasion, to have attempted any reply to the people: 'they went from the presence of the assembly,' and cast themselves upon the living God. They could not possibly have done better. Who but the God of all grace could meet the ten thousand necessities of wilderness life? God's treasury is absolutely inexhaustible. He can never fail a trusting heart. Let us remember this. God delights to be used. He never grows weary of ministering to the need of His people. If this were ever kept in the remembrance of the thoughts of our hearts, we should hear less of the accents of impatience and discontent, and more of the sweet language of thankfulness and praise. But, as we have had frequent occasion to remark, desert life tests every one. It proves what is in us; and thanks be to God, it brings out what is in *Him* for us." — *C. H. Mackintosh.*

4. THE DIVINE COMMAND, vs. 7, 8. 7. **And Jehovah spake unto Moses, saying, 8. Take the rod, and assemble the congregation, thou, and Aaron thy brother, and speak ye unto the rock before their eyes, that it give forth its water; and thou shalt bring forth to them water out of the rock; so thou shalt give the congregation and their cattle drink.** "Unlike the injunction on a similar occasion, which now lay back in the haze of years, Moses was bidden, though he took the rod, not to use it; but to speak to the rock with a certainty that the accents of his voice, smiting on its flinty face, would have as much effect as ever the rod had had previously, and would be followed by a rush of crystal water. Yes, when God is with you, words are equivalent to rods; the gentlest whisper spoken in His name will unlock the secrets of rocky chambers, and roll away great stones, and splinter sepulchres where entombed life awaits a summons. Rods are well enough to use at the commencement of faith's nurture, and when its strength is small; but they may be laid aside without hesitance in the later stages of the education of the soul. For as faith grows, the

9. And Moses took the rod from before Jehovah, as he commanded him.
10. And Moses and Aaron gathered the assembly together before the rock, and he said unto them, Hear now, ye rebels; shall we bring you forth water out of this rock?
11. And Moses lifted up his hand, and smote the rock with his rod twice: and water came forth abundantly, and the congregation drank, and their cattle.
12. And Jehovah said unto Moses and Aaron, Because ye believed not in me, to sanctify me in the eyes of the children of Israel, therefore ye shall not bring this assembly into the land which I have given them.

---

mere machinery and apparatus it employs becomes ever less; and its miracles are wrought with the sligchest possible introduction of the material. Years ago you were bidden to use the rod because your faith was untried; but by this time the greater faith should work through a slighter and more fragile means." — *F. B. Meyer.*

5. THE INCOMPLETE OBEDIENCE OF MOSES, VS. 9, 10. 9. **And Moses took the rod from before Jehovah, as he commanded him.** 10. **And Moses and Aaron gathered the assembly together before the rock, and he said unto them, Hear now, ye rebels; shall we bring you forth water out of this rock?** "Hitherto, in following the march of Israel through the wilderness, we have been called to deplore the iniquity of the *people.* The scene, in a single instance, is now changed; and instead of regarding the *rulers* of the host as men 'more sinned against than sinning,' we behold Moses and Aaron, the prophet and the priest, overpowered by temptation and falling into sin. 'Hear now, ye rebels.' No such language of rebuke entered into the commission with which Moses was now entrusted, and therefore it was wholly unwarranted. He was commanded to speak to the rock, and not to the people; and though they undoubtedly deserved censure, and were acting the part of rebels, yet it was not his duty now to upbraid them therewith. . . . They did not probably so much claim the ability to bring forth water themselves, as cherish a doubt whether the Lord would do it in behalf of such gross offenders. Therefore they speak distrustfully, and they may have discovered in other ways an uncertainty in their own minds whether water would come forth or not. This was a prominent part of the offense which they soon learned was to cost them so dear." — *George Bush.* 11. **And Moses lifted up his hand, and smote the rock with his rod twice: and water came forth abundantly, and the congregation drank, and their cattle.** Moses was not directly commanded to strike the rock, even once. Here we find him smiting it twice, undoubtedly the result of passionate excitement and unjustified anger.

Rock Meribah-Kadesh-barnea.

Where "Moses struck the rock and the waters gushed forth."

6. THE PUNISHMENT OF MOSES FOR HIS UNBELIEF, VS. 12, 13. 12. **And Jehovah said unto Moses and Aaron, Because ye believed not in me, to sanctify me in the eyes of the children of Israel, therefore ye shall not bring this assembly into the land which I have given them.** The words of F. B. Meyer here are exceptionally rich, probably the best of any exposition of this particular passage. Meyer brings out three reasons for the punishment that is here announced. "(1) There was distinct disobedience. No doubt was possible as to the divine command; and it had been distinctly infringed. He was not to strike, but to speak; and he had twice smitten

13. These are the waters of Meribah; because the children of Israel strove with Jehovah, and he was sanctified in them.

the rock. In this way he had failed to sanctify God in the eyes of the people. He who ought to have set the example of implicit obedience to every jot and tittle, had inserted his own will and way as a substitute for God's. This could not be tolerated in one who was set to lead and teach the people. God is sanctified whenever we put an inviolable fence around Himself and His words; treating them as unquestionable and decisive; obeying them with instinct and utter loyalty; daring to place them high above all dispute as the supreme rule and guide of conduct. Therefore, when Moses set them aside to follow the behest of his own whim, it was equivalent to a desecration of the holy name of God. 'Ye did not sanctify me in the eyes of the children of Israel.' . . . (2) There was unbelief. It was as if he had felt that a word was not enough. As if there must be something more of human might and instrumentality. There was a too evident reliance upon his own share in the transaction, or on the mysterious power of the rod which had so often wrought great wonders. He thought too much of these, to the exclusion or dwarfing of God's eternal power. He did not realize how small an act on his part was sufficient to open the sluice-gates of Omnipotence. A touch is enough to set Omnipotence in action. . . . Let us especially set a watch at our strongest point. Just because we are so confident of being strong there, we are liable to leave it unguarded and unwatched, and therefore open to the foe. So shall we be saved from a fall that shall shut the gates of Canaan against us, and consign us to an unknown and untimely grave. . . . (3) There was the spoiling of the type. 'That Rock was Christ'; from whose heart, smitten in death on Calvary, the river of water of life has flowed to make glad the city of God, and to transform the deserts into Edens. But death came to Him, and can come to Him but once. 'Christ was once offered to bear the sins of many.' 'The death that he died, he died unto sin once; but the life that he liveth, he liveth unto God.' 'I am he that was dead; and behold, I am alive forevermore.' These texts prove how important it was to keep clear and defined the fact of the death of Christ being a finished act, once for all. It is evident that for the completeness of the likeness between substance and shadow, the rock should have been stricken but once. Instead of that, it was smitten at the beginning and at the close of the desert march. But this was a misrepresentation of an eternal fact; and the perpetrator of the heedless act of iconoclasm must suffer the extreme penalty, even as Uzzah died for trying to steady the swaying ark." 13. **These are the waters of Meribah; because the children of Israel strove with Jehovah, and he was sanctified in them.** The word Meribah means strife, or contention. "The same name, originating in the same cause, had been previously bestowed upon the locality of Rephidim, where the former miracle had occurred (Exod. 17 : 7). But this place is sufficiently distinguished from that, being called 'The waters of Meribah-Kadesh in the wilderness of Zin' (Deut. 32 : 51). Not a word is said here about giving the name Meribah to the place. Elsewhere only the *waters of strife* at Kadesh are spoken of. That the author uses the expression *waters of strife* is intentional. The repetition of the designation, which, on the former occasion, became a proper name, here serves as an allusion to it, and therefore sets in a more conspicuous light the unbelief of the people and of their leader." — *George Bush.* Perhaps, because the teacher will wish to make this difficult passage as clear as possible, we ought to add the following helpful words of that fine scholar, Professor Thomas Whitelaw. "It was the fact of a bad impression made upon the people which was the ground of the divine rebuke. We come back, therefore, to the simple conclusion expressed by the Psalmist (Ps. 106 : 32, 33), that Moses lost his temper, and in the irritation of the moment, spoke and acted in such a way and in such a spirit as to dishonor his Master and to impair the good effect of the divine beneficence. It is quite likely that the repeated striking of the rock was one sign of the anger to which Moses gave way, but we could hardly have attached any serious character to the act if it stood alone. It is in the words of Moses, words in which he associated Aaron with himself, that we must find the explanation of the displeasure he incurred. That he called the people 'rebels' was unseemly, not because it was untrue, or because it was an uncalled-for term of reproach, but because he himself was at that very moment a rebel, and disloyal in heart to his Master (cf. v. 24). That he should say, 'Must we fetch you water out of this rock?' showed how completely he was carried away. . . . Moses had fallen at least once before into a similar error, one so natural to an angry man; but this was the first time that he had made his error public, and thereby dishonored the Master whom it was his special duty to uphold and glorify. This was the sin, and if the punishment seem disproportionate, it must be remembered that the heinousness of a sin depends quite as much on the position of the sinner as upon its intrinsic enormity."

II. **THE EDOMITES REFUSE TO ALLOW THE ISRAELITES TO PASS THROUGH THEIR BORDER,** 20 : 14–22. The forty years of wandering almost at an end, Moses knew that it was time for Israel to begin to plan at last to actually enter into the land of promise. So he asks permission from the king of Edom to go up into Palestine through his territory, promising that his people would not in any way impoverish the country, by taking the crops from the fields or drinking from their wells, nor would they turn either to the right hand or to the left until they had all gone through the land and had reached that territory which God had promised would be theirs (see Deut. 2 : 6, 7). "The boundaries of Edom may be traced with some approach to accuracy. On the east of the Arabah, the northern border ran from the Dead Sea, and was marked by Wady el-Kurahi, or Wady el-Hasa. On the east it marched with the desert. The southern border ran by Elath and Ezion-geber (Deut. 2 : 8). In the west of the Arabah the north boundary of Edom is determined by the south border of Israel, as indicated in Numbers 34 : 3 f.: a line running from the Salt Sea southward of the ascent of Akrabbim to Zin and Kadesh-barnea. This last, we are told, lay in the uttermost of the border of Edom (Num. 20 : 16)." — *W. Ewing.* Edom, as you will remember, was a name applied to Esau because of the color of his skin (Gen. 25 : 25), and in Genesis 36 : 8, 9 he is said to dwell with Edom in Mount Seir, and is called the father of the Edomites. Thus we find that the Edomites are descendants of Abraham, and for this reason they should have had some sympathy with the Israelites in the request which they now made. This relationship Moses refers to in his phrase, "Thy brother Israel." The request was denied, and this accounts for the fact that Israel did not enter Palestine by the easiest way, and the nearest, that is, going up through the south, but had to go east, around the Dead Sea, and enter Palestine from the east by way of Jericho. George Bush, in his remarkably rich commentary on the book of Numbers, one of the best we have for the interpretation of the deeper significance of these events, probably is not exaggerating when he says that the refusal of Edom symbolizes the hostility of the world to the Church, which we see everywhere exemplified. The main theme of the entire prophecy of Obadiah is judgment denounced against Edom, primarily because of Edom's shameful treatment of Israel.

From a photograph by Wilson.

By the Gulf of Akabah.

One of the wildest wadies in Arabia known as Wady Arabah. The Northern End of the East Branch of the Red Sea, near which the Israelites turned Northward toward Canaan.

III. **THE DEATH OF AARON,** 20 : 23–29. While Israel no doubt remained at Kadesh, Moses and Aaron, for reasons not named, are found in the last part of this chapter at Mount Hor. Exactly where Mount Hor was is not definitely known. "From Numbers 20 : 22; 33 : 37, we may perhaps infer that Mount Hor, 'in the edge of the land of Edom,' was about a day's journey from Kadesh. The name 'Hor the mountain' suggests a prominent feature of the landscape. Aaron was buried there (Num. 20 : 28; Deut. 32 : 50). It was therefore not in Mount Seir (Deut. 2 : 5), of which not even a foot breadth was given to Israel. . . . A hill meeting sufficiently all these conditions is *Jebel Maderah,* which rises to the northeast of *Ain kadis* (Kadesh-barnea). It stands at the extreme northwest boundary of the land of Edom, yet not within that boundary. Above the barrenness of the surrounding

27. And Moses did as Jehovah commanded: and they went up into mount Hor in the sight of all the congregation.

28. And Moses stripped Aaron of his garments, and put them upon Eleazar his son; and Aaron died there on the top of the mount: and Moses and Eleazar came down from the mount.

---

plain, this 'large, singular-looking, isolated, jagged hill' rises 'alone like a lofty citadel,' 'steep-sided,' and 'quite naked.' Here the solemn transactions described in Numbers 20 : 22 ff. could have been carried out literally 'in the sight of all the congregation.'" — *W. Ewing.* Throughout these forty years, Aaron had been the mouthpiece for Moses, his colleague in ruling and directing and controlling this vast multitude of people released from the bondage of Egypt. As Canon Liddon says: "Aaron was no doubt involved with Moses in the sin which we have just studied and which brought such divine condemnation upon Moses. Aaron's share in the sin at Meribah was due to the want of firmness, which, as has been seen, was a feature of his character. The sin of Meribah was primarily the sin of Moses, when the people murmured at the want of water, and Moses, wearied by their perverseness, in the very act of relieving them, betrayed, both by what he said and did, a temper unworthy of his high office, so that he 'did not sanctify God in the eyes of the people.' As a later psalmist reflects: 'The people angered God at the waters of strife, so that He punished Moses for their sakes; because they provoked his spirit, so that he spake unadvisedly with his lips' (Ps. 106 : 32). As for Aaron, he not only did not check Moses: he acquiesced in what he must have known to be dishonorable to God; and this in a man with his spiritual responsibilities was a grave failure of duty — so grave as to forfeit his entry into the land of promise. Moses too, much more, had forfeited that high privilege: but the work which Moses had to do in the world was not yet done. Moses must lead God's people round the southern point of Mount Seir: he must conquer the Amorite kings, Sihon at the battle of Jahaz, and Og at the battle of Edrei, and take possession of the country east of the Jordan, from the Arnon to Mount Hermon: he must rule Israel a while from the plains of Moab — from the very brink of the Jordan, ere he may mount on Pisgah and behold the land which it is forbidden him to enter, and go to his rest. But Aaron's appointed work was done: and there was no reason for delaying his summons." 27. **And Moses did as Jehovah commanded: and they went up into mount Hor in the sight of all the congregation.** 28. **And Moses stripped Aaron of his garments, and put them upon Eleazar his son; and Aaron died there on the top of the mount: and Moses and Eleazar came down from the mount.** "As to Aaron himself, the whole tenor of the narrative would imply that he went up to the summit of the holy mount with unfaltering step, and composed himself to die with as much serenity as if he were but laying himself down upon his bed to sleep. There is no intimation but that he was in perfect health at the very time, though he had reached the very extended term of 123 years. It was not in the waste of age, or through decays of sickness, or by a sudden stroke, that he was to pass away from among men, but at the call of heaven. As there is a place where to die, as well as a time when to die, both of which are in the divine appointment, so to both of these the high priest of Israel was now brought. He had reached his last stage in the wilderness, beyond which he could not pass. He had finished his priestly functions, he had made his last offering, he had left the sanctuary on earth, never again to enter it or to minister before the Lord. Many eyes were doubtless upon him as he went forth, eager to catch the last glimpse of his receding person, their many hearts invoking many blessings. Father, son, and brother went up together, and this was the last of their intercourse on earth. What passed on the way is not said, but we may well believe their conversation savored of heaven, and was serious, holy, and pleasant. In such circumstances, when the brightest scenes of earth fade away from the view, and the heart sickens at worldly thoughts, nothing but divine manifestations and the spiritual realities of another life, can possibly sustain the soul. These supports we cannot doubt that Aaron enjoyed as he went up the mount to die; for to him dying was ascending, as it will be to all the Lord's people, whatever be the circumstances of their departure. Some die in seclusion, unnoticed and unknown; some die embosomed in a circle of sorrowing friends. Yet it matters little where the saints depart, whether on a mount or in a vale, except as symbolical or typical considerations give one place a preference over another. Both Aaron and Moses died on a mountainous elevation, and we may not question that some rich significancy was veiled under the fact. In frequent cases recorded in Scripture things of a very important and memorable nature are said to have occurred on mountains, with which we are prone to connect what is conspicuous, remarkable, and involving high and heavenly mysteries. Our Lord died on Mount Calvary and ascended from the Mount of Olives, and in this respect the departure of his forerunners conformed to His." — *George Bush.*

John MacBeath, in his fine chapter on the burial of Aaron, makes the following beautiful comment on the stripping of Aaron and the placing of his garments upon his son Eleazar. "There is a radiant glow upon the mount where Aaron is privileged to see his son Eleazar assume the priestly succession. The old man's work does not die with himself. He shall have a grave but his work shall have no sepulchre. The workman passes, but the work survives. That was worth continuing. It is certain that every father would not like to see his son repeat his career, or prolong his influence, and it is equally certain that every father's work is not worth a longer life than himself. God tempered the disappointment of Aaron in His own way. He takes the robes from the worn shoulders and places them on younger energy, and ordains his successor. The new ministry begins where the old ends, among the hills of God. It was not a stranger who came back to the camp wearing the priestly robes, but the son of the high priest. That was the old man's comfort; that was the young man's peace; that was the people's consolation: that secured for Israel the continuity of priestly service. Will every father do his utmost that his son shall stand in his place in the service of God and carry the divine work forward to a new generation? Shall we all find our succession in the youth of today? Shall we build the bridge for the feet of youth?"

What different attributes of God are revealed to us in this particular lesson? What reasons can you give for explaining the fact that Moses is found to be more easily provoked now at the end of this long period of wandering in the wilderness than at the beginning? Why do you think the Edomites would not allow the Israelites to go through their territory? How many manifestations of grace or mercy do you find in the account of Aaron's death? How can we watch ourselves so that the criticisms of other people toward us or their failure toward us will not lead to bitterness or to placing anger in our own lives? Why did God Himself not strike the rock and totally eliminate the necessity of Moses being involved in this act in any way? Inasmuch as all of us must some day come to the hour of death (unless Christ Himself shall return before we die) what influence ought this imminent event exercise over our daily conduct?

LESSON XIII. — September 26.

ABIDING VALUES FROM ISRAEL'S HISTORY.
Deuteromony 1—3, 11.

PRINTED TEXT, Deuteronomy 11 : 13-25.

GOLDEN TEXT. — ***Righteousness exalteth a nation; but sin is a reproach to any people.*** PROVERBS 14 : 34.

Devotional Reading: Deuteronomy 10 : 12–22.
Beginner Topic: THE WORLD WE LIVE IN.
  Lesson Material: Deuteronomy 11 : 13–15; Genesis 1.
  Memory Verse: He hath made everything beautiful in its time. Ecclesiastes 3 : 11.
Primary Topic: MOSES' GOODBY.
  Lesson Material: Deuteronomy 11 : 13–32.
  Memory Verse: All that Jehovah hath spoken will we do, and be obedient. Exodus 24 : 7.
Junior Topic: MOSES' FAREWELL CHALLENGE.
  Lesson Material: Deuteronomy 11 : 13–32.
  Memory Verse: Choose you this day whom ye will serve . . . as for me and my house, we will serve Jehovah. Joshua 24 : 15.
Intermediate and Senior Topic: WHAT MAKES A NATION GREAT?
Topic for Young People and Adults: OUR PART IN THE MAKING OF OUR NATION.

THE TEACHER AND HIS CLASS.

The Younger Classes might be reminded that in building a playhouse out of blocks, they must follow certain laws, or the walls will fall down before the house is finished. They cannot build it anyway they please. If they are going to make a wall ten blocks high, and if they want the wall to stay up, they must put one block squarely upon another. If, instead, they put the second block off the edge of the first one a quarter of an inch, and the third one off the edge of the second a quarter of an inch, by the time they get to the fifth block, the whole thing will fall. So in our own lives, there are great laws of God to follow: if we obey them our life will be long, full of joy, and we will succeed in the things we undertake. If we go against these laws, then life will go to pieces, everything will go down in a heap.

The Older Classes will find one particular passage in the printed text which is particularly relevant to our time; that is, the promise that obedience to the laws of God will bring victory over our enemies. Now there are many things in the Old Testament not for us, but there are many things that are for us, and is it not reasonable to believe that even now, if our nation should turn about and begin sincerely and truly to obey the great commandments of God regarding the major spheres of life, God would keep His Word by giving us an overwhelming victory against our enemies? And this we need — God's gift of victory.

THE TEACHER'S LIBRARY.

A great and satisfactory commentary on the Book of Deuteronomy for the English reader is yet to be written. Harper's work in the *Expositor's Bible* is quite unsatisfactory in places. The volume by George Adam Smith in the *Cambridge Bible for Schools and Colleges* is very scholarly, filled with geographical and philological details, but without any spiritual interpretation or application whatever. The notes by Waller in the *Bible Commentary for English Readers* are fair, as are also the notes by Espin, in the *Bible Commentary* series. The only satisfactory devotional chapters the editor has seen on this portion of Deuteronomy are in C. H. Mackintosh's inimitable *Notes on the Book of Deuteronomy*, Vol. 1. I know of no homiletical material of any value on the chapter except a sermon by Hugh Black, on 11 : 15, in his *My Gospel*, 234 ff. There is a very good article on Deuteronomy, by Dr. George L. Robinson, in the *International Standard Bible Encyclopedia*, Vol. 2, 835–840.

THE PLAN OF THE LESSON.

SUBJECT: Some Fundamental Reasons for Obeying the Commandments of God and Some Promises That We May Claim if We Are Thus Obedient.

I. MOSES REVIEWS FOR ISRAEL HER FORTY YEARS OF WANDERING, Deut. 1 : 1—3 : 29.

1. Introduction, 1 : 1, 2.
2. Israel's history from Sinai to Kadesh-barnea, 1 : 3–46.
   - *a.* The command to possess Palestine, vs. 3–8.
   - *b.* Appointment of seventy elders, vs. 9–18.
   - *c.* The report of the spies and Israel's unbelief, vs. 19–46.
3. The thirty-eight years of wandering, 2 : 1.
4. The last (fortieth) year of the Exodus, 2 : 2—3 : 29.
   - *a.* The Israelites are refused permission to pass through Edom, 2 : 2–8.
   - *b.* From Kadesh over the brook Zered, 2 : 9–15.
   - *c.* From the brook Zered to the river Arnon, 2 : 16–37.
   - *d.* The defeat of Og of Bashan, 3 : 1–17.
   - *e.* Moses rehearses his former admonitions to Israel, 3 : 18–29.

II. THE PRIMACY OF OBEYING GOD'S COMMANDMENTS, Deut. 11 : 1–32.

1. His commandments should be obeyed because of His great kindness to Israel, vs. 1–7.
2. Obedience to God's commandments leads to long life and prosperity, vs. 8–15.
3. A warning about idolatry, vs. 16, 17.
4. The obligations to teach these commandments to their children, vs. 18–21.
5. Obedience would assure them of victory over their enemies, vs. 22–28.
6. The command concerning Gerizim and Ebal, vs. 29–32.

THE LESSON IN ITS SETTING.

Time. — 1406–05 B.C.

Place. — That part of the Jordan valley which was immediately north of the Red Sea and below the Dead Sea.

THE BOOK OF DEUTERONOMY.

In the Hebrew Bible the title for this book is taken from its opening phrase, "These are the words," but the title given in the translation is *Deuteronomon*, composed of two Greek words, meaning, "the second law." From this word comes the title used in the English Bible. "The Greek title is due to a mistranslation by the Septuagint of the clause in Deuteronomy 17 : 18, rendered, 'and he shall write for himself this *repetition* of the law.' The Hebrew really means 'and he shall write out for himself a *copy* of this law.' However, the error on which the English title rests is not serious, as Deuteronomy is in a very true sense a *repetition* of the law. Deuteronomy is the last of the five books of the Pentateuch, or 'five-fifths of the Law.' In Exodus and Numbers, Jehovah is represented as speaking unto Moses, whereas in Deuteronomy, Moses is represented as speaking at Jehovah's command to Israel (1 : 1–4; 5 : 1; 29 : 1). It is a hortatory recapitulation of various addresses delivered at various times and places in the desert wanderings. It is 'a Book of Reviews'; a translation of Israel's redemptive history into living principles; not as much a history as a commentary. There is much of retrospect in it, but its main outlook is forward. The rabbins speak of it as 'the Book of Reproofs.' It is the text of all prophecy; a manual of evangelical oratory; possessing 'all the warmth of a St. Bernard, the flaming zeal of a Savonarola, and the tender, gracious sympathy of a St. Francis of Assisi.' The author's interest is entirely moral. His one supreme purpose is to arouse Israel's loyalty to Jehovah and to His revealed law. Taken as a whole the book is an exposition of the great commandment, 'Thou shalt love Jehovah thy God with all thy heart, and with all thy soul, and with all thy might.' It was from Deuteronomy that Jesus summarized the whole of the Old Covenant in a single sentence (Matt. 22 : 37; cf. Deut. 6 : 5), and from it He drew His weapons with which to vanquish the tempter (Matt. 4 : 4, 7, 10; cf. Deut. 8 : 3; 6 : 16, 13)." — *George L. Robinson.*

I. MOSES REVIEWS FOR ISRAEL HER FORTY YEARS OF WANDERING, Deut. 1 : 1—3 : 29.

1. INTRODUCTION, 1 : 1, 2. It is commonly understood that these two verses form a connecting link between the previous four books of the Pentateuch and the Book of Deuteronomy. The geographical area defined here is the east side of the Jordan, first the desert of Arabia generally, and then "the sterile track which stretches along the lower Jordan to the Dead Sea, and is continued thence to the gulf of Akaba." In the Authorized Version, we find the phrase, "against the Red Sea," but in the Revised Version the phrase reads "against Suph," a word meaning "red." It is always used in the Hebrew Bible in the phrase when the Red Sea is referred to, though some believe, because the word sea is omitted, it must refer to some other place. The question is too difficult to be entered into here. The other places mentioned in the verse are southeast of the Dead Sea, Paran being the western limit of a district referred to in 33 : 2.

2. ISRAEL'S HISTORY FROM SINAI TO KADESH-BARNEA, 1 : 3–46. The first discourse of Moses in this book, beginning with verse 3 of the first chapter, extends to 4 : 40. Moses is here not recording the events taking place at the particular time when he is speaking, but is referring to events that took place thirty-eight years before this, *i.e.*, he is reviewing Israel's history for a new generation. He begins by reminding the Israelites that at the very beginning of the exodus, God had told them to go up and possess Palestine, the land of promise, which the Lord had sworn unto their fathers "to give unto them and to their seed after them." Professor C. H. Waller reminds us that the Hebrew word translated *declare* (verse 5) means, in the two other places where it occurs (17 : 8; Hab. 2 : 2), *writing*, and thus "it would seem that at this period, Moses began to throw the discourses and laws that he had delivered into a permanent form." Thus the beginning of the Book of Deuteronomy takes us back as far as the twelfth chapter of the Book of Genesis.

Moses next brings to the attention of this vast multitude, two occasions when a great number of helpers were appointed to assist him in the vast task of caring for and disciplining these people. First, there was the election of captains, referred to in Exodus 18 : 25 ff., when 78,600 men of captain rank were assigned certain duties and powers among this moving multitude. Later, seventy elders were appointed to assist Moses in the burden of legislating for the Israelites, and settling disputes among these murmuring people. (This particular event we find recorded in Num. 11 : 16 ff.)

Finally, with great detail, the great lawgiver rehearses before the people the sending up of spies into Palestine, their glowing report of what they had discovered, and the refusal of Israel because of fear and unbelief, to go up into this glorious land as God commanded them to do. This entire episode is recorded at the time of its actual occurrence in Numbers 13, 14. Mr. Espin has met an objection sometimes heard, in an excellent way when he says: "It is frivolous to object that the generation which had sinned thus was dead; and that Moses was addressing men who had had no concern in the events to which he is referring. That this fact was present to the speaker's mind is clear from vs. 34, 35; nay, it was the very aim he had in view, to warn the present generation not to follow their fathers in their perversity, and so defraud themselves of the promised blessing, as their fathers had done. It is but natural that Moses, who had been the leader of the congregation all along, should, when addressing it collectively, treat it as the same which he had brought forth from Egypt, and had now, for the second time, conducted to the threshold of the Promised Land."

3. THE THIRTY-EIGHT YEARS OF WANDERING, 2 : 1. Practically nothing is said in Exodus, Leviticus, Numbers or Deuteronomy about the experiences of Israel during the thirty-eight years of her fruitless wanderings in the wilderness, but we have many details of the events occurring the first year after Israel left Egypt. Then, we have a narrative of great detail concerning the last year before Israel entered the Land of Promise. But concerning the other thirty-eight years we know practically nothing. The only reference to this period in this entire section of review is in this one phrase. (See also Num. 13 : 26.)

4. THE LAST (FORTIETH) YEAR OF THE EXODUS, 2 : 2—3 : 29. The Israelites are refused permission to pass through Edom. Now, anxious to get into the land which God had promised them, and somehow conscious of the imminency of that great event when they would actually enter into Canaan, the Israelites ask permission of the Edomites, who dwelled at Mount Seir, and the surrounding territory north of the Red Sea, if they might pass through their land, and go on up northwest of the Dead Sea into the land God had promised them. The Edomites refused the permission, but they did allow them to buy bread and water for money. (See Num. 20 : 18–20.)

From Kadesh over the brook Zered. This is the second time Israel has been at Kadesh-barnea, once at the beginning of her wanderings, now again toward the end of them. It is located about eighty kilometers southwest of Beersheba, a territory which few tourists in the Holy Land now ever visit. The command of God was that the Israelites were not to disturb or war against the Moabites who lived directly east of the Dead Sea, and north of the Edomites. But a definite command was received from God that they should rise up and pass over the brook Zered, an event which did not take place, as verse 14 says, until all those who had come out of Egypt had passed away, thus fulfilling the sentence declared in Numbers 14 : 23. The word Zered does not occur again in the Old Testament, nor is it found in Josephus, and exactly where it was located we are not able now to determine. Where once was a great population and many geographical names familiar to those who lived at that time, there is now only for the most part a sparsely populated wilderness, and many names known three thousand years ago and more, are lost.

From the brook Zered to the river Arnon. Though this is a long section, there is not much need to go into it for our particular lesson, except to observe that God now speaks of things which up to this time had not been declared to Israel, especially when he says: " This day will I begin to put the dread of thee and the fear of thee upon the peoples that are under the whole heaven, who shall hear the report of thee, and shall tremble, and be in anguish because of thee." There is an extended reference here to the opposition of Sihon, king of Heshbon, to the advancing Israelitish host. The original account of this will be found in Numbers 21 : 21–31. The river Arnon, every one agrees, is the stream now called the Wady el Nojeb. " The greatest of all the canyons that cut the plateau of Mo'ab, one understands how it has so often been a political frontier. A little west of the Hajj road a valley is formed some 250 feet below the plateau by the conjunction of several wadies, which have risen among the desert hills to the east of the road. Under the successive names of W. Sa'ideh, Seil es-sefei, and W. el-Mojeb, it runs with a mainly western direction, and a rapidly increasing depth (at 'Aro'er 1800 or 2000 feet below the plateau) between almost precipitous walls to the Dead Sea, about 3500 feet below the plateau. The valley is entered from the north and south by other canyons, of which two are almost as long as itself. . . . The valley of Arnon in the present verse is probably the direct east and west canyon on its upper stretch, W. Sa'ideh." — *George Adam Smith.*

The defeat of Og of Bashan. It is interesting to note that the next event described by Moses in his remarkable review of Israel's history, is given in greater detail in the review, than in the earlier record of the event itself (Num. 21 : 32–35). In fact, the conquest mentioned in verses 4, 5 is not even referred to in the Book of Numbers. Bashan, which is famous in poetry and in earlier works on Biblical archaeology, because of the giant cities that were there, includes the territory immediately north of the Yarmuk River on the east side of the Jordan, and extending north as far as Mount Hermon. Verse 11, for some reason, is often referred to in books of questions about the Bible, and in some of the earlier works on Old Testament history, and perhaps the quotation of this verse and a comment upon it would not be out of place. " For only Og king of Bashan remained of the remnant of the Rephaim; behold, his bedstead was a bedstead of iron; is it not in Rabbah of the children of Ammon? nine cubits was the length thereof, and four cubits the breadth of it, after the cubit of a man." Mr. Waller makes the following excellent remark concerning these few but interesting lines: " The word for *bedstead* and the word for *iron* have given rise to some discussion and difficulty. An iron bedstead and an iron coffin are almost equally improbable. *Basalt* has been suggested as an alternative. But though there is basalt in Argob, there is none in Rabbath-Ammon. Conder, who has recently explored Rabbath, has discovered a remarkable throne of stone on the side of a hill there, and he suggests that the Hebrew word rendered bedstead, which properly signifies a couch with a canopy may apply to this. The word for iron (*barzil*) in Talmudical language means also ' a prince,' and this meaning has been suggested for the name *Barzillai*, which we find in the same district in later times. ' His canopied throne was a princely one, and yet remains in Rabbath of the Ammonites,' would be the meaning of the passage, on this hypothesis. The dimensions of the throne recently discovered are said to be nearly those given in this verse." On verses 13–17, compare Numbers 32 : 33–42.

Moses rehearses his former admonitions to Israel. For the original account of this particular episode of exhortation, see Numbers 32 : 20–42, and, for the appointment of Joshua as the successor of Moses, Numbers 27 : 18–23. On Moses' request to be allowed to enter the Land of Promise, and God's refusal to grant this request, see Numbers 20 : 12; 27 : 12–14. However, Moses did get into Palestine, many centuries later, when he stood with the Lord Jesus and Elijah and three of the apostles on the Mount of Transfiguration (Luke 9 : 31).

Before proceeding to the second part of our lesson, we ought to consider for a moment three or four of the fundamental lessons to be gathered from this brief résumé of the first three chapters of the Book of Deuteronomy. In the first place, note carefully how God is revealed as continually and definitely guiding His people. What they did, where they went, how they treated the peoples through whose territory they desired to go — these things were not left to their own wisdom and discretion, but they were instructed concerning them by a definite and divine revelation. In the second place, Israel's abnormally long period of wandering, so unnecessary considering the short distance from Egypt to Palestine, was due, not to any failure of God to foresee difficulties that would arise, but to Israel's refusal to believe God's promises; thus, it was the result of her own unbelief. The third truth comes directly out of the second, *i.e.*, that God will never force His purposes and plans for blessing and prosperity upon an unbelieving people. He is concerned not alone with their outward conditions, but with their inward life of faith and trust. The two go together, and He will not bestow great external blessings upon those who deliberately determine to distrust Him.

II. THE PRIMACY OF OBEYING GOD'S COMMANDMENTS, Deut. 11 : 1–32.

1. HIS COMMANDMENTS SHOULD BE OBEYED BECAUSE OF HIS GREAT KINDNESSES TO ISRAEL, VS. 1–7. Chapter divisions in the Bible are not of divine origin, but were inserted by men, centuries after the sacred canon of the Scriptures was finished. Some of them are excellent, some prevent us from getting as full a grasp of the significance of some statements as we ought. Thus, if one will take the last verse of Deuteronomy 10 and read it just before beginning Deuteronomy 11, he will then understand why this chapter should begin with such a phrase as it does. Let us read these verses together: " Thy fathers went down into Egypt with threescore and ten persons; and now Jehovah thy God hath made thee as the stars of heaven for multitude. Therefore thou shalt love Jehovah thy God, and keep his charge, and his statutes, and his ordinances, and his commandments, alway." This entire chapter concerns obeying the commandments of God. The first reason that Moses gives why the children of Israel should be glad to obey the Lord and to love Him is because of all the wonderful things God had done for Israel. " Whether the attention was called to the divine actings without or within, abroad or at home, it was all for the purpose of impressing their hearts and minds with a deep sense of the moral importance of obedience. This was the one grand aim of all the rehearsals, all the comments, all the exhortations, of the faithful servant of God who was so soon to be removed from their midst. All is brought to bear, with marvelous force and clearness, upon the conscience of the people, in order to strengthen the basis of Jehovah's claim upon their unqualified obedience to His holy commandments." — *C. H. Mackintosh.* In commenting on verse 6, Mr. Espin has well said: " The omission of Korah and the Levites seems intelligible enough when we remember that Moses was addressing and admonishing, not the Levites, but the congregation at large. The rebellion of Korah evidently included an attack on both the ecclesi-

DEUTERONOMY 11 : 13. And it shall come to pass, if ye shall hearken diligently unto my commandments which I command you this day, to love Jehovah your God, and to serve him with all your heart and with all your soul,

14. That I will give the rain of your land in its season, the former rain and the latter rain, that thou mayest gather in thy grain, and thy new wine, and thine oil.

15. And I will give grass in thy fields for thy cattle, and thou shalt eat and be full.

---

astical and civil arrangements of Moses; see note on Numbers 16. The former were assailed by Korah and certain of the Levites, the latter by Dathan, Abiram, and On, with 250 other 'princes of the assembly' (Num. 16 : 2). This latter was the only portion of the sedition which it was relevant to Moses' present purpose to name; and he therefore naturally omits the former."

2. OBEDIENCE TO GOD'S COMMANDMENTS LEADS TO LONG LIFE AND PROSPERITY, vs. 8–15. Moses, in urging upon the people the necessity, the obligation, the privilege of obeying God's commandments, turns now from the great things God *did do* for Israel, as a reason for such obedience, to the things that God *will do* for each one of them, if their life is marked by a loving adherence to the statutes which they had had continually rehearsed before them. The eighth verse has a beautiful phrase in it: "Therefore shall ye keep all the commandment . . . that ye may be strong." Mr. Mackintosh well says, "There is great strength gained by unreserved obedience to the Word of God. It will not do to pick and choose. What business has a servant to decide as to which of his master's commands he will obey? Surely none whatever; each commandment stands clothed with the master's authority, and therefore claims the servant's attention; and, we may add, the more implicitly the servant obeys, the more he bends his respectful attention to every one of his master's commands, be it ever so trivial, the more does he strengthen himself in his position and grow in his master's confidence and esteem."

A great deal has been written on verses 10–12, contrasting the land of Canaan with the land of Egypt, out of which they had come. "Canaan as a mountainous country was well watered, but by the rains of heaven, on which it absolutely depended for its crops. Without the autumn rain to quicken the newly sown seed, and the spring rain to give the grain bulk and substance, the harvest of Palestine would totally fail. Hence it was a land on which, so long as God's people were faithful and consequently prosperous, 'the eyes of the Lord' would always be, *i.e.*, He would supply at each successive season the needful conditions of productiveness. But Egypt, fit emblem here as elsewhere of the world of nature in distinction from the world of grace, though of course deriving its all ultimately from the Giver of all good things, yet directly and immediately owed its riches and plenty to human ingenuity and capital. It enjoyed no rain worth speaking of, but drew its water supply from the annual overflowing of the Nile, rendered available for agricultural purposes throughout the year by an elaborate and costly system of tanks, canals, forcing machines, etc. To these mechanical appliances allusion is made in this verse: 'Egypt where thou sowedst thy seed, and wateredst it with thy foot.' The inhabitants of Egypt probably watered 'with the foot' in two ways, viz., by means of tread-wheels working sets of pumps, and by means of artificial channels connected with reservoirs, and opened, turned, or closed by the feet. Both methods are still in use in Egypt and other similar districts of country." — *T. E. Espin.* 13. **And it shall come to pass, if ye shall hearken diligently unto my commandments which I command you this day, to love Jehovah your God, and to serve him with all your heart and with all your soul,** 14. **that I will give the rain of your land in its season, the former rain and the latter rain, that thou mayest gather in thy grain, and thy new wine, and thine oil.** 15. **And I will give grass in thy fields for thy cattle, and thou shalt eat and be full.** "The agricultural year in Palestine consisted of two seasons, a rainy and a dry. 'Toward the end of October heavy rains begin to fall, at intervals, for a day or several days at a time. These are what the English Bible calls the early or former rain. It opens the agricultural year; the soil, hardened and cracked by the long summer, rainless since May, is loosened, and the farmer begins ploughing. Till the end of November the average rainfall is not large, but it increases through December,

16. Take heed to yourselves, lest your heart be deceived, and ye turn aside, and serve other gods, and worship them;

17. And the anger of Jehovah be kindled against you, and he shut up the heavens, so that there shall be no rain, and the land shall not yield its fruit; and ye perish quickly from off the good land which Jehovah giveth you.

18. Therefore shall ye lay up these my words in your heart and in your soul; and ye shall bind them for a sign upon your hand, and they shall be for frontlets between your eyes.

19. And ye shall teach them your children, talking of them, when thou sittest in thy house, and when thou walkest by the way, and when thou liest down, and when thou risest up.

20. And thou shalt write them upon the door-posts of thy house, and upon thy gates;

21. That your days may be multiplied, and the days of your children, in the land which Jehovah sware unto your fathers to give them, as the days of the heavens above the earth.

January, and February, begins to abate in March, and is practically over by the end of April. The latter rains (Heb. *malkosh*), from a root meaning *to be late*, are the heavy showers of March and April. Coming as they do when the grain is ripening, and being the last before the long summer drought, they are of far more importance to the country than all the rains of the winter months." — *George Adam Smith.* God *is* concerned with the physical welfare, the material prosperity, of His people. God does not desire His own chosen people to live in constant hardship, nor any nation that follows Him to have to suffer long years of poverty or famine. What God first wants is the heart to be yielded to Him, and then all the things that man can desire will God lovingly bestow. Of course, there are exceptions to this. The New Testament says that the godly will suffer persecution, and that those who follow Christ will be tried as gold is tried in the fire, and as Christians we have spiritual blessings which the Israelites never had. What is referred to here is not luxury, but the ordinary comforts of life.

3. A WARNING ABOUT IDOLATRY, VS. 16, 17. 16. **Take heed to yourselves, lest your heart be deceived, and ye turn aside, and serve other gods, and worship them; 17. and the anger of Jehovah be kindled against you, and he shut up the heavens, so that there shall be no rain, and the land shall not yield its fruit; and ye perish quickly from off the good land which Jehovah giveth you.** Once again we must turn to Mr. Mackintosh for a rich comment on these lines: "Sad progress downward! The heart deceived. This is the beginning of all declension. 'And ye turn aside.' The feet are sure to follow the heart. Hence the deep need of keeping the heart with all diligence; it is the citadel of the whole moral being, and so long as it is kept for the Lord, the enemy can gain no advantage; but when once it is surrendered, all is really gone — there is the turning aside; the secret departure of the heart is proved by the practical ways — 'other gods' are served and worshiped. The descent down along the inclined plane is terribly rapid. 'And then' — mark the sure and solemn consequences — 'the Lord's wrath be kindled against you.' . . . What barrenness and desolation there must be when heaven is shut up! No refreshing showers coming down, no dewdrops falling, no communication between heaven and the earth. Alas! how often had Israel tasted the awful reality of this! There cannot be anything more miserable in all this world than a soul in this condition."

4. THE OBLIGATION TO TEACH THESE COMMANDMENTS TO THEIR CHILDREN, VS. 18–21. 18. **Therefore shall ye lay up these my words in your heart and in your soul; and ye shall bind them for a sign upon your hand, and they shall be for frontlets between your eyes.** 19. **And ye shall teach them your children, talking of them, when thou sittest in thy house, and when thou walkest by the way, and when thou liest down, and when thou risest up.** 20. **And thou shalt write them upon the door-posts of thy house, and upon thy gates;** 21. **that your days may be multiplied, and the days of your children, in the land which Jehovah sware unto your fathers to give them, as the days of the heavens above the earth.** Obedience

22. For if ye shall diligently keep all this commandment which I command you, to do it, to love Jehovah your God, to walk in all his ways, and to cleave unto him;

23. Then will Jehovah drive out all these nations from before you, and ye shall dispossess nations greater and mightier than yourselves.

24. Every place whereon the sole of your foot shall tread shall be yours: from the wilderness, and Lebanon, from the river, the river Euphrates, even unto the hinder sea shall be your border.

25. There shall no man be able to stand before you: Jehovah your God shall lay the fear of you and the dread of you upon all the land that ye shall tread upon, as he hath spoken unto you.

---

to the law of God does not come *naturally* to fallen man. Man's tendency is downward, not upward; away from God, not toward God. Man does not have to be reminded to eat or sleep or read. Man does not have to be urged to fall in love with some one (if he does, let us not call it love), but man must be continually reminded of the laws and commandments and will of God, or else he will forget them and live in disobedience to them. Therefore the Israelites are told that they should first lay up the words of the law of God in their heart and in their soul, and then bind them upon their hand and on their forehead between their eyes. The Jews have literally fulfilled this, by binding in little boxes, on their arms and foreheads, written portions of the book of the law. What really is meant here is that whatever one does, and whatever one thinks, should be controlled by the law of God. If keeping the law in the heart and soul were only as simple as binding pieces of paper on the hand and forehead! Then they were to teach their children these laws, speaking of them in the house and on the highway when resting and when rising up. It is not so important for us to have little pieces of paper nailed up on the doorpost, on which the law is inscribed, as it is for us to have a home recognized by those who enter it as belonging to the Lord. What is the use of having the law tacked up on the outside of the door if the evening is to be spent in carousing and in unkind or coarse conversation? It is the home that is to be sanctified. Obedience to these laws was that the days of the Israelites, yes, and our days, might be "as the days of heaven upon the earth."

5. OBEDIENCE WOULD ASSURE THEM OF VICTORY OVER THEIR ENEMIES, vs. 22–28. 22. **For if ye shall diligently keep all this commandment which I command you, to do it, to love Jehovah your God, to walk in all his ways, and to cleave unto him;** 23. **then will Jehovah drive out all these nations from before you, and ye shall dispossess nations greater and mightier than yourselves.** 24. **Every place whereon the sole of your foot shall tread shall be yours: from the wilderness, and Lebanon, from the river, the river Euphrates, even unto the hinder sea shall be your border.** 25. **There shall no man be able to stand before you: Jehovah your God shall lay the fear of you and the dread of you upon all the land that ye shall tread upon, as he hath spoken unto you.** (See also Josh. 1 : 3; 14 : 9.) Here is a definite promise that no matter how powerful the inhabitants of Canaan should be at the time of Israel's entrance into the promised land, God would give the Israelites a sweeping victory over all of them if they would but continue to walk in His commandments. Now, some one will say, how then do you account for the defeats suffered in the Book of Joshua, for the fact that Israel never occupied all the land that God originally assigned for her possession, and that, ultimately, Judah went down in disastrous defeat before Nebuchadnezzar, and her people were taken captive to Babylon? These tragic defeats are the result of the very law of obedience and disobedience here mentioned. When Israel was in obedience to God her victories were assured and continuous; when she disobeyed God, either as a people or as individuals, defeat overtook her. There is no greater illustration than this, that the tragedy that occurred to Israel in her early days of advance into Palestine was because of the sin of Achan (Josh. 7), and the glorious victory that came to her against the very same city which had defeated her when this sin was put away (Josh. 8). That the Lord desires to bestow blessings upon us is revealed so clearly in all the many beatitudes of the New Testament, and in no place more clearly than at the very beginning of the Sermon on the Mount (Matt. 5 : 1–12).

6. THE COMMAND CONCERNING GERIZIM AND EBAL, vs. 29–32. "The word

Gerizim is probably derived from a root *garaz*, "to shear" or "cut off." Mount Gerizim was and is as barren as Ebal, and was probably selected as the hill of benediction because it was the southernmost of the two, the south being the region, according to Hebrew ideas, of light, and so of life and blessing. On the ceremony of the solemn benediction and commination, see 27 : 14. . . . The words 'by the way where the sun goeth down,' should run, 'beyond the road of the west'; *i.e.*, on the further side of the main track which ran from Syria and Damascus to Jerusalem and Egypt through the center of Palestine. This is called 'the way of the west' in contrast to the other main route from Damascus to the south which passed through the district east of Jordan." — *T. E. Espin.*

What attributes of God are revealed to us in the four chapters assigned for our lesson? What were the principle sins of Israel, as revealed in these chapters, which brought to her so much suffering, and prevented her from entering fully upon the blessings which God intended for her (unbelief and idolatry)? What happens when believing parents are not at all concerned to teach their children the great spiritual truths, the facts concerning Christ, and the Word of God, through which they themselves have been saved? Do you think that God would ever allow a pagan, blaspheming, brutal nation to bring into defeat a country that only nominally worships Him, but which was not truly and thoroughly a nation that was giving glory to God? (The answer is, Yes, God used the pagan, brutal Assyrian host to humble in defeat His own chosen people of Judah.) If a nation is to obey God's commandments, when is the time when they should start to walk in such obedience? Do you think God can use the area known as the United States for a field of discipline for His people here, as much as He could use the wilderness of Sinai for disciplining His people of old? After all, what is the great difference between the promises to Israel of old and the promises to Christian believers today? (The great difference is that most of the promises to Israel were concerning material things, while the promises to us concern spiritual blessings, but both are obtained through faith.)

Phylacteries. Worn on the Forehead.

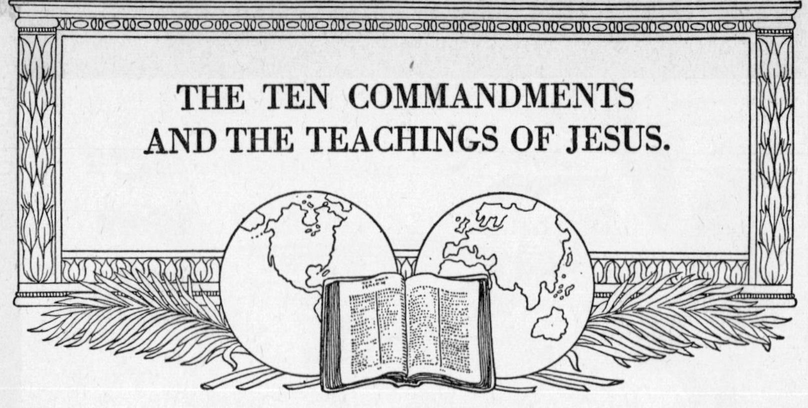

FOURTH QUARTER.

OCTOBER 3 — DECEMBER 26, 1943.

AIM: To help the student interpret the Ten Commandments in the light of the teachings of Jesus and to apply them in personal and social relationships.

LESSON I. — October 3.

JESUS AND THE TEN COMMANDMENTS. — Matthew 5 : 17–20; 19 : 16–22; John 5 : 39, 40.

GOLDEN TEXT. — ***Think not that I came to destroy the law or the prophets: I came not to destroy, but to fulfil.*** MATTHEW 5 : 17.

Devotional Reading: Matthew 7 : 21–27.
Beginner Topic: GOD'S BOOK.
  Lesson Material: Matthew 5 : 17–19; John 5 : 39; 2 Chronicles 34.
  Memory Verse: I was glad when they said unto me, Let us go into the house of Jehovah. Psalm 122 : 1.
Primary Topic: AN UNHAPPY RICH MAN.
  Lesson Material: Matthew 19 : 16–22.
  Memory Verse: The word of Jehovah is right; and all his work is done in faithfulness. Psalm 33 : 4.
Junior Topic: AN UNHAPPY RICH MAN.
  Lesson Material: Matthew 19 : 16–22.
  Memory Verse: There is that maketh himself rich, yet hath nothing: there is that maketh himself poor, yet hath great wealth. Proverbs 13 : 7.
Intermediate and Senior Topic: CHRIST'S WAY OF LIFE.
Topic for Young People and Adults: JESUS AND THE TEN COMMANDMENTS.

THE TEACHER AND HIS CLASS.

The Younger Classes should be reminded that every day there arises the problem of choices. Perhaps some day we feel lazy, and would like to spend time loafing, playing, or taking a trip. But it is school time, and we know if we are to pass our grade, and advance in knowledge, we *have* to go to school. Now let us say we have the privilege of making our own choice that day. So much depends upon the right choice, on refusing to take the easy way and choosing that which, though hard, ultimately wins the trophy of knowledge and advancement. Every day is a day of choices. In our lesson we have the sad story of a man who made the wrong choice. He chose to keep his wealth, instead of following the Lord Jesus.

The Older Classes will find here a remarkable illustration of Christ's conviction concerning His own absolute preeminence. The law of God, given throughout the Old Testament, is, He

BURNE-JONES

THE STAR OF BETHLEHEM

asserts, fulfilled in Him. It is toward Him supremely that the loyalties of life must be directed, and He declares that if we turn from Him we have actually lost eternal life, for no one else possesses the power to bestow it. Either these claims are true or false. If they are false, Christ is not our Saviour; but, if they are true, we cannot afford to neglect them.

THE LESSON IN ITS SETTING.

Time. — The Sermon on the Mount was delivered in the summer of A.D. 28; the interview with the rich young ruler was in February, A.D. 30; the two verses from John's Gospel are a part of a message given the first week of April, A.D. 28.

Place. — The Sermon on the Mount, on a mountain near Capernaum; the interview with the ruler took place in Perea; the events of John 5 occurred in Jerusalem.

THE PLAN OF THE LESSON.

SUBJECT: Christ Is the One in Whom Alone All the Preceding Messages of God Meet Their Fulfillment, and from Whom Alone Proceeds Eternal Life.

I. CHRIST'S RELATIONSHIP TO THE OLD TESTAMENT LAW, Matt. 5 : 17–20.

1. Christ came to fulfill the law and the prophets, vs. 17, 18.
2. Christ's estimate of the high value of the commandments, v. 19.
3. The necessity for true righteousness, v. 20.

II. THE MAN WHO BOASTED HE HAD KEPT ALL THE COMMANDMENTS BUT WOULD NOT DO WHAT JESUS TOLD HIM TO DO, Matt. 19 : 16–22.

1. The question he asked of Jesus, v. 16.
2. Christ's first answer, vs. 17–19.
3. The young man's assertion of his own righteousness, v. 20.
4. Christ's twofold command, v. 21.
5. The young man sorrowfully refuses to obey, v. 22.

III. CHRIST THE SECRET OF ETERNAL LIFE, John 5 : 39, 40.

THE TEACHER'S LIBRARY.

On the general subject of Christ and the law, see an article by A. S. Peake, "Law," and an article by H. H. Currie, "Law of God," in James Hastings's *Dictionary of Christ and the Gospels*, Vol. 2, 11–17; on the words of the Sermon on the Mount, there is nothing so superb as the exposition in G. Campbell Morgan: *The Gospel According to Matthew*, 50–53; other commentaries on Matthew's Gospel may be consulted. See also B. B. Warfield: *Bible Doctrines*, 293–299. On Matthew 5 : 17, see J. S. Holden: *The Confidence of Faith*, 138–144; James Hastings's *Great Tests of the Bible, Matthew*, 114–128; Joseph Parker: *The City Temple Pulpit*, Vol. 7, 118–126; on verse 18, James M. Gray: *The Fundamentals*, Vol. 3, 29–31; v. 20, Joseph Parker as above, Vol. 2, 13–20; and a profound sermon by G. Campbell Morgan, in the *Westminster Pulpit*, Vol. 6, 361–368. On the rich young ruler, see G. Campbell Morgan: *Westminster Pulpit*, Vol. 2, 113–120; A. T. Robertson: *Some Minor Characters in the New Testament*, 63–73; James Jeffrey: *The Personal Ministry of the Son of Man*, 133–144; L. R. Scarborough: *How Jesus Won Men*, 107–114; A. B. Davidson: *The Called of God*, 301–316; James Hastings's *Great Texts of the Bible, Matthew*, 360–375; on verse 17, see the article, "Good," in James Hastings's *Dictionary of Christ and the Gospels*, Vol. 1, 657–658; on verse 16, H. W. Morrow: *Questions Asked and Answered by Our Lord*, 210–215; on verse 19, J. D. Jones: *The Inevitable Christ*, 65–83; on verse 20, James Denney: *Gospel Questions and Answers*, 1 ff. (a volume the editor has never been able to consult). On John 5 : 39, see J. D. Jones: *The Gospel of the Sovereignty*, 173–186; F. F. Shannon: *The Enchanted Universe*, 106–124; on verse 40, Hugh Black: *Edinburgh Sermons*, 55 ff.

MATTHEW 5 : 17. Think not that I came to destroy the law or the prophets: I came not to destroy, but to fulfil.

I. **CHRIST'S RELATIONSHIP TO THE OLD TESTAMENT LAW,** Matt. 5 : 17–20.

1. CHRIST CAME TO FULFILL THE LAW AND THE PROPHETS, vs. 17, 18. 17. **Think not that I came to destroy the law or the prophets: I came not to destroy, but to fulfil.** By the phrase, " the law and the prophets," our Lord meant the whole of the Old Testament, the law referring to the five books of Moses, and the prophets referring to all the rest of the Old Testament. " Observe it is the law *or* the prophets. Not merely were the requirements of Moses to continue in force, which some Jews regarded as more sacred than the rest of the Old Testament, but also all that was taught by the other inspired writers, the prophets. No part of the existing Scriptures was to be set aside. And we know from Josephus and early Christian writers, that all Jews of our Lord's time would understand ' the Scriptures ' or ' the law and the prophets ' as meaning a well known and well defined collection of sacred books, the same as our Old Testament." — *J. A. Broadus.* The Jewish people of our Lord's day, who, of course, believed the law and the prophetical books to be divine messages, no doubt frequently declared that Christ was *breaking* the law, and if He had come to denounce and repudiate the law, then they could repudiate Him, for the law was of God. To answer this objection, our Lord frankly declared that instead of destroying the testament of these divine messages, instead of encouraging the

18. For verily I say unto you, Till heaven and earth pass away, one jot or one tittle shall in no wise pass away from the law, till all things be accomplished.

19. Whosoever therefore shall break one of these least commandments, and shall teach men so, shall be called least in the kingdom of heaven: but whosoever shall do and teach them, he shall be called great in the kingdom of heaven.

---

people to repudiate them, He Himself actually came to fulfill them. " Through the law and the prophets He has revealed His will, and it is impossible that His Son should attempt to pull down or undo this revelation of the Father's will, or that His will, in the smallest particular, should fail of fulfillment. Not until the whole of the divine purpose has been accomplished can the smallest expression of the divine will be abolished." — *Alfred Plummer.* " He carried into effect what was already definitely prescribed in the law and promised in the prophets, but He penetrated into their essential principles, discarding what was alien to them, deepening them and extending their range, yet developing them along the lines already laid down. He did actually disannul certain elements in the law (cf. vs. 34, 39), but He did so not as a destructive critic but as the consummator of the genius of Israel." — *E. E. Anderson.* 18. **For verily I say unto you, Till heaven and earth pass away, one jot or one tittle shall in no wise pass away from the law, till all things be accomplished.** " *Jot,* in the Greek *iota,* signifies the Hebrew letter *iod* (pronounced *yod*), corresponding to the English *i.* It is much smaller than the other Hebrew letters, so that it is liable to be overlooked; and besides, in many words it can be either inserted or omitted without affecting the sound or the sense, somewhat like the *u* in favour or honour. No part of the law, not the most insignificant letter, was to be set aside. And this statement is further strengthened by adding *tittle* — in the Greek ' horn ' — denoting a very slight projection at the corner of certain Hebrew letters, which distinguishes them from others that are rounded (cf. Luke 16 : 17). The word ' horn ' in this sense would not be understood among us, and so ' tittle ' (a very small object) was wisely used by Wycliff, and retained by all subsequent translators. The whole expression has been aptly compared to our English saying, ' Not the dot of an *i* nor the cross of a *t.*' We also frequently employ in the same way the Greek *iota* (Every iota of it). The things predicted in the law must all occur; the entire substance foreshadowed by any ceremony or type must have come into existence; the civil regulations for the Jewish State, after lasting while it lasts, must continue to serve as the germ and basis of much Christian legislation; the moral (ethical) precepts must be obeyed by every new generation. Not till all this has taken place, shall the least particle of the law be annulled." — *J. A. Broadus.*

Sermon on the Mount. Hofmann.

2. CHRIST'S ESTIMATE OF THE HIGH VALUE OF THE COMMANDMENTS, v. 19. 19. **Whosoever therefore shall break one of these least commandments, and shall**

20. For I say unto you, that except your righteousness shall exceed *the righteousness* of the scribes and Pharisees, ye shall in no wise enter into the kingdom of heaven.

teach men so, shall be called least in the kingdom of heaven: but whosoever shall do and teach them, he shall be called great in the kingdom of heaven. "We do not understand the nature of the mission which Jesus here ascribes to Himself until we clearly see that it finds its end in the perfecting of men. His purpose in coming is not accomplished in merely completing the law: it finds its fulfillment in bringing men completely to keep the completed law. If we speak of Him as legislator, then, we mean that He claims plenary authority with respect to the law. The law is His, and He uses it as an instrument in the accomplishment of His great end, the making of men righteous. He knows what is in the law, and He brings all its content out, with the most searching analysis. But this is but the beginning. He came to make this law, thus nobly expounded, the actual law of human lives. Abrogate it? Nothing could be further from His purpose. He came rather to fulfill it, to work it out into its most wide-reaching applications, and to work it, thus worked out, into men's lives. Those who are His disciples will not be behind the scribes and Pharisees themselves in the perfection of their obedience to its very jots and tittles. But their righteousness will not be the righteousness of the scribes and Pharisees. The difference will be that their obedience will not be confined to these jots and tittles. In their lives there will be 'accomplished' the whole law of God in its highest and profoundest meaning. Their lives will be a perfect transcript in act of the law of God, a perfect reflection of the will of God in life. It is for this that Jesus says that He came." — *B. B. Warfield.* "Dignity in the kingdom depends on Christlikeness, and Christlikeness depends on fulfilling, as He did, all righteousness. Small flaws are most dangerous because least noticeable. More Christian men lose their chance of promotion in the kingdom by a multitude of little sins than by single great ones." — *Alexander Maclaren.* "Notice carefully, 'break' and 'teach.' You never find a man teaching that any commandment of God is unimportant, but that behind his teaching is the fact that he himself is breaking that commandment. 'Whosoever shall break, and teach men so.' That is a close connection, and the issue for that man is that he is to be least in the kingdom. It is not a question of being cast out of the kingdom; it is a question of his losing the honors and the rewards. But mark also on the other side, in which the same philosophy is manifest: 'Whosoever shall do and teach them.' The only power of teaching is that of the doing which precedes it. No man ever teaches a commandment with power, if he is breaking it in his own life." — *G. Campbell Morgan.*

3. THE NECESSITY FOR TRUE RIGHTEOUSNESS, v. 20. 20. **For I say unto you, that except your righteousness shall exceed *the righteousness* of the scribes and Pharisees, ye shall in no wise enter into the kingdom of heaven.** The words of Dr. Campbell Morgan in his sermon in the *Westminster Pulpit* on this verse will probably not be available to any of the readers of this volume, and for that reason, the editor is taking the liberty of quoting two or three passages in detail. "Our word *righteousness*, as you will remember in its ancient form read *right-wise-ness*. That is to say it came from a word right-wise; and that had as its main value the word right. Instead of righteousness, say righteous; and instead of righteous, say right; and you are touching the very central thought. Yet immediately you discover that this is not definition. So we press the question further. What is right? If we take this actual word of ours, we find that its simplest meaning is *no crookedness*. The root word is a word which means to stretch, so that if you will take in your hand a piece of string looped, twisted, and stretch it, that is righteousness, that which is perfectly straight. The straightest course is the right course. Go back to your school days and remind yourselves of this phrase, a right line, a straight line. What is a straight line? The one that goes most directly from point to point. Right is that in which there is no loop, no crookedness, no doubling, no deviation from the truly straight. God is the absolute and eternal standard of right. Consequently, human conduct is righteous, as it conforms to His will and approximates to His character. . . . He is the one eternal, final standard of what is right; consequently righteousness in human life is conformity to His will and approximation to His character. . . . The Pharisees were religious, orthodox, and the base of their morality was their belief that man must conform to the will of God. Wherein then lay their failure? Three things characterized their righteousness; it was first

MATTHEW 19 : 16. And behold, one came to him and said, Teacher, what good thing shall I do, that I may have eternal life?

17. And he said unto him, Why askest thou me concerning that which is good? One there is who is good: but if thou wouldest enter into life, keep the commandments.

external; secondly, it was exclusive; finally, therefore, it was evasive of essential righteousness. . . . The result was the degradation of all life; the degradation of their own spirit to the hard, harsh, critical, cynical, self-satisfied temper which they manifested; the degradation of all their disciples, upon whom they laid burdens that they themselves would not lift. . . . Who is sufficient for these things? The answer is: None other than the child of God, or he alone knows Him, or is able to obey Him. . . . I can never have the righteousness that exceeds the righteousness of the scribes and Pharisees save only as He will take me, dwell in me, and make me love with His love; and see with His eyes; and be compassionate with His compassion; and angry with His anger; compassionate toward the sinner, but angry with his sin. May we know that righteousness, through the Lord Himself."

II. **THE MAN WHO BOASTED HE HAD KEPT ALL THE COMMANDMENTS BUT WOULD NOT DO WHAT JESUS TOLD HIM TO DO,** Matt. 19 : 16–22. To begin with, we should notice that this is not a parable, but an actual, historic episode in the life of our Lord. It is one of the most remarkable stories in all the Bible, and, though it occupies not more than a half column, yet it is so rich in meaning that it can never be fully exhausted in interpretation. A. T. Robertson has called it, "A True Soul's Tragedy." (The story is also to be found in Mark 10 : 17–30 and Luke 18 : 18–30.) If we compare the other Gospel records of this episode, we will note that this man had the following assets: (1) he was young; (2) he was a ruler, that is, probably, he had a very high place among the Jews, which meant that he had an excellent reputation; (3) he was rich; (4) he had kept all the commandments; (5) he was not a man debased with selfish indulgences, but was one in whom there strove a great desire for the higher things of life.

1. THE QUESTION HE ASKED OF JESUS, v. 16. 16. **And behold, one came to him and said, Teacher, what good thing shall I do, that I may have eternal life?** "At the very outset some of the noblest spirits and some of the best young men felt the influence of Jesus. Men like Nicodemus and Joseph of Arimathea became His disciples, though secretly, and gave Him their love and loyalty. His teaching contained the truth of which they were in quest. The narrative introduces us to a young man with life before him, with great advantages, and with splendid prospects. He was a cultured and educated man, trained in the knowledge of the law. He knew what God required of one who desired life, and endeavored to do what was right, so far as he himself understood it. But evidently he was not satisfied with himself. His conscience was uneasy, something was wrong. He was not happy. He was not conscious of enjoying the divine favor, and longed for that perfect peace in which God had promised to keep those who trusted in Him. While in this state of mind he met Jesus. He no doubt heard Him speak of His mission to seek and to save the lost, and of His offer of rest to the heavyladen. He came running out of the crowd to Jesus, as one who had suddenly made up his mind to this decision, and kneeling before Him poured out what was in his mind, in the eager question: 'Good Master, what good thing shall I do to inherit eternal life?' . . . Jesus had spoken of eternal life as a blessing He had come to bestow, for no one can read the Gospel of John without perceiving how frequently the words of life, and eternal life, were on the Saviour's lips, and how He conditioned the enjoyment of that blessing upon believing in Himself. That was what the young man could not understand. He felt as if he had failed in some part of his duty, and so he wished to have a clear statement from Jesus as to what was needed on his part to make him partaker of eternal life." — *James Jeffrey.*

2. CHRIST'S FIRST ANSWER, vs. 17–19. 17. **And he said unto him, Why askest thou me concerning that which is good? One there is who is good: but if thou wouldest enter into life, keep the commandments.** "When Christ said: 'Why callest thou me good? None is good, save One, even God,' He meant one of two things. He either meant I am not good, or, I am God. I do not think you can escape the alternative. I do not believe that here Jesus denied that He was good. I therefore believe that He claimed deity. Looking into the face of this man He knew that what he wanted was a Master. Man has only one Master — God.

18. He saith unto him, Which? And Jesus said, Thou shalt not kill, Thou shalt not commit adultery, Thou shalt not steal, Thou shalt not bear false witness,

19. Honor thy father and thy mother; and, Thou shalt love thy neighbor as thyself.

20. The young man saith unto him, All these things have I observed: what lack I yet?

There is only one King able to realize the kingdom of human life, and that is God. . . . When Christ asked that question, it is as though He had said to the man, You are after life. Your discernment is great because you have linked life with goodness. Why do you call Me good? Think what you are saying. If you have seen goodness in Me, you have seen God. If you have recognized goodness as you have looked into My face, watched My deeds, and listened to My words, your life has come into the

Christ and the Rich Young Ruler. Hofmann.

light of the Divine, into the light of God Himself." — *G. Campbell Morgan.* 18. **He saith unto him, Which? And Jesus said, Thou shalt not kill, Thou shalt not commit adultery, Thou shalt not steal, Thou shalt not bear false witness,** 19. **Honor thy father and thy mother; and, Thou shalt love thy neighbor as thyself.** Our Lord simply summarizes here what is called the Decalogue, that is, the Ten Commandments, naming five of them, and then adding a command from another part of the book of the law (Lev. 19 : 18), that a man should love his neighbor as himself. These laws, though ancient, were just as fundamentally necessary in the lives of men, and obedience to them just as imperative when Jesus spoke, as when they were declared by God through Moses. They are just as imperative today. Salvation has not delivered anybody from the need for obeying these laws. Disobedience to them on the part of any man in the world, Christian or non-Christian, means sin in the sight of God.

3. THE YOUNG MAN'S ASSERTION OF HIS OWN RIGHTEOUSNESS, V. 20. 20. **The young man saith unto him, All these things have I observed: what lack I yet?** "There is a touch of impatience in the rejoinder, 'All these have I kept,' with more than a touch of self-satisfaction. The law has failed to accomplish one of its chief purposes in the young man, in that it has not taught him his sinfulness. No doubt he had a right to say that his outward life had been free from breaches of such very elementary morality, which any old woman could have taught him. He had yet

21. Jesus said unto him, If thou wouldest be perfect, go, sell that which thou hast, and give to the poor, and thou shalt have treasure in heaven: and come, follow me.

22. But when the young man heard the saying, he went away sorrowful; for he was one that had great possessions.

---

to learn that whoever says, 'All these have I kept,' thereby convicts himself of understanding neither them nor himself. Still he was not at rest, although he had, as he fancied, kept them all. His last question is a plaintive, honest acknowledgment of the hungry void within, which no round of outward obediences can ever fill. He knows that he has not the inner fountain springing up into eternal life. He is dimly aware of something wanting, whether in his obedience or no, at all events in his peace; and he is right in believing that the reason for the conscious void is something wanting in his conduct." — *Alexander Maclaren.* We must not in any way condemn the man for keeping these commandments. Far better for a young man to say he has kept them from his youth than to confess that he had broken them all. At least, the man lived a clean life, and that is a great asset for any man at any time. The fact that he turned here from Jesus makes it a double tragedy.

4. CHRIST'S TWOFOLD COMMAND, V. 21. 21. **Jesus said unto him, If thou wouldest be perfect, go, sell that which thou hast, and give to the poor, and thou shalt have treasure in heaven: and come, follow me.** We should first clearly note, what is sometimes missed by teachers, that Christ did not tell this man to do *one* thing, but he told him to do *two* things, with the understanding that if he did both of these things he would have that which his heart longed for. First, he was to sell all he had, and give it to the poor. Having done that, he was to come and follow the Lord Jesus Christ. Of course, we should understand at once, this command of our Lord's to this young man to sell all that he had, is not necessarily what Christ says to every other person, or indeed, even to every one who is wealthy. The reason it was insisted upon for this certain man was that he had made wealth his idol. He was so attached to it that his life had become dependent upon it, his interests were centered in his wealth, and all that wealth could obtain. "The one thing needful for entrance into life is at bottom the self-surrender, and the casting away of all else for its sovereign sake. 'I do count them but dung,' must be the language of every one who will win Christ. The hands must be emptied of treasures, and the heart swept clear of lesser loves, if He is to be grasped by our hands, and to dwell in our hearts. More of us than we are willing to believe are kept from entire surrender to Jesus Christ by money and worldly possessions; and many professing Christians are kept shrivelled and weak and joyless because they love their wealth more than their Lord, and would think it madness to do as this man was bidden to do. When ballast is thrown out, the balloon shoots up." — *Alexander Maclaren.* "If there is anything in our life which is keeping us back from a full acceptance of Jesus, then we must part with it. We might take the Saviour's command literally and be as unhappy as ever. We might part with our wealth and yet not find eternal life, as was the case with many who entered the cloister." — *James Jeffrey.* By following Christ, our Lord did not mean what we might call a mere "geographical" following; that is, He did not mean that the young man was to accompany Him wherever He went. It was a following in his own heart. He was to do what the Lord wanted him to do; live as the Lord commanded him to live; go where the Lord sent him. In other words, he was to relinquish the sovereignty of money and take into its place the sovereignty of the Lord Jesus Christ. This is the struggle in every man's soul, to give up obedience to the idol of one's heart, and to yield obedience to the only begotten Son of God.

5. THE YOUNG MAN SORROWFULLY REFUSES TO OBEY, V. 22. 22. **But when the young man heard the saying, he went away sorrowful; for he was one that had great possessions.** This is one of the saddest sentences in all the Scriptures. The young man would not do what the Lord asked him to do, and therefore he went away without that for which he came, and, more than that, with a sorrow deeper than any he had known before. He did not know what he should do to have eternal life, when he came to Christ. He now knows what he would have to do, and he knows also that in not doing it he would never have this desire of his heart. Just why did he go away? Because he decided that his wealth, and all that it would buy, was more necessary for him than eternal life. "Without his property he would be

JOHN 5 : 39. Ye search the scriptures, because ye think that in them ye have eternal life; and these are they which bear witness of me;
40. And ye will not come to me, that ye may have life.

as a common day-laborer if not a pauper and a beggar. He took it all in after a moment of intellectual illumination as he faced his opportunity and crisis. He felt sure that Jesus had misjudged him. It was true that he was very rich, but that was no crime. Job had been very wealthy, as was King David. Jesus Himself had rich disciples, like the Bethany family and, later, Joseph of Arimathea. The Jews looked on wealth as proof of the favor of God and poverty as a curse. The young man was puzzled beyond expression. The new Teacher had cut across the path of all his training and conviction. He did not know that he was covetous. He probably gave alms regularly. He did not know that he worshipped mammon. . . . Many people today do not consider covetousness a vice at all, but rather a virtue. When did you ever know a man to be excluded from church on the charge of covetousness? And yet few sins are more blighting to the soul. The finer traits shrivel up under the blasting effect of the exaggerated love of money. Jesus evidently means the young man who posed so near perfection to see that he had violated the very first of the commandments. He loved money more than he did God. . . . He was willing to give up all the sins of which he was not guilty." — *A. T. Robertson.* " The young man seems to speak no word, to take no time for reflection. He stands for a moment as if stunned, and then silently turns away. What a moment! His fate hung on it. Once more we see the awful mystery enacted before our eyes, of a soul gathering up its power to put away life. Who will say that the decision of a moment, which is the outcome of all the past, may not fix the whole future? " — *Alexander Maclaren.*

WATTS.

" For He Had Great Possessions."

" My will not my own
 Till Thou hast made it Thine;
If it would reach the monarch's throne
 It must its crown resign;
It only stands unbent
 Amid the clashing strife,
When on Thy bosom it has leant,
 And found in Thee its life." — *G. Campell Morgan.*

III. **CHRIST THE SECRET OF ETERNAL LIFE,** John 5 : 39, 40. 39. **Ye search the scriptures, because ye think that in them ye have eternal life ; and these are they which bear witness of me ;** 40. **and ye will not come to me, that ye may have life.** In the Revised Version the opening clause of this sentence is in the indicative, simply meaning, " You do search the Scriptures, because you think that in them you have eternal life." But the margin of the Revised Version makes the sentence to begin, " Search the scriptures," which throws the entire sentence into the imperative mood, *i.e.*, a command, " You must search the Scriptures." Commentators greatly differ on this point. Bishop Ryle, together with Alford, Luther, Calvin, and others, take it to be a command; Tollock, Barnes, Westcott, Reith, and others, take it to be a simple statement of fact. Either way, the word rendered *search* means to search minutely and diligently. It appears intentionally used to show that the Jews should not be content with mere reading. The Septuagint phrase of Proverbs 2 : 4 has an expression like it. " This sentence is a strong and weighty declaration of the value of the Old Testament Scriptures. It was to them exclusively, of course, that our Lord referred. He says, ' They testify of me.' In direct prophecies, in promises, in typical persons, in typical ceremonies, the Old Testament Scriptures all through testify of Christ. We read them to very little purpose if we do not discern this. . . . Let us note in this verse the high honor which our Lord puts on the Old Testament Scriptures. He distinctly endorses the Jewish canon of inspired writings. Much infidelity begins with an ignorant contempt of the Old

Testament. Let us note further what a plain duty it is to read the Scriptures. Men have no right to expect spiritual light if they neglect the great treasury of all light. If even of the Old Testament our Lord said, 'Search, it testifies of me,' how much more it is a duty to search the whole Bible! An idle neglect of the Bible is one secret of the ignorant formal Christianity which is so widely prevalent in these latter days. God's blessing on a diligent study of the Scripture is strikingly illustrated in the case of the Bereans (Acts 17 : 11)." — *J. C. Ryle.* We have heard some teachers affirm that our Lord here means to correct the Jewish habit of a constant searching of the Scriptures, as though that in this Book they would find eternal life. I do not believe our Lord is rebuking such study at all. Rather the opposite, for does He not say that they speak of Himself? I think the simple meaning here is that, if in searching, they found Him, the Sent One of God, the Holy One of God, the One who would give His life for their sins, the Bestower of life, then, indeed, would they find Him who would be able to impart eternal life to their souls. But our Lord says they would not come to Him that they might have life. They sat by the Scriptures, constantly studying them, mastering the history, the prophecy, the typology, the theology, the anthropology of its holy pages, but they would not yield themselves to the person of Christ, of whom the Scriptures speak. Knowing the Word, they refuse to come to Him of whom the Word spoke, and this certainly means that Bible study in itself never bestows eternal life. Only Christ can do that. There is a wonderful illustration of this passage in Matthew 2 (vs. 1–11), where we find that the chief priests and scribes were able to tell the inquiring wise men and the frightened Herod exactly where Christ should be born according to the prophets, but when they heard that the Christ had been born in Bethlehem, they never went out to see if these things were true. The need of the human heart is just this of which our Scriptures are speaking — eternal life. It is that which the rich young ruler longed for, but so clung to his idol wealth that he could not receive it. It is that which our Lord insisted upon as being absolutely essential, but it could not be found outside of Him. This is as true today as ever. Fullness of life, life that satisfies, life from God, a life of peace and power, a life of joy and liberty, a life that can be truly called eternal life, a life that death can never interrupt, a life that will be consummated and glorified in heaven above, that life is derived from only one source in all the world, one Person in all history, only one, because He is the only begotten Son of God, and in Him alone is life indeed.

Would you say, from a study of the verses we have been considering, that Christ spoke with finality and with authority, or that He, like other men, was searching about for the truth? In what ways do the passages reveal Christ's love for man? In how many different ways does Christ in this lesson declare His own absolute pre-eminence over all others who have ever lived on this earth? What are some of the differences between a life, however rich and full, lived by any man or woman on this earth, apart from Christ, and the life of one lived in daily communion with Christ? Do you think from the story in our lesson that the rich young ruler came back to Christ again, and did what Christ told him to do? (The answer is probably, No. He reached the turning-point of his life, and took the wrong road.) Do you think that this urge to have eternal life would be as great in the heart of the young man after turning away from Christ as the day when he came to our Lord?

LESSON II. — October 10.

REVERENCE FOR GOD. — Exodus 20 : 3–7; Matthew 4 : 10; 6 : 9; John 4 : 23, 24.

GOLDEN TEXT. — ***God is a Spirit: and they that worship him must worship in spirit and truth.*** JOHN 4 : 24.

Devotional Reading: John 4 : 21–26.
Beginner Topic: LITTLE SAMUEL.
  Lesson Material: John 4 : 23, 24; 1 Samuel 1 : 20–28.
  Memory Verse: I was glad when they said unto me, Let us go unto the house of Jehovah. Psalm 122 : 1.

Primary Topic: BESIDE A WELL.
Lesson Material: Exodus 20 : 3–7; Matthew 4 : 10; 6 : 9; John 4 : 23, 24.
Memory Verse: I will give thanks unto thy name, O Jehovah, for it is good. Psalm 54 : 6.
Junior Topic: WHERE CAN WE WORSHIP?
Lesson Material: Exodus 20 : 3–7; Matthew 4 : 10; 6 : 9; John 4 : 23, 24.
Memory Verse: God is a Spirit: and they that worship him must worship in spirit and truth. John 4 : 24.
Intermediate and Senior Topic: WHAT IS REVERENCE?
Topic for Young People and Adults: VALUES OF REVERENCE AND WORSHIP.

THE TEACHER AND HIS CLASS.

The Younger Classes might begin a study of this lesson by being asked why we behave differently in a church than in a store, a factory, or in a lecture room? Well, the difference is that in a church we go to worship God, while in other places we only meet men, and God is so great and holy, so perfect and powerful and eternal, that He deserves the fear, the adoration, the worship, the reverence of our hearts. In fact, the word of our lesson *reverence* simply means a deep or due respect for a person because of that person's might and lofty character and position. Our whole lesson is occupied with the important subject of how we should live that we may truly *revere* and *worship* God.

The Older Classes will find here a much needed admonition regarding the holiness, the sanctity of our relationship to God, our worship of God, and our use of God's name. The world is so crude in itself, the sanctities of life are so easily lost sight of, that our very religious practices become, as it were, artificial, superficial, and sometimes blasphemous. For the right approach to God, and the right thoughts of God, we need to know truly who God is, and that in particular is what our lesson attempts to set forth.

THE LESSON IN ITS SETTING.

Time. — The commandments were given in 1445 B.C.; our Lord's Temptation took place in January, A.D. 27; the Sermon on the Mount was delivered in the summer of A.D. 28; our Lord's words with the woman at the well took place in December, A.D. 27.

Place. — The commandments were given on Mount Sinai; our Lord's temptation in the wilderness near the Jordan; the Se mon on the Mount was given somewhere on a mountain in northern Palestine; the discourse with the woman of Samaria was at Sychar.

THE PLAN OF THE LESSON.

SUBJECT: The Reverence Which Should Mark All of Our Thought of God, Our Worship of God, and Our Speaking of God.

I. THE FIRST THREE COMMANDMENTS, Exodus 20 : 3–7.
1. God the Lord is to be our only God, v. 3.
2. The prohibition of all forms of idolatrous worship, vs. 4–6.
3. The reverent use of God's name, v. 7.

II. OUR LORD'S TRIUMPH OVER SATAN'S MOST SUBTLE TEMPTATION IN THE TRUTH CONCERNING THE WORSHIP OF GOD, Matthew 4 : 10.

III. THE HALLOWING OF GOD'S NAME, Matthew 6 : 9.

IV. HOW TO WORSHIP GOD ACCEPTABLY, John 4 : 23, 24.

THE TEACHER'S LIBRARY.

Apart from the principal books dealing with the Ten Commandments, not much sermonic material will be found on the first three commandments. However, on Exodus 20 : 3, see a sermon by James Vaughan, in the *Contemporary Pulpit, Second Series*, Vol. 9, 52–61; and a sermon by the same author, on verse 7, in the same volume, 109–122. All volumes dealing with our Lord's Temptation will be found to have helpful material on Matthew 4 : 10. All volumes devoted to an exposition of the Lord's prayer will be found to have chapters on Matthew 6 : 9. See, also, Andrew Murray: *Christ in the School of Prayer*, 24–31. On John 4 : 23, 24, see, in addition to commentaries on John's Gospel, Andrew Murray, as above, 9–15; F. F. Shannon: *The Infinite Artist*, 52–65; R. A. Torrey: *Fundamental Doctrines of the Christian Faith*, 42–48; and, if one wishes to consider the subject theologically, W. G. T. Shedd: *Dogmatic Theology*, Vol. 1, 151–171.

I. **THE FIRST THREE COMMANDMENTS,** Exod. 20 : 3–7. "The first commandment guards the unity of God; the second commandment His spirituality; the third His deity or essence." — *J. G. Murphy*. Dr. G. Campbell Morgan expresses it this way: "The first commandment brings us face to face with the object of worship; the second commandment reveals the true mode of worship; the third states that this relationship of man to God — that of worship — is to be a perpetual one, governing all his life."

EXODUS 20 : 3. Thou shalt have no other gods before me.

4. Thou shalt not make unto thee a graven image, nor any likeness *of any thing* that is in heaven above, or that is in the earth beneath, or that is in the water under the earth:

---

1. GOD THE LORD IS TO BE OUR ONLY GOD, v. 3. 3. **Thou shalt have no other gods before me.** Dr. Charles Hodge, in his magnificent interpretation of this commandment, has well said that "this commandment includes, first, the injunction to recognize Jehovah as the true God. As this recognition must be intelligent and sincere, it includes: 1. Knowledge. We must know who, or what Jehovah is. This implies a knowledge of His attributes, of His relation to the world as its creator, preserver, and governor, and especially His relation to His rational creatures and to His own chosen people. This, of course, involves a knowledge of our relation to Him as dependent and responsible creatures and as the objects of His redeeming love. 2. Faith. We must believe that God is, and that He is what He declares Himself to be; and that we are His creatures and His children. 3. Confession. It is not enough that we secretly in our hearts recognize Jehovah as the true God; we must openly and under all circumstances and despite of all opposition, whether from magistrates or from philosophers, avow our faith in Him as the only living and true God. . . . The second or negative aspect of the command is the condemnation of the failure to recognize Jehovah as the true God; failing to believe in His existence and attributes, in His government and authority; failing to confess Him before men; and failing to render Him the inward reverence and the outward homage which are His due, that is, the first commandment forbids atheism whether theoretical or practical. It moreover forbids the recognition of any other than Jehovah as God. This includes the prohibition of ascribing to any other being divine attributes; rendering to any creature the homage or obedience due to God alone; or exercising toward any other person or object those feelings of love, confidence, and submission which belong of right only to God."

"If God is what He claims to be — He that will be, He that is, He that was— then He must be the supreme object of worship. If it be true that He is Jehovah, man's God, then the commandment is a reasonable one, and it must be a very unreasonable thing to have any other God beside Him. In the very necessity of the case, if the word spoken by God be true, then God is sufficient, and God *is God.* There cannot be two who fulfill that description of limitless life. Point to another god, and he must be limited. Every man needs a god. There is no man who has not, somewhere in his heart, in his life, in the essentials of his being, a shrine in which is a deity whom he worships. It is as impossible for a man to live without having an object of worship as it is for a bird to fly if it is taken out of the air. The very composition of human life, the mystery of man's being, demands a center of worship as a necessity of existence. All life is worship. There may be a false god at the center of the life; but every activity of being, all the energy of life, the devotion of powers — these things are all worship. The question is whether the life and powers of man are devoted to the worship of the true God or to that of a false one." — *G. Campbell Morgan.* "The most important thought a man has is his thought of God. In the rush and hurry of our lives we have few enough thoughts about Him. Days pass without the turning of our minds to Him. And yet it is true that our thought of God is the main formative thought we have. It determines our ideas of duty. If our thought leaves Him yonder, far away from the world, then our duty becomes a mechanical obedience to a system of laws. If our thought makes Him Father to us, always about us, always interested in us, then our duty becomes not mechanical, but the seeking and the doing of His will. Our thought of God determines our outlook on the world." — *C. B. McAfee.* Dr. McAfee adds that "this commandment involves three things which collide with much current thought. First, that God is a person, not an impersonal force; secondly, that there is a possibility of personal connection between God and man; thirdly, God has a claim upon the entire devotion of man."

2. THE PROHIBITION OF ALL FORMS OF IDOLATROUS WORSHIP, vs. 4–6. 4. **Thou shalt not make unto thee a graven image, nor any likeness *of any thing* that is in heaven above, or that is in the earth beneath, or that is in the water under the earth : 5. thou shalt not bow down thyself unto them, nor serve them ; for I Jehovah thy God am a jealous God, visiting the iniquity of the fathers upon the children, upon**

5. Thou shalt not bow down thyself unto them, nor serve them; for I Jehovah thy God am a jealous God, visiting the iniquity of the fathers upon the children, upon the third and upon the fourth generation of them that hate me,

6. And showing lovingkindness unto thousands of them that love me and keep my commandments.

---

the third and upon the fourth generation of them that hate me, 6. **and showing lovingkindness unto thousands of them that love me and keep my commandments.** The following magnificent interpretation of Professor Murphy should be carefully studied. "The second commandment refers to the worship of God. It guards the immateriality, or spirituality, of His nature. It opposes idolatry, that is, the worship of an idol or image of God, or of God through an idol. We are not to make, worship, or serve an idol. . . . The reason here assigned applies equally to the first and second commandments, and warrants the Masoretes in placing the verses (2–6) containing them in close contiguity. *A jealous God.* The passions of a moral being have their right as well as their wrong use. Hence anger, jealousy, hatred, and revenge are ascribed to God, not as passions, but as the feelings of a holy being in regard to that which is evil (Deut. 32 : 21, 22, 35). As the Judge of the universe, God has the supreme right not only to entertain these feelings, but also to carry out their holy behests in the administration of His everlasting dominion. The *iniquity* here spoken of is that of polytheism or idolatry, of having or making any other God. For the idol, or the being it represents, is not the true God, but another god, after the fashion of a vain imagination (Rom. 1 : 21–25). He that makes and worships an idol has lost the knowledge of the true God. This iniquity is called the iniquity of *the fathers*, inasmuch as it originates with them, and is only perpetuated in the sons who adhere to it. The history of the world shows that the ungodliness of the fathers is, as a rule of fallen nature, followed by the sons. Only grace interrupts the succession of sin. *Upon the sons, upon the third and upon the fourth generation.* This is a timely guard against a common error to which men have been prone in all ages, namely, that the opinions and customs of their forefathers, even though they be wrong, are an excuse or justification for the sons walking in the same errors of judgment and conduct. The fathers will have to account for their own iniquity, not only as men, but as fathers setting a bad example to their household. But the sons who, on arriving at the exercise of a natural judgment, walk in the same iniquity will be treated as responsible beings, and visited for the iniquity which they have made their own. Many evil consequences, indeed, such as poverty, disease, and infamy, befall the children of ungodly and vicious parents. . . . Mercy is that form of the divine goodness which reason dare not affirm and revelation alone can proclaim. And to show mercy or do kindness, not to requite merit or reward righteousness, is the most favorable language that can be employed concerning any portion of a fallen race. It forms the contrast here to 'visiting iniquity.' . . . The comforting promise is that God will never fail to show mercy to all successive generations that humbly and thankfully own Him for their God. The objects of the divine mercy are those who have the Lord for their God, and worship Him in spirit and in truth. They meet His mercy with an earnest, confiding gratitude; and this feeling displays itself in 'loving him and keeping his commandments.' There is an intense interest connected with the expression 'them that love me.' It plainly intimates that those who have no other God before the true God, and make no other God beside Him, are those who at the same time love Him." — *James G. Murphy.*

"There is in the human mind a perilous tendency to worship idols, which needs to be incessantly resisted. Israel was constantly starting aside into idolatry like a broken bow. Even in the wilderness they took up the tabernacle of Moloch and the star of their god Remphan, images which they had made to worship. . . . All Scripture rings with denunciations of idolatry. Its poets and prophets pursue every form of idol with a burning storm of irony and indignation. If idolatry were an extinct temptation, half of Scripture would only retain an historic interest. Alas! the temptation to idolatry, objective and subjective, open and secret, is still powerful. Men are too carnal, too sensuous, too inherently superstitious to be content with a pure, simple, spiritual religion. They always try to explain away the one fundamental message of Scripture, that religion means 'a good mind and a good life.' It is so much easier to bow the head than to cleanse the heart; so much easier to

7. Thou shalt not take the name of Jehovah thy God in vain; for Jehovah will not hold him guiltless that taketh his name in vain.

multiply services than to be kind, and truthful, and humble. Hence the eternal Pharisaism which tempts them to teach that what God cares for is sacrifice, not mercy; fasting, not charity; orthodoxy, not goodness; instrumentals, not fundamentals; rites, ceremonies, genuflexions, shibboleths, scrupulosities of outward observance, not the being meek, and pure, and just." — *F. W. Farrar*. "It is a solemn thing thus to pass on to children a wrong conception of God; it is the most awful thing a man can do. Men often take lower ground, and talk about passing to their children evil forces and habits. Nothing can minimize the awfulness of such conduct; but here is the root of it all. When a man puts something, as the object of his worship, in the place of God, he passes on the same practice to his offspring. What a terrible heritage he is thus handing down to the child!" — *G. Campbell Morgan*. "Why is it right for God to be jealous, and very wrong for us to be jealous? I will show you. Supposing anybody gets more good things than you, and you feel jealous about it, it is as much as to say, 'I ought to have all that.' But *you* ought not to have all that. But *God* ought to have everything. Therefore, if you are displeased because you have not got something that you have no business to have, you have no right to be so. But God has a right to have everything. Therefore, if anybody does not give anybody what he has a right to have, he has a right to be 'jealous'; but if we do not give somebody what he has not a right to receive, he has no right to be jealous. 'God is jealous.' 'Thou shalt have none other gods but me.'" — *James Vaughn*.

3. THE REVERENT USE OF GOD'S NAME, v. 7. 7. **Thou shalt not take the name of Jehovah thy God in vain; for Jehovah will not hold him guiltless that taketh his name in vain.** "The word *name* is used in reference to God in a very comprehensive sense. It often means a personal or individual designation; as when God says, 'This is my name,' *i.e.*, Jehovah. Frequently the name of God is equivalent to God Himself. To call on the name of the Lord, and to call on God, are synonymous forms of expression. As names are intended to distinguish one person or thing from another, anything distinguishing or characteristic may be included under the term. The name of God, therefore, includes everything by which He makes Himself known. This commandment, therefore, forbids all irrèverence toward God; not only the highest act of irreverence in calling on Him to bear witness to falsehood, but also all irreverent use of His name; all careless, unnecessary reference to Him, or His attributes; all indecorous conduct in His worship; and in short, every indication of the want of that fear, reverence, and awe due to a Being infinite in all His perfections, on whom we are absolutely dependent, and to whom we are accountable for our character and conduct. The third commandment, therefore, specially forbids not only perjury, but also all profane, or unnecessary oaths, all careless appeals to God, and all irreverent use of His name. All literature, whether profane or Christian, shows how strong is the tendency in human nature to introduce the name of God even on the most trivial occasions. Not only are those formulas, such as Adieu, Goodby, or God be with you, and God forbid, which may have had a pious origin, constantly used without any recognition of their true import, but even persons professing to fear God often allow themselves to use His name as a mere expression of surprise. God is everywhere present. He hears all we say. He is worthy of the highest reverence; and He will not hold him guiltless who on any occasion uses His name irreverently." — *Charles Hodge*.

"When Jesus lays on our lip the prayer, 'Hallowed be thy name,' He teaches us to 'sanctify God in our hearts' that He alone may be our 'fear.' I cannot resist a painful impression that much of our current religion errs through want of reverence. We come with unprepared minds to the holiest services. . . . We prattle glibly, with an easy familiarity, about the names of Persons before whom archangels bow. We are not ashamed sometimes to mimic in our worship the artifices of the showman, and to rival the attractions of the music hall. . . . A spirit inwardly sensitive to the real solemnity of God — a heart that secretly bows down in earnest awe before the holiness of Him who is utterly and inconceivably above us — a silent shrinking of the soul from any rash or light familiarity with One, the latchet of whose shoes, even while He walked the earth, none of us was worthy to untie — this would be a happy improvement on much that offends in modern Protestantism." — *J. O. Dykes*.

"I have read of a poor heathen woman, who was being taught to read, when she

MATTHEW 4 : 10. Then saith Jesus unto him, Get thee hence, Satan: for it is written, Thou shalt worship the Lord thy God, and him only shalt thou serve.

was very old. It was a long time before she could read. At last she was able to pronounce one-syllable words. And one day she came to the name of God, and she looked up to the missionary, who was teaching her, and she said, 'Is that the Great Name? Is that the Name of the *Great Massa* of us all?' 'Yes, it is,' he replied. She lifted up her hands, tears came down her cheeks, and she said, 'Oh, to think that such a poor, wicked, ignorant woman as I am should be allowed to live to read that Great Name of God! Thank God that I can read the Great Name of God.' See how she reverenced the Name. . . . What would you say is about the most horrible thing in all the world? I should say swearing. I hope I am not speaking to any one who swears! Horrible! Why, if it was only your own father, and you were to hear people taking your father's name in vain, speaking irreverently and blasphemously of your father, could you bear such a person? But when it is the great God of us all — it is horrible! Other sins which a person does may bring him something or other, but what good does swearing do to anybody? I will tell you what I have heard. A gentleman heard another one swearing. And he came to him and said, 'Sir, what does the Devil pay you for swearing?' He said, 'I do not know that the Devil pays me anything.' 'Does not he pay you anything, and you give up being a gentleman, and give up being respectable, and pain everybody that hears you, and you lose your own soul, and the Devil gives you nothing! You do work cheap.'" — *James Vaughan.*

The editor believes that the teacher, if he himself is living according to these commandments, and can therefore speak on them with conviction, ought to drive home with all the force and power he has the need for reverence in all those experiences of life which directly involve our worship of God and our speaking of holy things. One can never be too reverent in his own life; one can never be too careful in using reverent language. This is especially true as we speak before children. The editor had this whole matter most powerfully brought to his own attention just recently. About a year ago he was invited to the home of a well-known merchant, in the suburbs of the city where he lives. While visiting during the afternoon, it was necessary for the head of the home to drive into the village on an errand, and he took along his four-year-old daughter. The editor hesitates to confess this, but he must, to make use of the illustration. While in the car, for some reason now forgotten, the editor used the word "gosh," and at once the little girl said, "Oh, you shouldn't use that word. My mother says that is a bad word." Of course, I was rebuked, and justly so. But, a year later, I went back to that home, and the moment I got out of the car, the little five-year-old said, "You are the man that said 'gosh.'" How tragic that the little ones so clearly remember our weaknesses, and our mistakes, and identify us with them!

Christ Tempted by Satan. Cornicelius.

II. **OUR LORD'S TRIUMPH OVER SATAN'S MOST SUBTLE TEMPTATION IN THE TRUTH CONCERNING THE WORSHIP OF GOD,** Matt. 4 : 10. 10. **Then saith Jesus unto him, Get thee hence, Satan: for it is written, Thou shalt worship the Lord thy God, and him**

MATTHEW 6 : 9. After this manner therefore pray ye: Our Father who art in heaven, Hallowed be thy name.

only shalt thou serve. These words occurred in the third and last of the series of temptations which Satan used during this long forty-day period in the wilderness in attempting to draw Christ the Son of God from perfect obedience to the divine will on the threshold of the Saviour's ministry. If Satan had succeeded n any one of these temptations, the work of the Saviour could never even be undertaken. He would have been a sinning man. In this last temptation Satan told the Lord that he would give Him all the kingdoms of the world if the Lord would fall down and worship him. Christ immediately answered him, crushingly so, with finality, without any argument, by quoting the commandment of Deuteronomy 6 : 13. Of course, He could not bow down and worship Satan. The Word of God says that God only is to be worshiped. Not only men knew that, but Christ knew it, supremely, for He was the Son of God. I sometimes think that Satan here attempted the most foolish thing he ever undertook in all of his foul career, for if there was one thing above everything else that Christ would insist upon, it would be that no one but God should be worshiped. Whenever we do what Satan wants us to do, then Satan has taken the place of God for us, and we have put Satan's will before God's will. Whenever we bow down to anything, that are we the servant of.

III. **THE HALLOWING OF GOD'S NAME,** Matt. 6 : 9. 9. **After this manner therefore pray ye: Our Father who art in heaven, Hallowed be thy name.** The Lord's prayer, like the Ten Commandments, divides into two parts. The first part refers to God, the second part to men. Of the seven petitions in the Lord's prayer, it is the first three that fundamentally have to do with God, His name, His kingdom, His will. The first thing that our Lord would have us utter in our prayer is this line of adoration, which He puts first, because it is of first importance. As Luther said: " It is indeed a short saying, but its sense is as broad as the world: it speaks against all false doctrine and all false living." Dr. P. T. Forsyth somewhere says: " If we take the Lord's prayer alone, God's holiness is the interest which all the rest of it serves." Now, as we have noted before, the name of anything is that by which we know that particular object. It is that which differentiates it from all other objects or characteristics. The name of God is that by which God has chosen to reveal Himself to us. El Shaddai means Almighty God; Jehovah-Nissi means the Lord our banner; the Father means a God of love and tenderness. Christ came to reveal the Father's name to us (John 17 : 6). This English word *hallowed* is from an Anglo-Saxon word meaning " holy," " to make holy," and is found only here in the New Testament. In the Greek the word means the same thing, " to render, or to declare sacred or holy," and thus, to consecrate. It is found in many places in the New Testament (*e.g.*, Matt. 23 : 17, 19; John 17 : 17, 19). This means then that the name of God is to be considered as holy, and is to be hallowed or sanctified in our own life; that is, in every aspect of life wherein God's name is used, either in prayer, or in public speech, or in even our thinking of God, the name is to be used with utmost reverence. But more than that, we are to hallow His name in every relationship of life, in our homes, social life, public life, every place we go, and in everything we undertake. Our life, if we are Christians, either defiles the name of God before others, or sanctifies it. Either we honor God, or we dishonor Him. If then we mean this when we are praying, we are asking God that in all we do we may exalt, revere, and honor His holy name. " Of the petitions which are included in this prayer, none has been less prayed than this which our Lord sets first. Many a man has cried earnestly and sincerely enough, ' Give me this day my daily bread '; many with deeper earnestness, and out of a more appalling helplessness, have cried, ' Deliver us from evil '; but few have learned to have this petition deepest in the heart and readiest on the lip, ' Hallowed be thy name.' At all times we recognize it as very proper, but rather as a doing of homage to Him we invoke than as the first soaring petition, in which the spirit, feeling its liberty and rejoicing in the wealth of its prospect, rises at once to the very summit of all desire." — *Marcus Dods.* " There is something here that strikes us at once. While we ordinarily first bring our own needs to God in prayer, and then think of what belongs to God and His interests, the Lord reverses the order. First, *Thy* name, *Thy* kingdom, *Thy* will; then, give *us*, forgive *us*, lead *us*, deliver *us*. The lesson is of more importance than we think. In true worship the Father must be first, must be all. The sooner I learn to forget myself in the desire that He may be glorified, the richer will the

JOHN 4 : 23. But the hour cometh, and now is, when the true worshippers shall worship the Father in spirit and truth: for such doth the Father seek to be his worshippers.

24. God is a Spirit: and they that worship him must worship in spirit and truth.

---

blessing be that prayer will bring to myself. No one ever loses by what he sacrifices for the Father." — *Andrew Murray.*

IV. **HOW TO WORSHIP GOD ACCEPTABLY,** John 4 : 23, 24. 23. **But the hour cometh, and now is, when the true worshippers shall worship the Father in spirit and truth: for such doth the Father seek to be his worshippers.** 24. **God is a Spirit: and they that worship him must worship in spirit and truth.** The words of that great scholar, Dr. James Hope Moulton, are especially valuable here. "It is difficult to exhaust the meaning of these words, but we must start from the two thoughts of the verses which immediately precede: the first and chief points in the interpretation are — not in sacred place but in spirit (v. 21), not in imperfection of knowledge but in truth (v. 22). The very name by which Jesus indicates the object of all worship, 'the Father' (a name no longer used of a chosen *nation*, but offering to *each man* a *personal* relation to God), had prepared the way for the abolition of all limitations of place: the teaching is completed here, when man's spirit is declared to be the 'hallowed ground' where he may approach his Father and his God. The law had been but a shadow of the good things to come, and not the very image of the things (Heb. 10 : 1); type and figure concealed while they revealed the future blessing. But 'the hour now is' when the truth of God is revealed — 'truth' as well as 'grace' has come (1 : 17); and (in the full knowledge of it) worship may now be offered to the Father. The Son appearing as the revealer of the Father, Himself the Truth, Himself giving to men the Holy Spirit who alone can hallow man's spirit as the sanctuary of worship — all these thoughts cannot but press on us as we read this verse. . . . No other worship than that which is offered in spirit and truth can possibly be actual worship of God. . . . Not the outward action of the worshiper, not the forms he uses or the gifts he brings, but his spirit alone can be brought to meet the spiritual presence of God. Where this is done, God Himself meets the spirit which He has sought and prepared, and to which He has made known the truth lying at the foundation of all worship, the truth which reveals Himself. In this wonderful passage are concentrated many of the most essential truths of New Testament teaching. The historical development of God's plan, the preparation for Christianity made by Judaism, the idea of progress from the outward to the inward, from the sensuous to the spiritual (cf. 1 Cor. 15 : 46), the independence of forms which marks the essence of religion, and yet its freedom to clothe itself in form so long as the spirit is not lost — these are the lessons taught here; and however special the form in which they are presented, they are in perfect accord with the whole course of New Testament doctrine. The main principles of these verses would be understood by the woman to whom our Lord was speaking."

"As God is Spirit, not bound by space or time, but in His infinite perfection always and everywhere the same, so His worship would henceforth no longer be confined by place or form, but spiritual as God Himself is spiritual. How much our Christianity suffers from this, that it is confined to certain times and places. Our worship must be in spirit and truth: His worship must be the spirit of our life; our life must be worship in spirit as God is Spirit. . . . Jesus is 'the only begotten of the Father, *full* of grace and *truth*.' In the Old Testament all was shadow and promise; Jesus brought and gives the reality, the substance, of things hoped for. In Him the blessings and powers of the eternal life are our actual possession and experience. Jesus is full of grace and truth; the Holy Spirit is the Spirit of truth; through Him the grace that is in Jesus is ours in deed and truth, a positive communication out of the divine life. And so worship in spirit is worship in truth; actual living fellowship with God, a real correspondence and harmony between the Father, who is a Spirit, and the child praying in the spirit." — *Andrew Murray.*

In looking over this lesson, it seems to the editor that the three main sins here condemned are these: First, leaving God out of our life, denying to Him the place, the honor and worship due His holy name; secondly, the wrong kind of worship, an artificial, superficial, mechanical, materialistic worship, involving all forms of liberty and ritual, leading to the worship of images, pictures, and icons; the dependence upon the senses, incense for the nostrils, the rosary for the fingers, gorgeous adornments for the eyes, and the tinkling of altar bells for the ears, etc., etc., so that ultimately, worship is attached to material exercises, and God Himself is never reached; finally, the careless, irreverent, coarse, common, degrading use of all the divine names and substitutes for them, coarsening our talk, lowering our conception of Deity, and weakening our very capacity for true spiritual communion.

What reasons would you suggest why the commandments relating to our adoration of God appear in the Decalogue before the commandments which deal with our relation to our fellow men? Do you see any significance in the fact that the Lord's Prayer begins with the truth of God as it relates to our own life, just as the Ten Commandments begin with this truth? What one book in the Bible begins with the word God? (The Epistle to the Hebrews.) How can a man make the things of this world to be his God, and when he does, what happens to that man? (One should carefully read the last half of the first chapter of Romans on this.) Do you think a person can go through all the forms of worship, singing audibly, prayer, bowing the knee, listening to a sermon, putting something in the collection plate, being faithful in the house of God, and still not truly worship God? How does hallowing the name of God lead to the sanctifying of all of life? In what way are even little children frequently irreverent? Do you think that silence on our part in church after we are seated just preceding the beginning of the service, is a help toward the reverent worship of God?

LESSON III. — October 17.

JESUS AND THE SABBATH. — Exodus 20 : 8–11; Isaiah 58 : 13, 14; Mark 2 : 23—3 : 6.

GOLDEN TEXT. — *And he said unto them, The sabbath was made for man, and not man for the sabbath.* MARK 2 : 27.

Devotional Reading: Psalm 1.
Beginner Topic: THE FRIEND IN GOD'S HOUSE.
Lesson Material: Mark 3 : 1–5.
Memory Verse: Jehovah is good to all. Psalm 145 : 9.
Primary Topic: GOD'S HOLY DAY.
Lesson Material: Exodus 20 : 8–11; Mark 2 : 23—3 : 6.
Memory Verse: Remember the sabbath day, to keep it holy. Exodus 20 : 8.
Junior Topic: ON GOD'S HOLY DAY.
Lesson Material: Exodus 20 : 8–11; Mark 2 : 23—3 : 6.
Memory Verse: The Son of man is Lord even of the sabbath. Mark 2 : 28.
Intermediate and Senior Topic: WHAT TO DO ON THE SABBATH.
Topic for Young People and Adults: THE SABBATH IN OUR COMMUNITY.

THE TEACHER AND HIS CLASS.

The Younger Classes will enter into the meaning of this lesson more easily if they are reminded that all of us have bodies which need care, minds which need instruction, and souls made for God. We take care of our bodies by exercise, food, and sleep, at certain appointed times; and we provide the necessities of food, shelter, and clothing by hours of work. We cultivate our minds by long years at school, and by reading and studying in the years that follow. Now, our souls are made for God, and they too need certain set times when they approach God, when they are in communion with Him. Just as our life has certain times for work, sleep, recreation, and social fellowship, so do we need certain times for the special worship of God and meditation upon His Word. That is what the *Sabbath* day is for.

The Older Classes will especially need this lesson, because of the many tremendous forces now at work in our country, directly or indirectly, invading the *Lord's Day.* Movies are now open on Sunday all over the country; the necessities for vast production during this time of war is compelling men to work seven days a week; the strain of life seems to persuade men that on the seventh day they should give themselves almost entirely to rest and sport, and consequently church is eliminated. Furthermore, the decline in worthwhile preaching, and the insipidity and shallowness of many of our services, are keeping people away from church, because they do not seem to get anything there that they find necessary for life. Soon, if the tire shortage continues, many people will not be able to drive to church, and they will then use this as an excuse for not going up to the house of the Lord. So, with these enemies of the Lord's Day at work, we need soberly to remember what the Word of God has to say about this day.

THE PLAN OF THE LESSON.

SUBJECT: The One Day of the Week Which God Has Given to Men for Release from Work and for Worship, and What This Day Meant in the Life of the Son of God.

I. THE LAW OF THE SABBATH, Exod. 20 : 8–11; Isa. 58 : 13, 14.

1. The holiness with which the day should be kept, Exod. 20 : 8.
2. Freedom from labor should mark the Sabbath day, 20 : 9, 10.
3. The relation of the Sabbath to the creation, 20 : 11.
4. The joy that we should have in the true observance of the Sabbath, Isa. 58 : 13.
5. Promises relating to the true observance of this day, 58 : 14.

II. JESUS AND THE SABBATH DAY, Mark 2 : 23—3 : 6.

1. Some teachings about the Sabbath, 2 : 23–27.
2. The Son of Man is the Lord of the Sabbath, 2 : 28.
3. A miracle performed on the Sabbath, 3 : 1–6.

THE LESSON IN ITS SETTING.

Time. — The Ten Commandments were delivered in 1445 B.C.; the prophecy taken from Isaiah was spoken about 698 B.C.; the words here quoted from our Lord were uttered in the early summer of A.D. 28.

Place. — The Ten Commandments were given on Mount Sinai; Isaiah's prophecy, in Jerusalem; our Lord's discourse on the Sabbath took place not far from Capernaum.

THE TEACHER'S LIBRARY.

On the entire subject of the Sabbath, one should consult all books on the Ten Commandments, and the more important commentaries on the Book of Exodus. See, especially, John Calvin's *Commentaries on the Last Four Books of Moses*, Vol. 2, 432–472, and articles in all Biblical encyclopedias under the subject, "Sabbath." In addition, the following books might be consulted with profit: R. H. Horton: *The Day;* W. W. Davis: *The Day of Worship;* Paul Cotton: *From Sabbath to Sunday;* R. J. Floody: *Scientific Basis of Sabbath and Sunday;* James Gilfilian: *The Sabbath in the Light of Recent Revelation and History;* J. A. Hessey: *Sunday: Its Origin, History, and Present Obligation.* There is a good chapter on the Sabbath Day in George Boardman: *The Creative Week*, 251–272. On the passage taken from Isaiah, see, especially, the commentaries by Delitzsch, Calvin, and Bush, and, in addition, Thomas Chalmers: *Sermons and Addresses*, 51–59; D. J. Burrell: *The Golden Passional*, 306–317.

On the passage taken from Mark's Gospel, all commentaries on that Gospel will be found helpful, and most lives of Christ. Especially one should consult F. W. Farrar's *Life of Christ*, chapter 31. Likewise, most books on Christ's miracles will be found helpful here. On 2 : 23, see F. F. Shannon: *The New Greatness*, 18–31; on verses 1–5, D. J. Burrell: *The Wondrous Cross*, 23–46; on verse 4, H. W. Morrow: *Questions Asked and Answered by Our Lord*, 179–184; G. Campbell Morgan: *Westminster Pulpit*, Vol. 6, 377–384; Joseph Parker: *The City Temple Pulpit*, Vol. 4, 184–191; on verse 3 : 5, J. H. Jowett: *The Friend on the Road*, 73–75; Alexander Maclaren: *Expositions of Holy Scripture, Mark 1–8*, 94–104. On Jewish laws and the Sabbath, see Alfred Edersheim: *The Life and Times of Jesus the Messiah*, Vol. 2, 777–787; on our Lord's teachings on the Sabbath, see R. C. Trench: *Notes on the Miracles*, 330–338; D. J. Burrell: *The Wonderful Teacher*, 209–219; and an excellent article, "Sabbath," by F. E. Robinson, in James Hastings: *Dictionary of Christ and the Gospels*, Vol. 2, 540–542.

EXODUS 20 : 8. Remember the sabbath day, to keep it holy.

I. **THE LAW OF THE SABBATH,** Exod. 20 : 8–11; Isa. 58 : 13, 14. "This grand compendium of law now descends from the personal rights of God to the day of His rest. The former precepts are purely moral; the fourth is partly moral and partly positive. The principle that man's time should be divided between labor under the eye of God and leisure for the solemnities of His worship is moral. The apportionment according to the example of God is positive. The first three precepts are of universal obligation whenever and wherever there is a rational creature. The fourth is specially binding on man, being founded on the six days' work and the seventh day's rest in that creation of which he formed the crowning part. It is therefore to him of perpetual significance and obligation. Referring to a day of rest for appearing before God, it inculcates religion and prohibits secularity." — *James G. Murphy.*

1. THE HOLINESS WITH WHICH THE DAY SHOULD BE KEPT, Exod. 20 : 8. 8. **Remember the sabbath day, to keep it holy.** The fourth commandment begins with the significant word, *Remember*, and Dr. Cleland McAfee has well said that this "is frank recognition that there will be diverting arguments. It will be easy to forget, easy to become engrossed with other matters and so lose our sense of the holiness of the day. Whatever your theory about the Sabbath day and what you

9. Six days shalt thou labor, and do all thy work;
10. But the seventh day is a sabbath unto Jehovah thy God: *in it* thou
shalt not do any work, thou, nor thy son, nor thy daughter, thy man-servant,
nor thy maid-servant, nor thy cattle, nor thy stranger that is within thy
gates:

---

may or may not do in it, be sure that you remember that it is a day to be kept holy to God. It is striking that no other commandment opens in this way. There is no danger that we will forget that we must not kill and steal and lie. We know with no one's reminder that we must not. But we are strangely ready to confuse ourselves regarding the Sabbath day." To "hallow" the seventh day means to set it apart from the rest of time for sacred rest and recreation. The word Sabbath itself means *seventh*, and that is why the name was given to the seventh day.

2. FREEDOM FROM LABOR SHOULD MARK THE SABBATH DAY, 20 : 9, 10. 9. **Six days shalt thou labor, and do all thy work;** 10. **but the seventh day is a sabbath unto Jehovah thy God:** ***in it*** **thou shalt not do any work, thou, nor thy son, nor thy daughter, thy man-servant, nor thy maid-servant, nor thy cattle, nor thy stranger that is within thy gates.** "There is here an injunction to labor in so far as it is necessary for the support of life. There is at the same time a permission to employ six successive days in labor. Experience proves that this is more than sufficient for raising from the ground the sustenance needful for man. Work or business is a more extensive term than labor. The latter refers to outdoor work, or manual labor, requiring effort and entailing toil; the former includes, moreover, the routine of domestic operations, the management of affairs, the transactions of buying and selling, and all that is usually meant by the term 'business.' While six days are allowed for business, the seventh is assigned to leisure. The number seven has acquired a typical sacredness from its application to the Sabbath. The rest of God after six days of creative activity, in which a habitation was prepared, and man, the intended inhabitant, created, is the historical foundation for the Sabbath. But the proportion of time for labor and for rest is not only derived from the history but adapted to the nature of man. The operations of the corporeal frame consist of three parts: first, that which is involuntary and without intermission, as the action of the heart and other internal functionaries of the vital organism; second, that which is instinctive, as the travail of the animal powers in search of food, shelter, and other natural requirements; and third, that which is rational, as the effort to attain a certain end beyond the merely animal wants. The first part of the movement is kept in constant vigor by the regular supply of food. The second has its recompense in the natural repose of sleep. The third remains over, to be relieved by a recurring period of rest to be determined by reason. As on the whole about a third part of the exertion of our powers may be due to this last source, and that for the half of the natural day, it follows that a sixth part of each natural day needs its compensating repose. After six days, therefore, a seventh day of rest seems needful to repair the waste and weariness accruing from voluntary rational effort. At all events the special activity of the rational powers evidently stands in need of being recruited by a third provision, not of the animal, but of the rational nature, and that is plainly the Sabbath. *A Sabbath to the Lord thy God.* Rest and dedication to God are the properties here assigned to the Sabbath. The observance of the Sabbath connects man with the origin of his race, with the six days' creation, and with the Creator Himself. The connection is manifestly an historical one. The Sabbath thus becomes a sign by which the believers in an historical revelation are distinguished from those who have allowed these great facts to fade from their remembrance (31 : 13). The leisure of the Sabbath day, moreover, affords the opportunity for the holy convocation, and for the public and private exercises of praise, prayer, reading, expounding, and applying the Word of God." — *J. G. Murphy.* "That *rest* was the primary conception of Sabbath observances may be seen in the following passages: Exodus 16 : 22–30; 23 : 12; 31 : 13–17; 35 : 1–3; Leviticus 23 : 3; Deuteronomy 5 : 15; 16 : 8. The rest was to be from field work, vine-dressing, bearing burdens, buying and selling, gathering wood (Num. 15 : 32–36), and kindling fires (Exod. 35 : 3; Jeremiah 18 : 21; Amos 8 : 5). See further Nehemiah 13 : 15–22; Isaiah 56 : 2, 6, 7; 58 : 13, 14; Jeremiah 17 : 21–27; Ezekiel 20 : 12, 20." — *F. W. Farrar.* "He who never works is unfitted for worship, and he who never pauses to worship is rendered incapable of work." — *G. Campbell Morgan.*

11. For in six days Jehovah made heaven and earth, the sea, and all that in them is, and rested the seventh day: wherefore Jehovah blessed the sabbath day, and hallowed it.

3. THE RELATION OF THE SABBATH TO THE CREATION, 20 : 11. 11. **For in six days Jehovah made heaven and earth, the sea, and all that in them is, and rested the seventh day: wherefore Jehovah blessed the sabbath day, and hallowed it.** "God requires a rational service. The reason is historical. It refers to the original division of time into six days of work and a seventh day of rest on the occasion of the creation of man (Gen. 2 : 1–3). Reminding him of his exalted origin and bringing him into contact with his Maker, it awakens in his breast all those feelings of joy and thankfulness which the possession of conscious being naturally evokes. From the essence of God we naturally pass to his action. As the former three precepts indicate his intrinsic essence, so the fourth reveals the foundation of his authority over the creature. The act of creation is the origin of all title to the creature and to the obedience of the intelligent creation. The creation of man is commemorated in the fourth commandment. Hence it contains the fountain-head of all authority in God and all duty in man. The former three are negative. This is affirmative. The former regard eternity. This refers to time. The former three commands relate exclusively to God. The fourth introduces man on the stage of existence. It forms, therefore, the natural transition from the rights of God to those of man." — *J. G. Murphy.*

THE SABBATH DAY SHOULD BE A TIME WHEN WE ARE SPIRITUALLY OCCUPIED.

"Let our Sunday rest be neither sensual, nor frivolous, nor selfish, but gladly spiritual: a day of Christian worship and Christian thought; a day not only to rest but to ennoble; a day to remind us who we are, and whither we go, and whence we come. 'Hallow my Sabbaths,' saith the Lord, 'and they shall be a sign between

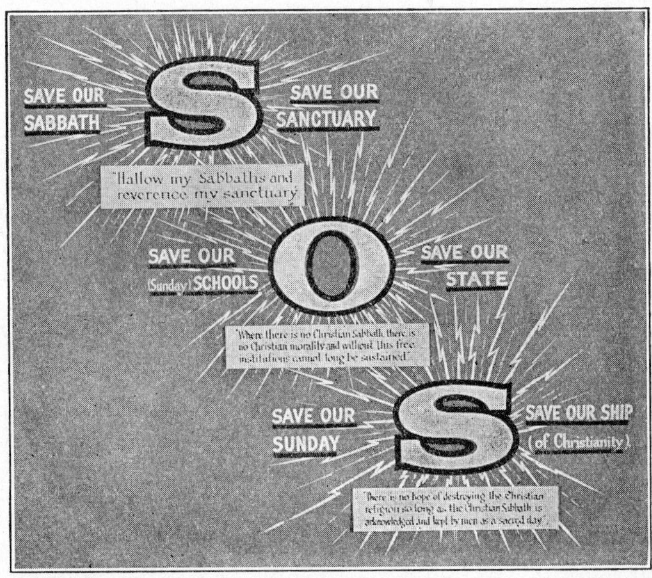

me and you, that I am the Lord your God.' We are all the children of the Most High, and the spiritual life, with its divine aspirations and bright-winged hopes, is, it has been truly said, 'not the one which we habitually lead. Beside and around us is the world, with its labors and cares, and pomps and vanities; before us is Virtue, Duty, Eternity. The Sabbath is a bridge thrown across life's troubled waters, over which we may pass to reach the opposite shore. For as the Sabbath calls on

ISAIAH 58 : 13. If thou turn away thy foot from the sabbath, from doing thy pleasure on my holy day; and call the sabbath a delight, *and* the holy of Jehovah honorable; and shalt honor it, not doing thine own ways, nor finding thine own pleasure, nor speaking *thine own* words:

the worldly to give place to the spiritual, and to lay aside the cares and labors of earth for the repose and holiness of heaven, so it is but a type of the eternal day, when the freed spirit, if it be true to itself and to God, shall put on forever its robe of immortal holiness and joy." — *F. W. Farrar.*

THE PURPOSE OF GOD IN GIVING US THE SEVENTH DAY FOR WORSHIP AND REST.

"The design of the fourth commandment was (1) to commemorate the work of creation. (2) To preserve alive the knowledge of the only living and true God. If heaven and earth, that is, the universe, were created, they must have had a creator. So long, therefore, as men believe in creation, they must believe in God. This accounts for the fact that so much stress is laid upon the right observance of the Sabbath. (3) This command was designed to arrest the current of the outward life of the people and to turn their thoughts to the unseen and spiritual. It was of the highest importance that there should be one day of frequent occurrence on which they were forbidden to think of the things of the world, and forced to think of the things unseen and eternal. (4) It was intended to afford time for the instruction of the people, and for the public and special worship of God. (5) By the prohibition of all servile labor, whether of man or beast, it was designed to secure recuperative rest for those on whom the primeval curse had fallen: 'In the sweat of thy face shalt thou eat bread.' (6) As a day of rest and as set apart for intercourse with God, it was designed to be a type of that rest which remains for the people of God, as we learn from Psalm 95 : 11, as expounded by the apostle in Hebrews 4 : 1–10." — *Charles Hodge.*

HOW TO OBSERVE THE SEVENTH DAY.

"Let each of us lay this well to heart that our Sabbaths are a gift from our kind Father of quite unspeakable value. They do make stepping-stones for our feet to walk to heaven by. They open to us at the wayside so many oratories and Bethel-like retreats where we may refresh our jaded spiritual nature, cultivate closer acquaintance with Christ, offer to God a less hurried praise, clear ourselves from the dust of time, re-examine the foundations of our confidence, scrutinize our motives, repair our faults, and revive our drooping ardor in a task of self-discipline for eternal bliss." — *J. O. Dykes.* "Let it be said very earnestly to young men and women, that the Sabbath stands at the parting of the ways in the lives of such as they are. Its observance measures the development of the spiritual life. Usually the non-observance of the day begins very gradually, and seems defensible, but it is the beginning, and the end is not far away. Guard all the hours of the day jealously. You can afford to be over-cautious rather than careless. Keep the day for the purpose for which it was given — for rest and for the culture of real manhood." — *C. McAfee.*

4. THE JOY THAT WE SHOULD HAVE IN THE TRUE OBSERVANCE OF THE SABBATH, Isa. 58 : 13. 13. **If thou turn away thy foot from the sabbath, from doing thy pleasure on my holy day.** "The foot is spoken of as the instrument of motion and travel. 'Ponder the paths of thy feet' (Prov. 4 : 26). That is, observe attentively thy goings. 'Remove thy foot from evil' (Prov. 4 : 27). That is, abstain from evil; do not go to execute evil. So here, to restrain the foot *from* the Sabbath, is not to have the foot employed on the Sabbath; not to be engaged in traveling, or in the ordinary active employments of life, either for business or for pleasure. . . . We are not to do our own pleasure on that day. That is, we are not to pursue our ordinary plans of amusement; we are not to devote it to feasting, to riot, or to revelry. It is true that they who love the Sabbath as they should will find pleasure in observing it — for they have happiness in the service of God. But the idea is, here, that we are to do the things which God requires, and to consult His will in the observance. It is remarkable that the thing here adverted to is the very way in which the Sabbath is commonly violated. It is not extensively a day of business — for the propriety of a periodical cessation from toil is so obvious that men *will* have

14. Then shalt thou delight thyself in Jehovah; and I will make thee to ride upon the high places of the earth; and I will feed thee with the heritage of Jacob thy father: for the mouth of Jehovah hath spoken it.

MARK 2 : 23. And it came to pass, that he was going on the sabbath day through the grainfields; and his disciples began, as they went, to pluck the ears.

24. And the Pharisees said unto him, Behold, why do they on the sabbath day that which is not lawful?

---

such days recurring at moderate intervals. But it is a day of pastime and amusement; a day not merely of relaxation from the restraints of temperance and virtue. And while the Sabbath is God's great ordinance for perpetuating religion and virtue, it is also, by perversion, made Satan's great ordinance for perpetuating intemperance, dissipation, and sensuality." — *Albert Barnes.* **And call the sabbath a delight, *and* the holy of Jehovah honorable; and shalt honor it, not doing thine own ways, nor finding thine own pleasure, nor speaking *thine own* words.** "This word *delight* must be viewed as referring to God, and not to men; because nothing can be more pleasing or acceptable to God than the observation of the Sabbath and sincere worship. Whoever wishes to serve God in a proper manner, must altogether renounce his flesh and his will. And hence we see the reason why God so highly recommends, in the whole Scripture, the observation of the Sabbath; for He contemplated something higher than the outward ceremony, that is, indolence and repose, in which the Jews thought that the greatest holiness consisted. On the contrary, He commanded the Jews to renounce the desires of the flesh, to give up their sinful inclinations, and to yield obedience to Him; as no man can meditate on the heavenly life, unless he be dead to the world and to himself. Now, although that ceremony has been abolished, nevertheless the truth remains; because Christ died and rose again, so that we have a continual sabbath; that is, we are released from our works, that the Spirit of God may work mightily in us." — *John Calvin.*

The Biggest Step in Any Man's Life.

5. PROMISES RELATING TO THE TRUE OBSERVANCE OF THIS DAY, Isa. 58 : 14. 14. **Then shalt thou delight thyself in Jehovah; and I will make thee to ride upon the high places of the earth; and I will feed thee with the heritage of Jacob thy father: for the mouth of Jehovah hath spoken it.** "It is on that day, set apart by His own authority for His own service, that He chooses to meet with His people, and to commune with them and bless them; and no one ever properly observed the Sabbath who did not find as a consequence that he had augmented pleasure in the existence, the character, and the service of Jehovah. . . . The general idea of prosperity and security is undoubtedly the main thing intended." — *Albert Barnes.*

II. **JESUS AND THE SABBATH DAY,** Mark 2 : 23—3 : 6.

1. SOME TEACHINGS ABOUT THE SABBATH, 2 : 23–27. 23. **And it came to pass, that he was going on the sabbath day through the grainfields; and his disciples began, as they went, to pluck the ears.** 24. **And the Pharisees said unto him, Behold, why do they on the sabbath day that which is not lawful?** "Perhaps these spying Pharisees had followed Jesus on this Sabbath day to watch whether He would go more than the prescribed Sabbath-day's journey of two thousand cubits; but here they had been fortunate enough to light upon a far more heinous and flagrant scandal — an act of the disciples, which, strictly and technically speaking, rendered them liable to death by stoning. Jesus Himself had not indeed shared in the offense. If we may press the somewhat peculiar expression of Mark, He was walking along through the cornfields by the ordinary path, bearing His hunger as best He might, while the disciples were pushing for themselves a road through the standing corn by plucking the ears as they went along. Now there was no harm whatever in plucking the ears; *that* was not only sanctioned by custom, but even distinctly per-

25. And he said unto them, Did ye never read what David did, when he had need, and was hungry, he, and they that were with him?
26. How he entered into the house of God when Abiathar was high priest, and ate the showbread, which it is not lawful to eat save for the priests, and gave also to them that were with him?
27. And he said unto them, The sabbath was made for man, and not man for the sabbath:
28. So that the Son of man is lord even of the sabbath.

---

mitted by the Mosaic law. But the heinous fact was that this should be done on a Sabbath. Instantly the Pharisees are round our Lord, pointing to the disciples with an angry question, ' See! why do *they* ' — with a contemptuous gesture towards the disciples — ' do that which is not lawful on the Sabbath day? ' " — *F. W. Farrar.* 25. **And he said unto them, Did ye never read what David did, when he had need, and was hungry, he, and they that were with him?** 26. **How he entered into the house of God when Abiathar was high priest, and ate the showbread, which it is not lawful to eat save for the priests, and gave also to them that were with him?** The emphasis here is laid by our Lord upon David's *need*, the necessity for food. All the laws of God were given for man's welfare, and his ultimate sustentation. The story which our Lord repeats here is recorded in 1 Samuel 21 : 1–6. The twelve cakes of fine, unleavened flour sprinkled with frankincense and set on the golden table reserved for the priest is what is referred to by the showbread. " Our Lord quotes a fact, a deed of David's, their favorite hero, to show that mercy is better than sacrifice. If hunger made David, and them that were with him, blameless in eating the consecrated showbread, may not the same plea of necessity be urged to justify the disciples, although they had transgressed a rabbinical tradition? " — *T. M. Lindsay.* 27. **And he said unto them, The sabbath was made for man, and not man for the sabbath.** The noblest thing on earth, the last of God's creation, is man, and he is the only creature on earth who has the capacity for communion with God. The earth was made for man, the very velocity of the wind is tempered for man's welfare, the amount of rainfall, the chemical composition of water, the nutritious values of fruits and vegetables, the alternating of day and night, and the seasons of the year — all these were made for man's welfare, his enjoyment, his sustenance, his health. So also the moral laws of God are made for man's welfare, and not man for the adorning of some law. So the Sabbath day was made for man's spiritual and physical welfare. Consequently, when men are hungry and need food, and the time for eating is come, no law pertaining to any one day should be so interpreted as to prevent this man from having that which means his physical welfare, in a legitimate, honorable, divinely-ordained way. The Sabbath was not made to bring about a state of suffering, but to provide for man's rest and communion with God.

Christ and His Disciples in the Wheatfield.

2. THE SON OF MAN IS THE LORD OF THE SABBATH, 2 : 28. 28. **So that the Son of man is lord even of the sabbath.** " Let it be observed that in this saying Christ claims a proprietary right in the Sabbath. Time belongs to Him, since He made it. All days are God's: but He is pleased to set apart one day in seven as peculiarly His own." — *D. J. Burrell.* By declaring that He is Lord of the Sabbath, Christ means frankly to say that He has in His power the dispensation and allocation of all time, that He Himself is not a slave to the Sabbath, but, because He is the Son

MARK 3 : 1. And he entered again into the synagogue; and there was a man there who had his hand withered.

2. And they watched him, whether he would heal him on the sabbath day; that they might accuse him.

3. And he saith unto the man that had his hand withered, Stand forth.

4. And he saith unto them, Is it lawful on the sabbath day to do good, or to do harm? to save a life, or to kill? But they held their peace.

5. And when he had looked round about on them with anger, being grieved at the hardening of their heart, he saith unto the man, Stretch forth thy hand. And he stretched it forth; and his hand was restored.

---

of God, He can declare what the Sabbath truly was meant to be, in the sight of God and in God's program for men. In other words, we must look to Christ for the ultimate and final interpretation of the observance of the Sabbath day for ourselves. And what He says about it should be for us the final word. Christ does not contradict the law of the Old Testament, but He came to fufill that law in His life and in His teachings, and so He brushes away on this occasion all the binding, unreasonable, unjustified, accumulated traditions of Jewish rabbis and brings out once again, free from encrustations, the true significance and meaning and beauty of this day.

3. A MIRACLE PERFORMED ON THE SABBATH, 3 : 1–6. 1. **And he entered again into the synagogue ; and there was a man there who had his hand withered.** 2. **And they watched him, whether he would heal him on the sabbath day ; that they might accuse him.** 3. **And he saith unto the man that had his hand withered, Stand forth.** 4. **And he saith unto them, Is it lawful on the sabbath day to do good, or to do harm ? to save a life, or to kill ? But they held their peace.** 5. **And when he had looked around about on them with anger, being grieved at the hardening of their heart, he saith unto the man, Stretch forth thy hand. And he stretched it forth ; and his hand was restored.** We find the words of Dr. W. Graham Scroggie exceptionally helpful and rich on this passage, and we quote him. "Seven miracles were wrought on the Sabbath, of which this one is the fourth. They are (1) the cripple at the pool of Bethesda (John 5 : 1–16); (2) the demoniac in the synagogue at Capernaum (Mark 1 : 21–28); (3) the healing of Peter's mother-in-law (Mark 1 : 29–31); (4) the incident before us; (5) the blind man at Siloam (John 9 : 1–41); (6) the paralytic woman (Luke 13 : 11–17); and (7) the man with the dropsy (Luke 14 : 1–6). This man had met with an accident to his right hand (Luke 6 : 6), and the effect was a withering arm. It is the Sabbath, and Jesus and the man are in the synagogue. The man is in the right place to be blessed; he is in the recognized place of worship. And the critics were there too. People go to church from manifold motives; some moved by curiosity, some by concern, and some by criticism. These long-bearded hypocrites kept watching Jesus, that they might accuse Him. The act was justifiable, but not the motive, and actions must be interpreted and judged by motives. Actions in themselves have no moral value; moral quality is given to them by the intention. Seemingly virtuous acts may have behind them vicious motives, and vice versa. But these men had met their master this time. Said Jesus to the afflicted man — Stand in the middle of the room where all can see you. That was an exciting moment. The man obeyed, for his legs were all right. Thank God for the faculties you have. The next word was to the religious spies, and a devastating word it was. On the Sabbath day, to do good, or evil, to save, or to kill, which is lawful? By that searching question He tears the drapery from hypocrisy, and the masque from humbug, and shows it to be what it is. This is not a question of doing or not doing, but of what one does; and it is made plain that all negatives are positives; that not to do good when one can is to do evil; that not to save life when one can is to kill."

Professor Chadwick has a fine word when he reminds us that these men interrogating Jesus, " believed that Jesus could work the cure, since this is the very basis of their plot; and yet their hostility is not shaken, for belief in a miracle is not conversion; to catch a protégé is one thing and to surrender the will is quite another."

" The word *anger* here suggests the sudden stretching out of the hand in a passion that is active and moves toward punishment. The Greek word translated ' being grieved ' is a striking word, and this is the only place in the New Testament where it occurs. The only word by which you can convey its meaning is our word *condo-*

6. And the Pharisees went out, and straightway with the Herodians took counsel against him, how they might destroy him.

---

lence. What is condolence? Just *grief with.* Condolence is in its truest sense that which I feel with you when you are in the midst of grief. He was grieved with whom? They were not grieved. They had no sense of shame. He was in sympathy with all that must inevitably come in the moment of their awaking to the unutterable folly and failure of their own attitudes. Grief with them was His fathoming of their sin to its deadly depth and its unutterable darkness. Now observe the reason of that anger and grief. Because of the hardening of their heart; not because of the hardness of their heart, as the Authorized Version rendered it, but far more accurately, because of the hardening of their heart. It was not merely grief over a condition; it was grief over a process. The word hardening there is a word that describes a process; the process by which the extremities of a fractured bone are united by a callus. They were hardening their own heart." — *G. Campbell Morgan.* 6. **And the Pharisees went out, and straightway with the Herodians took counsel against him, how they might destroy him.** " The enormity of this reaction speaks for itself. Luke adds that the Pharisees were filled with madness. In their rage they proceeded at once to take measures against Jesus. They met with the Herodians, some of the Jews who supported the rulership of Herod Antipas under the dominion of the Roman empire. This faction was comparatively small, and was considered unpatriotic by the other Jews, who desired complete independence and no imperial dominance. Yet this political difference did not deter the Pharisees from enlisting the Herodians in their plan to destroy Jesus. In Galilee the Pharisees could do nothing by themselves; in Jerusalem they had their Sanhedrin. So the Pharisees stirred up the following of Herod, who ruled Galilee, hoping that he would take sides with them at the solicitation of his followers. Mark alone reports this coalition with the Herodians." — *R. C. H. Lenski.*

The editor, of course, has heard a great deal of discussion as to whether the Sabbath is binding on man, and there are certain groups in our country that are preaching and teaching that the Christian Church is still bound to observe the Jewish Sabbath, that is, the seventh day of the week and not the Christian Sunday which occurs on the first day of the week. The editor firmly believes that Sunday is the day on which Christians should rest and worship, the day on which our Lord arose from the dead, and the day which has been observed in the Christian Church for 1800 years. What the editor is really concerned about is that there should be some one day for such rest and worship. Sometimes we get to discussing the technicalities and forget the great principle of one day out of seven for a time of rest and congregational fellowship before the throne of grace. Furthermore, in orthodox circles where it is especially emphasized that Christians are under grace and not under law, there is a great danger of treating Sunday carelessly, of engaging in business as we do on the other six days, of neglecting the house of God, of simply entertaining friends or staying at home, regularly absenting ourselves from the house of God, or engaging in many things which when the day is over have not spiritually profited us. All arguments against keeping Sunday as a sacred day are utterly smashed to bits in this great undeniably historical fact, that where Sunday is truly observed, the devotion of people to God, the strength and growth of the Christian Church and the fervor of religious life are always found in greater manifestation, intensity, and consistency than where the Sunday is carelessly considered. Its observance does mean a deeper spiritual life if it is observed sincerely.

How many different blessings are promised to those who give one day out of seven to God? How many different things did Jesus Himself say about the Sabbath day? Did Christ Himself in the New Testament attend divine worship on the seventh day? (The answer is a most emphatic Yes. See e.g. Luke 4 : 16.) Can you name any good reason why Christian people should not set apart Sunday for rest and for divine worship? Do you think that playing golf all day Sunday is honoring to God? Do you find that men on the golf course say this themselves? Do you think that the hours of divine worship should be set on the Lord's day so as to accommodate those who intend to spend it in travel and pleasure and picnicking and sport, or do you think we ought to arrange our day according to the hours set in our community for divine worship? Would you rather live in a community where business ceases, and churches are full on the Lord's day, or where all stores are open and churches are practically empty on that day, and what reason do you have for your preference?

LESSON IV. — October 24.

HONORING OUR PARENTS. — Exodus 20 : 12; Luke 2 : 48–51; Mark 7 : 6–13; John 19 : 25–27.

GOLDEN TEXT. — ***Children, obey your parents in the Lord: for this is right.*** EPHESIANS 6 : 1.

Devotional Reading: Proverbs 4 : 10–18.
Beginner Topic: JESUS AND THE TEACHERS.
Lesson Material: Luke 2 : 41–51.
Memory Verse: Oh give thanks unto Jehovah; for he is good. Psalm 136 : 1.
Primary Topic: IN GOD'S BOOK.
Lesson Material: Exodus 20 : 12; Luke 2 : 48–51; Mark 7 : 6–13; John 19 : 25–27.
Memory Verse: My son, keep the commandment of thy father, and forsake not the law of thy mother. Proverbs 6 : 20.
Junior Topic: AS JESUS GREW UP.
Lesson Material: Exodus 20 : 12; Luke 2 : 48–51; Mark 7 : 6–13; John 19 : 25–27.
Memory Verse: And Jesus advanced in wisdom and stature, and in favor with God and men. Luke 2 : 52.
Intermediate and Senior Topic: HOW MAY WE HONOR OUR PARENTS?
Topic for Young People and Adults: RESPONSIBILITY TO PARENTS.

THE TEACHER AND HIS CLASS.

The Younger Classes will not be too young to understand that there are three spheres to every person's life — first, the world within, our own individual selves, where character is formed; secondly, the world of others, and our relationship to them, at school, at home, at play, among neighbors, and, later, in business relationships of every description. The third sphere of life is that embracing God, and our relationship to Him. When any of these relationships are wrong, life becomes a tragedy; when they are right, life becomes a benediction and joy. Our lesson today is concerning one particular relationship, that of children to their parents, which can be wrong, and often is, but which, when right, bestows on life a true gladness of heart.

The Older Classes will find here a lesson which, if it is not to instruct them regarding their relationship to their parents, for their parents may be dead, yet will be found a most profitable lesson in teaching them what respect and honor their children ought to have for them, and thus should lead them to live that kind of a life which will elicit from their children the honor and reverence which the Word of God commands.

THE LESSON IN ITS SETTING.

Time. — The Ten Commandments were given about 1445 B.C.; the incident taken from our Lord's boyhood occurred in April, A.D. 8; our Lord's condemnation of Jewish men who dishonor their parents was spoken in April, A.D. 29; and the word from the cross was uttered on Friday, April 7, A.D. 30.

Place. — The Ten Commandments were given at Mount Sinai; the incident from our Lord's boyhood took place in the Temple in Jerusalem and later at Nazareth; the discourse about unfaithfulness to parents was given at Capernaum; our Lord was crucified outside the city wall of Jerusalem.

THE PLAN OF THE LESSON.

SUBJECT: What God Demands of Children in Their Regard for Parents, and How This Command of God Was Perfectly Fulfilled in the Life of Jesus of Nazareth.

I. THE FIFTH COMMANDMENT, Exodus 20 : 12.

II. HOW JESUS HONORED HIS PARENTS, Luke 2 : 48–51.
1. His mother's unjustified rebuke, v. 48.
2. Christ's early consciousness of His divine mission, vs. 49, 50.
3. His obedience to Joseph and Mary, v. 51.

III. JESUS DENOUNCES THE DECEITFUL WAYS MEN WERE USING IN ATTEMPTING TO ESCAPE THEIR RESPONSIBILITY FOR CARING FOR THEIR PARENTS, Mark 7 : 6–13.

IV. CHRIST'S WORD TO HIS MOTHER FROM THE CROSS, John 19 : 25–27.

THE TEACHER'S LIBRARY.

For an exposition of the fifth commandment, see, especially, J. O. Dykes: *The Law of the Ten Words*, 105–121; R. W. Dale: *The Ten Commandments*, 113–137; F. W. Farrar: *The Voice from Sinai*, 171–188; Andrew Murray: *The Children for Christ*, 108–115; Cleland B. McAfee: *The Mosaic Law in Modern Life*, 119–137; G. Campbell Morgan: *The Ten Commandments*, 52–65; Charles Hodge: *Systematic Theology*, Vol. 3, 348–362; William Masselink: *Sermons on the Commandments*, 115–131. On Luke's account of the one incident given from the life of our Lord when He was twelve years old, see, of course, all the commentaries on Luke's Gospel; a very long article by George Farrar, "Boyhood of Jesus," in James Hastings's *Dictionary of Christ and the Gospels*, Vol. 1, 224–230; J. Stuart Holden: *Supposition and Certainty*, 11–26; Phillips Brooks: *Visions and Tasks and Other Sermons*, 20–41; Alexander Whyte: *The Walk, Conversation, and Character of Jesus Christ Our Lord*, 59–75; James Hastings: *Great Texts of the Bible, St. Luke*, 104–142; T. Vincent Tymms: *The Private Relationships of Christ*, 164–180. On Christ's denunciation of the practice of children deceiving their parents in the matter of support, see the works on St. Mark by R. C. H. Lenski, W. Graham Scroggie, and Thomas M. Lindsay.

On our Lord's words to Mary and John from the cross, see, in addition to standard commentaries on John's Gospel, W. R. Nicoll: *The Seven Words from the Cross*, 29–44; F. W. Krummacher: *The Suffering Saviour*, 402–412; James Stalker: *The Trial and Death of Jesus Christ*, 231–242; A. Tholuck: *Light from the Cross*, 262–278; John A. Hutton: *There They Crucified Him*, 148–162; William Alexander: *Verbum Crucis*, 51–64; W. M. Clow: *The Day of the Cross*, 271–282; J. H. Bernard: *Verbum Crucis*, 28 ff.; some very fine things in F. W. Robertson: *The Mother of Jesus;* T. V. Tymms, as above, 55–72.

EXODUS 20 : 12. Honor thy father and thy mother, that thy days may be long in the land which Jehovah thy God giveth thee.

I. **THE FIFTH COMMANDMENT,** Exod. 20 : 12. 12. **Honor thy father and thy mother, that thy days may be long in the land which Jehovah thy God giveth thee.**

1. THE MEANING OF THE WORD HONOR. "The word *honor* involves reverence (Lev. 19 : 32); obedience (Col. 3 : 20); gratitude (1 Tim. 5 : 4); the following of advice (Prov. 1 : 8; 23 : 22); and, of course, the exclusion of all the feelings and actions opposite to these (Deut. 27 : 16; Exod. 21 : 15, 17). . . . The honor for our parents is love combined with reverence; the love must be honor touched with emotion. There can be no true honor without love. Of course the reciprocal duty is implied. If the commandment only says to every child, 'Honor thy father and thy mother,' it means no less distinctly, 'And ye, fathers, provoke not your children to wrath, but nurture them in the chastening and admonition of the Lord.' Into that side of duty there is less need to enter, because the love of parents to their children is far more intense and permanent than that of children to their parents." — *F. W. Farrar.*

2. THE COMMAND ITSELF. "If they are in after life to do what is so difficult, to honor all men, by recognizing even in the degraded and the lost the worth that belongs to them as created in the image of God, children must be carefully prepared for it in the home-school of family life. It is not only to secure a happy home, and place the intercourse of parent and child on a right footing, but to fit the child for all his future relations to God and his fellow men, and to lay in him one of the foundation stones of a noble character and a holy life, that God has placed this commandment the first of those on the second table. The child must honor the parent in obedience. 'Obey your parents' is the New Testament version of 'Honor thy father and thy mother.' God created men, with his wonderful liberty of will, that he might obey Him. Obedience to God was to lead to the enjoyment of God. By disobedience sin entered; in obedience, the twofold obedience, of Christ and to Christ (Heb. 5 : 8, 9), salvation comes. And on the parent the sacred charge is laid of training the child to obey, teaching it to link all the memories of happiness and love in home life with obedience, working the principle into the very life of mind and heart, not so much by instruction or reasoning, as by training and securing the habit of obedience. The will of the child, no less than his mind and affections, is given into the parent's hands to mold and guide. It is in yielding his will to the will of the parent that the child acquires that mastery over it and over himself which will afterward be its strength and safety, and make it an instrument for doing God's will. The will of the child is not free — passion and prejudice, selfishness and ignorance, seek to influence the child in the wrong direction. The superior judgment, the calmer deliberation, the fuller experience of the parent, are to decide for the child whose will has been entrusted to his care. . . . Above all, let parents remember that honor really comes from God. Let them honor Him in the eyes of their children, and He will honor them there too. The parent who teaches his child to obey the fifth commandment has guided his feet into the way of all God's commandments." — *Andrew Murray.*

LUKE 2 : 48. And when they saw him, they were astonished; and his mother said unto him, Son, why hast thou thus dealt with us? behold, thy father and I sought thee sorrowing.

49. And he said unto them, How is it that ye sought me? knew ye not that I must be in my Father's house.

3. THE PROMISE. " This promise first of all had a national significance. Israel as a nation was in the wilderness journeying to the promised land when God spake this precept. It would mean for Israel as a nation that it would live long in Canaan. However, the promise is not confined to the Hebrew nation. Paul repeats it in the New Testament in his letter to the Ephesians. Young men, and young women, tell me whether you are obedient to your parents and I will tell you your future. If you honor father and mother, depend upon it that God's favor will accompany you, and you will enjoy temporal and eternal blessings; but if you dishonor your parents depend upon it that God's hand shall be lifted up against you." — *Wm. Masselink.* " The nation whose homes are godly, orderly, and happy, whose successive generations are linked together by holy ligaments of love and respect from child to parent: that nation possesses the surest safeguard for prosperity and permanence. Men who revere their ancestry and prize their families will fight for the graves of the one and the hearths of the other, just as they will fight for the altars of that God whose authority has sanctified the ties of blood. When the family is dissolved, on the contrary, patriotism becomes a jest, and public spirit expires; and the distracted people, having lost the sense of unity and the habit of subordination, lies open an inviting prey to foreign assault as well as domestic discord. Such a people will not dwell long in the land which God gave them to inherit." — *J. O. Dykes.*

4. THE PERPETUAL OBLIGATION OF THIS COMMAND. This commandment " was not addressed originally to a Sabbath school class, nor to children. It was addressed to the same men who were bid to keep the other commandments. It was addressed to men who were gray as well as to men who were young. No man ever grows so wise or so great that it is not incumbent upon him to honor his father and his mother. The coming-of-age in a legal sense is a wise limitation upon certain lines of obedience. There is a period in our lives when our parents have the right to command us. After that, they lose the right to command and demand obedience, but they never lose the right to claim our honor." — *C. B. McAfee.*

II. **HOW JESUS HONORED HIS PARENTS,** Luke 2 : 48-51. This exquisite story, beautiful though sad, of an episode in the life of our Lord when he was twelve years of age, is recorded only by Luke. It was the custom with all pious Jews of that day to go up every year to Jerusalem, at the feast of the Passover, in April. When the Lord Jesus was twelve years of age, as was also the custom among the Jews, they took Him with them to Jerusalem, which probably was the first time our Lord had been in the holy city since the time when Mary His mother presented Him as a babe in the Temple. When the Passover was over, Joseph and Mary turned away, to go north to the city of Nazareth, where Joseph was a carpenter. For some strange reason, thinking the boy was in the company, they went on a whole day's journey before they missed Him. They immediately turned back to Jerusalem to seek Him. On the third day, Luke says: " They found him in the temple, sitting in the midst of the teachers, both hearing them, and asking them questions."
48. **And when they saw him, they were astonished; and his mother said unto him, Son, why hast thou thus dealt with us? behold, thy father and I sought thee sorrowing.** " The verb for the effect upon the parents is still stronger than the one for the hearers; they were actually struck as by a blow at seeing their boy in this place and so occupied. It is too cheap an application to say that parents often fail to perceive the wealth of nature in their children — here was something far different from nature wealth. This shocked condition betrays how quietly Jesus had acted up to this time, never opening His mouth in the synagogue — and here all at once He sits in the very Temple itself amid prominent rabbis, all eyes and ears fixed upon Him. The shock had ample reason. We do not think that the parents broke in on the scene, but that at sight of His parents the boy at once got up and walked away with them. Whether Joseph said anything we do not know — no word of His is recorded. It is Mary's mother-heart that speaks for both of them." — *R. C. H. Lenski.*
49. **And he said unto them, How is it that ye sought me? knew ye not that I must be in my Father's house?** " These words are very memorable as being the first

50. And they understood not the saying which he spake unto them.
51. And he went down with them, and came to Nazareth; and he was
subject unto them: and his mother kept all *these* sayings in her heart.

recorded words of Jesus. They bear with them the stamp of authenticity in their half-vexed astonishment, and perfect mixture of dignity and humility. It is remarkable, too, that He does not accept the phrase ' Thy father ' which Mary had employed. ' Did ye not know? ' recalls their fading memory of who He was; and the ' I must ' lays down the law of devotion to His Father by which He was to walk even to the cross (Ps. 40 : 7–9). ' My meat is to do the will of Him that sent me and to finish his work ' (John 4 : 34)." — *F. W. Farrar.* " For eighteen years, He applied Himself in silence to the business of His earthly father at Nazareth, where He is called the Carpenter (Mark 6 : 3)." — *F. Godet.* It is transparently clear from this utterance that our Lord's consciousness of His divine mission did not come to Him late in life, say, *e.g.*, at His baptism, but was powerfully present in all of His thoughts, even when a boy of twelve, and, we can believe, even before this. Furthermore, He is the only one who is conscious of His mission; that is, he was not told this by His mother, or by Joseph, for they were astonished when they heard His words. He was not told it by some rabbi, or some devoted nurse, or sainted prophetess, for none of them were aware of it. This was an inner consciousness of Christ, received in that precious, holy communion which, without any momentary interruption, He enjoyed from the moment of His birth to the last hour on the cross. 50. **And they understood not the saying which he spake unto them.** 51. **And he went down with them, and came to Nazareth; and he was subject unto them: and his mother kept all *these* sayings in her heart.** The word here translated *subject unto them*, " sums up the condition of the Messiah during the next seventeen years. This is the last mention of Joseph. He was almost certainly dead before Christ's public ministry began; but His statement of continued subjection to him and Mary probably covers some years. The main object of the statement, however, may be to remove the impression that in His reply, Jesus resents, or henceforth repudiates, their authority over Him." — *Alfred Plummer.* " In this simple word *submitting himself*, Luke has summed up the entire work of Jesus until His baptism. But why did not God permit the child to remain in the Temple of Jerusalem, which during the feast days had been His Eden? The answer is not difficult. He must inevitably have been thrown too early into the theologico-political discussions which agitated the capital; and after having excited the admiration of the doctors, He would have provoked their hatred by His original and independent turn of thought. If the spiritual atmosphere of Nazareth was heavy, it was at least calm; and the labors of the workshop in the retirement of this peaceful valley under the eye of the father, was a more favorable sphere for the development of Jesus than the ritualism of the Temple and the rabbinical discussions of Jerusalem." — *F. Godet.* The verb here translated *kept* means to group together a great number of circumstances, to combine, or collect them, and the prefix of the word denotes " the permanence of the recollection, notwithstanding circumstances which might have effaced it. She carefully kept in her possession this profound saying as an unexplained mystery." — *F. Godet.* " Christ knew Himself as the Son of the Father, knew as man that His person was divine, and

The Child Jesus in the Temple. Hofmann.

MARK 7 : 6. And he said unto them, Well did Isaiah prophesy of you
hypocrites, as it is written,
This people honoreth me with their lips,
But their heart is far from me.
7. But in vain do they worship me,
Teaching *as their* doctrines the precepts of men.
8. Ye leave the commandment of God, and hold fast the tradition of men.
9. And he said unto them, Full well do ye reject the commandment of
God, that ye may keep your tradition.
10. For Moses said, Honor thy father and thy mother; and, He that
speaketh evil of father or mother, let him die the death:
11. But ye say, If a man shall say to his father or his mother, That
wherewith thou mightest have been profited by me is Corban, that is to
say, Given *to God;*
12. Ye no longer suffer him to do aught for his father or his mother;
13. Making void the word of God by your tradition, which ye have
delivered: and many such like things ye do.

---

yet, not in contradiction to but in harmony with this knowledge, He went on as an obedient child to Joseph and Mary. This, He realized, was part of His Father's affairs. His obedience and subjection according to the fourth commandment was thus on a higher plane and far more significant than that of any other child." — *R. C. H. Lenski.* The editor has never seen it so stated, but he dares to suggest here that it may well be that parents whose children recognize Jesus Christ as their Saviour, and yet have found their children very difficult to handle, manifesting an increasingly stubborn spirit of disobedience, should call their attention to the submissiveness of Jesus (though He was the only begotten Son of God!) to His own parents in Nazareth, until He grew to be a man.

III. **JESUS DENOUNCES THE DECEITFUL WAYS MEN WERE USING IN ATTEMPTING TO ESCAPE THEIR RESPONSIBILITY FOR CARING FOR THEIR PARENTS,** Mark 7 : 6–13. The words of rebuke which are recorded here from the lips of Jesus were precipitated by the Pharisees themselves, who came to find fault with the methods of Jesus and His disciples. They came all the way up to Capernaum from Jerusalem, declaring that Jesus and His disciples were breaking the law, because they were eating bread with unwashed hands. There is nothing specifically said in the Scriptures about this matter, but the tradition of the Jewish leaders was that before every meal, hands were to be thoroughly washed, for the sake of cleanliness and for removing all ceremonial impurity. No matter how clean the hands might be, the ceremonial washing had to be performed anyway. Of course, there is nothing wrong with washing hands before eating, in fact, it is to be preferred; but these traditionalists actually said it was a *sin* not to go through these ceremonial purifications, at every period specified by their complicated laws. 6. **And he said unto them, Well did Isaiah prophesy of you hypocrites, as it is written, This people honoreth me with their lips, but their heart is far from me.** This leads our Lord to quote from the prophet Isaiah (29 : 13) that these ritualists of Jerusalem, like the Israelites of Isaiah's day, were honoring God with their lips, but their heart was far from them; that is, their religion was an external one, not an internal one. 7. **But in vain do they worship me, teaching *as their* doctrines the precepts of men.** 8. **Ye leave the commandment of God, and hold fast the tradition of men.** It must have been a terrible thing for them to hear that all these commandments they were multiplying, were manufactured by men and were not of divine origin. 9. **And he said unto them, Full well do ye reject the commandment of God, that ye may keep your tradition.** 10. **For Moses said, Honor thy father and thy mother; and, He that speaketh evil of father or mother, let him die the death:** 11. **but ye say, If a man shall say to his father or his mother, That wherewith thou mightest have been profited by me is Corban, that is to say, Given *to God;*** 12. **ye no longer suffer him to do aught for his father or his mother;** 13. **making void the word of God by your tradition, which ye have delivered: and many such like things ye do.** Our Lord now actually confronts these hypocritical Pharisees, these hardened ritualists, with

JOHN 19 : 25. These things therefore the soldiers did. But there were standing by the cross of Jesus his mother, and his mother's sister, Mary the *wife* of Clopas, and Mary Magdalene.

26. When Jesus therefore saw his mother, and the disciple standing by whom he loved, he saith unto his mother, Woman, behold, thy son!

---

an actual case which they could not deny, of a trick frequently practiced by them, and many others in Israel, whereby they quieted their conscience even when they were scheming to avoid taking care of their needy parents. The picture is of a father, or mother, being in actual need, informing the son of the need, only to hear the son say, " Corban," which means, " It is offered to God." In this case the parent could not expect the son to use this particular money, or property, or merchandise, for the support which was so needed. How awful for a man to have such a love for money that, instead of using some of it for the support of his parents, he pretends, with a false piety, so hateful to God, that he has dedicated this to a holy God in heaven! This is not religion but sophistry; not love but selfishness; not obedience to the command of God, but the most wicked form of the transgression of God's commandments. " There is a washing which leaves one unclean, and there is a purification which is not dependent on water. Clean hands can never compensate for an unclean heart; washing can never atone for wickedness, nor lip-honor for heart-hypocrisy. It is righteousness that God requires, not religiosity. God's truth and man's traditions do not agree. The latter are not of simple human origin, but of sinful human device. Pretending to observe the law, the Pharisees outraged it; so do people who sing the praises of God on Sunday, and cheat or slander their neighbors all the week. It is easy to neutralize by one's life what is confessed by one's lips. It is amazing what tricks people will play with themselves, and how, in doing so, they will trifle with God! . . . Our duties never clash, so that we are never under the necessity to outrage one to fulfill another; nor can we ever find justification in the Word of God for the neglect of any obvious duty: the Bible is on the side of practical righteousness. Then, away with postures and pious platitudes and pretenses, and let us get down, or, shall I say *up* to prayer and practice." — *W. Graham Scroggie.* " That the case with the fourth commandment is only a single illustration Jesus declares by adding that the Pharisees and scribes keep doing many such like things, *i.e.*, things that in like manner rob the divine Word of its authority for the conscience. Thus these men who imagined they had a case against Jesus not only have their answer, a complete vindication of Jesus and His disciples, but have an indictment launched against themselves, one fortified with crushing absolute proof, against which no defense is possible on their part. The severity of this indictment indicates that Jesus is done with them. They are not merely silenced, they are actually overwhelmed." — *R. C. H. Lenski.*

IV. **CHRIST'S WORD TO HIS MOTHER FROM THE CROSS,** John 19 : 25–27. 25. **These things therefore the soldiers did. But there were standing by the cross of Jesus his mother, and his mother's sister, Mary the *wife* of Clopas, and Mary Magdalene.** Previous to our Lord's crucifixion, the other ten disciples had fled, but the women, remaining faithful to our Lord through all of His hours of suffering, stand not far off (Matt. 27 : 56). Nearer than any of the other groups were the mother of our Lord, and John, the apostle whom Jesus loved. The particular incident now about to be described is not found in any of the other Gospel records, though the fact of several women standing and beholding our Lord on the cross from afar is mentioned by the Synoptists (Matt. 27 : 55, 56; etc.). Strange to say, Mary, our Lord's mother, is not in the records of His passion alluded to by any of the other Synoptic writers. 26. **When Jesus therefore saw his mother, and the disciple standing by whom he loved, he saith unto his mother, Woman, behold, thy son!** " There had been a moment when the mother's instincts and the love of the disciple urged them, at any personal risk, to steal nearer the cross. The evangelist does not attempt to tell us what his feelings at that awful hour were, much less to expose the mother's agony. At the same time, writing after the resurrection and the ascension, not to speak of the many years of triumphant progress of the gospel, the remembrance of these moments of intolerable grief must have been toned down — lost in profound joy and thankfulness to the God of such a salvation. . . . To His mother, the words, ' Woman, behold thy son! ' were meant in merciful compassion, advising her withdrawal from the cross, sparing her the anguish of the last moments; were meant

27. Then saith he to the disciple, Behold, thy mother! And from that hour the disciple took her unto his own *home*.

to suggest to her with all tenderness that the earthly tie between Him and her was now broken forever (the new wonderful tie binding sinner and Saviour would take its place, as wonderful, as precious and necessary to her as to any other redeemed soul); and yet that with the thoughtfulness which did not seek its own even in the last extremity He had provided for her loneliness and grief, and was giving her a son in His own place; for when Christ sunders old ties, He often forms new for His disciples." — *George Reith.* Archbishop Alexander makes a very fine comment on this precious verse, when he says that this gift of Christ to His mother at the cross was, in the first place, just the right gift, and in the second place, it was the right gift given at the right moment. "It is an unreal spirituality which affects to think little of making such loving provision as may be in our power for those who are nearest to us in blood and affection. But we cannot doubt that there was more here than food and shelter. There was provision for moral affinities of heart, thought, character, temperament, faith. . . . 'And from that hour that disciple took her unto his own home.' Simeon had said to Mary long ago, 'a sword shall pierce through thine own soul.' The sword must pierce. But no selfish yearning for sympathy shall cause it to be turned in the wound which it has made." — *William Alexander.* "He had no money to leave her; His earthly all, when He was crucified, consisted of the clothes He wore; and these fell to the soldiers. But it is one of the privileges of those who, though they may be poor themselves, make many rich with the gifts of truth, that they thereby win friends who are proud and eager to serve them or theirs. In committing His mother to John, Jesus knew that the charge would be accepted not as a burden but a gift. . . . This sermon, delivered from the pulpit of the cross, has a wider range. It informs us that our Saviour has a concern for our temporal as well as for our eternal interests. Even on the cross, where He was expiating the sin of the world, He was thinking of the comfort of His widowed mother. Let the needy and the deserted take courage from this, and cast all their care upon Him, for He careth for them." — *James Stalker.* 27. **Then saith he to the disciple, Behold, thy mother! And from that hour the disciple took her unto his own *home*.** "The near relationship of John, as well as Jesus' peculiar love to him, may explain this last proof of confidence in his loyalty and affection, when Jesus intrusted His mother to his care. Besides, John was the only one to whom Jesus could at that hour commit so dear and sacred a charge. His devotion to his dying Lord had earned the honorable and enviable distinction of being singled out to pay these tender, filial offices which Jesus had faithfully fulfilled, but could fulfill no more. His cross is the place where new and lasting ties are formed, more enduring than those which concern this world only. Also — and the lesson is applicable to all — the words meant that a check must be put even on grief so natural as a mother's for a son, and that in the discovery of fresh and new duties for God's sake must life be spent, not in helpless bewailing over the irrevocable past, however precious that

Mary and St. John. Plockhörst.

has been. Jesus might have committed His mother simply to God; but the place and the value of human sympathy are nowhere more fully recognized than in His own life." — *George Reith.* "The mother-love that was poured out on John flowed into the expression of John's Gospel. Surely he must have received some impression of Christ through the long intimate years when he cared for her as a son. It is significant that the apostle who knew Mary most intimately is the one who breathes his absolute assurance of the deity of Jesus into every paragraph of his book." — *M. T. Shelford.*

The words of the saint and scholar, A. Tholuck, seem to form the most perfect conclusion for this lesson which we have been studying. "Beloved in Christ, ye men, ye women, ye youths, He has left us all an example that we should follow His footsteps, an example which, in all our dealings with those we love, we should keep before our eye. Let us love those who belong to us with that considerate and thoughtful love which discovers and provides for every one what is best suited for his peculiar case. We must go more out of ourselves than we do, we must go deeper into the feelings of those with whom God has bound us in the ties of nature, in order that we may learn more fully to understand what each wants, what would give them joy. The apostle says, 'Let not every one mind his own things, but each one also the things of others.' We all look too much to our own things, are too much lost in our own sorrows, interests, and wants, and live too little in that which concerns others; hence we understand far too little the men with whom we associate, and it is because we do not properly understand them, that there is so little delicacy and consideration in our love. . . . It is a sign of tenderness of your love that you should seek at all to supply the spiritual wants of those that belong to you, but further, in doing so you must act with tenderness. Mere violent declamation, mere sermonizing will not gain your object. In the first place, you must gain over hearts by deeds, before you attempt to win them by words. That is done by tender, ministering love. Beloved, such a tender, ministering, self-forgetful love, a love which goes entirely out of itself, and out towards others, such a love has in it something so unearthly, so heavenly, that the heart must be of stone indeed which it fails to touch. Would you that men would lend a willing and attentive ear to your exhortations, then see to it, in the first place, that you succeed in taking possession of their hearts, and making them your own, and a love like this conquers hearts. This is a sermon such as the least eloquent among you may preach, even though he can urge no other testimony in favor of the truth of his cause; by this means many a Christian woman has exercised a greater and a deeper influence in the world on behalf of the kingdom of God than many settled clergymen. Now, after you have found for yourself a way to the heart, by such works — which are indeed infinitely more difficult than words — you will then find an entrance there for your words also. Tenderness of love is necessary in order to become in one's words all things to all men. Every human heart is a little world, and each is approached by a way of its own. Learn to know those who belong to you, to know them in their deepest and truest nature, in order that you may speak to each of them of the truth in the very way that is best fitted for each."

What natural reasons are there why children who gladly, habitually, honor and revere their parents, other things being equal, should enjoy a much longer life than those whose early days are marked by a stubborn resistance toward their parents and a spirit of disobedience? How are Christ's deity and His humanity found to be perfectly blended in the story given to us of the incident occurring when He was twelve years old? Do genius, or unusual intellectual brilliance, or great artistic gifts, manifest even in childhood, excuse a boy or girl from rendering implicit obedience to parents? How can parents make themselves unworthy of the honor and respect of their children? (One way is by frequently uttered falsehoods concerning business, social, or church relationships, etc., etc.) Why did Christ not make provision for Mary before He was crucified rather than wait until that dreadful day? How can a grown man, if either or both of his parents are living, somewhat make up for his early years of disobedience? (We mean by this, he can make provision for his parents in their need; he can be kind and thoughtful toward them even if they have no material needs; and if far away he can keep in touch with them by correspondence and by tokens of his love sent to them in one way or another.) What are some of the reasons that you can suggest why children these days are becoming so disrespectful toward parents?

LESSON V. — October 31.

BIBLE TEACHINGS ON ABSTINENCE. — Leviticus 10 : 1, 2, 8–11; Proverbs 31 : 4, 5; Luke 1 : 13–16.

GOLDEN TEXT. — ***Beware, I pray thee, and drink no wine nor strong drink.*** Judges 13 : 4.

Devotional Reading: Psalm 4.
Beginner Topic; The Baby's Name.
Lesson Material: Luke 1.
Memory Verse: Let us love one another. 1 John 4 : 7.
Primary Topic: A Name to Make.
Lesson Material: Luke 1 : 13–16, 25–80.
Memory Verse: A good name is rather to be chosen than great riches, and loving favor rather than silver and gold. Proverbs 22 : 1.
Junior Topic: A Name to Earn.
Lesson Material: Luke 1 : 13–16, 25–80.
Memory Verse: A good name is rather to be chosen than great riches, and loving favor rather than silver and gold. Proverbs 22 : 1.
Intermediate and Senior Topic: Keeping Fit for Christian Living.
Topic for Young People and Adults: Why Total Abstinence?

THE TEACHER AND HIS CLASS.

The Younger Classes may be introduced to this lesson in a very simple way. Let us say that on the shelf of a cabinet in our home there are a number of bottles containing different liquids. The labels are turned toward the wall, away from the one standing in front of the cabinet. What a difference it makes, however, which bottle is taken and used for medicine! One might be a cough syrup, which would be beneficial; another might be some simple remedy for quieting the nerves; another, however, might be carbolic acid, which, if taken orally, would burn out the tissues of the throat and stomach. How are we to tell what the consequences would be of taking what is in one bottle or another? Why, by the labels, of course. Now, the Word of God does that for every major part of life — it labels things, to tell us which will help and strengthen us, and make us spiritually sound and joyful. It tells us the things that will destroy our spiritual life, and lead us into iniquities, and perhaps into crimes. These labels have been put there by the Holy Spirit of God, and by the Lord Jesus, who knows man, and what is good for man, because He made him. Our lesson is one in which the label "Poison" is put on certain things which men seem so prone to indulge in, always to their harm. The label is there for our warning, and we do well to heed it.

The Older Classes must recognize that some things in life *have* to be *first*, if we are to get anywhere, and other things must be assigned to a subsidiary place, a place of less importance, even though the things that are given a minor place may be, for us, the more delightful. For instance, when we awaken in the morning, on a lovely spring day, we would *like* to work in the garden or take a drive in a car, or go out under the trees and read. That is what we would like to do. But instead of that, we have to go to work; we must go into the city, or walk behind a plow. That is what *must* be done. Now, in a higher realm, there are some things that must come first — physical health must be first considered, when we are thinking of any of the physical pleasures of life, and we must do nothing to injure our health. Likewise, we must fundamentally consider our spiritual life. One thing *must* be kept right — our relationship to God, and the spiritual sensitiveness of our souls. Anything that mars that relationship is wrong, and we will put it out of our lives. Our lesson tells us of things which, for some men, in themselves, mean pleasure and relaxation, things which we must deny ourselves, if we are to live in the will of God, to be strong spiritually, to do the work God has called us to do. First things must come first. A man may drink and enjoy it, but in doing so he will weaken his whole life. What is the use of taking pleasure in intoxicating beverages when the great and major spheres of life are being impaired by it? That is putting something low on a high plane, and something that ought to be minor in a major place.

THE LESSON IN ITS SETTING.

Time. — The Levitical code was given for the most part at Sinai about 1444 B.C.; the Book of Proverbs was written about 1000 B.C.; the words of the angel to Zacharias were spoken in 7 B.C.

Place. — The Levitical code was given at Sinai; Solomon wrote Proverbs probably in Jerusalem; the angel appeared to Zacharias also in Jerusalem, while he was ministering in the Temple.

THE PLAN OF THE LESSON.

SUBJECT: The Necessity of Abstinence from All Intoxicants by Those Who Are Called to Be Spiritual Leaders or Rulers Among Men.

I. THE OFFERING OF STRANGE FIRE BY NADAB AND ABIHU, Lev. 10:1, 2.

II. THE PROHIBITION OF STRONG DRINK FOR ALL WHO ARE ABOUT TO ENGAGE IN PRIESTLY SERVICE, Lev. 10:8–11.

III. WHY RULERS SHOULD ABSTAIN FROM ALL STRONG DRINK, Prov. 31:4, 5.

IV. HEAVEN'S DESCRIPTION OF THE LIFE TO BE LIVED BY JOHN THE BAPTIST, Luke 1:13–16.

THE TEACHER'S LIBRARY.

On the passage taken from Leviticus, one should especially consult the volumes on this book by A. A. Bonar and C. H. Mackintosh. For expository material, which is quite scarce, see Alexander Maclaren: *Expositions of Holy Scripture — Exodus, Leviticus, Numbers*, 240–247; and G. Campbell Morgan, in *The Westminster Pulpit*, Vol. 8, 41–48. Also, one may consult F. R. Lees and Dawson Burns: *The Temperance Bible Commentary*, 36–39.

On Proverbs 31:4, 5, commentaries are almost worthless. The only thing of real value the editor has seen is the material in the old but ever-dependable work, by Matthew Henry. See also, however, the *Temperance Bible Commentary*, 143–146. As far as the editor knows, there are no available, worthwhile sermons on these verses.

On Luke 1:13–16, one might consult the larger commentaries on Luke's Gospel, especially the one by R. C. H. Lenski; and, for those who can handle the Greek, the indispensable work by Alfred Plummer, in the *International Critical Commentary* series. On verse 15, see Hugh Black: *According to My Gospel*, 62–72; G. F. Pentecost: *The Birth and Boyhood of Jesus*, 18 ff.; likewise one should also consult all of the larger works on the life of John the Baptist. For these particular verses, the best one is the volume by A. T. Robertson. For temperance material, see the bibliography, in the Introduction to this volume.

LEVITICUS 10:1. And Nadab and Abihu, the sons of Aaron, took each of them his censer, and put fire therein, and laid incense thereon, and offered strange fire before Jehovah, which he had not commanded them.
2. And there came forth fire from before Jehovah, and devoured them, and they died before Jehovah.

I. THE OFFERING OF STRANGE FIRE BY NADAB AND ABIHU, Lev. 10:1, 2. 1. **And Nadab and Abihu, the sons of Aaron, took each of them his censer, and put fire therein, and laid incense thereon, and offered strange fire before Jehovah, which he had not commanded them.** 2. **And there came forth fire from before Jehovah, and devoured them, and they died before Jehovah.** One must give careful attention to this passage and its context to understand exactly what crime was here committed. Moses and Aaron had entered into the tabernacle of the congregation and had then come forth and bestowed a blessing upon the people, followed immediately by the manifestation of the glory of God, and by the descent of fire from heaven consuming on the altar the burnt offering which had just been presented. Two sons of Aaron, Nadab and Abihu, certainly of the priestly order, and certainly with a right, at the proper time, and in the proper way, to minister in the tabernacle, took censers, put some fire in them, the origin of which is not revealed, put incense on the fire, and offered this before the Lord, an offering which is here designated "strange fire." For this they were destroyed by a judgment of fire from God. What was it that these men did which was so terribly wrong? As Dr. Andrew Bonar has said, these men were immediately guilty of a threefold violation of the divine commandment. First, they offered this fire "at a time not commanded. Aaron should have been consulted for this. Secondly, it was offered in the wrong place, or in a part of the tabernacle not commanded; for they were in an open court (v. 4), where Uzziel's sons, who were only Levites, found them, not at the golden altar. Thirdly, they offered this fire in a manner contrary to the Lord's declared will: for the priests understood that the only fire to be used in the tabernacle was to be fire from the altar — fire that had come from heaven. The Lord had commanded neither the time, place, nor manner. But if the sinner's eye be blind to God, it sees not anything to be reverenced in the Lord's authority. And neither education, nor station, nor privileges are sufficient to keep men from this presumption. The heart

8. And Jehovah spake unto Aaron, saying,
9. Drink no wine nor strong drink, thou, nor thy sons with thee, when ye go into the tent of meeting, that ye die not: it shall be a statute for ever throughout your generations:
10. And that ye may make a distinction between the holy and the common, and between the unclean and the clean;
11. And that ye may teach the children of Israel all the statutes which Jehovah hath spoken unto them by Moses.

---

may continue unrenewed amid all such blessings. The Lord forthwith vindicated His own honor. These are priests, and they stand in the holy courts, and they hold the censers of the tabernacle in their hands, and the cloud of incense is ascending from them; but the Lord is dishonored under that cloud of incense, and therefore He must go forth in majesty. The stroke comes 'from the Lord' — the fire shoots across the mercy seat, and through the Holy Place, and finds the sinners under their cloud of incense! How awful to observe that it crosses the mercy seat to reach them: And though their cry reaches His ear over the mercy seat, it is *too late now!* The Lord has risen up. It is like the events that will attend Christ's second coming, when from Himself (the mercy seat itself), fire shall consume His foes, and their cry, though the Lamb Himself shall hear it, shall be in vain. He consumes all that have defiled Him; and many among these shall be found in the act of holding up the incense of vain worship to the Lord." — *Andrew Bonar.*

"Here was their sin. They departed in their worship from the plain word of Jehovah, who had fully and plainly instructed them as to the mode of their worship. We have already alluded to the divine fullness and sufficiency of the word of the Lord, in reference to every branch of priestly service. There was no room left for man to introduce what he might deem desirable or expedient. 'This is the thing which the Lord hath commanded,' was quite sufficient. It made all very plain and very simple. Nothing was needed on man's part save a spirit of implicit obedience to the divine command. But herein they failed. Man has always proved himself ill-disposed to walk in the narrow path of strict adherence to the plain Word of God. The bypath has ever seemed to present resistless charms to the poor human heart. 'Stolen waters are sweet, and bread eaten in secret is pleasant' (Prov. 9 : 17). Such is the enemy's language; but the lowly, obedient heart knows full well that the path of subjection to the Word of God is the only one that leads to 'waters' that are really 'sweet,' or to 'bread' that can be rightly called 'pleasant.' Nadab and Abihu might have deemed one kind of fire as good as another, but it was not their province to decide as to that. They should have acted according to the Word of the Lord; but instead of this, they took their own way and reaped the awful fruits thereof." — *C. H. Mackintosh.*

"What Nadab and Abihu did that day must be measured by these larger issues; for a disobedient priesthood means a corrupted nation, and a corrupted nation means a wronged world. This indeed is the story of the ultimate failure of the Hebrew people. Corrupted in its priesthood, therefore in its national life, therefore failing to fulfil its mission in the world. The final example of the failure is that of the refusal of the Messiah. The whole story of it is written in those brief, striking words of John: 'He came unto his own, and his own received him not.' A corrupted priesthood, Sadducean, demoralized, departed from the place of loyalty to God; a corrupted nation under the influence of such a priesthood resulted in the refusal of the One toward whom the whole economy had moved and therefore, so far as the Hebrew people were concerned, the world was wronged and robbed and degraded." — *G. Campbell Morgan.*

II. **THE PROHIBITION OF STRONG DRINK FOR ALL WHO ARE ABOUT TO ENGAGE IN PRIESTLY SERVICE,** Lev. 10 : 8–11. 8. **And Jehovah spake unto Aaron, saying,** 9. **Drink no wine nor strong drink, thou, nor thy sons with thee, when ye go into the tent of meeting, that ye die not: it shall be a statute for ever throughout your generations:** 10. **and that ye may make a distinction between the holy and the common, and between the unclean and the clean;** 11. **and that ye may teach the children of Israel all the statutes which Jehovah hath spoken unto them by Moses.** It is not quite clear why this divine command prohibiting intoxicating drink for all those who were to minister in holy things should appear directly

PROVERBS 31 : 4.
It is not for kings, O Lemuel, it is not for kings to drink wine;
Nor for princes *to say*, Where is strong drink?
5. Lest they drink, and forget the law,
And pervert the justice *due* to any that is afflicted.

after the account of the sin of Nadab and Abihu. Some have thought that these two men committed this transgression while in a state of intoxication, but the Word does not say so. May it not be that the connection is in this, that, when a person comes under the influence of intoxicants, that person becomes self-opinionated, unwise in his decisions, and rash in his actions, ignoring the importance of the law of God, and rushes in to do as he pleases? Thus, in setting forth the necessity for priests to abstain from intoxicating liquors, may it not be that the Lord is warning them to deny themselves that which, if indulged in, would turn their holy ministry into a series of transgressions? (Compare 1 Timothy 3 : 2, 3; and, especially, Ephesians 5 : 18.) " The effect of wine is to excite nature, and all natural excitement hinders that calm, well-balanced condition of soul which is essential to the proper discharge of the priestly office. So far from using any means to excite nature, we should treat it as a thing having no existence. Thus only shall we be in a moral condition to serve in the sanctuary, to form a dispassionate judgment between clean and unclean, and to expound and communicate the mind of God. It devolves upon each one to judge for himself what, in his special case, would act as ' wine or strong drink.' The things which excite mere nature are manifold indeed — wealth, ambition, politics, the varied objects of emulation around us in the world. If the heart be swollen with feelings of pride, covetousness, or emulation, it is utterly impossible that the pure air of the sanctuary can be enjoyed, or the sacred functions of priestly ministry discharged. The most versatile genius that was ever possessed could not enable a man to pass from an unhallowed arena of literary, commercial, or political competition, into the holy retirement of the sanctuary of the divine presence; nor could it ever adjust the eye that had become dimmed by the influence of such scenes, so as to enable it to discern, with priestly accuracy, the difference ' between holy and unholy, and between clean and unclean.' No, God's priests must keep themselves apart from wine and strong drink. Theirs is a path of holy separation and abstraction. They are to be raised far above the influence of earthly joy as well as earthly sorrow. The joy of God's priests is not the joy of earth, but the joy of heaven — the joy of the sanctuary. ' The joy of the Lord is their strength.' " — *C. H. Mackintosh.*

" As legitimate inferences from the whole passage, we may conclude (1) that God regards the use of intoxicating liquor as pregnant with danger to His servants, whatever their rank and attainments; (2) that the avoidance of this danger, by means of abstinence from such drink, having been a rule of His appointment, is still a cross worthy of general meditation; (3) that the adoption of this abstinence as a habit of life is specially approved by Him in the case of those who are required as a holy priest, to offer up without ceasing, ' spiritual sacrifices, acceptable to him by Jesus Christ.' " — *Bible Temperance Commentary.*

" Nothing has more power to blur the sharpness of moral and religious insight than even a small amount of alcohol. God must be worshiped with clear brain and naturally beating heart. Not the fumes of wine, in which there lurks almost necessarily the tendency to excess, but the being filled with the Spirit supplies the only legitimate stimulus to devotion. Lips stained from the wine cup would not be fit to speak holy words. Words spoken by such would carry no power. God's servants can never impress on the sluggish conscience of society their solemn messages from God, unless they are conspicuously free from self-indulgence, and show by their example, the gulf, wide as between heaven and hell, which bars cleanness from uncleanness. Our lives must witness to the eternal distinction between good and evil, if we are to draw men to ' abhor that which is evil, and cleave to that which is good.' " — *A. Maclaren.*

III. **WHY RULERS SHOULD ABSTAIN FROM ALL STRONG DRINK,** Prov. 31 : 4, 5. 4. **It is not for kings, O Lemuel, it is not for kings to drink wine; nor for princes *to say*, Where is strong drink?** 5. **Lest they drink and forget the law, and pervert the justice *due* to any that is afflicted.** (Compare 1 Kings 16 : 9; 20 : 16; Isa. 5 : 22, 23). " The indecency of drunkenness in a king; however some

LUKE 1 : 13. But the angel said unto him, Fear not, Zacharias: because thy supplication is heard, and thy wife Elisabeth shall bear thee a son, and thou shalt call his name John.

14. And thou shalt have joy and gladness; and many shall rejoice at his birth.

15. For he shall be great in the sight of the Lord, and he shall drink no wine nor strong drink; and he shall be filled with the Holy Spirit, even from his mother's womb.

---

may call it a fashionable accomplishment and entertainment, it is not for kings to allow themselves that liberty; it is a disparagement to their dignity, and profanes their crown, by confusing the head that wears it; that which for the time unmans them, does for the time unking them. Shall we say they are gods? No, they are worse than the beasts that perish. All Christians are made to our God kings and priests, and must apply this to themselves. . . . It is a sad complaint which is made of the priests and prophets (Isa. 28 : 7) that 'they have erred through wine, and through strong drink they are out of the way'; and the effect is as bad in kings, who, when they are drunk, or intoxicated, cannot but stumble in judgment. Judges must have clear heads, which those cannot have, who so often make themselves giddy, and incapacitate themselves to judge of the most common things." — *Matthew Henry*. We believe that these two verses in themselves need no further explanation, and that our readers would prefer that we devote such space as we have for this lesson, to additional temperance facts at the conclusion of the exposition of the Scripture passages assigned.

IV. **HEAVEN'S DESCRIPTION OF THE LIFE TO BE LIVED BY JOHN THE BAPTIST,** Luke 1 : 13-16. This passage stands at the threshhold of a new era in human history, indeed, at the turning point of the history of the whole world; that is, the coming of the Son of God to earth. Our lesson introduces us to that significant preliminary event, the birth of John the Baptist, ordained of God to be the forerunner of the Messiah, who, by His preaching, was to bring the first great revival Israel had known for many centuries, who would turn thousands to the Lord, and lead them to repentance and to baptism for the remission of sins. The words of our lesson are part of the communication by the angel Gabriel to Zacharias, the father of John the Baptist, even before the conception of this child. This is heaven's description of the life that heaven's servant was to live, and, as far as we can discover, it is a perfect picture of any true servant of God, or at least what God wants that servant to be. 13. **But the angel said unto him, Fear not, Zacharias: because thy supplication is heard, and thy wife Elisabeth shall bear thee a son, and thou shalt call his name John.** 14. **And thou shalt have joy and gladness; and many shall rejoice at his birth.** Professor Plummer says, and we think rightly, that when the angel told Zacharias that his prayer has been heard, it does not of necessity mean that Zacharias at this time was actually praying for a son. If it was such a prayer that was heard, then it was a prayer offered many years before this, for certainly Zacharias, as a true priest of God, would not be selfishly asking for God *now* to perform a miracle for him merely that he should have a son, and a miracle it would be if a son were born at this time, for Elisabeth was a woman long past the time of life when a son would be expected. "It is much more probable that he and the people were praying for the redemption of Israel — for the coming of the Messiah's kingdom; and it is this supplication which was heard. The joy at the appearance of a prophet after centuries of need was immense, although not universal. The Pharisees did not dare to say that John was not a prophet (Matt. 21 : 26), and Herod, until driven to it, did not dare to put him to death (Matt. 14 : 5). The word here translated *rejoice* means 'extreme joy,' or exaltation, and is never found in classical writings but occurs elsewhere in the New Testament in Luke 1 : 44; Acts 2 : 46; Heb. 1 : 9; Jude 24." — *Alfred Plummer*.

15. **For he shall be great in the sight of the Lord, and he shall drink no wine nor strong drink; and he shall be filled with the Holy Spirit, even from his mother's womb.** "The angel is describing John to his father as the prophet he is to be. He states first, the striking outward feature of avoidance of all intoxicants — not an ordinary but a very exceptional prophet is he to be. Secondly, his spiritual equipment. All prophets have the Holy Spirit, for there can be no divine prophecy

16. And many of the children of Israel shall he turn unto the Lord their God.

without Him. But John shall not merely have the Spirit when he comes to do his work, 'he shall be filled with the Holy Spirit already from his mother's womb.' So great will this prophet be (Matt. 11 : 9–11), exceeding all others, that his whole existence shall be under the direct control of the Holy Spirit. . . . Too little attention is paid to the striking fact that the person of the Holy Spirit and His divine work are mentioned to Jews as perfectly known to them." — *R. C. H. Lenski.* There is an obvious contrast here between "strong drink," and "the Holy Spirit." In place of the physical excitement of strong drink, he is to have the supernatural inspiration of the Holy Spirit. Why was he not to partake of strong drink? For two reasons: First, that his own spiritual vision might be unimpaired, that all of the faculties of his personality might be constantly under the sovereign control of the Spirit of God, and never under the clouding, coarsening, artificial stimulation of intoxicants. A man who is a heavy drinker will never be sensitive to the will of God, nor rise to great spiritual heights. In the second place, John was to preach repentance from sin, a life of temperance, of self-denial, of obedience to the laws of God, and it was absolutely necessary for him, as for all preachers, first to live that which he was to preach, to practice daily that which he would be proclaiming to others as the will of God. How many thousands and thousands of ministers, true in their doctrinal convictions, and definitely called into the ministry, have made shipwreck of themselves and become spiritual dwarfs, barren laborers, because liquor has been allowed to lay its fiendish fangs upon them and strangled their spiritual life. 16. **And many of the children of Israel shall he turn unto the Lord their God.** "The two personal characteristics — subjection of the flesh and sovereignty of the Spirit — will manifest themselves in two external effects, a great religious revival and the preparation for the Messianic kingdom. The first of these was the recognized work of every prophet. Israel, through sin, was constantly being alienated from God; and it was one of the chief functions of a prophet to convert his people to God again (Jer. 3 : 7, 10, 14; 18 : 8; Ezek. 3 : 19; Dan. 9 : 13)." — *A. Plummer.*

A DISTINGUISHED PHYSIOLOGIST ON THE EFFECT OF ALCOHOL ON THE HIGHER LIFE OF MAN.

One of the greatest physiologists of America today is Dr. A. C. Ivy, head of the Department of Physiology and Pharmacology of Northwestern University, Chicago. He recently made the following clear, comprehensive declaration concerning the consequence of imbibing intoxicating liquors: "Alcohol gives temporary relief from worry; abolishes mental tension, disguises difficulties, relieves a feeling of inferiority; makes a weak person feel strong, an ignorant person feel smart, a poor person feel rich, an oppressed person feel free, a bad person feel good, and makes one imagine himself a good driver who may be potentially a motor car murderer. But it is a very poor policy to play with fire or 'fire-water.' It is dangerous to play with a habit-forming poison or narcotic such as alcohol. Alcohol depresses the critical and most sensitive faculties of the brain. Alcohol disturbs normal motor control. Alcohol affects memory and learning. Alcohol is a direct and principal cause of several types of mental disease. The drink habit is usually formed in early adult life and continues for several years before the mental breakdown, principally between the ages of forty to forty-five, the prime of life. A person should have a more intelligent and less dangerous way to escape and relax. I do not have to take a narcotic like alcohol to forget my worries and to relax from the tensions of the day. I would suggest that the ideal substitute for alcohol is a hobby, by which I mean a pursuit which absorbs one's interest without unduly exciting the emotions. . . . Everyone knows of several pursuits which cause them to relax and escape from the worries and anxieties of the day. Sports and nature, a walk in the woods or park, are usually best because they exercise the body and free the mind from care."

THE EFFECT OF ALCOHOL ON THE NERVOUS SYSTEM OF MAN.

Dr. Alfred Salter, a distinguished surgeon of Great Britain, and a member of the British Parliament, in a very fine booklet, *The Nation Challenged*, gives an illuminating discussion, which even children can understand, of the disastrous effects on our nervous system of imbibing intoxicating liquors, and we believe the teacher will do well to master this brief discussion, and present it to the class in a way they will never forget. "Very few people, except medical men, have ever seen the brain of a human being and few doctors have seen the brain of a monkey. Suppose I submitted to you the brain of a newborn baby and that of an adult chimpanzee on the same dish, practically none of you would notice much difference in appearance. They are almost exactly the same in size and shape. Supposing, however, that I made microscopic sections of the two brains and showed them to you, you would notice certain cell groups in the human organ that are absent from that of the ape. I can demonstrate the difference by an illustration. Assume that my closed fist represents the brain of an adult chimpanzee. I then envelop it in a handkerchief. It would now represent the brain of a human infant. That is to say, in addition to the nervous structure which constitutes the simian brain there is a covering layer or cloak of cell tissue over the surface, or cortex, of the human brain, which is not present in the chimpanzee — this is called the neopallium. What is the function of this layer? Its groups of nerve centers are the seat of the highest human faculties and mental functions — judgment, self-control, the sense of values and self-criticism. . . . Now what is the first effect of alcohol on the human system? (I am not talking of excessive quantities, but just moderate or so-called dietetic quantities.) The first effect of alcohol in small doses is to narcotize the cells and centers of this highest level of the brain. Alcohol is primarily a narcotic drug. That is not a matter of opinion but a fact. Any authoritative textbook will tell you that. A narcotic is a substance that sends you to sleep, that depresses and dulls the highest faculties, that puts out of action, wholly or in part and for the time being, certain portions of the central nervous organization — the degree of suspension being dependent upon the quantity and concentration of the drug. When you take a moderate dose of alcohol you are affecting and putting out of action in whole or in part that very portion of your anatomy which is distinctively human. . . . You may say that is a strong statement and that it is an exaggeration of the position. 'Do we not know,' you say, 'as a matter of every day experience, that many people take their glass with their meals and no one can notice any difference? They appear to be and behave precisely the same afterward as before.' What is to be the reply to that? Suppose I have two bags of equal weight in my hands with three hundred marbles in each. I hand them to you and you can detect no difference in the weight. I take three marbles out of one bag and then hand both back to see if you can decide from which I have abstracted the marbles. Again you cannot tell any difference. If I take eight marbles out of one of the bags you still could not tell from which I had taken them. An experiment like this does not require a highly equipped laboratory — you may try it for yourself at home; but the fact is that the human nervous system is not sufficiently sensitive to enable you to discriminate between two weights unless the difference is at least *one-thirtieth of the total.* That is to say, I must remove at least ten marbles before you can appreciate which bag has been tampered with. For some people, I might have to take twelve, fifteen, or even twenty. Put the bags on the scales, however, and I have only to take out one marble and the scales will immediately show the difference. You see the man before he has taken his alcoholic drink at lunch and after, and you recognize no difference. But put him on the scales, *i.e.*, subject him to exact scientific investigation and you will see that something has gone from him. In a dozen different respects he is an altered man. His reaction time is increased. For example, before he takes a drink if he is driving a car and sees another car coming, a 'latent period' of one-fifth of a second has to elapse before his muscles can respond to the brain stimulus to contract and to operate the steering gear, brake or accelerator, as the case may be. Let him have his glass and then check his reaction time again. It is definitely increased, it is perhaps two, three or even four fifths of a second before his muscles can respond to the brain stimulus. His accuracy is impaired. His 'choice reactions' are delayed. Thousands of experiments have been conducted in various parts of the world, and all have shown that operations requiring correlation of hand and eye and brain are impaired, that is, they are slower and less accurate after taking alcohol, although the man himself *believes* he is doing things more quickly and accurately than before. This means that if you take alcohol you are reducing your efficiency, unknown to yourself, and unobserved by others. This reduction in the case of a motor driver in an emergency may mean the difference between life and death."

How many different reasons have been set forth in our lesson showing why men engaged in spiritual work should be extremely careful to abstain from all beverages

which can be called intoxicating? Do you know any one good argument why ministers of the gospel, persons of any faith, why clergymen should be addicted to the cup and should have intoxicating liquors around the house? Frankly, do you think a congregation can listen as profitably to the sermons of a minister on the Lord's Day, who they know regularly partakes of intoxicants, as they can to one who is a total abstainer? Do you think that a Christian gains anything at all by partaking with others with whom he happens to be in association, in the drinking of intoxicating beverages? What do you think would be some of the consequences in this country if every true believer would from this day on, say for the next five years, privately practice and publicly proclaim total abstinence from intoxicants?

LESSON VI. — November 7.

THE SACREDNESS OF HUMAN LIFE. — Exodus 20 : 13; Matthew 5 : 21–26, 38–45.

GOLDEN TEXT. — ***Whosoever hateth his brother is a murderer.*** 1 JOHN 3 : 15.

Devotional Reading: James 4 : 1–10.
Beginner Topic: GOD'S GIFT OF WATER.
Lesson Material: Exodus 15 : 22–27.
Memory Verse: Jehovah sendeth rain upon the earth. 1 Kings 17 : 14.
Primary Topic: WHILE THE KING SLEPT.
Lesson Material: Exodus 20 : 13; Matthew 5 : 21–26, 38–45; 1 Samuel 26.
Memory Verse: Be ye kind one to another, tenderhearted, forgiving each other, even as God also in Christ forgave you. Ephesians 4 : 32.
Junior Topic: SAUL'S SPEAR.
Lesson Material: Exodus 20 : 13; Matthew 5 : 21–26, 38–45; 1 Samuel 26.
Memory Verse: Depart from evil, and do good; seek peace, and pursue it. Psalm 34 : 14.
Intermediate and Senior Topic: WHY IS HUMAN LIFE SACRED?
Topic for Young People and Adults: MODERN SINS AGAINST HUMAN LIFE.

THE TEACHER AND HIS CLASS.

The Younger Classes will not be too young to understand the meaning of personal affront; that is, to know the meaning of an insult, of the experience of some one being mean or unkind, or unfair to them, and they will know, even in their young hearts, how quickly the fever of revenge arises. It is especially true with little children that, on the least provocation, in the school yard or on the street, they seem to enjoy striking back at some other child who has stepped on their toes, as it were. In this lesson our Lord is not condemning the defense of one's own person, but He is revealing the inconsistency of a person who loves Him, letting his actions be dominated by a revengeful spirit. Such a person is rather to suffer an insult, and thus escape the feverishness of anger, and a stream of bitterness and hatred in his life.

The Older Classes will be, in this time, face to face with the question of war, but, as we shall see when the lesson is expounded, this passage has nothing to do with war, but with personal relationships. Christianity works out in human life in a most practical and vital way, and men who have accepted Christ, and follow His teachings, are different from those who have not, in every sphere of life, and in no sphere more than in that which has to do with their relationship to men and women about them. If the relationship between individual men and women was always right, then we would have no such thing as war on earth. But let us begin with the individual relationship. War is a consequence, not a root; and it is the root of which our Lord is here speaking.

THE LESSON IN ITS SETTING.

Time. — The Ten Commandments were delivered in 1445 B.C.; the Sermon on the Mount was given in the summer of A.D. 28.

Place. — The Decalogue was given on Mount Sinai; the Sermon on the Mount was uttered not far from Capernaum.

THE PLAN OF THE LESSON.

SUBJECT: Christ's Standard for His Followers Regarding Their Thought

and Conduct Toward Those Who Have Intended to Injure or Insult Them.

I. THE ANCIENT COMMANDMENT FORBIDDING MURDER, Exod. 20 : 13.

II. CHRIST'S BROAD APPLICATION OF THIS COMMANDMENT, Matt. 5 : 21–26.

1. The sin of contemptuous speech concerning others, vs. 21, 22.
2. The necessity of being reconciled to our brother before any act of worship, vs. 23, 24.
3. The necessity for agreeing with our adversary, vs. 25, 26.

III. THE ATTITUDE CHRISTIANS SHOULD TAKE TOWARD THEIR ENEMIES, Matt. 5 : 38–45.

1. The Old Testament law of revenge, v. 38.
2. The Christian doctrine of non-resistance in regard to personal insults, v. 39.
3. The obligation to go the second mile, vs. 40–42.
4. Love for our enemies, vs. 43–45.

THE TEACHER'S LIBRARY.

In addition to books on the Ten Commandments, and commentaries on Matthew's Gospel, one should also consult the larger volumes on the Sermon on the Mount, especially the volume by J. O. Dykes, and Vol. 1 in a series simply entitled, *The Sermon on the Mount* (Manchester, 1903), containing sermons by a number of outstanding preachers of that generation. On 21 : 26, see T. Zahn: *Bread and Salt from the Word of God*, 245–263; on verse 23, D. J. Burrell: *The Verilies of Jesus*, 77–81; on verses 23, 24, F. B. Meyer: *Expository Preaching*, 131–141; and a sermon on "The Way to the Altar," by G. Campbell Morgan, in the *Westminster Pulpit*, Vol. 8, 393–400; on verses 38–41, Alexander Maclaren: *Expositions of Holy Scripture, Matthew 1–8*, 210–214; on verse 38, Phillips Brooks: *Seeking Life*, 224–240; on verse 39, James Moffatt: *The Second Things of Life*, 21–47; verse 41, J. H. Hutton: *Victory Over Victory*, 132–141; J. S. Holden: *The Pre-eminent Lord*, 121–127; J. D. Jones: *The Unfettered Word*, 68–74; J. Wilbur Chapman: *Another Mile*, 128–143; H. E. Fosdick: *The Second Mile;* verses 44, 45, J. H. Jowett: *Brooks by the Traveler's Way*, 129–140. On the subject of non-resistance, see Robert E. Speer: *The Principles of Jesus*, 123–127; H. E. Montgomery: *Christ's Social Remedies*, 139–156; and an article, "Retaliation," by R. B. Taylor, in Hastings's *Dictionary of Christ and the Gospels*, Vol. 2, 517, 518.

EXODUS 20 : 13. Thou shalt not kill.

I. **THE ANCIENT COMMANDMENT FORBIDDING MURDER,** Exod. 20 : 13. 13. **Thou shalt not kill.** " With the second table of the Decalogue begins our duty to our neighbor. The laws of probity follow the laws of piety, ' that the river of justice may be derived from the fountain of love to God.' The second table shows the immense importance of social life. It surrounds with eternal safeguards the undefeatable rights of all mankind. It is meant to bring home to us the truth that none of us liveth to himself and no man dieth to himself." — *F. W. Farrar.*

THE FUNDAMENTAL TEACHING OF THIS COMMANDMENT.

" This commandment protects life, and is against all endeavors that endanger the life of our neighbor. As there is no object expressed, it prohibits suicide as well as homicide. It also forbids violence, passion, lust, intemperance in eating or drinking, or anything that tends to shorten life. The peculiar sacredness of human life lies in this, that man is a responsible being, liable to be rewarded or punished according to his deeds. Life is a reward of obedience, and death is the penalty of disobedience. On the circumstance that this life is to the sinner the season of invitation to return to God, who will have mercy on him, depends immeasurably the crime of cutting short his life in the midst of his impenitence. All these considerations are wrapped up in a paramount reflection that man was created in the image of God." — *J. G. Murphy.*

SOCIAL ETHICS BASED ON RELIGIOUS TRUTHS.

" Social ethics, then, have a religious sanction. It is the constant duty and effort of the Church of God to saturate the whole life of man, all his conduct and his thought, with a sense of sacredness; and as the world is forever desecrating what is holy, so is religion forever consecrating what is secular. . . . It is when we see in our fellow man a divine creature of the Divine, made by God in His own image, marred and defaced by sin, but not beyond recovery, when his actions are regarded as wrought in the sight of a Judge whose presence supersedes utterly the slightness, heat, and inadequacy of our judgment and our vengeance, when his pure affections tell us of the love of God which passeth knowledge, when his errors affright us as dire and melancholy apostasies from a mighty calling, and when his death is solemn as the unveiling of unknown and unending destinies, then it is that we discern the sacredness of life, and the awful presumption of the deed which quenches it." — *G. A. Chadwick.*

THE RELATION OF THIS COMMANDMENT TO WAR.

Scripture must always be interpreted by Scripture. No one passage in the Word of God can be interpreted to the exclusion of other passages that relate to the same subject, nor fundamentally can one Scripture be made to contradict another. When, then, we remember that God, in the Old Testament, clearly told the Israelites to go up to battle against the Philistines and the Amorites and the Canaanites, when God Himself gave victory over these enemies, when He is called at times the God of war (Ex. 15 : 3) we cannot then expect to find in the Bible a verse which categorically, universally condemns war. The Bible does not do such. The Bible does tell us that war comes from a lust for things that nations do not have, but the Bible never says that a nation should not protect itself against an invading force. "Clearly the commandment was not intended to forbid war. The nation to which it was given had a strict military organization, constituted by the very authority from which the commandment came. The wars in which it engaged were, many of them, conducted by men who cannot be supposed to have been ignorant of what the commandment meant. Moses himself prayed to God that the hosts of Israel might be victorious over their enemies. Man is made in the image of God; has received a life which invests him with mysterious greatness, and therefore he must not be killed. But, for the unfolding and development of that life — for the existence of all those virtues, and the free culture, and exercise of all those powers, which constitute the glory of human nature — it is necessary that nations should exist with their definite territories, their social order, their systems of law, their recognized governments. Man, without the institutions of national life, would cease to be man. He would have no true history. Break up all national organizations, and he must drift back into a condition like that of the brutes.

Bringing of Heads after a Battle. From Maspero.

Scribes, standing before their tent doors, registered the number of heads cut off.

The stability of national institutions is necessary for man to be truly himself, for the development of his intelligence and the formation and exercise of all moral virtues. Hence the greatness which belongs to man himself passes on to the nation, which is indispensable to man's dignity. The nation, too, is sacred and inviolable. To defend its soil against invasion, to protect its independence, becomes a duty which cannot be abandoned without exposing to fatal injury that higher life which alone makes us superior to the brutes around us. Wars of ambition, wars of revenge — these are crimes. Wars to avenge a real or fancied insult, or to achieve or maintain political supremacy, are crimes; wars originated to save a dynasty, or prolonged to humiliate a vanquished enemy, are crimes. But the moral sense of the purest and noblest of mankind has sanctioned and honored the courage and heroism which repel by force of arms an assault on a nation's integrity, and the great principle which underlies this commandment sanctions and honors them too." — *R. W. Dale.*

THE RELATION OF THIS LAW TO CAPITAL PUNISHMENT.

"God Himself commanded, 'Whosoever sheddeth man's blood, by man shall his blood be shed, for in the image of God made he man' (Gen. 9 : 6). The claim that this precept belongs to the Mosaic ritual which was abrogated in the New Testament is certainly wrong. This commandment was given by God to Noah in connection with the covenant of nature. That this covenant has a permanent significance is evident from the context. God promised not to destroy the world again by a flood as long as summer and winter, cold and heat, sowing and reaping

MATTHEW 5 : 21–26. 21. Ye have heard that it was said to them of old time, Thou shalt not kill; and whosoever shall kill shall be in danger of the judgment:

22. But I say unto you, that every one who is angry with his brother shall be in danger of the judgment; and whosoever shall say to his brother, Raca, shall be in danger of the council; and whosoever shall say, Thou fool, shall be in danger of the hell of fire.

---

continued. The reason annexed to this commandment, 'For in the image of God made he man,' is also of permanent duration. It is just as true today as when it was given. . . . Paul declared in Romans 13 that the magistrate bears not the sword in vain. The bearing of the sword is equivalent to saying that the magistrate has the power over life and death. Think of the thief on the cross. Christ did not miraculously deliver the thieves from the gibbet. This is even true of the converted thief. Why not? Because they deserved to die. The converted thief said that they received just recompense for their reward. That capital punishment is legal is also confirmed by experience. There is no civilized nation on the face of the earth where more murders are committed and more banditry found than in the United States of America. Only one murderer out of four in our land is ever brought to trial. Only one of every ten of those brought to trial is ever sentenced to prison for the crime of murder. Only one accused murderer of every eighty is executed. A few years ago, there were more than three thousand murders committed in New York City in one year. Of these three thousand, only 10 per cent were convicted. During the same year there were twenty-six murders in the city of London. Thirteen of the murderers committed suicide and the other thirteen were executed. Not one escaped. The trouble is that men are turning away from the old Biblical doctrine of punishment." — *W. Masselink.*

II. **CHRIST'S BROAD APPLICATION OF THIS COMMANDMENT,** Matt. 5 : 21–26.

1. THE SIN OF CONTEMPTUOUS SPEECH CONCERNING OTHERS, VS. 21, 22. 21. **Ye have heard that it was said to them of old time, Thou shalt not kill; and whosoever shall kill shall be in danger of the judgment:** 22. **but I say unto you, that every one who is angry with his brother shall be in danger of the judgment; and whosoever shall say to his brother, Raca, shall be in danger of the council; and whosoever shall say, Thou fool, shall be in danger of the hell of fire.** The phrase, " whosoever shall kill shall be in danger of the judgment," is not found in the Old Testament, and it is generally assumed that our Lord is here speaking of traditional comments on the law. In this passage the " I " is emphasized in the Greek. Rabbinical teachers would refer to their famous masters. The Lord Jesus refers to Himself. The one difficult word of this passage is *Raca.* " As far as the dictionary sense of the word goes, it is the same as that of the '*vain* fellows' of Judges 9 : 4; 11 : 3; Prov. 12 : 11; but all words of abuse depend for their full force on popular association, and *raca,* like words of kindred meaning among ourselves, was in common use as expressing not anger only but insolent contempt. The temper condemned is that in which anger has so far gained the mastery that we no longer recognize a 'brother' in the man who has offended us, but look on him with malignant scorn. Offenses of this kind are placed by our Lord on the same level as those which came before the great court of the Sanhedrin. . . . The court consisted of seventy or seventy-two members, with a president and vice-president, and was made up of the heads of the twenty-four courses of the priests, with forty-six or forty-eight (how chosen it is not known) from the 'elders' and 'scribes.' . . . The point of our Lord's teaching was, therefore, that to scorn God's image in man is to do dishonor to God Himself. We cannot truly fear God unless we also honor all men (1 Pet. 2 : 17). The reverence for humanity as such must extend even to the man who has most provoked us. In the unseen eternal world the want of that reverence has its own appropriate punishment. To say, 'Thou fool,' embodied the temper, not, like that represented be *raca,* of petulant contempt, but of fixed and settled hatred. That it was the temper and not the utterance of the mere syllables which our Lord condemned is seen in that He Himself used the word of the scribes and Pharisees (Matt. 23 : 17, 19), and Paul of the skeptical Greek materialist (1 Cor. 15 : 36). The selfsame word might spring from a righteous indignation or from malignant hatred." — *E. H. Plumptre.*

23. If therefore thou art offering thy gift at the altar, and there rememberest that thy brother hath aught against thee,

24. Leave there thy gift before the altar, and go thy way, first be reconciled to thy brother, and then come and offer thy gift.

25. Agree with thine adversary quickly, while thou art with him in the way; lest haply the adversary deliver thee to the judge, and the judge deliver thee to the officer, and thou be cast into prison.

26. Verily I say unto thee, Thou shalt by no means come out thence, till thou have paid the last farthing.

Gehenna here refers originally to a place in the valley of Hinnom, a narrow gorge, south of Jerusalem, where fires were kept burning to consume the refuse of the city. On the lips of our Lord, the phrase came to refer to everlasting fire, to the fire of a judgment descending from God. This lesson is not assigned for teaching the doctrine of hell, but one cannot escape its awful significance in a verse like this. "The reckless use of opprobrious epithets Jesus regarded as the supreme offense against the law of humanity. The man guilty of this crime deserves to go not to the seven or the seventy, but to hell, his sin altogether damnable. These words are the strong utterance of one in whom all forms of inhumanity roused feelings of passionate abhorrence." — *Marcus Dods.*

2. THE NECESSITY OF BEING RECONCILED TO OUR BROTHER BEFORE ANY ACT OF WORSHIP, VS. 23, 24. 23. **If therefore thou art offering thy gift at the altar, and there rememberest that thy brother hath aught against thee,** 24. **leave there thy gift before the altar, and go thy way, first be reconciled to thy brother, and then come and offer thy gift.** It is when we come into the presence of God, that most delicate relationship of all of life, the most sacred communion that is possible to a human soul, that things that are wrong stand out in their true light. So our Lord says, if when bringing an offering, a gift, to the altar, one remembers that his brother has something against him, his gift is to be immediately left, and the offerer is to go and find his brother, be reconciled to him, and then go back and offer his gift. "It is impossible to read any text which is ushered in by the word 'therefore' without inquiring, Wherefore? What, then, is the simple meaning of the text in its first application? Because these mental moods of anger and contempt and malice are forbidden, *therefore,* if any man have given his brother occasion for such moods, he is at once to act so as to remove them. . . . If when thou art coming to the altar thou rememberest thy brother has something against thee which may inspire the feeling of anger, contempt, or malice in his breast, go and be reconciled to him, not for thy sake only, but for his sake, lest he become guilty of sin. . . . Moreover, coming to the altar is approach to God. Coming to the altar is coming to the hour and place of worship. Coming to the altar is finding our way into fellowship with God by means of mediation and sacrifice. Coming to the altar is the recognition of the sovereignty of God, of the supremacy of His will. Without any further argument, it is perfectly evident that coming to the altar produces recollection of any violation of that will. No man ever seriously draws near to the altar without remembering. . . . The altar is the way into purity, not an excuse for impurity. The intention of the altar is loosing from sin, not hiding it. The altar calls upon man to co-operate with God to the utmost of his ability in this moral restoration. The very first value of the altar is that it reminds a man of his sin. The very first value of Christian worship is that it starts the activity of conscience, and compels men to think of the actuality of sin. . . . Coming to the altar — for 'we have an altar' — we remember the things of wrong, the things of evil. A consequent value of the altar is that it absolutely refuses to harbor the man who is not prepared to co-operate to the utmost of his ability with God for his own moral restoration. 'Leave there thy gift before the altar, and go thy way, first be reconciled to thy brother.'" — *G. Campbell Morgan.*

3. THE NECESSITY FOR AGREEING WITH OUR ADVERSARY, VS. 25, 26. 25. **Agree with thine adversary quickly, while thou art with him in the way; lest haply the adversary deliver thee to the judge, and the judge deliver thee to the officer, and thou be cast into prison.** 26. **Verily I say unto thee, Thou shalt by no means come out thence, till thou have paid the last farthing.** "The imagery is changed and returns to that of human tribunals, which has met us in verse 22. The man whom

38. Ye have heard that it was said, An eye for an eye, and a tooth for a tooth:
39. But I say unto you, Resist not him that is evil: but whosoever smiteth thee on thy right cheek, turn to him the other also.

we have wronged appears as the adversary, the prosecutor bringing his charge against us. The impulse of the natural man at such a time, even if conscious of wrong, is to make the best of his case, to prevaricate, to recriminate. The truer wisdom, Christ teaches, is to agree — better, to be on good terms with — show our own good will, and so win his. The whole teaching, it is obvious, is addressed to one who *has* done wrong. The treatment of a false charge involves different considerations. . . . In the application of the words, the judge is clearly God, and the officers, those (angels or others) who execute His judgment, and the adversary those whom we have wronged, leaving the wrong unredressed. The Greek word translated *farthing* is derived from the Latin *quadrans*, the fourth part of the Roman *as*, a small copper or bronze coin which had become common in Palestine. The 'mite,' half the *quadrans* (Mark 12 : 42), was the smallest coin in circulation. The farthing of Matthew 10 : 29 is a different word, and was applied to the tenth part of the drachma." — *E. H. Plumptre.* There is not the slightest hint in this verse that our Lord is laying down any principle of judgment in life after death. He is talking, in this particular passage, about conditions here on earth. It is simply impossible for a man to pay God the last farthing that he owes, spiritually, to God. There is nothing in the Scriptures that would indicate a purgatorial state for man, in which he makes amends for the iniquities and transgressions of his life. How could a man, disembodied, a mere spirit in the darkness of some purgatorial region, ever even begin to pay back to God what he owes! We ask God to forgive us our debts, and it is only by His forgiveness through Jesus Christ that we can ever hope to be brought into the presence of God. This passage has to do then with relationships here on earth between men.

III. **THE ATTITUDE CHRISTIANS SHOULD TAKE TOWARD THEIR ENEMIES,** Matt. 5 : 38–45.

1. THE OLD TESTAMENT LAW OF REVENGE, v. 38. 38. **Ye have heard that it was said, An eye for an eye, and a tooth for a tooth.** This passage is quoted from Exodus 21 : 24 (cf. Lev. 24 : 20; Deut. 19 : 21). "The verses we have now before us correct and read backwards a misused principle of public law — the so-called *jus talionis*. The criminal code which God gave to the free Hebrew people fully recognized the principle of equivalent retaliation. It must be carefully remembered — what the Jewish lawyers forgot, and their forgetting it explains their whole blunder — that this statute was part of the criminal code of a commonwealth, and had for its end the satisfaction of public justice. It was no rule for private revenge. It put no license to retaliate into the hand of any private person. The law of the state only, acting for public ends of justice and through its own officers, exacted this stern retribution. . . . But the *jus talionis*, or principle of retaliation, is quite different. It belongs not to civil, but to criminal law. It deals with misdemeanors, not injuries. It awards, not damages, but punishment; and therefore (which is the vital point) it is a rule, not for private plaintiffs, but for the public prosecutor." — *J. O. Dykes.*

2. THE CHRISTIAN DOCTRINE OF NON-RESISTANCE IN REGARD TO PERSONAL INSULTS, v. 39. 39. **But I say unto you, Resist not him that is evil: but whosoever smiteth thee on thy right cheek, turn to him the other also.** First, we must get clear in our mind what it means for one man to smite another "on the cheek." This is the most insulting act among Oriental peoples, and among many Germanic peoples in Central Europe. For ages, just a slap in the face has been an invitation to dueling. The editor believes that this particular act is not at all what we would call an *assault* upon a person's being. It is not an attack with murderous intent. In fact, it is not even intended to hurt the person receiving the blow, but to insult that person. It is not a blow with a stick; it is not the thrust of a sword; it is not the hard striking of a fist. It is simply a blow on the cheek, and therefore to be taken as an insult. Now our Lord says when some one thus strikes us on one cheek, to insult us, to show his contempt for us, to arouse our anger, to drag us into a quarrel, we are to turn the other cheek. "Nothing will enable us to meet evil with a patient yielding love which does not bring the faintest tinge of anger even into the cheek reddened by a rude hand, but the 'love of God shed abroad in the heart,' and when that love fills a man,

40. And if any man would go to law with thee, and take away thy coat, let him have thy cloak also.

41. And whosoever shall compel thee to go one mile, go with him two.

'out of him will flow a river of living water,' which will bury evil below its clear, gentle abundance, and, perchance, wash it of its foulness. There is something hid away somewhere in most men's hearts which makes them ashamed of smiting the offered left cheek, and then ashamed of having smitten the right one. 'It is a shame to hit him, since he does not defend himself,' comes into many a ruffian's mind. The safest way to travel in savage countries is to show oneself quite unarmed. He that meets evil with evil is 'overcome of evil'; he that meets it with patient love is likely in most cases to 'overcome evil with good.' And even if he fails, he has, at all events, used the only weapon that has any chance of beating down the evil, and it is better to be defeated when fighting hate with love than to be victorious when fighting it with itself, or demanding an eye for an eye." — *Alexander Maclaren.* But there is another side to this, and the author we have just quoted, brings it out well. "If we take the right view of this precept, its limitations are in itself. Since it is love confronting, and seeking to transform evil into its own self not to yield. If turning the other cheek would but make the assaulter more angry, or if yielding the cloak would but make the legal robber more greedy, or if going the second mile would but make the press-gang more severe and exacting, resistance becomes a form of love and a duty for the sake of the wrongdoer. It may also become a duty for the sake of others, who are also objects of love, such as helpless persons, who otherwise would be exposed to evil, or society as a whole. But while clearly that limit is prescribed by the very nature of the precept, the resistance which it permits must have love to the culprit or to others as its motive, and not be tainted by the least suspicion of passion or vengeance."

"Jesus accepted the reproaches and injustice of men. When people threatened to stone Him or to maltreat Him, He made no resistance. He simply went away (Luke 4 : 29, 30; John 8 : 59; 10 : 39). He reproved His disciples for using violence in defending Him at the time of His arrest (Matt. 26 : 52). He Himself refrained from making use of the terrible power at His command to annihilate His enemies (Matt. 26 : 53, 54). At His trial He endured insult and wrong unmurmuringly (Matt. 26 : 67; Mark 14 : 65; Matt. 27 : 30); and went to His death without resistance or complaint (John 19 : 17); . . . On the other hand, when He was smitten on the cheek before the high priest, Jesus did not offer the other cheek. To have done so would not have been a display of love. It would have been a temptation to the evil man who smote Him to repeat his horrible offense." We do not believe that this rule has anything at all to do with war. This is a personal matter, between man and man, not between nation and nation. Neither does this have anything to do with the invasion of our homes, or a personal attack upon our bodies. It is sheer nonsense for anybody to draw out of this sentence such a principle of conduct as that one must not defend himself from personal injury, or defend women and children from the attack of brutes, or that a nation must not defend itself from the invasion of a cruel and monstrous evil-planning enemy. There is nothing like that in the New Testament. Soldiers have their place in the New Testament, and are used for the protection of persons, as, for instance, of Paul. Jesus never condemned a soldier for being a soldier. Governments have their place, and in Romans 13 it is clear that they are ordained to punish evildoers.

3. THE OBLIGATION TO GO THE SECOND MILE, VS. 40–42. 40. **And if any man would go to law with thee, and take away thy coat, let him have thy cloak also.** "Spoliation, whether under forms of law, as Matthew gives the next case, or by private violence, as in Luke's version, is a less serious wrong, because it only affects property. Our Lord urges His hearer to be prepared, before the case of extortion goes to court, to yield not merely the cheap linen under-tunic which is claimed, but over and above, if needful, the large outer plaid which is the Oriental's chief article of dress, both by night and by day. The verse is Eastern in coloring and concrete in form; but it really covers the whole principle which rules the litigation of Christians. It is under all circumstances not perhaps wrong, but at least a defect of charity, to go to law either for mere personal pique, or for the single end of private selfish gain." — *J. O. Dykes.* 41. **And whosoever shall compel thee to go one mile, go with him two.** The word here translated *compel* means, probably, to compel to carry one's baggage. "An instance in the New Testament of the use of the word

42. Give to him that asketh thee, and from him that would borrow of thee turn not thou away.
43. Ye have heard that it was said, Thou shalt love thy neighbor, and hate thine enemy:
44. But I say unto you, Love your enemies, and pray for them that persecute you;
45. That ye may be sons of your Father who is in heaven: for he maketh his sun to rise on the evil and the good, and sendeth rain on the just and the unjust.

---

in this sense occurs in Matthew 27 : 32 and Mark 15 : 21, in reference to Simon compelled to carry Christ's cross. We may conceive the compulsion in the present case to proceed from a military man. A Roman mile was about 1,600 yards. The sense of oppression is involved, subject to arbitrary military power. Christ's counsel is: do not submit to the inevitable in a slavish, sullen spirit, harboring thoughts of revolt. Do the service cheerfully and more than you are asked. The counsel is far-reaching, covering the case of the Jewish people subject to the Roman yoke, and of slaves serving hard masters. The three cases of nonresistance are not meant to foster an abject spirit. They point out the higher way to victory. He that magnanimously bears, forgives." — *Marcus Dods.* "The doctrine of the second mile demands that we shall not only be honest in our business dealings but generous also, measuring duty not by financial consideration but in the spirit of Christian service. It means that we look beyond second causes and gladly acknowledge God's will in all life's restrictions and burdens. It is the transformation of statutes into songs in the house of our pilgrimage." — *J. S. Holden.* 42. **Give to him that asketh thee, and from him that would borrow of thee turn not thou away.** "Here again our Lord teaches us by the method of a seeming paradox, and enforces a principle binding upon every one in the form of a rule which in its letter is binding upon no man. Were we to give to all men what they ask, we should in many cases be cursing, not blessing, them with our gifts. Not so does our Father give us what we ask in prayer: not so did Christ grant the prayers of His disciples. That which the words really teach as the ideal of the perfect life which we ought to aim at, is the loving and the giving temper that sees in every request made to us the expression of a want of some kind, which we are to consider as a call to thoughtful inquiry how best to meet the want, giving what is asked for if we honestly believe that it is really for the good of him who asks, giving something else if that would seem to be really better for him. Rightly understood, the words do not bid us idly give alms to the idle or the impostor: and Paul's rule, 'If a man will not work, neither let him eat' (2 Thess. 3 : 10), is not a departure from the law of Christ, but its truest application and fulfillment. . . . The higher law of Christ treats all men as brothers, and bids us, if it is right to lend, as an act of charity, to do so for love, and not for profit. Cases where the business of the world calls for loans not for the relief of want, but as a matter of commercial convenience, lie obviously outside the range of the precept." — *E. H. Plumptre.*

4. LOVE FOR OUR ENEMIES, vs. 43–45. 43. **Ye have heard that it was said, Thou shalt love thy neighbor, and hate thine enemy:** 44. **but I say unto you, Love your enemies, and pray for them that persecute you;** 45. **that ye may be the sons of your Father who is in heaven: for he maketh his sun to rise on the evil and the good, and sendeth rain on the just and the unjust.** The quotation here is from Leviticus 19 : 18, but the phrase, 'hate thine enemy,' is not to be found anywhere in the Old Testament, but was an addition erroneously added by the Rabbinical teachers of subsequent generations. "Our Lord's answer there shows, as He teaches here, that in the sense of the law even an enemy is our neighbor. But the Jewish teachers held that an enemy was not a neighbor, and that the command to love the latter implied permission to withhold it from the former. So as they publicly repeated and expounded the law, they would make the addition, 'Thou shalt love thy neighbor — and hate thine enemy.' This they would perhaps seek to justify by pointing to the severe treatment of the Canaanites which God enjoined upon Israel; but that was an exceptional case. The commandment to love the neighbor was extended in Leviticus 19 : 33, 34 to strangers sojourning in Israel. With such teachings prevalent as Jesus here describes, we can understand how the Jews came to be charged by Tacitus with 'hatred to the human race.'" — *J. A. Broadus.* The admonition to love

our enemies is often found in the Scriptures (see *e.g.*, Luke 6 : 27, 28; Acts 7 : 60, etc.). Even the Old Testament teaches kindness to enemies (Exod. 23 : 4, 5; Prov. 24 : 17, 29, etc.). It is possible for one to be in war and still to love one's enemies. This does not mean we are not to engage in conflict with an invading host, with all the force and power we can muster, but it does mean when an invading force is suppressed, and the danger of conquest is over, we are to do nothing toward our enemies but what would be for their welfare, which, after all, is the deepest implication of love for others. Even now, while we are at war, we should pray for our enemies, not that they may win the war, but that the awful passions and desires which have brought about this war may be removed, that the brutality and the hatred which are manifest in such a war may be done away with; that nations which have turned away from God may turn back to God. We can use all the power we have to defeat our enemies in physical combat, and at the same time exercise the power of prayer in praying for their conversion, and their ultimate welfare. "Sunshine and rain are chosen as among the chief providential blessings (cf. Acts 14 : 17). One element and proof of sonship is resemblance, as it is said, 'Be ye therefore followers (imitators) of God as dear children, and we are urged to love our enemies and treat them kindly, in order that we may be acting like our heavenly Father, for He loves His enemies, and sends natural blessings upon them as well as upon His friends (cf. Luke 6 : 35), 'for he is kind toward the unthankful and evil.'" — *J. A. Broadus.*

What does anger do to the spiritual and moral life of the one becoming angry? What are some of the things that normally arouse our anger? Why should not an individual take upon himself the punishment of wrong, as the state assumes the obligation of punishing wrongdoers? Do you think a judge sitting in a court is liable to be fairer in his verdict concerning any case of personal affront, or insult, or damage, than the one suffering harm, who is involved in the case himself? If we love our enemies, what will be some manifestations of this love? What happens within our own natures when we speak contemptuously of other people? In how many different ways does our entire lesson uphold the Biblical teaching that man is made in the image of God, and his person therefore is sacred in God's sight and should be sacred in man's sight? Do you think those who deal unjustly and unfairly with us, even to the point of insult, would know we were followers of Christ in refusing to retaliate at such a time?

LESSON VII. — November 14.

THE SANCTITY OF THE HOME. — Exodus 20 : 14; Matthew 5 : 27–30; Mark 10 : 2–12.

GOLDEN TEXT. — ***Blessed are the pure in heart: for they shall see God.*** MATTHEW 5 : 8.

Devotional Reading: Proverbs 2 : 11–22.
Beginner Topic: BREAD FOR RUTH.
  Lesson Material: Ruth 2.
  Memory Verse: O give thanks unto Jehovah; for he is good. Psalm 136 : 1.
Primary Topic: THE FIRST FAMILY.
  Lesson Material: Mark 10 : 2–12; Genesis 1 : 27; 2 : 18–24.
  Memory Verse: God setteth the solitary in families. Psalm 68 : 6.
Junior Topic: GOD'S PLAN FOR A HOME.
  Lesson Material: Mark 10 : 2–12; Genesis 1 : 27; 2 : 18–24.
  Memory Verse: God setteth the solitary in families. Psalm 68 : 6.
Intermediate and Senior Topic: CLEAN THINKING FOR CLEAN LIVING.
Topic for Young People and Adults: CHRISTIAN IDEALS OF LOVE AND MARRIAGE.

THE TEACHER AND HIS CLASS.

The Younger Classes are not too young to be taught the necessity for purity in thought and in deed — the editor has seen and heard children, five, six, and seven years old, even in better neighborhoods where the highest type of people live, do and say things that were in themselves shocking, a manifestation of the inward wickedness of the human heart even among little ones. If possible, boys and girls in the earlier ages should be taught this lesson separately. Among adults it does not make much difference. How to begin this lesson with children it is difficult to say. Perhaps one might commence by showing that as impurity in food causes us pain, and impurity in some liquid medicine might work for death, instead of healing, so impurity in human relationships always works for the ultimate destruction of those relationships.

The Older Classes especially need this lesson. We are living in a time of dreadful moral license, which will get much worse, because of the war. The human heart is itself so wicked, and the tides of sensuality in modern life are so powerful, that nothing but a recognition of a word from God, a divine commandment, and faith in Jesus Christ, will be able to keep men and women of our day clean and right. So we turn in this lesson not to the verdicts of the medical profession, nor to philosophy, or theories of sociology, but to the clear teaching of the Word of God, to which every normal man should bow.

THE PLAN OF THE LESSON.

SUBJECT: The Absolute Necessity for Purity and Faithfulness in the Relationships of Men and Women.

I. THE COMMANDMENT FORBIDDING PERSONAL IMPURITY, Exodus 20 : 14.

II. CHRIST'S INTERPRETATION OF THIS SEVENTH COMMANDMENT, Matthew 5 : 27–30.

1. The old law, v. 27.
2. The new interpretation, v. 28.
3. The accompanying admonitions, vs. 29, 30.

III. CHRIST'S TEACHING REGARDING DIVORCE, Mark 10 : 2–12.

1. The question He was asked, v. 2.
2. His reiteration of the Mosaic law, vs. 3–5.
3. The divine institution of marriage, vs. 6–9.
4. The only true ground for divorce, vs. 10–12.

THE LESSON IN ITS SETTING.

Time. — The Ten Commandments were delivered in 1445 B.C.; the Sermon on the Mount was given in the summer of A.D. 28; the passage taken from Mark is a part of a discourse delivered in February, A.D. 30.

Place. — The Ten Commandments were given on Mount Sinai; the Sermon on the Mount was preached near Capernaum; the discourse on divorce was spoken in Peræa.

THE TEACHER'S LIBRARY.

Most of the books on the Ten Commandments are unsatisfactory in their treatment of the seventh commandment, exceptions being the chapters by G. Campbell Morgan, George D. Boardman, and Masselink. On the entire subject of adultery, one should consult the long article by J. R. Willis, in James Hastings's *Dictionary of Christ and the Gospels*, Vol. 1, 29–32; Newman Smyth: *Christian Ethics*, 405–415; the article by M. L. Margolis, in the *International Standard Bible Encyclopedia*, Vol. 1, 63, 64; and a very interesting article, especially for its spiritual applications, in the older, little-known, but invaluable *Englishman's Critical and Expository Bible Cyclopedia*, by R. A. Fausset, p. 19. On the very difficult subject of the teaching of the New Testament on divorce, see the article on that subject by W. C. Allen, in James Hastings's *Dictionary of Christ and the Gospels*, Vol. 1, 483–485; James Stalker: *The Ethics of Jesus*, 331–348; Shailer Matthews: *The Social Teaching of Jesus*, 79–106; E. H. Hughes: *The Bible and Life*, 83–89; R. H. Charles: *The Teaching of the New Testament on Divorce* (London, 1921); A. H. Strong: *The Philosophy of Religion*, 431–442; and a very powerful sermon, in pamphlet form, by Dr. C. E. Macartney, of the First Presbyterian Church, of Pittsburgh, *Broken Marriage—Divorce*. There is a very good chapter, "The Bible and the Family," in W. L. Lingle's, *The Bible and Social Problems*, 131–151.

On the four verses taken from the Sermon on the Mount, commentaries on the Gospel of Mark, and the larger expositions of this particular portion of the Gospels, will be found helpful, but one should especially consult J. Oswald Dykes: *The Manifesto of the King*, 245–261; and Boardman's work, *Ten Commandments*, 229–233. On Mark 10 : 2–12, in addition to commentaries on this Gospel, one should consult, on verse 6, Joseph Parker: *Studies on Texts*, Vol. 1, 84–94; and a beautiful sermon, "Our Lord's Estimate of Human Love," in W. R. Nicoll: *Sunday Evening*, 75–82; on verses 10, 11, George Jackson: *The Table-Talk of Jesus*, 205 ff.

There are only two kinds of personalities on earth — men, and women — and true fellowship, real communion (we are not speaking about communion with God) is limited to these two types of personality. Furthermore, men and women are distinctly different from each other; neither is absolutely complete without the other. This is the way God has made us. Therefore, by our very creation, and our very individual natures, there is, inevitably, a powerful attraction between the two sexes, the most powerful single force on earth (spiritual forces not here being considered, for the time being). God Himself has endowed men and women with personalities which complement each other, which result in this powerful drawing toward each other, and God has also provided a holy, pure, sacred institution, in which men and women may dwell together in all the fullness of life, for their mutual joy, edification, enrichment, and strengthening of life. This institution is known as marriage. Within the boundaries of marriage the profoundest relationships of men and women are honorable and right. Outside of the marriage relationship, any intimate, personal, physical relationship between men and women, of the most extreme kind, is

Exodus 20 : 14. Thou shalt not commit adultery.

definitely wrong, and divinely prohibited. In other words, God has ordained that in marriage men and women should live together, and outside of marriage God has ordained that men and women should not live together in mutual physical intercourse. That which the marriage relationship allows is known outside of that relationship by the two horrible words — adultery and fornication. Our lesson concerns this crime, and our Lord's larger teaching about impurity of life.

THE SACREDNESS OF MARRIAGE.

In these days when marriage is so often lightly entered upon, into which many young people seem to be swept by some temporary emotional experience of the hour, some superficial attraction, or, worse, a state of intoxication, when men and women are returning to the dreadful state of Roman society in our Lord's time, when one divorce follows another, and many have been married five or six times before their life is lived out — all these things are tending to destroy in the minds of men the idea of sanctity which God always attaches to marriage in His Holy Word. Let us think for a moment of what makes marriage so sacred. In the first place, it was actually instituted by God (Gen. 2 : 24). It is the first institution embracing human personalities to be established on earth. It precedes government and social laws. Ordained of God, it receives from Him the approval of His own holy nature. In the second place, marriage involves love, and love is the highest human experience of which any one will ever be capable. Of course, it is possible for love to be known outside of marriage. Many people love others apart from the marriage relationship, but love reaches its greatest fulness, its richest meaning, exhibits its most beautiful manifestations, in the marriage relationship. If then there is something wrong in this relationship of men and women, then love itself begins to deteriorate, and that which ought to be beautiful becomes ugly, the finest and most sensitive and delicate things of life are Satanically transmuted into things that are coarse, that harden life, and that allow for every other conceivable sin to enter in. When the factor of love in the life of men and women is tampered with, and this divine stream becomes polluted, life itself loses its glory and its beauty. In the third place, marriage has to do, not in whole, of course, but certainly in part, with physical relationships involving the human body, and, in the sight of God, our bodies are holy, and have an enormous influence over our mental and spiritual experiences. Again and again in the New Testament the body is spoken of as the temple of the Holy Ghost. What we see, what we hear, what we feel — all this must come to us through the body. Our work is the expression of the body. Preaching must be with the lips; all literature is written with the hands; musical instruments are played with the fingers; children are born from the sacred body of the mother, and partake of the very physical characteristics of the father and the mother. In these bodies we live, through these bodies we are taught, and from these bodies our personalities go out. How important to keep them clean, and noble, and on a lofty level — the passions of our body being held in constant restraint, the soul being kept from being clouded by the steam of unrestrained living. Furthermore, marriage in the Word of God is often used, symbolically, for expressing spiritual truths, and in this way God once again reveals the sacredness of this relationship. "The union of God and His one Church, in His everlasting purpose, is the archetype and foundation on which rests the union of man and wife (Eph. 5 : 22–33). As he (*ish*) gave Eve (*isha*) his name, signifying her formation from him, so Christ gives a new name to the Church (Rev. 2 : 17; 3 : 12). Hence idolatry, covetousness, and apostasy are adultery spiritually (Jer. 3 : 6, 8, 9; Ezek. 16 : 32; Hos. 1, 2, 3; Rev. 2 : 22). An apostate church, the daughter of Jerusalem, becoming the daughter of Babylon, is an adulteress (Isa. 1 : 21; Ezek. 23 : 4, 7, 37). So Jesus calls the Jews 'an adulterous generation' (Matt. 12 : 39)." — *A. R. Faunet.*

I. THE COMMANDMENT FORBIDDING PERSONAL IMPURITY, Exod. 20 : 14. 14. **Thou shalt not commit adultery.** The sin of adultery is mentioned *by name* thirty-four times in the Old Testament, and thirty times in the New. Fornication is found five times in the Old Testament, and thirty-nine times in the New. This is in itself significant. When one realizes, however, that the New Testament is less than one-third the length of the Old, yet contains nearly twice as many references to this sin as the Old Testament does, one is aware of the definite bearing Christianity has on this vice, and how utterly intolerant it must be of all of its manifestations. Adultery is in itself simply sexual relationship between a married man and a woman not his wife, or a married woman and a man not her husband. Adultery in itself is only possible when the one accused is married, but fornication covers all forms of this sin, and an unmarried person can be guilty of it as well as a married one. In other words, all that can be called adultery can also be called fornication, but not vice versa. Because the editor of this book has sometimes been asked this question, he thinks it might be well to state it and answer it here: Is there anywhere in the Bible permission for sexual relationship outside of the marriage state? The answer is an absolute, unequivocal, uncompromising No, not from the first of Genesis to the end of Revelation, and any one teaching otherwise is perverting and distorting the clear teaching of the Word of God.

Dr. G. Campbell Morgan, in his excellent book on the Ten Commandments, has a remarkable discussion of the terribleness of this sin, and we take the liberty of freely quoting from it. " A sevenfold vice is this sin of unchaste conduct, being sin against the individual, the family, society, the nation, the race, the universe, and God. Nature visits the sin with the heaviest penalties in every department of the complex being of man. The terrible results of unchaste life in the purely physical realm are such as cannot be named here. They are well known. Every man of science will bear testimony to the awful demand that nature makes for purity, and will assert that she has no pity for the unclean. The statistics of lunacy in this and all lands could tell horrible tales of the effect of unclean life upon the mental side of man's nature. The perfect unity and balance of spirit, soul, and body, is destroyed by this vice, and that man or woman surely and irrevocably commits suicide who falls into and persists in unchaste habits and life. It is a sin against the family. The sacredness of motherhood and childhood, and all the demands they make upon the care and thought of all, are secured and met in the divine institution of marriage. Wherever the rights of the marriage relationship are violated and set aside, God's provision for both is broken down, and the disastrous result of the breakdown of the family circle and entity results. . . . It is a sin against society. This follows from the previous consideration. The family is a unity of individuals sharing a common life and governed by a common love. Society is the accumulation of families, and all the human interrelations of property, of reputation, and of character break down with the breakdown of the family. The sin which blights the marriage relation and destroys the family is the enemy of all true socialism. . . . It is a sin against the nation. This, again, moves out as a logical sequence from the former considerations. The adulterer is the enemy of the state, and as such, after being divorced in the divorce court, should be imprisoned by the criminal courts. The man or woman upon whose guilt the marriage tie is broken, no Christian minister of any denomination has a right to remarry. It is an act of treason to the state to allow such persons to go free. . . . It is a sin against the race. Every life is contributing its quota of force to the forces that make or mar. All are hindering or hastening the perfect day. The crime of prolonging sorrow and agony lies at the door of every impure human being. The agony and wrong of degraded humanity is a curse upon the unchastity of the past, and every licentious and bestial man or woman is inflicting new wounds, not only upon the immediate present, but also upon the years yet unborn. The voice of the human race, so often, alas, unheard in the clamor of the interests of the passing moment, is thundering perpetually the divine command, ' Thou shalt not commit adultery.' It is a sin against the universe. The life of the universe is love. The origin of all is love, for ' God is love.' The propagation of all is love. From the highest form, that of the unity of the marriage relation, through all the lower spaces of action, love is the law of growth. The lair of the wild beast is fiercely guarded by the love that holds it sacred. The nestling of the birds is token of the impulse of the love-life that throbs through all creation. The bee that carries the pollen from flower to flower is the messenger of the same instinct. Love is everywhere. The sin of lustful unchastity is the violation of love, blighting and destroying it. Let every adulterer and adulteress know then, that their impurity sins against all the genius of the universe, and if they but listen, every pure and holy love of man and maiden, every devotion of the beasts to their mates, every song of bird, and every hum of the wing of summer bee, proclaims the heinousness of their offence against the whole creation. It is a sin against God. The race is His own to its utmost limit. The love law of the universe is the will of God for all. Thus, lastly and consequently, every impure act or person strikes a blow at the very heart

MATTHEW 5 : 27. Ye have heard that it was said, Thou shalt not commit adultery:

---

of God. By an eternal necessity He excludes the ' abominable . . . and fornicators ' (Rev. 21 : 8) from the new heaven and the new earth, and gives them ' their part in the lake that burneth with fire and brimstone, which is the second death.' "

SOME REASONS WHY SOCIAL IMPURITY IS INCREASING IN OUR TIME.

To discuss why sexual impurity is increasing is not of itself to expose its wickedness, which is what the Word of God does, but nevertheless it ought to be thought of for a few moments, that we may the more clearly recognize the increasing seriousness and extent of this problem. In the first place, opportunities for sins relating to sexual life are multiplylng: the enormous increase in travel, especially travel in automobiles, the vast multiplication of hotels in our large cities, and the abuse of tourist camps — all these simply throw open the doors to those who wish to multiply opportunities for temptation for our young people. In the second place, we are living in a time when men and women are thrown together in unfavorable conditions; especially is this true in regard to our commercial life. Millions of our women are employed in offices and factories, and more will be while the war is on, and everyone knows that the conversation in the majority of factories, where large groups of unsaved men and women are together, is simply rotten. Thousands of women in our country have been dragged into wicked practices because they were under constant deteriorating influences of corrupt conversation. In the third place, the tenseness of modern life excites all these more delicate factors of human relationship, and, as always happens when under great mental and nervous strain, temptations along these lines become more powerful. In the fourth place, we are living in a world which, as it were, glorifies, one is sorry to say, sexual license. This is particularly true in filthy movies, and in most of our modern fiction. Again and again, has the editor heard fine Christian people, not ascetic snobs, not religious fanatics, but men and women of culture, college graduates, occupying big places in the world, say that they simply have not been able to finish reading certain widely-advertised books because of their filthiness. Drop these volumes into the hands of our young people, force them to read them in college courses of literature, and what can you expect but excitement to the same type of uncleanness? Again, we are being continually confronted with bad examples of loose sexual living on the part of those in high places in our land, who ought to exert a wholesome influence over the generation to come, but do not. Every scandal attaching to a man in high office, every divorce occurring in a family that ought to be looked up to, because some member of the family is an outstanding leader of the nation, tends to destroy high ideals relating to marriage among our younger people. Finally, and the editor is no fanatic on this subject, he is compelled to say that he believes our modern bathing beaches and dance halls, without going into particulars, have a terribly polluting influence over the thoughts, and, ultimately, the actions of our young people.

The Bible is full of illustrations of the terrible consequences of the violation of the marriage vow, the most famous of which is the sin of David (2 Sam. 11, 12). But in the editor's mind, one of the most terrible chapters recording the consequences of the violation of the seventh commandment is the one that immediately follows, the story of Amnon, recorded in 2 Samuel 13. There is nothing truer to human experience in all the Scriptures than the verse that follows the announcement of this wicked act of Amnon: " Then Amnon hated her with exceeding great hatred; for the hatred wherewith he hated her was greater than the love wherewith he had loved her. And Amnon said unto her, Arise, be gone." And there is nothing more tragic, more pitiful, in all the Scriptures than the very next verse: " And she said unto him, Not so, because this great wrong in putting me forth is worse than the other that thou didst unto me." You cannot prevent such consequences as these. The way to avoid spoiling life, and bringing perpetual darkness into a woman's heart, is to have some sense of decency, of self-control, of uprightness, and to look up into the face of God and vow that you for one are not going to sink into this kind of life.

II. **CHRIST'S INTERPRETATION OF THIS SEVENTH COMMANDMENT,** Matt. 5 : 27–30. 27. **Ye have heard that it was said, Thou shalt not commit adultery:** 28. **but I say unto you, that every one that looketh on a woman to lust**

28. But I say unto you, that every one that looketh on a woman to lust after her hath committed adultery with her already in his heart.

29. And if thy right eye causeth thee to stumble, pluck it out, and cast it from thee: for it is profitable for thee that one of thy members should perish, and not thy whole body be cast into hell.

30. And if thy right hand causeth thee to stumble, cut it off, and cast it from thee: for it is profitable for thee that one of thy members should perish, and not thy whole body go into hell.

---

after her hath committed adultery with her already in his heart. After quoting the old Mosaic law, our Lord (see also Deut. 5 : 18) gives it a deeper application than was ever possible under the old dispensation. "The English word *lust* originally signified desire of any kind, good or bad; in the Scriptures it is used only for evil desires, and at the present day is confined to one particular class of evil desires. The Greek word here used signifies desire in general and is used in a good sense in 13 : 17; Luke 22 : 15, and some other passages. More frequently it is a bad sense, as in Mark 4 : 19, etc., denoting evil desires in general (human desires being so often evil). The specific sense of sexual desire is found (in the New Testament) only here and in Romans 1 : 24, though of course included, along with other desires, in most cases of the bad sense. . . . Jesus condemns not merely the outward act of sin, the cherishing of sinful desire. 'He who experiences at a first glance this desire, and then instead of turning away and withdrawing from sin, throws a second glance with lustful intent, and in order to retain and increase that impulse, *commits* the sin' (Stier). As in 1 John 3 : 15, 'whosoever hateth his brother is a murderer,' so here, every one that cherishes lust by a look is an adulterer." — *John A. Broadus.* "Beneath a law so scrutinizing, so subtly penetrative, which expects our loyalty for the sanctities of marriage to be so scrupulous, which demands that the soul's purity shall repel the very first approach of prohibited desire, and calls the briefest impure glance a crime — beneath such a law, who shall say there is any one chaste? Dare any of us have the secret history of his heart ransacked? This moralist on the mount is to be our Judge. How shall we answer Him for the imaginations which have defiled our private hours, for the prurience to which we gave houseroom, for the warmth of look, the desire which dared not betray itself by a gesture? There is no one who does not need to dread the entrance of unhallowed affection into those secret recesses of the nature which ought to be the home or shrine for God's most pure Spirit." — *J. O. Dykes.* 29. **And if thy right eye causeth thee to stumble, pluck it out, and cast it from thee : for it is profitable for thee that one of thy members should perish, and not thy whole body be cast into hell.** 30. **And if thy right hand causeth thee to stumble, cut it off, and cast it from thee : for it is profitable for thee that one of thy members should perish, and not thy whole body go into hell.** Of course, our Lord here is speaking figuratively. He does not actually want us to take out our eyes, or to cut off our hands, but is simply laying down the *principle* that it would be much better to be deprived of these organs if, in this deprivation, we would be delivered from the sins of impurity, than to have all of our faculties, our complete bodies, and to be a slave to impurity. Physically cutting off both hands and plucking out both eyes would not make a man pure within. "If Jesus can alter our disposition, what is the need of discipline? Yet in these verses our Lord puts very stern discipline, to the parting with the right arm or eye. The reason is this, that our physical cases, *i.e.*, mortal bodies, have been used by the wrong disposition, and when the new disposition is put in, the old physical case is not taken away, it is left there for us to discipline and make it an obedient servant to the new disposition. In 5 : 48, Jesus describes an absolutely different life, not a maimed life, but a perfect life, but in the beginning it is maimed, meaning by that there are a hundred and one things you dare not do and you do not want to do when you are introduced to the new disposition, things that are to you and also in the eyes of the world that knew you, as your right arm and your eye, and the worldly person comes to you and says, 'What an absurd idea!' There never was a saint yet who did not have to start with Jesus a maimed life. Jesus says it is better that you should enter into this life, this Christian life, maimed, lovely in God's sight and lame in man's, than that you should be lovely in man's sight and lame in God's. You will find that principle runs all through, and at the beginning Jesus Christ, by His Spirit in you, has to check

MARK 10 : 2. And there came unto him Pharisees, and asked him, Is it lawful for a man to put away *his* wife? trying him.
3. And he answered and said unto them, What did Moses command you?
4. And they said, Moses suffered to write a bill of divorcement, and to put her away.
5. But Jesus said unto them, For your hardness of heart he wrote you this commandment.
6. But from the beginning of the creation, Male and female made he them.
7. For this cause shall a man leave his father and mother, and shall cleave to his wife;
8. And the two shall become one flesh: so that they are no more two, but one flesh.
9. What therefore God hath joined together let not man put asunder.
10. And in the house the disciples asked him again of this matter.
11. And he saith unto them, Whosoever shall put away his wife, and marry another, committeth adultery against her:
12. And if she herself shall put away her husband, and marry another, she committeth adultery.

---

your doing a great many things that are perfectly right for everybody else but you." — *Oswald Chambers.*

III. **CHRIST'S TEACHING REGARDING DIVORCE,** Mark 10 : 2–12.
2. **And there came unto him Pharisees, and asked him, Is it lawful for a man to put away *his* wife? trying him.** 3. **And he answered and said unto them, What did Moses command you?** 4. **And they said, Moses suffered to write a bill of divorcement, and to put her away.** 5. **But Jesus said unto them, For your hardness of heart he wrote you this commandment.** 6. **But from the beginning of the creation, Male and female made he them.** 7. **For this cause shall a man leave his father and mother, and shall cleave to his wife;** 8. **and the two shall become one flesh: so that they are no more two, but one flesh.** 9. **What therefore God hath joined together let not man put asunder.** 10. **And in the house the disciples asked him again of this matter.** 11. **And he saith unto them, Whosoever shall put away his wife, and marry another, committeth adultery against her:** 12. **and if she herself shall put away her husband, and marry another, she committeth adultery.** Inasmuch as the editor has felt that in this lesson he ought to emphasize the sin of impurity, there does not remain much space for a discussion of Christ's teaching on divorce, which, however, frequently comes up in other lessons. Our Lord did not open this discussion himself, but it arose because of the question of the Pharisees, whether it was lawful for a man to put away his wife. In answering this question, our Lord directed them back to the Mosaic law, which they, as Pharisees, prided themselves on knowing so well and obeying so perfectly. "The question was one which divided the Pharisees. The disciples of Hillel wished to make divorce easy, and said that a man could divorce his wife for any dislike he might have to her. The followers of Shammai held that only notorious unchastity could be the ground of divorce. The words recorded in Matthew, 'for every cause,' are most important. The whole question is about that unlimited right to divorce which was undermining morals in Judæa as well as throughout the Roman empire at that time. . . . The Pharisees admit what Jesus seeks to bring out, that Moses did not command, but only permitted divorce; the Mosaic legislation presupposed the existence of divorce, and tried to regulate it. The husband who wished to divorce had to go to a learned scribe to get the bill of divorcement written for him, and therefore divorce could never be made in the heat of passion; and he had to state the grounds on which he wished the separation, and according to the law quoted they could not be quite trivial. The Mosaic law further provided for two cases of marriage where divorce was impossible — (1) where a man had dishonored a virgin, and (2) where he had slanderously denied the virginity of his young wife (Deut. 22 : 19, 20). The Mosaic law, therefore, did not permit unlimited divorce for every cause, and its aim was benevolent. Moses had found heathen practices among the Jews, and his laws were

meant to restrain and to point them to a still better and purer state of matters; and therefore the right way to deal with the law is not to keep merely within the letter and evade the spirit, but to make it full by seeing in it the moral principles which it embodies, and by acting up to them." — *T. M. Lindsay.* (See Deut. 24 : 1, 2.)

But our Lord did not stop with the Mosaic commandment. He went back to the very time of creation, and quoted from Genesis 2 : 21–25, where marriage itself as a divine institution is first referred to. "The description commonly given both in the New Testament and the Old of the married state, is contained in the phrase that husband and wife are one flesh. The term has two principle uses in the New Testament: (1) it denotes the matter of the body as opposed to the soul, which meaning is absurd in the present case; and (2) the embodied spirit, man, as opposed to the unembodied spirit, God, which seems to be the meaning here. The phrase will therefore mean that the husband and wife have such a community of end and aim in life that they are one ethical person. In the New Testament this identity of interest and aim is usually expressed as consisting in a peculiar double reciprocal relation in which the husband and wife stand to each other. It is the duty of the husband to love his wife; and it is the duty of the wife to obey her husband (Col. 3 : 18, 19; Eph. 5 : 22–28; 1 Pet. 3 : 1–7). Thus the unity described in the phrase *one flesh* is one of function, each one of the married pair bringing its own element — love and obedience — out of which the union of common ends and aims is compacted. This scriptural idea of marriage given in verses 6–8, with its phrases 'male and female,' 'man and wife,' 'they twain,' implies (1) that 'marriage is to be between one man and one woman, and that it is not lawful for any man to have more than one wife, nor for any woman to have more than one husband at the same time'; and (2) that when a marriage has once been formed, it must not be arbitrarily broken; there must be no easy way of divorce." — *T. M. Lindsay.* "The plain implication is that any man who divides what God has thus, by His own creation, united into one, flies in the face of God and His will — a serious opposition indeed. How indissoluble marriage is according to God's own creation is thus made clear. Did these Pharisees never read these divine words in Scripture and think on what they obviously declare?" — *R. C. H. Lenski.*

Finally, our Lord says that the only ground for divorce is adultery, and whenever a man puts away his wife for any other reason than adultery, or a wife puts away her husband for any other cause, and is married again, the new relationship is an adulterous one. Again we turn to Professor Lindsay for a compact presentation of this entire subject. "Verses 11 and 12 form one of the four passages which record our Lord's statement about divorce. The other three are found in Matthew 5 : 31, 32; 19 : 3–9; Luke 16 : 18; and refer evidently to the same occasion when Jesus answers a tempting question put by the Pharisees, and record the one utterance. . . . The statements He makes in these verses seem to be (1) that the man who, in conformity with the permission accorded to him in the Mosaic law, puts away his wife by giving her a bill of divorcement, 'save for fornication,' and marries another commits adultery against his wife (Matthew, Mark, Luke). (2) He also causes her to commit adultery, because he puts it into her power to marry again (Matthew). (3) The man who marries a wife so put away, also commits adultery (Matthew, Luke). (4) The woman who in like fashion puts away her husband, and is married again to another, commits adultery (Mark). From these statements Protestant theologians conclude that (1) divorce *a vinculo* is permitted, because the case brought forward is such separation as permits of the divorced marrying again. (2) That the dissolution of the marriage bond is permissible only because of adultery on the part of one of the married pair, or because of what is equivalent to adultery — such wilful desertion as cannot be remedied by the Church or by the civil magistrate."

In how many different ways would you say the impurity of relationship between men and women harm both parties, and, ultimately, the state, and the whole social fabric? What are some of the ways in which men and women can think, and live, and act, so as to be increasingly victorious over the subtle temptations of our day along this line? If the Word of God is clear on this subject, and impurity is definitely and constantly revealed as abhorrent to God, deserving of the severest punishment, what conclusion ought we to come to in our own heart regarding our own relationship to sin of this kind? Do you think the habits of impurity become more binding, or less binding, as they are continually practiced through the years? (They become tragically more binding until that is about all one thinks of, and life becomes a terrible and perpetual experience of disappointment and darkness.) Did our Lord in His words honor marriage? (The answer is certainly, Yes.) Thinking of men

and women you know, recalling such pages of history as you are most familiar with, and remembering some of the great examples of the Scriptures, do you know of anybody who, through the years, living in this kind of sin, has enjoyed peace or power or joy or true communion with God?

LESSON VIII. — November 21.

HONESTY IN ALL THINGS. — Exodus 20 : 15; Leviticus 19 : 11, 13; Luke 19 : 1–10, 45, 46.

GOLDEN TEXT. — *Thou shalt not steal.* EXODUS 20 : 15.

Devotional Reading: Matthew 6 : 24–33.
Beginner Topic: WHEN COMPANY COMES.
Lesson Material: Luke 19 : 1–10.
Memory Verse: Thou, Jehovah, hast made me glad. Psalm 92 : 4.
Primary Topic: AT ZACCHÆUS' HOUSE.
Lesson Material: Exodus 20 : 15; Leviticus 19 : 11, 13; Luke 19 : 1–10, 45, 46.
Memory Verse: We pray to God that ye do no evil . . . but that ye may do that which is honorable. 2 Corinthians 13 : 7.
Junior Topic: THE CHANGE IN ZACCHÆUS.
Lesson Material: Exodus 20 : 15; Leviticus 19 : 11, 13; Luke 19 : 1–10, 45, 46.
Memory Verse: We pray to God that ye do no evil . . . but that ye may do that which is honorable. 2 Corinthians 13 : 7.
Intermediate and Senior Topic: WHY IS STEALING WRONG?
Topic for Young People and Adults: THE CHRISTIAN STANDARD OF HONESTY.

THE TEACHER AND HIS CLASS.

The Younger Classes may be asked how they feel when some one gives them a good book, or a bicycle, or a train — why, of course, they feel delighted and pleased. Then, how do they feel when they have done so many hours of work for a neighbor, with the promise that they would be paid for it, and when the task was finished the money was put into their hands — they would feel proud of their labor. These are two ways of getting things. Then, ask how they would feel, down deep in their hearts, if they saw a group of children playing, and came upon a box of pencils and crayons of one who was playing, and they stole it, and ran away with it — they would have a sense of guilt and shame in their hearts. Now why the difference? Because receiving something as a gift, and receiving something as wages is honorable, but stealing is against the laws of God, and these laws God has written in our hearts, and no man can ever escape them. They are just as much there as the mechanical laws which control the erection of a building, or the chemical laws that determine the results of a combination of certain fluids. And yet, this is a sin we are so prone to be guilty of that God has had to tell us again and again, in different ways, that we must not sin by stealing. This is what our lesson is concerned about.

The Older Classes should come away from the study of this lesson with a deeper sense of the wrongness of cheating, or falsifying, in commercial life, the wrongness of underpaying employees, the wrongness of not giving one's strength and time according to the stipulations of a financial arrangement concerning any job or task. If ever this country needed to know what it is to steal and not to steal, the difference between honesty and dishonesty, it needs to know it now.

THE LESSON IN ITS SETTING.

Time. — The Decalogue was given 1445 B.C.; our Lord met Zacchæus in Jerusalem in March, A.D. 30; the second cleansing of the Temple took place on Monday of Passion Week, April 3, A.D. 30.

Place. — The Ten Commandments were delivered from Mount Sinai; the event recorded concerning Zacchæus took place in Jericho, at the lower end of the Jordan River; the cleansing of the Temple, of course, took place in Jerusalem.

THE PLAN OF THE LESSON.

SUBJECT: How the Christian Religion Continually Demands Honesty in Every Relationship of Life Among Those Who Are Its Adherents.

I. THE EIGHTH COMMANDMENT — THE CONDEMNATION OF ALL THEFT, Exod. 20 : 15; Lev. 19 : 11, 13.

1. The fundamental law itself, Exod. 20 : 15.
2. Some applications of the law, Lev. 19 : 11, 13.

II. THE STORY OF A MAN WHO HAD STOLEN MUCH BUT WHEN CONVERTED LONGED TO MAKE FULL RESTORATION, Luke 19 : 1–10.

1. The man described, vs. 1, 2.
2. The man's eagerness to see Jesus, vs. 3, 4.
3. The man hears a gracious word from Jesus, v. 5.
4. The man welcomes Jesus to his home, v. 6, 7.
5. The man manifests true repentance, v. 8.
6. Christ's twofold declaration.
   a. Concerning the household of Zacchæus, v. 9.
   b. Concerning His own mission to save men, v. 10.

III. THE SIN OF MAKING A TEMPLE OF GOD TO SERVE AS A DEN OF THIEVES, Luke 19 : 45, 46.

THE TEACHER'S LIBRARY.

All books on the Ten Commandments will be found to have helpful chapters for the study of our lesson. For the study of the passage taken from Luke's Gospel, in addition to commentaries on the Gospel, which by the way will generally be found rather unsatisfactory for this lesson, one should consult the following chapters on Zacchæus: R. C. Trench: *Studies in the Gospel*, 262–272; J. G. Greenhough: *Men of the New Testament*, 183–192; George Matheson: *Representative Men of the New Testament*, 196–216; Adolph Saphir: *Conversion Illustrated by Examples Recorded in the Bible*, 331–350; James Jeffrey: *The Personal Ministry of the Son of Man*, 205–215; F. A. Noble: *Typical New Testament Conversions*, 121–134; A. B. Davidson: *The Called of God*, 273–297; E. C. Comfort: *The Partiality of Jesus*, 9–30; W. Y. Fullerton: *Christ and Men*, 14 ff.; Alexander Whyte: *Bible Characters, Joseph and Mary to James the Lord's Brother*, 72–77; Alexander Maclaren: *Expositions of Holy Scripture, St. Luke, 13–24*, 151–163. On 19 : 9, see J. D. Jones: *The Gospel of the Sovereignty*, 147–159; on verse 10, one should especially consult B. B. Warfield: *Bible Doctrines*, 304–308; W. R. Nicol: *Sunday Evening*, 29–37; W. L. Watkinson: *The Fatal Barter*, 156–169; on verses 45, 46, see H. P. Liddon: *Sermons on Some Words of Christ*, 284–293.

EXODUS 20 : 15. Thou shalt not steal.

I. THE EIGHTH COMMANDMENT — THE CONDEMNATION OF ALL THEFT, Ex. 20 : 15; Lev. 19 : 11, 13.

1. THE FUNDAMENTAL LAW ITSELF, Ex. 20 : 15. 15. **Thou shalt not steal.** As far as the editor knows, and this will no doubt surprise many, the best fundamental treatment of this commandment with which he is acquainted is not in a book of sermons, or in a book of the Ten Commandments, but in the great Systematic Theology of Charles Hodge, and it is from this book that we make the following extended quotation because we believe it covers the entire subject thoroughly and is worthy of the most careful study. " This commandment forbids all violations of the rights of property. The right of property in an object is the right to its exclusive possession and use. The foundation of the right of property is the will of God. By this is meant: (1) that God has so constituted man that he desires and needs this right of the exclusive possession and use of certain things. (2) Having made man a social being, He has made the right of property essential to the healthful development of human society. (3) He has implanted a sense of justice in the nature of man, which condemns as morally wrong everything inconsistent with the right in question. (4) He has declared in His Word that any and every violation of this right is sinful. This doctrine of the divine right of property is the only security for the individual or for society. If it be made to rest on any other foundation, it is insecure and unstable. It is only by making property sacred, guarded by the fiery sword of divine justice, that it can be safe from the dangers to which it is everywhere and always exposed. . . . It may well be doubted whether society is more in danger from the destructive principles of communism, than from the secret or tolerated frauds which, to so great an extent, pervade almost all the departments of social life. If this commandment forbids all unfair or unjust appropriation of the property of others to our own use or advantage, if every such appropriation is stealing in the sight of God, then theft is the most common of all the outward transgressions of the Decalogue. It includes not merely vulgar theft such as the law can detect and punish, but (1) all false pretences in matters of business; representing an article proposed for purchase or exchange to be other and better than it is. This includes a multitude of sins. Articles produced at home are sold as foreign productions, and the price asked and given is determined by this fradulent representation. . . . (2) Another class of violations of the eighth commandment comprises attempts to take undue advantage

LEVITICUS 19 : 11. Ye shall not steal; neither shall ye deal falsely, nor lie one to another.

13. Thou shalt not oppress thy neighbor, nor rob him: the wages of a hired servant shall not abide with thee all night until the morning.

LUKE 19 : 1. And he entered and was passing through Jericho.

2. And behold, a man called by name Zacchæus; and he was a chief publican, and he was rich.

---

of the ignorance or of the necessities of our fellow men. It is of the nature of theft if a man sells an article knowing it to be of less value than he to whom he offers it for sale takes it to be. If a man is aware that the credit of a bank is impaired, or that the affairs of a railroad, or of any other corporation, are embarrassed, and takes advantage of that knowledge, to dispose of the stock or notes of such corporations to those ignorant on the subject, demanding more for them than their actual worth, he is guilty of theft."

The most important recent book on the Ten Commandments is by Dr. William Masselink, of Grand Rapids, Mich., and his application of this commandment to modern conditions is excellent indeed. "This commandment clearly forbids oppression. The demanding of exorbitant rent of houses or lands; and still more, by seizing their goods for rent, which without their fault, they are unable to pay. 'To grind the faces of the poor' is a sin which God will punish. This commandment is also transgressed when more is expected of the hireling than is reasonable, and he is deprived of the necessary comforts of life. Unjust lawsuits violate the precept before us. It is a great privilege and blessing to live in a country where law governs, and where no tyrant or mob can injure the property. Our Saviour, however, teaches us that many offences must be suffered in silence without appeal to law. Paul teaches us that Christians should endeavor to settle their difficulties and controversies without going to law. 'Dare any of you, having a matter against another, go to the law before the unjust, and not before the saints? . . . If then ye have judgments of things pertaining to this life, set them to judge who are least esteemed in the church' (1 Cor. 6 : 1, 4)."

We believe that Dr. Cleland McAfee's interpretation of this commandment as involving stewardship is not at all a strained one. "I have no right to waste any money. I have no right to throw it in the river, because that robs society which it ought to serve through me. I have no right to use it for the worst part of my life, to buy with it anything that degrades me or develops the lower side of my life, because that robs my better life and again robs society which has right to have me at my best and not at my worst. But I have no right to hold it for my own low pleasures because that robs God who has higher claim on it and on me. The old prophet called out over the people of Israel: 'Will a man rob God?' And when the people indignantly replied that they had not robbed God, the prophet replied with words true to this day, 'Ye have robbed me in tithes and in offerings.' The commandment covers the regard we owe to the rights of God in ourselves and our possessions. There are many followers of Christ who are scrupulously honest with their grocers and their bakers who keep no fair standing with God who has first claim on them. The time which He claims, the money which He calls for, the strength which He demands in His kingdom, the very life of the servant whom He has redeemed — these are withheld from Him. In all our reckoning of our honesty, let us not deceive ourselves that fairness in the small things of human relations will compensate for unfairness in the higher things."

2. SOME APPLICATIONS OF THE LAW, Lev. 19 : 11, 13. 11. **Ye shall not steal; neither shall ye deal falsely, nor lie one to another.** 13. **Thou shalt not oppress thy neighbor, nor rob him: the wages of a hired servant shall not abide with thee all night until the morning.** Inasmuch as these very verses were fully commented upon in the lesson for September 5 of this year, we believe it is unnecessary to make further comments. The full exposition of the eighth commandment above will include everything that is here specifically referred to.

II. THE STORY OF A MAN WHO HAD STOLEN MUCH BUT WHEN CONVERTED LONGED TO MAKE FULL RESTORATION, Luke 19 : 1–10.

1. THE MAN DESCRIBED, vs. 1, 2. 1. **And he entered and was passing through Jericho.** 2. **And behold, a man called by name Zacchæus; and he was a chief publican, and he was rich.** The story of our Lord's interview with Zacchæus is recorded

3. And he sought to see Jesus who he was; and could not for the crowd, because he was little of stature.

4. And he ran on before, and climbed up into a sycomore tree to see him: for he was to pass that way.

only in this Gospel. Some one has said that here the Good Shepherd of the sheep and a truly lost sheep met each other, the one seeking the lost, and the other conscious of the need of salvation. Perhaps if our Lord had met Zacchæus a year or two before this, the publican would not have been ready for the glorious experience for which his heart was prepared on this day. The clock of God is never slow and never fast. One thing is sure, when a man longs to be saved by Christ, Christ is there to save him. Jericho is in a double way the nearest to hell of any city on earth — geographically, because it is hundreds of feet below the level of the sea; and morally because it is so notoriously wicked. In this wicked city lived a Jew who had sold himself to the Roman government, as a tax-gatherer. "The fact that he was a publican *and* a Jew says a good deal about his character. There are some trades which condemn, to a certain extent, the men who engage in them. You would not expect to find a man of sensitive honor acting as a professional spy; or one of earnest religious character keeping a public house. You would not expect to find a very good Jew condescending to be the tool of the Roman government. Zacchæus was at the head of the revenue office in Jericho, a position of considerable importance, inasmuch as there was a large volume of trade through that city from its situation near the fords of the Jordan, and from the fertility of the plain in which it stood. He had made some money, and probably made it by very questionable means. He was the object, not undeservedly, of the execration and suspicion of his countrymen. Italians did not love Italians who took service under Austria. Irishmen did not love Irishmen who in the bad old days used to collect church cess. And so Jews had no kind feeling toward Jews who became Cæsar's servants. That a man should be in such a position indicated that he cared more for money than for patriotism, religion, or popular approval. His motto was the motto of that Roman emperor who said, 'Money has no smell,' out of whatever cesspool it may have been fished up. But the consciousness of being encompassed by universal hatred would induce the object of it to put on an extra turn of the screw, and avenge upon individuals the general hostility. So we may take it for granted that Zacchæus, the head of the Jericho's custom house, and rich to boot, was by no means a desirable character." — *Alexander Maclaren.*

Zacchæus in the Sycomore. From an old print.

2. MAN'S EAGERNESS TO SEE JESUS, VS. 3, 4. 3. **And he sought to see Jesus who he was; and could not for the crowd, because he was little of stature.** 4. **And he ran on before, and climbed up into a sycomore tree to see him: for he was to pass that way.** Of course, any significant event taking place, or about to take place, in Jericho, would not only be known to all in the city, but would be particularly known to such an important personage as Zacchæus. How Jericho knew that Jesus would be passing that way we are not informed, but the fact that a great crowd was gathering to see Him indicates something of the tremendous stir which our Lord made throughout all of Palestine during His earthly ministry. This man Zacchæus could have done many different things when he heard that Christ was coming: he could have thought, this is the one Man he did not want to see, and he could have left town to return in a day or two; he could have stayed at home; he could have

5. And when Jesus came to the place, he looked up, and said unto him, Zacchæus, make haste, and come down; for to-day I must abide at thy house.

6. And he made haste, and came down, and received him joyfully.

7. And when they saw it, they all murmured, saying, He is gone in to lodge with a man that is a sinner.

---

encouraged some official opposition to His coming into the city, though no doubt this would have been opposed by the multitude; he could have gone out with the rest of the crowd, merely to be a watcher among hundreds of others, just to see the great Man go by. But no, because of the shortness of his stature, Zacchæus feared that in the press of the multitude he might be prevented from actually seeing Christ. Something deep in his heart told him that this day when Christ was passing through Jericho, would be a turning point in his life. I do not mean to say that he thought he would be converted. He knew nothing about such an experience. But I am sure something deep within kept saying that all of his former weak or strong desires to be a different man, and to live an honest life, would powerfully manifest themselves once again, and whatever he did this day would determine his destiny. He knew if there was any one who could help him it was Jesus, and, no matter what the cost might be, Jesus he must see.

3. THE MAN HEARS A GRACIOUS WORD FROM JESUS, v. 5. 5. **And when Jesus came to the place, he looked up, and said unto him, Zacchæus, make haste, and come down; for to-day I must abide at thy house.** This is one of the most beautiful verses in all the New Testament. "Are we not reminded by this story, that Jesus is on the outlook for those who seek Him? One of the most striking features of this visit to Jericho was that among the crowds who were watching His progress, and among the many curious onlookers, our Lord should have fixed on this publican, and have addressed him by name. Is it not another proof of His wonderful insight into the human heart? While multitudes were looking on, some from mere curiosity, some kindly disposed to Jesus, some with feelings of contempt, or even of hatred, He was examining their faces, He was reading the hearts of the thousands who were lining the roads, and apparently the only one in whom He saw any real desire for spiritual blessing, was this outcast publican, who, sick of the past, was anxious to enter on a new life. And so when He came beneath the branches where Zacchæus was seated, He looked up into the face gazing down so intently on Himself, and addressed the man in words that surprised and thrilled him. What wonderful condescension! What an unexpected honor! Many houses in Jericho, the publican may have thought, were at His disposal. In this city of the priests, this abode of the Pharisees, were surely many who would feel it an honor to have Jesus as their guest. But in none of them will He stay. 'He did not come to call the righteous.' He knew too well the character of these formalists. In none of their homes was a welcome provided for Him. In the house of this despised publican He would make His abode, for He 'delights to dwell with him who is of a humble and contrite spirit, and who trembleth at His word.' So is it always. No sinner ever yet sought Jesus for whom Jesus was not on the outlook, and whom He was not prepared to welcome." — *James Jeffrey.*

4. THE MAN WELCOMES JESUS TO HIS HOME, vs. 6, 7. 6. **And he made haste, and came down, and received him joyfully.** The words of Dr. Maclaren here are excellent. "Did you ever think that it was now or never with this publican; that Jesus Christ was never to go through the streets of Jericho any more; that it was Zacchæus' last chance; and that, if he had not made haste, he would have lost Christ forever? And so it is yet. There may be some in this place at this moment to whom Jesus Christ is making His last appeal. I know not; no man knows. A rabbi said, when they asked him when a man should repent: 'Repent on the last day of your lives,' and they said: 'But we do not know when that will be.' And he said: 'Then repent *now.*' So I say, because some of you may never hear Christ's gospel again, and because none of us know whether we shall or not, make sure work of it now, and do not let Jesus Christ go out of the city and up the road between the hills yonder; for if once the folds of the ravine shut Him from sight He will never be back in Jericho, or seen by Zacchæus any more forever." 7. **And when they saw it, they all murmured, saying, He is gone in to lodge with a man that is a sinner.** "Jericho was a city of priests as well as a city of publicans. The Talmudists tell

8. And Zacchæus stood, and said unto the Lord, Behold, Lord, the half of my goods I give to the poor; and if I have wrongfully exacted aught of any man, I restore fourfold.

9. And Jesus said unto him, To-day is salvation come to this house, forasmuch as he also is a son of Abraham.

10. For the Son of man came to seek and to save that which was lost.

---

us that there were almost as many priests there as at Jerusalem itself; so that it is a stroke from the life to introduce in the parable of the Good Samaritan the priest and the Levite, as passing exactly along that road which led from one of these cities where they dwelt, to the other where their duties lay (Luke 10 : 31, 32). With such a choice of hosts from whom to select, would it not have better become a preacher of righteousness to select some other than this sinner, whose house to honor with His presence? Surely, it was ill done by a favor so signal to reverse that just sentence of social ex-communication under which the publicans, and Zacchæus among the number, lay (Luke 15 : 2)." — *R. C. Trench.*

5. THE MAN MANIFESTS TRUE REPENTANCE, v. 8. 8. **And Zacchæus stood, and said unto the Lord, Behold, Lord, the half of my goods I give to the poor; and if I have wrongfully exacted aught of any man, I restore fourfold.** Undoubtedly, a considerable conversation was carried on by the Lord Jesus with Zacchæus, which is not recorded here. As Lenski has well said: " Before the evening meal could be prepared, Jesus, the Twelve, Zacchæus, and whoever else was present, sat in oriental fashion while Jesus spoke. When He ceased, Zacchæus stood up. Great things were taking place in his soul, and he acts with grave formality in thus rising from the rug or divan on which he had been sitting. Jesus had made his house a church of God, and now he stands as in the presence of God and makes his response to Jesus. He is making a weighty statement, hence the exclamation 'lo.' First a vow or promise of thanksgiving: 'the half of my possessions I give to the poor.' This is the man's thankoffering for the pardon, comfort of conscience, and peace of soul he has just received from Jesus. A priceless gift has been given to him, and he thus acknowledges the gift. The act is wholly voluntary. Jesus made no demand upon him to give any of his wealth away. Why he gave half and not a different fraction is hard to say. Love has and always will have its own generous measure, as those best know who have been prompted by love. Beside the confession of faith with thanksgiving Zacchæus places a confession of sin coupled with restitution. The verb *exacted* (as in 3 : 14) means by false assertions to press money out of some-one. That was the sin of these publicans. To what extent Zacchæus was guilty cannot be determined. He cannot have oppressed right and left, for then he could not, after giving away half of his wealth, have made fourfold restitution. The law required that in cases like this only a fifth more than the sum should be returned (Lev. 6 : 5; Num. 5 : 6, 7, etc.). But Zacchæus voluntarily offers to treat any peculations of his as plain and simple theft, for which the law stipulated fourfold or fivefold restitution (Ex. 22 : 1; 1 Sam. 12 : 3). In the fullest possible measure Zacchæus makes amends for his wrongs. Not that amends wipe out guilt. Proper amends are the evidence of a changed heart, and the amends of Zacchæus must be treated as such evidence."

6. CHRIST'S TWOFOLD DECLARATION, vs. 9, 10. 9. **And Jesus said unto him, To-day is salvation come to this house, forasmuch as he also is a son of Abraham.** This verse seems to be generally ignored by the standard commentators on Luke's Gospel. First of all, it is a direct declaration that salvation, the salvation which God alone can give, the salvation which Christ came to provide, real salvation in the sight of heaven, salvation which really saves, had that day come into this house where heretofore it had never been experienced. Salvation can come quickly, instantaneously, but it never comes unless it is wanted. Salvation is never thrust upon any one. The heart of this man yearned for that which God also yearned to bestow. Any house can have salvation any day it sincerely desires it and is willing to depart from sin. In the second place, we must not interpret this verse by making it to mean Zacchæus that day received salvation because he was a Jew, but rather that even to this benighted, despised man, who had forfeited every right to the consideration of his fellow men, even this despised man, despised with all other Jews and more, could receive salvation from God. 10. **For the Son of man came to seek and to save that which was lost.** The words of the late Dr. Warfield, the distin-

45. And he entered into the temple, and began to cast out them that sold,
46. Saying unto them, It is written, And my house shall be a house of
prayer: but ye have made it a den of robbers.

guished theologian, sets forth with his customary keenness, the real meaning of this precious assertion of the Son of Man. "The term 'lost' here is simply taken over in this form from Ezekiel 34:16, where Jehovah declares: 'I will seek that which was lost.' . . . Obviously 'the lost' which He declares that He came to seek and to save were not merely neglected people but veritably lost people, lost beyond retrieval save only as He not merely sought them but in some great sense saved them. The solemnity with which Jesus speaks of having come as the Saviour of 'the lost' will not permit us to think lightly of their condition, which necessarily carries with it thinking lightly also of His mission and achievement. . . . To say 'I came' may mean nothing more than a claim to divine appointment. But to say, 'the Son of Man came' transports the mind back into the pre-temporal, heavenly existence of the Son of Man and conveys the idea of His voluntary descent to earth. . . . The stress lies on the greatness of the agent, which carries with it the greatness of the achievement, and that in turn carries with it the hopelessness, apart from this achievement by this agent, of the condition of the 'lost.'"

"How low Zacchæus was in the moral scale! And yet how high he rose! From being hard, he became very merciful; and from being niggard and unjust — a true child of Abraham, the friend of God. Think of him as he was and as he became; born again, his flesh came as the flesh of a little child; and his were a child's feelings, a child's repentance, a child's ingenuousness of confession, a child's heart and liberality, a child's resolutions. Oh! delicate hand of the Son of Man, that could grope its way around the dead heart-strings of this hardened man, and make them tingle, and enervate them into humanity and into godliness again! Think of this, and be persuaded; and let no consideration drive the persuasion from you, that Christ has something in common with you — some sight of Him with some sight of you — whereby He can reach you, can find you — can seek and save the lost." — *A. B. Davidson.*

III. **THE SIN OF MAKING A TEMPLE OF GOD TO SERVE AS A DEN OF THIEVES,** Luke 19:45, 46. 45. **And he entered into the temple, and began to cast out them that sold,** 46. **saying unto them, It is written, And my house shall be a house of prayer: but ye have made it a den of robbers.** A number of days separate our Lord's conversation with Zacchæus in Jericho and the event which is here briefly described. This is one of the incidents that occurred on Monday of Passion Week (described also in Matthew 21:12–16 and Mark 11:15–18). Once again, as before during these unusually sacred days immediately preceding His passion, our Lord enters the Temple. The words of the gifted Biblical scholar, Dr. Cunningham Geikie, are especially rich in the description and interpretation of these two verses. "Two years before, He had purified its outer court from the sordid abuses which love of gain had dexterously cloaked under an affectation of piously serving the requirements of worship. Since then, they had been restored in all their hatefulness. The lowing of oxen, the bleating of sheep, the cries of the money-changers, and the noisy market chaffering of buyers and sellers of doves or other accessories to a ceremonial worship, filled the air with discordant sounds of the outside world, which had no right in these sacred precincts. The scene roused the same deep indignation in Jesus, as when He formerly rose in His grand protest against it. He had now, in His triumphal entry, formally proclaimed His kingship, and would forthwith vindicate its rights, by once more restoring the Temple to its becoming purity; for while it stood, it should be holy. His command sufficed to clear the spacious court of its motley crowd. By this cleansing of the outer Temple spaces, Jesus meant to show, among other things, to the multitudes round Him, by an act which they could not mistake, that the holy house was already desecrated by the sanctioned intrusion of the spirit of common gain, and made no better than a huge bazaar, with all its abuses, doubly unworthy in such a place. He wished to teach them, by the sight of such insensibility to the ideal of a Temple of God, that the fall of the theocracy, with its scoffing high priests and worn out ceremonial, was a fact already begun. The very texts He had quoted were from lamentations over the religious decay of the nation, which the prophets predicted would bring the stranger into the house of Jehovah, as more worthy than the Jew; a decay which demanded, instead of mere outward service, a reform of the heart and life. It was the knell of the Jewish economy at its center, for a Temple thus publicly marked as given over to greed and gain, under a pretense of zeal for religion, was doomed to perish, as all hypocrisies must, in the end."

The passage which our Lord quotes here is, fundamentally, Isaiah 56 : 7, though the last clause is from Jeremiah 7 : 11.

Why was Zacchæus so joyful when Jesus told him He would that day be a guest in his house? What factors do you think were prominent at this particular time in Zacchæus' life, bringing about this keen desire to see the Lord Jesus? Why did he want to see Jesus more than anybody else? How many different things were true about Zacchæus that day which, in themselves, would lead one to believe salvation would not come to his house at that time? Why did not some of the so-called righteous, ecclesiastical leaders of Jericho invite Jesus to their homes that day? What conclusion do you draw from the fact that our Lord, instead of simply ignoring the wicked commercialism that had come to take up its abode in the Temple, actually went in and drove out these money-changers, and powerfully denounced the whole nefarious business? Do you think Jesus wants us to be silent in the face of ecclesiastical wrongs, or should we speak up and let our testimony be clear and definite?

LESSON IX. — November 28.

TRUTHFULNESS AT ALL TIMES. — Exodus 20 : 16; 23 : 1, 7; Matthew 5 : 33–37; John 8 : 42–45.

GOLDEN TEXT. — ***Wherefore, putting away falsehood, speak ye truth each one with his neighbor: for we are members one of another.*** EPHESIANS 4 : 25.

Devotional Reading: Revelation 22 : 10–17.
Beginner Topic: A MAN WHO SAID THANK YOU.
  Lesson Material: Luke 17 : 11–19.
  Memory Verse: Thou, Jehovah, hast made me glad. Psalm 92 : 4.
Primary Topic: THE BOY SAMUEL.
  Lesson Material: John 8 : 42–45; 1 Samuel 3 : 1–18.
  Memory Verse: Jehovah our God will we serve, and unto his voice will we hearken. Joshua 24 : 24.
Junior Topic: SAMUEL'S ANSWER.
  Lesson Material: John 8 : 42–45; 1 Samuel 3 : 1–18.
  Memory Verse: Speak, Jehovah; for thy servant heareth. 1 Samuel 3 : 9.
Intermediate and Senior Topic: WHY IS LYING WRONG?
Topic for Young People and Adults: TELLING THE TRUTH IN SPEECH AND IN PRINT.

THE TEACHER AND HIS CLASS.

The Younger Classes should be reminded that while poison taken accidentally can be counteracted by some powerful antidote and the person's life saved, or, when a fire starts in some large building it can almost always be put out by fire extinguishers and the lavish use of water, when a lie about a person escapes our lips who can ever stop it? In fact, words that we once speak, whether true or false, can never fully be overtaken and slain. They pass so rapidly from one to another. Things we hear from others somehow lodge so permanently in our hearts, that almost nothing in the world can take them out. How careful then we ought to be about the truthfulness of words that escape our lips, even in seemingly inconsequential matters.

The Older Classes should make a careful study of the tragic consequences that flow from falsehoods of different types: false testimony about a man being tried for life can send him, though innocent, to the electric chair; lies about a young man seeking employment in a certain institution can forever keep that man from finding the place he is entitled to in his generation. Lies about a minister can follow him all over the country, and prevent him from ever exercising the influence which his gifts, and loyalty to the truth, and uprightness of character warrant. Lies can smash homes; lies in business can ruin thousands of people, swallowing up their life's savings, leaving them, though thrifty in all the years before, destitute for life. This business of falsehood is a serious one. Let us make it so as we teach this lesson.

THE PLAN OF THE LESSON.

SUBJECT: The Law of Truthfulness; the Cultivation of Truthfulness; the Enemy of the Truth.

I. THE COMMANDMENT FORBIDDING ALL FORMS OF LYING, Exod. 20 : 16; 23 : 1, 7.

II. OUR LORD'S WORDS ABOUT USING OATHS IN SPEAKING TO OTHERS, Matt. 5 : 33–37.

III. CHRIST THE TRUTH — AND WHY SOME REFUSE TO BELIEVE HIM, John 8 : 42–45.

1. The divine origin of Christ, v. 42.
2. The twofold condemnation of the unbelieving Jews, vs. 43, 44 *a*.
   a. They could not understand Christ's words.
   b. They were under the power of Satan.
3. The fivefold characterization of Satan in relation to falsehood, v. 44 *b*.
   a. He is a murderer from the beginning.
   b. He abode not in the truth.
   c. There is no truth in him.
   d. He is a liar.
   e. He is the father of all falsehood.
4. The reason why men will not believe the truth Christ declares, v. 45.

THE LESSON IN ITS SETTING.

Time. — The Ten Commandments were given in 1445 B.C.; the Sermon on the Mount was delivered in the summer of A.D. 28; our Lord's words about those who refuse to believe in Him were uttered in mid-October, A.D. 29.

Place. — The commandments were given on Mount Sinai; the Sermon on the Mount was preached not far from Capernaum; the discourse from John 8 was spoken in Jerusalem.

THE TEACHER'S LIBRARY.

Of course, on the ninth commandment, all books expounding the Decalogue will be found helpful, a list of which is given in the bibliography in the Introduction to this volume. On Exodus 20 : 16 there is a wonderful sermon for children, by Dr. James Vaughan, in the *Contemporary Pulpit*, Second Series, Vol. 10, 226–238. All commentaries on the Gospels of Matthew and John will be somewhat helpful for the study of the passages taken therefrom, as likewise most books on the Sermon on the Mount. On Matthew 5 : 37, there is a sermon by Phillips Brooks, "The Glory of Simplicity," in his *New Starts in Life*, 158–175; especially on this passage see a sermon by Dr. A. Rowland, in *The Sermon on the Mount — A Practical Exposition of St. Matthew*, Vol. 1, 295–304. There is very little sermonic material on the passage from John. Maclaren's sermons on verse 42 have no particular reference to the subject of falsehood and truth. On the entire subject of truth, however, see articles on Truth in various Bible dictionaries, Henry Clay Trumbull: *A Lie Never Justifiable;* Robert E. Speer: *The Marks of a Man*, 15–46; and a very excellent outline study, "The Christian's Relationship to Truth," in Henry W. Frost: *Outline Bible Studies*, 148–154.

THE WICKEDNESS OF FALSE SPEAKING.

The editor of this volume too well realizes that he does not have as much material week to week for children as he ought. This week is going to be an exception. There is a remarkable sermon for children by Dr. Vaughan on the ninth commandment, found in a volume so obscure that the editor believes few will be able to consult it, and for this reason he takes the liberty of quoting the first two pages in full, as an introduction to this lesson.

"What a very pretty thing the mouth is, is it not? Those two beautiful little bits of red coral; and then inside the two bits of red coral a white regiment, standing like soldiers, shoulder to shoulder, in two such neat ranks; and then such a pretty little thing inside, that has to dart about in its little cave, and go so quickly on its easy hinges. What a pretty thing the mouth is, is it not?

"What an *ugly* thing the mouth is — those pouting lips! those greedy teeth! that tongue, that red tongue of fire! God calls it 'fire.' In the third chapter of James and the sixth verse it is called 'fire.' Where does it get its fire from? From hell! And it sets all nature on fire, as says James. Let us look at it. 'The tongue is a fire, a world of iniquity . . . it setteth on fire the course of nature; and it is set on fire of hell!' What an ugly thing the mouth is! What a pity it is that such a pretty thing can become so ugly!

"When you look at a clock, you do not see the works, you see only the face; and there is something on the face of the clock that tells you how the works are going; there are the two hands, and they tell you how the works are going. I cannot see your heart; but you have got a face; your two eyes and your mouth are as the hands to the face of the clock; and I can tell by your two hands (your face) how the works are going. I mean your two eyes and your mouth. And if I look at your two eyes and your mouth, I can pretty well tell how the works inside are going.

"God says, at the last day we shall be judged by our words. It is in Matthew 12 : 37, 'By thy words thou shalt be justified, and by thy words thou shalt be condemned.' Why? Because they are as the hands on the face of a beautiful clock; they show how the works are going; your words show the state of your heart. I can tell your heart from your words. 'Thou shalt not bear false witness against thy neighbor.'

EXODUS 20 : 16. Thou shalt not bear false witness against thy neighbor.

" Do you know what it is to bear witness? Supposing you saw a man stealing something, and supposing a policeman came up at the time and took the man, and the man is taken before a judge. As you saw him steal that thing they would send for you to come into court, that you might say what you had seen. That is bearing witness. And you would have to stand up in the witness-box, and they would put a Testament into your hand, and the clerk of the court would say to you, ' The witness that you shall bear between our sovereign lady the queen and the prisoner at the bar shall be the truth, the whole truth, and nothing but the truth '; and you would kiss the book, to show you love the Bible, and you say that you don't expect God will ever help you if you tell a lie, because you add, ' So help me God! ' that means, bearing witness in court. Perhaps some of you have borne witness. Now we must be very careful indeed if we are in court that we do not bear false witness.

" There was once a Man (oh, such a Man!) and He was in court, and they brought false witness against Him, very false! Do you know whom I mean? It is in the New Testament in the Gospels, at the end of them. He was a Man, but He was God! They bore false witness against Him. They said: ' We heard him say, I will destroy this temple that is made with hands, and within three days I will build another made without hands.' Did He ever say so? No. He said: ' If you destroy this temple, in three days I will raise it up.' It was false witness. And there are accounts of other false witnesses in the Bible. I hope if we are ever called upon to give witness in court, we shall give true witness."

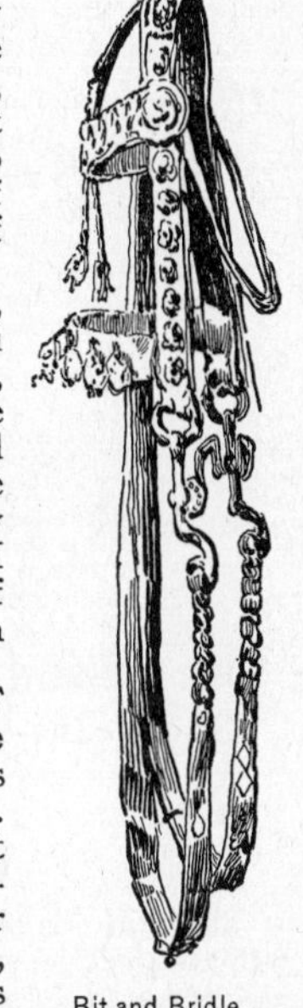
Bit and Bridle. (Roman.)
(The tongue to be bridled. Jas. 3 : 3.)

I. **THE COMMANDMENT FORBIDDING ALL FORMS OF LYING,** Ex. 20 : 16; 23 : 1, 7. 20 : 16. **Thou shalt not bear false witness against thy neighbor.** The finest words the editor knows of anywhere, on this particular commandment, are those of Dr. G. Campbell Morgan, and he believes they will be found sufficient for a full understanding of the fundamental meaning and applications of this particular verse. " The words, ' Thou shalt not bear false witness against thy neighbor,' demand truth in the statement, directly or indirectly, made by man, to man, concerning man. As the third commandment forbade the taking of the name of God in vain, and so conditioned the relation of man to God in sincerity and truth; so the ninth reveals the fact that man in his relation to his fellow is to be actuated by the same principles, and proceed on the same lines. God ever deals with man upon the basis of His full and accurate knowledge of what man is. . . . The intercourse of men with each other is to depend upon actual facts of character, conduct, and capability. The whole social fabric is based upon testimony that one bears to another, and in order that that fabric may be established in truth and righteousness, such testimony is to be true. No man must be helped or harmed by statements made concerning him, which are not exactly in accordance with the facts as far as they are known. Beyond knowledge, therefore, no testimony may be borne, and in the giving of testimony, no facts are to be withheld that would alter the decision. In order that men may approximate in their dealings with each other, to the same law of rectitude which characterizes the divine dealing with them, the opinions which one man produces in the mind of a second concerning the character of a third are to be simple, exact, true.

" The first and simplest application of the commandment is to evidence given in courts of justice. The very name just used indicates the true function of such courts. They are tribunals for the execution of justice. Justice is based upon truth, and any false testimony borne is a violation of truth and produces a miscarriage of justice. For this reason, therefore, perjury is made a criminal offence, and rightly so, because through perjury other forms of crime may go unpunished, and the innocent be made to suffer. To stay here, however, would be to rob the commandment of more than half its force, and because the majority of men may never have had to give evidence in a court of human law, and yet are daily in danger of breaking this word of the divine law, they should carefully examine the sevenfold way in which false witness may be borne. The most bare and unblushing form of the sin is that of

23 : 1. Thou shalt not take up a false report: put not thy hand with the wicked to be an unrighteous witness.

7. Keep thee far from a false matter; and the innocent and righteous slay thou not: for I will not justify the wicked.

MATTHEW 5 : 33. Again, ye have heard that it was said to them of old time, Thou shalt not forswear thyself, but shalt perform unto the Lord thine oaths:

---

slander, the lie invented and distributed with malicious intention. Perhaps no form of injury done by man to man is more despicable than this. The person who makes use of it is one compared with whom the highwayman is a gentleman, and the assassin almost kind. . . . Again, false witness is borne by tale-bearing, that is, by repetition of some report without careful investigation. It is a very great question whether the law of libel is not based on righteousness when it provides that not even the truth is to be circulated to the detriment of any person. This, at any rate, is certain, that to repeat a story, if it reflects upon the honor or character of any man, without the most careful inquiry, is to violate the commandment. . . . False witness, moreover, may also be borne by silence. When one man utters a calumny and another for some personal reason or dislike, or it may be from fear, remains silent, that person is as guilty of the breach of the law as is the one uttering the calumny. Then again, the imputation of motive is a prolific source of evil. Some deed done, or some gift bestowed, is called in question, not because they in themselves are wrong, but because it is hinted there was a reason for doing this other than that appearing — an ulterior, selfish, sordid motive. Some sentences that mark the methods of imputed motives are so commonly in use that to mention them is to reveal how prevalent is this form of sin. 'Ah, yes; he knows what he is doing.' 'The gift was only a sprat to catch a mackerel.' 'He knows which side his bread is buttered on.'"

Our lesson does not mention some of the great verses in the Bible dealing with the subject of falsehood, but the editor himself has these days discovered two, which he must confess, are quite new to him, and perhaps to his readers. One is, "So is the man that deceiveth his neighbor, and saith, Am not I in sport?" (Prov. 26 : 19). Another is a beautiful line from Isaiah, "Surely they are my people; children that will not lie" (63 : 8). Then, of course, there is the classic passage in Ephesians (4 : 25), which we might call the New Testament interpretation of the ninth commandment. Some important passages on the wickedness of a lying tongue are Psalm 5 : 9; 140 : 3; Romans 3 : 13–16; James 3 : 1–18.

23 : 1. **Thou shalt not take up a false report: put not thy hand with the wicked to be an unrighteous witness.** 7. **Keep thee far from a false matter; and the innocent and righteous slay thou not: for I will not justify the wicked.** "The ninth commandment is here expanded and developed. The line, 'Thou shalt not raise a false report,' forbids the origination of a calumny; the other clause prohibits the joining with others in spreading one. Both clauses have a special reference to bearing witness in a court, but neither would seem to be confined to it. Verse 7 admonishes us to hold aloof from anything like a false accusation. Neither bring one, nor countenance one, lest thou mayest cause the death of an innocent and righteous man, and bring down on thyself the vengeance of Him who will not justify the wicked." — *George Rawlinson.* Our true relationship to our fellow men is just about the most sacred relationship in all of life, except that to God Himself. Surely if we are the children of God, who is Himself the absolute truth, we will be truthful to those who are about us.

II. **OUR LORD'S WORDS ABOUT USING OATHS IN SPEAKING TO OTHERS,** Matt. 5 : 33–37. 33. **Again, ye have heard that it was said to them of old time, Thou shalt not forswear thyself, but shalt perform unto the Lord thine oaths.** The quotation here is not from the ninth commandment, which we have just been studying, but, in the first clause, from Leviticus 19 : 12, and, in the second clause, from Numbers 30 : 2. "The verb here rendered 'perform' is translated by 'pay' in verse 26, and 18 : 25–34; 'recompense' in 6 : 4, 6, 18, Revised Version; 'render' in 16 : 27, Revised Version; 21 : 41; 22 : 21; and signifies to give back, or to give in full, and hence to repay or to pay off. The idea here is that an oath becomes a debt to the Lord, and we must be sure to pay it. This conception is especially appropriate to a vow." — *John Broadus.* 34. **But I say unto you, Swear**

34. But I say unto you, Swear not at all; neither by the heaven, for it is the throne of God.
35. Nor by the earth, for it is the footstool of his feet; nor by Jerusalem, for it is the city of the great King.
36. Neither shalt thou swear by thy head, for thou canst not make one hair white or black.
37. But let your speech be, Yea, yea; Nay, nay: and whatsoever is more than these is of the evil *one*.

---

not at all; neither by the heaven, for it is the throne of God. "The Jewish teachers correctly interpreted the law as prohibiting false swearing. Every assertion accompanied by an oath must be true; every promise accompanied by an oath must be kept. But this cannot be if men use many oaths; and they sought to evade the difficulty in their usual fashion by a quibble of interpretation. The third commandment spoke of swearing in the name of Jehovah; and the law elsewhere expressly required that they should 'swear by his name,' *i.e.*, not by the name of any false deity. So the rabbis held that the law made binding only those oaths which contained some name or peculiar attribute of God, or something else that was eminently sacred. Other oaths, not naming or directly suggesting God, they held to be not binding. . . . Accordingly the Jews were remarkable for their frequent use of oaths in ordinary conversation, swearing by the temple, by the altar, by the lamb, by the dishes, by the law, by Moses, by the prophets, by the life of the rabbis, as well as the oaths here mentioned and countless others, and reckoning such oaths to be 'nothing.' . . . In this, as in the previous examples, our Lord is enjoining, not merely an outward and literal obedience to the law, but that regard be had to the principle involved. The command not to swear falsely was a great restriction upon the familiar use of oaths: Jesus does not abrogate that command, but goes farther in the same direction. Yet as the prohibition of killing and of anger is not to be taken without any exception, it being lawful to kill and to be angry, upon sufficient occasion, so, we might conclude by parity of reasoning, must be the case here. And accordingly we find our Lord Himself consenting to speak when formally put upon oath before the supreme court (see on 26:63); and the apostle Paul repeatedly using, where there was special occasion, such expressions as 'God is my witness,' 'I call God for a witness upon my soul,' 'Before God I lie not' (Rom. 1:9; 2 Cor. 1:23; Gal. 1:20, Revised Version), which are strong oaths; and the angel in Revelation 10:6, swearing a very solemn oath. So in the Old Testament, men being accustomed to swear, 'As Jehovah liveth,' God Himself is said to swear, 'As I live' (Ezek. 33:11); and the Epistle to the Hebrews appeals to God's oath 'by myself' (Gen. 22:16), as given to strengthen our confidence in the faithfulness of His promise (Heb. 6:13). An oath, therefore, is not inherently and necessarily wrong, and there are occasions which justify its use, as in judicial proceedings (our Lord's example), and where some very solemn asseveration in speech or writing is required by the circumstances (Paul's example). But as anger, even when legitimate, is in great danger of becoming sinful (see on v. 22), so with oaths, which are often administered in courts of justice with such irreverence as to be highly sinful, and which in individual assertions or promises ought to be confined to very rare and solemn occasions, and to be used, as the apostle does, in the most reverential spirit." — *John Broadus*. 35. **Nor by the earth, for it is the footstool of his feet; nor by Jerusalem, for it is the city of the great King.** 36. **Neither shalt thou swear by thy head, for thou canst not make one hair white or black.** "There are two sins which our Lord did condemn very emphatically, namely, profanity and untruthfulness. The oaths referred to in verses 35 and 36 were what we should call conversational oaths. Instead of a simple asseveration, it was a common thing for a Jew to say, 'By Jerusalem,' or 'By heaven, this is true.' He maintained that there was no harm in this, because the name of Jehovah was not used, but only a place which was associated with Him. Jesus, however, showed that so far as these words had any force at all, they derived it from their association of 'heaven,' or of 'earth,' or of 'Jerusalem,' with God, and this, therefore, in spirit, was taking God's name in vain." — *Alfred Rowland*. 37. **But let your speech be, Yea, yea; Nay, nay: and whatsoever is more than these is of the evil *one*.** It is strange how most modern commentators simply ignore this verse. What our Lord means here is that a man should so live,

JOHN 8:42. Jesus said unto them, If God were your Father, ye would love me: for I came forth and am come from God; for neither have I come of myself, but he sent me.

43. Why do ye not understand my speech? *Even* because ye cannot hear my word.

44. Ye are of *your* father the devil, and the lusts of your father it is your will to do. He was a murderer from the beginning, and standeth not in the truth, because there is no truth in him. When he speaketh a lie, he speaketh of his own: for he is a liar, and the father thereof.

---

and his reputation for truth should be so sound, that all he would need to do is to say "No," or, "Yes," in answer to any question, whether it be in a public courtroom, or in a private conversation, and he would be implicitly believed and no oath would be necessary, for it would be superficial in his case. When our Lord says that what is more than this cometh of the evil one, He does not mean that to take an oath is in itself evil, but it is only a revelation of man's distrust of man, and a testimony to the history of human falsehood, which seems to make it necessary in modern society to require an oath, because, normally speaking, it is understood that a man would be prone to lie without the oath. The Quakers and the Moravians interpret this verse literally, and refuse to take an oath in court; and English and American law, even today, makes an exception in their faith.

III. **CHRIST THE TRUTH — AND WHY SOME REFUSE TO BELIEVE HIM,** John 8:42-45.

1. THE DIVINE ORIGIN OF CHRIST, V. 42. 42. **Jesus said unto them, If God were your Father, ye would love me: for I came forth and am come from God; for neither have I come of myself, but he sent me.** "Jesus now asserts (1) that personally God is the source of His existence; and (2) that God is the author of His mission to earth. They should love Him instead of hating and seeking to slay Him. Even if they felt it difficult to believe, they might still have this affection of love excited in their hearts. One needs must love the highest when he sees it. The preposition 'out of' (different from the 'from' of clause second) is that which denotes closest relation, and here that of father and son. The words 'came forth' refer, therefore, to what is called the eternal generation of the Son of God; the following 'and am come' seem to refer also to this, with the implicit meaning, 'and so, such being my origin, I am here'; so that this remarkable expression would cover both facts of the eternal generation and the incarnation. Veiled in human form though He was, they might know, and would if God were their Father, that His connection with God was something unique." — *George Reith.* "Christ's argument is this: whoever is a child of God will acknowledge His first-born Son; but you hate me, and therefore you have no reason to boast that you are God's children. We ought carefully to observe in this passage, that there is no piety and no fear of God where Christ is rejected. Hypocritical religion presumptuously shelters itself under the name of God; but how can they agree with the Father, who disagree with His only Son." — *John Calvin.*

2. THE TWOFOLD CONDEMNATION OF THE UNBELIEVING JEWS, VS. 43, 44 *a*. 43. **Why do ye not understand my speech?** ***Even*** **because ye cannot hear my word.** 44 *a*. **Ye are of** ***your*** **father the devil, and the lusts of your father it is your will to do.** Our Lord's listeners "were continually misunderstanding, misinterpreting, and stumbling at, the expressions and language that He used in teaching them. . . . Any one who preaches the gospel now must often observe that precisely the same thing happens in the present day. Hearers, who are strongly prejudiced against the gospel, are constantly perverting, wresting, and misinterpreting the language of the preacher. None are so blind as those who will not see, and none so stupid as those who do not want to understand." — *J. C. Ryle.* "Jesus may as well talk to deaf men. These Jews claim indeed that they are God's children; but when Jesus talks to them in the language of God and God's house, they act like deaf men. His meaning is lost upon them. That is subject to only one explanation: they do not even recognize the language, that it is that of God. That proves how much God is their father. Children know their father's language, it is their mother-tongue. These Jews belong to a foreign land, where a different mother-tongue is used. No need to say what land that is." — *R. C. H. Lenski.*

45. But because I say the truth, ye believe me not.

3. THE FIVEFOLD CHARACTERIZATION OF SATAN, v. 44 *b*. 44 *b*. **He was a murderer from the beginning.** See Genesis 3; 1 John 3 : 8, 12, 15. "The Devil compassed man's sin, and so his death, by the lie against his Maker." — *George Reith.* Godet profoundly says: "Whence did this hatred of Satan against man arise? Undoubtedly from the fact that he had discerned in him the future organ of divine truth and the destroyer of his own lies. Thus the two features of his character are united: hatred of man and enmity to the truth. And we may understand how this double hatred must be concentrated in the highest degree upon Jesus, in whom at length was perfectly realized the idea of man, and of man as the organ of divine truth." **And standeth not in the truth, because there is no truth in him.** "It is implied that the Devil once existed in the truth, and is not an originally and eternally evil personality or principle. He fell from a true condition. The untrue in act must proceed from the untrue in thought and in will. Of no man living can it be affirmed that there is not truth in him, for in no case, so far as we can tell, is that surrender made of the will absolutely into the possession of sin, that no possibility is left for its conquest by Christ. But of the Devil Jesus says not only that he does evil, that he hates and lies, but that he begets these lusts, wherever found; for in him truth is not. He is not simply untrue, he is the untrue one; not wicked only, but the wicked one. He has therefore surrendered his will over to evil, so as to have his nature simply and solely evil." — *George Reith.* **When he speaketh a lie, he speaketh of his own: for he is a liar, and the father thereof.** The first words we have from Satan in the Word of God are those found in Genesis 3, and they are words of absolute falsehood, because he not only here lies about God, and the consequences of sin, but he actually insinuates that God Himself has lied, which is the greatest lie of all. In fact, the very name which our Lord uses here in designating this evil one, the word translated Devil, is the Greek word *diabolos*, meaning, one who slanders, who falsely accuses. All lies, therefore, proceed from the great liar himself, that is, he taught men to lie by lying to men. All falsehoods are thus the children of this original lie. Once man is deceived, falls into sin, distrusts God, and believes the Devil, he has a tendency in his nature to deceive others, to lie concerning himself and others, and, most tragic of all, to turn from the truth and to believe a lie. In fact, there is hardly anything more terrible in all the Bible than the statement of the Apostle Paul in his earliest and last epistles, where he tells us that in the last days men will turn away their ears from the truth and will actually "believe a lie" (2 Thess. 2 : 11; 2 Tim. 4 : 4). The implication of this terrible verse from our Lord is too clear to need any argument. A man who lies aligns himself with the evil one. A man who lies is doing what the Devil wants him to do. A man who lies is an enemy of God, is taking sides against God.

4. THE REASON WHY MEN WILL NOT BELIEVE THE TRUTH CHRIST DECLARES, v. 45. 45. **But because I say the truth, ye believe me not.** Look long at this verse and keep on looking at it. "If I say the truth" — what ought to follow a phrase like that? Something like this — "Every man will believe Me," or, "ye will recognize what I say to be right," or, "ye will believe Me." But the very opposite is here. Christ says, if He speaks the truth they will *not* believe Him. Can anything be more terrible than that? When a boy, studying arithmetic, is told that two and two make four, and says he does not believe it, and will never believe it, then he can never go on in arithmetic, he will never be able to add and subtract. When a boy in school hears that *h-a-t* spells *hat*, but says he does not believe it, and never will believe it, he will never be able to read and he will never be able to write with accuracy. When an army officer, looking through a telescope, sees a great body of enemy tanks approaching, and says, I see it, but I do not believe it, he is doomed. The only thing that we can believe (and keep from disaster) is the truth. The only thing that is solid and permanent and worthwhile in life is the truth. If we reject the truth, we are going to believe a lie, and if Christ is the truth and men are going to follow the Devil, and do his work, they have rejected what is true and will receive what is false. What a day of accounting that will be when, either in the hour of crisis, or at the time of death, or in the day of judgment, they will know that the great Deceiver has deluded them, and the truth which could save them they forever spurned. The editor of this volume knows of nothing that our Lord ever said so penetrating and dreadful, in exposing the iniquity of the human heart, the darkness that rests upon fallen humanity, than this, that when He came as the

truth, living the truth, speaking the truth, offering the truth to men, then, and today, men say no to Him, and, turning from the Son of God who can save them, embrace the wicked one, who will only destroy and disappoint.

What are some of the reasons why men, normally speaking, resort to falsehood? What do you think would be the most powerful force working in our lives to keep us from telling lies? What does falsehood do to the one uttering it? What are some of the things falsehood can do to others who hear it? What are some of the lies which the world now holds concerning Christ, which keep men from receiving Him as their Lord and Saviour? How does such a passage as Matthew 28: 11–15 illustrate the Satanic determination to deceive mankind regarding the truth of the Lord Jesus Christ and His work? Why do you think so many people today prefer the falsehood of Christian Science and the delusions of Mormonism to the truth of the gospel of the Lord Jesus Christ? If men will not believe the truth Christ declares, what can you and I do in the power of God to lead them out of this state of darkness into the light where God dwells, to persuade them to turn from the falsehoods which are deceiving them to embrace the truth which can save them?

LESSON X. — December 5.

THE SIN OF COVETOUSNESS. — Exodus 20 : 17; Luke 12 : 13–34.

PRINTED TEXT, Exodus 20 : 17; Luke 12 : 13-25.

GOLDEN TEXT. — *Thou shalt not covet . . . anything that is thy neighbor's.* EXODUS 20 : 17.

Devotional Reading: Luke 18 : 18–27.
Beginner Topic: GOOD FOOD FOR ALL.
 Lesson Material: Luke 12 : 6, 7, 22–30.
 Memory Verse: God . . . careth for you. 1 Peter 5 : 7.
Primary Topic: A POOR RICH MAN.
 Lesson Material: Exodus 20 : 17; Luke 12 : 13–34.
 Memory Verse: And the King shall answer and say unto them, Verily I say unto you, Inasmuch as ye did it unto one of these my brethren, even these least, ye did it unto me. Matthew 25 : 40.
Junior Topic: GIFTS TO SHARE.
 Lesson Material: Exodus 20 : 17; Luke 12 : 13–34.
 Memory Verse: And the King shall answer and say unto them, Verily I say unto you, Inasmuch as ye did it unto one of these my brethren, even these least, ye did it unto me. Matthew 25 : 40.
Intermediate and Senior Topic: THE SIN OF GREED.
Topic for Young People and Adults: WHEN IS COVETING WRONG?

THE TEACHER AND HIS CLASS.

The Younger Classes may be asked, what is the difference between a young girl looking into a store window and seeing a beautiful dress, and asking her mother, who can afford to buy it for her (which the mother does), and a girl of the same age, looking at a dress worn by some other girl, which the one beholding cannot afford, and then constantly wishing she had it until she plots and schemes to get such a garment, no matter by what means? Well, the difference is this, that the first gets her desire in a legitimate and right way, which leads to no ultimate wrong-doing, whereas in the second case there is first jealousy, then bitterness, and, if it is continued, the person may want to do something to destroy that dress which she cannot have, or to go down to the store and steal such a dress, or get money in some unfair way for the purchase of the dress. This mood is what is called *covetousness*, which we will further define in our lesson.

The Older Classes will actually find in this lesson the one sin which has prompted every great war of aggression in the history of the world, the desire to have what is not one's own, and the determination to take it by force. That is covetousness, and that is the *root* of the terrible war in which we are now engaged.

THE LESSON IN ITS SETTING.

Time. — The Ten Commandments were delivered in 1445 B.C.; our Lord's teachings concerning covetousness in this lesson were uttered in December, A.D. 29.

Place. — The Ten Commandments were given on Mount Sinai; the passage taken from Luke is from a discourse delivered in Peræa, on the east of the Jordan River.

THE PLAN OF THE LESSON.

SUBJECT: The Nature and Manifestations of Covetousness, and the Doom of a Life Ever Bent on the Acquisition of the Mere Things of This World.

I. THE CONDEMNATION OF COVETOUSNESS, Ex. 20 : 17.

II. THE COVETOUS BROTHER, Luke 12 : 13–15.

III. THE PARABLE OF THE FOOLISH RICH MAN, Luke 12 : 16–21.

1. His abundant wealth, v. 16.
2. His selfish plans regarding his possession, vs. 17, 18.
3. His foolish scheme for satisfying his soul's needs, v. 19.
4. The terrible and unexpected end of all his plans, v. 20.
5. The application, v. 21.

IV. HOW TO LIVE A LIFE OF VICTORY OVER COVETOUSNESS, Luke 12 : 22–34.

1. The life free from anxiety, vs. 22, 23.
2. We should always be assured of God's care for us, vs. 24, 27, 28.
3. We should remind ourselves of the folly of anxiety, vs. 25, 26.
4. We should remember God knows all our needs, vs. 29, 30.
5. If we seek God's kingdom, material things will follow, v. 31.
6. We should ever be storing up treasure in heaven, vs. 32–34.

THE TEACHER'S LIBRARY.

For some strange reason, most books on the Ten Commandments become weak when the last one is reached. This is amazingly true with Hodge, Chadwick, and some others. However, the passage in Murphy is good, and the chapters by Dale, Farrar, and McAfee are commendable. In addition, one may consult various articles on Covetousness in Biblical encyclopedias (but even here one will be disappointed). See, on the entire subject of covetousness, J. B. Mozley: *University Sermons*, 275–290; J. C. Massee: *Conflict and Conquest in Holiness*, 120–128; and James Stalker: *Seven Daily Sins*, 19–38. There is not a great deal of good material on this long passage taken from Luke. In addition to commentaries on Luke's Gospel, one should especially read the works on the parables by Trench, Marcus Dods, and William Taylor. On verses 13–21, see Alexander Maclaren: *The Gospel of St. Luke*, 152–158; and, on 22 : 34, the same, 159–165; on vs. 13–23, the same author: *Expositions of Holy Scripture, Luke 1–12*, 337–342; on vs. 22–31, the same, 343–349. On verse 15, see James Hastings: *The Great Texts of the Bible, St. Luke*, 236–272; G. Campbell Morgan, in the *Westminster Pulpit*, Vol. 9, 233–240; H. P. Liddon: *Passiontide Sermons*, 259–275. On the entire passage, especially on the rich fool, see an excellent chapter in James Jeffrey: *The Personal Ministry of the Son of Man*, 157–168.

EXODUS 20 : 17. Thou shalt not covet thy neighbor's house, thou shalt not covet thy neighbor's wife, nor his man-servant, nor his maid-servant, nor his ox, nor his ass, nor anything that is thy neighbor's.

I. **THE CONDEMNATION OF COVETOUSNESS,** Ex. 20 : 17. **Thou shalt not covet thy neighbor's house, thou shalt not covet thy neighbor's wife, nor his man-servant, nor his maid-servant, nor his ox, nor his ass, nor anything that is thy neighbor's.**

SOME DEFINITIONS.

The Oxford English Dictionary defines covetousness as "inordinate and culpable desire of possessing that which belongs to another to which one has no right." Archbishop Trench says that the Greek word translated covetousness in the New Testament means, primarily, "the having more," and then, in a secondary and more usual sense, "the desire after the having more. It is the drawing and snatching by the sinner to himself of the creature in every form and kind as it lies out of and beyond himself. It is the fiercer and ever fiercer longing of the creature which has forsaken God to fill itself with the lower objects of sense."

THE MEANING OF THE COMMANDMENT ITSELF.

"This commandment refers to the thoughts, inculcates disinterestedness, and prohibits indulging a desire after that which belongs to another. . . . The improper desire is the root of all evil. It can seldom be reached by human legislation. But it is open to the Searcher of hearts. The intent is that which, in the last resort, determines the moral character of the act. This last 'word' is, therefore, the interpreting clause of the whole Decalogue (Rom. 7 : 7). It raises the code immeasurably above every code of man, who looketh on the outward appearance of conduct, and at once renders it worthy of the Lord who looketh on the heart. Covetousness here includes envy, malice, and every other selfish or unholy state of the feelings. Its prohibition involves the inculcation not merely of disinterestedness, but of all the forms of unselfish benevolence. This commandment is, therefore, virtually the law of love, and in this positive sense gives that loftier aspect of the Decalogue, the traces of which have been already noticed." — *James G. Murphy.*

SOME WAYS IN WHICH COVETOUSNESS IS MANIFEST.

"Individuals, as well as nations, may violate this law. It is violated by the ambition which looks with a restless and hungry heart upon the fame and the power of a successful rival, and longs to secure his greatness for itself. It is violated by the discontent and envy with which we are apt to think of the pleasant homes and the luxurious comfort of men who are wealthier than ourselves. It is violated by the desire to win from another man the love which is the pride and joy of his life. It is violated by the evil passion which has appropriated to itself the word 'lust,' which once had a much wider meaning, a passion which, unless subdued, will lead us to invade the sanctity of marriage, and involve what may be a happy household in misery and disgrace. It is violated by the desire to put ourselves into the place of a fellow servant who has an easier or more remunerative position than ourselves; if we yield to that desire, instead of crushing it, it will lead us to resort to mean and disgraceful methods of destroying the confidence reposed in him, to base insinuations, to slander, and to treachery." — *R. W. Dale.*

COVETOUSNESS IN RELATION TO WAR.

"The history of the world is stained and darkened by the crimes to which nations have been driven by the spirit of covetousness. A great and prosperous people with a beautiful country rich in all the material resources which contribute to national wealth and splendor, cannot endure that the cornfields, and the vineyards, and the noble river which can be seen from its frontiers should belong to a neighboring power. Or an inland state with hardly any seaboard looks upon the indented coast of some insignificant and feeble neighbor, and dreams of the formidable navies which could ride in safety in those secure harbors, and of the vast commercial cities which might be built if those convenient seaports were its own. Or a strong and masculine and enterprising race speculates on the wealth it might win if it could appropriate by policy or by force rich and fertile territories on the other side of the world, governed by a decaying empire and possessed by an unwarlike and imperfectly civilized people. Sooner or later, it is almost certain that in every case this national covetousness will end in a war of aggression and conquest. Some pretext will be found for a quarrel; there will be an insult to avenge; or an ancient wrong to redress, or a frontier to rectify; or the idea of national unity to vindicate; or punishment to inflict and compensation to claim for the violation of a commercial treaty; by some means or other there will be a justification discovered or created for seizing, by force of arms, what the heart of the nation longed for." — *R. W. Dale.*

COVETOUSNESS IN RELATION TO THE OTHER COMMANDMENTS.

"Coveting tempts us into violation of the fourth commandment, or Sabbath-breaking; it is covetousness which encroaches on God's appointed day of sacred rest, tempting us to run trains for merely secular purposes, to vend tobacco and liquors, to hawk newspapers. Again, coveting tempts us into violation of the fifth commandment, or disrespect for authority; tempting the young man to deride his early parental counsels; the citizen to trample on civic enactments. Again, covetousness tempts us into violation of the sixth commandment, or murder; recall how Judas' love of money drove him into the sacrilegious betrayal of his divine Friend into the hands of His murderers; his lure being the paltry sum of — say — fifteen dollars. Again, covetousness tempts us into violation of the seventh commandment, or adultery; observe how Scripture combines greed and lust. The Gentiles, being past feeling, gave themselves up to lasciviousness, 'to work all uncleanness with greediness (covetousness)'; fornication, and all uncleanness, or covetousness, let it not even be named among you, as becometh saints; for this ye know of a surety, that no fornicator, nor unclean person, nor covetous man, who is an idolater, hath any inheritance in the kingdom of Christ and God (Eph. 4 : 19; 5 : 3, 5; Col. 3 : 5). Again, cov-

Luke 12 : 13. And one out of the multitude said unto him, Teacher bid my brother divide the inheritance with me.
14. But he said unto him, Man, who made me a judge or a divider over you?
15. And he said unto them, Take heed, and keep yourselves from all covetousness: for a man's life consisteth not in the abundance of the things which he possesseth.

---

etousness tempts us into violation of the eighth commandment, or theft; recall how it tempted Achan to steal a goodly Babylonish mantle, and two hundred shekels of silver, and a wedge of gold of fifty shekels weight. Again, covetousness tempts us into violation of the ninth commandment, or bearing false witness against our neighbor; recall how the covetousness of Ahab instigated his wife Jezebel to employ two sons of Belial to bear blasphemous and fatal testimony against Naboth, saying, 'Thou didst curse God and the king.'" — *G. D. Boardman.*

SOME MANIFESTATIONS OF COVETOUSNESS IN THE BIBLE.

Among the famous cases of covetousness in the Scriptures, one will recall the stories of Achan (Josh. 7), Saul (1 Sam. 15 : 9, 19); Ahab (1 Kings 21); Judas (Matt. 26 : 14, 15), and Ananias and Sapphira (Acts 5 : 1–11).

THE UNIQUENESS OF THIS COMMANDMENT.

Canon Farrar begins his fine chapter on the tenth commandment by saying: "This is a unique commandment. Search all the laws of all the world, and you will not find one which resembles it. The sixth, seventh, eighth, and ninth commandments you will find in all codes, though only as prohibitions of crimes amenable to judicial punishment. The tenth commandment is the complement of all the rest. It shows that God requires of us not only outward virtue, but inward holiness; that He demands in us the sacrifice of the will, from which wicked actions spring; that sinful imaginations are a crime against Him as well as wicked acts. Human laws can only prohibit those crimes of which human eyes can take cognizance; the thoughts of men are beyond their reach."

II. **THE COVETOUS BROTHER,** Luke 12 : 13–15. 13. **And one out of the multitude said unto him, Teacher, bid my brother divide the inheritance with me.** "This incident forms the historical introduction to the parable of the rich fool just as the lawyer's questions in chapter 10 form the historical introduction to the parable of the Good Samaritan. We are not told whether the man was making an unjust claim on his brother or not; probably not: but he was certainly making an unjust claim on Jesus, whose work did not include settling disputes about property. The man grasped at any means of obtaining what he desired, invading Christ's time and trying to impose upon his brother an extraneous authority." — *Alfred Plummer.* Is it not strange that this man should think of nothing but an estate, property, an inheritance, when coming into the presence of the very Son of God? This shows the fearful grip of a passion for possessions on his whole being. 14. **But he said unto him, Man, who made me a judge or a divider over you?** The form of address which our Lord uses here is severe, and as Plummer says, "implies disapprobation or a desire to stand aloof. Jesus abstains from invading the office of constituted authority. No one appointed Him to any such office" (cf. Ex. 2 : 14). Though our Lord refused to enter into this legal question, He did speak concerning a much more important matter, a profounder theme, not external possessions, but internal principles. 15. **And he said unto them, Take heed, and keep yourselves from all covetousness: for a man's life consisteth not in the abundance of the things which he possesseth.** Our Lord now "was reaching the heart of the man who ventured to submit this request to Him. Wronged he might be, he was doing himself a far greater wrong: he could think of nothing but the loss he had sustained. His happiness was bound up in its possession; and since deprived of it he could think of nothing else. Life had lost its flavor because he had lost a portion of this world's goods. That is the general experience of the men of this world, who have set their hearts on possessions — when they fail they have nothing left to occupy their minds." — *James Jeffrey.* The words here of Archbishop Trench are profound, and should be studied carefully. "While

16. And he spake a parable unto them, saying, The ground of a certain rich man brought forth plentifully:
17. And he reasoned within himself, saying, What shall I do, because I have not where to bestow my fruits?
18. And he said, This will I do: I will pull down my barns, and build greater; and there will I bestow all my grain and my goods.

---

we have but one word for 'life,' the Greek possesses two — one to express the life *which we live*, another to express that life *by which we live;* and it is of this latter which Christ is speaking here. A man may have his living, the sustenance of his lower life, out of his earthly goods; nay more, they may themselves be called by this very name (Mark 12 : 44; Luke 8 : 43; 15 : 8; 21 : 4; 1 John 3 : 17); but his life itself, he cannot draw from them. The breath of his nostrils is of God; not all his worldly possessions, be they ever so large, will retain his spirit an instant if that breath be withdrawn. And if this be true of life, merely as the animating principle of man's earthly existence, how much less can life, as identical with peace, joy, blessedness here, and with immortality hereafter, consist in these things which are at once outside of a man and beneath him? They may overlay, hinder, strangle this life; they were threatening to do so in one who evidently cared so much more for a patch of earth than for the kingdom of heaven; but they cannot produce it. This life is *from* God, as it is *to* God. In this double meaning of life lies the key to this passage, whose force they fail to educe who accept life either exclusively in the lower, or exclusively in a higher, sense." Our Lord is now about to illustrate the principal He has just enunciated, by one of the most pointedly powerful parables He ever uttered, occupying only five verses in the text, and yet a parable about which whole books could be written.

III. **THE PARABLE OF THE FOOLISH RICH MAN,** Luke 12 : 16–21.

1. HIS ABUNDANT WEALTH, v. 16. 16. **And he spake a parable unto them, saying, The ground of a certain rich man brought forth plentifully.** There is nothing wrong in what is here stated. In fact, everything is right. The man of whom our Lord is about to speak was not only rich, but his crops were abundant, which means that he had good land, an asset indeed, and that he was careful to make the most of the land, which involves careful planning and hard work.

"I will pull down my barns and build greater."

2. HIS SELFISH PLANS REGARDING HIS POSSESSIONS, VS. 17, 18. 17. **And he reasoned within himself, saying, What shall I do, because I have not where to bestow my fruits?** 18. **And he said, This will I do: I will pull down my barns, and build greater; and there will I bestow all my grain and my goods.** "How clear and deep an insight Jesus had into the misery of wealth, when He made the first effect of prosperity on this man to be reasoning within himself and perplexity as to what he was to do! How many rich men cannot sleep for wondering how they are to invest their money! But the perplexity is not altogether displeasing to the farmer. Observe how delicately the pride of ownership is hinted at in the 'my's' with which his talk is so plentifully sprinkled — 'my fruits,' 'my barns,' 'my corn,' 'my goods,' and even 'my soul.' 'My' is the devil's pronoun. Its continual use hardens against the claims of brotherhood and the recognition of God, the giver and owner of all." — *Alexander Maclaren.* There is an unpardonable selfishness in this man's schemes. With more possessions than he knows what to do with, he does not

19. And I will say to my soul, Soul, thou hast much goods laid up for many years; take thine ease, eat, drink, be merry.

20. But God said unto him, Thou foolish one, this night is thy soul required of thee; and the things which thou hast prepared, whose shall they be?

---

say that he is going to help the poor, or share what he has. There is no expression of thanks to God for favorable weather, sufficient rain, or abundant harvest. He does not even contemplate sending his family away on a journey. All his desires concentrate in the further accumulation of material things, of which he has more now than he will ever need. Marcus Dods brings out vividly the tragic fact that there is no reckoning here with the mercy, the grace, and the goodness of God, and adds: " Can anything be more pitiable than the man who stands at his counting-house door and forbids God's entrance while his balance is being struck, who does not care that God should know how much he made last year, but goes and prays that this God would give him success this year? Is it not astonishing how religious men who profess to live for God, should so carefully keep Him from interfering in their money matters, that is, in those matters round which their life really revolves? If we cannot go before God and frankly say, That is what I have made this year, and I could not have made it but for Thee and Thy help — this is because we fear God will claim too much, and prompt us to use it as we are not prepared to do. Must there not be something wrong if we are not letting God's eye and judgment fully and freely into every transaction we engage in, and every gain we make? "

3. HIS FOOLISH SCHEME FOR SATISFYING HIS SOUL'S NEEDS, v. 19. 19. **And I will say to my soul, Soul, thou hast much goods laid up for many years; take thine ease, eat, drink, be merry.** " How unconsciously he acknowledges that wealth has hitherto failed to bring peace! ' Take thine ease ' confesses that there has been no ease yet in his life; and unless he has really ' many years ' to live, there will have been none. That is the experience of thousands of prosperous men, who toil and fret till old age, to amass wealth, before they begin to get the good of it, even according to their own poor notions of good, and then have but a year or two at the fag-end of their days in which to enjoy it. Toil in getting and anxiety in keeping far outweigh the pride of possessing, and to be able to say ' my goods ' is but a poor result of slaving for years. All the pleasure that he can think of in his leisure is eating and drinking. His case is that of many prosperous men nowadays, who have no tastes but the coarsest, and, when they go out of business, are miserable. They cannot eat and drink all day, and they have killed so much in themselves, by their course of life, that they care for nothing, books, or thought, or nature, or God, and so live empty lives, and try to fancy they like it." — *Alexander Maclaren.* " There is again an irony as melancholy as profound in making him address this speech, not to his body, but to his soul; for that soul, though capable of being thus dragged down to a basest service of the flesh, embodied and imbruted, was also capable of being quickened by the divine Spirit, of knowing and loving and glorifying God." — *R. C. Trench.*

4. THE TERRIBLE AND UNEXPECTED END OF ALL HIS PLANS, v. 20. 20. **But God said unto him, Thou foolish one, this night is thy soul required of thee; and the things which thou hast prepared, whose shall they be?** Somewhere Dr. John Hutton has very brilliantly remarked that this man thought there were only three acts to life, and that, having played all three of them very well, he could now retire from the stage. But just as he was completely disrobed, behind the stage, a bell rang, calling him to the fourth act, which he had never even thought of. There he stood, naked and shivering, in the presence of God. " There is a grim contrast between what the rich man said and what God said. The man's words were empty breath; God's are powers, and what He says is a deed. The divine decree comes crushing into the abortive human plans like a thunderclap into a wood full of singing birds, and they are all stricken silent. So little does life consist in possessions that all the abundance cannot keep the breath in man for one moment. His life is required of him, not only in the sense that he has to give it up, but also inasmuch as he has to answer for it. In that requirement the selfishly used wealth will be a ' swift witness against him,' and instead of ministering to life or ease, will ' eat his flesh as fire.' " — *Alexander Maclaren.* " How much are you worth? That is a revised form of the question which is easily asked in the third person after a man is dead. So-and-

21. So is he that layeth up treasure for himself, and is not rich toward God.

22. And he said unto his disciples, Therefore I say unto you, Be not anxious for *your* life, what ye shall eat; nor yet for your body, what ye shall put on.

23. For the life is more than the food, and the body than the raiment.

24. Consider the ravens, that they sow not, neither reap; which have no store-chamber nor barn; and God feedeth them: of how much more value are ye than the birds!

---

so died yesterday, says one business man to another as they travel to the city. Yes, what was he worth? What are you worth? If tonight thy soul be required of thee, what art thou worth? According to men of like passions with yourself, and like limited outlook, you are worth what you leave behind. According to Christ you are worth what you take with you. 'This night is thy soul required of thee; and the things which thou hast prepared, whose shall they be?' " — *G. Campbell Morgan.*

5. THE APPLICATION, V. 21. 21. **So is he that layeth up treasure for himself, and is not rich toward God.** "Self and God are here contemplated as the two poles between which the soul is placed, for one or other of which it must determine, and then constitute that one the end and object of all its aims and efforts. If for the first, then the man 'layeth up treasure for himself,' and what the issue of this is, we have seen; the man and his treasure come to nothing together. He has linked himself to the perishable in his inmost being, and he must perish with it. The very enriching of himself outwardly, being made the purpose of his existence, is an impoverishing of himself inwardly, that is, toward God, and in those things which are the true riches: for there is a continual draining off to worldly objects, of those affections which should have found their only satisfying object in God; where his treasure is, there his heart is also. . . ." — *R. C. Trench.* "Suppose we never got back to our homes, suppose we were by some great natural catastrophe at this hour separated from all that we have provided for this life, should we still be rich? Is there something so belonging to you that you can say, This is mine for evermore — mine through every change, through health and sickness, in life and death — mine though I be stripped of all that can be separated from my person, though I stand a bare spirit without connection with material things? Will you honestly give yourselves an answer to this question? What *have* I towards God? What that is certain to increase the nearer I go to Him?" — *Marcus Dods.*

IV. HOW TO LIVE A LIFE OF VICTORY OVER COVETOUSNESS, Luke 12 : 22–34. The sequence in our lesson is both beautiful and logical: first, there is the conversation with the covetous man, then there is a parable concerning the awful tragedy awaiting the man who is held in the grip of covetousness, and now, finally, our Lord tells His followers how they may live triumphantly over this besetting sin. He begins with an admonition that we are to live free from anxiety, and then He goes on giving reasons *why* our minds should be free from anxious care.

1. THE LIFE FREE FROM ANXIETY, VS. 22, 23. 22. **And he said unto his disciples, Therefore I say unto you, Be not anxious for *your* life, what ye shall eat; nor yet for your body, what ye shall put on.** 23. **For the life is more than the food, and the body than the raiment.** In our Authorized Version, the text reads, "Take no thought," which has given some the idea that our Lord is here commending carelessness of life, which is not at all the case. In the seventeenth century (when the Authorized Version appeared) the word "thought" was used to express "care." The word here really means a turning from one side to the other, resulting in exhaustion, friction, and fear. Our Lord does not say that we should not take care for the securing of the necessities of life. He is not saying we should not work, and plan, and make provision for the future. But He is saying that, concerning these material things, we should not be *anxious*, we should not get fretful, we should not be living under a shadow of fear, for such a state of mind is destructive of inward peace, and it is the inward peace that we must seek for and live for.

2. WE SHOULD ALWAYS BE ASSURED OF GOD'S CARE FOR US, VS. 24, 27, 28. 24. **Consider the ravens, that they sow not, neither reap; which have no store-chamber nor barn; and God feedeth them: of how much more value are ye than the birds!** Our Lord now gives some reasons why we *should* thus live free from

25. And which of you by being anxious can add a cubit unto the measure of his life?

anxiety. First, He reminds them that ravens themselves do not sow crops and do not reap; do not have barns, but God in His mercy feeds them. "The word here translated raven covers the whole of the crow tribe, which is strongly represented in Palestine. Like the vulture, the raven acts as a scavenger: but it is a fable that it turns its young out of the nest, leaving them to feed themselves, and that this is the point of our Lord's mention of them. The raven is very careful of its young; and God feeds both old and young." "Consider the lilies, how they grow: they toil not, neither do they spin: yet I say unto you, Even Solomon in all his glory was not arrayed like one of these. But if God doth so clothe the grass in the field, which today is and tomorrow is cast into the oven; how much more shall he clothe you, O ye of little faith?" In a similar way, our Lord illustrates His point by pointing to the lilies which toil not, nor spin, but provide a glory and beauty which Solomon himself could not reach. Our Lord does not mean that we are not to have barns, that we are not to toil or spin. That is not the point. He means that if in nature there is real provision for their needs, even though the birds do not build barns nor the lilies toil and spin, how much more certain will be the provision for man's needs, when God has given to him the ability to work, and to build barns, and to put away things for the future. If nature, without this foresight, is provided for, how much more man, who is called to labor daily that he might honestly provide the things needed. Man can do, by the grace of God, what birds and flowers cannot do. Thus has God arranged for the necessities of his life.

"Consider the lilies of the field."

3. WE SHOULD REMIND OURSELVES OF THE FOLLY OF ANXIETY, VS. 25, 26.
25. **And which of you by being anxious can add a cubit unto the measure of his life?** There is no advantage in such anxiety, so afflicting men and women. Professor Plummer believes that the phrase, "the measure of his life," refers to the length of man's life, that is, the use of his life and not its stature, and probably this is right, for one hardly comes across a person attempting to add eighteen inches to his height. But almost all people are anxious about longer life, and this can easily be understood. The point here is that worry will not prolong life; in fact, it will shorten life. You do not add years to your existence by worrying about this and that.

4. WE SHOULD REMEMBER GOD KNOWS ALL OUR NEEDS, VS. 29, 30. Furthermore, our Lord says that our earthly father knows what things we have need of, and certainly our heavenly Father knows what we have need of much more, long before the need arises. We should keep in mind that these words are directed not to the world in general, but to followers of the Lord, to the children of the heavenly Father. "He recognizes our claims on Him. He made the needs, and will send the supply. My wants, so far as God has made me to feel them, are prophecies of God's gifts. He has made them as doors by which He will come in and bless me. Trust is the only reasonable temper for a child of such a Father. Anxious care is a denial of His love or knowledge or power." — *Alexander Maclaren.*

5. IF WE SEEK GOD'S KINGDOM, MATERIAL THINGS WILL FOLLOW, V. 31. Finally, our Lord gives a promise, *e.g.*, that if we first seek the things of God's kingdom,

these things will be added unto us. This does not mean that we will necessarily get rich if we are good Christians. Our Lord is not talking about wealth, the vast accumulation of material possessions. He is simply talking about the necessities of life. When a man so orders his life, our Lord promises, that God is first, and the ways of God are the ways in which he wishes to walk, which means he is living honestly, sincerely, that he is diligently employing his time, that he is kind and gracious to others, that he is not extravagant, that he gives a portion of his earnings to the things that pertain to God, that he is diligent in prayer, that he is seeking to glorify the name of Christ. When these things are true, this man's life is of such a nature, the material things which he needs will be available, legitimately, and in sufficient abundance.

6. WE SHOULD EVER BE STORING UP TREASURE IN HEAVEN, VS. 32–34. The entire passage closes with an admonition, " Where your treasure is there will your heart be also " (cf. Matt. 6 : 21). Our Lord does not mean that everything a man possesses should be disposed of, but He does mean that our material possessions should be used for doing good, for distributing to the poor, and contributing to those things which tend to the proclamation of the gospel and the distribution of His Word. We store up treasure there by doing on earth the things that God in heaven approves. Secondly, if sincerely we have a desire to honor God with all of our substance, if our mind is on the things of God, if we ultimately center our affection not on a great mansion, or a huge barn, or a large estate, or hunting dogs, or racing horses, or a great art gallery, or a collection of rare books (many of these being in themselves all right), if we do not set our deepest affection on these things, but on the things of God, then our life will be simple, God will be honored, men will be blessed, and in the life to come we will find ourselves abundantly rewarded.

Why is the sin of covetousness so comprehensive, and at the same time so destructive of the finer things of life? What is the relation of the sin of covetousness to political corruption, which prevails so largely in our country today? What great criminal instructions in America exist primarily because men are covetous? Why is covetousness a sin so easily fallen into? How many different truths does our Lord set forth, which, if we believed, would deliver us from a life of anxiety? Can a person be anxious and not be covetous? (The answer is, Yes.) Do you think real Christians are more susceptible to anxiety than they are to covetousness? How does this vice of covetousness manifest itself in the life of some Christian churches and some outstanding Christian leaders? Do you think a person can wickedly covet another person's spiritual influence and power?

LESSON XI. — December 12.

CHRIST'S NEW COMMANDMENT. — Mark 12 : 28–34; John 13 : 34, 35; 15 : 10–14.

GOLDEN TEXT. — ***A new commandment I give unto you, that ye love one another; even as I have loved you, that ye also love one another.*** JOHN 13 : 34.

Devotional Reading: 1 John 4 : 7–16.
Beginner Topic: MARY'S HAPPY SONG.
  Lesson Material: Luke 1 : 26–56.
  Memory Verse: I will sing unto Jehovah. Exodus 15 : 1.
Primary Topic: WHAT MAKES CHRISTMAS.
  Lesson Material: Mark 12 : 28–34.
  Memory Verse: Let us love one another: for love is of God. 1 John 4 : 7.
Junior Topic: WHAT MAKES CHRISTMAS.
  Lesson Material: Mark 12 : 28–34.
  Memory Verse: Let us love one another: for love is of God. 1 John 4 : 7.
Intermediate and Senior Topic: WHAT CHRIST'S NEW COMMANDMENT MEANS.
Topic for Young People and Adults: THE SUPREME TEST OF DISCIPLESHIP.

THE TEACHER AND HIS CLASS.

The Younger Classes might be asked first, how many would like to live every day in a joyful way? Then let them be asked, what takes away joy? Doing something we know we ought not to do, disobeying parents, not being prepared for our lessons, telling a lie, hurting some one's feelings, fear, etc. And what makes joy? Doing what we know we ought to do, being kind to others, finding the things we like to do, and doing them with all our heart. Now in this lesson, Jesus Himself tells us how we may have fullness of joy. Let us see what He tells us is the secret of this kind of life.

The Older Classes should have emphasized the fact that in the Word of God we not only have God's commandments to us, but we also have one person, the Son of God, who is also called the Word of God, who lived out on earth a life in which God's commandments were perfectly obeyed. In our lesson, we not only have Jesus teaching commandments, but living them so perfectly that He could say He was our example for life. Thus, in following Christ as our example, we will find ourselves at the same time fulfilling the commandments of God as Jesus fulfilled them.

THE LESSON IN ITS SETTING.

Time. — The passage taken from Mark was uttered on Tuesday of Passion Week, April 4, A.D. 30. The discourses in John were uttered two days later, Thursday, April 6.

Place. — All the words of our Lord recorded in this lesson were spoken in Jerusalem.

THE PLAN OF THE LESSON.

SUBJECT: The One Commandment Which, if Obeyed, Will Mean Keeping All the Commandments, and a Life of Perfect Joy and Blessing.

I. THE FIRST TWO COMMANDMENTS ACCORDING TO THEIR GREATNESS, Mark 12 : 28–34.

1. The question asked of Jesus, v. 28.
2. "The first of all the commandments," vs. 29, 30.
3. The second greatest commandment, v. 31.
4. The scribe's hearty acceptance of Jesus' verdict, vs. 32, 33.
5. Christ's verdict concerning the scribe, v. 34.

II. THE NEW COMMANDMENT, John 13 : 34, 35; 15 : 10–14.

1. The commandment itself — to love one another, 13 : 34 *a*.
2. The great example — Christ's love for us, 34 *b*.
3. Love — the disciples' distinguishing mark, v. 35.
4. The consequences of obeying Christ's commandments, 15 : 10, 11, 14.
   a. Abiding in Christ's love, v. 10.
   b. Fullness of joy, v. 11.
   c. Friendship with Christ, v. 14.
5. The commandment reiterated, v. 12.
6. The supreme manifestation of love, v. 13.

THE TEACHER'S LIBRARY.

In addition to commentaries on the Gospels of Mark and John, for good discussions of "the new commandment" see J. O. Dykes: *The Law of the Ten Words*, 209–241; G. Campbell Morgan: *The Ten Commandments*, 118–126; J. D. Boardman: *The Ten Commandments*, 335–365; James Stalker: *The Ethics of Jesus*, 289–305; the relevant pages in James Moffatt: *Love in the New Testament;* and the rather rare pamphlet by Dr. Henry Clay Trumbull: *The Ten Commandments as a Covenant of Love* (Philadelphia, 1895). On the passage from Mark, see D. J. Burrell: *Christ and Man*, 269 ff.; on verse 28, J. A. Bain: *Questions Answered by Christ*, 88–97; on verses 29–31, James Hastings: *Great Texts of the Bible, St. Mark*, 296–331; on verse 34, F. W. Boreham: *A Bunch of Everlastings*, 198 ff.; W. L. Watkinson: *The Bane and the Antidote*, 23–37; J. Wilbur Chapman: *Revival Sermons*, 132 ff.; R. J. Drummond: *Faith's Perplexities*, 259–274; James Hastings, as above, 334–350; G. H. Morrison: *The Afterglow of God*, 264–273; F. W. Farrar: *In the Days of Thy Youth*, 265 ff.; and, on the entire episode, an excellent chapter in W. M. Mackay: *Bible Types of Modern Men*, 196–210. On John 13 : 34, 35, R. F. Horton: *The Commandments of Jesus*, 319–341; J. G. Greenhough: *Great Texts of the New Testament*, 99–107; James Hastings: *Great Texts of the Bible, St. John, 13–21*, 26–37; Alexander Maclaren: *Expositions of Holy Scripture, John 9–14*, 226–235; on 15 : 9–11, Alexander Maclaren: the same, *15–21*, 20–28. On verse 11, George H. Morrison: *Highways of the Heart*, 79 ff.; Andrew Murray: *Abide in Christ*, 173–179; J. H. Jowett: *The Friend on the Road*, 190–197; on verses 12 and 13, Alexander Maclaren: the same, 28–38; on verse 12, A. J. Gossip: *The Galilean Accent*, 221–234; Andrew Murray: as above, 180–186; on verse 13, P. C. Ainsworth: *A Throneless World*, 164–171; on verse 14, J. H. Jowett: *Things That Matter Most*, 144–153; James I. Vance: *The Breaking of the Bread*, 69–75.

MARK 12 : 28. And one of the scribes came, and heard them questioning together, and knowing that he had answered them well, asked him, What commandment is the first of all?

I. **THE FIRST TWO COMMANDMENTS ACCORDING TO THEIR GREATNESS,** Mark 12 : 28–34.

While in the event immediately preceding the one here recorded, our Lord is approached by Sadducees who do not believe in Him, who wish to trap Him, and while, in the event immediately following, Christ is talking to antagonistic Pharisees, in this brief episode it would seem that we are listening to a scribe who was not fundamentally antagonistic to our Lord, but was truly sincere in his questions (see for parallel accounts, Matt. 22 : 34–40; Luke 10 : 25–37). 28. **And one of the scribes came, and heard them questioning together, and knowing that he had answered them well, asked him, What commandment is the first of all?** The Lord

29. Jesus answered, The first is, Hear, O Israel; The Lord our God, the Lord is one:

30. And thou shalt love the Lord thy God with all thy heart, and with all thy soul, and with all thy mind, and with all thy strength.

---

is not asked to select one commandment out of the ten, but to specify a class of commandments or a particular commandment as representative of a class to which the priority belongs. 29. **Jesus answered, The first is, Hear, O Israel; The Lord our God, the Lord is one:** 30. **and thou shalt love the Lord thy God with all thy heart, and with all thy soul, and with all thy mind, and with all thy strength.** The quotation here is from the Septuagint translation of Deuteronomy 6 : 4, 5, and Leviticus 19 : 18, the former passage summing up the first table of the law, the latter summing up the second table. "The first quotation is the famous *Shema* of the Jewish worship, so called from its first word meaning *hear*, and constantly repeated as a sort of creed or summary of all religion. There is no need of attempting any nice distinction between *heart* and *soul* and *mind*, the obvious design of the accumulated synonyms being to exhaust the one idea of the whole man with all his powers and affections. . . . Self-love, as being an original principle of our nature, and therefore not subject to the caprices of the will, is wisely made the standard of men's love to one another, which would otherwise be ever sinking far below the level of our natural regard to our own welfare." — *J. A. Alexander.*

"Love is the duty of man toward God, and this is in itself a revelation of the nature of God. It is only one who loves who demands love, and only one in whom love is supreme demands love as the supreme duty. He requires of man what is consonant with his own being. In the phrase, *from all the heart*, the preposition denotes the source of the love. It is to be from all the heart on the same principle of the unity of God. Being one, he requires an undivided love." — *E. P. Gould.* "It is as impossible for a man to be under the sway of two opposite principles at the same time, as it is for a ship to have her deck and her keel uppermost at the same instant. And not only must man be under the one governing principle: man can only be under one governing principle at a given time. And this governing principle, whatever it be, if steadily obeyed, gives directness and coherence and unity to his plans and conduct of life." — *George D. Boardman.* "Before we do anything else, and in everything else we do, our whole thinking must be inspired with love for the Lord our God. Otherwise, we cannot keep any of His commandments, as God counts keeping. Otherwise, we cannot do anything good, as God counts good. Do what we may, that appears to men to be righteous — fast twice in a week, mortify ourselves by our own stern strength of will, till our life is joyless and passionless; observe a thousand and one traditions of men, till we are ready to drop with fatigue; deny ourselves all things in a spirit of ascetic pride — God is not pleased in the least unless our heart and mind and soul are full of love for Him, as the sole motive of all that we do. Bow and posture as we will, unless our hearts swell with a full tide of love for God it profiteth nothing." — *James Hastings.* "God appeals to every element of our personality. For these four words, heart, soul, mind, strength, include every essential element in our personal nature. He appeals to our heart through the revelation of His Fatherhood. . . . God appeals to our heart through the gift of Christ. 'Herein is love, not that we loved God, but that he loved us, and sent his Son to be the propitiation for our sins.' God appeals to our heart by the satisfying fellowship He offers. Love is maintained and strengthened by satisfying intercourse. . . . God appeals to our heart by the abiding home He promises us. . . . God appeals for the love of our soul, of what we may call in a special sense the spiritual element in our nature, to that side of us which looks toward what is spiritual. God makes this appeal through His holiness. . . . God appeals to the love of the soul in His revelation of the moral law. . . . God appeals to the love of the soul in His offer of salvation through Christ. . . . God appeals for the supreme love of our minds. Words of Christ's and Paul's about the relation of the wise to religion have led some to despise the part the intellect should play in religious life. And the excessive intellectualism that has often characterized those who have dealt with the subject has seemed to justify the suspicion with which the incursion of the intellect into the department of spiritual things has been regarded. But the intellect is an essential part of man's nature, and man can never find religion satisfactory and adequate if it does not in a measure call forth intellectual interest, the love of the mind. As a matter of fact, there is scarcely any subject on which so much intellec-

31. The second is this, Thou shalt love thy neighbor as thyself. There is none other commandment greater than these.

32. And the scribe said unto him, Of a truth, Teacher, thou hast well said that he is one; and there is none other but he:

33. And to love him with all the heart, and with all the understanding, and with all the strength, and to love his neighbor as himself, is much more than all whole burnt-offerings and sacrifices.

34. And when Jesus saw that he answered discreetly, he said unto him, Thou art not far from the kingdom of God. And no man after that durst ask him any question.

---

tual energy has been spent as on Christianity and Christ. The greater part of the New Testament was written by two men of supreme intellectual gifts. . . . But God appeals also to our logical faculties. God has created these faculties, and does not despise the influence they exercise even on spiritual life. . . . God appeals also to the will. Man's strength is his will. The strong man is the man of strong will. Great emotional and intellectual gifts are often possessed by a man whose will is weak, and the results are frequently tragical. God appeals to the will as the regal element in man. All other appeals are in vain if they do not lead to the question, 'Lord, what wilt thou have me to do?'" — *J. A. Bain.* 31. **The second is this, Thou shalt love thy neighbor as thyself. There is none other commandment greater than these.** "The scribe did not ask for the second commandment, but the statement is incomplete without it. Our Lord wishes to show that this first commandment did not stand at the head of a long list of heterogeneous commands, among which it was simply one among many, but that it was one of two homogeneous commands, which exhausted the idea of righteousness. This second commandment does not stand in the Old Testament in the commanding position of the first, but is brought in only incidentally in Leviticus 19, where moreover, *neighbor* is evidently restricted to a brother Jew. Jesus puts it in a commanding position, and widens the meaning of *neighbor* to *fellowman*. . . . The love of God includes in itself all other affections, but this love of the neighbor has over against it a love of self, with which Jesus allows it to divide the man. This self-love is already there, monopolizing the man, and the command is to subordinate it to the love of God, and to co-ordinate it with the love of man." — *E. P. Gould.* 32. **And the scribe said unto him, Of a truth, Teacher, thou hast well said that he is one; and there is none other but he:** 33. **and to love him with all the heart, and with all the understanding, and with all the strength, and to love his neighbor as himself, is much more than all whole burnt-offerings and sacrifices.** "The scribe's answer is made of quotations from the prophets which exalt the moral over the ceremonial law (Ps. 51 : 16; Hos. 6 : 6; Mic. 6 : 6–8). That ceremonial law is now abrogated, but the moral law as Jesus quoted it from the Old Testament is still of universal application. The scribe's enthusiastic appreciation of Jesus' answer, and our Lord's reply, are recorded by Mark only, and are extremely interesting. The scribe's admiration was evidently quite sincere. He addresses Jesus with the title of rabbi, and thereby admits Him to be one of the order of teachers; his address is really an answer to the question of the deputation from the Sanhedrin. His words seem to imply that some of the scribes were beginning to understand not merely our Lord's teaching about the spiritual meaning of the law, and the difference between its essence and accidents, but also that there was a distinct sympathy between the ideas of Jesus and those of the greater prophets. He expresses all this with earnestness and rapid eloquence. He seems almost the firstfruits of those of the sect of the Pharisees who afterward believed." — *T. M. Lindsay.* 34. **And when Jesus saw that he answered discreetly, he said unto him, Thou art not far from the kingdom of God. And no man after that durst ask him any question.** "He answered as one having intelligence or intellect, not only as a natural endowment, but in active exercise, and on the highest subjects. This high praise is followed by a still more interesting statement, namely, that he was not far from the kingdom of God, the best explanation of which language is the simplest and most obvious, to wit, that he was almost on the same ground with our Lord's disciples. The reference is not so much to moral dispositions as to intellectual and doctrinal perceptions. This is no assurance that the scribe was then a true believer or would finally be saved. It was rather a warning to come nearer

JOHN 13 : 34. A new commandment I give unto you, that ye love one another; even as I have loved you, that ye also love one another.
35. By this shall all men know that ye are my disciples, if ye have love one to another.

---

still or rather actually enter, lest he should have cause to wish that he had still remained afar off. There is the same reticency, as to this man's subsequent career, as in the case of the young ruler, but with far more positive encouragement to hope that he was ultimately saved." — *J. A. Alexander.* "Half of the world at the present moment lies in darkness, but some parts are nearer the dawn than others. So all men out of Christ are in darkness, but some are nearer the light than others. If there is tenderness in this word of Christ, there is severity too. Not far — no, but not *in.* And though not far, a man may yet be never in. Just as a ship that has buffeted the oceans of half the globe may be wrecked on the last night when the passengers are making up their baggage, and perish almost in sight of home, so there are men who come very near Christ and then drift away, and never have the same holy contiguity again." — *W. M. Mackay.*

II. **THE NEW COMMANDMENT,** John 13 : 34, 35; 15 : 10–14.

1. THE COMMANDMENT ITSELF — TO LOVE ONE ANOTHER, 13 : 34 *a.* 34 *a.* **A new commandment I give unto you, that ye love one another.** "The Lord claims to be the lawgiver for His people. This particular commandment already prescribed in the Old Testament (Lev. 19 : 18) is designated new, not because it is another, additional to that of the foot-washing, a commandment most recent, always new, as Calvin says; renewing, as Augustine says; or the latest as others claim, but because it enjoins an altogether new love, as the next clause explains." — *Thomas Whitelaw.* "The commandment was not entirely strange to the Old Testament (Lev. 19 : 18), but the example embodied in the Lord Jesus Christ of a love seeking not its own, and going to the extreme of self-sacrifice for its object — and its object unworthy — was new. Hence the 'as' includes both fact, measure, manner, and motive. He had just given them an instance (v. 15). To love God with all the heart, and the neighbor as oneself, is the sum of the old covenant. To love one another as Christ has loved us, is the sum of the new covenant. The two are essentially one; but love, God's love, has been now manifested (1 John 3 : 16; 4 : 10). The departure of their Lord should therefore become the means of drawing them into a closer brotherhood, as if to make some amends for their loss. They should grow spiritually. That mutual love, after the pattern of Christ's, should be a witness to themselves of their Lord's continual presence with them. The more they loved one another for Christ's sake, and in Christ's way, they should realize Himself as among them." — *George Reith.*

2. THE GREAT EXAMPLE — CHRIST'S LOVE FOR US, 13 : 34 *b.* 34 *b.* **Even as I have loved you, that ye also love one another.** "Jesus has brought a new love into the world, a love not only faultless and perfect as love, but one intelligently bent on salvation for the one loved. Only the disciples know from Jesus what this love is, only they have made the experience of His love; hence this precept is for them alone — it would be useless to give it to the world. So also this love is to be for each other, in the circle of the disciples." — *R. C. H. Lenski.* Jesus loved these men in permitting them to companion with Him, in teaching them, in delivering them from the superstitions and errors of the day, in emancipating them from fear, in washing away their sins, in desiring day by day to make them men of strong character, in making an open way for them to approach the throne of God, in dying for them that their sins might be forgiven, in rising again that they might forever be alive. His love is shown in His coming again for all of us, that we might be with Him forever, and in preparing a home for us above.

3. LOVE — THE DISCIPLES' DISTINGUISHING MARK, John 13 : 35. 35. **By this shall all men know that ye are my disciples, if ye have love one to another.** (See 1 John 3 : 10, 14.) One can never read this verse without thinking of the famous passage in Tertullian's *Apology* (ch. 34) written at the end of the second century, in which he draws a beautiful picture of Christian conduct in his day. "I shall at once go on, then, to exhibit the peculiarities of the Christian society, that, as I have refuted the evil charged against it, I may point out its positive good. We are a body knit together as such by a common religious profession, by unity of discipline, and by the bond of a common hope. We meet together as an assembly and congregation, that, offering up prayer to God as with united force, we may wrestle with

JOHN 15 : 10. If ye keep my commandments, ye shall abide in my love; even as I have kept my Father's commandments, and abide in his love.
11. These things have I spoken unto you, that my joy may be in you, and *that* your joy may be made full.

Him in our supplications. This violence God delights in. We pray, too, for the emperors, for their ministers, and for all in authority, for the welfare of the world, for the prevalence of peace, for the delay of the final consummation. We assemble to read our sacred writings, if any peculiarity of the times makes either forewarning or reminiscence needful. However it be in that respect, with the sacred words we nourish our faith, we animate our hope, we make our confidence more stedfast; and no less by inculcations of God's precepts we confirm good habits. . . . On the monthly day, if he likes, each puts in a small donation; but only if it be his pleasure, and only if he be able: for there is no compulsion, all is voluntary. These gifts are, as it were, piety's deposit fund. For they are not taken thence and spent on feasts, and drinking-bouts, and eating houses, but to support and bury poor people, to supply the wants of boys and girls destitute of means and parents, and of old persons confined now to the house; such, too, as have suffered shipwreck; and if there happen to be any in the mines, or banished to the islands, or shut up in the prisons, for nothing but their fidelity to the cause of God's Church, they become the nurslings of their confession. But it is mainly the deeds of a love so noble that lead many to put a brand upon us. 'See,' they say, 'how they love one another, for themselves are animated by mutual hatred; how they are ready even to die for one another, for they themselves will sooner put to death. And they are wroth with us, too, because we call each other brethren; for no other reason, as I think, than because among themselves names of consanguinity are assumed in mere pretence of affection. But we are your brethren as well, by the law of our common mother nature, though you are hardly men, because brothers so unkind. At the same time, how much more fittingly they are called and counted brothers who have been led to the knowledge of God as their common Father, who have drunk in one spirit of holiness, who from the same womb of a common ignorance have agonized into the same light of truth!" — *Tertullian.*

"Jesus believed and foresaw that in proportion as mutual love pervaded His divine society and ruled there, would it give forth a mighty witness to the world and draw men to it. A world full of hatred, envies, and dissensions would be sure to feel the attractive force and the fascinating spell of this wonderful new thing planted down in the midst of it — a society in which love was the predominant element, and in which all sorts and conditions of men clave together as brothers. And that, as we know from unimpeachable testimony, was what actually took place in the early days of our faith. A score of pagan writers have borne their witness to the fact, while professing their utter inability to account for it. It was a wonderful thing, strange, novel, and inexplicable. For the first time in the world's history a society appeared in which men of all races and of the most diverse conditions, cultured and illiterate, rich and poor, master and slave, buried their distinctions in the grave of a sweet forgetfulness, or rather, as we should say, in the grave of their risen Lord; and clung to each other through evil and good repute, through suffering and persecution, with an intense affection almost surpassing that of family life, an affection which nothing short of death could quench." — *J. G. Greenhough.*

4. THE CONSEQUENCES OF OBEYING CHRIST'S COMMANDMENTS, 15 : 10, 11, 14.
10. **If ye keep my commandments, ye shall abide in my love; even as I have kept my Father's commandments, and abide in his love.** (Cf. John 14 : 15, 21, 24.) We keep the commandments of the Lord Jesus not by locking up a Bible in a box, not by writing the commandments on a piece of paper and putting them into our pocket, not even necessarily by memorizing them, but by *obeying* them. Jesus kept His Father's commandments by His obedience to them, and we keep Christ's commandments by doing the things He tells us to do. One keeps one's word by doing what one has promised to do. When we obey the commandments of our Lord we continue to abide in His love. Sickness can never terminate our abiding in Christ's love, neither can poverty, nor reverses, defeats, frailties, or infirmities. One thing we *can* do by His grace. We can determine to keep His commandments; and if we do, this proves to Him that we truly love Him, if we do not, it proves as clearly that our love for Him is not first. 11. **These things have I spoken unto you, that my joy may be in you, and *that* your joy may be made full.** "This does not mean

12. This is my commandment, that ye love one another, even as I have loved you.

'that I may have pleasure in you'; but that the joy which Christ experienced through consciousness of His fellowship with the Father, and which supported Him in His sufferings, might be in His disciples and support them in theirs. Here first, on the eve of His sufferings, does Christ speak of His joy. This expression of joy being fulfilled is peculiar to John (cf. 3 : 29; 16 : 24; 17 : 13; 1 John 1 : 4; 2 John 12)." — *A. Plummer.* "'My joy' must be interpreted in the same way as 'my peace' (14 : 27). It is the joy which Jesus possesses as anointed with the oil of gladness above His fellows, which flowed from the uninterrupted possession of His Father's love (v. 9), which was ever and again renewed as He felt that He was accomplishing His Father's will (v. 10), which was crowned in that uninterrupted intercourse with His Father, in which He asked and received whatsoever He desired (11 : 42), and which filled His heart amid all the trials and sorrows of His work on earth (cf. Luke 10 : 21). That very joy He will communicate to His disciples and their joy will be then forever. Like Him who went before them, they shall 'see of the travail of their soul and shall be satisfied.' The arrangement of the words in the original of this phrase by which 'my' is brought into the closest juxtaposition with 'in you,' is worthy of notice (cf. 14 : 1, 3)." — *George Milligan.* "Why, O why is it that this joy has so little power to attract? The reason simply is that men, yea, even God's children, do not believe in it. Instead of the abiding in Christ being looked upon as the happiest life that ever can be led, it is regarded as a life of self-denial and of sadness. They forget that the self-denial and the sadness are owing to the not abiding, and that to those who once yield themselves unreservedly to abide in Christ as a bright and blessed life, their faith comes true — the joy of the Lord is theirs. Child of God, who seekest to abide in Christ, remember what the Lord says. At the close of the parable of the vine, He adds these precious words: '*These things* have I spoken unto you, that my joy might abide in you, and that your joy might be full.' Claim the joy as part of the branch life, not the first or chief part, but as the blessed proof of the sufficiency of Christ to satisfy every need of the soul. Be happy. Cultivate gladness. If there are times when it comes of itself, and the heart feels the unutterable joy of the Saviour's presence, praise God for it, and seek to maintain it." — *Andrew Murray.* 14. **Ye are my friends if ye do the things which I command you.** This is one of the most precious declarations that ever came from the lips of the Lord Jesus, that we may be His friends. A true friend is one in whom you can confide the deepest secrets, and problems, and hopes of your life. A true friend is one who will never betray you. In real friendship each will be concerned with the interests and welfare of the other. True friends harmoniously agree on the fundamental principles of life. Thus, *e.g.*, a coarse person can never be a friend of a refined person; a sensualist can never be a friend of a truly holy person; there must be a harmony of nature. *We* do not ask the Lord if we can be His friends. He *invites* us to become His friends, and declares that we will be. The secret is — if we keep His commandments. It is not the result of sentimentality; it is not one-sided; it is not based on mere emotion; it is not even based on our conviction of Christ's deity. We are saved by believing in Christ, and receiving His sacrifice for our sins. Friendship is a privilege of those who are saved, but many who are saved do not experience the privilege. If every night we can kneel down and talk to the Lord Jesus with the assurance that that day, as far as we know, we have obeyed Him, we abide in His friendship, and we know it. You can hurt and alienate your closest friend by doing something degrading, in the mind of that friend, or expressing something treasonable concerning that friend. When you persistently and deliberately violate the principles on which your friendship is based, the friendship goes. Do we think Christ is less sensitive than people here on earth?

5. THE COMMANDMENT REITERATED, 15 : 12. 12. **This is my commandment, that ye love one another, even as I have loved you.** "Amid all diversity of character or of creed, of language or of station, they are to prove that love has made them members of one body, and of each other, and has taught them each to forget and sacrifice self for the sake of the other. Their life of love is the chief evidence of Christianity, the proof to the world that God sent Christ, and that He has shed abroad in them the same love with which He loved Him. Of all the evidences of Christianity, this is the mightiest and most convincing. The love to one unseen

13. Greater love hath no man than this, that a man lay down his life for his friends.
14. Ye are my friends, if ye do the things which I command you.

may so easily be a mere sentiment, or even an imagination; in the intercourse with God's children, love to God is really called into exercise, and shows itself in deeds that the Father accepts as done to Himself. The love to the brethren is the flower and fruit of the root, unseen in the heart, of love to God. And this fruit again becomes the seed of love to all men: intercourse with each other is the school in which believers are trained and strengthened to love their fellow men, who are yet out of Christ, not simply with the liking that rests on points of agreement, but with the holy love that takes hold of the unworthiest, and bears with the most disagreeable for Jesus' sake. He who gave the command in such close connection with His teaching about the vine and the abiding in Him, gave us in that the assurance that we have only to abide in Him to be able to love like Him. Regard the abiding in Him more than ever as an abiding in His love; rooted and grounded daily in a love that passeth knowledge, you receive of its fullness, and learn to love. With Christ abiding in you, the Holy Spirit sheds abroad the love of God in your heart, and you love the brethren, the most trying and unlovable, with a love that is not your own, but the love of Christ in you." — *Andrew Murray.* "This is why the appearance of a really good man is such a godsend to us. He makes us look up. He shows us what can be made of life. Face to face with him our way of it looks squalid and uninviting and dull. But who does that for us like Jesus, or who flashes before us so ennobling an ideal as this Christ who measures our life by His cross — aye, and compels us when we see it to adopt that as our standard too? With Christ's eyes upon us, we are bigger and better than we are elsewhere; many things just cannot be done there in His presence. So long as the shadow of the cross is on us, so long as we remember that our norm is Jesus, so long as we recall that we are meant to love as He loved us, and to use life as He used it, and to act as He would act, faults that are natural to us fall off from us and are left behind, become impossible, there upon Calvary — As I, as I, as I." — *A. J. Gossip.*

Legend of St. Christopher.

A modern conception of an ancient interpretation of the Christ spirit. "To serve men is to serve God."

6. THE SUPREME MANIFESTATION OF LOVE, 15 : 13. 13. **Greater love hath no man than this, that a man lay down his life for his friends.** "We must resist the tendency to crowd too much into the comparison here made. Jesus, we note, says nothing in this connection about taking up again the life laid down for others. This act places His sacrifices absolutely in a class by itself, as we see in 10 : 17, 18. He here contents Himself with the sacrifice as such. He does not even mention Himself as giving this supreme proof of His own love, and that just as we make this application to our own love. This means furthermore that in the present connection the redemptive effect of the sacrifice of His own life for us is left out, for none of us by laying down His life for the sake of the brethren could possibly duplicate this redemptive effect. Furthermore, Jesus here does not mean to say that we must all lay down our lives for the brethren, and that unless we do, our love will not be like His. For the supreme sacrifice is demanded only in rare instances, such as that of Aquila and Priscilla in Romans 16 : 4; and even these two were not required actually to die.

What Jesus says is that our love for our brethren must be willing to rise to this height, thus following His own example. On the expression, 'lay down the life,' see 10 : 11, 17, 18. It is peculiar to John. The tense here is properly the aorist, punctiliar because this is a single act." — *R. C. H. Lenski.*

I think at the close of such a lesson as this on love for one another, we ought to remind ourselves of one thing, that love in the life of Christ was something active, something that went out in deliberate, determined, definite work for those who were loved. Love brought Christ down out of heaven, love kept Him among the crowds that disbelieved and denied Him, love led Him to pray earnestly for the welfare of those who loved; love constrained Him to suffer all things, even death itself, that the ones loved might come into a life of blessing, fullness, forgiveness of sin, power, and communion with God. Christ's love stooped even to the washing of the disciples' feet. Christ's love was manifested in His patience, His forgiveness, His tenderness, His compassion. Christ's love drove Him into the out-of-the-way places of the great city of Jerusalem and the little towns of Palestine, looking for those who needed Him, revealing their hearts' deepest thoughts, bestowing upon them the blessings which could come from Him alone. This is the kind of a love we need for others — active, sacrificial, compassionate, forgiving; a love that bestows blessings, that enriches others, that lifts and ennobles life, that makes others speak of Christ; a love that is a testimony to the world, a love which is part of the stream of that divine life which has ever flowed to us.

How many reasons can you give why in your opinion the two commandments which appear at the beginning of the Decalogue were placed first among the ten great Words? Why does a wrong opinion of God and an unworthy worship of God lead to a life of disobedience in relation to the laws that follow? Do you think that the order of the Ten Commandments implies that if one is right with God he will inevitably be right with his fellow men, or that if one will strive to be right with man he will gradually get to be right with God? In how many different ways can we truly manifest our love for other people? How did Christ prove His love for us? Why will the world always be so quick to recognize sincere love among men? Why is it impossible for us to be close friends with Christ if we live in disobedience to Him? Where does the Apostle Paul speak of "the proof of love," and to what is he referring? (This passage does not come in our lesson but it certainly has direct bearing upon it and is one we rarely ever hear quoted — 2 Cor. 8: 8.) Do you think that a life of disobedience to God inevitably results in a definite, ever-deepening decrease in our love for our fellow men?

LESSON XII.—December 19.

CHRIST THE FULFILLMENT OF THE LAW. — Hebrews 1 : 1–9; Romans 10 : 4–10.

GOLDEN TEXT. — ***God . . . hath at the end of these days spoken unto us in his Son.*** HEBREWS 1 : 1, 2.

Devotional Reading: Romans 5 : 1–11.
Beginner Topic: THE FIRST CHRISTMAS.
  Lesson Material: Luke 2; Hebrews 1 : 1–3.
  Memory Verse: God . . . loved us, and sent his Son. 1 John 4 : 10.
Primary Topic: THE FIRST CHRISTMAS.
  Lesson Material: Hebrews 1 : 1–9; Romans 10 : 4–10; Luke 2.
  Memory Verse: Glory to God in the highest, and on earth peace among men in whom he is well pleased. Luke 2 : 14.
Junior Topic: THE FIRST CHRISTMAS.
  Lesson Material: Hebrews 1 : 1–9; Romans 10 : 4–10; Luke 2.
  Memory Verse: Glory to God in the highest, and on earth peace among men in whom he is well pleased. Luke 2 : 14.
Intermediate and Senior Topic: GOD'S PURPOSE IN CHRIST'S COMING.
Topic for Young People and Adults: GOD'S MESSAGE IN HIS SON.

THE TEACHER AND HIS CLASS.

The Younger Classes might be introduced to this lesson by a brief consideration of what makes for greatness in men. Take, for instance, the vicinity of the White House in Washington. Why is the man in the White House (whatever we think of some of his policies) such a great man in his ability to influence others, in the revolutionary policies he has introduced into our country, in his enormous capacity for work, in his grasp of modern problems, whereas the man on the street corner nearby, selling peanuts, is not in any way "great" — except, of course, his soul is most precious in the sight of God? We admire great men; we follow great men; great men dominate the age in which they live. Our lesson concerns One greater than any one else who ever lived on this earth, and there are things said about Him in this lesson, not one of which could be said about any mere man, however great, who has ever lived on this earth. What a privilege to be loved by, redeemed by, changed by, prayed for by such a Person as the Lord Jesus Christ who is here revealed!

The Older Classes should receive from this lesson a deep conviction of the truth of the Christian faith as a final revelation, beyond which no revelation from God will be given in this age. When once we firmly believe this, then none of these humanly-conceived cults that arise like mushrooms in the night, only to disappear with the blazing sun of the next day, will even appear to us serious enough to be given consideration. We will never think of them as even possibly being able to contribute something new concerning eternal truth, for eternal truth concerning God, sin, salvation, and the life to come, have been perfectly revealed to us in Christ. Why need we any other? When the sun shines on us, why carry about a lighted candle?

THE PLAN OF THE LESSON.

SUBJECT: The Absolute Pre-eminence of the Lord Jesus Christ, and Especially as the Consummation of God's Revelation.

I. CHRIST PRE-EMINENT OVER THE ENTIRE UNIVERSE, Hebrews 1 : 1–9.

1. In His being God's final revelation, vs. 1, 2 *a*.
2. In His eternal glory and power, vs. 2 *b*, 3 *a*.
   a. He is heir of all things.
   b. He is the One through whom all things were made.
   c. He is the outshining of God's glory.
   d. He is the image of God's substance.
   e. He upholds the universe.
3. In the work He accomplished in purifying men of sins, v. 3 *b*.
4. In His exaltation at the right hand of God, v. 3 *c*.
5. In His superiority over the angels, vs. 4–9.
   a. Called by a more excellent name than they, vs. 4, 5.
   b. The recipient of worship from them, v. 6.
   c. The possessor of an eternal throne and kingdom, vs. 7–9.

II. CHRIST IS THE END OF THE LAW, Romans 10 : 4–10.

1. The truth declared, v. 4.
2. The truth expounded, vs. 5–10.

THE LESSON IN ITS SETTING.

Time. — The Epistle to the Hebrews was written, it would seem, before the fall of Jerusalem, and, therefore, between A.D. 65 and A.D. 68. The Epistle to the Romans was written about A.D. 60.

Place. — We do not know in what locality the Epistle to the Hebrews was written. Paul wrote his Epistle to the church at Rome, the Eternal City, from Corinth, where he spent many months during his missionary journeys.

THE TEACHER'S LIBRARY.

On the Epistle to the Hebrews one should first of all consult the remarkable exposition on our lesson (of 100 pages) in Adolph Saphir's wonderfully rich exposition, *The Epistle to the Hebrews;* for minute analysis see the volume by A. B. Davidson, in the *Handbooks for Bible Classes and Private Students;* and F. W. Farrar, in the *Cambridge Bible for Schools and Colleges*. For more general exposition one should consult the volume by T. C. Edwards, in the *Expositor's Bible*, and Bishop G. A. Chadwick, in the *Devotional Commentary* series. For devotional material, see Andrew Murray: *The Holiest of All;* and F. B. Meyer: *The Way into the Holiest*. On verses 1–3, see A. W. Pink: *The Sovereignty of God*, 49–64; L. A. Banks: *Paul and His Friends*, 13–25; on verses 1, 2, James Hastings: *Great Texts of the Bible, Thessalonians to Hebrews*, 272–285; Charles F. Thwing in *Modern Sermons by World Scholars*, Vol. 10, 3–14; and a sermon on, "The Voice of God in the Old Testament," in S. R. Driver's *Sermons on Subjects Connected with the Old Testament*, 119–142. On verse 1, B. F. Westcott: *The Incarnation and Common Life*, 277–292; especially should one consult, on verses 2, 3, a magnificent sermon by J. D. Jones in his *The Inevitable Christ*, 132–160. On the Epistle to the Romans, first of all one should consult the two volumes by Bishop Moule, one in the *Expositor's Bible* series, and the other in the *Cambridge Bible for Schools and Colleges*. Then, for detailed, analytical study, Charles Hodge: *Commentary on the Epistle to the Romans*, and R. C. H. Lenski: *Interpretation of Romans*. W. R. Newell's book, *Romans Verse by Verse*, is not so good for this particular passage. There is some helpful material for teachers, however, in the second volume of W. H. Griffith Thomas' work on Romans in the *Devotional Commentary* series. There are scores of other volumes on this Epistle, but not so helpful for this lesson. On verse 10, see W. E. Biederwolf: *Evangelistic Sermons*, 173 ff.; James Hastings: *Great Texts of the Bible, Romans 8–16*, 188–199; and Charles G. Finney: *The Way of Salvation*, 313–331. On the work of Christ before His incarnation, one should see the magnificent chapter in Alexander Patterson's *The Greater Life and Work of Christ*, 27–68. Strange to say, there is nothing at all in Maclaren's volumes on any verse in the two chapters we are studying in this lesson.

HEBREWS 1:1. God, having of old time spoken unto the fathers in the prophets by divers portions and in divers manners,

2. Hath at the end of these days spoken unto us in *his* Son, whom he appointed heir of all things, through whom also he made the worlds;

The verses assigned for our lesson are some of the profoundest, and, especially in relation to the passage taken from Romans, some of the most difficult in the New Testament. However, they are in the Word of God: thus, they are given for our admonition; they concern the Lord Jesus Christ, and we ought to give them the most serious consideration, the most careful and prayerful thought, of which we are capable. The reason these verses will be found somewhat difficult is because we are not accustomed in these days to think theologically, or even to think profoundly on religious questions. If, however, men can master the intricacies of radio, and the mechanics of airplanes, men can also grasp these precious things concerning the Lord Jesus Christ.

I. **CHRIST PRE-EMINENT OVER THE ENTIRE UNIVERSE,** Heb. 1:1-9.

1. IN HIS BEING GOD'S FINAL REVELATION, vs. 1, 2 *a*. 1. **God, having of old time spoken unto the fathers in the prophets by divers portions and in divers manners.** This is the only book in the Bible which begins with the Word *God*. It begins with a glorious declaration, that God has spoken to men. This Epistle was written, as its title indicates, to the Hebrews, that is, to Hebrew people who had been won to Jesus Christ, and had received Him as their Messiah and Saviour. At this time some of these Jews were being tempted to go back to their old faith, to the Levitical sacrifices, to the Mosaic law, for righteousness, and to all the forms and rituals which held them in legalistic bondage. This Epistle is written to show to Jewish Christians the infinite superiority of Christ to the old dispensation, to every created thing in the world, and to every other individual of history, however great and holy they might be. In beginning to speak to them, the author begins, as it were, where they and their forefathers had lived, that is, in the Old Testament Scriptures, recognizing these writings to be indeed divinely inspired. "The phrase, 'in sundry portions and in divers manners,' *i.e.*, in various parts and in many forms, does not indicate any inferiority of the Old Testament revelation to the New, arising from its fragmentariness and the color it received from circumstances and the many prophetic minds through whom it came. The expression rather signalizes the variety and fullness of the Old Testament Word of God. In another point of view, indeed, these words might indicate defect: the Old Testament revelation being given in sundry portions was not final and complete; and being given under diverse forms, it was not simple and homogeneous." — *A. B. Davidson.* 2 *a*. **Hath at the end of these days.** Certainly a great dispensation had just closed, *i.e.*, the dispensation of the Law, and a new one was now opening, a dispensation of grace. Nothing shows more definitely that people in the first century were living at the end of one age and at the beginning of another, than the fact that all events occurring before the birth of Christ are now designated by the letters B.C., while all events occurring since His birth are indicated, chronologically, by numerals preceded by the letters A.D., an abbreviation of the Latin phrase meaning, "In the year of our Lord." **Spoken unto us in *his* Son.** "Look now at the contrast. The whole contrast is in one word — in our language in one syllable — 'by the *Son*.' The prophets were many: the Son is one. The prophets were servants: the Son is the Lord. The prophets were temporary: the Son abideth forever. The prophets were imperfect: the Son is perfect, even as the Father is perfect. The prophets were guilty: the Son is not merely pure, but able to purify those that are full of sin and pollution. The prophets point to the future: the Son points to Himself, and says, 'Here am *I*.' As the Sonship is the beginning of the gospel, so it is also the end and purpose of God's message. God, speaking to us by His Son, shows unto us that we also are to become the sons of God." — *Adolph Saphir.*

2. IN HIS ETERNAL GLORY AND POWER, 2 *b*, 3 *a*. 2 *b*. **Whom he appointed heir of all things.** "The whole human race is given unto Him. Since He took upon Him our flesh and blood, God has given unto Him the whole human race — power over all flesh. And out of this whole human race, which belongs unto Him by eternal right, and by the right of His incarnation, by the right of His perfect and holy humanity, by the right of His unspeakable love, and of His death — out of this whole world of humanity God has chosen in Him a people, that the Son should give eternal life to 'as many as thou hast given him.' 'Thine they were, and thou gavest

3. Who being the effulgence of his glory, and the very image of his substance, and upholding all things by the word of his power, when he had made purification of sins, sat down on the right hand of the Majesty on high;

them me.' All these are His in a special sense. That innumerable multitude which no man can number from among all nations, peoples, and kindreds, and tongues — the chosen family in whom God has manifested His love, who have been renewed by the Holy Ghost, who have been washed in the blood of Jesus, who have been trained, educated, sanctified — all the lively stones, who by the Spirit have been built on the only foundation, who have been chiseled, beautified, perfected by the all-loving divine Spirit, through experiences and sufferings most precious, appointed by perfect wisdom and grace, who have become the members of His wonderful mystical body, they all are His." — *Adolph Saphir.* **Through whom also he made the worlds.** (Cf. John 1 : 1, 3.) In the first chapter of Genesis, we read that " God spake, and it was done." This must be taken as closely related to the fact that Christ is the Eternal Word. If God is the originator of creation, the architect of creation, then we may speak of Christ Jesus as the executor of God's will, the One who framed the worlds according to God's eternal plans. Christ is all powerful and eternal, and therefore He was before anything was ever created. Either we believe that the world thus came into existence, by the will of God, through the power and work of Christ, or we do not know how the world came into existence. Scientists everywhere recognize that they cannot tell, by all their manifold investigations, how the world was created. They know something about the world as created, but not about the creation itself. Thus our precious Bible gives us truth which the heart of man yearns to know, but which man can never himself discover. 3 *a.* **Who being the effulgence of his glory.** " ' Glory ' is not any external halo that surrounds the divine nature; it is the divine nature itself in its majesty and as manifested to the world. The expression *effulgence* suggests perhaps three ideas: (1) That the nature of the Son is derived from God; (2) that it has distinct subsistence of its own; and (3) that it resembles the nature of God. The word effulgence seems to mean not rays of light streaming from a body in their connection with that body or as part of it, still less the reflection of these rays caused by their falling upon another body, but rather rays of light coming out from the original body and forming a similar light-body themselves." — *A. B. Davidson.* **And the very image of his substance.** " The allusion here is to the impression made by a seal on molten wax; and as the image made on the wax is the exact resemblance, though on another substance, of the die, so is Christ the exact resemblance of the Father in our human flesh. And thus He was able to say, ' He that hath seen me hath seen the Father.' The life of Jesus is the life of God rendered into the terms of our human life; so that we may understand the very being and nature of God by seeing it reproduced before us, so far as it is possible, in the character and life of Jesus. These two images complete each other." — *F. B. Meyer.* " By the time this letter came to be written, the Christian Church thought of Jesus in terms of God, and spoke of Him as being on an equality with God. I cannot see how any one with this particular Scripture in his hand can contend that the claim of deity for Jesus was not made till after a long process of idealization had taken place. It doesn't matter who was the author of this epistle — it may have been Apollos, it may have been Priscilla, it may have been one of Paul's companions — scholars tell us it was written probably as early as A.D. 64, certainly not later than A.D. 80. All of which goes to prove beyond possibility of challenge or dispute that to the first Christian disciples Jesus was not simply a Galilean prophet, the carpenter from Nazareth, as we moderns delight to speak of Him. He was something infinitely greater. He was the supreme and exalted Lord. He was the everlasting Son. God and Christ are, with them, almost convertible terms." — *J. D. Jones.* **And upholding all things by the word of his power.** (Cf. Col. 1 : 16, 17.) " Things have not been started, and then left to run on their own material or moral momentum, but all things are under the constant control of the divine Creator, in whom all things have their center of unity, who appoints to everything its place, who determines the relation of things to one another, and who combines all into an ordered whole so that this universe is a cosmos and not a chaos. Remove Christ from the universe, and everything would go to pieces. The laws which govern all things, and which it is the work of science to discover, and understand, are His laws; they are non-existent out of Him. In Him, and in

4. Having become by so much better than the angels, as he hath inherited a more excellent name than they.

5. For unto which of the angels said he at any time,

Thou art my Son,
This day have I begotten thee?

and again,

I will be to him a Father,
And he shall be to me a Son?

Him alone, all things find their bond of union and their orderly arrangement into one whole. The very scheme of nature and the whole government of the world must be in accordance with what we know of Christ. It is not law ultimately which rules this universe, but God, and He rules it through Christ. Human history is not in the grip of fate, but in the hands of Him who was pierced for us on Calvary. There is infinite comfort in this truth, of the absolute sovereignty of God, resident in and exercised by Christ, for it applies equally to the moral as to the material world. As we think of tyrannies which for ages have crushed the powers of nations, of ambitions which have squandered them with prodigal selfishness, of what seems, from age to age, to be the blind tumults of the peoples, we may at times have wondered whether aback and above all is active an infinitely wise Providence. But upon further reflection we shall see that reason as well as faith demands God for the true interpretation of human history." — *W. G. Scroggie.*

3. IN THE WORK HE ACCOMPLISHED IN PURIFYING MEN OF SINS, 3 *b*. 3 *b*. **When he had made purification of sins.** Before one even considers the deeper meaning of this phrase, one should recognize here a very remarkable fact, *i.e.*, that the only line in this entire paragraph concerning the greatness and glory and majesty of Jesus Christ, beginning back in eternity and extending on into eternity — the only line referring to anything done *on earth* by Christ is this, that He made purification for our sins, which certainly implies that that for which He came was this, and that the first great work He was to undertake and to accomplish on earth was this. If we do not know Christ as the sin-bearer, we do not know Him truly. (On the purification of our sins, see Hebrews 9 : 12; 10 : 12; 1 Pet. 2 : 24; 2 Pet. 1 : 9.) In the Septuagint of Exodus 29 : 36, the day of atonement is called " the day of purification." " Think of our sins as defilement. Think of their number, of their heinousness! Who will remove this fearful and utterly loathsome iniquity which separates us hopelessly and infinitely from God in His holy and righteous love? Who will touch the leprosy? Who can take it out of the way, and cleanse the sinners, so that they appear pure and spotless in God's sight? The Son of God came to make the purification of our sins; and this, oh marvel of marvels! by Himself. Not like the high priest in Israel, offering something as a sacrifice; not with the blood, the life of another, but by Himself. He came into contact with this sin. He was the only one who could properly understand the true nature, depth, and guilt of sin. God of God, Son of the Father, He perfectly sympathized with the Father in His loathing and abhorrence of sin; but having befriended us, and having become one with us, He could not bear the thought of our being lost. So this loathsomeness of our iniquity, as loathsome to Jesus as to the Father, He takes upon Himself." —*A. Saphir.*

4. IN HIS EXALTATION AT THE RIGHT HAND OF GOD, V. 3 *c*. 3 *c*. **Sat down on the right hand of the Majesty on high.** " The ' sitting down,' besides implying that His attaining the honor was an event of history, again expresses the honor itself rather than any condition of repose, for He actively performs the duties of a high priest (7 : 25; cf. 10 : 13). The 'right hand' is a place of influence, and also of rule. He is King, and over the house of God. He is appointed heir of all things and set over the world to come." — *A. B. Davidson.* " The Lamb is in the midst of the throne. Behold His majesty, and worship Him with angels and archangels, and all the throng of the redeemed. Prostrate yourself at his feet, consecrating to Him all you are and all you have. Comfort yourself also by remembering that He would not sit to rest from His labors in redemption, and in the purging away of sins, unless they were so completely finished that there was nothing more to do. It is all accomplished; and it is all very good. He has ceased from His works, because they are done; and therefore He is entered into His rest." — *F. B. Meyer.*

5. IN HIS SUPERIORITY OVER THE ANGELS, VS. 4–9. 4. **Having become by so much better than the angels, as he hath inherited a more excellent name than they.**

6. And when he again bringeth in the firstborn into the world he saith,
And let all the angels of God worship him.
7. And of the angels he saith,
Who maketh his angels winds,
And his ministers a flame of fire:
8. But of the Son *he saith*,
Thy throne, O God, is for ever and ever;
And the sceptre of uprightness is the sceptre of thy kingdom.
9. Thou hast loved righteousness, and hated iniquity;
Therefore God, thy God, hath anointed thee
With the oil of gladness above thy fellows.

---

5. **For unto which of the angels said he at any time, Thou art my Son, this day have I begotten thee? and again, I will be to him a Father, and he shall be to me a Son?** In the first century there was a very powerful, speculative, philosophical system known as Gnosticism, which insisted that because God was absolutely holy, and man was truly sinful, God could not in any way reach out toward man to save him, could not touch him, could not come near him; in fact, could not even create such a being as man. So, according to these gnostics, there had to be a series of emanations from God, " every additional link in the chain being less divine, until we arrive at the material universe, where the element of divinity is entirely lost." Some held that, " angels are the only possible mediators between God and man. Thus the angels were regarded as messengers or apostles from God and reconcilers or priests for men. Our author acknowledges the existence of angels. He declares that the law was given through angels, but he begins his epistle by maintaining the superiority of the Son to the angels." — *T. C. Edwards*. The two passages here quoted are Psalm 2 : 7 and 2 Samuel 7 : 14. " God in Scripture calls the Messiah Son; at no time has He given such a name to any angel. In some parts of the English Bible the angels are called ' sons of God ' (*e.g.*, Job 1 : 6; 38 : 7). The Hebrew is ' sons of Elohim ' or ' Elim ' (Ps. 29 : 1; 89 : 6). The word *Elohim* commonly means God. But it had a more general sense. In this secondary meaning it describes what is superhuman or, as might be said, ' divine.' In this sense the angels receive the name Elohim, or sons (*i.e.*, members of the race) of Elohim. No relation to God is intimated by the name: it describes the angels as a class in contrast with man. This sense of the word was well understood in early times." — *A. B. Davidson*. 6. **And when he again bringeth in the firstborn into the world he saith, And let all the angels of God worship him.** The passage here quoted is the Septuagint of Deuteronomy 32 : 43 (cf. Ps. 97 : 7). " The apostles and evangelists always describe Christ as returning ' with the holy angels ' (Matt. 25 : 31; Mark 8 : 38), and describe ' all angels and authorities ' as ' subject unto him ' (1 Pet. 3 : 22; Rev. 5 : 11-13)." — *F. W. Farrar*. 7. **And of the angels he saith, Who maketh his angels winds, and his ministers a flame of fire:** 8. **but of the Son *he saith*, Thy throne, O God, is for ever and ever; and the sceptre of uprightness is the sceptre of thy kingdom.** The quotations here are from Psalm 104 : 4; 45 : 6. " To the Son He has given His own name: the angels are called by the name of the wild and strong forces of the universe, storm and fire. For God is in nature: His agents work the changes which we call elemental: our faith needs only to be a little stronger, and we should own the work of mysterious and holy beings in the tornado that sweeps the ocean, and the volcano that shakes the world. Wind and fire, so intermittent, changeful, and with such mixed result, while they change, He is forever; and while they are messengers, He sitteth on the throne judging aright. He is eternal, but they are created things. ' He *maketh* his angels winds.' " — *G. A. Chadwick*. 9. **Thou hast loved righteousness and hated iniquity; therefore God, thy God, hath anointed thee with the oil of gladness above thy fellows.** " As kings were anointed when called to the throne, the phrase means, made King. ' Gladness ' describes the height and joy of the rule to which this King is called (cf. 12 : 2; 7 : 2). His ' fellows ' in the psalm are probably other princes; if any special force be attached to the expression here, it no doubt means the angels, as dwellers in the city of God (12 : 22), and thus the fellows of the Son." — *A. B. Davidson*.

Saphir has a remarkable conclusion to his own discussion of these verses, which we should take to our hearts. " Have we this first chapter? Is it ours? Do we

ROMANS 10 : 4. For Christ is the end of the law unto righteousness to every one that believeth.

5. For Moses writeth that the man that doeth the righteousness which is of the law shall live thereby.

6. But the righteousness which is of faith saith thus, Say not in thy heart, Who shall ascend into heaven? (that is, to bring Christ down:)

7. Or, Who shall descend into the abyss? (that is, to bring Christ up from the dead.)

---

possess it? Can we say, 'I will go with this into eternity'; I believe it from my heart; it is a treasure to my own soul; I stand upon this rock; I hear His voice in *the Son*, and therefore I can go to Him with childlike confidence. Let me sum up, and apply the teaching of this chapter in three questions. Do we worship Jesus? In this chapter He is called by divine names, the Son, Lord, God. Divine works are assigned to Him. Divine attributes are given to Him; He is omniscient, He is omnipotent, He is unchangeable, He is eternal. Divine worship is accorded to Him. Do you worship Jesus, Jesus the Son of David, who was crucified upon the cross? Have you learned like Thomas to say unto Him, 'My Lord and my God'?"

II. **CHRIST IS THE END OF THE LAW,** Rom. 10 : 4–10.

1. THE TRUTH DECLARED, v. 4. 4. **For Christ is the end of the law unto righteousness to every one that believeth.** "The word *end* may mean the object to which anything leads. Christ is in this sense the end of the law, inasmuch as the law was a schoolmaster to lead us to Him (Gal. 3 : 24); and as all its types and prophecies pointed to Him (Col. 2 : 17; Heb. 9 : 9). The word may be taken in the sense of completion or fulfillment. Then Christ is the end of the law because He fulfills all its requisitions, all its types and ceremonies, and satisfies its demands. The sense is scriptural but is not consistent with the meaning of the word. Preferably we may take the word in its more ordinary sense of end or termination and understand it for the one who terminates or puts an end to something. The meaning and connection would be then, 'the Jews mistake the true method of justification, because they seek it from the law, whereas Christ has abolished the law, in order that all who believe may be justified.' Christ has abolished the law, not by destroying it, but by fulfilling it. He has abolished the law as a rule of justification, or covenant of works, and the whole Mosaic economy, having made its completion in Him, has by Him been brought to an end. (See Luke 16 : 16.) When Christ came, the old legal system was abolished and a new era commenced. The same idea is presented in Galatians 3 : 23. . . . It is because Christ is the fulfiller of the law, that He is the end of it. The word *law* is obviously here used, in its prevalent sense throughout this epistle, for the whole duty prescribed to man, including for the Jews the whole of the Mosaic institutions. The *law* is intended which has been fulfilled, satisfied, or abrogated by Jesus Christ." — *Charles Hodge.*

2. THE TRUTH EXPOUNDED, vs. 5–10. 5. **For Moses writeth that the man that doeth the righteousness which is of the law shall live thereby.** The quotation here is from Leviticus 18 : 5. "Moses is quoted because he was the Jews' own lawgiver. The only trouble with the law as a means for attaining righteousness is that it requires complete doing on our part, the plural 'them,' its antecedent understood, quietly points to the many things that must thus be done, as does also the final phrase: 'Shall live in (in connection with) them, *i.e.*, all of them completely done. A single break in the doing, or a single omission in the many things to be done, is fatal. Man is in a sinful condition from the start, and thus could not hope to achieve righteousness by doing the law. . . . The way to righteousness by means of law and our doing is forever closed to us because of our sin." — *R. C. H. Lenski.* 6. **But the righteousness which is of faith saith thus, Say not in thy heart, Who shall ascend into heaven? (that is, to bring Christ down:) 7. or, Who shall descend into the abyss? (that is, to bring Christ up from the dead.)** The Old Testament passage here quoted is Deuteronomy 30 : 12–14. "'The righteousness of faith' is here equivalent to 'the righteousness of God.' So in 4 : 11, 13 — here, by a striking personification, not unlike that of the divine wisdom in the Proverbs, justification is said to speak, in the words of Deuteronomy. . . . Paul assumes that the Old Testament is full of Christ; and so it is no wonder to him to see in this Mosaic passage a divinely-designed suggestion of His exaltation, humiliation, and gospel, under words having another immediate reference." — *H. C. G. Moule.* "Israel in Deuteronomy 30

8. But what saith it? The word is nigh thee, in thy mouth, and in thy heart: that is, the word of faith, which we preach:
9. Because if thou shalt confess with thy mouth Jesus *as* Lord, and shalt believe in thy heart that God raised him from the dead, thou shalt be saved:
10. For with the heart man believeth unto righteousness; and with the mouth confession is made unto salvation.

---

was no longer the people of God, and God was addressing them, not on the ground of law, but on the basis of faith. This being the case, says the apostle, it is Christ who is its object, and in Him Israel was intended to gain what they had lost by disobedience to law. Thus the Old Testament bears witness at once to righteousness by law and righteousness by faith, and this exactly corresponds with Paul's earlier statement that righteousness by faith was witnessed to by the law and the prophets (3 : 21, 22)." — *W. H. Griffith Thomas.*

The editor believes that the teacher should not undertake to discuss Christ's descent into hades from the phrase, "To bring Christ up from the dead." The whole argument here is that salvation is not far from us, as up in heaven, or down in the underworld, but it is nigh to us, and to get away from this main line of truth and into a discussion of Christ's descent into hades will be to miss the whole meaning of our lesson.

8. **But what saith it? The word is nigh thee, in thy mouth, and in thy heart: that is, the word of faith, which we preach.** The quotation here is from Deuteronomy 30 : 14. "As the expressions 'to be hidden, to be far off,' imply that the thing to which they refer is inaccessible or difficult, so 'to be near, to be in the mouth' and 'in the heart,' mean to be accessible, easy, and familiar. They are frequently thus used; see Joshua 1 : 8: 'This law shall not depart out of thy mouth,' *i.e.*, it shall be constantly familiar to thee; Exodus 13 : 9: 'That the law may be in thy mouth,' Psalm 37 : 31; 40 : 8. The meaning of this passage then is, 'The gospel instead of directing us to ascend into heaven, or to go down to the abyss, tells us the thing required is simple and easy. Believe with thy heart and thou shalt be saved.' 'The word is nigh thee,' *i.e.*, the doctrine or truth contemplated, and by implication, what that doctrine demands. Paul, therefore, represents the gospel as speaking of itself. The method of justification by faith says: 'The word is near thee, in thy mouth, *i.e.*, the word or doctrine of faith is thus easy and familiar.' This is Paul's own explanation. The expression 'word of faith,' is the gospel, or doctrine of justification." — *Charles Hodge.* 9. **Because if thou shalt confess with thy mouth Jesus *as* Lord, and shalt believe in thy heart that God raised him from the dead, thou shalt be saved.** See, for the demand of such confession, Matthew 10 : 32; Luke 12 : 8. "For all adult converts, this was an important feature of baptism. In all cases, it is to be a test of the intelligence and reality of the faith of which it is a fruit. Confession is here put before believing, because in Deuteronomy 'the mouth' had been named before the heart. In the order of experience, of course, faith precedes confession. . . . The belief in the resurrection here is not merely historical belief (which yet is indispensable to all other belief in it), but 'heart' belief; the perception and cordial embrace of what the resurrection reveals and imports as to the risen One and His work." — *H. C. G. Moule.*

From a photograph.

Thorwaldsen's Statue of Christ.

10. **For with the heart man believeth unto righteousness; and with the mouth confes-**

sion is made unto salvation. "In relation to the past, it is salvation from the penalty of sin. In relation to the present, it is salvation from the power of sin. In relation to the future, it is salvation from the presence of sin." — *W. H. Griffith Thomas.* "Faith is 'unto righteousness'; confession is 'unto salvation.' Why is this? Is faith after all not enough for our union with the Lord, and for our safety in Him? Must we bring in something else, to be a more or less meritorious makeweight in the scale? No; it is eternally true that we are justified, that we are accepted, that we are incorporated, that we are kept, through faith only; that is, that Christ is all for all things in our salvation, and our part and work in the matter is to receive and hold Him in *an empty hand.* But then this empty hand, holding Him, receives life and power from Him. The man is vivified by his Rescuer. He is rescued that he may live, and that he may serve as living. He cannot truly serve without loyalty to his Lord. He cannot be truly loyal while he hides his relation to Him. In some articulate way he must confess Him; or he is not treading the path where the Shepherd walks before the sheep. The 'confession with the mouth' here in view is, surely, nothing less than the believer's open loyalty to Christ. It is no mere recitation of even the sacred catholic creed; which may be recited as by an automaton. It is the witness of the whole man to Christ, as his own discovered life and Lord. And thus it means in effect the path of faithfulness along which the Saviour actually leads to glory those who are justified by faith." — *Bishop Moule.*

Our study of these difficult passages has come to an end. The teacher in this lesson should be careful to constantly emphasize the utter, absolute uniqueness and supremacy of the Lord Jesus Christ. Beginning far back in creation, when Christ created the world, coming down through the ages, recognizing the world as upheld by Christ, seeing Him on the cross making purification for our sins, beholding Him at the right hand of God, ever making intercession for us, called Son by the Father, prophesied by the prophets, raised from the dead, believed on with our hearts and confessed with our lips — how can we help but believe in such a glorious One as He; how can we help but confess Him before men, who have, in all the annals of human history, no one to exalt and glorify and worship like the Lord Jesus?

How many different titles are assigned to the Lord Jesus in our lesson? How many different phrases are uttered by the Father concerning His Son in our passage? Making a list of all that Christ is said to have accomplished, and is accomplishing, can you divide these phrases into what Christ did before He came to earth, what Christ did while He was on earth, and what Christ is now doing in His glorified place in heaven? Can you find phrases in this lesson which indicate Christ's work as a prophet, as a priest, and as a king? Why should we not worship and pray to angels? Is confession with the mouth something to meditate upon in our quiet hours of devotion, or is it something definitely to do before men? Why does Christ want us to publicly confess Him before men?

LESSON XIII. — December 26.

GOD'S GREAT LOVE AND HIS GIFT. — Matthew 2 : 1–12.

GOLDEN TEXT. — ***For God so loved the world, that he gave his only begotten Son, that whosoever believeth on him should not perish, but have eternal life.*** JOHN 3 : 16.

Devotional Reading: Isaiah 9 : 1–7.
Beginner Topic: GIFTS FOR BABY JESUS.
  Lesson Material: Matthew 2 : 1–11.
  Memory Verse: God . . . loved us, and sent his Son. 1 John 4 : 10.
Primary Topic: GIFTS FOR LITTLE JESUS.
  Lesson Material: Matthew 2 : 1–12.
  Memory Verse: And they came into the house and saw the young child with Mary his mother . . . and opening their treasures they offered unto him gifts. Matthew 2 : 11.
Junior Topic: GIFTS OF THE WISE MEN.
  Lesson Material: Matthew 2 : 1–12.
  Memory Verse: And they came into the house and saw the young child with Mary his mother . . . and opening their treasures they offered unto him gifts. Matthew 2 : 11.
Intermediate and Senior Topic: OUR RESPONSE TO GOD'S GIFT.
Topic for Young People and Adults: OUR RESPONSE TO GOD'S GIFT.

THE TEACHER AND HIS CLASS.

The Younger Classes may be asked what is the one word that would most fully express the mood in which people are found at the Christmas season, generally, and the mood in which all people long to be found at that season, above every other time of the year. That word is *joy*. It so happens that the very word joy occurs in our lesson for today. As we study these verses we will try to discover who found this joy, and why they found it, and then we will have the secret for joy in our own hearts, at this Christmas season, and in every season of the year.

The Older Classes will know this lesson intimately, and will think that there is nothing new to be learned from this brief portion of the Word of God, just twelve verses, so would it not be profitable for the teacher to try to show just how these verses reveal the great truth that the innermost nature of the hearts and characters of men are revealed as they come into the presence of Jesus, and how their reaction to Christ indicates the condition of their hearts? Herod was a great sinner, and when he heard that Jesus was near he was troubled and tried to destroy Him. The wise men were really seeking for the truth, and as they came near to Christ their hearts rejoiced.

THE PLAN OF THE LESSON.

SUBJECT: How the Birth of Jesus Reveals That the Genuine Searchers for the Truth Will Ultimately Be Drawn to Christ to Bow Down and Worship Him Alone.

I. The Search for the Newborn King by the Wise Men, Matt. 2 : 1, 2.

II. The Verdict of the Scribes and Chief Priests Regarding the Birthplace of the Messiah, vs. 3–6.

III. The Command of the Scheming Herod, vs. 7, 8.

IV. The Guiding Star, vs. 9, 10.

V. The Adoration of the Magi, v. 11.

VI. The Warning Dream, v. 12.

THE LESSON IN ITS SETTING.

Time. — 5 B.C.

Place. — The city of Bethlehem, six miles south of Jerusalem.

Photograph by Bonfils.

The Well of the Magi.

THE TEACHER'S LIBRARY.

All lives of Christ will be found somewhat helpful for the study of this lesson, as well as larger commentaries on the Gospel of Matthew. By far the most important treatment of these twelve verses will be found in the very old work; *The Star of the Wise Men*, by the distinguished scholar, Archbishop R. C. Trench (1850). We need a great encyclopedic work on every aspect of the birth of our Lord, and why no one has published it is a mystery. One may consult the articles in the better Bible dictionaries on Bethlehem, Frankincense, Herod, Magi, Myrrh, and Star, and the very scholarly article, by R. J. Knowling: "The Birth of Christ," in James Hastings's *Dictionary of Christ and the Gospels*, Vol. 1, 202–208.

On the city of Bethlehem, which derives its fame from this holy event, see J. R. MacDuff: *The City of Bethlehem;* D. J. Burrell· *In David's Town;* Louis Gaston Leary: *The Christmas City: Bethlehem Across the Ages;* J. M. P. Otts: *The Fifth Gospel*, 35–68; G. Dallmann: *Sacred Sites and Ways*, 17–66; and two articles, by the editor of this volume: "Why Was Bethlehem the Birthplace of Our Lord," in *Revelation*, December, 1936; and "The Miraculous Choice of Bethlehem," in the *Sunday School Times*, December 5, 1936. There is an interesting article on the Magi in W. R. Ramsay's *The Bearing of Recent Discovery on the Trustworthiness of the New Testament*, 140–149.

Sermonic material on this famous and constantly-used passage is, for some strange reason, for the most part very poor. However, on verses 1, 2, see H. P. Liddon: *Christmastide Sermons*, 348–367; on verse 2, Joseph Parker: *The City Temple Pulpit*, Vol. 5, 2–10; and, the same, *Studies in Texts*, Vol. 1, 37–46. Especially should one consult, for verse 11, a splendid sermon by George H. Morrison: *The Unlighted Lustre*, 252–258. Some years ago Dr. Frances W. Upham published quite an exhaustive work: *The Wise Men, Who They Were, and How They Came to Jerusalem* (1873), which the teacher will find quite interesting reading, if he has time for it.

MATTHEW 2 : 1. Now when Jesus was born in Bethlehem of Judæa in the days of Herod the king, behold, Wise-men from the east came to Jerusalem, saying,

SOME CHARACTERISTICS OF MATTHEW'S STORY OF THE BIRTH OF OUR LORD WHICH REVEAL ITS TRUSTWORTHINESS.

"This one chapter contains all that Matthew records of the infancy. Mark and John tell us nothing, and Luke very little. This singular reticence has often been remarked upon, and it certainly is most noteworthy, and a manifest sign of genuineness and truthfulness, a token that what these men wrote was in the deepest sense not their own. For if they had been left to themselves in the performance of the task assigned them, they could not have restrained themselves as they have done. The Jews of the time attached the greatest importance to child life, as is evident from the single fact that they had no less than eight different words to mark the successive stages of development from the newborn babe up to the young man; and to omit all reference to these stages, except the slight notice of the infancy in this chapter, was certainly not 'according to Matthew' the Jew — not what would have been expected of him had he been left to himself. It can only be explained by the fact that he spoke or was silent according as he was moved or restrained by the Holy Spirit. This view is strikingly confirmed by comparison with the spurious Gospels afterwards published, by men who thought they could improve on the original records with their childish stories as to what the boy Jesus said and did. These awkward fictions reflect the spirit of the age; the simple records of the four evangelists mirror for us the Spirit of Truth. To the vulgar mind, they may seem bare and defective, but all men of culture and mature judgment recognize in their simplicity and naturalness a note of manifest superiority." — *J. M. Gibson.*

I. **THE SEARCH FOR THE NEWBORN KING BY THE WISE MEN,** vs. 1, 2.

1. **Now when Jesus was born in Bethlehem of Judæa.** Because we have so much material to study in our lesson today, we are not going to dwell at length, as in previous Christmas lessons, on Bethlehem itself. The town was very ancient, and is mentioned as far back as Genesis 35 : 19. It was here that David was born, and spent the early years of his life, which gave to Bethlehem the name of "the city of David" (Luke 2 : 11; 1 Sam. 16 : 1). Of the great prophecy concerning Bethlehem we will speak later. Bethlehem was a small village, six miles south of Jerusalem, in beautiful rolling country, a place famous for its natural beauty, and, during the Christian ages, famous for the beauty of its women. The word *Bethlehem* means *house of bread*, and, as Archbishop Trench has said, with the birth of Jesus here, "Bethlehem indeed became that which its name had promised from the first; for He who had been always the bread of angels, and who, in His incarnation, became also the bread of men, found His earliest earthly habitation there." We might even go further than this and say that the name has an even deeper fulfillment, for Christ said the bread that He would give was His flesh, which He would give for the life of the world, bread coming down from heaven, and it was in Bethlehem that His body of flesh first appeared in the world (John 6 : 48–58). As far as we know, the Lord Jesus never returned to Bethlehem, during His adult life; it has no part whatever in the apostolic history, leading us to conclude that when Christ was born there it had fulfilled its mission. **In the days of Herod the king.** This was "Herod the Great, son of Antipater, an Idumæan, by an Arabian mother, made king of Judæa on occasion of his having fled to Rome, being driven from his tetrarchy by the pretender Antigonus. This title was confirmed to him after the battle of Actium by Octavianus. He sought to strengthen his throne by a series of cruelties and slaughters, putting to death even his wife Mariamne, and his sons, Alexander and Aristobulus. His cruelties, and his affectation of Gentile customs, gained for him a hatred among

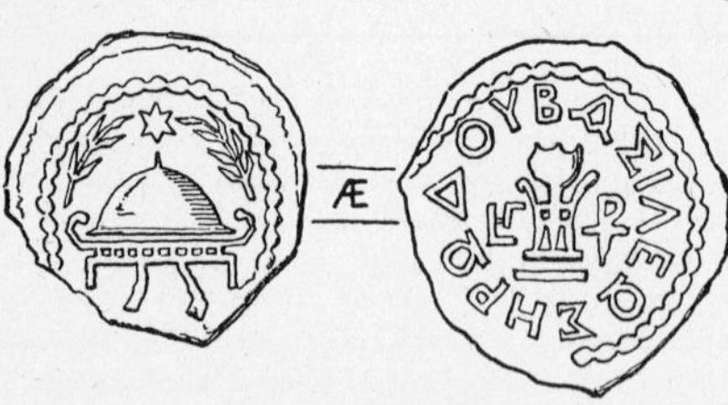

Coin of Herod the Great.

A helmet with cheek-pieces and above it a star, which is remarkable, as the birth of Christ was announced by a star.

2. Where is he that is born King of the Jews? for we saw his star in the east, and are come to worship him.

the Jews, which neither his magnificent rebuilding of the temple, nor his liberality in other public works, nor his provident care of the people during a severe famine, could mitigate. He died miserably, five days later after having put to death his son Antipater, in the seventieth year of his age, the thirty-eighth of his reign, and the 750th year of Rome. The events here related took place a short time before his death, but necessarily more than forty days; for he spent the last forty days of his life at Jericho and the baths of Callirrhoe, and therefore would not be found by the Magi at Jerusalem." — *Henry Alford.* **Behold, Wise-men from the east.** The phrase *wise men* is a translation of the Greek word *magi*, and this explains why we speak of "the visit of the Magi." The word *magi* is the root of our word *magic.* "The wise men, or Magi, were originally the priestly tribe or caste among the Medes, and afterwards the Medo-Persians, being the recognized teachers of religion and science. In the great Persian empire they wielded the highest influence and power. As to science, they cultivated astronomy, especially in the form of astrology, with medicine, and every form of divination and incantation. Their name gradually came to be applied to persons of similar position and pursuits in other nations, especially to diviners, enchanters. It is used in the Greek translation of Daniel 1 : 20; 2 : 27; 5, 7, 11, 15, to render a word signifying 'diviner,' etc. So in the New Testament it is employed to describe Barjesus (Acts 13 : 6, 8, translated 'sorcerer'), and words derived from it applied to Simon at Samaria (Acts 8 : 9, 11), who is commonly spoken of as Simon Magus, and from it come our words *magic, magician*, etc. It is, however, probable that these Magi from the East were not mere ordinary astrologers or diviners, but belonged to the old Persian class, many members of which still maintained a high position and an elevated character. So it is likely, but of course not certain, that they came from Persia or from Babylonia; in the latter region Jews were now very numerous and influential, and in Persia also they had been regarded with special interest, as far back as the time of Cyrus." — *J. A. Broadus.* Canon Liddon, in calling attention to the prophecies of Psalm 86 : 9; 22 : 27, 28; Isa. 49 : 6; 11 : 1, 10, that all the kingdoms of the nations should worship the Lord, and that God would give the Messiah for a light unto the Gentiles, says that "the first step to the fulfillment of these predictions was made when the wise men crossed the desert on their visit to the cradle at Bethlehem. That visit opens a new era in the religious history of the world." **Came to Jerusalem saying.**
2. **Where is he that is born King of the Jews.** "They had taken for granted that the royal child would have been born in the royal city, and that they should find him there." — *R. C. Trench.* **For we saw his star in the east, and are come to worship him.** "If we place together (*a*) the prophecy in Numbers 24 : 17, which could hardly be unknown to the eastern astrologers, and (*b*) the assertion of Suetonius 'that there prevailed an ancient and consistent opinion in all the East, that it was fated that at that time those should go forth from Judæa who should rule the empire': and of Tacitus, to the same effect and nearly in the same words — and (*c*) the prophecy, also likely to be known in the East, of the seventy weeks in Daniel 9 : 24, we can, I think, be at no loss to understand how any remarkable celestial appearance at this time should have been interpreted as it was. There was no ground for supposing the Magi to have been three in number, or to have been kings. The first tradition appears to have arisen from the number of their gifts; the second, from the prophecy in Isaiah 60 : 3." — *H. Alford.* "The gold indicates wealth; the frankincense and myrrh point to the East, more particularly to Arabia. Frankincense, a resin of bitter taste, but fragrant odor, was used chiefly in sacrifices and in the services of the temple. Myrrh, an aromatic of a similar kind, was produced from a shrub, which, indigenous in Arabia and Ethiopia, grows also in Palestine. Myrrh was employed for fumigation and for improving the taste of wine, but especially as an ingredient of a very precious ointment." — *J. P. Lange.* "We know too little of the astrology of that period to determine what star might or might not seem to those who watched the heavens as the precursor of a great king. Without building too much on uncertain data, we may, however, at least believe that the wise men were Gentiles. They do not ask for *our* king, but for the king of the Jews; and yet, though Gentiles, they were sharers in the Messianic hopes of the Jews." — *E. H. Plumptre.* Trench makes a very fine point when he says: "It is not uninstructive to compare the guidance by which the Magi and the shepherds respectively are

3. And when Herod the king heard it, he was troubled, and all Jerusalem with him.
4. And gathering together all the chief priests and scribes of the people, he inquired of them where the Christ should be born.
5. And they said unto him, In Bethlehem of Judæa: for thus it is written through the prophet,
6. And thou Bethlehem, land of Judah,
Art in no wise least among the princes of Judah:
For out of thee shall come forth a governor,
Who shall be shepherd of my people Israel.

---

brought to the presence of the newborn King. The shepherds, as of Jewish extraction, are guided by an angel; but the wise men, as Gentiles, by a star — those by revelation which was familiar to them; these by nature with the aspects of which they were familiar. There was a fitness, too, in the fact of the shepherds, who were the representatives of the Jews, of them therefore that were near, making their appearance on the very day of the nativity, while the wise men who, like the whole Gentile world, came from afar, certainly did not appear till a much later date."

II. **THE VERDICT OF THE SCRIBES AND CHIEF PRIESTS REGARDING THE BIRTHPLACE OF THE MESSIAH,** vs. 3–6. 3. **And when Herod the king heard it, he was troubled, and all Jerusalem with him.** "When we remember the recent agitations at Jerusalem through the refusal of the Pharisees, to the number of six thousand, to take the oath of allegiance to him, with their prophecy of the divinely-intended transfer of the kingdom from him and his race to a favorite of their own, we can easily understand how much less a thing would have been sufficient to terrify him than this anouncement of the Star and of the King; as these will also help to explain the bloody precautions which presently he took. 'He was troubled,' for the wicked fear where no fear is, even as in one sense there was none even for him. For this King that was born was candidate for quite another crown than any which Herod would have cared to wear (Matt. 27 : 29). But though not exactly in the shape that he imagined, in another sense there was most truly fear. The King of righteousness was born, and the whole kingdom of unrighteousness felt itself already tottering to its base." — *R. C. Trench.* 4. **And gathering together all the chief priests and scribes of the people, he inquired of them where the Christ should be born.** "The chief priests were probably the heads of the twenty-four courses into which the sons of Aaron were divided (2 Chron. 23 : 8; Luke 1 : 5), but the term may have included those who had, though only for a time, held the office of high priest. The scribes were the interpreters of the law, casuists and collectors of the traditions of the elders, for the most part Pharisees. The meeting thus convened was not necessarily a formal meeting of the Sanhedrin or Great Council, and may have been only as a committee of notables called together for a special purpose. With a characteristic subtlety, as if trying to gauge the strength of their Messianic hopes, Herod acts as if he himself shared them, and asks where the Christ, the expected Messiah, the anointed of the Lord was to be born." — *E. H. Plumptre.* 5. **And they said unto him, In Bethlehem of Judæa: for thus it is written through the prophet,** 6. **And thou Bethlehem, land of Judah, art in no wise least among the princes of Judah: for out of thee shall come forth a governor, who shall be shepherd of my people Israel.** The prophecy here quoted is found in Micah 5 : 2, a passage which the editor has always felt was one of the most remarkable in the entire Word of God. It is admitted on every hand that Micah uttered these words about 700 B.C. That the passage in Micah definitely, clearly refers to the Messiah to come all Biblical students, Jews and Gentiles, before Christ and since Christ, have admitted. The amazing thing is that Micah did not put the birth of the great King of the Jews in the city of Jerusalem, where all the kings of Judah, from the time of David's sons, were born, for it was indeed "the city of the great king," the royal city, the greatest of all cities in Palestine. Just to show the remarkableness of this prophecy, let us recognize, say, the simple fact that in all the millions of pages printed in America, down to 1809, not one page contains a line that even gives a hint that there would be born, in Harlan County, Kentucky, a man who would some day be the President of the United States. In fact, the man who will be the President of our nation forty years from now has already been born, but we would not dare say

7. Then Herod privily called the Wise-men, and learned of them exactly what time the star appeared.
8. And he sent them to Bethlehem, and said, Go and search out exactly concerning the young child; and when ye have found *him*, bring me word, that I also may come and worship him.
9. And they, having heard the king, went their way; and lo, the star, which they saw in the east, went before them, till it came and stood over where the young child was.
10. And when they saw the star, they rejoiced with exceeding great joy.

---

in what city that birth had taken place, for we do not know who the President will be. How did Micah come to put his finger on this one little town of the whole ancient world, and say that *there* the Messiah would be born? He did it by divine inspiration. There are some variations between the quotation in Matthew and the original text in Micah, but they are slight, and all the changes of phraseology made by Matthew "do not introduce any idea foreign to the original, but bring out more plainly its actual meaning. It was common among the Jews of that day to interpret in quoting." — *John A. Broadus.*

III. **THE COMMAND OF THE SCHEMING HEROD,** vs. 7, 8. 7. **Then Herod privily called the Wise-men, and learned of them exactly what time the star appeared.** 8. **And he sent them to Bethlehem, and said, Go and search out exactly concerning the young child; and when ye have found *him*, bring me word, that I also may come and worship him.** It is remarkable that the chief priests and scribes did not even discuss whether *they* perhaps ought not to go down to Bethlehem also, to see this thing which had taken place. Here, at the very threshold of our Lord's incarnate life, begins the fulfillment of that tragic sentence: "He came unto his own, and they that were his own received him not" (John 1 : 11). The only person in the whole city who took an interest in Christ was this wicked king, and his only desire, as later events revealed, was to put Him to death. Thus we see two tendencies among the people of Palestine at the time our Lord was born, unbelief and opposition. These tendencies will finally result in the crucifixion of the one whose birth we are now studying.

Worship of the Magi. Hofmann.

IV. **THE GUIDING STAR,** vs. 9, 10. 9. **And they, having heard the king, went their way; and lo, the star, which they saw in the east, went before them, till it came and stood over where the young child was.** 10. **And when they saw the star, they rejoiced with exceeding great joy.** "If it is to be understood as standing over the house, and thus indicating to the Magi the position of the object of their search, the whole incident must be regarded as miraculous. But this is not necessarily implied, even if the words of the text be literally understood; and in a matter like astronomy, where popular language is so universally broad, and the Scriptures so generally use popular language, it is surely not the letter, but the spirit of the narrative with which we are concerned." — *Henry Alford.* "They express the joy of those Eastern seers, not at the mere seeing of the star, which they had often seen before, but at seeing

11. And they came into the house and saw the young child with Mary his mother; and they fell down and worshipped him; and opening their treasures they offered unto him gifts, gold and frankincense and myrrh.

it stand over where the young Child was, having at length fulfilled its mission, and having brought them there where they would be. It is the joy of men that have the haven in sight; that are just about to grasp the good expected so long." — *R. C. Trench.*

V. **THE ADORATION OF THE MAGI,** v. 11. 11. **And they came into the house and saw the young child with Mary his mother; and they fell down and worshipped him; and opening their treasures they offered unto him gifts, gold and frankincense and myrrh.** Inasmuch as some weeks had elapsed between the birth of Jesus in the manger and the arrival of the wise men, the implication of this text, that the holy family were not any longer in the stable of the inn, can easily be understood. Whether it is significant or not, we should note that the baby Jesus is referred to before His mother. But certainly there is tremendous significance in the fact that these wise men, in falling down to worship, did not worship the mother, or the mother and child, but they "worshiped *him.*" Nowhere in all the Scriptures is there the slightest hint that any one but the Three Persons of the Trinity should be worshiped. Christians should have great respect for the Virgin Mary, and sermons should be preached concerning her character and place in the Word of God, but she is not to be worshiped. In commenting on the words, "they fell down," Canon Liddon says: "They did not sit up, as if nothing great was before them; or on the foolish supposition that the body has no relation to the soul, and that while the soul is cleaving unto the dust before the majesty of God, there is no reason why the body should not lounge and loll on a chair in a posture of easy, if not of studied, indifference. They fell down and worshiped; the outward act corresponding to, and being dictated by, the inward self-prostration, just as the Hebrew word for adoration implies the prostration of the adoring soul. Say you that this prostration was only oriental? Was it not rather profoundly human, and should we not do well to note it? Ah! brethren, methinks we have much to learn of these Eastern sages; we who, like them, come into the presence of the King of kings, but who, unlike them, think it perhaps proof of a high spirituality to behave before Him as we should not think of behaving in the presence of our earthly superiors. Do we murmur that God looks not at the bowed head or at the bent knee, but at the heart? No doubt He does look at the heart; but the question is whether it is possible for the heart to be engaged in worship while the posture of the body suggests irreverent sloth." On the gifts of the wise men, Archbishop Trench remarks, "Thus we have continual mention of such gifts, as made to kings and other great persons on earth, and to the King of kings in heaven (1 Sam. 10 : 27; 1 Kings 10 : 2; Gen. 32 : 13; 43 : 11, 25; 1 Sam. 9 : 7; 25 : 18, 27; Job 42 : 11). . . . The frankincense, the choicest of all odors, was offered to the Son of God, who as such was Himself also God, and to whom therefore the sweet odors of prayer and all other sacrifices were rightly due: the myrrh to the *son* of Mary, who, as man, was subject to mortality, while at the same time he should be free from corruption; the myrrh, therefore, used in burial, and yet preserving from decay, containing a latent prophecy, not of His death and burial only, as it is sometimes explained, but the

Karl Schönherr.

The Nativity.

12. And being warned *of God* in a dream that they should not return to Herod, they departed into their own country another way.

pledge also of His resurrection; and the gold to the Son of David, the King of Israel, to whom all other kings and people should yield tribute of the most precious things which they had."

Dr. George H. Morrison draws a very fine lesson from the journey of these wise men, which can be used for blessing to all of our hearts: "The secret of the perseverance of these wise men is not hard to find. It sprang from this, that they were following a star. Had they been guided by anything less than that, they would have sunk down wearied long ago. Do you think, now, if they had read about this king in some of their Chaldean or Babylonian libraries — do you think that that literary discovery would have buoyed them up and carried them at last into the manger? It needed more than earth to carry them through; it needed the bright and beckoning radiance of the sky. They were strong because their guidance was a star. They looked to the lamp of heaven and not to earth's taper. And if they battled bravely, and journeyed with zeal unquenchable, and if nothing could turn them from their unheard-of quest, it was because they followed, not a light of earth, but a light that was hung aloft by God. . . . Do you observe why the wise men saw the King when all others that night at Bethlehem were blind to Him? The simple reason is that they were seeking Him, and just because they were seeking Him, they saw. Where is He that is born King of the Jews — they had troubled all Jerusalem with their questions. They were more than star-gazers, they were anxious searchers not to be beaten off in their endeavor. And so where others saw nothing but a child, they saw, because they had searched for Him, a king."

VI. **THE WARNING DREAM,** v. 12. 12. **And being warned *of God* in a dream that they should not return to Herod, they departed into their own country another way.** "Following the order of events in our minds, it seems probable that after their homage on the evening of their arrival, they retired, possibly to the inn of Bethlehem, and were then, in their sleep, warned not to return to Jerusalem the following day, but to make their way to the fords of Jordan, and so to escape from the tyrant's jealous pursuit. So ends all that we know of the visit of the Magi. Matthew, writing for Hebrews, recorded it apparently as testifying to the kingly character of Jesus. Christendom, however, has rightly seen in it a yet deeper significance, and the wise men have been regarded as the firstfruits of the outlying heathen world, the earnest of the future ingathering." — *E. H. Plumptre.* We thus have in this lesson three miracles, each used as a means of revelation and guidance to men — the miracle of the moving star leading to Bethlehem; the miracle of Micah's prophecy, also leading to Bethlehem; and the miracle of warning, in a divinely-sent dream.

How many different persons do you find in this lesson, and what would you say are the chief characteristics of each, as far as the lesson reveals? What reasons did Herod the king have for being afraid when he heard that a king of the Jews had been born? How many reasons did the Magi have for the joy which flooded their hearts when they found the Babe? What is the significance of the fact that these wise men brought gifts — would not their visit have been just as genuine and just as important if no gifts had been brought? What attitudes toward Christ taken by men through the ages, and held by different men today, do you find immediately taken by men at the very beginning of our Lord's life on earth?

INDEX.

The titles of the lessons are printed in SMALL CAPITALS.

INDEX.